To Celia Kepic
in loving memory of your
sister Eulalia Totten

Given By
The Women's Fellowship
of Old South Church

Presented August 2009

*I can do all things through him
who gives me strength.*
Phillippians 4:13

Belongs to

Given by

Date

Occasion

MY TIME *with* GOD

NEW CENTURY VERSION®

MY TIME with GOD

15 MINUTE DEVOTIONS *for the* ENTIRE YEAR

NASHVILLE DALLAS MEXICO CITY RIO DE JANEIRO BEIJING

MY TIME WITH GOD

The preliminary research and development on the *New Century Version*® was done by the World Bible Translation Center, Inc., Fort Worth, TX 76182.

Printed in China

12 13 - 09 08

INTRODUCTION

Would you like to know God better . . . to explore exciting Scriptural truths each day and still meet your other demands and responsibilities . . . to be challenged (at a comfortable pace) to grow deeper in your faith?

My Time with God has been designed for you! In fifteen minutes a day, you can systematically explore the treasures of Scripture. You may begin any time you wish, and at the end of the year you will have read the entire New Testament and related sections from the Old Testament. Plus you will have received insights from classical and contemporary writers.

There's a reading for Monday, Tuesday, Wednesday, Thursday, Friday, and one for Saturday/Sunday. (We know how busy weekends can be.)

Each two-page reading begins with the New Testament passage for the day and is followed by at least one Old Testament passage that reinforces the theme. This unique format allows you to see Scripture's truths unfold and to gain a new understanding of God's love and mercy throughout history.

If you wish, you may read thematically. Maybe you're wrestling with a problem at work, an issue of faith, or some type of suffering. Or maybe you would like to study a particular biblical theme. Whatever your need, the index on page 627 will guide you to just the right reading.

Not only is *My Time with God* a valuable aid in personal growth and meditative study, it is helpful for small groups and Sunday school classes.

My Time with God features the New Century Version, an accurate and readable translation that is well suited to devotional reading. In fact, because of its ease of reading, you may find it hard to stop at just one reading a day.

Most likely, you will recognize many of the authors' quotations we've included. Their insights—gleaned from more than one hundred seventy books—will challenge your thinking, broaden your understanding, and guide you to an even deeper relationship with God. The credits at the end of the book show the source of each quotation so you may pursue further reading.

Questions at the end of each reading will help you evaluate and apply what you've read. They are also excellent discussion starters for small group settings. We invite you now to spend time with God and discover what He has in store for you!

Amanda and Stephen Sorenson
Editors

MONDAY

The Savior of God's People Is Born

Matthew 1:1–25

The Family History of Jesus

1 This is the family history of Jesus Christ. He came from the family of David, and David came from the family of Abraham.

2 Abraham was the father of Isaac.
Isaac was the father of Jacob.
Jacob was the father of Judah and his brothers.
3 Judah was the father of Perez and Zerah.
(Their mother was Tamar.)
Perez was the father of Hezron.
Hezron was the father of Ram.
4 Ram was the father of Amminadab.
Amminadab was the father of Nahshon.
Nahshon was the father of Salmon.
5 Salmon was the father of Boaz.
(Boaz's mother was Rahab.)
Boaz was the father of Obed.
(Obed's mother was Ruth.)
Obed was the father of Jesse.
6 Jesse was the father of King David.
David was the father of Solomon.
(Solomon's mother had been Uriah's wife.)
7 Solomon was the father of Rehoboam.
Rehoboam was the father of Abijah.
Abijah was the father of Asa.
8 Asa was the father of Jehoshaphat.
Jehoshaphat was the father of Jehoram.
Jehoram was the ancestor of Uzziah.
9 Uzziah was the father of Jotham.
Jotham was the father of Ahaz.
Ahaz was the father of Hezekiah.
10 Hezekiah was the father of Manasseh.
Manasseh was the father of Amon.
Amon was the father of Josiah.
11 Josiah was the grandfather of Jehoiachin and his brothers.
(This was at the time that the people were taken to Babylon.)
12 After they were taken to Babylon:
Jehoiachin was the father of Shealtiel.
Shealtiel was the grandfather of Zerubbabel.
13 Zerubbabel was the father of Abiud.
Abiud was the father of Eliakim.
Eliakim was the father of Azor.
14 Azor was the father of Zadok.
Zadok was the father of Akim.
Akim was the father of Eliud.
15 Eliud was the father of Eleazar.
Eleazar was the father of Matthan.
Matthan was the father of Jacob.
16 Jacob was the father of Joseph.
Joseph was the husband of Mary, and Mary was the mother of Jesus.
Jesus is called the Christ.

17 So there were fourteen generations from Abraham to David. And there were fourteen generations from David until the people were taken to Babylon. And there were fourteen generations from the time when the people were taken to Babylon until Christ was born.

The Birth of Jesus Christ

This is how the birth of Jesus Christ came about. His mother Mary was

engaged to marry Joseph, but before they married, she learned she was pregnant by the power of the Holy Spirit.
[19] Because Mary's husband, Joseph, was a good man, he did not want to disgrace her in public, so he planned to divorce her secretly.

[20] While Joseph thought about these things, an angel of the Lord came to him in a dream. The angel said, "Joseph, descendant of David, don't be afraid to take Mary as your wife, because the baby in her is from the Holy Spirit.
[21] She will give birth to a son, and you will name him Jesus, because he will save his people from their sins."

[22] All this happened to bring about what the Lord had said through the prophet:
[23] "The virgin will be pregnant. She will have a son, and they will name him Immanuel," which means "God is with us."

[24] When Joseph woke up, he did what the Lord's angel had told him to do. Joseph took Mary as his wife,
[25] but he did not have sexual relations with her until she gave birth to the son. And Joseph named him Jesus.

OLD TESTAMENT READING

Then Isaiah said, "Ahaz, descendant of David, listen carefully! Isn't it bad enough that you wear out the patience of people? Do you also have to wear out the patience of my God?
[14] The Lord himself will give you a sign: The virgin will be pregnant. She will have a son, and she will name him Immanuel."

Isaiah 7:13–14

INSIGHTS

The doctrine of the virgin birth is crucial to our faith. The incarnation of the Son of God was accomplished by a creative act of the Holy Spirit in the body of Mary, a virgin. It was a special miracle performed by the third person of the Holy Trinity—the Holy Spirit—which enabled the second person of the Trinity—the eternal Son of God—to take upon Himself a genuine, although sinless, human nature. He was born of a virgin, as a man, without surrendering any aspect of His deity. . . .

. . . One with us, yet one with God. He had to become man because man was the one who had sinned. He had to be God because God was the only One who could do anything about the sin of man. Humanity had tried for centuries, and the situation only got worse! The only way God could bring about the salvation of the fallen human race was to assume the form of the race He was to redeem.

God has given us the means to know the truth. Jesus is the way to the Father, because He is our Redeemer. He is the truth because He is the fulfillment of all the prophecies concerning Him. He is the life because He overcame death. . . . Jesus has the fullness of God dwelling in Him bodily forever and ever. The Son of God became the Son of man so that the sons of men might become the sons of God.

Terry Fullam

PAUSE FOR REFLECTION

What does the virgin birth of Jesus signify for all people? In what ways have you and all nations been blessed through the children of Abraham?

TUESDAY

God Guides and Protects Us

Matthew 2:1–23

Wise Men Come to Visit Jesus

2 Jesus was born in the town of
Bethlehem in Judea during the
time when Herod was king. When
Jesus was born, some wise men
from the east came to Jerusalem.
2 They asked, "Where is the baby
who was born to be the king of the
Jews? We saw his star in the east and
have come to worship him."
3 When King Herod heard this, he
was troubled, as well as all the
people in Jerusalem. 4 Herod called
a meeting of all the leading priests
and teachers of the law and asked
them where the Christ would be
born. 5 They answered, "In the town
of Bethlehem in Judea. The prophet
wrote about this in the Scriptures:

6 'But you, Bethlehem, in the land
of Judah,
are important among the tribes
of Judah.
A ruler will come from you
who will be like a shepherd for
my people Israel.'" *Micah 5:2*

7 Then Herod had a secret meeting with the wise men and learned
from them the exact time they first
saw the star. 8 He sent the wise men
to Bethlehem, saying, "Look carefully for the child. When you find
him, come tell me so I can worship
him too."
9 After the wise men heard the
king, they left. The star that they had
seen in the east went before them
until it stopped above the place
where the child was. 10 When the
wise men saw the star, they were
filled with joy. 11 They came to the
house where the child was and saw
him with his mother, Mary, and
they bowed down and worshiped
him. They opened their gifts and
gave him treasures of gold, frankincense, and myrrh. 12 But God
warned the wise men in a dream
not to go back to Herod, so they returned to their own country by a
different way.

Jesus' Parents Take Him to Egypt

13 After they left, an angel of the Lord
came to Joseph in a dream and said,
"Get up! Take the child and his
mother and escape to Egypt, because Herod is starting to look for
the child so he can kill him. Stay in
Egypt until I tell you to return."
14 So Joseph got up and left for
Egypt during the night with the child
and his mother. 15 And Joseph stayed
in Egypt until Herod died. This happened to bring about what the Lord
had said through the prophet: "I called
my son out of Egypt."

Herod Kills the Baby Boys

16 When Herod saw that the wise
men had tricked him, he was furious.
So he gave an order to kill all the
baby boys in Bethlehem and in the
surrounding area who were two
years old or younger. This was in
keeping with the time he learned
from the wise men. 17 So what God
had said through the prophet
Jeremiah came true:

18 "A voice was heard in Ramah
of painful crying and deep
sadness:

Rachel crying for her children.
She refused to be comforted,
because her children are
dead." *Jeremiah 31:15*

Joseph and Mary Return

After Herod died, an angel of the Lord spoke to Joseph in a dream while he was in Egypt. 20 The angel said, "Get up! Take the child and his mother and go to the land of Israel, because the people who were trying to kill the child are now dead."

21 So Joseph took the child and his mother and went to Israel. 22 But he heard that Archelaus was now king in Judea since his father Herod had died. So Joseph was afraid to go there. After being warned in a dream, he went to the area of Galilee, 23 to a town called Nazareth, and lived there. And so what God had said through the prophets came true: "He will be called a Nazarene."

OLD TESTAMENT READING

But you, Bethlehem Ephrathah,
though you are too small to be
among the army groups
from Judah,
from you will come one who will
rule Israel for me.
He comes from very old times,
from days long ago."
3 The LORD will give up his people
until the one who is having a
baby gives birth;
then the rest of his relatives will
return
to the people of Israel.
4 At that time the ruler of Israel will
stand
and take care of his people
with the LORD's strength
and with the power of the
name of the LORD his God.
The Israelites will live in safety,
because his greatness will
reach all over the earth.
5 He will bring peace.

Micah 5:2–5a

INSIGHTS

God has led. This is history's testimony. Looking back over lives, we can see how beautifully, wonderfully, lovingly God has led. "As for me, the LORD has led me," testified the servant of Abraham (Genesis 24:27).

God will lead. This is the testimony of doctrine. The Scriptures teach it by precept and example throughout Old and New Testaments. The word of God declares it to be so. Looking ahead—before the need, before the crunch—we can testify that God will lead.

God is leading! This is the testimony of faith, where the rubber meets the road. God has promised to lead, and I seek to be led—an unbeatable combination. God's promise, my submission.

God has led, for which I am grateful.

I know God will lead, and for this I praise and thank Him.

God is leading! This is my confidence and joy . . . my rest.

Richard Halverson

PAUSE FOR REFLECTION

Note the instances in which God protected the child Jesus and how each of those also fulfilled prophecy. What does this reveal to you about God's sovereignty and faithfulness in protecting his own?

WEDNESDAY

Change Your Hearts and Lives

Matthew 3:1—4:11

The Work of John the Baptist

3 About that time John the Baptist began preaching in the desert area of Judea. 2 John said, "Change your hearts and lives because the kingdom of heaven is near." 3 John the Baptist is the one Isaiah the prophet was talking about when he said:

"This is a voice of one
  who calls out in the desert:
'Prepare the way for the Lord.
  Make the road straight for
  him.' " *Isaiah 40:3*

4 John's clothes were made from camel's hair, and he wore a leather belt around his waist. For food, he ate locusts and wild honey. 5 Many people came from Jerusalem and Judea and all the area around the Jordan River to hear John. 6 They confessed their sins, and he baptized them in the Jordan River.

7 Many of the Pharisees and Sadducees came to the place where John was baptizing people. When John saw them, he said, "You are all snakes! Who warned you to run away from God's coming punishment? 8 Do the things that show you really have changed your hearts and lives. 9 And don't think you can say to yourselves, 'Abraham is our father.' I tell you that God could make children for Abraham from these rocks. 10 The ax is now ready to cut down the trees, and every tree that does not produce good fruit will be cut down and thrown into the fire.

11 "I baptize you with water to show that your hearts and lives have changed. But there is one coming after me who is greater than I am, whose sandals I am not good enough to carry. He will baptize you with the Holy Spirit and fire. 12 He will come ready to clean the grain, separating the good grain from the chaff. He will put the good part of the grain into his barn, but he will burn the chaff with a fire that cannot be put out."

Jesus Is Baptized by John

At that time Jesus came from Galilee to the Jordan River and wanted John to baptize him. 14 But John tried to stop him, saying, "Why do you come to me to be baptized? I need to be baptized by you!"

15 Jesus answered, "Let it be this way for now. We should do all things that are God's will." So John agreed to baptize Jesus.

16 As soon as Jesus was baptized, he came up out of the water. Then heaven opened, and he saw God's Spirit coming down on him like a dove. 17 And a voice from heaven said, "This is my Son, whom I love, and I am very pleased with him."

The Temptation of Jesus

4 Then the Spirit led Jesus into the desert to be tempted by the devil. 2 Jesus ate nothing for forty days and nights. After this, he was very hungry. 3 The devil came to Jesus to tempt him, saying, "If you are the Son of God, tell these rocks to become bread."

[4]Jesus answered, "It is written in
the Scriptures, 'A person does not
live by eating only bread, but by everything God says.'"
[5]Then the devil led Jesus to the
holy city of Jerusalem and put him
on a high place of the Temple. [6]The
devil said, "If you are the Son of God,
jump down, because it is written in
the Scriptures:

'He has put his angels in charge
of you.
They will catch you in their
hands
so that you will not hit your foot
on a rock.'" *Psalm 91:11-12*

[7]Jesus answered him, "It also
says in the Scriptures, 'Do not test
the Lord your God.'"
[8]Then the devil led Jesus to the
top of a very high mountain and
showed him all the kingdoms of the
world and all their splendor. [9]The
devil said, "If you will bow down and
worship me, I will give you all these
things."
[10]Jesus said to the devil, "Go away
from me, Satan! It is written in the
Scriptures, 'You must worship the
Lord your God and serve only him.'"
[11]So the devil left Jesus, and angels came and took care of him.

OLD TESTAMENT READING

Children, come and listen to me.
I will teach you to worship the
Lord.
[12]You must do these things
to enjoy life and have many
happy days.
[13]You must not say evil things,
and you must not tell lies.
[14]Stop doing evil and do good.
Look for peace and work for it.

Psalm 34:11–14

INSIGHTS

Jean, a small shopkeeper in Bordeaux, worked long hours with virtually nothing to show for his labors. Even his best efforts to beguile the Paris tax collector left him very little for his family. His life was depressing and without purpose, until the day when a missionary entered his shop to make a purchase.

Before leaving the shop, this foreigner shared his faith with Jean, and for the first time the shopkeeper realized that there was more to life than he had ever supposed. . . .

As he grew in faith, Jean became convinced that his lifestyle must be radically altered and that he could no longer lie about how much income he was making at his little shop. When the time came to submit his tax forms, he filled them out in full and paid the required amount of taxes. The local tax clerk was stunned, and word spread like wildfire among the shopkeepers. Jean's wife was outraged, and his neighbors were convinced that he had lost his mind. When they inquired about his foolish actions, he could only explain that God had made him a different man.

Ruth Tucker

PAUSE FOR REFLECTION

What message from God did John bring to the people of his day? Was it different from the message of the Old Testament? Was it different from Jesus' message? What does it mean to have a changed heart and live a changed life today?

THURSDAY

"Come, Follow Me"

Matthew 4:12—5:12

Jesus Begins Work in Galilee

When Jesus heard that John had
been put in prison, he went back to
Galilee. 13 He left Nazareth and went
to live in Capernaum, a town near
Lake Galilee, in the area near
Zebulun and Naphtali. 14 Jesus did
this to bring about what the prophet
Isaiah had said:

15 "Land of Zebulun and land of
Naphtali
along the sea,
beyond the Jordan River.
This is Galilee where the non-
Jewish people live.
16 These people who live in darkness
will see a great light.
They live in a place covered with
the shadows of death,
but a light will shine on them."

Isaiah 9:1-2

Jesus Chooses Some Followers

From that time Jesus began to
preach, saying, "Change your hearts
and lives, because the kingdom of
heaven is near."

18 As Jesus was walking by Lake
Galilee, he saw two brothers, Simon
(called Peter) and his brother Andrew. They were throwing a net into
the lake because they were fishermen. 19 Jesus said, "Come follow me,
and I will make you fish for people."
20 So Simon and Andrew immediately
left their nets and followed him.

21 As Jesus continued walking by
Lake Galilee, he saw two other
brothers, James and John, the sons
of Zebedee. They were in a boat with
their father Zebedee, mending their
nets. Jesus told them to come with
him. 22 Immediately they left the boat
and their father, and they followed
Jesus.

Jesus Teaches and Heals People

Jesus went everywhere in Galilee,
teaching in the synagogues, preaching the Good News about the kingdom of heaven, and healing all the
people's diseases and sicknesses.
24 The news about Jesus spread all
over Syria, and people brought all the
sick to him. They were suffering from
different kinds of diseases. Some
were in great pain, some had demons, some were epileptics, and
some were paralyzed. Jesus healed all
of them. 25 Many people from Galilee,
the Ten Towns, Jerusalem, Judea,
and the land across the Jordan River
followed him.

Jesus Teaches the People

5 When Jesus saw the crowds, he
went up on a hill and sat down.
His followers came to him, 2 and he
began to teach them, saying:

3 "Those people who know they
have great spiritual needs
are happy,
because the kingdom of
heaven belongs to them.
4 Those who are sad now are
happy,
because God will comfort them.
5 Those who are humble are happy,
because the earth will belong
to them.

[6]Those who want to do right more
than anything else are
happy,
because God will fully satisfy
them.
[7]Those who show mercy to others
are happy,
because God will show mercy
to them.
[8]Those who are pure in their
thinking are happy,
because they will be with God.
[9]Those who work to bring peace
are happy,
because God will call them his
children.
[10]Those who are treated badly for
doing good are happy,
because the kingdom of
heaven belongs to them.
[11] "People will insult you and hurt
you. They will lie and say all kinds
of evil things about you because you
follow me. But when they do, you
will be happy. [12] Rejoice and be glad,
because you have a great reward
waiting for you in heaven. People did
the same evil things to the prophets
who lived before you."

OLD TESTAMENT READING

The LORD said to Abram, "Leave
your country, your relatives, and
your father's family, and go to the
land I will show you.
[2]I will make you a great nation,
and I will bless you.
I will make you famous,
and you will be a blessing to
others."
[4] So Abram left Haran as the LORD
had told him, and Lot went with him.
At this time Abram was seventy-five
years old.

Genesis 12:1, 2, 4

INSIGHTS

Today, in principle, the call of the Lord Jesus has not changed. He still says 'Follow me', and adds, 'whoever of you does not renounce all that he has cannot be my disciple'. In practice, however, this does not mean for the majority of Christians a physical departure from their home or their job. It implies rather an inner surrender of both, and a refusal to allow either family or ambition to occupy the first place in our lives.

First, there must be a renunciation of sin. This, in a word, is repentance. It is the first part of Christian conversion. It can in no circumstances be bypassed. Repentance and faith belong together. We cannot follow Christ without forsaking sin. . . .

Second, there must be a renunciation of self. In order to follow Christ we must not only forsake isolated sins, but renounce the very principle of self-will which lies at the root of every act of sin. To follow Christ is to surrender to him the rights over our own lives. It is to abdicate the throne of our heart and do homage to him as our King. . . .

The full, inexorable demand of Jesus Christ is now laid bare. He does not call us to a sloppy half-heartedness, but to a vigorous, absolute commitment. He calls us to make him our Lord.

John Stott

ACTION POINT

What have you had to forsake in order to follow Jesus? Think about what occupies first place in your life now. Pray that you will make following Jesus most important.

FRIDAY

Take God's Light into the World

Matthew 5:13–37

You Are like Salt and Light

You are the salt of the earth. But if
the salt loses its salty taste, it cannot be made salty again. It is good
for nothing, except to be thrown out
and walked on.
14 "You are the light that gives
light to the world. A city that is built
on a hill cannot be hidden. 15 And
people don't hide a light under a
bowl. They put it on a lampstand so
the light shines for all the people in
the house. 16 In the same way, you
should be a light for other people.
Live so that they will see the good
things you do and will praise your
Father in heaven.

The Importance of the Law

Don't think that I have come to destroy the law of Moses or the teaching of the prophets. I have not come
to destroy them but to bring about
what they said. 18 I tell you the truth,
nothing will disappear from the law
until heaven and earth are gone. Not
even the smallest letter or the smallest part of a letter will be lost until
everything has happened. 19 Whoever refuses to obey any command
and teaches other people not to obey
that command will be the least important in the kingdom of heaven.
But whoever obeys the commands
and teaches other people to obey
them will be great in the kingdom
of heaven. 20 I tell you that if you are
no more obedient than the teachers
of the law and the Pharisees, you will
never enter the kingdom of heaven.

Jesus Teaches About Anger

You have heard that it was said to our
people long ago, 'You must not murder anyone. Anyone who murders another will be judged.' 22 But I tell you,
if you are angry with a brother or sister, you will be judged. If you say bad
things to a brother or sister, you will
be judged by the council. And if you
call someone a fool, you will be in danger of the fire of hell.
23 "So when you offer your gift to
God at the altar, and you remember
that your brother or sister has something against you, 24 leave your gift
there at the altar. Go and make peace
with that person, and then come and
offer your gift.
25 "If your enemy is taking you to
court, become friends quickly, before
you go to court. Otherwise, your enemy might turn you over to the judge,
and the judge might give you to a
guard to put you in jail. 26 I tell you the
truth, you will not leave there until you
have paid everything you owe.

Jesus Teaches About Sexual Sin

You have heard that it was said,
'You must not be guilty of adultery.'
28 But I tell you that if anyone looks
at a woman and wants to sin sexually with her, in his mind he has already done that sin with the woman.
29 If your right eye causes you to sin,
then take it out and throw it away. It
is better to lose one part of your
body than to have your whole body
thrown into hell. 30 If your right hand
causes you to sin, cut it off and throw
it away. It is better to lose one part

of your body than for your whole
body to go into hell.

Jesus Teaches About Divorce

It was also said, 'Anyone who divorces his wife must give her a written divorce paper.' 32 But I tell you
that anyone who divorces his wife
forces her to be guilty of adultery.
The only reason for a man to divorce
his wife is if she has sexual relations
with another man. And anyone who
marries that divorced woman is
guilty of adultery.

Make Promises Carefully

You have heard that it was said to
our people long ago, 'Don't break
your promises, but keep the promises you make to the Lord.' 34 But I
tell you, never swear an oath. Don't
swear an oath using the name of
heaven, because heaven is God's
throne. 35 Don't swear an oath using
the name of the earth, because the
earth belongs to God. Don't swear
an oath using the name of Jerusalem, because that is the city of the
great King. 36 Don't even swear by
your own head, because you cannot
make one hair on your head become
white or black. 37 Say only yes if you
mean yes, and no if you mean no. If
you say more than yes or no, it is
from the Evil One."

OLD TESTAMENT READING

People who love the LORD hate evil.
The LORD watches over those
who follow him
and frees them from the
power of the wicked.
11 Light shines on those who do
right;
joy belongs to those who are
honest.

Psalm 97:10–11

LORD, you give light to my lamp.
My God brightens the darkness around me.

Psalm 18:28

INSIGHTS

Nowhere in the Bible are we commanded to bring non-Christians into the church to get saved. In fact, there is not one instance in the Bible of anyone who ever got converted in a church or synagogue. For instance, in Luke 19, our Lord did not ask Zaccheus to meet Him at the synagogue on the Sabbath. Instead, he went to Zaccheus' home. The misconception is that the pagan is supposed to come and hear; the Biblical mandate for the believer is to go and tell.

If we are to be salt and light in our world, we need to go where the lost are. That might mean inviting them into your home for dinner, going next door to visit with them, playing miniature golf together, or doing something else with them. The Holy Spirit will start working in their lives as they watch our lives and try to figure out why we are different.

Robert Tamasy

APPLICATION

Think about what it means to be salt and light in the world today. What kind of lifestyle shines as a light to the world and shows people how to be saved? How do you need to change your life in order to be the salt and light God wants you to be?

WEEKEND

The Wonder of God's Forgiveness

Matthew 5:38—6:15

Don't Fight Back

You have heard that it was said, 'An eye for an eye, and a tooth for a tooth.' 39 But I tell you, don't stand up against an evil person. If someone slaps you on the right cheek, turn to him the other cheek also. 40 If someone wants to sue you in court and take your shirt, let him have your coat also. 41 If someone forces you to go with him one mile, go with him two miles. 42 If a person asks you for something, give it to him. Don't refuse to give to someone who wants to borrow from you.

Love All People

You have heard that it was said, 'Love your neighbor and hate your enemies.' 44 But I say to you, love your enemies. Pray for those who hurt you. 45 If you do this, you will be true children of your Father in heaven. He causes the sun to rise on good people and on evil people, and he sends rain to those who do right and to those who do wrong. 46 If you love only the people who love you, you will get no reward. Even the tax collectors do that. 47 And if you are nice only to your friends, you are no better than other people. Even those who don't know God are nice to their friends. 48 So you must be perfect, just as your Father in heaven is perfect.

Jesus Teaches About Giving

6 Be careful! When you do good things, don't do them in front of people to be seen by them. If you do that, you will have no reward from your Father in heaven.

2 "When you give to the poor, don't be like the hypocrites. They blow trumpets in the synagogues and on the streets so that people will see them and honor them. I tell you the truth, those hypocrites already have their full reward. 3 So when you give to the poor, don't let anyone know what you are doing. 4 Your giving should be done in secret. Your Father can see what is done in secret, and he will reward you.

Jesus Teaches About Prayer

When you pray, don't be like the hypocrites. They love to stand in the synagogues and on the street corners and pray so people will see them. I tell you the truth, they already have their full reward. 6 When you pray, you should go into your room and close the door and pray to your Father who cannot be seen. Your Father can see what is done in secret, and he will reward you.

7 "And when you pray, don't be like those people who don't know God. They continue saying things that mean nothing, thinking that God will hear them because of their many words. 8 Don't be like them, because your Father knows the things you need before you ask him. 9 So when you pray, you should pray like this:

'Our Father in heaven,
may your name always be kept
holy.

[10]May your kingdom come
and what you want be done,
here on earth as it is in heaven.
[11]Give us the food we need for each day.
[12]Forgive us for our sins,
just as we have forgiven those
who sinned against us.
[13]And do not cause us to be tempted,
but save us from the Evil One.'
[14]Yes, if you forgive others for their
sins, your Father in heaven will also
forgive you for your sins. [15]But if you
don't forgive others, your Father in
heaven will not forgive your sins."

OLD TESTAMENT READING

LORD, tell me your ways.
Show me how to live.
[5]Guide me in your truth,
and teach me, my God, my Savior.
I trust you all day long.
[6]LORD, remember your mercy and love
that you have shown since long ago.
[7]Do not remember the sins
and wrong things I did when I was young.
But remember to love me always
because you are good, LORD.

Psalm 25:4–7

INSIGHTS

Scripture is realistic in its treatment of sin, whether in the believer or unbeliever. It recognizes that sin is a continuing problem, even for the believer. He is not forever done with sin when he is converted, because he never gets beyond the reach of temptation. True, he has experienced the joy of forgiveness. He revels in the assurance that his guilt has been removed, but he is nowhere promised exemption from the lure of temptation or the possibility of sinning. . . .

Then how is it possible for a God who hates sin and requires purity, to continue having dealings with a sin-prone believer, to say nothing of permitting a deepening intimacy? The answer is that in the multi-faceted death of His Son, provision is made for a cleaning so deep, so radical, so continuous that a believer can walk with God in unbroken communion and deepening fellowship.

J. Oswald Sanders

ACTION POINT

In your own words, describe how God wants his people to pray. Why do you think seeking God's forgiveness is an essential part of prayer? Approach God now in prayer. Make yourself pure before him and share with him all that is in your heart.

MONDAY

God Wants Us to Seek, Honor, and Trust Him

Matthew 6:16—7:6

Jesus Teaches About Worship

When you give up eating, don't
put on a sad face like the hypocrites.
They make their faces look sad to
show people they are giving up eating. I tell you the truth, those hypocrites already have their full reward.
17 So when you give up eating, comb
your hair and wash your face.
18 Then people will not know that
you are giving up eating, but your
Father, whom you cannot see, will
see you. Your Father sees what is
done in secret, and he will reward
you.

God Is More Important than Money

Don't store treasures for yourselves here on earth where moths
and rust will destroy them and
thieves can break in and steal them.
20 But store your treasures in
heaven where they cannot be destroyed by moths or rust and where
thieves cannot break in and steal
them. 21 Your heart will be where
your treasure is.

22 "The eye is a light for the body.
If your eyes are good, your whole
body will be full of light. 23 But if your
eyes are evil, your whole body will
be full of darkness. And if the only
light you have is really darkness,
then you have the worst darkness.

24 "No one can serve two masters.
The person will hate one master and
love the other, or will follow one master and refuse to follow the other.
You cannot serve both God and
worldly riches.

Don't Worry

So I tell you, don't worry about
the food or drink you need to live,
or about the clothes you need for
your body. Life is more than food,
and the body is more than clothes.
26 Look at the birds in the air. They
don't plant or harvest or store food
in barns, but your heavenly Father
feeds them. And you know that
you are worth much more than
the birds. 27 You cannot add any
time to your life by worrying about
it.

28 "And why do you worry about
clothes? Look at how the lilies in the
field grow. They don't work or make
clothes for themselves. 29 But I tell
you that even Solomon with his
riches was not dressed as beautifully
as one of these flowers. 30 God
clothes the grass in the field, which
is alive today but tomorrow is
thrown into the fire. So you can be
even more sure that God will clothe
you. Don't have so little faith! 31 Don't
worry and say, 'What will we eat?'
or 'What will we drink?' or 'What will
we wear?' 32 The people who don't
know God keep trying to get these
things, and your Father in heaven
knows you need them. 33 The thing
you should want most is God's kingdom and doing what God wants.
Then all these other things you need
will be given to you. 34 So don't worry
about tomorrow, because tomorrow
will have its own worries. Each day
has enough trouble of its own.

Be Careful About Judging Others

7 Don't judge other people, or
you will be judged. 2 You will
be judged in the same way that
you judge others, and the amount
you give to others will be given
to you.
3 "Why do you notice the little
piece of dust in your friend's eye, but
you don't notice the big piece of
wood in your own eye? 4 How can
you say to your friend, 'Let me take
that little piece of dust out of your
eye'? Look at yourself! You still have
that big piece of wood in your own
eye. 5 You hypocrite! First, take the
wood out of your own eye. Then you
will see clearly to take the dust out
of your friend's eye.
6 "Don't give holy things to dogs,
and don't throw your pearls before
pigs. Pigs will only trample on
them, and dogs will turn to attack
you."

OLD TESTAMENT READING

On the twenty-fourth day of that
same month, the people of Israel
gathered. They did not eat, and they
wore rough cloth and put dust on
their heads to show their sadness.
2 Those people whose ancestors
were from Israel had separated
themselves from all foreigners. They
stood and confessed their sins and
their ancestors' sins. 3 For a fourth
of the day they stood where they
were and read from the Book of the
Teachings of the LORD their God. For
another fourth of the day they confessed their sins and worshiped the
LORD their God.

Nehemiah 9:1–3

The LORD says, "Even now,
come back to me with all
your heart.
Go without food, and cry and
be sad."
13 Tearing your clothes is not
enough to show you are sad;
let your heart be broken.
Come back to the LORD your God,
because he is kind and shows
mercy.
He doesn't become angry quickly,
and he has great love.

Joel 2:12–13c

INSIGHTS

Our problem is that we want to test God rather than trust him. We want to experiment with him rather than rely on him. We're like the boy who tests the doubtful ice instead of skating confidently where God is leading. What is our faith worth if we don't trust completely? It is perfectly natural to trust in our own understanding, to rely on our own natural strengths, gifts, or talents (and indeed some modern prophets tell us to do so!). But it is the walk of faith to trust his teaching and direction. Give him first place and let him have precedence. This is the secret of safe guidance and peaceful progression. Simple dependence upon him, committing our all to him, obeying him implicitly—this is how to acknowledge him "in all thy ways."

Al Bryant

APPLICATION

Describe the kind of life that truly honors God. In what ways do you trust and seek God on a daily basis?

TUESDAY

There Is Wisdom and Goodness in Walking in God's Ways

Matthew 7:7—8:4

Ask God for What You Need

Ask, and God will give to you. Search, and you will find. Knock, and the door will open for you. [8]Yes, everyone who asks will receive. Everyone who searches will find. And everyone who knocks will have the door opened.

[9]"If your children ask for bread, which of you would give them a stone? [10]Or if your children ask for a fish, would you give them a snake? [11]Even though you are bad, you know how to give good gifts to your children. How much more your heavenly Father will give good things to those who ask him!

The Most Important Rule

Do to others what you want them to do to you. This is the meaning of the law of Moses and the teaching of the prophets.

The Way to Heaven Is Hard

Enter through the narrow gate. The gate is wide and the road is wide that leads to hell, and many people enter through that gate. [14]But the gate is small and the road is narrow that leads to true life. Only a few people find that road.

People Know You by Your Actions

Be careful of false prophets. They come to you looking gentle like sheep, but they are really dangerous like wolves. [16]You will know these people by what they do. Grapes don't come from thornbushes, and figs don't come from thorny weeds. [17]In the same way, every good tree produces good fruit, but a bad tree produces bad fruit. [18]A good tree cannot produce bad fruit, and a bad tree cannot produce good fruit. [19]Every tree that does not produce good fruit is cut down and thrown into the fire. [20]In the same way, you will know these false prophets by what they do.

[21]"Not all those who say that I am their Lord will enter the kingdom of heaven. The only people who will enter the kingdom of heaven are those who do what my Father in heaven wants. [22]On the last day many people will say to me, 'Lord, Lord, we spoke for you, and through you we forced out demons and did many miracles.' [23]Then I will tell them clearly, 'Get away from me, you who do evil. I never knew you.'

Two Kinds of People

Everyone who hears my words and obeys them is like a wise man who built his house on rock. [25]It rained hard, the floods came, and the winds blew and hit that house. But it did not fall, because it was built on rock. [26]Everyone who hears my words and does not obey them is like a foolish man who built his house on sand. [27]It rained hard, the floods came, and the winds blew and hit that house, and it fell with a big crash."

[28]When Jesus finished saying
these things, the people were amazed
at his teaching, [29]because he did not
teach like their teachers of the law.
He taught like a person who had authority.

Jesus Heals a Sick Man

8 When Jesus came down from the
hill, great crowds followed him.
2 Then a man with a skin disease
came to Jesus. The man bowed
down before him and said, "Lord,
you can heal me if you will."
3 Jesus reached out his hand and
touched the man and said, "I will. Be
healed!" And immediately the man
was healed from his disease. 4 Then
Jesus said to him, "Don't tell anyone
about this. But go and show yourself
to the priest and offer the gift Moses
commanded for people who are
made well. This will show the people
what I have done."

OLD TESTAMENT READING

Happy are those who don't
listen to the wicked,
who don't go where sinners go,
who don't do what evil people do.
2 They love the LORD's teachings,
and they think about those
teachings day and night.
3 They are strong, like a tree
planted by a river.
The tree produces fruit in season,
and its leaves don't die.
Everything they do will succeed.

Psalm 1:1–3

When a person's steps follow
the LORD,
God is pleased with his ways.
24 If he stumbles, he will not fall,
because the LORD holds his
hand.

Psalm 37:23, 24

INSIGHTS

It must be admitted that, in its first stages, the broad way is generally easy and rather delightful. The boat launched on the flowing stream sweeps merrily and pleasantly along, the gradient of the road slopes so as to make walking easy, the sun shines, and the path is filled with bright flowers. But to a life given up to self-indulgence, there is only one end—destruction.

There is a more excellent way, but it is too narrow to admit the trailing garments of passionate desire, too narrow for pride, self-indulgence, greed, and avarice—it is the Way of the Cross, but it leads to Life! We all want to see life—and the remarkable thing is that those who expect to get most out of it by self-indulgence miss everything; whilst those who seem to curtail their lives by following Christ, win everything. Few find and enter this path, is the lament of our Lord. Let us put our hand in His, that He may lead us into the path of life, "that shineth more and more unto the perfect day."

F. B. Meyer

APPLICATION

What good things does God promise to those who search for him and walk in his ways? What kind of person makes the decision to walk through the narrow gate and build on the Rock? What kind of person are you? On what path do you walk? What will be the reward of that path?

WEDNESDAY:
Jesus' Amazing Authority

Matthew 8:5–27

Jesus Heals a Soldier's Servant

When Jesus entered the city of
Capernaum, an army officer came to
him, begging for help. 6 The officer
said, "Lord, my servant is at home
in bed. He can't move his body and
is in much pain."
7 Jesus said to the officer, "I will
go and heal him."
8 The officer answered, "Lord, I
am not worthy for you to come into
my house. You only need to command it, and my servant will be
healed. 9 I, too, am a man under the
authority of others, and I have soldiers under my command. I tell one
soldier, 'Go,' and he goes. I tell another soldier, 'Come,' and he comes.
I say to my servant, 'Do this,' and my
servant does it.
10 When Jesus heard this, he was
amazed. He said to those who were
following him, "I tell you the truth,
this is the greatest faith I have found,
even in Israel. 11 Many people will
come from the east and from the
west and will sit and eat with
Abraham, Isaac, and Jacob in the
kingdom of heaven. 12 But those
people who should be in the kingdom will be thrown outside into the
darkness, where people will cry and
grind their teeth with pain."
13 Then Jesus said to the officer,
"Go home. Your servant will be
healed just as you believed he
would." And his servant was healed
that same hour.

Jesus Heals Many People

When Jesus went to Peter's house,
he saw that Peter's mother-in-law
was sick in bed with a fever. 15 Jesus
touched her hand, and the fever left
her. Then she stood up and began
to serve Jesus.
16 That evening people brought to
Jesus many who had demons. Jesus
spoke and the demons left them, and
he healed all the sick. 17 He did these
things to bring about what Isaiah the
prophet had said:

"He took our suffering on him
and carried our diseases."

Isaiah 53:4

People Want to Follow Jesus

When Jesus saw the crowd around
him, he told his followers to go to the
other side of the lake. 19 Then a
teacher of the law came to Jesus and
said, "Teacher, I will follow you any
place you go."
20 Jesus said to him, "The foxes
have holes to live in, and the birds
have nests, but the Son of Man has
no place to rest his head."
21 Another man, one of Jesus' followers, said to him, "Lord, first let
me go and bury my father."
22 But Jesus told him, "Follow me,
and let the people who are dead bury
their own dead."

Jesus Calms a Storm

Jesus got into a boat, and his followers went with him. 24 A great storm
arose on the lake so that waves covered the boat, but Jesus was sleeping. 25 His followers went to him and
woke him, saying, "Lord, save us!
We will drown!"

26 Jesus answered, "Why are you afraid? You don't have enough faith." Then Jesus got up and gave a command to the wind and the waves, and it became completely calm.

27 The men were amazed and said, "What kind of man is this? Even the wind and the waves obey him!"

OLD TESTAMENT READING

My whole being, praise the
LORD.
LORD my God, you are very
great.
You are clothed with glory and
majesty;
2 you wear light like a robe.
You stretch out the skies like a
tent.
3 You build your room above the
clouds.
You make the clouds your
chariot,
and you ride on the wings of
the wind.
4 You make the winds your messengers,
and flames of fire are your
servants.
31 May the glory of the LORD be
forever.
May the LORD enjoy what he
has made.
32 He just looks at the earth, and it
shakes.
He touches the mountains, and
they smoke.

33 I will sing to the LORD all my life;
I will sing praises to my God as
long as I live.

Psalm 104:1–4, 31–33

INSIGHTS

When Jesus was on earth He displayed remarkable powers. He raised Lazarus from the dead and performed many other miracles. His contemporaries noted an element of His power that we sometimes do not—the power of His speaking. The gospel writers reported that Jesus did not speak like the scribes and the Pharisees but as one "having authority" (see Matt. 7:29). . . .

Behind the authority of Jesus stood the omnipotent power of God, the link to Jesus' divine authority. The very word authority hints at a connection to the word authorship. God is the omnipotent author of His creation. He is the omnipotent redeemer of His creation. He exercises omnipotent authority over His creation.

R. C. Sproul

PAUSE FOR REFLECTION

In what ways did Jesus' followers see his powerful authority demonstrated? In what did the psalmist recognize his authority? What reveals his authority to you? Is his authority as real to you as to the army officer?

THURSDAY

God Forgives and Saves

Matthew 8:28—9:17

Jesus Heals Two Men with Demons

When Jesus arrived at the other
side of the lake in the area of the
Gadarene people, two men who had
demons in them met him. These
men lived in the burial caves and
were so dangerous that people could
not use the road by those caves.
29 They shouted, "What do you want
with us, Son of God? Did you come
here to torture us before the right
time?"
30 Near that place there was a
large herd of pigs feeding. 31 The
demons begged Jesus, "If you make
us leave these men, please send us
into that herd of pigs."
32 Jesus said to them, "Go!" So the
demons left the men and went into
the pigs. Then the whole herd rushed
down the hill into the lake and were
drowned. 33 The herdsmen ran away
and went into town, where they told
about all of this and what had happened to the men who had demons.
34 Then the whole town went out to
see Jesus. When they saw him, they
begged him to leave their area.

Jesus Heals a Paralyzed Man

9 Jesus got into a boat and went
back across the lake to his own
town. 2 Some people brought to
Jesus a man who was paralyzed and
lying on a mat. When Jesus saw the
faith of these people, he said to the
paralyzed man, "Be encouraged,
young man. Your sins are forgiven."
3 Some of the teachers of the law
said to themselves, "This man speaks
as if he were God. That is blasphemy!"
4 Knowing their thoughts, Jesus
said, "Why are you thinking evil
thoughts? 5 Which is easier: to say,
'Your sins are forgiven,' or to tell
him, 'Stand up and walk'? 6 But I will
prove to you that the Son of Man has
authority on earth to forgive sins."
Then Jesus said to the paralyzed
man, "Stand up, take your mat, and
go home." 7 And the man stood up
and went home. 8 When the people
saw this, they were amazed and
praised God for giving power like
this to human beings.

Jesus Chooses Matthew

When Jesus was leaving, he saw a
man named Matthew sitting in the
tax collector's booth. Jesus said to
him, "Follow me," and he stood up
and followed Jesus.
10 As Jesus was having dinner at
Matthew's house, many tax collectors and "sinners" came and ate with
Jesus and his followers. 11 When the
Pharisees saw this, they asked Jesus'
followers, "Why does your teacher
eat with tax collectors and sinners?"
12 When Jesus heard them, he
said, "It is not the healthy people
who need a doctor, but the sick. 13 Go
and learn what this means: 'I want
kindness more than I want animal
sacrifices.' I did not come to invite
good people but to invite sinners."

Jesus' Followers Are Criticized

Then the followers of John came to
Jesus and said, "Why do we and the

Pharisees often give up eating for a
certain time, but your followers
don't?"
15 Jesus answered, "The friends of
the bridegroom are not sad while he
is with them. But the time will come
when the bridegroom will be taken
from them, and then they will give
up eating.
16 "No one sews a patch of
unshrunk cloth over a hole in an old
coat. If he does, the patch will shrink
and pull away from the coat, making
the hole worse. 17 Also, people never
pour new wine into old leather bags.
Otherwise, the bags will break, the
wine will spill, and the wine bags will
be ruined. But people always pour
new wine into new wine bags. Then
both will continue to be good."

OLD TESTAMENT READING

The LORD shows mercy and is
kind.
He does not become angry
quickly, and he has great
love.
9 He will not always accuse us,
and he will not be angry forever.
10 He has not punished us as our
sins should be punished;
he has not repaid us for the
evil we have done.
11 As high as the sky is above the
earth,
so great is his love for those
who respect him.
12 He has taken our sins away from
us
as far as the east is from west.
13 The LORD has mercy on those
who respect him,
as a father has mercy on his
children.

Psalm 103:8–13

INSIGHTS

Other faiths assume our ability to secure and retain God's favor by right action and give us detailed guidance as to how to do it; but Christianity has said that sin has so ruined us that we cannot do this. It is beyond our power to keep the law of God as we should; we are guilty and helpless, wholly unable to save ourselves, and so must be saved, if at all, by the action of another.

Other faiths direct us to follow the teaching of their founders—famous men long deceased; but Christianity, identifying its founder as God incarnate, who died for our sins and rose again to bestow forgiveness, proclaims him as alive and calls on us to trust him and his atoning work, making him the object of our worship and service. Redemption through the love of the Son of God, who became man, bore his Father's judgment on our sins, and rose from death to reign forever, is a theme without parallel in the world's religions.

Christianity proclaims that those who repent of sin and trust in Jesus Christ are created anew at the heart of their being by the Holy Spirit. They are united to Jesus Christ in his risen life, their inner nature is changed, so that their deepest impulse is not now to disobey God and serve self, but to deny self and obey God. There is nothing like this in any other religion.

J. I. Packer

APPLICATION

If Jesus is our example, what should our attitude toward sinners be?

FRIDAY

Jesus' Great Compassion for His Lost Sheep

Matthew 9:18—10:10

Jesus Gives Life to a Dead Girl and Heals a Sick Woman

While Jesus was saying these things, a leader of the synagogue came to him. He bowed down before Jesus and said, "My daughter has just died. But if you come and lay your hand on her, she will live again." 19 So Jesus and his followers stood up and went with the leader.

20 Then a woman who had been bleeding for twelve years came behind Jesus and touched the edge of his coat. 21 She was thinking, "If I can just touch his clothes, I will be healed."

22 Jesus turned and saw the woman and said, "Be encouraged, dear woman. You are made well because you believed." And the woman was healed from that moment on.

23 Jesus continued along with the leader and went into his house. There he saw the funeral musicians and many people crying. 24 Jesus said, "Go away. The girl is not dead, only asleep." But the people laughed at him. 25 After the crowd had been thrown out of the house, Jesus went into the girl's room and took hold of her hand, and she stood up. 26 The news about this spread all around the area.

Jesus Heals More People

When Jesus was leaving there, two blind men followed him. They cried out, "Have mercy on us, Son of David!"

28 After Jesus went inside, the blind men went with him. He asked the men, "Do you believe that I can make you see again?"

They answered, "Yes, Lord."

29 Then Jesus touched their eyes and said, "Because you believe I can make you see again, it will happen." 30 Then the men were able to see. But Jesus warned them strongly, saying, "Don't tell anyone about this." 31 But the blind men left and spread the news about Jesus all around that area.

32 When the two men were leaving, some people brought another man to Jesus. This man could not talk because he had a demon in him. 33 After Jesus forced the demon to leave the man, he was able to speak. The crowd was amazed and said, "We have never seen anything like this in Israel."

34 But the Pharisees said, "The prince of demons is the one that gives him power to force demons out."

35 Jesus traveled through all the towns and villages, teaching in their synagogues, preaching the Good News about the kingdom, and healing all kinds of diseases and sicknesses. 36 When he saw the crowds, he felt sorry for them because they were hurting and helpless, like sheep without a shepherd. 37 Jesus said to his followers, "There are many people to harvest but only a few workers to help harvest them. 38 Pray to the Lord, who owns the harvest, that he will send more workers to gather his harvest."

Jesus Sends Out His Apostles

10 Jesus called his twelve followers together and gave them
authority to drive out evil spirits and
to heal every kind of disease and
sickness. 2 These are the names of
the twelve apostles: Simon (also
called Peter) and his brother Andrew; James son of Zebedee, and
his brother John; 3 Philip and
Bartholomew; Thomas and Matthew, the tax collector; James son of
Alphaeus, and Thaddaeus; 4 Simon
the Zealot and Judas Iscariot, who
turned against Jesus.
5 Jesus sent out these twelve men
with the following order: "Don't go
to the non-Jewish people or to any
town where the Samaritans live.
6 But go to the people of Israel, who
are like lost sheep. 7 When you go,
preach this: 'The kingdom of
heaven is near.' 8 Heal the sick, raise
the dead to life again, heal those
who have skin diseases, and force
demons out of people. I give you
these powers freely, so help other
people freely. 9 Don't carry any
money with you—gold or silver or
copper. 10 Don't carry a bag or extra clothes or sandals or a walking
stick. Workers should be given
what they need."

OLD TESTAMENT READING

I will feed my flock and lead them
to rest, says the Lord GOD. 16 I will
search for the lost, bring back those
that strayed away, put bandages on
those that were hurt, and make the
weak strong. But I will destroy those
sheep that are fat and strong. I will
tend the sheep with fairness.'"

Ezekiel 34:15–16

INSIGHTS

The nature of God is to seek and to save sinners. From the opening pages of human history, it was God who sought the fallen couple in the garden. . . . The Almighty was portrayed as a Savior throughout the Old Testament (Psalm 106:21; Isaiah 43:11; Hosea 13:4), so it is appropriate that when Christ entered the world of men as God in human flesh, He was known first of all as a Savior.

Even His name was divinely chosen to be the name of a Savior. An angel told Joseph in a dream, "You shall call His name Jesus, for it is He who will save His people from their sins" (Matthew 1:21). The very heart of all redemptive teaching is that Jesus entered this world on a search-and-rescue mission for sinners. That truth is what characterizes the gospel as good news.

But it is good news only for those who perceive themselves as sinners. The unequivocal teaching of Jesus is that those who will not acknowledge and repent of their sin are beyond the reach of saving grace. All are sinners, but not all are willing to admit their depravity. If they do, He becomes their friend (cf. Matthew 11:19). Those who will not can know Him only as a Judge.

John F. MacArthur, Jr.

ACTION POINT

In what ways is God's compassion for the lost expressed in these passages of Scripture? How does God want to care for his people? Thank him for the ways he has shown his compassion to you.

WEEKEND

The Price of Following Jesus

Matthew 10:11–40

When you enter a city or town,
find some worthy person there and
stay in that home until you leave.
12 When you enter that home, say,
'Peace be with you.' 13 If the people
there welcome you, let your peace
stay there. But if they don't welcome
you, take back the peace you wished
for them. 14 And if a home or town
refuses to welcome you or listen to
you, leave that place and shake its
dust off your feet. 15 I tell you the
truth, on the Judgment Day it will be
better for the towns of Sodom and
Gomorrah than for the people of that
town.

Jesus Warns His Apostles

Listen, I am sending you out like
sheep among wolves. So be as smart
as snakes and as innocent as doves.
17 Be careful of people, because they
will arrest you and take you to court
and whip you in their synagogues.
18 Because of me you will be taken
to stand before governors and kings,
and you will tell them and the non-
Jewish people about me. 19 When you
are arrested, don't worry about what
to say or how to say it. At that time
you will be given the things to say.
20 It will not really be you speaking
but the Spirit of your Father speaking through you.
21 "Brothers will give their own
brothers to be killed, and fathers will
give their own children to be killed.
Children will fight against their own
parents and have them put to death.
22 All people will hate you because
you follow me, but those people who
keep their faith until the end will be
saved. 23 When you are treated badly
in one city, run to another city. I tell
you the truth, you will not finish going through all the cities of Israel
before the Son of Man comes.
24 "A student is not better than his
teacher, and a servant is not better
than his master. 25 A student should
be satisfied to become like his
teacher; a servant should be satisfied
to become like his master. If the head
of the family is called Beelzebul,
then the other members of the family will be called worse names!

Fear God, Not People

So don't be afraid of those people,
because everything that is hidden
will be shown. Everything that is
secret will be made known. 27 I tell
you these things in the dark, but I
want you to tell them in the light.
What you hear whispered in your
ear you should shout from the
housetops. 28 Don't be afraid of
people, who can kill the body but
cannot kill the soul. The only one
you should fear is the one who can
destroy the soul and the body in hell.
29 Two sparrows cost only a penny,
but not even one of them can die
without your Father's knowing it.
30 God even knows how many hairs
are on your head. 31 So don't be
afraid. You are worth much more
than many sparrows.

Tell People About Your Faith

All those who stand before others
and say they believe in me, I will say

before my Father in heaven that they
belong to me. 33 But all who stand
before others and say they do not
believe in me, I will say before my
Father in heaven that they do not
belong to me.
34 "Don't think that I came to bring
peace to the earth. I did not come to
bring peace, but a sword. 35 I have
come so that

'a son will be against his father,
a daughter will be against her
mother,
a daughter-in-law will be against
her mother-in-law.
36 A person's enemies will be
members of his own family.'

Micah 7:6

37 "Those who love their father or
mother more than they love me are
not worthy to be my followers.
Those who love their son or daughter more than they love me are not
worthy to be my followers. 38 Whoever is not willing to carry the cross
and follow me is not worthy of me.
39 Those who try to hold on to their
lives will give up true life. Those who
give up their lives for me will hold
on to true life. 40 Whoever accepts
you also accepts me, and whoever
accepts me also accepts the One
who sent me."

OLD TESTAMENT READING

I tell the people about the
message I received from the
LORD,
but this only brings me insults.
The people make fun of me all
day long.
9 Sometimes I say to myself,
"I will forget about the LORD.
I will not speak anymore in his
name."
But then his message becomes
like a burning fire inside me,
deep within my bones.
I get tired of trying to hold it
inside of me,
and finally, I cannot hold it in.

Jeremiah 20:8c–9

INSIGHTS

In the Sermon on the Mount Jesus said that those who suffer unjust treatment will have a "great" reward in heaven (see Matt. 5:10). The elect who have been abused, abandoned, stolen from, taken advantage of—all will be rewarded for their pain. . . .

God knows when we suffer unjustly. . . . God has not abandoned you to the whims and wishes of those who are more powerful. He knows when His children are overlooked for advancement because of their religious views. Young lady, He knows when less talented women are advanced past you because you refuse to compromise morally. He sees the abandoned mother who never knows from month to month if her estranged husband is going to send a check. God is taking it all in. He has already appointed a prosecuting attorney, a jury, and a judge. And they are all the same person—the Lord Jesus. On that court date He will bring about justice for His elect.

Charles Stanley

PAUSE FOR REFLECTION

How intensely does the desire to speak about Jesus burn within you? What price are you willing to pay to follow Jesus? What gives you comfort as you seek to follow him? What is your reward?

MONDAY

God Has Sent His Kingdom; Don't Reject It Foolishly!

Matthew 10:41—11:24

Whoever meets a prophet and accepts him will receive the reward of
a prophet. And whoever accepts a
good person because that person is
good will receive the reward of a
good person. 42 Those who give one
of these little ones a cup of cold water because they are my followers
will truly get their reward."

Jesus and John the Baptist

11 After Jesus finished telling
these things to his twelve followers, he left there and went to the
towns in Galilee to teach and preach.
2 John the Baptist was in prison,
but he heard about what Christ was
doing. So John sent some of his followers to Jesus. 3 They asked him,
"Are you the One who is to come,
or should we wait for someone else?"
4 Jesus answered them, "Go tell
John what you hear and see: 5 The
blind can see, the crippled can walk,
and people with skin diseases are
healed. The deaf can hear, the dead
are raised to life, and the Good News
is preached to the poor. 6 Those who
do not stumble in their faith because
of me are blessed."
7 As John's followers were leaving,
Jesus began talking to the people
about John. Jesus said, "What did
you go out into the desert to see? A
reed blown by the wind? 8 What did
you go out to see? A man dressed in
fine clothes? No, those who wear
fine clothes live in kings' palaces.
9 So why did you go out? To see a
prophet? Yes, and I tell you, John is
more than a prophet. 10 This was
written about him:

'I will send my messenger ahead
of you,
who will prepare the way for
you.' *Malachi 3:1*

11 I tell you the truth, John the Baptist is greater than any other person
ever born, but even the least important person in the kingdom of heaven
is greater than John. 12 Since the time
John the Baptist came until now, the
kingdom of heaven has been going
forward in strength, and people have
been trying to take it by force. 13 All
the prophets and the law of Moses
told about what would happen until
the time John came. 14 And if you will
believe what they said, you will believe that John is Elijah, whom they
said would come. 15 You people who
can hear me, listen!
16 "What can I say about the people
of this time? What are they like? They
are like children sitting in the marketplace, who call out to each other,
17 'We played music for you, but
you did not dance;
we sang a sad song, but you
did not cry.'
18 John came and did not eat or drink
like other people. So people say, 'He
has a demon.' 19 The Son of Man
came, eating and drinking, and
people say, 'Look at him! He eats too
much and drinks too much wine,
and he is a friend of tax collectors
and sinners.' But wisdom is proved
to be right by what it does."

Jesus Warns Unbelievers

Then Jesus criticized the cities

where he did most of his miracles,
because the people did not change
their lives and stop sinning. 21 He
said, "How terrible for you, Korazin!
How terrible for you, Bethsaida! If
the same miracles I did in you had
happened in Tyre and Sidon, those
people would have changed their
lives a long time ago. They would
have worn rough cloth and put ashes
on themselves to show they had
changed. 22 But I tell you, on the
Judgment Day it will be better for
Tyre and Sidon than for you. 23 And
you, Capernaum, will you be lifted
up to heaven? No, you will be thrown
down to the depths. If the miracles
I did in you had happened in Sodom,
its people would have stopped sinning, and it would still be a city today.
24 But I tell you, on the Judgment Day
it will be better for Sodom than for
you."

OLD TESTAMENT READING

You fools, how long will you be
    foolish?
24 I called, but you refused to
    listen;
  I held out my hand, but you
    paid no attention.
25 You did not follow my advice
  and did not listen when I
    corrected you.
26 So I will laugh when you are in
    trouble.

28 "Then you will call to me,
  but I will not answer.
You will look for me,
  but you will not find me.
29 It is because you rejected knowl-
    edge
  and did not choose to respect
    the LORD.
30 You did not accept my advice,
  and you rejected my correction.
31 So you will get what you deserve;
  you will get what you planned
    for others."

Proverbs 1:22a, 24–26a, 28–31

INSIGHTS

Generally speaking, God's kingdom is a synonym for God's rule. Those who choose to live in His kingdom (though still very much alive on Planet Earth) choose to live under His authority. . . .

. . . The kingdom is the invisible realm where God rules as supreme authority. That's helpful news. The bad news is that we, by nature, don't want Him to rule over us; we much prefer to please ourselves. . . .

. . . To put it bluntly, we don't want anybody other than ourselves ruling over us! Much like those people in a story Jesus once told, "We do not want this man to reign over us!" (Luke 19:14). Not until we experience a spiritual rebirth will we submit to God's rule.

Charles Swindoll

PAUSE FOR REFLECTION

What is the penalty for rejecting God's wisdom and knowledge? What does God promise to those who listen to him? What change occurs in those who accept God's kingdom? Has that change occurred in you?

TUESDAY

God Wants Faithful Love More than Sacrifices

Matthew 11:25—12:21

Jesus Offers Rest to People

At that time Jesus said, "I praise you, Father, Lord of heaven and earth, because you have hidden these things from the people who are wise and smart. But you have shown them to those who are like little children. 26 Yes, Father, this is what you really wanted.

27 "My Father has given me all things. No one knows the Son, except the Father. And no one knows the Father, except the Son and those whom the Son chooses to tell.

28 "Come to me, all of you who are tired and have heavy loads, and I will give you rest. 29 Accept my teachings and learn from me, because I am gentle and humble in spirit, and you will find rest for your lives. 30 The teaching that I ask you to accept is easy; the load I give you to carry is light."

Jesus Is Lord of the Sabbath

12 At that time Jesus was walking through some fields of grain on a Sabbath day. His followers were hungry, so they began to pick the grain and eat it. 2 When the Pharisees saw this, they said to Jesus, "Look! Your followers are doing what is unlawful to do on the Sabbath day."

3 Jesus answered, "Have you not read what David did when he and the people with him were hungry? 4 He went into God's house, and he and those with him ate the holy bread, which was lawful only for priests to eat. 5 And have you not read in the law of Moses that on every Sabbath day the priests in the Temple break this law about the Sabbath day? But the priests are not wrong for doing that. 6 I tell you that there is something here that is greater than the Temple. 7 The Scripture says, 'I want kindness more than I want animal sacrifices.' You don't really know what those words mean. If you understood them, you would not judge those who have done nothing wrong.

8 "So the Son of Man is Lord of the Sabbath day."

Jesus Heals a Man's Hand

Jesus left there and went into their synagogue, 10 where there was a man with a crippled hand. They were looking for a reason to accuse Jesus, so they asked him, "Is it right to heal on the Sabbath day?"

11 Jesus answered, "If any of you has a sheep, and it falls into a ditch on the Sabbath day, you will help it out of the ditch. 12 Surely a human being is more important than a sheep. So it is lawful to do good things on the Sabbath day."

13 Then Jesus said to the man with the crippled hand, "Hold out your hand." The man held out his hand, and it became well again, like the other hand. 14 But the Pharisees left and made plans to kill Jesus.

Jesus Is God's Chosen Servant

Jesus knew what the Pharisees were

doing, so he left that place. Many
people followed him, and he healed
all who were sick. 16 But Jesus
warned the people not to tell who he
was. 17 He did these things to bring
about what Isaiah the prophet had
said:

18 "Here is my servant whom I have chosen.
I love him, and I am pleased with him.
I will put my Spirit upon him,
and he will tell of my justice to all people.
19 He will not argue or cry out;
no one will hear his voice in the streets.
20 He will not break a crushed blade of grass
or put out even a weak flame
until he makes justice win the victory.
21 In him will the non-Jewish people find hope."

Isaiah 42:1–4

OLD TESTAMENT READING

The sacrifice God wants is a broken spirit.
God, you will not reject a heart that is broken and sorry for sin.

Psalm 51:17

INSIGHTS

"Lord," I said, "I want to be your man, not my own.
So to you I give my money, my car—even my home."
Then, smug and content, I relaxed with a smile
And whispered to God, "I bet it's been a while,
Since anyone has given so much—so freely?"

His answer surprised me. He replied, "Not really."

"Not a day has gone by since the beginning of time,
That someone hasn't offered meager nickels and dimes,
Golden altars and crosses, contributions and penance,
Stone monuments and steeples; but why not repentance?

"Your lips know no prayers. Your eyes, no compassion.
But you will go to church (when church-going's in fashion).

"Just give me a tear—a heart ready to mold.
And I'll give you a mission, a message so bold—
That a fire will be stirred where there was only death,
And your heart will be flamed by my life and my breath."

I stuck my hands in my pockets and kicked at the dirt.
It's tough to be corrected (I guess my feelings were hurt).
But it was worth the struggle to realize the thought.
That the cross isn't for sale and Christ's blood can't be bought.

Max Lucado

APPLICATION

What does God want from his people? Be specific! Think about what it means for God to want those things from you. Pray that you will understand what he wants and that your heart will be open to obey him.

WEDNESDAY

Our Words Reveal What Is in Our Hearts

Matthew 12:22–45

Jesus' Power Is from God

Then some people brought to Jesus a man who was blind and could not talk, because he had a demon. Jesus healed the man so that he could talk and see. 23 All the people were amazed and said, "Perhaps this man is the Son of David!"

24 When the Pharisees heard this, they said, "Jesus uses the power of Beelzebul, the ruler of demons, to force demons out of people."

25 Jesus knew what the Pharisees were thinking, so he said to them, "Every kingdom that is divided against itself will be destroyed. And any city or family that is divided against itself will not continue. 26 And if Satan forces out himself, then Satan is divided against himself, and his kingdom will not continue. 27 You say that I use the power of Beelzebul to force out demons. If that is true, then what power do your people use to force out demons? So they will be your judges. 28 But if I use the power of God's Spirit to force out demons, then the kingdom of God has come to you.

29 "If anyone wants to enter a strong person's house and steal his things, he must first tie up the strong person. Then he can steal the things from the house.

30 "Whoever is not with me is against me. Whoever does not work with me is working against me. 31 So I tell you, people can be forgiven for every sin and everything they say against God. But whoever speaks against the Holy Spirit will not be forgiven. 32 Anyone who speaks against the Son of Man can be forgiven, but anyone who speaks against the Holy Spirit will not be forgiven, now or in the future.

People Know You by Your Words

If you want good fruit, you must make the tree good. If your tree is not good, it will have bad fruit. A tree is known by the kind of fruit it produces. 34 You snakes! You are evil people, so how can you say anything good? The mouth speaks the things that are in the heart. 35 Good people have good things in their hearts, and so they say good things. But evil people have evil in their hearts, so they say evil things. 36 And I tell you that on the Judgment Day people will be responsible for every careless thing they have said. 37 The words you have said will be used to judge you. Some of your words will prove you right, but some of your words will prove you guilty."

The People Ask for a Miracle

Then some of the Pharisees and teachers of the law answered Jesus, saying, "Teacher, we want to see you work a miracle as a sign."

39 Jesus answered, "Evil and sinful people are the ones who want to see a miracle for a sign. But no sign will be given to them, except the sign of the prophet Jonah. 40 Jonah was in the stomach of the big fish for three days and three nights. In the same way, the Son of Man will

be in the grave three days and three
nights. 41 On the Judgment Day the
people from Nineveh will stand up
with you people who live now, and
they will show that you are guilty.
When Jonah preached to them,
they were sorry and changed their
lives. And I tell you that someone
greater than Jonah is here. 42 On the
Judgment Day, the Queen of the
South will stand up with you people
who live today. She will show that
you are guilty, because she came
from far away to listen to Solomon's
wise teaching. And I tell you that
someone greater than Solomon is
here.

People Today Are Full of Evil

When an evil spirit comes out of a
person, it travels through dry places,
looking for a place to rest, but it
doesn't find it. 44 So the spirit says, 'I
will go back to the house I left.'
When the spirit comes back, it finds
the house still empty, swept clean,
and made neat. 45 Then the evil spirit
goes out and brings seven other spirits even more evil than it is, and they
go in and live there. So the person
has even more trouble than before.
It is the same way with the evil
people who live today."

OLD TESTAMENT READING

The words of a good person are
 like pure silver,
 but an evil person's thoughts
 are worth very little.
21 Good people's words will help
 many others,
 but fools will die because they
 don't have wisdom.

Proverbs 10:20–21

INSIGHTS

The tongue is the indicator of the person. What we talk about all the time is what we love. The words we use and the words we don't use define what we are thinking, feeling, and becoming. . . .

We Christians must learn to undergo rigorous self-examination; we must honestly discern what we are really saying if we are going to understand who we are. . . .

We must listen closely to the inner reminder of this Holy Spirit. In essence, what we are doing is sticking out our tongues for the Great Physician to examine. . . . If some symptoms indicate mouth disease, we must confess to him the words that were unpleasing to him and ask forgiveness. Then we should take a dose of medicine and read from those Scriptures that emphasize healthy mouth habits. We should place the medicinal verses dealing with word usage under our tongues nightly, and let them accomplish a cathartic cleaning as we sleep so that tomorrow we can begin the day with renewed strength to speak words of life.

Karen Burton Mains

ACTION POINT

Are you intimidated by the thought of explaining every careless word you have said? Listen to your words today and write down what they reveal about your heart. Pray that your words will prove your heart to be innocent before God.

THURSDAY

Not Everyone Who Hears Understands

Matthew 12:46—13:17

Jesus' True Family

While Jesus was talking to the
people, his mother and brothers
stood outside, trying to find a way
to talk to him. 47 Someone told Jesus,
"Your mother and brothers are
standing outside, and they want to
talk to you."
48 He answered, "Who is my
mother? Who are my brothers?"
49 Then he pointed to his followers
and said, "Here are my mother and
my brothers. 50 My true brother and
sister and mother are those who do
what my Father in heaven wants."

A Story About Planting Seed

13 That same day Jesus went out
of the house and sat by the
lake. 2 Large crowds gathered
around him, so he got into a boat and
sat down, while the people stood on
the shore. 3 Then Jesus used stories
to teach them many things. He said:
"A farmer went out to plant his seed.
4 While he was planting, some seed
fell by the road, and the birds came
and ate it all up. 5 Some seed fell on
rocky ground, where there wasn't
much dirt. That seed grew very fast,
because the ground was not deep.
6 But when the sun rose, the plants
dried up, because they did not have
deep roots. 7 Some other seed fell
among thorny weeds, which grew
and choked the good plants. 8 Some
other seed fell on good ground
where it grew and produced a crop.
Some plants made a hundred times
more, some made sixty times more,
and some made thirty times more.
9 You people who can hear me, listen."

Why Jesus Used Stories to Teach

The followers came to Jesus and
asked, "Why do you use stories to
teach the people?"
11 Jesus answered, "You have
been chosen to know the secrets
about the kingdom of heaven, but
others cannot know these secrets.
12 Those who have understanding
will be given more, and they will
have all they need. But those who do
not have understanding, even what
they have will be taken away from
them. 13 This is why I use stories to
teach the people: They see, but they
don't really see. They hear, but they
don't really hear or understand. 14 So
they show that the things Isaiah said
about them are true:

'You will listen and listen, but you
will not understand.
You will look and look, but you
will not learn.
15 For the minds of these people
have become stubborn.
They do not hear with their
ears,
and they have closed their
eyes.
Otherwise they might really
understand
what they see with their eyes
and hear with their ears.
They might really understand in
their minds
and come back to me and be
healed.' *Isaiah 6:9-10*

[16] But you are blessed, because you
see with your eyes and hear with
your ears. [17] I tell you the truth, many
prophets and good people wanted to see the things that you now see, but they did not see them. And they wanted to hear the things that you now hear, but they did not hear them."

OLD TESTAMENT READING

How I love your teachings!
I think about them all day long.
[101] I have avoided every evil way
so I could obey your word.
[103] Your promises are sweet to me,
sweeter than honey in my mouth!
[104] Your orders give me understanding,
so I hate lying ways.

[105] Your word is like a lamp for my feet
and a light for my path.
[106] I will do what I have promised
and obey your fair laws.

Psalm 119:97, 101, 103–106

But they refused to pay attention; they were stubborn and did not want
to listen anymore. [12] They made their
hearts as hard as rock and would not listen to the teachings of the LORD All-Powerful. And they would not hear the words he sent by his Spirit through the earlier prophets. So the LORD All-Powerful became very angry."

Zechariah 7:11–12

INSIGHTS

Our Lord warns that the human heart can be so pounded and beaten down with the traffic of sin that it becomes completely insensitive to the gospel. This is the heart that knows no repentance, no sorrow over sin, no guilt, and no concern for the things of God. It allows itself to be trampled by an endless procession of evil thoughts, cherished sins, and ungodly activities. It is careless, callous, indifferent, never broken up or softened by conviction or sorrow for wrongdoing. This is the heart of the fool described in Proverbs. The fool hates knowledge, and resists instruction. The fool despises wisdom and says in his heart there is no God. He will not hear. His mind is closed. And he does not want to be bothered with a gospel invitation.

Many people have hearts like that. You can shower them with seed, but it just lies there. It does not penetrate. And it does not stay very long before Satan comes and takes it away completely. Each time you try to witness to such a person, you must start again at the beginning.

Dry, hard, soil on the edge of the field does not necessarily signify someone who is anti-religious. Some of the hardest individuals in the world remain on the fringes of true religion. But because sin has so hardened their hearts, they are utterly unproductive and unresponsive to God.

John F. MacArthur, Jr.

ACTION POINT

How are the teachings of Jesus received by those who follow him? Why is it that some people are unable to understand God's words? Pray for a soft heart that wants to understand all that God teaches.

FRIDAY

Hide God's Teachings in Your Heart

Matthew 13:18–43

Jesus Explains the Seed Story

So listen to the meaning of that
story about the farmer. 19 What is the
seed that fell by the road? That seed
is like the person who hears the
message about the kingdom but
does not understand it. The Evil One
comes and takes away what was
planted in that person's heart. 20 And
what is the seed that fell on rocky
ground? That seed is like the person
who hears the teaching and quickly
accepts it with joy. 21 But he does not
let the teaching go deep into his life,
so he keeps it only a short time.
When trouble or persecution comes
because of the teaching he accepted,
he quickly gives up. 22 And what is
the seed that fell among the thorny
weeds? That seed is like the person
who hears the teaching but lets worries about this life and the temptation of wealth stop that teaching
from growing. So the teaching does
not produce fruit in that person's life.
23 But what is the seed that fell on the
good ground? That seed is like the
person who hears the teaching and
understands it. That person grows
and produces fruit, sometimes a
hundred times more, sometimes
sixty times more, and sometimes
thirty times more."

A Story About Wheat and Weeds

Then Jesus told them another story:
"The kingdom of heaven is like a
man who planted good seed in his
field. 25 That night, when everyone
was asleep, his enemy came and
planted weeds among the wheat and
then left. 26 Later, the wheat sprouted
and the heads of grain grew, but the
weeds also grew. 27 Then the man's
servants came to him and said, 'You
planted good seed in your field.
Where did the weeds come from?'
28 The man answered, 'An enemy
planted weeds.' The servants asked,
'Do you want us to pull up the
weeds?' 29 The man answered, 'No,
because when you pull up the weeds,
you might also pull up the wheat.
30 Let the weeds and the wheat grow
together until the harvest time. At
harvest time I will tell the workers,
"First gather the weeds and tie them
together to be burned. Then gather
the wheat and bring it to my barn."'"

Stories of Mustard Seed and Yeast

Then Jesus told another story:
"The kingdom of heaven is like a
mustard seed that a man planted in
his field. 32 That seed is the smallest
of all seeds, but when it grows, it is
one of the largest garden plants. It
becomes big enough for the wild
birds to come and build nests in its
branches."

33 Then Jesus told another story:
"The kingdom of heaven is like yeast
that a woman took and hid in a large
tub of flour until it made all the
dough rise."

34 Jesus used stories to tell all
these things to the people; he always
used stories to teach them. 35 This is
as the prophet said:

"I will speak using stories;

I will tell things that have been
secret since the world was
made." *Psalm 78:2*

Jesus Explains About the Weeds

Then Jesus left the crowd and went into the house. His followers came to him and said, "Explain to us the meaning of the story about the weeds in the field."

[37]Jesus answered, "The man who
planted the good seed in the field is
the Son of Man. [38]The field is the
world, and the good seed are all of
God's children who belong to the
kingdom. The weeds are those
people who belong to the Evil One.
[39]And the enemy who planted the
bad seed is the devil. The harvest
time is the end of the world, and the
workers who gather are God's angels.

[40]"Just as the weeds are pulled up
and burned in the fire, so it will be
at the end of the world. [41]The Son of
Man will send out his angels, and
they will gather out of his kingdom
all who cause sin and all who do evil.
[42]The angels will throw them into
the blazing furnace, where the
people will cry and grind their teeth
with pain. [43]Then the good people
will shine like the sun in the kingdom of their Father. You people who can hear me, listen."

OLD TESTAMENT READING

Remember my words with your whole being. Write them down and tie them to your hands as a sign; tie them on your foreheads to remind
you. [19]Teach them well to your children, talking about them when you sit at home and walk along the road, when you lie down and when you get
up. [20]Write them on your doors and
gates [21]so that both you and your children will live a long time in the land the LORD promised your ancestors, as long as the skies are above the earth.

Deuteronomy 11:18–21

INSIGHTS

H. A. Ironside told of a godly man named Andrew Frazer who had come to southern California to recover from a serious illness. Though this Irishman was quite weak, he opened his worn Bible and began expounding the truths of God's Word in a way that Ironside had never heard before. So moved by Frazer's words was Ironside that his curiosity drove him to ask, "Where did you learn these things? Did you learn them in some college or seminary?" The sickly man said, "My dear young man, I learned these things on my knees on the mud floor of a little sod cottage in the north of Ireland. There with my open Bible before me I used to kneel for hours at a time and ask the Spirit of God to reveal Christ to my soul and to open the Word to my heart. He taught me more on my knees on that mud floor than I ever could have learned in all the seminaries or colleges in the world."

Woodrow Kroll

APPLICATION

What happens when a person understands and lives by God's teaching? What are you willing to do in order to remember God's Word with your whole heart?

WEEKEND

Jesus Tells His Followers About God's Kingdom

Matthew 13:44—14:12

Stories of a Treasure and a Pearl

The kingdom of heaven is like a
treasure hidden in a field. One day
a man found the treasure, and then
he hid it in the field again. He was
so happy that he went and sold everything he owned to buy that field.
45 "Also, the kingdom of heaven is
like a man looking for fine pearls.
46 When he found a very valuable
pearl, he went and sold everything
he had and bought it.

A Story of a Fishing Net

Also, the kingdom of heaven is like
a net that was put into the lake and
caught many different kinds of fish.
48 When it was full, the fishermen
pulled the net to the shore. They sat
down and put all the good fish in baskets and threw away the bad fish. 49 It
will be this way at the end of the
world. The angels will come and
separate the evil people from the
good people. 50 The angels will throw
the evil people into the blazing furnace, where people will cry and
grind their teeth with pain."
51 Jesus asked his followers, "Do
you understand all these things?"
They answered, "Yes, we understand."
52 Then Jesus said to them, "So
every teacher of the law who has
been taught about the kingdom of
heaven is like the owner of a house.
He brings out both new things and
old things he has saved."

Jesus Goes to His Hometown

When Jesus finished teaching with
these stories, he left there. 54 He
went to his hometown and taught
the people in the synagogue, and
they were amazed. They said,
"Where did this man get this wisdom and this power to do miracles?
55 He is just the son of a carpenter.
His mother is Mary, and his brothers are James, Joseph, Simon, and
Judas. 56 And all his sisters are here
with us. Where then does this man
get all these things?" 57 So the people
were upset with Jesus.
But Jesus said to them, "A
prophet is honored everywhere except in his hometown and in his own
home."
58 So he did not do many miracles
there because they had no faith.

How John the Baptist Was Killed

14 At that time Herod, the ruler
of Galilee, heard the reports
about Jesus. 2 So he said to his servants, "Jesus is John the Baptist, who
has risen from the dead. That is why
he can work these miracles."
3 Sometime before this, Herod had
arrested John, tied him up, and put
him into prison. Herod did this because of Herodias, who had been the
wife of Philip, Herod's brother. 4 John
had been telling Herod, "It is not lawful for you to be married to Herodias."
5 Herod wanted to kill John, but he
was afraid of the people, because they
believed John was a prophet.
6 On Herod's birthday, the daughter of Herodias danced for Herod

and his guests, and she pleased him.
7 So he promised with an oath to give
her anything she wanted. 8 Herodias
told her daughter what to ask for, so
she said to Herod, "Give me the head
of John the Baptist here on a platter."
9 Although King Herod was very sad,
he had made a promise, and his dinner guests had heard him. So Herod
ordered that what she asked for be
done. 10 He sent soldiers to the prison
to cut off John's head. 11 And they
brought it on a platter and gave it to
the girl, and she took it to her mother.
12 John's followers came and got his
body and buried it. Then they went
and told Jesus.

OLD TESTAMENT READING

LORD, everything you have made
will praise you;
those who belong to you will
bless you.
11 They will tell about the glory of
your kingdom
and will speak about your power.
12 Then everyone will know the
mighty things you do
and the glory and majesty of
your kingdom.
13 Your kingdom will go on and on,
and you will rule forever.

Psalm 145:10–13a

INSIGHTS

During the Civil War, the army of the Union and the army of the Confederacy were locked in a vicious battle to the death just outside the city of Richmond. As night fell after the first day of the battle, cheers were heard from the Confederate lines. When General Grant asked what was going on behind the enemy's line, he was told that the wife of General George Pickett had given birth to a baby boy, and that his troops were celebrating. . . .

Upon receiving the news, General Grant ordered bonfires to be lit and a toast to be given. Cheers and hoorahs rang out all night long. For a few hours, the shooting stopped and warring soldiers were drawn together for a birthday party. The birth of Pickett's son only temporarily stopped a war. But it stands as evidence of what a good birthday party can do. . . .

The good news is that another Son was born, and there were some who stopped what they were doing and enjoyed a little bit of peace for just a little while. There was singing in the sky—at least some shepherds said there was. And some strange visitors came looking for a baby whom they nicknamed the Prince of Peace. Everyone has not gotten the message, so not everyone knows about the baby. But the baby started a movement and we know that someday everyone will come to His party and call Him the Lord of the feast.

There's a great day coming when the world will change. What started as a birthday party will end with a wedding feast. We will call it the "Kingdom of God." We must pray for it, and we must work for it.

Tony Campolo

PAUSE FOR REFLECTION

What do you understand about God's kingdom from the three images Jesus presented to his followers? Is the coming of God's kingdom exciting enough for you to stop doing your own thing and celebrate?

MONDAY

Trust in God to Meet Our Needs

Matthew 14:13–36

More than Five Thousand Fed

When Jesus heard what had happened to John, he left in a boat and
went to a lonely place by himself. But
the crowds heard about it and followed him on foot from the towns.
14 When he arrived, he saw a great
crowd waiting. He felt sorry for
them and healed those who were
sick.
15 When it was evening, his followers came to him and said, "No one
lives in this place, and it is already
late. Send the people away so they
can go to the towns and buy food for
themselves."
16 But Jesus answered, "They
don't need to go away. You give them
something to eat."
17 They said to him, "But we have
only five loaves of bread and two
fish."
18 Jesus said, "Bring the bread and
the fish to me." 19 Then he told the
people to sit down on the grass. He
took the five loaves and the two fish
and, looking to heaven, he thanked
God for the food. Jesus divided the
bread and gave it to his followers,
who gave it to the people. 20 All the
people ate and were satisfied. Then
the followers filled twelve baskets
with the leftover pieces of food.
21 There were about five thousand
men there who ate, not counting
women and children.

Jesus Walks on the Water

Immediately Jesus told his followers to get into the boat and go ahead
of him across the lake. He stayed
there to send the people home. 23 After he had sent them away, he went
by himself up into the hills to pray.
It was late, and Jesus was there
alone. 24 By this time, the boat was
already far away from land. It was
being hit by waves, because the wind
was blowing against it.
25 Between three and six o'clock
in the morning, Jesus came to them,
walking on the water. 26 When his followers saw him walking on the water, they were afraid. They said, "It's
a ghost!" and cried out in fear.
27 But Jesus quickly spoke to
them, "Have courage! It is I. Do not
be afraid."
28 Peter said, "Lord, if it is really
you, then command me to come to
you on the water."
29 Jesus said, "Come."
And Peter left the boat and
walked on the water to Jesus. 30 But
when Peter saw the wind and the
waves, he became afraid and began
to sink. He shouted, "Lord, save
me!"
31 Immediately Jesus reached out
his hand and caught Peter. Jesus
said, "Your faith is small. Why did
you doubt?"
32 After they got into the boat, the
wind became calm. 33 Then those
who were in the boat worshiped
Jesus and said, "Truly you are the
Son of God!"
34 When they had crossed the
lake, they came to shore at
Gennesaret. 35 When the people
there recognized Jesus, they told

people all around there that Jesus had come, and they brought all their sick to him. 36 They begged Jesus to let them touch just the edge of his coat, and all who touched it were healed.

OLD TESTAMENT READING

You, LORD, give true peace
to those who depend on you,
because they trust you.
4 So, trust the LORD always,
because he is our Rock forever.

Isaiah 26:3–4

The LORD is kind and does what is right;
our God is merciful.
6 The LORD watches over the foolish;
when I was helpless, he saved me.
7 I said to myself, "Relax,
because the LORD takes care of you."
8 LORD, you saved me from death.
You stopped my eyes from crying;
you kept me from being defeated.
9 So I walk with the LORD
in the land of the living.

Psalm 116:5–9

INSIGHTS

Today many fears fill our lives. We fear poverty, sickness, loneliness, death. We fear the dangers of the night and the pressures of the day.

David learned that the only way to be released from fears was to TRUST the Lord. "What time I am afraid, I will trust in thee." He changed the focus of his eyes from his situation to the Lord. Faith replaced fear. He PUT his trust in the Lord. This was an act of his will. "In God have I put my trust: I will not be afraid what man can do unto me" (Ps. 56:11).

Freedom from fear is the result of confidence and trust in God. We may be helpless against fear, but God is not. When trusting God, there is nothing to fear.

Faith is more than believing what God can do. It is trust in the Person of God Himself. "But without faith it is impossible to please him: for he that cometh to God must believe that He IS, and that He is a rewarder of them that diligently seek Him" (Heb. 11:6). . . .

One day a father discovered his little boy had climbed an old tree. The limbs were beginning to break under the boy's weight. The father held up his arms and called, "Jump! I'll catch you." The little son considered the offer for a moment. Then, as more limbs began to break, he said, "Shall I let go of everything, Daddy, and trust you?"

What a lesson for us. Our Heavenly Father wants us to let go of everything and trust Him.

Millie Stamm

PAUSE FOR REFLECTION

Think about the fears and needs in your life. In what ways have you "let go of everything" and put your trust in God to meet those needs? Pray or write your own psalm of trust to God. Praise him for his faithfulness to you.

TUESDAY

Warnings Against Hypocrisy

Matthew 15:1–31

Obey God's Law

15 Then some Pharisees and teachers of the law came to Jesus from Jerusalem. They asked him, 2 "Why don't your followers obey the unwritten laws which have been handed down to us? They don't wash their hands before they eat."

3 Jesus answered, "And why do you refuse to obey God's command so that you can follow your own teachings? 4 God said, 'Honor your father and your mother,' and 'Anyone who says cruel things to his father or mother must be put to death.' 5 But you say a person can tell his father or mother, 'I have something I could use to help you, but I have given it to God already.' 6 You teach that person not to honor his father or his mother. You rejected what God said for the sake of your own rules. 7 You are hypocrites! Isaiah was right when he said about you:

8 'These people show honor to me
with words,
but their hearts are far from
me.
9 Their worship of me is worthless.
The things they teach are
nothing but human rules.' "

Isaiah 29:13

10 After Jesus called the crowd to him, he said, "Listen and understand what I am saying. 11 It is not what people put into their mouths that makes them unclean. It is what comes out of their mouths that makes them unclean."

12 Then his followers came to him and asked, "Do you know that the Pharisees are angry because of what you said?"

13 Jesus answered, "Every plant that my Father in heaven has not planted himself will be pulled up by the roots. 14 Stay away from the Pharisees; they are blind leaders. And if a blind person leads a blind person, both will fall into a ditch."

15 Peter said, "Explain the example to us."

16 Jesus said, "Do you still not understand? 17 Surely you know that all the food that enters the mouth goes into the stomach and then goes out of the body. 18 But what people say with their mouths comes from the way they think; these are the things that make people unclean. 19 Out of the mind come evil thoughts, murder, adultery, sexual sins, stealing, lying, and speaking evil of others. 20 These things make people unclean; eating with unwashed hands does not make them unclean."

Jesus Helps a Non-Jewish Woman

Jesus left that place and went to the area of Tyre and Sidon. 22 A Canaanite woman from that area came to Jesus and cried out, "Lord, Son of David, have mercy on me! My daughter has a demon, and she is suffering very much."

23 But Jesus did not answer the woman. So his followers came to Jesus and begged him, "Tell the woman to go away. She is following us and shouting."

24 Jesus answered, "God sent me only to the lost sheep, the people of Israel."

25 Then the woman came to Jesus

again and bowed before him and
said, "Lord, help me!"
[26]Jesus answered, "It is not right
to take the children's bread and give
it to the dogs."
[27]The woman said, "Yes, Lord,
but even the dogs eat the crumbs
that fall from their masters' table."
[28]Then Jesus answered, "Woman,
you have great faith! I will do what
you asked." And at that moment the
woman's daughter was healed.

Jesus Heals Many People

After leaving there, Jesus went
along the shore of Lake Galilee. He
went up on a hill and sat there.
[30]Great crowds came to Jesus,
bringing with them the lame, the
blind, the crippled, those who could
not speak, and many others. They
put them at Jesus' feet, and he
healed them. [31]The crowd was
amazed when they saw that people
who could not speak before were
now able to speak. The crippled
were made strong. The lame could
walk, and the blind could see. And
they praised the God of Israel for
this.

OLD TESTAMENT READING

Those who hate you may try to
fool you with their words,
but in their minds they are
planning evil.
[25]People's words may be kind, but
don't believe them,
because their minds are full of
evil thoughts.
[26]Lies can hide hate,
but the evil will be plain to
everyone.

Proverbs 26:24–26

INSIGHTS

In the ancient Greek plays, the actors were called hypocrites. On the stage they professed to be something they weren't. Unfortunately, there are many people who go through life playacting. They profess to be something they are not. They are hypocrites. They fool no one with this false veneer, this facade, this hypocrisy, except themselves. What they really are is well-known to God and their acquaintances with the result that they are displeasing to both. . . .

. . . Through the years innumerable people have gone to a Christless grave to spend eternity in hell because of the hypocrisy of many who call themselves Christians.

It is said that Thomas K. Beecher could not stand deceit of any kind. When he discovered that the clock in his church ran habitually either too slow or too fast, he reportedly put a placard on the wall above it that read in large letters, "Don't blame my hands—the trouble lies deeper." Don't make the mistake of promising to be a better Christian. The trouble is not on the outside; it is in the inner recesses of a person's being. Only Christ can cure this malady. This He will do if a person in genuine repentance seeks His forgiveness and turns himself over to Him in simple childlike faith.

Harold Fickett

APPLICATION

Why is hypocrisy so displeasing to God? Where does hypocrisy originate? What hypocrisy in your life needs to be healed?

WEDNESDAY

Jesus Offers Real Food

Matthew 15:32—16:20

More than Four Thousand Fed

Jesus called his followers to him and
said, "I feel sorry for these people,
because they have already been with
me three days, and they have nothing to eat. I don't want to send them
away hungry. They might faint while
going home."
33 His followers asked him, "How
can we get enough bread to feed all
these people? We are far away from
any town."
34 Jesus asked, "How many loaves
of bread do you have?"
They answered, "Seven, and a few
small fish."
35 Jesus told the people to sit on
the ground. 36 He took the seven
loaves of bread and the fish and
gave thanks to God. Then he divided the food and gave it to his followers, and they gave it to the
people. 37 All the people ate and
were satisfied. Then his followers
filled seven baskets with the leftover pieces of food. 38 There were
about four thousand men there who
ate, besides women and children.
39 After sending the people home,
Jesus got into the boat and went to
the area of Magadan.

The Leaders Ask for a Miracle

16 The Pharisees and Sadducees
came to Jesus, wanting to trick
him. So they asked him to show
them a miracle from God.
2 Jesus answered, "At sunset you
say we will have good weather, because the sky is red. 3 And in the
morning you say that it will be a
rainy day, because the sky is dark
and red. You see these signs in the
sky and know what they mean. In
the same way, you see the things
that I am doing now, but you don't
know their meaning. 4 Evil and sinful people ask for a miracle as a sign,
but they will not be given any sign,
except the sign of Jonah." Then
Jesus left them and went away.

Guard Against Wrong Teachings

Jesus' followers went across the
lake, but they had forgotten to bring
bread. 6 Jesus said to them, "Be careful! Beware of the yeast of the Pharisees and the Sadducees."
7 His followers discussed the
meaning of this, saying, "He said
this because we forgot to bring
bread."
8 Knowing what they were talking
about, Jesus asked them, "Why are
you talking about not having bread?
Your faith is small. 9 Do you still not
understand? Remember the five
loaves of bread that fed the five thousand? And remember that you filled
many baskets with the leftovers?
10 Or the seven loaves of bread that
fed the four thousand and the many
baskets you filled then also? 11 I was
not talking to you about bread. Why
don't you understand that? I am telling you to beware of the yeast of the
Pharisees and the Sadducees."
12 Then the followers understood
that Jesus was not telling them to
beware of the yeast used in bread
but to beware of the teaching of the
Pharisees and the Sadducees.

Peter Says Jesus Is the Christ

When Jesus came to the area of
Caesarea Philippi, he asked his followers, "Who do people say the Son
of Man is?"
14 They answered, "Some say you
are John the Baptist. Others say you
are Elijah, and still others say you are
Jeremiah or one of the prophets."
15 Then Jesus asked them, "And
who do you say I am?"
16 Simon Peter answered, "You are
the Christ, the Son of the living God."
17 Jesus answered, "You are
blessed, Simon son of Jonah, because no person taught you that. My
Father in heaven showed you who I
am. 18 So I tell you, you are Peter. On
this rock I will build my church, and
the power of death will not be able
to defeat it. 19 I will give you the keys
of the kingdom of heaven; the things
you don't allow on earth will be the
things that God does not allow, and
the things you allow on earth will be
the things that God allows." 20 Then
Jesus warned his followers not to tell
anyone he was the Christ.

OLD TESTAMENT READING

The LORD says, "All you who are
thirsty,
come and drink.
Those of you who do not have
money,
come, buy and eat!
Come buy wine and milk
without money and without
cost.
2 Why spend your money on
something that is not real
food?
Why work for something that
doesn't really satisfy you?
Listen closely to me, and you will
eat what is good;
your soul will enjoy the rich
food that satisfies."

Isaiah 55:1–2

INSIGHTS

Our Lord's mission of grace and truth was at its height. His help was sought with the utmost eagerness. Large numbers of sick were cast at his feet in hot haste. The crumb was given to the woman of Canaan, but whole loaves were distributed to the crowds of Jews, because it was befitting that they should have a full chance to appreciate and accept Christ. For a brief moment they glorified the God of Israel, but the spasm of gratitude was transient. "His own" rejected Jesus. They would have his miracles, but would not own his claims. Take care that you do not become content with getting his help; love him for himself.

Do not suppose that these miracles were confined to his earthly life. He is still the great storehouse of divine and healing energy. He is still moved with compassion, and longs to help each weary and sin-sick soul. His thought still is "lest they faint in the way." The wilderness can place no bar on "the saving strength of his right hand."

F. B. Meyer

APPLICATION

What does the "real food" that Jesus offers satisfy? How does a person receive that food? Why do you want to be close to Jesus? Do you want his miracles or his claims? Physical food or spiritual food?

THURSDAY

Jesus' Suffering Will Be Followed by His Judgment

Matthew 16:21—17:13

Jesus Says that He Must Die

From that time on Jesus began telling his followers that he must go to
Jerusalem, where the older Jewish
leaders, the leading priests, and the
teachers of the law would make him
suffer many things. He told them he
must be killed and then be raised
from the dead on the third day.
22 Peter took Jesus aside and told
him not to talk like that. He said,
"God save you from those things,
Lord! Those things will never happen to you!"
23 Then Jesus said to Peter, "Go
away from me, Satan! You are not
helping me! You don't care about the
things of God, but only about the
things people think are important."
24 Then Jesus said to his followers, "If people want to follow me,
they must give up the things they
want. They must be willing even to
give up their lives to follow me.
25 Those who want to save their lives
will give up true life, and those who
give up their lives for me will have
true life. 26 It is worth nothing for
them to have the whole world if
they lose their souls. They could
never pay enough to buy back their
souls. 27 The Son of Man will come
again with his Father's glory and
with his angels. At that time, he will
reward them for what they have
done. 28 I tell you the truth, some
people standing here will see the
Son of Man coming with his kingdom before they die."

Jesus Talks with Moses and Elijah

17 Six days later, Jesus took Peter, James, and John, the
brother of James, up on a high
mountain by themselves. 2 While
they watched, Jesus' appearance
was changed; his face became
bright like the sun, and his clothes
became white as light. 3 Then Moses
and Elijah appeared to them, talking
with Jesus.
4 Peter said to Jesus, "Lord, it is
good that we are here. If you want,
I will put up three tents here—one
for you, one for Moses, and one for
Elijah."
5 While Peter was talking, a
bright cloud covered them. A voice
came from the cloud and said, "This
is my Son, whom I love, and I am
very pleased with him. Listen to
him!"
6 When his followers heard the
voice, they were so frightened they
fell to the ground. 7 But Jesus went
to them and touched them and said,
"Stand up. Don't be afraid." 8 When
they looked up, they saw Jesus was
now alone.
9 As they were coming down the
mountain, Jesus commanded them
not to tell anyone about what they
had seen until the Son of Man had
risen from the dead.
10 Then his followers asked him,
"Why do the teachers of the law say
that Elijah must come first?"
11 Jesus answered, "They are
right to say that Elijah is coming and
that he will make everything the
way it should be. 12 But I tell you that
Elijah has already come, and they

did not recognize him. They did to
him whatever they wanted to do. It
will be the same with the Son of
Man; those same people will make
the Son of Man suffer." 13 Then the
followers understood that Jesus was
talking about John the Baptist.

OLD TESTAMENT READING

We all have wandered away like
sheep;
each of us has gone his own way.
But the LORD has put on him the
punishment
for all the evil we have done.

7 He was beaten down and punished,
but he didn't say a word.
He was like a lamb being led to
be killed.
He was quiet, as a sheep is quiet
while its wool is being cut;
he never opened his mouth.
8 Men took him away roughly and
unfairly.
He died without children to
continue his family.
He was put to death;
he was punished for the sins of
my people.
9 He was buried with wicked men,
and he died with the rich.
He had done nothing wrong,
and he had never lied.

10 But it was the LORD who decided
to crush him and make him
suffer.
The LORD made his life a
penalty offering,
but he will still see his descendants and live a long life.
He will complete the things the
LORD wants him to do.

Isaiah 53:6–10

INSIGHTS

The New Testament proclaims that at some unforeseeable time in the future God will ring down the final curtain on history, and there will come a Day on which all our days and all the judgments upon us and all our judgments upon each other will themselves be judged. The judge will be Christ. In other words, the one who judges us most finally will be the one who loves us most fully.

Romantic love is blind to everything except what is lovable and lovely, but Christ's love sees us with terrible clarity and sees us whole. Christ's love so wishes our joy that it is ruthless against everything in us that diminishes our joy. The worst sentence Love can pass is that we behold the suffering which Love has endured for our sake, and that is also our acquittal. The justice and mercy of the judge are ultimately one.

Frederick Buechner

ACTION POINT

What was most important to Jesus when he suffered and died for us? What did he promise would follow? Think about the statement, "the one who judges us most finally will be the one who loves us most fully." Pray now and thank God that our Judge is also our Savior!

FRIDAY

Greatness in God's Kingdom Begins with Humility

Matthew 17:14—18:9

Jesus Heals a Sick Boy

When Jesus and his followers
came back to the crowd, a man came
to Jesus and bowed before him.
15 The man said, "Lord, have mercy
on my son. He has epilepsy and is
suffering very much, because he often falls into the fire or into the water. 16 I brought him to your followers, but they could not cure him."
17 Jesus answered, "You people
have no faith, and your lives are all
wrong. How long must I put up with
you? How long must I continue to be
patient with you? Bring the boy
here." 18 Jesus commanded the demon inside the boy. Then the demon
came out, and the boy was healed
from that time on.
19 The followers came to Jesus
when he was alone and asked, "Why
couldn't we force the demon out?"
20 Jesus answered, "Because your
faith is too small. I tell you the truth,
if your faith is as big as a mustard
seed, you can say to this mountain,
'Move from here to there,' and it will
move. All things will be possible for
you. 21 That kind of spirit comes out
only if you use prayer and give up
eating."

Jesus Talks About His Death

While Jesus' followers were gathering in Galilee, he said to them,
"The Son of Man will be handed
over to people, 23 and they will kill
him. But on the third day he will be
raised from the dead." And the followers were filled with sadness.

Jesus Talks About Paying Taxes

When Jesus and his followers
came to Capernaum, the men who
collected the Temple tax came to
Peter. They asked, "Does your
teacher pay the Temple tax?"
25 Peter answered, "Yes, Jesus
pays the tax."

Peter went into the house, but
before he could speak, Jesus said to
him, "What do you think? The kings
of the earth collect different kinds
of taxes. But who pays the taxes—
the king's children or others?"
26 Peter answered, "Other people
pay the taxes."

Jesus said to Peter, "Then the
children of the king don't have to pay
taxes. 27 But we don't want to upset
these tax collectors. So go to the lake
and fish. After you catch the first
fish, open its mouth and you will find
a coin. Take that coin and give it to
the tax collectors for you and me."

Who Is the Greatest?

18 At that time the followers
came to Jesus and asked,
"Who is greatest in the kingdom of
heaven?"
2 Jesus called a little child to him
and stood the child before his followers. 3 Then he said, "I tell you the
truth, you must change and become
like little children. Otherwise, you
will never enter the kingdom of
heaven. 4 The greatest person in the
kingdom of heaven is the one who
makes himself humble like this child.

[5]"Whoever accepts a child in my
name accepts me. [6]If one of these
little children believes in me, and
someone causes that child to sin, it
would be better for that person to
have a large stone tied around the
neck and be drowned in the sea.
[7]How terrible for the people of the
world because of the things that
cause them to sin. Such things will
happen, but how terrible for the one
who causes them to happen! [8]If your
hand or your foot causes you to sin,
cut it off and throw it away. It is better for you to lose part of your body
and live forever than to have two
hands and two feet and be thrown
into the fire that burns forever. [9]If
your eye causes you to sin, take it
out and throw it away. It is better for
you to have only one eye and live forever than to have two eyes and be
thrown into the fire of hell."

OLD TESTAMENT READING

Pride will ruin people,
but those who are humble will
be honored.

Proverbs 29:23

As Manasseh suffered, he begged
the LORD his God for help and
humbled himself before the God of
his ancestors. [13]When Manasseh
prayed, the LORD heard him and had
pity on him. So the LORD let him return to Jerusalem and to his kingdom. Then Manasseh knew that the
LORD is the true God.

2 Chronicles 33:12–13

INSIGHTS

I was once considering what the reason was our Lord loved humility in us so much. I suddenly remembered that He is essentially the supreme truth and that humility is just our walking in truth. For it is a very great truth that we have no good in us; we have only misery and nothingness. He who does not understand this walks in lies. But he who understands this the best is the most pleasing to the Supreme Truth. May God grant us this favor, sisters, never to be without the humbling knowledge of ourselves. . . .

His Majesty seeks and loves courageous souls. But they must be humble in all their ways and have no confidence in themselves. . . .

. . . I often used to think of those words of the Apostle Paul: "All things are possible with God" (Philippians 4:13). I saw clearly that I could do nothing of myself. This was of great help to me to see this. So also was the saying of Augustine: "Give me, Lord, what You command, and command what You desire." . . .

. . . But it is necessary that we should understand what this humility is like. For I believe Satan will try to do great harm. He hinders those who begin to pray from going forward by suggesting to them false notions of humility. He makes them think that it is pride to have spiritual ambitions, desires to imitate the saints, and longings to be like martyrs.

St. Teresa of Avila

ACTION POINT

How does God view pride? Why do you think he places such a high value on humility? Describe the attitudes and actions of true humility, and pray that God will cause you to want to be humble.

WEEKEND

The Magnitude of God's Forgiveness

Matthew 18:10–35

A Lost Sheep

Be careful. Don't think these little
children are worth nothing. I tell you
that they have angels in heaven who
are always with my Father in heaven.
11 The Son of Man came to save lost
people.
12 "If a man has a hundred sheep
but one of the sheep gets lost, he will
leave the other ninety-nine on the
hill and go to look for the lost sheep.
13 I tell you the truth, he is happier
about that one sheep than about the
ninety-nine that were never lost. 14 In
the same way, your Father in heaven
does not want any of these little children to be lost.

When a Person Sins Against You

If your fellow believer sins against
you, go and tell him in private what
he did wrong. If he listens to you,
you have helped that person to be
your brother or sister again. 16 But if
he refuses to listen, go to him again
and take one or two other people
with you. 'Every case may be proved
by two or three witnesses.' 17 If he refuses to listen to them, tell the
church. If he refuses to listen to the
church, then treat him like a person
who does not believe in God or like
a tax collector.
18 "I tell you the truth, the things
you don't allow on earth will be the
things God does not allow. And the
things you allow on earth will be
the things that God allows.
19 "Also, I tell you that if two of you
on earth agree about something and
pray for it, it will be done for you by
my Father in heaven. 20 This is true
because if two or three people come
together in my name, I am there
with them."

An Unforgiving Servant

Then Peter came to Jesus and
asked, "Lord, when my fellow believer sins against me, how many
times must I forgive him? Should I
forgive him as many as seven times?"
22 Jesus answered, "I tell you, you
must forgive him more than seven
times. You must forgive him even if
he does wrong to you seventy-seven
times.
23 "The kingdom of heaven is like
a king who decided to collect the
money his servants owed him.
24 When the king began to collect his
money, a servant who owed him several million dollars was brought to
him. 25 But the servant did not have
enough money to pay his master,
the king. So the master ordered that
everything the servant owned
should be sold, even the servant's
wife and children. Then the money
would be used to pay the king what
the servant owed.
26 "But the servant fell on his
knees and begged, 'Be patient with
me, and I will pay you everything I
owe.' 27 The master felt sorry for his
servant and told him he did not have
to pay it back. Then he let the servant go free.
28 "Later, that same servant found
another servant who owed him a
few dollars. The servant grabbed
him around the neck and said, 'Pay
me the money you owe me!'

29 "The other servant fell on his
knees and begged him, 'Be patient
with me, and I will pay you everything I owe.'
30 "But the first servant refused to
be patient. He threw the other servant into prison until he could pay
everything he owed. 31 When the
other servants saw what had happened, they were very sorry. So they
went and told their master all that
had happened.
32 "Then the master called his servant in and said, 'You evil servant!
Because you begged me to forget
what you owed, I told you that you
did not have to pay anything. 33 You
should have showed mercy to that
other servant, just as I showed
mercy to you.' 34 The master was
very angry and put the servant in
prison to be punished until he could
pay everything he owed.
35 "This king did what my heavenly Father will do to you if you do
not forgive your brother or sister
from your heart."

OLD TESTAMENT READING

But suppose the wicked stop doing
all the sins they have done and obey
all my rules and do what is fair and
right. Then they will surely live; they
will not die. 22 Their sins will be forgotten. Because they have done
what is right, they will live. 23 I do not
really want the wicked to die, says
the Lord GOD. I want them to stop
their bad ways and live."

Ezekiel 18:21–23

INSIGHTS

Forgiving and being forgiven are all of one piece. They cannot be separated. In giving we receive. In accepting those who have injured us we open ourselves to God's acceptance.

It is not a matter of which comes first. There is no sequence of time or priority. The two are one. Anyone who loves God must also love his neighbor. Anyone who hates another does not and cannot love God. Love of God and our neighbor are interlocking and indivisible. We only learn to love as we learn to know God. And we truly learn to know God as we learn to love our brother and sister. It's all of a piece. The life that is open to the love of God is loving to others. The person who truly receives the forgiveness of God is truly forgiving of others. . . .

God's forgiveness gives us the freedom to love and live creatively. The rush of God's strength, which brings forgiveness, gives in turn the ability to forgive, and forgive, and forgive, not just seven times, as the apostle Peter once volunteered, but seventy times seven. . . .

The contrast between our debt to God and the debts others may owe us is immeasurable.

And when God has forgiven us the debt we owe Him, how can we be unforgiving to others who owe us so little in comparison?

David Augsburger

APPLICATION

As you think about the parable of the servants, what debt that God has forgiven you can serve as a model of how you ought to forgive others? In what ways does Ezekiel 18 affect how you think about God?

MONDAY

Jesus Talks About Marriage and Divorce

Matthew 19:1–26

Jesus Teaches About Divorce

19 After Jesus said all these
things, he left Galilee and went
into the area of Judea on the other
side of the Jordan River. 2 Large
crowds followed him, and he healed
them there.
3 Some Pharisees came to Jesus
and tried to trick him. They asked,
"Is it right for a man to divorce his
wife for any reason he chooses?"
4 Jesus answered, "Surely you
have read in the Scriptures: When
God made the world, 'he made them
male and female.' 5 And God said, 'So
a man will leave his father and
mother and be united with his wife,
and the two will become one body.'
6 So there are not two, but one. God
has joined the two together, so no
one should separate them."
7 The Pharisees asked, "Why then
did Moses give a command for a
man to divorce his wife by giving her
divorce papers?"
8 Jesus answered, "Moses allowed
you to divorce your wives because
you refused to accept God's teaching, but divorce was not allowed in
the beginning. 9 I tell you that anyone who divorces his wife and marries another woman is guilty of adultery. The only reason for a man to
divorce his wife is if his wife has
sexual relations with another man."
10 The followers said to him, "If
that is the only reason a man can
divorce his wife, it is better not to
marry."
11 Jesus answered, "Not everyone
can accept this teaching, but God has
made some able to accept it. 12 There
are different reasons why some men
cannot marry. Some men were born
without the ability to become fathers.
Others were made that way later in life
by other people. And some men have
given up marriage because of the
kingdom of heaven. But the person
who can marry should accept this
teaching about marriage."

Jesus Welcomes Children

Then the people brought their little
children to Jesus so he could put his
hands on them and pray for them.
His followers told them to stop, 14 but
Jesus said, "Let the little children
come to me. Don't stop them, because the kingdom of heaven belongs to people who are like these
children." 15 After Jesus put his
hands on the children, he left there.

A Rich Young Man's Question

A man came to Jesus and asked,
"Teacher, what good thing must I do
to have life forever?"
17 Jesus answered, "Why do you
ask me about what is good? Only
God is good. But if you want to have
life forever, obey the commands."
18 The man asked, "Which commands?"

Jesus answered, "'You must not
murder anyone; you must not be
guilty of adultery; you must not steal;
you must not tell lies about your
neighbor; 19 honor your father and
mother; and love your neighbor as
you love yourself.'"

[20]The young man said, "I have obeyed all these things. What else do I need to do?"

[21]Jesus answered, "If you want to be perfect, then go and sell your possessions and give the money to the poor. If you do this, you will have treasure in heaven. Then come and follow me."

[22]But when the young man heard this, he left sorrowfully, because he was rich.

[23]Then Jesus said to his followers, "I tell you the truth, it will be hard for a rich person to enter the kingdom of heaven. [24]Yes, I tell you that it is easier for a camel to go through the eye of a needle than for a rich person to enter the kingdom of God."

[25]When Jesus' followers heard this, they were very surprised and asked, "Then who can be saved?"

[26]Jesus looked at them and said, "This is something people cannot do, but God can do all things."

OLD TESTAMENT READING

This is another thing you do. You cover the LORD's altar with your tears. You cry and moan, because he does not accept your offerings and is not pleased with what you bring. [14]You ask, "Why?" It is because the LORD sees how you treated the wife you married when you were young. You broke your promise to her, even though she was your partner and you had an agreement with her. [15]God made husbands and wives to become one body and one spirit for his purpose—so they would have children who are true to God.

So be careful, and do not break your promise to the wife you married when you were young.

[16]The LORD God of Israel says, "I hate divorce. And I hate people who do cruel things as easily as they put on clothes," says the LORD All-Powerful.

So be careful. And do not break your trust.

Malachi 2:13–16

INSIGHTS

The marriage law must conform with the purpose for which marriage was instituted by God. It was instituted to create a new unity of two persons, and no provision was made for the dissolving of that unity. Jesus does not idealize marriage. He does not say that every marriage is made in heaven; he says that marriage itself is made in heaven—that is, instituted by God. To the question, 'Is it lawful for a man to divorce his wife?' his answer, in effect, is 'No; not for any cause.' . . .

Is it wise to take Jesus's rulings on this or other practical issues and give them legislative force? Perhaps not. It is better probably, to let his words stand in the uncompromising rigour as the ideal at which his followers ought to aim. Legislation has to make provision for the hardness of men's hearts, but Jesus showed a more excellent way than the way of legislation and supplies the power to change the human heart and make his ideal a practical possibility.

F. F. Bruce

PAUSE FOR REFLECTION

In what ways does knowing God's purpose for marriage affect your view of marriage and divorce?

TUESDAY

God's View of Fairness

Matthew 19:27—20:19

Peter said to Jesus, "Look, we have
left everything and followed you. So
what will we have?"
28 Jesus said to them, "I tell you
the truth, when the age to come has
arrived, the Son of Man will sit on
his great throne. All of you who followed me will also sit on twelve
thrones, judging the twelve tribes of
Israel. 29 And all those who have left
houses, brothers, sisters, father,
mother, children, or farms to follow
me will get much more than they
left, and they will have life forever.
30 Many who have the highest place
now will have the lowest place in the
future. And many who have the lowest place now will have the highest
place in the future.

A Story About Workers

20 The kingdom of heaven is like
a person who owned some
land. One morning, he went out very
early to hire some people to work in
his vineyard. 2 The man agreed to
pay the workers one coin for working that day. Then he sent them into
the vineyard to work. 3 About nine
o'clock the man went to the marketplace and saw some other people
standing there, doing nothing. 4 So
he said to them, 'If you go and work
in my vineyard, I will pay you what
your work is worth.' 5 So they went
to work in the vineyard. The man
went out again about twelve o'clock
and three o'clock and did the same
thing. 6 About five o'clock the man
went to the marketplace again and
saw others standing there. He asked
them, 'Why did you stand here all
day doing nothing?' 7 They answered, 'No one gave us a job.' The
man said to them, 'Then you can go
and work in my vineyard.'
8 "At the end of the day, the owner
of the vineyard said to the boss of
all the workers, 'Call the workers
and pay them. Start with the last
people I hired and end with those I
hired first.'
9 "When the workers who were
hired at five o'clock came to get their
pay, each received one coin. 10 When
the workers who were hired first
came to get their pay, they thought
they would be paid more than the
others. But each one of them also
received one coin. 11 When they got
their coin, they complained to the
man who owned the land. 12 They
said, 'Those people were hired last
and worked only one hour. But you
paid them the same as you paid us
who worked hard all day in the hot
sun.' 13 But the man who owned the
vineyard said to one of those workers, 'Friend, I am being fair to you.
You agreed to work for one coin.
14 So take your pay and go. I want to
give the man who was hired last the
same pay that I gave you. 15 I can do
what I want with my own money. Are
you jealous because I am good to
those people?'
16 "So those who have the last
place now will have the first place in
the future, and those who have the
first place now will have the last
place in the future."

Jesus Talks About His Death

While Jesus was going to Jerusalem, he took his twelve followers

aside privately and said to them,
18 "Look, we are going to Jerusalem.
The Son of Man will be turned over
to the leading priests and the teachers of the law, and they will say that
he must die. 19 They will give the Son
of Man to the non-Jewish people to
laugh at him and beat him with
whips and crucify him. But on the
third day, he will be raised to life
again."

OLD TESTAMENT READING

There is no one holy like the
LORD.
There is no God but you;
there is no Rock like our God.

6 "The LORD sends death,
and he brings to life.
He sends people to the grave,
and he raises them to life
again.
7 The LORD makes some people
poor,
and others he makes rich.
He makes some people humble,
and others he makes great.
8 The LORD raises the poor up from
the dust,
and he lifts the needy from the
ashes.
He lets the poor sit with princes
and receive a throne of honor."

1 Samuel 2:2,6–8b

INSIGHTS

The message of the parable is that the revolution of God brought by Jesus is a marvellously generous revolution, offering a full place and reward even to the late-comer or outsider. For the rich and the religious such egalitarian salvation did not always seem good news, since it meant giving up their present advantage and special position. . . . In the parable those who had worked all day complained of the master's unfair generosity. But for those in need of employment at the eleventh hour the master's generosity was good news indeed. . . .

. . . The revolution of God is a levelling revolution; not, however, a negatively levelling revolution bringing everyone down, but a positively levelling revolution in which God's amazing generosity welcomes even late-comers . . . and gives them the full day's wage. . . .

. . . To put it simply: entry into the kingdom of God is through God's generosity to sinners; being in the kingdom of God entails running the race to obtain the prize (1 Cor 9:24). There is truth in the old saying that the entry fee to Christianity is completely free, but the annual subscription is everything we've got. No one will be in the coming kingdom of God on the basis of his or her own achievements, but only on the basis of God's generosity; but everyone will be called to account on the day of judgement and will be rewarded according to his or her response to the Lord's generosity.

David Wenham

ACTION POINT

Think about God's fairness and mercy. In what ways are you tempted to be jealous of his generosity shown to others? Pray for a greater understanding of his goodness, and extend his generosity to others.

WEDNESDAY

Jerusalem Honors Jesus as King

Matthew 20:20—21:11

A Mother Asks Jesus a Favor

Then the wife of Zebedee came to
Jesus with her sons. She bowed before him and asked him to do something for her.
21 Jesus asked, "What do you
want?"
She said, "Promise that one of my
sons will sit at your right side and
the other will sit at your left side in
your kingdom."
22 But Jesus said, "You don't understand what you are asking. Can
you drink the cup that I am about to
drink?"
The sons answered, "Yes, we can."
23 Jesus said to them, "You will
drink from my cup. But I cannot
choose who will sit at my right or my
left; those places belong to those for
whom my Father has prepared
them."
24 When the other ten followers
heard this, they were angry with the
two brothers.
25 Jesus called all the followers together and said, "You know that the
rulers of the non-Jewish people love
to show their power over the people.
And their important leaders love to
use all their authority. 26 But it should
not be that way among you. Whoever wants to become great among
you must serve the rest of you like
a servant. 27 Whoever wants to become first among you must serve
the rest of you like a slave. 28 In the
same way, the Son of Man did not
come to be served. He came to serve
others and to give his life as a ransom for many people."

Jesus Heals Two Blind Men

When Jesus and his followers were
leaving Jericho, a great many people
followed him. 30 Two blind men sitting by the road heard that Jesus was
going by, so they shouted, "Lord,
Son of David, have mercy on us!"
31 The people warned the blind
men to be quiet, but they shouted
even more, "Lord, Son of David,
have mercy on us!"
32 Jesus stopped and said to the
blind men, "What do you want me
to do for you?"
33 They answered, "Lord, we want
to see."
34 Jesus felt sorry for the blind
men and touched their eyes, and at
once they could see. Then they followed Jesus.

Jesus Enters Jerusalem as a King

21 As Jesus and his followers
were coming closer to Jerusalem, they stopped at Bethphage at
the hill called the Mount of Olives.
From there Jesus sent two of his followers 2 and said to them, "Go to the
town you can see there. When you
enter it, you will quickly find a donkey tied there with its colt. Untie
them and bring them to me. 3 If anyone asks you why you are taking the
donkeys, say that the Master needs
them, and he will send them at
once."
4 This was to bring about what the
prophet had said:
5 "Tell the people of Jerusalem,

'Your king is coming to you.
He is gentle and riding on a
donkey,
on the colt of a donkey.' "

Isaiah 62:11; Zechariah 9:9

6 The followers went and did
what Jesus told them to do. 7 They
brought the donkey and the colt
to Jesus and laid their coats on
them, and Jesus sat on them.
8 Many people spread their coats
on the road. Others cut branches
from the trees and spread them on
the road. 9 The people were walking ahead of Jesus and behind
him, shouting,

"Praise to the Son of David!
God bless the One who comes in
the name of the Lord!

Psalm 118:26

Praise to God in heaven!"

10 When Jesus entered Jerusalem,
all the city was filled with excitement. The people asked, "Who is
this man?"
11 The crowd said, "This man is
Jesus, the prophet from the town of
Nazareth in Galilee."

OLD TESTAMENT READING

Come, let's sing for joy to the
LORD.
Let's shout praises to the Rock
who saves us.
2 Let's come to him with thanksgiving.
Let's sing songs to him,
3 because the LORD is the great God,
the great King over all gods.

Psalm 95:1–3

This is the day that the LORD has
made.
Let us rejoice and be glad today!

Psalm 118:24

INSIGHTS

You can almost hear the roar of the crowds as Jesus proceeds slowly into Jerusalem, like a triumphant general returning from a great victory. . . .

From the dusty roads of this earth, where the lips of little children sang his praises, to the very throne of heaven where surely angel anthems rolled, this was Jesus' moment. . . .

Not only on this day of days, but down through the centuries, Jesus has reigned in triumph in the hearts of men and women who have accepted his glorious life and teaching. The Pharisees could hardly have realized how prophetic their words would be: "Look how the whole world has gone after him!"

And why wouldn't we follow Jesus? He leads us in triumph! Just when we think we have had all the trouble we can handle, Jesus reaches down and lifts us gently onto the colt he is riding into Jerusalem. Just when we think nobody cares, he opens our ears and we can hear the crowds shout, "Look who's riding with the King!" And just when we think there is no reward for being righteous, Jesus smiles and quietly reassures us, "My Father will honor the one who serves me."

F. LaGard Smith

ACTION POINT

List the ways Jesus has shown himself to be a king of triumph in your life. Spend some time in prayer, celebrating your praise to him. If you would like, write down your praises.

THURSDAY

God Seeks Sincere Worship

Matthew 21:12–32

Jesus Goes to the Temple

Jesus went into the Temple and threw out all the people who were buying and selling there. He turned over the tables of those who were exchanging different kinds of money, and he upset the benches of those who were selling doves. 13 Jesus said to all the people there, "It is written in the Scriptures, 'My Temple will be called a house for prayer.' But you are changing it into a 'hideout for robbers.' "

14 The blind and crippled people came to Jesus in the Temple, and he healed them. 15 The leading priests and the teachers of the law saw that Jesus was doing wonderful things and that the children were praising him in the Temple, saying, "Praise to the Son of David." All these things made the priests and the teachers of the law very angry.

16 They asked Jesus, "Do you hear the things these children are saying?"

Jesus answered, "Yes. Haven't you read in the Scriptures, 'You have taught children and babies to sing praises'?"

17 Then Jesus left and went out of the city to Bethany, where he spent the night.

The Power of Faith

Early the next morning, as Jesus was going back to the city, he became hungry. 19 Seeing a fig tree beside the road, Jesus went to it, but there were no figs on the tree, only leaves. So Jesus said to the tree, "You will never again have fruit." The tree immediately dried up.

20 When his followers saw this, they were amazed. They asked, "How did the fig tree dry up so quickly?"

21 Jesus answered, "I tell you the truth, if you have faith and do not doubt, you will be able to do what I did to this tree and even more. You will be able to say to this mountain, 'Go, fall into the sea.' And if you have faith, it will happen. 22 If you believe, you will get anything you ask for in prayer."

Leaders Doubt Jesus' Authority

Jesus went to the Temple, and while he was teaching there, the leading priests and the older leaders of the people came to him. They said, "What authority do you have to do these things? Who gave you this authority?"

24 Jesus answered, "I also will ask you a question. If you answer me, then I will tell you what authority I have to do these things. 25 Tell me: When John baptized people, did that come from God or just from other people?"

They argued about Jesus' question, saying, "If we answer, 'John's baptism was from God,' Jesus will say, 'Then why didn't you believe him?' 26 But if we say, 'It was from people,' we are afraid of what the crowd will do because they all believe that John was a prophet."

27 So they answered Jesus, "We don't know."

Jesus said to them, "Then I won't tell you what authority I have to do these things.

A Story About Two Sons

Tell me what you think about this: A man had two sons. He went to the first son and said, 'Son, go and work
today in my vineyard.' 29 The son an-
swered, 'I will not go.' But later the son changed his mind and went.
30 Then the father went to the other son and said, 'Son, go and work today in my vineyard.' The son answered, 'Yes, sir, I will go and work,'
but he did not go. 31 Which of the two sons obeyed his father?"

The priests and leaders answered, "The first son."

Jesus said to them, "I tell you the truth, the tax collectors and the prostitutes will enter the kingdom of God
before you do. 32 John came to show you the right way to live. You did not believe him, but the tax collectors and prostitutes believed him. Even after seeing this, you still refused to change your ways and believe him."

OLD TESTAMENT READING

LORD, I love the Temple where
you live,
where your glory is.

Psalm 26:8

If you do that, do you think you can come before me and stand in this place where I have chosen to be worshiped? Do you think you can say, "We are safe!" when you do all
these hateful things? 11 This place
where I have chosen to be worshiped is nothing more to you than a hideout for robbers. I have been watching you, says the LORD.
12 "'You people of Judah, go now to the town of Shiloh, where I first made a place to be worshiped. See what I did to it because of the evil things the people of Israel had done.
13 You people of Judah have done all these evil things too, says the LORD. I spoke to you again and again, but you did not listen to me. I called you,
but you did not answer. 14 So I will de-
stroy the place where I have chosen to be worshiped in Jerusalem.'"

Jeremiah 7:10–14a

INSIGHTS

In both the Old and New Testaments, God's purpose in revealing himself, in redeeming, and in bringing a people into existence was to create a worshiping community to be a sign of his redeeming work. For example, when God entered into a covenant with the people of Israel, they met him at Mt. Sinai in the first public meeting between God and his people. This meeting with God became the prototype for public worship in Israel. And it was through public worship that God's revelation, redemption, and covenant were remembered and passed down in history. . . .

. . . We go to worship in praise and thank God for what he has done, is doing, and will do.

Robert Webber

PAUSE FOR REFLECTION

In God's eyes, worship is no casual, Sunday-morning time filler! How does your worship experience stand as a continuing reminder of God's redeeming work in your life?

FRIDAY

The Kingdom of Heaven Is for All Who Obey

Matthew 21:33—22:14

A Story About God's Son

Listen to this story: There was a man who owned a vineyard. He put a wall around it and dug a hole for a winepress and built a tower. Then he leased the land to some farmers and left for a trip. 34 When it was time for the grapes to be picked, he sent his servants to the farmers to get his share of the grapes. 35 But the farmers grabbed the servants, beat one, killed another, and then killed a third servant with stones. 36 So the man sent some other servants to the farmers, even more than he sent the first time. But the farmers did the same thing to the servants that they had done before. 37 So the man decided to send his son to the farmers. He said, 'They will respect my son.' 38 But when the farmers saw the son, they said to each other, 'This son will inherit the vineyard. If we kill him, it will be ours!' 39 Then the farmers grabbed the son, threw him out of the vineyard, and killed him. 40 So what will the owner of the vineyard do to these farmers when he comes?"

41 The priests and leaders said, "He will surely kill those evil men. Then he will lease the vineyard to some other farmers who will give him his share of the crop at harvest time."

42 Jesus said to them, "Surely you have read this in the Scriptures:

'The stone that the builders
rejected
became the cornerstone.
The Lord did this,
and it is wonderful to us.'

Psalm 118:22-23

43 "So I tell you that the kingdom of God will be taken away from you and given to people who do the things God wants in his kingdom. 44 The person who falls on this stone will be broken, and on whomever that stone falls, that person will be crushed."

45 When the leading priests and the Pharisees heard these stories, they knew Jesus was talking about them. 46 They wanted to arrest him, but they were afraid of the people, because the people believed that Jesus was a prophet.

A Story About a Wedding Feast

22 Jesus again used stories to teach the people. He said, 2 "The kingdom of heaven is like a king who prepared a wedding feast for his son. 3 The king invited some people to the feast. When the feast was ready, the king sent his servants to tell the people, but they refused to come.

4 "Then the king sent other servants, saying, 'Tell those who have been invited that my feast is ready. I have killed my best bulls and calves for the dinner, and everything is ready. Come to the wedding feast.'

5 "But the people refused to listen to the servants and left to do other things. One went to work in his field, and another went to his business. 6 Some of the other people grabbed the servants, beat them, and killed them. 7 The king was furious and sent his army to kill the murderers and burn their city.

8 "After that, the king said to his

servants, 'The wedding feast is
ready. I invited those people, but
they were not worthy to come. [9]So
go to the street corners and invite
everyone you find to come to my
feast.' [10]So the servants went into the
streets and gathered all the people
they could find, both good and bad.
And the wedding hall was filled with
guests.

[11]"When the king came in to see
the guests, he saw a man who was
not dressed for a wedding. [12]The
king said, 'Friend, how were you allowed to come in here? You are not
dressed for a wedding.' But the man
said nothing. [13]So the king told some
servants, 'Tie this man's hands and
feet. Throw him out into the darkness, where people will cry and
grind their teeth with pain.'

[14]"Yes, many people are invited,
but only a few are chosen."

OLD TESTAMENT READING

Foreigners who have joined the
 Lord should not say,
"The Lord will not accept me
 with his people."
The eunuch should not say,
"Because I cannot have
 children, the Lord will not
 accept me."
[4]This is what the Lord says:
"The eunuchs should obey the
 law about the Sabbath
and do what I want
and keep my agreement.
[5]If they do, I will make their
 names remembered
within my Temple and its walls.
It will be better for them than
 children.
I will give them a name that will
 last forever,
that will never be forgotten."

Isaiah 56:3–5

INSIGHTS

Who can became a Christian? The answer in a nutshell is that anyone can. Anyone who wants to can "take the free gift of the water of life" (Revelation 22:17). Whosoever will may come. Everyone has an invitation to the marriage supper of the Lamb (Matthew 22:9). . . .

. . . It is certainly true that not all do make the decision to give their lives over to God. Some stubbornly insist on going their own way. "Whoever rejects the Son will not see life, for God's wrath remains on him" (John 3:36). Such people will not enjoy the salvation God has for the world. "Yet to all who received him, to those who believed in his name, he gave the right to become children of God" (John 1:12). . . .

Who can become a Christian? Anyone can, because God's grace closes nobody out. There are no limits to his grace except those that sinners impose upon themselves. Jesus Christ, our Advocate, has become "the atoning sacrifice for our sins, and not only for ours but also for the sins of the whole world" (1 John 2:2). Salvation is so broad as to encompass potentially the entire human race.

Clark H. Pinnock

APPLICATION

To whom is God's kingdom given? For what reasons do people refuse God's invitation? Are there ways by which you limit God's grace in your life?

WEEKEND

The Most Important Command

Matthew 22:15–40

Is It Right to Pay Taxes or Not?

Then the Pharisees left that place
and made plans to trap Jesus in saying something wrong. 16 They sent
some of their own followers and
some people from the group called
Herodians. They said, "Teacher, we
know that you are an honest man
and that you teach the truth about
God's way. You are not afraid of what
other people think about you, because you pay no attention to who
they are. 17 So tell us what you think.
Is it right to pay taxes to Caesar or
not?"

18 But knowing that these leaders
were trying to trick him, Jesus said,
"You hypocrites! Why are you trying
to trap me? 19 Show me a coin used
for paying the tax." So the men
showed him a coin. 20 Then Jesus
asked, "Whose image and name are
on the coin?"

21 The men answered, "Caesar's."

Then Jesus said to them, "Give to
Caesar the things that are Caesar's,
and give to God the things that are
God's."

22 When the men heard what
Jesus said, they were amazed and
left him and went away.

Some Sadducees Try to Trick Jesus

That same day some Sadducees
came to Jesus and asked him a question. (Sadducees believed that
people would not rise from the
dead.) 24 They said, "Teacher,
Moses said if a married man dies
without having children, his brother
must marry the widow and have
children for him. 25 Once there were
seven brothers among us. The first
one married and died. Since he had
no children, his brother married the
widow. 26 Then the second brother
also died. The same thing happened
to the third brother and all the other
brothers. 27 Finally, the woman died.
28 Since all seven men had married
her, when people rise from the dead,
whose wife will she be?"

29 Jesus answered, "You don't understand, because you don't know
what the Scriptures say, and you
don't know about the power of God.
30 When people rise from the dead,
they will not marry, nor will they be
given to someone to marry. They
will be like the angels in heaven.
31 Surely you have read what God
said to you about rising from the
dead. 32 God said, 'I am the God of
Abraham, the God of Isaac, and the
God of Jacob.' God is the God of the
living, not the dead."

33 When the people heard this,
they were amazed at Jesus' teaching.

The Most Important Command

When the Pharisees learned that
the Sadducees could not argue with
Jesus' answers to them, the Pharisees met together. 35 One Pharisee,
who was an expert on the law of
Moses, asked Jesus this question to
test him: 36 "Teacher, which command in the law is the most important?"

[37] Jesus answered, "'Love the Lord your God with all your heart, all your soul, and all your mind.' [38] This is the first and most important command. [39] And the second command is like the first: 'Love your neighbor as you love yourself.' [40] All the law and the writings of the prophets depend on these two commands."

OLD TESTAMENT READING

Listen, people of Israel! The LORD our God is the only LORD. [5] Love the LORD your God with all your heart, all your soul, and all your strength. [6] Always remember these commands I give you today. [7] Teach them to your children, and talk about them when you sit at home and walk along the road, when you lie down and when you get up. [8] Write them down and tie them to your hands as a sign. Tie them on your forehead to remind you, [9] and write them on your doors and gates.

Deuteronomy 6:4–9

Then Joshua called a meeting of all the people from the tribes of Reuben, Gad, and East Manasseh. [2] He said to them, "You have done everything Moses, the LORD's servant, told you to do. You have also obeyed all my commands. [5] But be careful to obey the teachings and laws Moses, the LORD's servant, gave you: to love the LORD your God and obey his commands, to continue to follow him and serve him the very best you can."

Joshua 22:1–2, 5

I love those who love me,
and those who seek me find me.

Proverbs 8:17

INSIGHTS

I have tried giving myself to other gods—the gods of education and knowledge, success and money, accomplishment and work. I have given good works First Place in my affection. I have tried to get other people to be god for me; I have even let the church assume top priority in my time and energy. I have placed my neck in other worldly nooses and yokes, but only the yoke of Christ grants me freedom.

Surrendering my will to His yoke is a constant process. As I continue to allow the presence of God to permeate the various parts of my life, I am understanding more clearly that anything or anyone, other than God, to whom I turn for meaning, purpose, or strength will ultimately disappoint me or destroy me. God affirmed the first commandment for my benefit; He knew I would never be whole as long as I worshiped anything or anyone besides Himself. I have tried to fill my life with other people, pleasure, work, and acquisition, but these things only partially satisfy.

. . . I am learning that the God of Abraham, Joseph, and Isaac is indeed the Source of everything I need and that His intent is always for good.

Jeanie Miley

APPLICATION

How do we demonstrate that we love God with all our heart, soul, and mind? How are you loving God today? How is he satisfying your soul?

MONDAY

Judgment Against False Spiritual Leaders

Matthew 22:41—23:22

Jesus Questions the Pharisees

While the Pharisees were together,
Jesus asked them, 42 "What do you
think about the Christ? Whose son
is he?"

They answered, "The Christ is
the Son of David."

43 Then Jesus said to them, "Then
why did David call him 'Lord'?
David, speaking by the power of the
Holy Spirit, said,

44 'The Lord said to my Lord:
Sit by me at my right side,
until I put your enemies under
your control.' *Psalm 110:1*

45 David calls the Christ 'Lord,' so
how can the Christ be his son?"

46 None of the Pharisees could
answer Jesus' question, and after
that day no one was brave enough
to ask him any more questions.

Jesus Accuses Some Leaders

23 Then Jesus said to the crowds
and to his followers, 2 "The teachers of the law and the Pharisees have
the authority to tell you what the law of
Moses says. 3 So you should obey and
follow whatever they tell you, but their
lives are not good examples for you to
follow. They tell you to do things, but
they themselves don't do them. 4 They
make strict rules and try to force people
to obey them, but they are unwilling to
help those who struggle under the
weight of their rules.

5 "They do good things so that
other people will see them. They
make the boxes of Scriptures that
they wear bigger, and they make
their special prayer clothes very
long. 6 Those Pharisees and teachers
of the law love to have the most important seats at feasts and in the
synagogues. 7 They love people to
greet them with respect in the marketplaces, and they love to have
people call them 'Teacher.'

8 "But you must not be called
'Teacher,' because you have only
one Teacher, and you are all brothers and sisters together. 9 And don't
call any person on earth 'Father,'
because you have one Father, who
is in heaven. 10 And you should not
be called 'Master,' because you have
only one Master, the Christ. 11 Whoever is your servant is the greatest
among you. 12 Whoever makes himself great will be made humble.
Whoever makes himself humble will
be made great.

13 "How terrible for you, teachers
of the law and Pharisees! You are
hypocrites! You close the door for
people to enter the kingdom of
heaven. You yourselves don't enter,
and you stop others who are trying
to enter.

14 "How terrible for you, teachers
of the law and Pharisees. You are
hypocrites! You take away widows'
houses, and you say long prayers so
that people will notice you. So you
will have a worse punishment.

15 "How terrible for you, teachers
of the law and Pharisees! You are
hypocrites! You travel across land
and sea to find one person who will
change to your ways. When you find
that person, you make him more fit
for hell than you are.

16 “How terrible for you! You
guide the people, but you are blind.
You say, ‘If people swear by the
Temple when they make a promise,
that means nothing. But if they
swear by the gold that is in the
Temple, they must keep that promise.’ 17 You are blind fools! Which is
greater: the gold or the Temple that
makes that gold holy? 18 And you say,
‘If people swear by the altar when
they make a promise, that means
nothing. But if they swear by the gift
on the altar, they must keep that
promise.’ 19 You are blind! Which is
greater: the gift or the altar that
makes the gift holy? 20 The person
who swears by the altar is really using the altar and also everything on
the altar. 21 And the person who
swears by the Temple is really using
the Temple and also everything in
the Temple. 22 The person who
swears by heaven is also using God’s
throne and the One who sits on that
throne.”

OLD TESTAMENT READING

A terrible and shocking thing
has happened in the land of
Judah:
31 The prophets speak lies,
and the priests take power into
their own hands,
and my people love it this way.
But what will you do when the
end comes?”

Jeremiah 5:30–31

INSIGHTS

From the Hallmark-card theology of a thousand churches to the nauseating nonsense of PTL, American evangelicalism is awash in a sloppy, sentimental, superficial theology that wouldn’t empower a clockwork mouse, let alone a disciple of Christ in the tough, modern world. . . .

. . . Having visited almost all the countries in the English-speaking world, I would say that I know none where the churches are more full and the sermons more empty than in America. There are magnificent exceptions, of course. But by and large, I am never hungrier and rarely angrier than when I come out of an American evangelical church after what passes for the preaching of the Word of God.

The problem is not just the heresy, though doubtless there is some of that. Nor is it just the degree of entertainment, and there is lots of that. Nor is it even the appalling gaps in the theology, for there is far too much of that. The real problem is that in what is said there is almost no sense of announcement from God; and in what is shown, there is almost no sense of anointing by God.

Jeremiah attacked the false prophets of his day with the damning question, “Which of them has stood in the council of the LORD, *seen him and heard his word?” (Jer 23:18). Are we who profess a high view of authority much better in practice? Is such a standard too demanding?*

Os Guinness

PAUSE FOR REFLECTION

Study these readings and list the things that God’s teachers are supposed to do. Why will God punish false spiritual leaders? How well do you think today’s religious leaders measure up?

TUESDAY

God Will Punish Those Who Persecute His Messengers

Matthew 23:23—24:8

How terrible for you, teachers of
the law and Pharisees! You are hypocrites! You give to God one-tenth of
everything you earn—even your
mint, dill, and cumin. But you don't
obey the really important teachings of
the law—justice, mercy, and being
loyal. These are the things you should
do, as well as those other things. 24 You
guide the people, but you are blind! You
are like a person who picks a fly out of
a drink and then swallows a camel!
25 "How terrible for you, teachers
of the law and Pharisees! You are
hypocrites! You wash the outside of
your cups and dishes, but inside they
are full of things you got by cheating others and by pleasing only yourselves. 26 Pharisees, you are blind!
First make the inside of the cup
clean, and then the outside of the
cup can be truly clean.
27 "How terrible for you, teachers
of the law and Pharisees! You are
hypocrites! You are like tombs that
are painted white. Outside, those
tombs look fine, but inside, they are
full of the bones of dead people and
all kinds of unclean things. 28 It is the
same with you. People look at you and
think you are good, but on the inside
you are full of hypocrisy and evil.
29 "How terrible for you, teachers
of the law and Pharisees! You are
hypocrites! You build tombs for the
prophets, and you show honor to the
graves of those who lived good lives.
30 You say, 'If we had lived during the
time of our ancestors, we would not
have helped them kill the prophets.'
31 But you give proof that you are
children of those who murdered the
prophets. 32 And you will complete
the sin that your ancestors started.
33 "You are snakes! A family of
poisonous snakes! How are you going to escape God's judgment? 34 So I
tell you this: I am sending to you
prophets and wise men and teachers.
Some of them you will kill and crucify. Some of them you will beat in
your synagogues and chase from
town to town. 35 So you will be guilty
for the death of all the good people
who have been killed on earth—from
the murder of that good man Abel to
the murder of Zechariah son of Bera-
kiah, whom you murdered between
the Temple and the altar. 36 I tell you
the truth, all of these things will happen to you people who are living now.

Jesus Feels Sorry for Jerusalem

Jerusalem, Jerusalem! You kill the
prophets and stone to death those
who are sent to you. Many times I
wanted to gather your people as a
hen gathers her chicks under her
wings, but you did not let me. 38 Now
your house will be left completely
empty. 39 I tell you, you will not see
me again until that time when you
will say, 'God bless the One who
comes in the name of the Lord.' "

The Temple Will Be Destroyed

24 As Jesus left the Temple and
was walking away, his followers came up to show him the
Temple's buildings. 2 Jesus asked,
"Do you see all these buildings? I tell
you the truth, not one stone will be

left on another. Every stone will be thrown down to the ground."

[3] Later, as Jesus was sitting on the Mount of Olives, his followers came to be alone with him. They said, "Tell us, when will these things happen? And what will be the sign that it is time for you to come again and for this age to end?"

[4] Jesus answered, "Be careful that no one fools you. [5] Many will come in my name, saying, 'I am the Christ,' and they will fool many people. [6] You will hear about wars and stories of wars that are coming, but don't be afraid. These things must happen before the end comes. [7] Nations will fight against other nations; kingdoms will fight against other kingdoms. There will be times when there is no food for people to eat, and there will be earthquakes in different places. [8] These things are like the first pains when something new is about to be born."

OLD TESTAMENT READING

Crooked leaders cannot be your
friends.
They use the law to cause
suffering.
[21] They join forces against people
who do right
and sentence to death the
innocent.
[22] But the LORD is my defender;
my God is the rock of my
protection.
[23] God will pay them back for their
sins
and will destroy them for their
evil.
The LORD our God will destroy
them.

Psalm 94:20–23

INSIGHTS

A young man came to D. L. Moody and said, "Mr. Moody, I want to be a Christian; but must I give up the world?" Moody characteristically replied, "Young man, if you live the out-and-out Christian life, the world will soon give you up." If we are popular with the crowd of worldlings, or if we are not penalised in some way for our attachment to Christ, we have good cause to inspect our discipleship. . . .

The world varies its ways of persecuting us. Sometimes it uses the sword, and sometimes the lip of scorn. Most of us can stand the sword far better than derision or sarcasm. . . .

Let us remember, also, that there is another side to this being penalised for Christian godliness. It is equally true that all who live ungodly, and persecute God's people, shall suffer punishment. Old Testament incidents, as Paul tells us, were recorded for our admonition, as warnings and examples to us. Under the old dispensation God frequently visited punishment upon persons immediately after their committing of wrongs, so that the connection between the sin and the punishment might be clearly seen. In this present age, the judgment of the ungodly may be deferred; but it is none the less certain, and will be awful when at last it falls.

J. Sydlow Baxter

PAUSE FOR REFLECTION

What are Jesus' accusations against the teachers and Pharisees? What are his warnings to them?

WEDNESDAY

The Unmistakable and Terrible Signs of the End Times

Matthew 24:9–35

Then people will arrest you, hand
you over to be hurt, and kill you.
They will hate you because you believe in me. 10 At that time, many will
lose their faith, and they will turn
against each other and hate each
other. 11 Many false prophets will
come and cause many people to believe lies. 12 There will be more and
more evil in the world, so most
people will stop showing their love
for each other. 13 But those people
who keep their faith until the end will
be saved. 14 The Good News about
God's kingdom will be preached in
all the world, to every nation. Then
the end will come.

15 "Daniel the prophet spoke
about 'the destroying terror.' You
will see this standing in the holy
place." (You who read this should
understand what it means.) 16 "At
that time, the people in Judea should
run away to the mountains. 17 If
people are on the roofs of their
houses, they must not go down to
get anything out of their houses. 18 If
people are in the fields, they must
not go back to get their coats. 19 At
that time, how terrible it will be for
women who are pregnant or have
nursing babies! 20 Pray that it will not
be winter or a Sabbath day when
these things happen and you have to
run away, 21 because at that time
there will be much trouble. There
will be more trouble than there has
ever been since the beginning of the
world until now, and nothing as bad
will ever happen again. 22 God has
decided to make that terrible time
short. Otherwise, no one would go
on living. But God will make that
time short to help the people he has
chosen. 23 At that time, someone
might say to you, 'Look, there is the
Christ!' Or another person might
say, 'There he is!' But don't believe
them. 24 False Christs and false
prophets will come and perform
great wonders and miracles. They
will try to fool even the people God
has chosen, if that is possible. 25 Now
I have warned you about this before
it happens.

26 "If people tell you, 'The Christ
is in the desert,' don't go there. If
they say, 'The Christ is in the inner
room,' don't believe it. 27 When the
Son of Man comes, he will be seen
by everyone, like lightning flashing
from the east to the west. 28 Wherever the dead body is, there the vultures will gather.

29 "Soon after the trouble of those
days,

'the sun will grow dark,
  and the moon will not give its
    light.
The stars will fall from the sky.
  And the powers of the heavens
    will be shaken.'

Isaiah 13:10; 34:4

30 "At that time, the sign of the Son
of Man will appear in the sky. Then
all the peoples of the world will cry.
They will see the Son of Man coming on clouds in the sky with great
power and glory. 31 He will use a loud
trumpet to send his angels all
around the earth, and they will
gather his chosen people from every
part of the world.

[32]"Learn a lesson from the fig tree: When its branches become green and soft and new leaves appear, you know summer is near. [33]In the same way, when you see all these things happening, you will know that the time is near, ready to come. [34]I tell you the truth, all these things will happen while the people of this time are still living. [35]Earth and sky will be destroyed, but the words I have said will never be destroyed."

OLD TESTAMENT READING

Look, the LORD's day of judging
is coming—
a terrible day, a day of God's
anger.
He will destroy the land
and the sinners who live in it.
[10]The stars will not show their
light;
the skies will be dark.
The sun will grow dark as it rises,
and the moon will not give its
light.

Isaiah 13:9–10

INSIGHTS

To a unique degree this generation has witnessed the universal and dramatic fulfillment of prophecy. Many of the signs Jesus said would herald His return have developed before our eyes.

There is the evangelistic sign: "This gospel of the kingdom will be preached in the whole world as a testimony to all nations, and then the end will come" (Matthew 24:14).

This prophecy has been fulfilled in our generation to a degree that has never before been the case. There is now no major nation in which there is no Christian witness. . . .

There is the religious sign: "That day will not come until the rebellion occurs and the man of lawlessness is revealed" (2 Thessalonians 2:3).

Unfortunately, we can see this sign being fulfilled all around us. As Jesus foretold, the love of the many is growing cold (Matthew 24:12). . . .

Political signs abound. Could prevailing world conditions have been more accurately and comprehensively described than in our Lord's words in Luke 21:25–26? "There will be signs. . . . On the earth, nations will be in anguish and perplexity. . . . Men will faint from terror, apprehensive of what is coming on the world."

There is the Jewish sign: "Jerusalem will be trampled on by the Gentiles until the times of the Gentiles are fulfilled" (Luke 21:24). . . .

. . . For the first time in 2,500 years, Jerusalem is not dominated by Gentiles. . . .

Whatever view we hold regarding the details surrounding the second coming of Christ, history is moving rapidly—not to cataclysm merely, but to consummation.

J. Oswald Sanders

PAUSE FOR REFLECTION

Why did Jesus warn his followers about the end times? What event will be perfectly clear to all people? Despite the horror of these events, what glorious hope does Jesus promise to his people at the end?

THURSDAY

Always Be Ready for the Lord's Coming

Matthew 24:36—25:13

When Will Jesus Come Again?

No one knows when that day or
time will be, not the angels in
heaven, not even the Son. Only the
Father knows. 37 When the Son of
Man comes, it will be like what happened during Noah's time. 38 In
those days before the flood, people
were eating and drinking, marrying
and giving their children to be married, until the day Noah entered the
boat. 39 They knew nothing about
what was happening until the flood
came and destroyed them. It will be
the same when the Son of Man
comes. 40 Two men will be in the
field. One will be taken, and the
other will be left. 41 Two women will
be grinding grain with a mill. One
will be taken, and the other will be
left.

42 "So always be ready, because
you don't know the day your Lord
will come. 43 Remember this: If the
owner of the house knew what time
of night a thief was coming, the
owner would watch and not let the
thief break in. 44 So you also must be
ready, because the Son of Man will
come at a time you don't expect him.

45 "Who is the wise and loyal servant that the master trusts to give
the other servants their food at the
right time? 46 When the master
comes and finds the servant doing
his work, the servant will be blessed.
47 I tell you the truth, the master will
choose that servant to take care of
everything he owns. 48 But suppose
that evil servant thinks to himself,
'My master will not come back soon,'
49 and he begins to beat the other
servants and eat and get drunk with
others like him? 50 The master will
come when that servant is not ready
and is not expecting him. 51 Then the
master will cut him in pieces and
send him away to be with the hypocrites, where people will cry and
grind their teeth with pain.

A Story About Ten Bridesmaids

25 At that time the kingdom of
heaven will be like ten bridesmaids who took their lamps and
went to wait for the bridegroom.
2 Five of them were foolish and five
were wise. 3 The five foolish bridesmaids took their lamps, but they did
not take more oil for the lamps to
burn. 4 The wise bridesmaids took
their lamps and more oil in jars. 5 Because the bridegroom was late, they
became sleepy and went to sleep.

6 "At midnight someone cried out,
'The bridegroom is coming! Come
and meet him!' 7 Then all the bridesmaids woke up and got their lamps
ready. 8 But the foolish ones said to
the wise, 'Give us some of your oil,
because our lamps are going out.'
9 The wise bridesmaids answered,
'No, the oil we have might not be
enough for all of us. Go to the people
who sell oil and buy some for yourselves.'

10 "So while the five foolish bridesmaids went to buy oil, the bridegroom came. The bridesmaids who
were ready went in with the bridegroom to the wedding feast. Then
the door was closed and locked.

11 "Later the others came back
and said, 'Sir, sir, open the door to
let us in.' 12 But the bridegroom answered, 'I tell you the truth, I don't
want to know you.'
13 "So always be ready, because
you don't know the day or the hour
the Son of Man will come."

OLD TESTAMENT READING

The LORD All-Powerful says, "I will
send my messenger, who will prepare the way for me. Suddenly, the
Lord you are looking for will come
to his Temple; the messenger of the
agreement, whom you want, will
come." 2 No one can live through
that time; no one can survive when
he comes. He will be like a purifying fire and like laundry soap. 5 The
LORD All-Powerful says, "Then I will
come to you and judge you. I will
be quick to testify against those
who take part in evil magic, adultery, and lying under oath, those
who cheat workers of their pay and
who cheat widows and orphans,
those who are unfair to foreigners,
and those who do not respect me."
16 Then those who honored the
LORD spoke with each other, and the
LORD listened and heard them. The
names of those who honored the LORD
and respected him were written in his
presence in a book to be remembered.
17 The LORD All-Powerful says,
"They belong to me; on that day they
will be my very own. As a parent
shows mercy to his child who serves
him, I will show mercy to my people.
18 You will again see the difference between good and evil people, between
those who serve God and those who
don't."

Malachi 3:1, 2, 5, 16–18

INSIGHTS

We look for the return of the Lord because He said many times that He would come—and because it is one of the most frequently mentioned subjects in the Bible. Christ is with us today through His Holy Spirit, and He will be with Christians and with the church down to the end of the age. When He ascended up into heaven, the disciples were told by two angels standing by that He would return again as they were now seeing Him go (see Acts 1:11).

The climactic event of history is yet in the future. It will be sudden and final—the culmination of the ages. It will take the unbelieving world by surprise, and people will try to hide from His holy presence. At the return of Christ the resurrection of believers will take place. They will be gathered together to be with the Lord forever. We can only speculate about the exact details of His return. The important thing is that He is coming again and that we yet have time to trust in Him as our Savior and Lord. The Bible says all people must face Him at that time—as either Savior or Judge: "When the Son of Man comes in his glory . . . he will sit on his throne in heavenly glory" (Matthew 25:31).

Billy Graham

APPLICATION

What do you want to be doing when Jesus comes again? Will you be with those who say it is useless to serve God, or will you stand with those who honor the Lord? Pray that you will remain faithful.

FRIDAY

God Rewards Kindness

Matthew 25:14–40

A Story About Three Servants

The kingdom of heaven is like a
man who was going to another place
for a visit. Before he left, he called
for his servants and told them to
take care of his things while he was
gone. 15 He gave one servant five
bags of gold, another servant two
bags of gold, and a third servant one
bag of gold, to each one as much as
he could handle. Then he left. 16 The
servant who got five bags went
quickly to invest the money and
earned five more bags. 17 In the same
way, the servant who had two bags
invested them and earned two more.
18 But the servant who got one bag
went out and dug a hole in the
ground and hid the master's money.

19 "After a long time the master
came home and asked the servants
what they did with his money. 20 The
servant who was given five bags of
gold brought five more bags to the
master and said, 'Master, you
trusted me to care for five bags of
gold, so I used your five bags to earn
five more.' 21 The master answered,
'You did well. You are a good and
loyal servant. Because you were
loyal with small things, I will let you
care for much greater things. Come
and share my joy with me.'

22 "Then the servant who had
been given two bags of gold came to
the master and said, 'Master, you
gave me two bags of gold to care for,
so I used your two bags to earn two
more.' 23 The master answered, 'You
did well. You are a good and loyal
servant. Because you were loyal
with small things, I will let you care
for much greater things. Come and
share my joy with me.'

24 "Then the servant who had
been given one bag of gold came to
the master and said, 'Master, I knew
that you were a hard man. You harvest things you did not plant. You
gather crops where you did not sow
any seed. 25 So I was afraid and went
and hid your money in the ground.
Here is your bag of gold.' 26 The master answered, 'You are a wicked and
lazy servant! You say you knew that
I harvest things I did not plant and
that I gather crops where I did not
sow any seed. 27 So you should have
put my gold in the bank. Then, when
I came home, I would have received
my gold back with interest.'

28 "So the master told his other
servants, 'Take the bag of gold from
that servant and give it to the servant who has ten bags of gold.
29 Those who have much will get
more, and they will have much more
than they need. But those who do
not have much will have everything
taken away from them.' 30 Then the
master said, 'Throw that useless servant outside, into the darkness
where people will cry and grind their
teeth with pain.'

The King Will Judge All People

The Son of Man will come again in
his great glory, with all his angels.
He will be King and sit on his great
throne. 32 All the nations of the world
will be gathered before him, and he
will separate them into two groups
as a shepherd separates the sheep

from the goats. 33 The Son of Man
will put the sheep on his right and
the goats on his left.
34 "Then the King will say to the
people on his right, 'Come, my Father has given you his blessing. Receive the kingdom God has prepared
for you since the world was made. 35 I
was hungry, and you gave me food. I
was thirsty, and you gave me something to drink. I was alone and away
from home, and you invited me into
your house. 36 I was without clothes,
and you gave me something to wear.
I was sick, and you cared for me. I was
in prison, and you visited me.'
37 "Then the good people will answer, 'Lord, when did we see you hungry and give you food, or thirsty and
give you something to drink? 38 When
did we see you alone and away from
home and invite you into our house?
When did we see you without clothes
and give you something to wear?
39 When did we see you sick or in
prison and care for you?'
40 "Then the King will answer, 'I
tell you the truth, anything you did
for even the least of my people here,
you also did for me.'"

OLD TESTAMENT READING

Happy is the person who thinks
about the poor.
When trouble comes, the LORD
will save him.
2 The LORD will protect him and
spare his life
and will bless him in the land.
He will not let his enemies take
him.
3 The LORD will give him strength
when he is sick,
and he will make him well again.

Psalm 41:1–3

INSIGHTS

One kind word can warm three winter months," says a Japanese proverb.

Kind words indeed warm the human spirit. Kindness is literally love in action, showing genuine friendship to others by regarding them as important in God's sight and worthy of dignity and respect. It involves treating others with courtesy, lending encouragement, and freely offering yourself or your resources to help a person in need, no strings attached. . . .

In the book of Proverbs, we read that kindness is a prime quality of a virtuous woman: "When she speaks, her words are wise, and kindness is the rule for everything she says" (Proverbs 31:26). Men, these virtues are for us, too!

Jim has discovered the pleasure of kindness. He makes a special effort to brighten someone's day with an unexpected kind word or gesture. . . . At work, he frequently expresses appreciation to others for the jobs they do. With his neighbors, he is quick to lend a helping hand or offer encouragement.

Imagine the impact Christians could have on the world if kindness were the rule in all we do!

Bill Bright

APPLICATION

What in these readings shows that God considers mistreatment of the poor, homeless, sick, and downtrodden to be a personal insult? How does that inspire you to be merciful, kind, and generous?

WEEKEND

Honoring God Is a Beautiful Thing

Matthew 25:41—26:19

Then the King will say to those on his left, 'Go away from me. You will be punished. Go into the fire that burns forever that was prepared for the devil and his angels. [42]I was hungry, and you gave me nothing to eat. I was thirsty, and you gave me nothing to drink. [43]I was alone and away from home, and you did not invite me into your house. I was without clothes, and you gave me nothing to wear. I was sick and in prison, and you did not care for me.'

[44]"Then those people will answer, 'Lord, when did we see you hungry or thirsty or alone and away from home or without clothes or sick or in prison? When did we see these things and not help you?'

[45]"Then the King will answer, 'I tell you the truth, anything you refused to do for even the least of my people here, you refused to do for me.'

[46]"These people will go off to be punished forever, but the good people will go to live forever."

The Plan to Kill Jesus

26 After Jesus finished saying all these things, he told his followers, [2]"You know that the day after tomorrow is the day of the Passover Feast. On that day the Son of Man will be given to his enemies to be crucified."

[3]Then the leading priests and the older Jewish leaders had a meeting at the palace of the high priest, named Caiaphas. [4]At the meeting, they planned to set a trap to arrest Jesus and kill him. [5]But they said, "We must not do it during the feast, because the people might cause a riot."

Perfume for Jesus' Burial

Jesus was in Bethany at the house of Simon, who had a skin disease. [7]While Jesus was there, a woman approached him with an alabaster jar filled with expensive perfume. She poured this perfume on Jesus' head while he was eating.

[8]His followers were upset when they saw the woman do this. They asked, "Why waste that perfume? [9]It could have been sold for a great deal of money and the money given to the poor."

[10]Knowing what had happened, Jesus said, "Why are you troubling this woman? She did an excellent thing for me. [11]You will always have the poor with you, but you will not always have me. [12]This woman poured perfume on my body to prepare me for burial. [13]I tell you the truth, wherever the Good News is preached in all the world, what this woman has done will be told, and people will remember her."

Judas Becomes an Enemy of Jesus

Then one of the twelve apostles, Judas Iscariot, went to talk to the leading priests. [15]He said, "What will you pay me for giving Jesus to you?" And they gave him thirty silver coins. [16]After that, Judas watched for the best time to turn Jesus in.

Jesus Eats the Passover Meal

On the first day of the Feast of Unleavened Bread, the followers came to Jesus. They said, "Where do you want us to prepare for you to eat the Passover meal?"

18 Jesus answered, "Go into the city to a certain man and tell him, 'The Teacher says: The chosen time is near. I will have the Passover with my followers at your house.' " 19 The followers did what Jesus told them to do, and they prepared the Passover meal.

OLD TESTAMENT READING

Manoah said to the angel of the LORD, "We would like you to stay awhile so we can cook a young goat for you."

16 The angel of the LORD answered, "Even if I stay awhile, I would not eat your food. But if you want to prepare something, offer a burnt offering to the LORD." (Manoah did not understand that the man was really the angel of the LORD.)

17 Then Manoah asked the angel of the LORD, "What is your name? Then we will honor you when what you have said really happens."

18 The angel of the LORD said, "Why do you ask my name? It is too amazing for you to understand." 19 So Manoah sacrificed a young goat on a rock and offered some grain as a gift to the LORD. Then an amazing thing happened as Manoah and his wife watched. 20 The flames went up to the sky from the altar. As the fire burned, the angel of the LORD went up to heaven in the flame. When Manoah and his wife saw that, they bowed facedown on the ground. 21 The angel of the LORD did not appear to them again. Then Manoah understood that the man was really the angel of the LORD. 22 Manoah said, "We have seen God, so we will surely die."

23 But his wife said to him, "If the LORD wanted to kill us, he would not have accepted our burnt offering or grain offering. He would not have shown us all these things or told us all this."

Judges 13:15–23

INSIGHTS

It was said of the soldiers of the first Napoleon that they were content to die in the ditch if only he rode over them to victory. With their last breath they cried, "Long live the Emperor!" It seemed as though they had lost all thought and care of their own interests, so long as glory was given to his name. So should it be of us. Higher than our own comfort, or success, or popularity, should be the one thought of the glory of our God. Let Christ be honored, loved, exalted, at whatever cost to us. . . .

. . . Live to please God, and He will breathe on you His peace. Seek His glory, and He will make your heart His home. Do His will, and thereby good shall come to you.

F. B. Meyer

ACTION POINT

Review the ways people honored God in these readings (including the Matthew 25 parable). Spend some time honoring God in prayer today. Then, list the ways you want to honor God. Start glorifying him today!

MONDAY

God Cares for His Scattered Sheep

Matthew 26:20–46

In the evening Jesus was sitting at
the table with his twelve followers.
21 As they were eating, Jesus said, "I
tell you the truth, one of you will turn
against me."
22 This made the followers very
sad. Each one began to say to Jesus,
"Surely, Lord, I am not the one who
will turn against you, am I?"
23 Jesus answered, "The man who
has dipped his hand with me into the
bowl is the one who will turn against
me. 24 The Son of Man will die, just
as the Scriptures say. But how terrible it will be for the person who
hands the Son of Man over to be
killed. It would be better for him if
he had never been born."
25 Then Judas, who would give
Jesus to his enemies, said to Jesus,
"Teacher, surely I am not the one, am
I?"
Jesus answered, "Yes, it is you."

The Lord's Supper

While they were eating, Jesus took
some bread and thanked God for it
and broke it. Then he gave it to his
followers and said, "Take this bread
and eat it; this is my body."
27 Then Jesus took a cup and
thanked God for it and gave it to the
followers. He said, "Every one of you
drink this. 28 This is my blood which
is the new agreement that God
makes with his people. This blood is
poured out for many to forgive their
sins. 29 I tell you this: I will not drink
of this fruit of the vine again until
that day when I drink it new with you
in my Father's kingdom."
30 After singing a hymn, they went
out to the Mount of Olives.

Jesus' Followers Will Leave Him

Jesus told his followers, "Tonight
you will all stumble in your faith on
account of me, because it is written
in the Scriptures:
'I will kill the shepherd,
and the sheep will scatter.'
Zechariah 13:7
32 But after I rise from the dead, I will
go ahead of you into Galilee."
33 Peter said, "Everyone else may
stumble in their faith because of you,
but I will not."
34 Jesus said, "I tell you the truth,
tonight before the rooster crows you
will say three times that you don't
know me."
35 But Peter said, "I will never say
that I don't know you! I will even die
with you!" And all the other followers said the same thing.

Jesus Prays Alone

Then Jesus went with his followers
to a place called Gethsemane. He
said to them, "Sit here while I go
over there and pray." 37 He took Peter and the two sons of Zebedee with
him, and he began to be very sad
and troubled. 38 He said to them, "My
heart is full of sorrow, to the point
of death. Stay here and watch with
me."
39 After walking a little farther
away from them, Jesus fell to the
ground and prayed, "My Father, if it
is possible, do not give me this cup

of suffering. But do what you want,
not what I want." 40 Then Jesus went
back to his followers and found them
asleep. He said to Peter, "You men
could not stay awake with me for one
hour? 41 Stay awake and pray for
strength against temptation. The
spirit wants to do what is right, but
the body is weak."
42 Then Jesus went away a second
time and prayed, "My Father, if it is
not possible for this painful thing to
be taken from me, and if I must do
it, I pray that what you want will be
done."
43 Then he went back to his followers, and again he found them asleep,
because their eyes were heavy. 44 So
Jesus left them and went away and
prayed a third time, saying the same
thing.
45 Then Jesus went back to his followers and said, "Are you still sleeping and resting? The time has come
for the Son of Man to be handed over
to sinful people. 46 Get up, we must
go. Look, here comes the man who
has turned against me."

OLD TESTAMENT READING

This is what the Lord GOD says: I,
myself, will search for my sheep and
take care of them. 12 As a shepherd
takes care of his scattered flock
when it is found, I will take care of
my sheep. I will save them from all
the places where they were scattered on a cloudy and dark day. I will
bring them out from the nations and
gather them from the countries. 16 I
will search for the lost, bring back
those that strayed away, put bandages on those that were hurt, and
make the weak strong.'"

Ezekiel 34:11–12, 16a

INSIGHTS

Lambs are wont to lag behind, prone to wander, and apt to grow weary, but from all the danger of these infirmities the Shepherd protects them with His arm of power. He finds new-born souls, like young lambs, ready to perish—He nourishes them till life becomes vigorous; He finds weak minds ready to faint and die—He consoles them and renews their strength. All the little ones He gathers, for it is not the will of our heavenly Father that one of them should perish. What a quick eye He must have to see them all! What a tender heart to care for them all! What a far-reaching and potent arm, to gather them all! In His lifetime on earth He was a great gatherer of the weaker sort, and now that He dwells in heaven, His loving heart yearns towards the meek and contrite, the timid and feeble, the fearful and fainting here below. How gently did He gather me to Himself, to His truth, to His blood, to His love, to His church! With what effectual grace did He compel me to Himself! Since my first conversion, how frequently has He restored me from my wanderings, and once again folded me within the circle of His everlasting arm! The best of all is, that He does it all Himself personally, not delegating the task of love, but condescending Himself to rescue and preserve His most unworthy servant.

Charles Spurgeon

APPLICATION

How do these readings comfort you? Thank God that he promises to care for you.

TUESDAY

The Pain of Being Betrayed by Friends

Matthew 26:47–68

Jesus Is Arrested

While Jesus was still speaking, Judas, one of the twelve apostles, came
up. With him were many people carrying swords and clubs who had
been sent from the leading priests
and the older Jewish leaders of the
people. 48 Judas had planned to give
them a signal, saying, "The man I
kiss is Jesus. Arrest him." 49 At once
Judas went to Jesus and said, "Greetings, Teacher!" and kissed him.

50 Jesus answered, "Friend, do
what you came to do."

Then the people came and
grabbed Jesus and arrested him.
51 When that happened, one of Jesus'
followers reached for his sword and
pulled it out. He struck the servant
of the high priest and cut off his ear.
52 Jesus said to the man, "Put your
sword back in its place. All who use
swords will be killed with swords.
53 Surely you know I could ask my
Father, and he would give me more
than twelve armies of angels. 54 But
it must happen this way to bring
about what the Scriptures say."

55 Then Jesus said to the crowd,
"You came to get me with swords
and clubs as if I were a criminal. Every day I sat in the Temple teaching,
and you did not arrest me there.
56 But all these things have happened
so that it will come about as the
prophets wrote." Then all of Jesus'
followers left him and ran away.

Jesus Before the Leaders

Those people who arrested Jesus
led him to the house of Caiaphas, the
high priest, where the teachers of
the law and the older Jewish leaders
were gathered. 58 Peter followed far
behind to the courtyard of the high
priest's house, and he sat down with
the guards to see what would happen to Jesus.

59 The leading priests and the
whole Jewish council tried to find
something false against Jesus so
they could kill him. 60 Many people
came and told lies about him, but the
council could find no real reason to
kill him. Then two people came and
said, 61 "This man said, 'I can destroy
the Temple of God and build it again
in three days.' "

62 Then the high priest stood up
and said to Jesus, "Aren't you going
to answer? Don't you have something to say about their charges
against you?" 63 But Jesus said nothing.

Again the high priest said to
Jesus, "I command you by the power
of the living God: Tell us if you are
the Christ, the Son of God."

64 Jesus answered, "Those are
your words. But I tell you, in the future you will see the Son of Man sitting at the right hand of God, the
Powerful One, and coming on
clouds in the sky."

65 When the high priest heard
this, he tore his clothes and said,
"This man has said things that are
against God! We don't need any
more witnesses; you all heard him
say these things against God. 66 What
do you think?"

The people answered, "He should
die."

[67]Then the people there spat in Jesus' face and beat him with their fists. Others slapped him. [68]They said, "Prove to us that you are a prophet, you Christ! Tell us who hit you!"

OLD TESTAMENT READING

It was not an enemy insulting me.
  I could stand that.
It was not someone who hated me.
  I could hide from him.
[13]But it is you, a person like me,
  my companion and good
    friend.
[14]We had a good friendship
  and walked together to God's
    Temple.

[20]The one who was my friend
  attacks his friends
  and breaks his promises.
[21]His words are slippery like butter,
  but war is in his heart.
His words are smoother than oil,
  but they cut like knives.

Psalm 55:12–14, 20–21

INSIGHTS

Have you ever been betrayed by a friend? If so, you know the pain of separation which resembles the grief of death. When Judas agreed to betray Jesus, he might as well have hammered the spikes that would later be driven through Jesus' hands.

Have you ever wondered how it was possible for one of the apostles (who had witnessed Jesus' power, teaching, and love) to turn him over to his enemies for any amount of money? This, of course, was not Judas' first act of betrayal. As treasurer for the disciples, Judas had been dipping into the till all along. He was a dishonest and greedy man. Even so, the mind races: How in the world could he have betrayed Jesus? . . .

Perhaps we have a clue when we are told about others who refused to accept Jesus as the Christ: "Even after Jesus had done all these miraculous signs in their presence, they still would not believe in him." Judas was not the only one to betray Jesus. All those who refused to believe on him despite the overwhelming evidence of his deity might as well have picked up their own 30 silver coins when Judas did.

Even today there are those who, despite the evidence, continue to betray Jesus through disbelief. How is it possible? Why do they choose to ignore him? . . .

. . . We can choose Christ, or we can choose the world with its false allure. Yet it is not a choice that we make just once in a lifetime. Each day that Judas robbed Jesus was a day of betrayal. And for those who heard Jesus teach, and watched his miracles, yet refused to believe—for them, every day was a day of betrayal.

Do we believe in Jesus, yet live our lives as if we didn't? If so, we too betray Jesus. Will today be a day of faith or a day of betrayal?

F. LaGard Smith

PAUSE FOR REFLECTION

When Jesus answered Judas' betrayal with the words, "Friend, do the thing you came to do," Jesus showed that he knew exactly what was in Judas' heart. If Jesus said the same thing today about your plans, how would you be affected?

WEDNESDAY

God Can Speak to Powerful Leaders Through Dreams

Matthew 26:69—27:20

Peter Says He Doesn't Know Jesus

At that time, as Peter was sitting in
the courtyard, a servant girl came to
him and said, "You also were with
Jesus of Galilee."

70 But Peter said to all the people
there that he was never with Jesus.
He said, "I don't know what you are
talking about."

71 When he left the courtyard and
was at the gate, another girl saw him.
She said to the people there, "This
man was with Jesus of Nazareth."

72 Again, Peter said he was never
with him, saying, "I swear I don't
know this man Jesus!"

73 A short time later, some people
standing there went to Peter and
said, "Surely you are one of those
who followed Jesus. The way you
talk shows it."

74 Then Peter began to place a curse
on himself and swear, "I don't know
the man." At once, a rooster crowed.
75 And Peter remembered what Jesus
had told him: "Before the rooster
crows, you will say three times that
you don't know me." Then Peter went
outside and cried painfully.

Jesus Is Taken to Pilate

27 Early the next morning, all the
leading priests and older leaders of the people decided that Jesus
should die. 2 They tied him, led him
away, and turned him over to Pilate,
the governor.

Judas Kills Himself

Judas, the one who had given Jesus
to his enemies, saw that they had
decided to kill Jesus. Then he was
very sorry for what he had done. So
he took the thirty silver coins back
to the priests and the leaders, 4 saying, "I sinned; I handed over to you
an innocent man."

The leaders answered, "What is
that to us? That's your problem, not
ours."

5 So Judas threw the money into
the Temple. Then he went off and
hanged himself.

6 The leading priests picked up
the silver coins in the Temple and
said, "Our law does not allow us to
keep this money with the Temple
money, because it has paid for a
man's death." 7 So they decided to
use the coins to buy Potter's Field
as a place to bury strangers who
died in Jerusalem. 8 That is why that
field is still called the Field of Blood.
9 So what Jeremiah the prophet had
said came true: "They took thirty
silver coins. That is how little the Israelites thought he was worth.
10 They used those thirty silver
coins to buy the potter's field, as the
Lord commanded me."

Pilate Questions Jesus

Jesus stood before Pilate the governor, and Pilate asked him, "Are you
the king of the Jews?"

Jesus answered, "Those are your
words."

12 When the leading priests and
the older leaders accused Jesus, he
said nothing.

13 So Pilate said to Jesus, "Don't
you hear them accusing you of all
these things?"

[14]But Jesus said nothing in answer to Pilate, and Pilate was very surprised at this.

Pilate Tries to Free Jesus

Every year at the time of Passover the governor would free one prisoner whom the people chose. [16]At
that time there was a man in prison, named Barabbas, who was known to
be very bad. [17]When the people
gathered at Pilate's house, Pilate said, "Whom do you want me to set free: Barabbas or Jesus who is called the
Christ?" [18]Pilate knew that the
people turned Jesus in to him because they were jealous.

[19]While Pilate was sitting there on the judge's seat, his wife sent this message to him: "Don't do anything to that man, because he is innocent. Today I had a dream about him, and it troubled me very much."

[20]But the leading priests and older leaders convinced the crowd to ask for Barabbas to be freed and for Jesus to be killed.

OLD TESTAMENT READING

The king asked Daniel, who was also called Belteshazzar, "Are you able to tell me what I dreamed and what it means?"

[27]Daniel answered, "No wise man, magician, or fortune-teller can explain to the king the secret he has asked
about. [28]But there is a God in heaven who explains secret things, and he has shown King Nebuchadnezzar what will happen at a later time."

Daniel 2:26–28a

INSIGHTS

On one occasion when I was in prayer, I had a vision in which I saw how all things are seen in God. I cannot explain what I saw, but what I saw remains to this day, deeply imprinted upon my soul. It was a great act of grace in God to give me that vision. It puts me to unspeakable confusion, shame, and horror whenever I recall that magnificent sight, and then think of my sin. I believe that had the Lord been pleased to send me that great revelation of Himself earlier in my life, it would have kept me back from much sin. . . .

Suppose the Godhead to be like a vast globe of light, a globe larger than the whole world, and that all our actions are seen in that all-embracing globe. . . . I saw all my most filthy actions gathered up and reflected back upon me from that world of light. I tell you it was the most pitiful and dreadful thing to see. I did not know where to hide myself, for that shining light, in which there was no darkness at all, held the whole world within it, and all worlds. . . .

. . . Oh that those who commit deeds of darkness could be made to see this! . . . Oh, the madness of committing sin in the immediate presence of a Majesty so great.

St. Teresa of Avila

PAUSE FOR REFLECTION

Why did Pilate ignore his wife's urgent warning? What important messages from God are you ignoring?

THURSDAY

The Wicked Insult the Righteous

Matthew 27:21–44

Pilate said, "I have Barabbas and
Jesus. Which do you want me to set
free for you?"
The people answered, "Barabbas."
22 Pilate asked, "So what should I
do with Jesus, the one called the
Christ?"
They all answered, "Crucify him!"
23 Pilate asked, "Why? What
wrong has he done?"
But they shouted louder, "Crucify
him!"
24 When Pilate saw that he could
do nothing about this and that a riot
was starting, he took some water
and washed his hands in front of the
crowd. Then he said, "I am not guilty
of this man's death. You are the ones
who are causing it!"
25 All the people answered, "We
and our children will be responsible
for his death."
26 Then he set Barabbas free. But
Jesus was beaten with whips and handed over to the soldiers to be crucified.
27 The governor's soldiers took
Jesus into the governor's palace, and
they all gathered around him.
28 They took off his clothes and put
a red robe on him. 29 Using thorny
branches, they made a crown, put it
on his head, and put a stick in his
right hand. Then the soldiers bowed
before Jesus and made fun of him,
saying, "Hail, King of the Jews!"
30 They spat on Jesus. Then they took
his stick and began to beat him on
the head. 31 After they finished, the
soldiers took off the robe and put his
own clothes on him again. Then they
led him away to be crucified.

Jesus Is Crucified

As the soldiers were going out of
the city with Jesus, they forced a
man from Cyrene, named Simon, to
carry the cross for Jesus. 33 They all
came to the place called Golgotha,
which means the Place of the Skull.
34 The soldiers gave Jesus wine
mixed with gall to drink. He tasted
the wine but refused to drink it.
35 When the soldiers had crucified
him, they threw lots to decide who
would get his clothes. 36 The soldiers
sat there and continued watching
him. 37 They put a sign above Jesus'
head with a charge against him. It
said: THIS IS JESUS, THE KING OF THE
JEWS. 38 Two robbers were crucified
beside Jesus, one on the right and
the other on the left. 39 People
walked by and insulted Jesus and
shook their heads, 40 saying, "You
said you could destroy the Temple
and build it again in three days. So
save yourself! Come down from that
cross if you are really the Son of
God!"
41 The leading priests, the teachers of the law, and the older Jewish
leaders were also making fun of
Jesus. 42 They said, "He saved others,
but he can't save himself! He says he
is the king of Israel! If he is the king,
let him come down now from the
cross. Then we will believe in him.
43 He trusts in God, so let God save
him now, if God really wants him. He
himself said, 'I am the Son of God.' "
44 And in the same way, the robbers
who were being crucified beside
Jesus also insulted him.

OLD TESTAMENT READING

But I am like a worm instead of
a man.
People make fun of me and
hate me.
7Those who look at me laugh.
They stick out their tongues
and shake their heads.
8They say, "Turn to the LORD for
help.
Maybe he will save you.
If he likes you,
maybe he will rescue you."

Psalm 22:6–8

Who would have believed what
we heard?
Who saw the LORD's power in
this?
2He grew up like a small plant
before the LORD,
like a root growing in a dry land.
He had no special beauty or form
to make us notice him;
there was nothing in his
appearance to make us
desire him.
3He was hated and rejected by
people.
He had much pain and suffering.
People would not even look at
him.
He was hated, and we didn't
even notice him.

5But he was wounded for the
wrong we did;
he was crushed for the evil we
did.
The punishment, which made us
well, was given to him,
and we are healed because of
his wounds.

Isaiah 53:1–3, 5

INSIGHTS

While Francis Xavier was preaching one day in one of the cities of Japan, a man walked up to him as if he had something to say to him privately. As the missionary leaned closer to hear what he had to say, the man spat on his face.

Without a word or the least sign of annoyance, Xavier pulled out a handkerchief and wiped his face. Then he went on with his important message as if nothing had happened. The scorn of the audience was turned to admiration.

The most learned doctor of the city happened to be present.

"A law which teaches men such virtue, inspires them with such courage, and gives them such complete mastery over themselves," he said, "could not but be from God."

Supernatural power and enablement by God's Holy Spirit make that kind of behavior possible for every believer. Furthermore, that kind of behavior probably will do more to attract and influence an unbelieving world than words ever can.

With Christ as our example, love as our motive, and humility as our covering, let us depend on God's Holy Spirit for the wisdom and strength required to respond to mistreatment in a Christlike way. Then, and only then, are we in a position to reflect honor and glory to the Lord Jesus Christ.

Bill Bright

ACTION POINT

Study the model of grace Christ provides. Pray for grace to bear whatever insults come your way.

FRIDAY

The Eternal Impact of Jesus' Death and Resurrection

Matthew 27:45—28:10

Jesus Dies

At noon the whole country became
dark, and the darkness lasted for
three hours. 46 About three o'clock
Jesus cried out in a loud voice, "Eli,
Eli, lama sabachthani?" This means,
"My God, my God, why have you
rejected me?"
47 Some of the people standing
there who heard this said, "He is calling Elijah."
48 Quickly one of them ran and got
a sponge and filled it with vinegar
and tied it to a stick and gave it to
Jesus to drink. 49 But the others said,
"Don't bother him. We want to see
if Elijah will come to save him."
50 But Jesus cried out again in a
loud voice and died.
51 Then the curtain in the Temple
was torn into two pieces, from the top
to the bottom. Also, the earth shook
and rocks broke apart. 52 The graves
opened, and many of God's people
who had died were raised from the
dead. 53 They came out of the graves
after Jesus was raised from the dead
and went into the holy city, where
they appeared to many people.
54 When the army officer and the
soldiers guarding Jesus saw this
earthquake and everything else that
happened, they were very frightened and said, "He really was the
Son of God!"
55 Many women who had followed
Jesus from Galilee to help him were
standing at a distance from the
cross, watching. 56 Mary Magdalene,
and Mary the mother of James and
Joseph, and the mother of James and
John were there.

Jesus Is Buried

That evening a rich man named Joseph, a follower of Jesus from the
town of Arimathea, came to Jerusalem. 58 Joseph went to Pilate and
asked to have Jesus' body. So Pilate
gave orders for the soldiers to give
it to Joseph. 59 Then Joseph took the
body and wrapped it in a clean linen
cloth. 60 He put Jesus' body in a new
tomb that he had cut out of a wall of
rock, and he rolled a very large
stone to block the entrance of the
tomb. Then Joseph went away.
61 Mary Magdalene and the other
woman named Mary were sitting
near the tomb.

The Tomb of Jesus Is Guarded

The next day, the day after Preparation Day, the leading priests and
the Pharisees went to Pilate. 63 They
said, "Sir, we remember that while
that liar was still alive he said, 'After
three days I will rise from the dead.'
64 So give the order for the tomb to
be guarded closely till the third day.
Otherwise, his followers might
come and steal the body and tell
people that he has risen from the
dead. That lie would be even worse
than the first one."
65 Pilate said, "Take some soldiers
and go guard the tomb the best way
you know." 66 So they all went to the
tomb and made it safe from thieves
by sealing the stone in the entrance
and putting soldiers there to guard it.

Jesus Rises from the Dead

28 The day after the Sabbath day
was the first day of the week.
At dawn on the first day, Mary
Magdalene and another woman
named Mary went to look at the tomb.
2 At that time there was a strong
earthquake. An angel of the Lord
came down from heaven, went to the
tomb, and rolled the stone away
from the entrance. Then he sat on
the stone. 3 He was shining as bright
as lightning, and his clothes were
white as snow. 4 The soldiers guarding the tomb shook with fear because of the angel, and they became
like dead men.
5 The angel said to the women,
"Don't be afraid. I know that you are
looking for Jesus, who has been crucified. 6 He is not here. He has risen
from the dead as he said he would.
Come and see the place where his
body was. 7 And go quickly and tell
his followers, 'Jesus has risen from
the dead. He is going into Galilee
ahead of you, and you will see him
there.'" Then the angel said, "Now I
have told you."
8 The women left the tomb
quickly. They were afraid, but they
were also very happy. They ran to
tell Jesus' followers what had happened. 9 Suddenly, Jesus met them
and said, "Greetings." The women
came up to him, took hold of his feet,
and worshiped him. 10 Then Jesus
said to them, "Don't be afraid. Go
and tell my followers to go on to Galilee, and they will see me there."

OLD TESTAMENT READING

I keep the LORD before me
always.
Because he is close by my side,
I will not be hurt.
9 So I rejoice and am glad.
Even my body has hope,
10 because you will not leave me in
the grave.
You will not let your holy one
rot.

Psalm 16:8–10

INSIGHTS

The power of the resurrection is the power of personal regeneration. Resurrection spells regeneration. The two things must always be kept together: the new world and the new person. Resurrection is not just a passport to heaven, but a power to change us now. Paul says he wants to know Christ and the power of his resurrection. The two are the same. To know Christ today is to come under the influence of the same power that raised Him from the dead. What a cruel thing an example is without the power to live it. Christ is the best of all examples, but more than that, He can come within us and give us His own Spirit to fulfill the example. The result is we actually become like Him, we are able to do the things He did, and most of all, we are able to love as He loved.

Lloyd Ogilvie

PAUSE FOR REFLECTION

Why did the Pharisees fear the possibility of Jesus' resurrection? When he rose again, what did Jesus destroy forever? What difference did his resurrection make in the lives of his followers? How has his resurrection regenerated your life?

WEEKEND

Tell the Good News!

Matthew 28:11—Mark 1:20

Soldiers Report to the Leaders

While the women went to tell
Jesus' followers, some of the soldiers
who had been guarding the tomb
went into the city to tell the leading
priests everything that had happened. 12 Then the priests met with
the older Jewish leaders and made
a plan. They paid the soldiers a large
amount of money 13 and said to them,
"Tell the people that Jesus' followers
came during the night and stole the
body while you were asleep. 14 If the
governor hears about this, we will
satisfy him and save you from
trouble." 15 So the soldiers kept the
money and did as they were told.
And that story is still spread among
the Jewish people even today.

Jesus Talks to His Followers

The eleven followers went to Galilee to the mountain where Jesus
had told them to go. 17 On the mountain they saw Jesus and worshiped
him, but some of them did not believe it was really Jesus. 18 Then
Jesus came to them and said, "All
power in heaven and on earth is
given to me. 19 So go and make followers of all people in the world.
Baptize them in the name of the Father and the Son and the Holy Spirit.
20 Teach them to obey everything
that I have taught you, and I will be
with you always, even until the end
of this age."

John Prepares for Jesus

1 This is the beginning of the Good
News about Jesus Christ, the
Son of God, 2 as the prophet Isaiah
wrote:

"I will send my messenger ahead
of you,
who will prepare your way."
Malachi 3:1

3 "This is a voice of one
who calls out in the desert:
'Prepare the way for the Lord.
Make the road straight for
him.' " *Isaiah 40:3*

4 John was baptizing people in the
desert and preaching a baptism of
changed hearts and lives for the forgiveness of sins. 5 All the people
from Judea and Jerusalem were going out to him. They confessed their
sins and were baptized by him in
the Jordan River. 6 John wore
clothes made from camel's hair, had
a leather belt around his waist, and
ate locusts and wild honey. 7 This is
what John preached to the people:
"There is one coming after me who
is greater than I; I am not good
enough even to kneel down and untie his sandals. 8 I baptize you with
water, but he will baptize you with
the Holy Spirit."

Jesus Is Baptized

At that time Jesus came from the
town of Nazareth in Galilee and was
baptized by John in the Jordan River.
10 Immediately, as Jesus was coming
up out of the water, he saw heaven
open. The Holy Spirit came down on
him like a dove, 11 and a voice came
from heaven: "You are my Son,
whom I love, and I am very pleased
with you."

[12]Then the Spirit sent Jesus into
the desert. [13]He was in the desert
forty days and was tempted by Satan. He was with the wild animals, and the angels came and took care of him.

Jesus Chooses Some Followers

After John was put in prison, Jesus went into Galilee, preaching the
Good News from God. [15]He said,
"The right time has come. The kingdom of God is near. Change your hearts and lives and believe the Good News!"

[16]When Jesus was walking by Lake Galilee, he saw Simon and his brother Andrew throwing a net into the lake because they were fishermen. [17]Jesus said to them, "Come follow me, and I will make you fish
for people." [18]So Simon and Andrew immediately left their nets and followed him.

[19]Going a little farther, Jesus saw two more brothers, James and John, the sons of Zebedee. They were in a boat, mending their nets.
[20]Jesus immediately called them, and they left their father in the boat with the hired workers and followed Jesus.

OLD TESTAMENT READING

Sing to the LORD, all the earth.
Every day tell how he saves us.
[24]Tell the nations about his glory;
tell all peoples the miracles he does.
[25]The LORD is great; he should be praised.
He should be respected more than all the gods.

1 Chronicles 16:23–25

INSIGHTS

For the New Testament Christians, witness was not a sales pitch.

They simply shared, each in his own way, what they had received. Theirs was not a formally prepared, carefully worked-out presentation with a gimmick to manipulate conversation, and a "closer" for an on-the-spot-decision . . . but the spontaneous, irrepressible, effervescent enthusiasm of those who had met the most fascinating Person who ever lived.

The gospel is not theology. It's a Person. Theology doesn't save. Jesus Christ saves. The first-century disciples were totally involved with a Person. They were followers of Jesus. They were learners of Jesus. They were committed to Jesus. They were filled with Jesus.

They had encountered Jesus Christ and it simply could not be concealed. They witnessed not because they had to, but because they could not help it.

Their school of witnessing was the school of the Spirit where they learned continuously. Authentic Christian witness is born of the Spirit.

Madison Avenue, with all its sophisticated know-how, can't improve on the strategy. Nothing is more convincing than the simple, unembellished word of a satisfied customer.

Richard Halverson

ACTION POINT

Pray that God's salvation will be so real to you that you cannot help but tell others.

MONDAY

God Is Compassionate and Brings Healing to Body and Soul

Mark 1:21–45

Jesus Forces Out an Evil Spirit

Jesus and his followers went to Capernaum. On the Sabbath day He went to the synagogue and began to teach. 22 The people were amazed at his teaching, because he taught like a person who had authority, not like their teachers of the law. 23 Just then, a man was there in the synagogue who had an evil spirit in him. He shouted, 24 "Jesus of Nazareth! What do you want with us? Did you come to destroy us? I know who you are—God's Holy One!"

25 Jesus commanded the evil spirit, "Be quiet! Come out of the man!" 26 The evil spirit shook the man violently, gave a loud cry, and then came out of him.

27 The people were so amazed they asked each other, "What is happening here? This man is teaching something new, and with authority. He even gives commands to evil spirits, and they obey him." 28 And the news about Jesus spread quickly everywhere in the area of Galilee.

Jesus Heals Many People

As soon as Jesus and his followers left the synagogue, they went with James and John to the home of Simon and Andrew. 30 Simon's mother-in-law was sick in bed with a fever, and the people told Jesus about her. 31 So Jesus went to her bed, took her hand, and helped her up. The fever left her, and she began serving them.

32 That evening, after the sun went down, the people brought to Jesus all who were sick and had demons in them. 33 The whole town gathered at the door. 34 Jesus healed many who had different kinds of sicknesses, and he forced many demons to leave people. But he would not allow the demons to speak, because they knew who he was.

35 Early the next morning, while it was still dark, Jesus woke and left the house. He went to a lonely place, where he prayed. 36 Simon and his friends went to look for Jesus. 37 When they found him, they said, "Everyone is looking for you!"

38 Jesus answered, "We should go to other towns around here so I can preach there too. That is the reason I came." 39 So he went everywhere in Galilee, preaching in the synagogues and forcing out demons.

Jesus Heals a Sick Man

A man with a skin disease came to Jesus. He fell to his knees and begged Jesus, "You can heal me if you will."

41 Jesus felt sorry for the man, so he reached out his hand and touched him and said, "I will. Be healed!" 42 Immediately the disease left the man, and he was healed.

43 Jesus told the man to go away at once, but he warned him strongly, 44 "Don't tell anyone about this. But go and show yourself to the priest. And offer the gift Moses commanded for people who are made well. This will show the people what I have done." 45 The man left there,

but he began to tell everyone that Jesus had healed him, and so he spread the news about Jesus. As a result, Jesus could not enter a town if people saw him. He stayed in places where nobody lived, but people came to him from everywhere.

OLD TESTAMENT READING

Come, let's go back to the LORD.
He has hurt us, but he will heal us.
He has wounded us, but he will bandage our wounds.
2 In two days he will put new life in us;
on the third day he will raise us up
so that we may live in his presence 3 and know him.
Let's try to learn about the LORD;
He will come to us as surely as the dawn comes.
He will come to us like rain,
like the spring rain that waters the ground."

Hosea 6:1–3

LORD, heal me, and I will truly be healed.
Save me, and I will truly be saved.
You are the one I praise.

Jeremiah 17:14

INSIGHTS

Bethlehem, Galilee, Gethsemane—He walked there. But today Christ walks the concrete sidewalks of Times Square, 47th Street, and Broadway. And as He walks, His feet are soiled—not with the sand of the seashore or the reddish dust of the Emmaus Road, but with the soot and filth of the city.

He walks the "Great White Way," and His face is lit by the gaudy neon signboards of materialism. He walks in the shadows of the dark alleyways, where faces are not lit at all. . . .

He is pushed and shoved through Grand Central Station, elbowed and ignored, yet in the crowd He feels a measure of virtue flow from His being and searches through the faces for an honest seeker passing by. . . .

Christ walks the city and . . . weaves the cloth that transforms rags into a lovely tapestry. . . . He acts the part that tells the story of how that Love invaded humankind, for only story tells the Story. Christ incarnate. Christ the living, walking parable, takes the stage to be the Story. . . .

. . . He is the broken, and He is the healer. He is the hungry, and He is the Bread of Life. He is the homeless, yet it is He who says "Come to Me all you who are overloaded, and I will be your resting place." He is the loser who makes losing the only way to win. He is the omnipotent who calls all who follow to choose powerlessness and teaches us by laying down all power in heaven and in earth. He is the sick, and He is the wholeness.

Gloria Gaither

ACTION POINT

Can there be any greater healing than that given by the Healer? Can you imagine any greater compassion than that shown in the love of his Son? Meditate on one of these readings and let it become your prayer of praise to God today.

TUESDAY

Jesus Has the Authority to Forgive

Mark 2:1–22

Jesus Heals a Paralyzed Man

2 A few days later, when Jesus
came back to Capernaum, the
news spread that he was at home.
2 Many people gathered together so
that there was no room in the house,
not even outside the door. And Jesus
was teaching them God's message.
3 Four people came, carrying a paralyzed man. 4 Since they could not get
to Jesus because of the crowd, they
dug a hole in the roof right above
where he was speaking. When they
got through, they lowered the mat
with the paralyzed man on it. 5 When
Jesus saw the faith of these people,
he said to the paralyzed man,
"Young man, your sins are forgiven."
6 Some of the teachers of the law
were sitting there, thinking to themselves, 7 "Why does this man say things
like that? He is speaking as if he were
God. Only God can forgive sins."
8 Jesus knew immediately what
these teachers of the law were thinking. So he said to them, "Why are
you thinking these things? 9 Which
is easier: to tell this paralyzed man,
'Your sins are forgiven,' or to tell
him, 'Stand up. Take your mat and
walk'? 10 But I will prove to you that
the Son of Man has authority on
earth to forgive sins." So Jesus said
to the paralyzed man, 11 "I tell you,
stand up, take your mat, and go
home." 12 Immediately the paralyzed
man stood up, took his mat, and
walked out while everyone was
watching him.
The people were amazed and
praised God. They said, "We have
never seen anything like this!"
13 Jesus went to the lake again.
The whole crowd followed him
there, and he taught them. 14 While
he was walking along, he saw a man
named Levi son of Alphaeus, sitting
in the tax collector's booth. Jesus
said to him, "Follow me," and he
stood up and followed Jesus.
15 Later, as Jesus was having dinner
at Levi's house, many tax collectors
and "sinners" were eating there with
Jesus and his followers. Many people
like this followed Jesus. 16 When the
teachers of the law who were Pharisees saw Jesus eating with the tax collectors and "sinners," they asked his
followers, "Why does he eat with tax
collectors and sinners?"
17 Jesus heard this and said to
them, "It is not the healthy people
who need a doctor, but the sick. I did
not come to invite good people but
to invite sinners."

Jesus' Followers Are Criticized

Now the followers of John and the
Pharisees often gave up eating for a
certain time. Some people came to
Jesus and said, "Why do John's followers and the followers of the Pharisees often give up eating, but your
followers don't?"
19 Jesus answered, "The friends of
the bridegroom do not give up eating
while the bridegroom is still with
them. As long as the bridegroom is
with them, they cannot give up eating.
20 But the time will come when the
bridegroom will be taken from them,

and then they will give up eating.
21 "No one sews a patch of
unshrunk cloth over a hole in an old coat. Otherwise, the patch will shrink and pull away—the new patch will pull away from the old coat. Then the hole will be worse.
22 Also, no one ever pours new wine
into old leather bags. Otherwise, the new wine will break the bags, and the wine will be ruined along with the bags. But new wine should be put into new leather bags."

OLD TESTAMENT READING

But it was the LORD who decided
to crush him and make him
suffer.
The LORD made his life a
penalty offering,
but he will still see his descendants and live a long life.
He will complete the things
the LORD wants him to do.
11 "After his soul suffers many
things,
he will see life and be satisfied.
My good servant will make many
people right with God;
he will carry away their sins.
12 For this reason I will make him a
great man among people,
and he will share in all things
with those who are strong.
He willingly gave his life
and was treated like a criminal.
But he carried away the sins of
many people
and asked forgiveness for
those who sinned."

Isaiah 53:10–12

INSIGHTS

Forgiveness is one of the first and most glorious blessings we receive from God. It is the transition from the old to the new life; the sign and pledge of God's love: with it we receive the right to all the spiritual gifts which are prepared for us in Christ. The believer can never forget, either here or in eternity, that he is a forgiven sinner. Nothing more inflames his love, awakens his joy, or strengthens his courage than the continually renewed experience of God's forgiving love. Every day, yes, every thought of God reminds him: I owe all to pardoning grace.

This forgiving love is one of the greatest manifestations of the divine nature. In it God finds His glory and blessedness and wants to share this with His redeemed people.

Andrew Murray

APPLICATION

What is the most important characteristic of the good servant promised in Isaiah 53? Is it then surprising that Jesus forgave sins while he was on earth? Has your spirit been healed by Jesus' forgiveness of your sins?

WEDNESDAY

Jesus Teaches About the Rules of the Sabbath

Mark 2:23—3:27

Jesus Is Lord of the Sabbath

One Sabbath day, as Jesus was walking through some fields of grain, his followers began to pick some grain to eat. [24]The Pharisees said to Jesus, "Why are your followers doing what is not lawful on the Sabbath day?"

[25]Jesus answered, "Have you never read what David did when he and those with him were hungry and needed food? [26]During the time of Abiathar the high priest, David went into God's house and ate the holy bread, which is lawful only for priests to eat. And David also gave some of the bread to those who were with him."

[27]Then Jesus said to the Pharisees, "The Sabbath day was made to help people; they were not made to be ruled by the Sabbath day. [28]So then, the Son of Man is Lord even of the Sabbath day."

Jesus Heals a Man's Hand

3 Another time when Jesus went into a synagogue, a man with a crippled hand was there. [2]Some people watched Jesus closely to see if he would heal the man on the Sabbath day so they could accuse him.

[3]Jesus said to the man with the crippled hand, "Stand up here in the middle of everyone."

[4]Then Jesus asked the people, "Which is lawful on the Sabbath day: to do good or to do evil, to save a life or to kill?" But they said nothing to answer him.

[5]Jesus was angry as he looked at the people, and he felt very sad because they were stubborn. Then he said to the man, "Hold out your hand." The man held out his hand and it was healed. [6]Then the Pharisees left and began making plans with the Herodians about a way to kill Jesus.

Many People Follow Jesus

Jesus left with his followers for the lake, and a large crowd from Galilee followed him. [8]Also many people came from Judea, from Jerusalem, from Idumea, from the lands across the Jordan River, and from the area of Tyre and Sidon. When they heard what Jesus was doing, many people came to him. [9]When Jesus saw the crowds, he told his followers to get a boat ready for him to keep people from crowding against him. [10]He had healed many people, so all the sick were pushing toward him to touch him. [11]When evil spirits saw Jesus, they fell down before him and shouted, "You are the Son of God!" [12]But Jesus strongly warned them not to tell who he was.

Jesus Chooses His Apostles

Then Jesus went up on a mountain and called to him the men he wanted, and they came to him. [14]Jesus chose twelve men and called them apostles. He wanted them to be with him, and he wanted to send them out to preach [15]and to have the authority to force demons out of people. [16]These are

the twelve men he chose: Simon
(Jesus named him Peter), [17]James
and John, the sons of Zebedee (Jesus
named them Boanerges, which
means "Sons of Thunder"), [18]An-
drew, Philip, Bartholomew, Matthew,
Thomas, James the son of Alphaeus,
Thaddaeus, Simon the Zealot, [19]and
Judas Iscariot, who later turned
against Jesus.

Some People Say Jesus Has a Devil

Then Jesus went home, but again a
crowd gathered. There were so many
people that Jesus and his followers
could not eat. [21]When his family
heard this, they went to get him because they thought he was out of his
mind. [22]But the teachers of the law
from Jerusalem were saying,
"Beelzebul is living inside him! He
uses power from the ruler of demons
to force demons out of people."

[23]So Jesus called the people together and taught them with stories.
He said, "Satan will not force himself
out of people. [24]A kingdom that is
divided cannot continue, [25]and a family that is divided cannot continue.
[26]And if Satan is against himself and
fights against his own people, he
cannot continue; that is the end of
Satan. [27]No one can enter a strong
person's house and steal his things
unless he first ties up the strong person. Then he can steal things from
the house."

OLD TESTAMENT READING

This is what the LORD says:
"Give justice to all people,
and do what is right,
because my salvation will come to
you soon.
Soon everyone will know that I
do what is right.
[2]The person who obeys the law
about the Sabbath
will be blessed,
and the person who does no evil
will be blessed."

Isaiah 56:1–2

INSIGHTS

Sabbath rest means worship with the Christian family. In proper worship we will have a chance to exercise all three aspects that lead to the rest of our private worlds: looking backward, upward, and ahead. Such worship is non-negotiable to the person committed to walking with God. . . .

. . . Sabbath means a deliberate acceptance of personal rest and tranquility within the individual life. Sabbath means a rest that brings peace into the private world. As Christ pressed stillness into a storm, order into a being of a demon-possessed maniac, health into a desperately sick woman, and life into a dead friend, so He seeks to press peace into the harried private world of the man or woman who has been in the marketplace all week. But there is a condition. We must accept this peace as a gift and take the time to receive it.

Gordon MacDonald

APPLICATION

Think about Jesus' statement that the Sabbath was meant to help people. In what ways do you think keeping the Sabbath is good for us? How do you think Jesus feels about the way you keep the Sabbath?

THURSDAY

Those Who Obey God Belong to Him

Mark 3:28—4:20

I tell you the truth, all sins that people do and all the things people say against God can be forgiven. 29 But anyone who speaks against the Holy Spirit will never be forgiven; he is guilty of a sin that continues forever."

30 Jesus said this because the teachers of the law said that he had an evil spirit inside him.

Jesus' True Family

Then Jesus' mother and brothers arrived. Standing outside, they sent someone in to tell him to come out. 32 Many people were sitting around Jesus, and they said to him, "Your mother and brothers are waiting for you outside."

33 Jesus asked, "Who are my mother and my brothers?" 34 Then he looked at those sitting around him and said, "Here are my mother and my brothers! 35 My true brother and sister and mother are those who do what God wants."

A Story About Planting Seed

4 Again Jesus began teaching by the lake. A great crowd gathered around him, so he sat down in a boat near the shore. All the people stayed on the shore close to the water. 2 Jesus taught them many things, using stories. He said, 3 "Listen! A farmer went out to plant his seed. 4 While he was planting, some seed fell by the road, and the birds came and ate it up. 5 Some seed fell on rocky ground where there wasn't much dirt. That seed grew very fast, because the ground was not deep. 6 But when the sun rose, the plants dried up because they did not have deep roots. 7 Some other seed fell among thorny weeds, which grew and choked the good plants. So those plants did not produce a crop. 8 Some other seed fell on good ground and began to grow. It got taller and produced a crop. Some plants made thirty times more, some made sixty times more, and some made a hundred times more."

9 Then Jesus said, "You people who can hear me, listen!"

Jesus Tells Why He Used Stories

Later, when Jesus was alone, the twelve apostles and others around him asked him about the stories.

11 Jesus said, "You can know the secret about the kingdom of God. But to other people I tell everything by using stories 12 so that:

'They will look and look, but they
will not learn.
They will listen and listen, but
they will not understand.
If they did learn and understand,
they would come back to me
and be forgiven.' " *Isaiah 6:9–10*

Jesus Explains the Seed Story

Then Jesus said to his followers, "Don't you understand this story? If you don't, how will you understand any story? 14 The farmer is like a person who plants God's message in people. 15 Sometimes the teaching falls on the road. This is like the people who hear the teaching of God, but Satan quickly comes and takes away the teaching that was planted in them. [16]Others are like the seed planted on rocky ground. They hear the teaching and quickly accept it with joy. [17]But since they don't allow the teaching to go deep into their lives, they keep it only a short time. When trouble or persecution comes because of the teaching they accepted, they quickly give up. [18]Others are like the seed planted among the thorny weeds. They hear the teaching, [19]but the worries of this life, the temptation of wealth, and many other evil desires keep the teaching from growing and producing fruit in their lives. [20]Others are like the seed planted in the good ground. They hear the teaching and accept it. Then they grow and produce fruit—sometimes thirty times more, sometimes sixty times more, and sometimes a hundred times more."

OLD TESTAMENT READING

Then Moses went up on the mountain to God. The LORD called to him from the mountain and said, "Say this to the family of Jacob, and tell the people of Israel: [4]'Every one of you has seen what I did to the people of Egypt. You saw how I carried you out of Egypt, as if on eagle's wings. And I brought you here to me. [5]So now if you obey me and keep my agreement, you will be my own possession, chosen from all nations.'"

Exodus 19:3–5

INSIGHTS

The source of Christ's victory, the secret of His power, and of ours, lies in obedience. . . . In an obedient heart there is a way prepared for God. There are many Christians who always seek pleasure and satisfaction for themselves. These have not yet learned that only obedient children are happy children. That which in truth brings abiding happiness is nothing else than obedience toward God. For a healthy soul there is only one thing that counts—to be obedient. . . .

Why have so many of God's lambs so little assurance of salvation? Why are their souls not satisfied with the peace of God? God gives us the answer in Isaiah 48:18: "Oh, that thou hadst hearkened to my commandments! Then had thy peace been as a river, and thy righteousness as the waves of the sea." People say, "I lack faith. I have too little faith; therefore I have no assurance of salvation, no peace." But in most instances it is not faith which is lacking, for even with a trembling hand one can receive costly gifts. It is rather obedience which is lacking. There is something in their lives which they will not let go, and which hinders the Holy Spirit from giving them the assurance that they are God's children. . . . No one who is disobedient to God can have confidence in Him. Confidence is a result of obedience.

G. Steinberger

APPLICATION

What one thing does God require of those who would be his people? What do those who obey God receive from him? How's your obedience? Is it obvious that you belong to God?

FRIDAY

Jesus Demonstrates His Power over All

Mark 4:21—5:10

Use What You Have

Then Jesus said to them, "Do you
hide a lamp under a bowl or under a
bed? No! You put the lamp on a
lampstand. 22 Everything that is hidden will be made clear and every
secret thing will be made known.
23 You people who can hear me, listen!
24 "Think carefully about what you
hear. The way you give to others is
the way God will give to you, but God
will give you even more. 25 Those who
have understanding will be given
more. But those who do not have understanding, even what they have will
be taken away from them."

Jesus Uses a Story About Seed

Then Jesus said, "The kingdom of
God is like someone who plants seed
in the ground. 27 Night and day,
whether the person is asleep or
awake, the seed still grows, but the
person does not know how it grows.
28 By itself the earth produces grain.
First the plant grows, then the head,
and then all the grain in the head.
29 When the grain is ready, the
farmer cuts it, because this is the
harvest time."

A Story About Mustard Seed

Then Jesus said, "How can I show
you what the kingdom of God is like?
What story can I use to explain it?
31 The kingdom of God is like a mustard seed, the smallest seed you
plant in the ground. 32 But when
planted, this seed grows and becomes the largest of all garden
plants. It produces large branches,
and the wild birds can make nests
in its shade."
33 Jesus used many stories like
these to teach the crowd God's message—as much as they could understand. 34 He always used stories to
teach them. But when he and his followers were alone, Jesus explained
everything to them.

Jesus Calms a Storm

That evening, Jesus said to his followers, "Let's go across the lake."
36 Leaving the crowd behind, they
took him in the boat just as he was.
There were also other boats with
them. 37 A very strong wind came up
on the lake. The waves came over
the sides and into the boat so that it
was already full of water. 38 Jesus was
at the back of the boat, sleeping with
his head on a cushion. His followers
woke him and said, "Teacher, don't
you care that we are drowning!"
39 Jesus stood up and commanded
the wind and said to the waves, "Quiet!
Be still!" Then the wind stopped, and
it became completely calm.
40 Jesus said to his followers,
"Why are you afraid? Do you still
have no faith?"
41 The followers were very afraid and
asked each other, "Who is this? Even
the wind and the waves obey him!"

A Man with Demons Inside Him

5 Jesus and his followers went to
the other side of the lake to the

area of the Gerasene people. 2 When
Jesus got out of the boat, instantly a
man with an evil spirit came to him
from the burial caves. 3 This man
lived in the caves, and no one could
tie him up, not even with a chain.
4 Many times people had used chains
to tie the man's hands and feet, but
he always broke them off. No one
was strong enough to control him.
5 Day and night he would wander
around the burial caves and on the
hills, screaming and cutting himself
with stones. 6 While Jesus was still
far away, the man saw him, ran to
him, and fell down before him.

7 The man shouted in a loud voice,
"What do you want with me, Jesus,
Son of the Most High God? I command you in God's name not to torture me!" 8 He said this because
Jesus was saying to him, "You evil
spirit, come out of the man."

9 Then Jesus asked him, "What is
your name?"

He answered, "My name is Legion, because we are many spirits."
10 He begged Jesus again and again
not to send them out of that area.

OLD TESTAMENT READING

The LORD's voice is heard over
 the sea.
The glorious God thunders;
 the LORD thunders over the
  ocean.
4 The LORD's voice is powerful;
 the LORD's voice is majestic.
5 The LORD's voice breaks the
  trees;
 the LORD breaks the cedars of
  Lebanon.
7 The LORD's voice makes the
  lightning flash.
10 The LORD controls the flood.
 The LORD will be King forever.

Psalm 29:3–5, 7, 10

INSIGHTS

There is a power that destroys. There is also a power that creates. The power that creates gives life and joy and peace. It is freedom and not bondage, life and not death, transformation and not coercion. The power that creates restores relationship and gives the gift of wholeness to all. The power that creates is spiritual power, the power that proceeds from God. . . .

In the crucifixion the power that creates reached its apex. At the cross Satan sought to use all the power at his disposal to destroy Christ, but God turned it into the ultimate act of creative power. The penalty for sin was paid; the justice of God was satisfied. Through the cross of Christ, you and I can receive forgiveness and know the restoring of our relationship to God. Christ died for our sins, and in that death we see the power that creates.

Our response to this supreme act of power is gratitude. It is "love divine, all loves excelling." We can never hope or want to duplicate this act of power. We simply thank God for what he has done.

Richard Foster

ACTION POINT

Think about the many kinds of awesome power God has at his disposal. How has he used his power to draw you to himself? Thank him for saving you by his power.

WEEKEND

The Power of Faith

Mark 5:11–36

A large herd of pigs was feeding on
a hill near there. 12 The demons
begged Jesus, "Send us into the pigs;
let us go into them." 13 So Jesus allowed them to do this. The evil spirits left the man and went into the pigs.
Then the herd of pigs—about two
thousand of them—rushed down the
hill into the lake and were drowned.

14 The herdsmen ran away and
went to the town and to the countryside, telling everyone about this. So
people went out to see what had happened. 15 They came to Jesus and
saw the man who used to have the
many evil spirits, sitting, clothed, and
in his right mind. And they were
frightened. 16 The people who saw
this told the others what had happened to the man who had the demons living in him, and they told
about the pigs. 17 Then the people began to beg Jesus to leave their area.

18 As Jesus was getting back into
the boat, the man who was freed from
the demons begged to go with him.

19 But Jesus would not let him. He
said, "Go home to your family and
tell them how much the Lord has
done for you and how he has had
mercy on you." 20 So the man left and
began to tell the people in the Ten
Towns about what Jesus had done
for him. And everyone was amazed.

Jesus Gives Life to a Dead Girl and Heals a Sick Woman

When Jesus went in the boat back
to the other side of the lake, a large
crowd gathered around him there.
22 A leader of the synagogue, named
Jairus, came there, saw Jesus, and
fell at his feet. 23 He begged Jesus,
saying again and again, "My daughter is dying. Please come and put
your hands on her so she will be
healed and will live." 24 So Jesus went
with him.

A large crowd followed Jesus and
pushed very close around him.
25 Among them was a woman who
had been bleeding for twelve years.
26 She had suffered very much from
many doctors and had spent all the
money she had, but instead of improving, she was getting worse.
27 When the woman heard about
Jesus, she came up behind him in
the crowd and touched his coat.
28 She thought, "If I can just touch his
clothes, I will be healed." 29 Instantly
her bleeding stopped, and she felt in
her body that she was healed from
her disease.

30 At once Jesus felt power go out
from him. So he turned around in
the crowd and asked, "Who touched
my clothes?"

31 His followers said, "Look at how
many people are pushing against
you! And you ask, 'Who touched
me?' "

32 But Jesus continued looking
around to see who had touched him.
33 The woman, knowing that she was
healed, came and fell at Jesus' feet.
Shaking with fear, she told him the
whole truth. 34 Jesus said to her,
"Dear woman, you are made well
because you believed. Go in peace;
be healed of your disease."

35 While Jesus was still speaking,
some people came from the house
of the synagogue leader. They said,

"Your daughter is dead. There is no need to bother the teacher anymore."

36 But Jesus paid no attention to what they said. He told the synagogue leader, "Don't be afraid; just believe."

OLD TESTAMENT READING

When Goliath looked at David and saw that he was only a boy, tanned and handsome, he looked down on David with disgust. 43 He said, "Do you think I am a dog, that you come at me with a stick?" He used his gods' names to curse David. 44 He said to David, "Come here. I'll feed your body to the birds of the air and the wild animals!"

45 But David said to him, "You come to me using a sword and two spears. But I come to you in the name of the LORD All-Powerful, the God of the armies of Israel! You have spoken against him. 46 Today the LORD will hand you over to me, and I'll kill you and cut off your head. Today I'll feed the bodies of the Philistine soldiers to the birds of the air and the wild animals. Then all the world will know there is a God in Israel! 47 Everyone gathered here will know the LORD does not need swords or spears to save people. The battle belongs to him, and he will hand you over to us."

50 So David defeated the Philistine with only a sling and a stone. He hit him and killed him. He did not even have a sword in his hand.

1 Samuel 17:42–47, 50

INSIGHTS

The doctrine of the Bible is that Christ saves His people from sin through faith; that Christ's Spirit is received by faith to dwell in the heart. It is faith that works by love. Love is wrought and sustained by faith. By faith, Christians "overcome the world, the flesh, and the devil." It is by faith that they "quench all the fiery darts of the wicked." It is by faith that they "put on the Lord Jesus Christ, and put off the old man, with his deeds." It is by faith that we "stand," by resolutions we fall. This is the victory that overcometh the world, even our faith.

It is by faith that the flesh is kept under and carnal desires subdued, and by faith that we receive the Spirit of Christ to work in us to will and to do, according to His good pleasure. He sheds abroad His own love in our hearts, and thereby enkindles ours. . . . Nothing but the life and energy of the Spirit of Christ can save us from sin, and trust is the universal condition for the working of His saving energy within us. . . . . . When we open the door by implicit trust, He enters in and takes up His abode with us and in us. By shedding abroad His love, He quickens our souls into sympathy with himself, and in this way, and in this way alone, He purifies our hearts through faith.

Charles Finney

PAUSE FOR REFLECTION

What has the Lord done for you? How has he shown himself to you? How has he responded to your faith in him? In what way does his mercy amaze you? With whom does he want you to share your faith?

MONDAY

The Consequences of Unbelief

Mark 5:37—6:20

Jesus let only Peter, James, and John the brother of James go with him. 38 When they came to the house of the synagogue leader, Jesus found many people there making lots of noise and crying loudly. 39 Jesus entered the house and said to them, "Why are you crying and making so much noise? The child is not dead, only asleep." 40 But they laughed at him. So, after throwing them out of the house, Jesus took the child's father and mother and his three followers into the room where the child was. 41 Taking hold of the girl's hand, he said to her, "Talitha, koum!" (This means, "Young girl, I tell you to stand up!") 42 At once the girl stood right up and began walking. (She was twelve years old.) Everyone was completely amazed. 43 Jesus gave them strict orders not to tell people about this. Then he told them to give the girl something to eat.

Jesus Goes to His Hometown

6 Jesus left there and went to his hometown, and his followers went with him. 2 On the Sabbath day he taught in the synagogue. Many people heard him and were amazed, saying, "Where did this man get these teachings? What is this wisdom that has been given to him? And where did he get the power to do miracles? 3 He is just the carpenter, the son of Mary and the brother of James, Joseph, Judas, and Simon. And his sisters are here with us." So the people were upset with Jesus.

4 Jesus said to them, "A prophet is honored everywhere except in his hometown and with his own people and in his own home." 5 So Jesus was not able to work any miracles there except to heal a few sick people by putting his hands on them. 6 He was amazed at how many people had no faith.

Then Jesus went to other villages in that area and taught. 7 He called his twelve followers together and got ready to send them out two by two and gave them authority over evil spirits. 8 This is what Jesus commanded them: "Take nothing for your trip except a walking stick. Take no bread, no bag, and no money in your pockets. 9 Wear sandals, but take only the clothes you are wearing. 10 When you enter a house, stay there until you leave that town. 11 If the people in a certain place refuse to welcome you or listen to you, leave that place. Shake its dust off your feet as a warning to them."

12 So the followers went out and preached that people should change their hearts and lives. 13 They forced many demons out and put olive oil on many sick people and healed them.

How John the Baptist Was Killed

King Herod heard about Jesus, because he was now well known. Some people said, "He is John the Baptist, who has risen from the dead. That is why he can work these miracles."

15 Others said, "He is Elijah."

Other people said, "Jesus is a prophet, like the prophets who lived long ago."

16 When Herod heard this, he
said, "I killed John by cutting off his
head. Now he has risen from the
dead!"
17 Herod himself had ordered his
soldiers to arrest John and put him
in prison in order to please his wife,
Herodias. She had been the wife of
Philip, Herod's brother, but then
Herod had married her. 18 John had
been telling Herod, "It is not lawful
for you to be married to your
brother's wife." 19 So Herodias hated
John and wanted to kill him. But she
couldn't, 20 because Herod was afraid
of John and protected him. He knew
John was a good and holy man. Also,
though John's preaching always
bothered him, he enjoyed listening
to John.

OLD TESTAMENT READING

But the LORD said to me, "Tell the
people, 'You must not go up there
and fight. I will not be with you, and
your enemies will defeat you.'"
43 So I told you, but you would not
listen. You would not obey the LORD's
command. You were proud, so you
went on up into the mountains, 44 and
the Amorites who lived in those
mountains came out and fought you.
They chased you like bees and
defeated you from Edom to Hormah.
45 So you came back and cried before
the LORD, but the LORD did not listen
to you; he refused to pay attention
to you.

Deuteronomy 1:42–45

INSIGHTS

God had told the people to enter and possess the land, but they preferred to spy it out just to see if God was really telling the truth! Well, He was—it was a rich land, a beautiful land, and a fruitful land. But there were giants! "We are not able to overcome!" This was the majority report.

The minority report came from Caleb and Joshua, and Moses agreed with them: "We are well able to overcome it!" This is the Old Testament version of Romans 8:31: "If God be for us, who can be against us?" The majority saw the obstacles, and they were bigger than their God. The minority saw God, and the obstacles disappeared!

Unbelief always cries and complains. It plays the same tune: "We are not able!" The nation had the promises of God to lean on and the presence of God to depend on, but they preferred to walk by sight. It cost them forty years in the wilderness, the world's longest funeral march!

Christians do not fight for victory; we fight from victory. Jesus said, "In the world ye shall have tribulation: but be of good cheer; I have overcome the world" (John 16:33). John said, "This is the victory that overcometh the world, even our faith" (1 John 5:4).

Either we are overcomers—or overcome.

Warren Wiersbe

APPLICATION

List the consequences of unbelief described in these Scripture readings. What are the rewards of faith? What about your life? Are you reaping consequences or rewards? Will you be an overcomer or be overcome?

TUESDAY

Trust God for His Provision

Mark 6:21–44

Then the perfect time came for Herodias to cause John's death. On Herod's birthday, he gave a dinner party for the most important government leaders, the commanders of his army, and the most important people in Galilee. 22 When the daughter of Herodias came in and danced, she pleased Herod and the people eating with him.

So King Herod said to the girl, "Ask me for anything you want, and I will give it to you." 23 He promised her, "Anything you ask for I will give to you—up to half of my kingdom."

24 The girl went to her mother and asked, "What should I ask for?"

Her mother answered, "Ask for the head of John the Baptist."

25 At once the girl went back to the king and said to him, "I want the head of John the Baptist right now on a platter."

26 Although the king was very sad, he had made a promise, and his dinner guests had heard it. So he did not want to refuse what she asked. 27 Immediately the king sent a soldier to bring John's head. The soldier went and cut off John's head in the prison 28 and brought it back on a platter. He gave it to the girl, and the girl gave it to her mother. 29 When John's followers heard this, they came and got John's body and put it in a tomb.

More than Five Thousand Fed

The apostles gathered around Jesus and told him about all the things they had done and taught. 31 Crowds of people were coming and going so that Jesus and his followers did not even have time to eat. He said to them, "Come away by yourselves, and we will go to a lonely place to get some rest."

32 So they went in a boat by themselves to a lonely place. 33 But many people saw them leave and recognized them. So from all the towns they ran to the place where Jesus was going, and they got there before him. 34 When he arrived, he saw a great crowd waiting. He felt sorry for them, because they were like sheep without a shepherd. So he began to teach them many things.

35 When it was late in the day, his followers came to him and said, "No one lives in this place, and it is already very late. 36 Send the people away so they can go to the countryside and towns around here to buy themselves something to eat."

37 But Jesus answered, "You give them something to eat."

They said to him, "We would all have to work a month to earn enough money to buy that much bread!"

38 Jesus asked them, "How many loaves of bread do you have? Go and see."

When they found out, they said, "Five loaves and two fish."

39 Then Jesus told his followers to have the people sit in groups on the green grass. 40 So they sat in groups of fifty or a hundred. 41 Jesus took the five loaves and two fish and, looking up to heaven, he thanked God for the food. He divided the bread and gave it to his followers for them to give to the people. Then he divided the two fish among them all. 42 All the people

ate and were satisfied. 43 The followers filled twelve baskets with the leftover pieces of bread and fish. 44 There were five thousand men who ate.

OLD TESTAMENT READING

I praise your greatness, my God
the King;
I will praise you forever and
ever.
2 I will praise you every day;
I will praise you forever and
ever.
3 The LORD is great and worthy of
our praise;
no one can understand how
great he is.

4 Parents will tell their children
what you have done.
They will retell your mighty acts,
5 wonderful majesty, and glory.
And I will think about your
miracles.
6 They will tell about the amazing
things you do,
and I will tell how great you are.

Psalm 145:1–6

Let them give thanks to the
LORD for his love
and for the miracles he does
for people.
9 He satisfies the thirsty
and fills up the hungry.

Psalm 107:8–9

INSIGHTS

It is better to trust in God than to accumulate riches. . . .

Trust in God gives clearness of vision. When we are thinking partly of doing God's work in the world, and partly of lining our own nest, we are in the condition of the man whose eyes do not look in the same direction. . . . We are endeavouring to serve two masters, and our judgment is therefore distorted. Who has not often experienced this? You have tried to ascertain God's will, or to form a right judgment about your life, but constantly your perception of duty has been obscured by the thought that, if you decided in a certain direction, you would interfere with your interests in another. Your eye has not been single, and you have walked in darkness. When, however, you feel so absorbed in God's interests that you are indifferent to your own, all becomes clear, and you leave Him to care for all results. . . .

Let us not think that God is niggardly and stinting in His gifts. He gives fish as well as bread when He feeds the crowds; colours as well as leaves when He clothes the flowers. You have been adopted into His Family, and may call Him "Abba, Father." Surely this act of grace shows a special love on His part. Would He have taken such care of the spiritual, and have none for the physical? The ungodly may worry about the maintenance; but a child of God may be sure that His needs will be supplied.

F. B. Meyer

APPLICATION

What is the difference between Jesus' perspective on feeding the crowd and his disciples' perspective? Do you face similar conflict between feeling a need to provide for yourself and trusting God to provide? Let these psalms be your prayer of trust and thanks for God's provision!

WEDNESDAY

God Is Merciful, Even to Those Who Do Not Understand

Mark 6:45—7:13

Jesus Walks on the Water

Immediately Jesus told his followers to get into the boat and go ahead
of him to Bethsaida across the lake.
He stayed there to send the people
home. 46 After sending them away, he
went into the hills to pray.
47 That night, the boat was in the
middle of the lake, and Jesus was
alone on the land. 48 He saw his followers struggling hard to row the
boat, because the wind was blowing
against them. Between three and six
o'clock in the morning, Jesus came
to them, walking on the water, and
he wanted to walk past the boat.
49 But when they saw him walking on
the water, they thought he was a
ghost and cried out. 50 They all saw
him and were afraid. But quickly
Jesus spoke to them and said, "Have
courage! It is I. Do not be afraid."
51 Then he got into the boat with
them, and the wind became calm.
The followers were greatly amazed.
52 They did not understand about the
miracle of the five loaves, because
their minds were closed.
53 When they had crossed the lake,
they came to shore at Gennesaret
and tied the boat there. 54 When they
got out of the boat, people immediately recognized Jesus. 55 They ran
everywhere in that area and began
to bring sick people on mats wherever they heard he was. 56 And everywhere he went—into towns, cities,
or countryside—the people brought
the sick to the marketplaces. They
begged him to let them touch just
the edge of his coat, and all who
touched it were healed.

Obey God's Law

7 When some Pharisees and some
teachers of the law came from
Jerusalem, they gathered around
Jesus. 2 They saw that some of Jesus'
followers ate food with hands that
were not clean, that is, they hadn't
washed them. 3 (The Pharisees and
all the Jews never eat before washing their hands in a special way according to their unwritten laws.
4 And when they buy something in
the market, they never eat it until
they wash themselves in a special
way. They also follow many other unwritten laws, such as the washing of
cups, pitchers, and pots.)
5 The Pharisees and the teachers of
the law said to Jesus, "Why don't your
followers obey the unwritten laws
which have been handed down to us?
Why do your followers eat their food
with hands that are not clean?"
6 Jesus answered, "Isaiah was
right when he spoke about you
hypocrites. He wrote,

'These people show honor to me
with words,
but their hearts are far from me.
7 Their worship of me is worthless.
The things they teach are
nothing but human rules.'

Isaiah 29:13

8 You have stopped following the
commands of God, and you follow
only human teachings."
9 Then Jesus said to them, "You
cleverly ignore the commands of

God so you can follow your own
teachings. [10] Moses said, 'Honor your
father and your mother,' and 'Anyone
who says cruel things to his father or
mother must be put to death.' [11] But
you say a person can tell his father
or mother, 'I have something I could
use to help you, but it is Corban—a
gift to God.' [12] You no longer let that
person use that money for his father
or his mother. [13] By your own rules,
which you teach people, you are rejecting what God said. And you do
many things like that."

OLD TESTAMENT READING

But they kept on sinning;
they did not believe even with
the miracles.
33 So he ended their days without
meaning
and their years in terror.
34 Anytime he killed them, they
would look to him for help;
they would come back to God
and follow him.
35 They would remember that God
was their Rock,
that God Most High had saved
them.
36 But their words were false,
and their tongues lied to him.
37 Their hearts were not really loyal
to God;
they did not keep his agreement.
38 Still God was merciful.
He forgave their sins
and did not destroy them.
Many times he held back his anger
and did not stir up all his anger.
39 He remembered that they were
only human,
like a wind that blows and does
not come back.

Psalm 78:32–39

INSIGHTS

In Christ, God has broken the cycle of judgment and retaliation. We have received mercy—undeserved and unearned love. In the fifth Beatitude, Jesus invites us to share His character trait of mercy. But inflow and outgo must be matched. Mercy must be given away if we want to live in its flow. . . .

The test of the greatness Christ offers us is to be merciful to those who do not return it. When we've endured disappointments, injustice, or hurts, we do not become bitter or sour but draw on and express mercy. This is not easy—not until we remember how merciful Christ has been to us. We are called to be a channel of divine mercy flowing through us to others. This is the source of the silent strength of greatness.

Lloyd Ogilvie

ACTION POINT

Did Jesus condemn his followers for their lack of faith and understanding? What did he do for those who want his healing and miracles, but little else? How was Jesus merciful to the Pharisees and teachers of the law? In what way is God merciful, even to those who don't live by his teachings? Write your own psalm of praise to God for his unending mercy.

THURSDAY

Evil Comes from Within

Mark 7:14–37

After Jesus called the crowd to him again, he said, "Every person should listen to me and understand what I am saying. 15 There is nothing people put into their bodies that makes them unclean. People are made unclean by the things that come out of them. 16 You people who can hear me, listen!"

17 When Jesus left the people and went into the house, his followers asked him about this story. 18 Jesus said, "Do you still not understand? Surely you know that nothing that enters someone from the outside can make that person unclean. 19 It does not go into the mind, but into the stomach. Then it goes out of the body." (When Jesus said this, he meant that no longer was any food unclean for people to eat.)

20 And Jesus said, "The things that come out of people are the things that make them unclean. 21 All these evil things begin inside people, in the mind: evil thoughts, sexual sins, stealing, murder, adultery, 22 greed, evil actions, lying, doing sinful things, jealousy, speaking evil of others, pride, and foolish living. 23 All these evil things come from inside and make people unclean."

Jesus Helps a Non-Jewish Woman

Jesus left that place and went to the area around Tyre. When he went into a house, he did not want anyone to know he was there, but he could not stay hidden. 25 A woman whose daughter had an evil spirit in her heard that he was there. So she quickly came to Jesus and fell at his feet. 26 She was Greek, born in Phoenicia, in Syria. She begged Jesus to force the demon out of her daughter.

27 Jesus told the woman, "It is not right to take the children's bread and give it to the dogs. First let the children eat all they want."

28 But she answered, "Yes, Lord, but even the dogs under the table can eat the children's crumbs."

29 Then Jesus said, "Because of your answer, you may go. The demon has left your daughter."

30 The woman went home and found her daughter lying in bed; the demon was gone.

Jesus Heals a Deaf Man

Then Jesus left the area around Tyre and went through Sidon to Lake Galilee, to the area of the Ten Towns. 32 While he was there, some people brought a man to him who was deaf and could not talk plainly. The people begged Jesus to put his hand on the man to heal him.

33 Jesus led the man away from the crowd, by himself. He put his fingers in the man's ears and then spit and touched the man's tongue. 34 Looking up to heaven, he sighed and said to the man, "Ephphatha!" (This means, "Be opened.") 35 Instantly the man was able to hear and to use his tongue so that he spoke clearly.

36 Jesus commanded the people not to tell anyone about what happened. But the more he commanded

them, the more they told about it.
37 They were completely amazed and said, "Jesus does everything well. He makes the deaf hear! And those who can't talk he makes able to speak."

OLD TESTAMENT READING

Some people are wicked and no
good.
They go around telling lies,
13 winking with their eyes, tapping
with their feet,
and making signs with their
fingers.
14 They make evil plans in their
hearts
and are always starting
arguments.
15 So trouble will strike them in an
instant;
suddenly they will be so hurt
no one can help them.

16 There are six things the LORD
hates.
There are seven things he
cannot stand:
17 a proud look,
a lying tongue,
hands that kill innocent
people,
18 a mind that thinks up evil
plans,
feet that are quick to do evil,
19 a witness who lies,
and someone who starts
arguments among families.

Proverbs 6:12–19

More than anything else, a
person's mind is evil
and cannot be healed.
No one truly understands it."

Jeremiah 17:9

INSIGHTS

A friend received a significant honor. I can't remember struggling with envy and jealousy before, but on that day, I was swept up into a whirlwind of envy. I drove back to my office in a complete state of shock. Where in creation did that come from? It leaked through the pinholes of my otherwise good character. A Christian's good character is the character of Jesus breathed into each of us by the Holy Spirit. Once we stop allowing the Spirit to fill us with power, the pinholes leak sin from our old nature.

Accepting our total depravity—our capacity to sin, that our character is filled with pinholes—is essential to living a victorious Christian life. If we presume that when we become Christian we are now good, we have missed the point. Jesus Christ shed His blood to forgive our sin, not to remove our sin. We have a continuing sinful nature which requires us to guard our heart and mind. We must post a twenty-four-hour guard at the gate to our mind.

Patrick Morley

APPLICATION

What evil things does Jesus say come from within a person? Why is it necessary to have a clean heart? Does your life show any evidence of "heart" trouble? What commitment will you make to guard those areas of weakness?

FRIDAY

Miracles Won't Soften Hard Hearts

Mark 8:1–26

More than Four Thousand Fed

8 Another time there was a great
crowd with Jesus that had nothing to eat. So Jesus called his followers and said, 2 "I feel sorry for these
people, because they have already
been with me for three days, and
they have nothing to eat. 3 If I send
them home hungry, they will faint on
the way. Some of them live a long
way from here."
4 Jesus' followers answered, "How
can we get enough bread to feed all
these people? We are far away from
any town."
5 Jesus asked, "How many loaves
of bread do you have?"
They answered, "Seven."
6 Jesus told the people to sit on the
ground. Then he took the seven
loaves, gave thanks to God, and divided the bread. He gave the pieces
to his followers to give to the people,
and they did so. 7 The followers also
had a few small fish. After Jesus gave
thanks for the fish, he told his followers to give them to the people
also. 8 All the people ate and were
satisfied. Then his followers filled
seven baskets with the leftover
pieces of food. 9 There were about
four thousand people who ate. After
they had eaten, Jesus sent them
home. 10 Then right away he got into
a boat with his followers and went
to the area of Dalmanutha.

The Leaders Ask for A Miracle

The Pharisees came to Jesus and
began to ask him questions. Hoping to trap him, they asked Jesus
for a miracle from God. 12 Jesus
sighed deeply and said, "Why do
you people ask for a miracle as
a sign? I tell you the truth, no sign
will be given to you." 13 Then
Jesus left the Pharisees and went
in the boat to the other side of the
lake.

Guard Against Wrong Teachings

His followers had only one loaf of
bread with them in the boat; they
had forgotten to bring more. 15 Jesus
warned them, "Be careful! Beware of
the yeast of the Pharisees and the
yeast of Herod."
16 His followers discussed the
meaning of this, saying, "He said this
because we have no bread."
17 Knowing what they were talking about, Jesus asked them, "Why
are you talking about not having
bread? Do you still not see or understand? Are your minds closed?
18 You have eyes, but you don't really see. You have ears, but you
don't really listen. Remember when
19 I divided five loaves of bread for
the five thousand? How many baskets did you fill with leftover pieces
of food?"
They answered, "Twelve."
20 "And when I divided seven
loaves of bread for the four thousand, how many baskets did you
fill with leftover pieces of food?"
They answered, "Seven."
21 Then Jesus said to them, "Don't
you understand yet?"

Jesus Heals a Blind Man

Jesus and his followers came to Bethsaida. There some people brought a blind man to Jesus and begged him to touch the man. 23 So Jesus took the blind man's hand and led him out of the village. Then he spit on the man's eyes and put his hands on the man and asked, "Can you see now?"

24 The man looked up and said, "Yes, I see people, but they look like trees walking around."

25 Again Jesus put his hands on the man's eyes. Then the man opened his eyes wide and they were healed, and he was able to see everything clearly. 26 Jesus told him to go home, saying, "Don't go into the town."

OLD TESTAMENT READING

They turned against God so
  often in the desert
  and grieved him there.
41 Again and again they tested God
  and brought pain to the Holy
   One of Israel.
42 They did not remember his power
  or the time he saved them
   from the enemy.
43 They forgot the signs he did in
   Egypt
  and his wonders in the fields of
   Zoan.

Psalm 78:40–43

INSIGHTS

For three years, day in and day out, he [Judas] occupied himself with Jesus Christ. He saw the Lord's miracles, heard His words, even participated in His ministry. In all that time, no one ever questioned his faith. He had the same status as the other disciples. Except for the Savior Himself, who knew the thoughts of Judas's heart, no one ever suspected that this man would betray Christ.

Yet, while the others were growing into apostles, Judas was quietly becoming a vile, calculating tool of Satan. Whatever his character seemed to be at the beginning, his faith was not real (John 13:10–11). He was unregenerate, and his heart gradually hardened so that he became the treacherous man who sold the Savior for a fistful of coins. . . .

It was not the will of God apart from Judas's own choice that he should betray Christ. At every opportunity, Jesus warned Judas and entreated him to repent and be saved, but at every point Judas turned away. Judas had heard the gospel according to Jesus, yet he refused to turn from his sin and selfishness. Jesus' words in John 13 represent His final, loving appeal to this man. In the end, however, the Savior's merciful entreaty would condemn Judas in the hardness of his heart.

John F. MacArthur, Jr.

PAUSE FOR REFLECTION

Who has witnessed more miracles of God than the Israelites or those who walked with Jesus while he was on earth? Do miracles lead people to salvation? What is more important than miracles in causing a person to turn toward God?

WEEKEND

Learn to Value What God Values

Mark 8:27—9:13

Peter Says Jesus Is the Christ

Jesus and his followers went to the towns around Caesarea Philippi. While they were traveling, Jesus asked them, "Who do people say I am?"

28 They answered, "Some say you are John the Baptist. Others say you are Elijah, and others say you are one of the prophets."

29 Then Jesus asked, "But who do you say I am?"

Peter answered, "You are the Christ."

30 Jesus warned his followers not to tell anyone who he was.

31 Then Jesus began to teach them that the Son of Man must suffer many things and that he would be rejected by the older Jewish leaders, the leading priests, and the teachers of the law. He told them that the Son of Man must be killed and then rise from the dead after three days. 32 Jesus told them plainly what would happen. Then Peter took Jesus aside and began to tell him not to talk like that. 33 But Jesus turned and looked at his followers. Then he told Peter not to talk that way. He said, "Go away from me, Satan! You don't care about the things of God, but only about things people think are important."

34 Then Jesus called the crowd to him, along with his followers. He said, "If people want to follow me, they must give up the things they want. They must be willing even to give up their lives to follow me. 35 Those who want to save their lives will give up true life. But those who give up their lives for me and for the Good News will have true life. 36 It is worth nothing for them to have the whole world if they lose their souls. 37 They could never pay enough to buy back their souls. 38 The people who live now are living in a sinful and evil time. If people are ashamed of me and my teaching, the Son of Man will be ashamed of them when he comes with his Father's glory and with the holy angels."

9 Then Jesus said to the people, "I tell you the truth, some people standing here will see the kingdom of God come with power before they die."

Jesus Talks with Moses and Elijah

Six days later, Jesus took Peter, James, and John up on a high mountain by themselves. While they watched, Jesus' appearance was changed. 3 His clothes became shining white, whiter than any person could make them. 4 Then Elijah and Moses appeared to them, talking with Jesus.

5 Peter said to Jesus, "Teacher, it is good that we are here. Let us make three tents—one for you, one for Moses, and one for Elijah." 6 Peter did not know what to say, because he and the others were so frightened.

7 Then a cloud came and covered them, and a voice came from the cloud, saying, "This is my Son, whom I love. Listen to him!"

8 Suddenly Peter, James, and John looked around, but they saw only Jesus there alone with them.

9 As they were coming down the mountain, Jesus commanded them

not to tell anyone about what they had seen until the Son of Man had risen from the dead.
[10] So the followers obeyed Jesus, but they discussed what he meant about rising from the dead.
[11] Then they asked Jesus, "Why do the teachers of the law say that Elijah must come first?"
[12] Jesus answered, "They are right to say that Elijah must come first and make everything the way it should be. But why does the Scripture say that the Son of Man will suffer much and that people will treat him as if he were nothing? [13] I tell you that Elijah has already come. And people did to him whatever they wanted to do, just as the Scriptures said it would happen."

OLD TESTAMENT READING

Anything I saw and wanted, I
got for myself;
I did not miss any pleasure I
desired.
I was pleased with everything I did,
and this pleasure was the reward
for all my hard work.
11 But then I looked at what I had done,
and I thought about all the hard
work.
Suddenly I realized it was useless,
like chasing the wind.
There is nothing to gain from
anything we do here on
earth.

Ecclesiastes 2:10–11

INSIGHTS

I will hear what God the Lord will speak" (Ps. 85:8). Blessed is the soul which hears the Lord speaking within, and from His mouth receives the word of consolation. Blessed are the ears that catch the pulses of the divine whisper (Matt. 13:16, 17), and give no heed to the whisperings of this world. Blessed indeed are those ears which listen not after the voice which is sounding without, but for the truth teaching inwardly. Blessed are the eyes that are shut to outward things, but intent on things inward. Blessed are they that enter far into things within, and endeavor to prepare themselves more and more, by daily exercises, for the receiving of heavenly secrets. Blessed are they who are glad to have time to spare for God, and who shake off all worldly hindrances.

Consider these things, O my soul, and shut up the door of your sensual desires, that you may hear what the Lord your God speaks in you (Ps. 85:8).

Thus says your Beloved, "I am thy salvation," your Peace, and your Life: keep yourself with Me, and you shall find peace. Let go all transitory things, and seek the things eternal. What are all transitory objects but seductive things? And what can all creatures avail, if you are forsaken by the Creator?

Renounce therefore all things, and labor to please your Creator, and to be faithful unto Him, that you may be able to attain unto true blessedness.

Thomas à Kempis

ACTION POINT

List and evaluate the things in your life that seem worth pursuing. If you want to follow Jesus, what priorities do you need to rearrange?

MONDAY

God Wants to Teach Us His Ways

Mark 9:14–37

Jesus Heals a Sick Boy

When Jesus, Peter, James, and John came back to the other followers, they saw a great crowd around them and the teachers of the law arguing with them. 15 But as soon as the crowd saw Jesus, the people were surprised and ran to welcome him.

16 Jesus asked, "What are you arguing about?"

17 A man answered, "Teacher, I brought my son to you. He has an evil spirit in him that stops him from talking. 18 When the spirit attacks him, it throws him on the ground. Then my son foams at the mouth, grinds his teeth, and becomes very stiff. I asked your followers to force the evil spirit out, but they couldn't."

19 Jesus answered, "You people have no faith. How long must I stay with you? How long must I put up with you? Bring the boy to me."

20 So the followers brought him to Jesus. As soon as the evil spirit saw Jesus, it made the boy lose control of himself, and he fell down and rolled on the ground, foaming at the mouth.

21 Jesus asked the boy's father, "How long has this been happening?"

The father answered, "Since he was very young. 22 The spirit often throws him into a fire or into water to kill him. If you can do anything for him, please have pity on us and help us."

23 Jesus said to the father, "You said, 'If you can!' All things are possible for the one who believes."

24 Immediately the father cried out, "I do believe! Help me to believe more!"

25 When Jesus saw that a crowd was quickly gathering, he ordered the evil spirit, saying, "You spirit that makes people unable to hear or speak, I command you to come out of this boy and never enter him again!"

26 The evil spirit screamed and caused the boy to fall on the ground again. Then the spirit came out. The boy looked as if he were dead, and many people said, "He is dead!" 27 But Jesus took hold of the boy's hand and helped him to stand up.

28 When Jesus went into the house, his followers began asking him privately, "Why couldn't we force that evil spirit out?"

29 Jesus answered, "That kind of spirit can only be forced out by prayer."

Jesus Talks About His Death

Then Jesus and his followers left that place and went through Galilee. He didn't want anyone to know where he was, 31 because he was teaching his followers. He said to them, "The Son of Man will be handed over to people, and they will kill him. After three days, he will rise from the dead." 32 But the followers did not understand what Jesus meant, and they were afraid to ask him.

Who Is the Greatest?

Jesus and his followers went to Capernaum. When they went into a house there, he asked them, "What were you arguing about on the road?" 34 But the followers did not answer, because their argument on the road was about which one of them was the greatest.

35 Jesus sat down and called the twelve apostles to him. He said, "Whoever wants to be the most important must be last of all and servant of all."

36 Then Jesus took a small child and had him stand among them. Taking the child in his arms, he said, 37 "Whoever accepts a child like this in my name accepts me. And whoever accepts me accepts the One who sent me."

OLD TESTAMENT READING

Moses used to take a tent and set it up a long way outside the camp; he called it the "Meeting Tent." Anyone who wanted to ask the LORD about something would go to the Meeting Tent outside the camp.
8 Whenever Moses went out to the Tent, all the people would rise and stand at the entrances of their tents, watching him until he entered the Meeting Tent.
9 When Moses went into the Tent, the pillar of cloud would always come down and stay at the entrance of the Tent while the LORD spoke with Moses.
10 Whenever the people saw the pillar of cloud at the entrance of the Tent, they stood and worshiped, each person at the entrance of his own tent.

11 The LORD spoke to Moses face to face as a man speaks with his friend. Then Moses would return to the camp, but Moses' young helper, Joshua son of Nun, did not leave the Tent.

Exodus 33:7–11

INSIGHTS

The Father in heaven is so interested in His child, and so longs to have his life in step with His will and His love, that He is willing to keep the child's guidance entirely in His own hand. He knows so well that we do not do what is really holy and heavenly, except when He works it in us, that He intends His very demands to become promises of what He will do, in watching over and leading us all day long. We may count on Him to teach us His way and show us His path not only in special trials and hard times, but in everyday life. . . .

. . . So simple and delightful can it become to a soul that has practiced waiting on God, to walk all day in the enjoyment of God's light and leading. What is needed to help us find such a life is one thing: the real knowledge and faith of God as the only source of wisdom and goodness, as always ready and longing to be to us all that we can possibly need. Yes, this is the one thing we need.

Andrew Murray

ACTION POINT

What special teaching did Jesus want to give his followers when they were alone? As you read Old Testament passages, think about how much God wants to teach his people. Thank him for his great outpouring of love. Pray that your heart will listen for his wisdom.

TUESDAY

Flee All Evil

Mark 9:38—10:16

Anyone Not Against Us Is for Us

Then John said, "Teacher, we saw someone using your name to force demons out of a person. We told him to stop, because he does not belong to our group."

[39] But Jesus said, "Don't stop him, because anyone who uses my name to do powerful things will not easily say evil things about me. [40] Whoever is not against us is with us. [41] I tell you the truth, whoever gives you a drink of water because you belong to the Christ will truly get his reward.

[42] "If one of these little children believes in me, and someone causes that child to sin, it would be better for that person to have a large stone tied around his neck and be drowned in the sea. [43] If your hand causes you to sin, cut it off. It is better for you to lose part of your body and live forever than to have two hands and go to hell, where the fire never goes out. [44] In hell the worm does not die; the fire is never put out. [45] If your foot causes you to sin, cut it off. It is better for you to lose part of your body and to live forever than to have two feet and be thrown into hell. [46] In hell the worm does not die; the fire is never put out. [47] If your eye causes you to sin, take it out. It is better for you to enter the kingdom of God with only one eye than to have two eyes and be thrown into hell. [48] In hell the worm does not die; the fire is never put out. [49] Every person will be salted with fire.

[50] "Salt is good, but if the salt loses its salty taste, you cannot make it salty again. So, be full of salt, and have peace with each other."

Jesus Teaches About Divorce

10 Then Jesus left that place and went into the area of Judea and across the Jordan River. Again, crowds came to him, and he taught them as he usually did.

[2] Some Pharisees came to Jesus and tried to trick him. They asked, "Is it right for a man to divorce his wife?"

[3] Jesus answered, "What did Moses command you to do?"

[4] They said, "Moses allowed a man to write out divorce papers and send her away."

[5] Jesus said, "Moses wrote that command for you because you were stubborn. [6] But when God made the world, 'he made them male and female.' [7] 'So a man will leave his father and mother and be united with his wife, [8] and the two will become one body.' So there are not two, but one. [9] God has joined the two together, so no one should separate them."

[10] Later, in the house, his followers asked Jesus again about the question of divorce. [11] He answered, "Anyone who divorces his wife and marries another woman is guilty of adultery against her. [12] And the woman who divorces her husband and marries another man is also guilty of adultery."

Jesus Accepts Children

Some people brought their little children to Jesus so he could touch them, but his followers told them to stop. [14] When Jesus saw this, he was

upset and said to them, "Let the little children come to me. Don't stop them, because the kingdom of God belongs to people who are like these
children. [15] I tell you the truth, you must accept the kingdom of God as if you were a little child, or you will
never enter it." [16] Then Jesus took the children in his arms, put his hands on them, and blessed them.

OLD TESTAMENT READING

Now Joseph was well built and
handsome. [7] After some time the wife of Joseph's master began to desire Joseph, and one day she said to him, "Have sexual relations with me."
[8] But Joseph refused and said to her, "My master trusts me with everything in his house. He has put me in charge of everything he owns.
[9] There is no one in his house greater than I. He has not kept anything from me except you, because you are his wife. How can I do such an evil thing? It is a sin against God."
[10] The woman talked to Joseph every day, but he refused to have sexual relations with her or even spend time with her.
[11] One day Joseph went into the house to do his work as usual and was the only man in the house at that
time. [12] His master's wife grabbed his coat and said to him, "Come and have sexual relations with me." But Joseph left his coat in her hand and ran out of the house.

Genesis 39:6b–12

INSIGHTS

Repentance is a definite turn from every thought, word, deed and habit which is known to be wrong. It is not sufficient to feel pangs of remorse or to make some kind of apology to God. Fundamentally, repentance is a matter neither of emotion nor of speech. It is an inward change of mind and attitude towards sin which leads to a change of behaviour.

There can be no compromise here. There may be sins in our lives which we do not think we ever could renounce; but we must be willing to let them go as we cry to God for deliverance from them. If you are in doubt regarding what is right and what is wrong, what must go and what may be retained, do not be too greatly influenced by the customs and conventions of Christians you may know. Go by the clear teaching of the Bible and by the prompting of your conscience, and Christ will gradually lead you further along the path of righteousness. When he puts his finger on anything, give it up. It may be some association or recreation, some literature we read, or some attitude of pride, jealousy or resentment, or an unforgiving spirit.

Jesus told his followers to pluck out their eye and cut off their hand or foot if these caused them to sin. We are not to obey this with dead literalism, of course, and mutilate our bodies. It is a vivid figure of speech for dealing ruthlessly with the avenues along which temptation comes to us.

John Stott

APPLICATION

How serious a problem does Jesus consider sin to be? Is there anything casual about his attitude? What about your attitude toward sin? Do you vigorously run from it or politely coexist with it?

WEDNESDAY

The Righteous Will Be Rewarded in Heaven

Mark 10:17–41

A Rich Young Man's Question

As Jesus started to leave, a man ran
to him and fell on his knees before
Jesus. The man asked, "Good teacher,
what must I do to have life forever?"
18 Jesus answered, "Why do you
call me good? Only God is good.
19 You know the commands: 'You
must not murder anyone. You must
not be guilty of adultery. You must
not steal. You must not tell lies about
your neighbor. You must not cheat.
Honor your father and mother.' "
20 The man said, "Teacher, I have
obeyed all these things since I was
a boy."
21 Jesus, looking at the man, loved
him and said, "There is one more
thing you need to do. Go and sell
everything you have, and give the
money to the poor, and you will have
treasure in heaven. Then come and
follow me."
22 He was very sad to hear Jesus
say this, and he left sorrowfully,
because he was rich.
23 Then Jesus looked at his followers and said, "How hard it will be for
the rich to enter the kingdom of
God!"
24 The followers were amazed at
what Jesus said. But he said again,
"My children, it is very hard to enter
the kingdom of God! 25 It is easier for
a camel to go through the eye of a
needle than for a rich person to enter
the kingdom of God."
26 The followers were even more
surprised and said to each other,
"Then who can be saved?"
27 Jesus looked at them and said,
"This is something people cannot
do, but God can. God can do all
things."
28 Peter said to Jesus, "Look, we
have left everything and followed you."
29 Jesus said, "I tell you the truth,
all those who have left houses, brothers, sisters, mother, father, children,
or farms for me and for the Good
News 30 will get more than they left.
Here in this world they will have a
hundred times more homes, brothers, sisters, mothers, children, and
fields. And with those things, they
will also suffer for their belief. But
in the age that is coming they will
have life forever. 31 Many who have
the highest place now will have the
lowest place in the future. And many
who have the lowest place now will
have the highest place in the future."

Jesus Talks About His Death

As Jesus and the people with him
were on the road to Jerusalem, he
was leading the way. His followers
were amazed, but others in the
crowd who followed were afraid.
Again Jesus took the twelve apostles
aside and began to tell them what
was about to happen in Jerusalem.
33 He said, "Look, we are going to
Jerusalem. The Son of Man will be
turned over to the leading priests
and the teachers of the law. They will
say that he must die, and they will
turn him over to the non-Jewish
people, 34 who will laugh at him and
spit on him. They will beat him with
whips and crucify him. But on the
third day, he will rise to life again."

Two Followers Ask Jesus a Favor

Then James and John, sons of Zebedee, came to Jesus and said, "Teacher, we want to ask you to do something for us."
[36] Jesus asked, "What do you want me to do for you?"
[37] They answered, "Let one of us sit at your right side and one of us sit at your left side in your glory in your kingdom."
[38] Jesus said, "You don't understand what you are asking. Can you drink the cup that I must drink? And can you be baptized with the same kind of baptism that I must go through?"
[39] They answered, "Yes, we can."
Jesus said to them, "You will drink the same cup that I will drink, and you will be baptized with the same baptism that I must go
through. [40] But I cannot choose who will sit at my right or my left; those places belong to those for whom they have been prepared."
[41] When the other ten followers heard this, they began to be angry with James and John.

OLD TESTAMENT READING

Then people will say,
"There really are rewards for
doing what is right.
There really is a God who
judges the world."

Psalm 58:11

INSIGHTS

Be not wearied by the labors which you have undertaken for my sake, nor let tribulations cast you down. But let My promise strengthen and comfort you under every circumstance. I am well able to reward you, above all measure and degree. . . .

Do in earnest what you do; labor faithfully in My vineyard (Matt. 20:7); I will be your recompense. Write, read, chant, mourn, keep silence, pray, endure crosses manfully. Life everlasting is worth all these battles, and greater than these. Peace shall come in one day which is known unto the Lord, and there shall be "not day, nor night" (Zech. 14:7) (that is, of this present time), but unceasing light, infinite brightness, steadfast peace, and secure rest. Then you shall not say: "Who shall deliver me from the body of this death?" (Rom. 7:24); nor cry: "Woe is me, that I sojourn in Mesech" (Ps. 120:5). For death shall be cast down headlong, and there shall be salvation which can never fail, no more anxiety, blessed joy, companionship sweet and noble. . . .

Lift up your face therefore to Heaven. Behold, I and all My saints with Me, who in this world had great conflict, do now rejoice, now are comforted, now secure, now at rest, and shall remain with Me everlastingly in the kingdom of My Father!

Thomas à Kempis

APPLICATION

What areas of personal commitment to God's kingdom do you find difficult? What is hard for you to leave behind? Pray that you will truly believe—deep inside—that God will reward your faithfulness far above what you can even imagine.

THURSDAY

Being a Servant of God

Mark 10:42—11:14

Jesus called them together and said, "The non-Jewish people have rulers. You know that those rulers love to show their power over the people, and their important leaders love to use all their authority. 43 But it should not be that way among you. Whoever wants to become great among you must serve the rest of you like a servant. 44 Whoever wants to become the first among you must serve all of you like a slave. 45 In the same way, the Son of Man did not come to be served. He came to serve others and to give his life as a ransom for many people."

Jesus Heals a Blind Man

Then they came to the town of Jericho. As Jesus was leaving there with his followers and a great many people, a blind beggar named Bartimaeus son of Timaeus was sitting by the road. 47 When he heard that Jesus from Nazareth was walking by, he began to shout, "Jesus, Son of David, have mercy on me!"

48 Many people warned the blind man to be quiet, but he shouted even more, "Son of David, have mercy on me!"

49 Jesus stopped and said, "Tell the man to come here."

So they called the blind man, saying, "Cheer up! Get to your feet. Jesus is calling you." 50 The blind man jumped up, left his coat there, and went to Jesus.

51 Jesus asked him, "What do you want me to do for you?"

The blind man answered, "Teacher, I want to see."

52 Jesus said, "Go, you are healed because you believed." At once the man could see, and he followed Jesus on the road.

Jesus Enters Jerusalem as a King

11 As Jesus and his followers were coming closer to Jerusalem, they came to the towns of Bethphage and Bethany near the Mount of Olives. From there Jesus sent two of his followers 2 and said to them, "Go to the town you can see there. When you enter it, you will quickly find a colt tied, which no one has ever ridden. Untie it and bring it here to me. 3 If anyone asks you why you are doing this, tell him its Master needs the colt, and he will send it at once."

4 The followers went into the town, found a colt tied in the street near the door of a house, and untied it. 5 Some people were standing there and asked, "What are you doing? Why are you untying that colt?" 6 The followers answered the way Jesus told them to answer, and the people let them take the colt.

7 They brought the colt to Jesus and put their coats on it, and Jesus sat on it. 8 Many people spread their coats on the road. Others cut branches in the fields and spread them on the road. 9 The people were walking ahead of Jesus and behind him, shouting,

"Praise God!
God bless the One who comes in
the name of the Lord!
Psalm 118:26
10 God bless the kingdom of our
father David!

That kingdom is coming!
Praise to God in heaven!"
11 Jesus entered Jerusalem and
went into the Temple. After he had
looked at everything, since it was
already late, he went out to Bethany
with the twelve apostles.
12 The next day as Jesus was leaving Bethany, he became hungry.
13 Seeing a fig tree in leaf from far
away, he went to see if it had any figs
on it. But he found no figs, only
leaves, because it was not the right
season for figs. 14 So Jesus said to the
tree, "May no one ever eat fruit from
you again." And Jesus' followers
heard him say this.

OLD TESTAMENT READING

After these things God tested
Abraham's faith. God said to him,
"Abraham!"
And he answered, "Here I am."
2 Then God said, "Take your only
son, Isaac, the son you love, and go
to the land of Moriah. Kill him there
and offer him as a whole burnt offering on one of the mountains I will
tell you about."
10 Then Abraham took his knife
and was about to kill his son.
11 But the angel of the LORD called
to him from heaven and said,
"Abraham! Abraham!"
Abraham answered, "Yes."
12 The angel said, "Don't kill your
son or hurt him in any way. Now I
can see that you trust God and that
you have not kept your son, your
only son, from me."

Genesis 22:1–2, 10–12

INSIGHTS

We must squarely face the fact that the thought of service, except as a token or temporary activity, is distasteful. To accept a lower place is bad enough, but to choose a lower place—preposterous!

Words like obey, submit, serve, or worse, the expression "know your place," are met with defiance from a people who are obsessed with their "rights." Of course these rights are not wrong, and it is appropriate that there is legislation to protect rights. The problem is that legislation can only protect us from the bad; it cannot produce good in us. And it certainly cannot suggest to us that there might be some value in renouncing our rights for something or someone else. The Cross is the best evidence that there is much more to love than justice, much more to right than rights. A person who has won a public battle for human rights has done a good thing. But a person who has won a personal battle and given up human rights in the interest of human obligation has done a great thing. More often than not, the action will be labeled demeaning or ridiculous. So was the Cross.

Thomas Schmidt

APPLICATION

Who is our greatest example of being a servant of God? How far was he willing to go in serving others? What did God call his servant Abraham to do? How is God calling you to serve him? Are you willing to be his servant?

FRIDAY

Pray with Conviction

Mark 11:15—12:12

Jesus Goes to the Temple

When Jesus returned to Jerusalem, he went into the Temple and began to throw out those who were buying and selling there. He turned over the tables of those who were exchanging different kinds of money, and he upset the benches of those who were selling doves. [16]Jesus refused to allow anyone to carry goods through the Temple courts. [17]Then he taught the people, saying, "It is written in the Scriptures, 'My Temple will be called a house for prayer for people from all nations.' But you are changing God's house into a 'hideout for robbers.' "

[18]The leading priests and the teachers of the law heard all this and began trying to find a way to kill Jesus. They were afraid of him, because all the people were amazed at his teaching. [19]That evening, Jesus and his followers left the city.

The Power of Faith

The next morning as Jesus was passing by with his followers, they saw the fig tree dry and dead, even to the roots. [21]Peter remembered the tree and said to Jesus, "Teacher, look! The fig tree you cursed is dry and dead!"

[22]Jesus answered, "Have faith in God. [23]I tell you the truth, you can say to this mountain, 'Go, fall into the sea.' And if you have no doubts in your mind and believe that what you say will happen, God will do it for you. [24]So I tell you to believe that you have received the things you ask for in prayer, and God will give them to you. [25]When you are praying, if you are angry with someone, forgive him so that your Father in heaven will also forgive your sins. [26]But if you don't forgive other people, then your Father in heaven will not forgive your sins."

Leaders Doubt Jesus' Authority

Jesus and his followers went again to Jerusalem. As Jesus was walking in the Temple, the leading priests, the teachers of the law, and the older leaders came to him. [28]They said to him, "What authority do you have to do these things? Who gave you this authority?"

[29]Jesus answered, "I will ask you one question. If you answer me, I will tell you what authority I have to do these things. [30]Tell me: When John baptized people, was that authority from God or just from other people?"

[31]They argued about Jesus' question, saying, "If we answer, 'John's baptism was from God,' Jesus will say, 'Then why didn't you believe him?' [32]But if we say, 'It was from other people,' the crowd will be against us." (These leaders were afraid of the people, because all the people believed that John was a prophet.)

[33]So they answered Jesus, "We don't know."

Jesus said to them, "Then I won't tell you what authority I have to do these things."

A Story About God's Son

12 Jesus began to use stories to teach the people. He said, "A

man planted a vineyard. He put a
wall around it and dug a hole for a
winepress and built a tower. Then he
leased the land to some farmers and
left for a trip. 2 When it was time for
the grapes to be picked, he sent a
servant to the farmers to get his
share of the grapes. 3 But the farmers grabbed the servant and beat
him and sent him away empty-
handed. 4 Then the man sent another
servant. They hit him on the head
and showed no respect for him. 5 So
the man sent another servant, whom
they killed. The man sent many
other servants. The farmers beat
some of them and killed others.

6 "The man had one person left to
send, his son whom he loved. He
sent him last of all, saying, 'They will
respect my son.'

7 "But the farmers said to each
other, 'This son will inherit the vineyard. If we kill him, it will be ours.'
8 So they took the son, killed him,
and threw him out of the vineyard.

9 "So what will the owner of the
vineyard do? He will come and kill
those farmers and will give the
vineyard to other farmers. 10 Surely
you have read this Scripture:

'The stone that the builders
rejected
became the cornerstone.
11 The Lord did this,
and it is wonderful to us.' "

Psalm 118:22-23

12 The Jewish leaders knew that the
story was about them. So they wanted
to find a way to arrest Jesus, but they
were afraid of the people. So the leaders left him and went away.

OLD TESTAMENT READING

The LORD is close to everyone
who prays to him,
to all who truly pray to him.
19 He gives those who respect him
what they want.
He listens when they cry, and
he saves them.

Psalm 145:18–19

INSIGHTS

How do you pray a prayer so filled with faith that it can move a mountain? By shifting the focus from the size of your mountain to the sufficiency of the mountain mover, and by stepping forward in obedience. . . .

While the children of Israel are perched on the edge of the Promised Land, twelve spies go out to survey it. Ten come back saying, "You wouldn't believe the size of the cities, the armies, the giants. We'd better look somewhere else." Two come back saying, "The God who is faithful promised he would give us the land, so let's go in his strength." Ten looked at the size of the mountain and fell back; only two looked at the sufficiency of the mountain mover and wanted to move forward. . . .

I challenge you to shift the focus of your prayer. Don't spend a lot of time describing your mountain to the Lord. He knows what it is. Instead, focus your attention on the mountain mover—his glory, power and faithfulness. Then start walking in faith, following his leading, and watch that mountain step aside.

Bill Hybels

ACTION POINT

How does God want us to ask him for what we need? In what remarkable ways has God answered your prayers? Make a list of them.

WEEKEND

The Wicked Persecute the Righteous

Mark 12:13–31

Is It Right To Pay Taxes or Not?

Later, the Jewish leaders sent some
Pharisees and Herodians to Jesus to
trap him in saying something wrong.
14 They came to him and said,
"Teacher, we know that you are an
honest man. You are not afraid of
what other people think about you,
because you pay no attention to who
they are. And you teach the truth
about God's way. Tell us: Is it right to
pay taxes to Caesar or not? 15 Should
we pay them, or not?"

But knowing what these men
were really trying to do, Jesus said
to them, "Why are you trying to trap
me? Bring me a coin to look at."
16 They gave Jesus a coin, and he
asked, "Whose image and name are
on the coin?"

They answered, "Caesar's."

17 Then Jesus said to them, "Give
to Caesar the things that are
Caesar's, and give to God the things
that are God's." The men were
amazed at what Jesus said.

Some Sadducees Try to Trick Jesus

Then some Sadducees came to
Jesus and asked him a question.
(Sadducees believed that people
would not rise from the dead.)
19 They said, "Teacher, Moses wrote
that if a man's brother dies, leaving
a wife but no children, then that man
must marry the widow and have
children for his brother. 20 Once
there were seven brothers. The first
brother married and died, leaving no
children. 21 So the second brother
married the widow, but he also died
and had no children. The same thing
happened with the third brother.
22 All seven brothers married her and
died, and none of the brothers had
any children. Finally the woman died
too. 23 Since all seven brothers had
married her, when people rise from
the dead, whose wife will she be?"

24 Jesus answered, "Why don't
you understand? Don't you know
what the Scriptures say, and don't
you know about the power of God?
25 When people rise from the dead,
they will not marry, nor will they be
given to someone to marry. They
will be like the angels in heaven.
26 Surely you have read what God
said about people rising from the
dead. In the book in which Moses
wrote about the burning bush, it
says that God told Moses, 'I am the
God of Abraham, the God of Isaac,
and the God of Jacob.' 27 God is the
God of the living, not the dead. You
Sadducees are wrong!"

The Most Important Command

One of the teachers of the law came
and heard Jesus arguing with the
Sadducees. Seeing that Jesus gave
good answers to their questions, he
asked Jesus, "Which of the commands is most important?"

29 Jesus answered, "The most important command is this: 'Listen,
people of Israel! The Lord our God
is the only Lord. 30 Love the Lord
your God with all your heart, all your
soul, all your mind, and all your
strength.' 31 The second command is

this: 'Love your neighbor as you love yourself.' There are no commands more important than these."

OLD TESTAMENT READING

Those who lead good people to
do wrong
will be ruined by their own evil,
but the innocent will be
rewarded with good things.
Proverbs 28:10

LORD, rescue me from evil people;
protect me from cruel people
2 who make evil plans,
who always start fights.
3 They make their tongues sharp
as a snake's;
their words are like snake
poison. *Selah*
4 LORD, guard me from the power
of wicked people;
protect me from cruel people
who plan to trip me up.
5 The proud hid a trap for me.
They spread out a net beside
the road;
they set traps for me. *Selah*
6 I said to the LORD, "You are my
God."
LORD, listen to my prayer for
help.
7 LORD God, my mighty savior,
you protect me in battle.
8 LORD, do not give the wicked
what they want.
Don't let their plans succeed,
or they will become proud.
Selah
Psalm 140:1–8

INSIGHTS

The reproach we experience is the natural resentment in the hearts of men toward all that is godly and righteous. This is the cross we are to bear. This is why Christians are often persecuted. . . .

Let us not forget that there is happiness and blessing in persecution. As George MacDonald puts it, we become "hearty through hardship." . . .

Our Lord instructs the persecuted to be happy. "Rejoice," He said, "and be exceeding glad: for great is your reward in heaven: for so persecuted they the prophets which were before you" (Matthew 5:12).

The word joy has all but disappeared from our current Christian vocabulary. One of the reasons is that we have thought that joy and happiness were found in comfort, ease and luxury. James did not say, "Count it all joy when you fall into an easy chair," but he said, "Count it all joy when you fall into divers temptations" (James 1:2).

The persecuted are happy because they are being processed for heaven. Persecution is one of the natural consequences of living the Christian life. It is to the Christian what "growing pains" are to the growing child. No pain, no development. No suffering, no glory. No struggle, no victory. No persecution, no reward! Jesus predicted that if they persecuted Him, they would persecute you who follow Him, too.

Billy Graham

APPLICATION

Have you ever felt that you've unwittingly walked into a trap designed to test your Christian commitment? If so, be glad—you must be an effective witness! Pray for strength to face such encounters.

MONDAY

Give Generously, Even Sacrificially, to God

Mark 12:32—13:10

The man answered, "That was a
good answer, Teacher. You were
right when you said God is the only
Lord and there is no other God besides him. 33 One must love God with
all his heart, all his mind, and all his
strength. And one must love his
neighbor as he loves himself. These
commands are more important than
all the animals and sacrifices we offer to God."

34 When Jesus saw that the man
answered him wisely, Jesus said to
him, "You are close to the kingdom
of God." And after that, no one was
brave enough to ask Jesus any more
questions.

35 As Jesus was teaching in the
Temple, he asked, "Why do the
teachers of the law say that the
Christ is the son of David? 36 David
himself, speaking by the Holy Spirit,
said:

'The Lord said to my Lord:
Sit by me at my right side,
until I put your enemies under
your control.' *Psalm 110:1*

37 David himself calls the Christ
'Lord,' so how can the Christ be his
son?" The large crowd listened to
Jesus with pleasure.

38 Jesus continued teaching and
said, "Beware of the teachers of the
law. They like to walk around wearing fancy clothes, and they love for
people to greet them with respect in
the marketplaces. 39 They love to have
the most important seats in the synagogues and at feasts. 40 But they cheat
widows and steal their houses and
then try to make themselves look
good by saying long prayers. They will
receive a greater punishment."

True Giving

Jesus sat near the Temple money
box and watched the people put in
their money. Many rich people gave
large sums of money. 42 Then a poor
widow came and put in two small
copper coins, which were only worth
a few cents.

43 Calling his followers to him,
Jesus said, "I tell you the truth, this
poor widow gave more than all those
rich people. 44 They gave only what
they did not need. This woman is
very poor, but she gave all she had;
she gave all she had to live on."

The Temple Will be Destroyed

13 As Jesus was leaving the
Temple, one of his followers
said to him, "Look, Teacher! How
beautiful the buildings are! How big
the stones are!"

2 Jesus said, "Do you see all these
great buildings? Not one stone will
be left on another. Every stone will
be thrown down to the ground."

3 Later, as Jesus was sitting on the
Mount of Olives, opposite the
Temple, he was alone with Peter,
James, John, and Andrew. They
asked Jesus, 4 "Tell us, when will
these things happen? And what will
be the sign that they are going to
happen?"

5 Jesus began to answer them, "Be
careful that no one fools you. 6 Many
people will come in my name, saying, 'I am the One,' and they will fool

many people. 7 When you hear about
wars and stories of wars that are
coming, don't be afraid. These
things must happen before the end
comes. 8 Nations will fight against
other nations, and kingdoms against
other kingdoms. There will be earthquakes in different places, and there
will be times when there is no food
for people to eat. These things are
like the first pains when something
new is about to be born.
9 "You must be careful. People will
arrest you and take you to court and
beat you in their synagogues. You
will be forced to stand before kings
and governors, to tell them about
me. This will happen to you because
you follow me. 10 But before these
things happen, the Good News must
be told to all people."

OLD TESTAMENT READING

The people continued to bring gifts
each morning because they wanted to.
4 So all the skilled workers left the work
they were doing on the Holy Tent, 5 and
they said to Moses, "The people are
bringing more than we need to do the
work the LORD commanded."
6 Then Moses sent this command
throughout the camp: "No man or
woman should make anything else
as a gift for the Holy Tent." So the
people were kept from giving more,
7 because what they had was already
more than enough to do all the work.

Exodus 36:3b–7

INSIGHTS

Many beloved saints are depriving themselves of wondrous spiritual blessing by not giving as stewards what is entrusted to them. They act as if it were their own, as if all belonged to them, as if already they were in possession of the inheritance incorruptible and undefiled; forgetting that they have nothing whatever which is their own, that they are bought by the precious blood of Christ, and all they possess—their bodily strength, their time, their talents, their business, their professions, their eyes, their hands, their feet, all belong to the Lord Jesus Christ; because He has bought them with his precious blood. . . .

Just as we are constrained by the love of Christ, so God condescends to use us; and as we give, He is pleased to entrust to us more and more. . . .

My advice is this: if the reader has as yet but little knowledge and little grace, let him accordingly begin with a small percentage, yea, though it were ever so small a percentage, only let him be true to God, and put aside for Him habitually as He may be pleased to prosper him. In this way blessing for the soul will be reaped, will be abundantly reaped, and soon will the desire spring up in the heart to increase the proportion of returns to the Lord. This way will more and more lead the heart to such a state to be only a steward for the Lord, and to be willing to stand with all we have and are before the Lord as His stewards.

George Müller

PAUSE FOR REFLECTION

What does God promise to those who give generously to him? To those who do not? Reread the Exodus passage. Can you imagine God's people today giving so much that they would have to be told to stop?

TUESDAY

Be Strong During the End Times

Mark 13:11–37

When you are arrested and judged,
don't worry ahead of time about
what you should say. Say whatever
is given you to say at that time, because it will not really be you speaking; it will be the Holy Spirit.
12 "Brothers will give their own
brothers to be killed, and fathers will
give their own children to be killed.
Children will fight against their own
parents and cause them to be put to
death. 13 All people will hate you because you follow me, but those
people who keep their faith until the
end will be saved.
14 "You will see 'the destroying terror' standing where it should not
be." (You who read this should
understand what it means.) "At that
time, the people in Judea should run
away to the mountains. 15 If people
are on the roofs of their houses, they
must not go down or go inside to get
anything out of their houses. 16 If
people are in the fields, they must
not go back to get their coats. 17 At
that time, how terrible it will be for
women who are pregnant or have
nursing babies! 18 Pray that these
things will not happen in winter,
19 because those days will be full of
trouble. There will be more trouble
than there has ever been since the
beginning, when God made the
world, until now, and nothing as bad
will ever happen again. 20 God has
decided to make that terrible time
short. Otherwise, no one would go
on living. But God will make that
time short to help the people he has
chosen. 21 At that time, someone
might say to you, 'Look, there is the
Christ!' Or another person might
say, 'There he is!' But don't believe
them. 22 False Christs and false
prophets will come and perform
great wonders and miracles. They
will try to fool even the people God
has chosen, if that is possible. 23 So
be careful. I have warned you about
all this before it happens.
24 "During the days after this
trouble comes,

'the sun will grow dark,
and the moon will not give its
light.
25 The stars will fall from the sky.
And the powers of the heavens
will be shaken.'

Isaiah 13:10; 34:4

26 "Then people will see the Son
of Man coming in clouds with great
power and glory. 27 Then he will send
his angels all around the earth to
gather his chosen people from every
part of the earth and from every part
of heaven.
28 "Learn a lesson from the fig
tree: When its branches become
green and soft and new leaves
appear, you know summer is near.
29 In the same way, when you see
these things happening, you will
know that the time is near, ready to
come. 30 I tell you the truth, all these
things will happen while the people
of this time are still living. 31 Earth
and sky will be destroyed, but the
words I have said will never be
destroyed.
32 "No one knows when that day
or time will be, not the angels in
heaven, not even the Son. Only the
Father knows. 33 Be careful! Always
be ready, because you don't know
when that time will be. 34 It is like a

man who goes on a trip. He leaves his house and lets his servants take care of it, giving each one a special job to do. The man tells the servant guarding the door always to be
watchful. 35 So always be ready, because you don't know when the owner of the house will come back. It might be in the evening, or at midnight, or in the morning while it is still dark, or when the sun rises.
36 Always be ready. Otherwise he might come back suddenly and find you sleeping.
37 I tell you this, and I say this to everyone: 'Be ready!' "

OLD TESTAMENT READING

Those who are wise will help the others understand what is happening. But they will be killed with swords, or burned, or taken captive, or robbed of their homes and possessions. These things will continue
for many days. 34 When the wise ones are suffering, they will get a little help, but many who join the wise ones will not help them in their time
of need. 35 Some of the wise ones will be killed. But the hard times must come so they can be made stronger and purer and without faults until the time of the end comes. Then, at the right time, the end will come."

Daniel 11:33–35

INSIGHTS

My hope is built on nothing less
Than Jesus' blood and righteousness;
I dare not trust the sweetest frame,
But wholly lean on Jesus' name.
On Christ, the solid Rock, I stand:
All other ground is sinking sand.

When darkness veils His lovely face,
I rest on His unchanging grace;
In ev'ry high and stormy gale,
My anchor holds within the veil.
On Christ, the solid Rock, I stand:
All other ground is sinking sand.

His oath, His covenant, His blood,
Support me in the whelming flood;
When all around my soul gives way,
He then is all my hope and stay.
On Christ, the solid Rock I stand:
All other ground is sinking sand.

When He shall come with trumpet sound,
O may I then in Him be found:
Dressed in His righteousness alone,
Faultless to stand before the throne.
On Christ, the solid Rock, I stand:
All other ground is sinking sand.

Edward Mote

PAUSE FOR REFLECTION

What are God's people to be and do during the end times? What is the purpose of their suffering during that time? On what can God's righteous ones depend during that time?

WEDNESDAY

The Passover and the Lord's Supper

Mark 14:1–26

The Plan to Kill Jesus

14 It was now only two days before the Passover and the Feast of Unleavened Bread. The leading priests and teachers of the law were trying to find a trick to arrest Jesus and kill him. 2 But they said, "We must not do it during the feast, because the people might cause a riot."

A Woman with Perfume for Jesus

Jesus was in Bethany at the house of Simon, who had a skin disease. While Jesus was eating there, a woman approached him with an alabaster jar filled with very expensive perfume, made of pure nard. She opened the jar and poured the perfume on Jesus' head.

4 Some who were there became upset and said to each other, "Why waste that perfume? 5 It was worth a full year's work. It could have been sold and the money given to the poor." And they got very angry with the woman.

6 Jesus said, "Leave her alone. Why are you troubling her? She did an excellent thing for me. 7 You will always have the poor with you, and you can help them anytime you want. But you will not always have me. 8 This woman did the only thing she could do for me; she poured perfume on my body to prepare me for burial. 9 I tell you the truth, wherever the Good News is preached in all the world, what this woman has done will be told, and people will remember her."

Judas Becomes an Enemy of Jesus

One of the twelve apostles, Judas Iscariot, went to talk to the leading priests to offer to hand Jesus over to them. 11 These priests were pleased about this and promised to pay Judas money. So he watched for the best time to turn Jesus in.

Jesus Eats the Passover Meal

It was now the first day of the Feast of Unleavened Bread when the Passover lamb was sacrificed. Jesus' followers said to him, "Where do you want us to go and prepare for you to eat the Passover meal?"

13 Jesus sent two of his followers and said to them, "Go into the city and a man carrying a jar of water will meet you. Follow him. 14 When he goes into a house, tell the owner of the house, 'The Teacher says: Where is my guest room in which I can eat the Passover meal with my followers?' 15 The owner will show you a large room upstairs that is furnished and ready. Prepare the food for us there."

16 So the followers left and went into the city. Everything happened as Jesus had said, so they prepared the Passover meal.

17 In the evening, Jesus went to that house with the twelve. 18 While they were all eating, Jesus said, "I tell you the truth, one of you will turn against me—one of you eating with me now."

19 The followers were very sad to hear this. Each one began to say to Jesus, "I am not the one, am I?"

[20]Jesus answered, "It is one of the twelve—the one who dips his bread into the bowl with me. [21]The Son of Man will die, just as the Scriptures say. But how terrible it will be for the person who hands the Son of Man over to be killed. It would be better for him if he had never been born."

The Lord's Supper

While they were eating, Jesus took some bread and thanked God for it and broke it. Then he gave it to his followers and said, "Take it; this is my body."

[23]Then Jesus took a cup and thanked God for it and gave it to the followers, and they all drank from the cup.

[24]Then Jesus said, "This is my blood which is the new agreement that God makes with his people. This blood is poured out for many. [25]I tell you the truth, I will not drink of this fruit of the vine again until that day when I drink it new in the kingdom of God."

[26]After singing a hymn, they went out to the Mount of Olives.

OLD TESTAMENT READING

You are always to remember this day and celebrate it with a feast to the LORD. Your descendants are to honor the LORD with this feast from now on.

[25]"Do this when you go to the land the LORD has promised to give you. [26]When your children ask you, 'Why are we doing these things?' [27]you will say, 'This is the Passover sacrifice to honor the LORD. When we were in Egypt, the LORD passed over the houses of Israel, and when he killed the Egyptians, he saved our homes.'" Then the people bowed down and worshiped the LORD.

Exodus 12:14, 25–27

INSIGHTS

Right down to the present, Jews reenact the Passover-event in celebration of their redemption from Egypt. . . .

In this service, words are connected with ritual, symbol, and gesture. It is a drama, a reenactment of the flight of Israel from the land of Pharaoh. It is not only a past event, but a present reality. For, although the Exodus happened in the past, its power and meaning reach down into history and change the lives of people now as did the original event. Reenactment of the action still has the power to change lives. . . .

The church has also retained the Old Testament principle that the event being celebrated becomes contemporaneous: Paul referred to the Table as a "participation" in Christ (1 Cor. 10:16). It is important to understand, though, that the death and resurrection of Jesus Christ is not an event which we memorialize. Its power, like that of the Exodus, reaches down through history and becomes a present reality to the people who celebrate it in faith.

Robert Webber

PAUSE FOR REFLECTION

Reread the full account of the Passover (Exodus 12:1–27) and try to feel the drama and significance of the Passover celebration. What feelings and awareness related to Jesus' celebration of the Lord's Supper (Mark 14:22–26) does this stir within you?

THURSDAY

Kneel Before God in Prayer

Mark 14:27–52

Jesus' Followers Will Leave Him

Then Jesus told the followers, "You
will all stumble in your faith, because
it is written in the Scriptures:

'I will kill the shepherd,
and the sheep will scatter.'

Zechariah 13:7

[28] But after I rise from the dead, I will
go ahead of you into Galilee."
[29] Peter said, "Everyone else may
stumble in their faith, but I will not."
[30] Jesus answered, "I tell you the
truth, tonight before the rooster
crows twice you will say three times
you don't know me."
[31] But Peter insisted, "I will never
say that I don't know you! I will even
die with you!" And all the other
followers said the same thing.

Jesus Prays Alone

Jesus and his followers went to a
place called Gethsemane. He said to
them, "Sit here while I pray." [33] Jesus
took Peter, James, and John with
him, and he began to be very sad
and troubled. [34] He said to them, "My
heart is full of sorrow, to the point
of death. Stay here and watch."
[35] After walking a little farther
away from them, Jesus fell to the
ground and prayed that, if possible,
he would not have this time of
suffering. [36] He prayed, "Abba, Father! You can do all things. Take
away this cup of suffering. But do
what you want, not what I want."
[37] Then Jesus went back to his followers and found them asleep. He
said to Peter, "Simon, are you sleeping? Couldn't you stay awake with
me for one hour? [38] Stay awake and
pray for strength against temptation.
The spirit wants to do what is right,
but the body is weak."
[39] Again Jesus went away and
prayed the same thing. [40] Then he
went back to his followers, and again
he found them asleep, because their
eyes were very heavy. And they did
not know what to say to him.
[41] After Jesus prayed a third time,
he went back to his followers and
said to them, "Are you still sleeping
and resting? That's enough. The
time has come for the Son of Man
to be handed over to sinful people.
[42] Get up, we must go. Look, here
comes the man who has turned
against me."

Jesus Is Arrested

At once, while Jesus was still speaking, Judas, one of the twelve
apostles, came up. With him were
many people carrying swords and
clubs who had been sent from the
leading priests, the teachers of the
law, and the older Jewish leaders.
[44] Judas had planned a signal for
them, saying, "The man I kiss is
Jesus. Arrest him and guard him
while you lead him away." [45] So Judas went straight to Jesus and said,
"Teacher!" and kissed him. [46] Then
the people grabbed Jesus and
arrested him. [47] One of his followers
standing nearby pulled out his sword
and struck the servant of the high
priest and cut off his ear.
[48] Then Jesus said, "You came to
get me with swords and clubs as if I
were a criminal. [49] Every day I was

with you teaching in the Temple, and
you did not arrest me there. But all
these things have happened to make
the Scriptures come true." 50 Then all
of Jesus' followers left him and ran
away.
51 A young man, wearing only a
linen cloth, was following Jesus, and
the people also grabbed him. 52 But
the cloth he was wearing came off,
and he ran away naked.

OLD TESTAMENT READING

Solomon prayed this prayer to the
LORD, kneeling in front of the altar
with his arms raised toward heaven.
When he finished praying, he got up.
55 Then, in a loud voice, he stood and
blessed all the people of Israel, saying: 56 "Praise the LORD! He promised
he would give rest to his people Israel, and he has given us rest. The
LORD has kept all the good promises
he gave through his servant Moses.
57 May the LORD our God be with us
as he was with our ancestors. 58 May
he never leave us, and may he turn
us to himself so we will follow him.
Let us obey all the laws and commands he gave our ancestors. 59 May
the LORD our God remember this
prayer day and night and do what is
right for his servant and his people
Israel day by day."

1 Kings 8:54–59

Three times each day Daniel would kneel down to pray and thank God, just as he always had done.

Daniel 6:10b

INSIGHTS

The powerful reality grips me, Lord
That when I kneel in Your presence
To ask Your forgiveness
I am utterly stripped of facade.
You accept no big-name references
No high-caliber recommendations.
Extenuating circumstances
Crumble to dust
In Your court of appeal . . .
I am forgiven never
Because of inherited tendencies
Or emotional discomfort
Or nagging weakness . . .
I can never plead
Corrupt environment
Or life's strange twistings
Or my own unbelievable stupidity . . .
Ultimately I have one solitary defense.
Only one—
But always one:
Forgive me, God
For Jesus' sake.
Like a song unending
The words keep singing . . .
I am totally forgiven
I am continually cleansed
Just for Jesus' sake.

Ruth Calkin

PAUSE FOR REFLECTION

What physical posture did these men of God assume when they offered their heartfelt prayers to God? Do you think there is a difference between kneeling, sitting, or standing before God in prayer? How do you pray most earnestly to God?

FRIDAY

Accused by the Wicked, the Blameless Stand Innocent Before God

Mark 14:53—15:5

Jesus Before the Leaders

The people who arrested Jesus led
him to the house of the high priest,
where all the leading priests, the
older Jewish leaders, and the teachers of the law were gathered. 54 Peter followed far behind and entered
the courtyard of the high priest's
house. There he sat with the guards,
warming himself by the fire.
55 The leading priests and the
whole Jewish council tried to find
something that Jesus had done
wrong so they could kill him. But the
council could find no proof of
anything. 56 Many people came and
told false things about him, but all
said different things—none of them
agreed.
57 Then some people stood up and
lied about Jesus, saying, 58 "We
heard this man say, 'I will destroy
this Temple that people made. And
three days later, I will build another
Temple not made by people.' " 59 But
even the things these people said did
not agree.
60 Then the high priest stood before them and asked Jesus, "Aren't
you going to answer? Don't you have
something to say about their
charges against you?" 61 But Jesus
said nothing; he did not answer.
The high priest asked Jesus another question: "Are you the Christ,
the Son of the blessed God?"
62 Jesus answered, "I am. And in
the future you will see the Son of
Man sitting at the right hand of God,
the Powerful One, and coming on
clouds in the sky."
63 When the high priest heard
this, he tore his clothes and said,
"We don't need any more witnesses!
64 You all heard him say these things
against God. What do you think?"
They all said that Jesus was guilty
and should die. 65 Some of the people
there began to spit at Jesus. They
blindfolded him and beat him with
their fists and said, "Prove you are a
prophet!" Then the guards led Jesus
away and beat him.

Peter Denies Knowing Jesus

While Peter was in the courtyard,
a servant girl of the high priest came
there. 67 She saw Peter warming himself at the fire and looked closely at
him.
Then she said, "You also were
with Jesus, that man from Nazareth."
68 But Peter said that he was never
with Jesus. He said, "I don't know or
understand what you are talking
about." Then Peter left and went
toward the entrance of the
courtyard. And the rooster crowed.
69 The servant girl saw Peter
there, and again she said to the
people who were standing nearby,
"This man is one of those who
followed Jesus." 70 Again Peter said
that it was not true.
A short time later, some people
were standing near Peter saying,
"Surely you are one of those who
followed Jesus, because you are
from Galilee, too."
71 Then Peter began to place a
curse on himself and swear, "I don't
know this man you're talking about!"
72 At once, the rooster crowed the

second time. Then Peter remembered what Jesus had told him: "Before the rooster crows twice, you will say three times that you don't know me." Then Peter lost control of himself and began to cry.

Pilate Questions Jesus

15 Very early in the morning, the leading priests, the older leaders, the teachers of the law, and all the Jewish council decided what to do with Jesus. They tied him, led him away, and turned him over to Pilate, the governor.

2 Pilate asked Jesus, "Are you the king of the Jews?"

Jesus answered, "Those are your words."

3 The leading priests accused
Jesus of many things. 4 So Pilate
asked Jesus another question, "You can see that they are accusing you of many things. Aren't you going to answer?"

5 But Jesus still said nothing, so Pilate was very surprised.

OLD TESTAMENT READING

LORD, defend me because I
have lived an innocent life.
I have trusted the LORD and
never doubted.
2 LORD, try me and test me;
look closely into my heart and
mind.

Psalm 26:1–2

INSIGHTS

Here is a secret to the spiritual strength that willingly suffers wrong: accustom yourself in everything that happens to recognize the hand and will of God. Whether it be some great wrong that is done you, or some little offense that you meet in daily life, before you consider the person who did it, first be still and remember, God allows me to come into this trouble to see if I will glorify Him in it. This trial, be it great or small, is allowed by God and is His will concerning me. Let me first recognize and submit to God's will in it. Then with the peace of God which this gives, I will receive wisdom to know how to behave in it. With my eye turned from man to God, suffering wrong takes on this new dimension.

. . . Jesus saw beyond the temporal injustice and was satisfied to leave the vindication of His rights and honor in God's hands; He knew they were safe with Him. Peter writes, "He committed himself to him that judgeth righteously" (2:23). It was settled between the Father and the Son: the Son was not to care for His own honor, but only for the Father's. The Father would care for the Son's honor. Let the believer follow Christ's example in this; it will give him such rest and peace. Commit your right and your honor into God's keeping. Meet every offense that man commits against you with the firm trust that God will watch over and care for you.

Andrew Murray

PAUSE FOR REFLECTION

How important is innocence in God's eyes? Think about the total trust Jesus had in his Father—a trust that enabled him to stand innocent before God without having to prove his innocence to his accusers.

WEEKEND

Jesus Suffered for Us

Mark 15:6–32

Pilate Tries to Free Jesus

Every year at the time of the Passover the governor would free one prisoner whom the people chose.
7 At that time, there was a man named Barabbas in prison who was a rebel and had committed murder during a riot.
8 The crowd came to Pilate and began to ask him to free a prisoner as he always did.
9 So Pilate asked them, "Do you want me to free the king of the Jews?"
10 Pilate knew that the leading priests had turned Jesus in to him because they were jealous.
11 But the leading priests had persuaded the people to ask Pilate to free Barabbas, not Jesus.
12 Then Pilate asked the crowd again, "So what should I do with this man you call the king of the Jews?"
13 They shouted, "Crucify him!"
14 Pilate asked, "Why? What wrong has he done?"

But they shouted even louder, "Crucify him!"
15 Pilate wanted to please the crowd, so he freed Barabbas for them. After having Jesus beaten with whips, he handed Jesus over to the soldiers to be crucified.
16 The soldiers took Jesus into the governor's palace (called the Praetorium) and called all the other soldiers together.
17 They put a purple robe on Jesus and used thorny branches to make a crown for his head.
18 They began to call out to him, "Hail, King of the Jews!"
19 The soldiers beat Jesus on the head many times with a stick. They spit on him and made fun of him by bowing on their knees and worshiping him.
20 After they finished, the soldiers took off the purple robe and put his own clothes on him again. Then they led him out of the palace to be crucified.

Jesus Is Crucified

A man named Simon from Cyrene, the father of Alexander and Rufus, was coming from the fields to the city. The soldiers forced Simon to carry the cross for Jesus.
22 They led Jesus to the place called Golgotha, which means the Place of the Skull.
23 The soldiers tried to give Jesus wine mixed with myrrh to drink, but he refused.
24 The soldiers crucified Jesus and divided his clothes among themselves, throwing lots to decide what each soldier would get.
25 It was nine o'clock in the morning when they crucified Jesus.
26 There was a sign with this charge against Jesus written on it: THE KING OF THE JEWS.
27 They also put two robbers on crosses beside Jesus, one on the right, and the other on the left.
28 "And the Scripture came true that says, 'They put him with criminals.'"
29 People walked by and insulted Jesus and shook their heads, saying, "You said you could destroy the Temple and build it again in three days.
30 So save yourself! Come down from that cross!"
31 The leading priests and the teachers of the law were also making fun of Jesus. They said to each other, "He saved other people, but he can't save himself.
32 If he is really the Christ, the king of Israel, let him come down now from the cross. When we see this, we

will believe in him." The robbers who were being crucified beside Jesus also insulted him.

OLD TESTAMENT READING

Evil people have surrounded me;
like dogs they have trapped me.
They have bitten my arms and legs.
17 I can count all my bones;
people look and stare at me.
18 They divided my clothes among them,
and they threw lots for my clothing.

Psalm 22:16–18

INSIGHTS

Think of the love that God must have had when He gave His son to die for the world! I used to think a good deal more of Christ than I did of the Father. Somehow or other I had the idea that God was a stern judge; that Christ came between me and God, and appeased the anger of God. But after I became a father, and for years had an only son, as I looked at my boy I thought of the Father giving His Son to die, and it seemed to me as if it required more love for the Father to give His Son than for the Son to die. Oh, the love that God must have had for the world when He gave His Son to die for it! "God so loved the world, that He gave His only begotten Son, that whosoever believeth in Him should not perish, but have everlasting life" (John 3:16). I have never been able to preach from that text. I have often thought I would, but it is so high that I can never climb to its height, I have just quoted it and passed on. Who can fathom the depth of those words: "God so loved the world"? We can never scale the heights of His love, or fathom its depths. Paul prayed that he might know the height, the depth, the length, and the breadth of the love of God; but it was past his finding out. . . .

Nothing speaks to us of the love of God like the Cross of Christ. Come with me to Calvary, and look upon the Son of God as He hangs there. Can you hear that piercing cry from His dying lips: "Father, forgive them; for they know not what they do!" and say that He does not love you? "Greater love hath no man than this, that a man lay down his life for his friends" (John 15:13). But Jesus Christ laid down His life for His enemies.

Another thought is this: He loved us long before we ever thought of Him. The idea that He does not love us until we first love Him is not to be found in Scripture. In 1 John 4:10 it is written: "Herein is love, not that we love God, but that He loved us, and sent His Son to be the propitiation for our sins." He loved us before we ever thought of loving Him. You loved your children before they knew anything about your love. And so, long before we ever thought of God, we were in His thoughts.

D. L. Moody

PAUSE FOR REFLECTION

How does your image of God's love change as you read about the way Jesus suffered injury, insult, and degradation in order to save you? Perhaps now would be a good time for a thoughtful prayer of thanks for God's love.

MONDAY

Jesus Dies, but Rises as He Promised

Mark 15:33—16:8

Jesus Dies

At noon the whole country became
dark, and the darkness lasted for
three hours. 34 At three o'clock Jesus
cried in a loud voice, "Eloi, Eloi, lama
sabachthani." This means, "My God,
my God, why have you rejected me?"
35 When some of the people standing there heard this, they said, "Listen! He is calling Elijah."
36 Someone there ran and got a
sponge, filled it with vinegar, tied it to
a stick, and gave it to Jesus to drink. He
said, "We want to see if Elijah will
come to take him down from the cross."
37 Then Jesus cried in a loud voice
and died.
38 The curtain in the Temple was
torn into two pieces, from the top to
the bottom. 39 When the army officer who was standing in front of the
cross saw what happened when
Jesus died, he said, "This man really
was the Son of God!"
40 Some women were standing at a
distance from the cross, watching;
among them were Mary Magdalene,
Salome, and Mary the mother of James
and Joseph. (James was her youngest
son.) 41 These women had followed
Jesus in Galilee and helped him. Many
other women were also there who had
come with Jesus to Jerusalem.

Jesus Is Buried

This was Preparation Day. (That
means the day before the Sabbath
day.) That evening, 43 Joseph from
Arimathea was brave enough to go
to Pilate and ask for Jesus' body. Joseph, an important member of the
Jewish council, was one of the
people who was waiting for the
kingdom of God to come. 44 Pilate
was amazed that Jesus would have
already died, so he called the army
officer who had guarded Jesus and
asked him if Jesus had already
died. 45 The officer told Pilate that
he was dead, so Pilate told Joseph
he could have the body. 46 Joseph
bought some linen cloth, took the
body down from the cross, and
wrapped it in the linen. He put the
body in a tomb that was cut out of
a wall of rock. Then he rolled a
very large stone to block the entrance of the tomb. 47 And Mary
Magdalene and Mary the mother
of Joseph saw the place where
Jesus was laid.

Jesus Rises from the Dead

16 The day after the Sabbath day,
Mary Magdalene, Mary the
mother of James, and Salome
bought some sweet-smelling spices
to put on Jesus' body. 2 Very early on
that day, the first day of the week,
soon after sunrise, the women were
on their way to the tomb. 3 They said
to each other, "Who will roll away for
us the stone that covers the entrance
of the tomb?"
4 Then the women looked and
saw that the stone had already been
rolled away, even though it was very
large. 5 The women entered the
tomb and saw a young man wearing
a white robe and sitting on the right
side, and they were afraid.

[6] But the man said, "Don't be afraid.
You are looking for Jesus from
Nazareth, who has been crucified.
He has risen from the dead; he is not
here. Look, here is the place they laid
him. [7] Now go and tell his followers
and Peter, 'Jesus is going into Galilee
ahead of you, and you will see him
there as he told you before.'"
[8] The women were confused and
shaking with fear, so they left the
tomb and ran away. They did not tell
anyone about what happened,
because they were afraid.

OLD TESTAMENT READING

The burning desert will have
pools of water,
and the dry ground will have
springs.
Where wild dogs once lived,
grass and water plants will grow.
[8] A road will be there;
this highway will be called
"The Road to Being Holy."
Evil people will not be allowed to
walk on that road;
only good people will walk on it.
No fools will go on it.
[9] No lions will be there,
nor will dangerous animals be
on that road.
They will not be found there.
That road will be for the people
God saves;
[10] the people the LORD has freed
will return there.
They will enter Jerusalem with joy,
and their happiness will last
forever.
Their gladness and joy will fill
them completely,
and sorrow and sadness will go
far away.

Isaiah 35:7–10

INSIGHTS

I will never forget the day that I looked into the tomb. It changed my whole ministry. It came to me that my Savior was really alive, that His work on the cross for sinners so satisfied divine justice and divine character and divine righteousness, that I would never see my sins again. God raised Him from the dead as a guarantee to me personally that death has no more authority over the man in Christ. It has been shorn of its power. . . . At the cross we see His love, but in resurrection we see His power.

We've been joined to a risen Savior. That is why the apostles gave witness with such great power in the book of Acts. Paul stood before Felix, before Festus, before Agrippa, before the Sanhedrin, before the philosophers of Athens, and before the corrupt Corinthians with only one message. He preached the risen Christ. . . . The cross is a tragedy if there is no resurrection. Would to God that His people would continually rejoice that our Savior is alive forevermore.

John G. Mitchell

ACTION POINT

Meditate on the Isaiah 35 reading until you begin to understand the awesome reality of Christ's resurrection. Pray now and thank God that Jesus not only died, but that he lives today!

TUESDAY

Those Who Don't Believe Will Be Judged Guilty

Mark 16:9—Luke 1:13

Some Followers See Jesus

After Jesus rose from the dead early on the first day of the week, he showed himself first to Mary Magdalene. One time in the past, he had forced seven demons out of her. 10 After Mary saw Jesus, she went and told his followers, who were very sad and were crying. 11 But Mary told them that Jesus was alive. She said that she had seen him, but the followers did not believe her.

12 Later, Jesus showed himself to two of his followers while they were walking in the country, but he did not look the same as before. 13 These followers went back to the others and told them what had happened, but again, the followers did not believe them.

Jesus Talks to the Apostles

Later Jesus showed himself to the eleven apostles while they were eating, and he criticized them because they had no faith. They were stubborn and refused to believe those who had seen him after he had risen from the dead.

15 Jesus said to his followers, "Go everywhere in the world, and tell the Good News to everyone. 16 Anyone who believes and is baptized will be saved, but anyone who does not believe will be punished. 17 And those who believe will be able to do these things as proof: They will use my name to force out demons. They will speak in new languages. 18 They will pick up snakes and drink poison without being hurt. They will touch the sick, and the sick will be healed."

19 After the Lord Jesus said these things to his followers, he was carried up into heaven, and he sat at the right side of God. 20 The followers went everywhere in the world and told the Good News to people, and the Lord helped them. The Lord proved that the Good News they told was true by giving them power to work miracles.

Luke Writes About Jesus' Life

1 Many have tried to report on the things that happened among us. 2 They have written the same things that we learned from others—the people who saw those things from the beginning and served God by telling people his message. 3 Since I myself have studied everything carefully from the beginning, most excellent Theophilus, it seemed good for me to write it out for you. I arranged it in order 4 to help you know that what you have been taught is true.

Zechariah and Elizabeth

During the time Herod ruled Judea, there was a priest named Zechariah who belonged to Abijah's group. Zechariah's wife, Elizabeth, came from the family of Aaron. 6 Zechariah and Elizabeth truly did what God said was good. They did everything the Lord commanded and were without fault in keeping his law. 7 But they had no children, because Elizabeth could not have a baby, and both of them were very old.

[8] One day Zechariah was serving
as a priest before God, because his
group was on duty. [9] According to
the custom of the priests, he was
chosen by lot to go into the Temple
of the Lord and burn incense.
[10] There were a great many people
outside praying at the time the incense was offered. [11] Then an angel
of the Lord appeared to Zechariah,
standing on the right side of the incense table. [12] When he saw the angel, Zechariah was startled and
frightened. [13] But the angel said to
him, "Zechariah, don't be afraid. God
has heard your prayer. Your wife,
Elizabeth, will give birth to a son,
and you will name him John."

OLD TESTAMENT READING

Joshua son of Nun and Caleb son of
Jephunneh, who had explored the
land, tore their clothes. [7] They said
to all of the Israelites, "The land we
explored is very good. [9] Don't turn
against the LORD! Don't be afraid of
the people in that land! We will chew
them up. They have no protection,
but the LORD is with us. So don't be
afraid of them."
[11] The LORD said to Moses, "How
long will these people ignore me?
How long will they not believe me
in spite of the miracles I have done
among them?"
[20] The LORD answered, "I have forgiven them as you asked. [21] But, as
surely as I live and as surely as my
glory fills the whole earth, I make
this promise: [22] All these men saw
my glory and the miracles I did in
Egypt and in the desert, but they disobeyed me and tested me ten times.
[23] So not one of them will see the
land I promised to their ancestors.
No one who rejected me will see that
land. [24] But my servant Caleb thinks
differently and follows me completely. So I will bring him into the
land he has already seen, and his
children will own that land."

Numbers 14:6–7, 9, 11, 20–24

INSIGHTS

You may ask how people wind up in hell if God is a loving God. People wind up in hell by trampling the love of God instead of treasuring it. They ignore it, spurn it, yawn over it, close their hearts to it, keep saying "someday, someday, someday."

The Bible says there will be a someday. It's a day of reckoning. To those who have spurned His love, God will say in effect, "I loved you every day of your life. I loved you with a perfect love. I extended Myself to you. I made My wisdom available to you. I made My comfort and My strength and My Spirit available to you. I made My offer of salvation to you. But you trampled and spurned My love. You had it your way on earth, so now you can have it your way in eternity."

Are you facing that scenario? Will you continue to trample the love of God? That's the question of the ages, and it is one you yourself must answer.

Bill Hybels

PAUSE FOR REFLECTION

What is the essential message of the Good News? After Jesus returned to heaven, how did he prove that the Good News was true? Is it really easier to believe God when we see his miracles? What is the fate of all those who—even though they have witnessed miracles—choose to reject God?

WEDNESDAY

God Sends Special Messengers

Luke 1:14–45

He will bring you joy and gladness, and many people will be happy because of his birth. 15 John will be a great man for the Lord. He will never drink wine or beer, and even from birth, he will be filled with the Holy Spirit. 16 He will help many people of Israel return to the Lord their God. 17 He will go before the Lord in spirit and power like Elijah. He will make peace between parents and their children and will bring those who are not obeying God back to the right way of thinking, to make a people ready for the coming of the Lord."

18 Zechariah said to the angel, "How can I know that what you say is true? I am an old man, and my wife is old, too."

19 The angel answered him, "I am Gabriel. I stand before God, who sent me to talk to you and to tell you this good news. 20 Now, listen! You will not be able to speak until the day these things happen, because you did not believe what I told you. But they will really happen."

21 Outside, the people were still waiting for Zechariah and were surprised that he was staying so long in the Temple. 22 When Zechariah came outside, he could not speak to them, and they knew he had seen a vision in the Temple. He could only make signs to them and remained unable to speak. 23 When his time of service at the Temple was finished, he went home.

24 Later, Zechariah's wife, Elizabeth, became pregnant and did not go out of her house for five months. Elizabeth said, 25 "Look what the Lord has done for me! My people were ashamed of me, but now the Lord has taken away that shame."

An Angel Appears to Mary

During Elizabeth's sixth month of pregnancy, God sent the angel Gabriel to Nazareth, a town in Galilee, 27 to a virgin. She was engaged to marry a man named Joseph from the family of David. Her name was Mary. 28 The angel came to her and said, "Greetings! The Lord has blessed you and is with you."

29 But Mary was very startled by what the angel said and wondered what this greeting might mean.

30 The angel said to her, "Don't be afraid, Mary; God has shown you his grace. 31 Listen! You will become pregnant and give birth to a son, and you will name him Jesus. 32 He will be great and will be called the Son of the Most High. The Lord God will give him the throne of King David, his ancestor. 33 He will rule over the people of Jacob forever, and his kingdom will never end."

34 Mary said to the angel, "How will this happen since I am a virgin?"

35 The angel said to Mary, "The Holy Spirit will come upon you, and the power of the Most High will cover you. For this reason the baby will be holy and will be called the Son of God. 36 Now Elizabeth, your relative, is also pregnant with a son though she is very old. Everyone thought she could not have a baby, but she has been pregnant for six months. 37 God can do anything!"

[38] Mary said, "I am the servant of
the Lord. Let this happen to me as
you say!" Then the angel went away.

Mary Visits Elizabeth

Mary got up and went quickly to a
town in the hills of Judea. [40] She
came to Zechariah's house and
greeted Elizabeth. [41] When Elizabeth
heard Mary's greeting, the unborn
baby inside her jumped, and Elizabeth was filled with the Holy Spirit.
[42] She cried out in a loud voice, "God
has blessed you more than any other
woman, and he has blessed the baby
to which you will give birth. [43] Why
has this good thing happened to me,
that the mother of my Lord comes
to me? [44] When I heard your voice,
the baby inside me jumped with joy.
[45] You are blessed because you believed that what the Lord said to you
would really happen."

OLD TESTAMENT READING

But I will send you Elijah the
prophet before that great and terri-
fying day of the LORD's judging.
[6] Elijah will help parents love their
children and children love their parents. Otherwise, I will come and put
a curse on the land."

Malachi 4:5–6

INSIGHTS

Reports continually flow to my attention from many places around the world telling of visitors of the angelic order appearing, ministering, fellowshiping and disappearing. They warn of God's impending judgment; they spell out the tenderness of His love; they meet a desperate need; then they are gone. Of one thing we can be sure: angels never draw attention to themselves but ascribe glory to God and press His message upon the hearers as a delivering and sustaining word of the highest order.

Demonic activity and Satan worship are on the increase in all parts of the world. The devil is alive and more at work than at any other time. The Bible says that since he realizes his time is short, his activity will increase. Through his demonic influences he does succeed in turning many away from true faith; but we can still say that his evil activities are countered for the people of God by His ministering spirits, the holy ones of the angelic order. They are vigorous in delivering the heirs of salvation from the strategems of evil men. They cannot fail.

Believers, look up—take courage. The angels are nearer than you think. For after all, God has given "his angels charge of you, to guard you in all your ways. On their hands they will bear you up, lest you dash your foot against a stone" (Psalm 91:11, 12 RSV).

Billy Graham

APPLICATION

When an angel delivers God's message to a person, what response does God expect? What are the consequences of believing or doubting God's message? Are you open to receiving his message for you?

THURSDAY

God Is Merciful to His People

Luke 1:46–77

Mary Praises God

Then Mary said,
"My soul praises the Lord;
47 my heart rejoices in God my Savior,
48 because he has shown his concern for his humble servant girl.
From now on, all people will say that I am blessed,
49 because the Powerful One has done great things for me.
His name is holy.
50 God will show his mercy forever and ever
to those who worship and serve him.
51 He has done mighty deeds by his power.
He has scattered the people who are proud
and think great things about themselves.
52 He has brought down rulers from their thrones
and raised up the humble.
53 He has filled the hungry with good things
and sent the rich away with nothing.
54 He has helped his servant, the people of Israel,
remembering to show them mercy
55 as he promised to our ancestors,
to Abraham and to his children forever."

56 Mary stayed with Elizabeth for about three months and then returned home.

The Birth of John

When it was time for Elizabeth to
give birth, she had a boy. 58 Her
neighbors and relatives heard how
good the Lord was to her, and they
rejoiced with her.

59 When the baby was eight days
old, they came to circumcise him.
They wanted to name him Zechariah
because this was his father's name,
60 but his mother said, "No! He will
be named John."

61 The people said to Elizabeth,
"But no one in your family has this
name." 62 Then they made signs to
his father to find out what he would
like to name him.

63 Zechariah asked for a writing
tablet and wrote, "His name is John,"
and everyone was surprised.
64 Immediately Zechariah could talk
again, and he began praising God.
65 All their neighbors became
alarmed, and in all the mountains of
Judea people continued talking
about all these things. 66 The people
who heard about them wondered,
saying, "What will this child be?"
because the Lord was with him.

Zechariah Praises God

Then Zechariah, John's father, was filled with the Holy Spirit and prophesied:

68 "Let us praise the Lord, the God of Israel,
because he has come to help his people and has given them freedom.
69 He has given us a powerful Savior from the family of God's servant David.
70 He said that he would do this through his holy prophets who lived long ago:

[71] He promised he would save us
from our enemies
and from the power of all those
who hate us.
[72] He said he would give mercy to
our fathers
and that he would remember
his holy promise.
[73] God promised Abraham, our
father,
[74] that he would save us from the
power of our enemies
so we could serve him without
fear,
[75] being holy and good before God
as long as we live.

[76] "Now you, child, will be called a
prophet of the Most High
God.
You will go before the Lord to
prepare his way.
[77] You will make his people know
that they will be saved
by having their sins forgiven."

OLD TESTAMENT READING

But I have hope
when I think of this:
[22] The LORD's love never ends;
his mercies never stop.
[23] They are new every morning;
LORD, your loyalty is great.
[24] I say to myself, "The LORD is mine,
so I hope in him."
[25] The LORD is good to those who
hope in him,
to those who seek him.
[26] It is good to wait quietly
for the LORD to save.

Lamentations 3:21–26

INSIGHTS

The Israelites were always worshiping the idols of the peoples around them in spite of the warning and the pleadings of the prophets. It wasn't until their captivity in Babylon that they were cured of these dangerous liaisons with "other gods." From the days of their captivity until now—two-and-a-half millennia—the Jews have never again been guilty of this sin. But in many places in Scripture, the Holy Spirit takes up the refrain to make sure the people of God would never slip back. . . .

God is still dealing mercifully with those who wander away in rebellion and pride, but return in humility and faith. We have our Golden Calves, our substitutes for the living God. We have things in our lives that seem more important because they promise more immediate gratification. We, too, grow discouraged in a wilderness—a treadmill of monotonous busyness without tangible or meaningful results. To banish our sense of emptiness and lostness in this secular world, we may have looked for satisfaction in lesser gods, although we would never call them Golden Calves. Even so, God is patiently waiting for us to forsake these idols. He may discipline us, but in His mercy, He will never forsake us.

William Stoddard

PAUSE FOR REFLECTION

Do you sense how greatly Mary, Elizabeth, and Zechariah felt God's mercy to them and to all of God's people? Thank God that no matter how greatly we sin he is merciful and forgiving to everyone who repents!

FRIDAY

Praise God for His Salvation!

Luke 1:78—2:26

With the loving mercy of our
God,
a new day from heaven will
dawn upon us.
79 It will shine on those who live in
darkness,
in the shadow of death.
It will guide us into the path of
peace."

80 And so the child grew up and became strong in spirit. John lived in the desert until the time when he came out to preach to Israel.

The Birth of Jesus

2 At that time, Augustus Caesar sent an order that all people in the countries under Roman rule must list their names in a register. 2 This was the first registration; it was taken while Quirinius was governor of Syria. 3 And all went to their own towns to be registered.

4 So Joseph left Nazareth, a town in Galilee, and went to the town of Bethlehem in Judea, known as the town of David. Joseph went there because he was from the family of David. 5 Joseph registered with Mary, to whom he was engaged and who was now pregnant. 6 While they were in Bethlehem, the time came for Mary to have the baby, 7 and she gave birth to her first son. Because there were no rooms left in the inn, she wrapped the baby with pieces of cloth and laid him in a box where animals are fed.

Shepherds Hear About Jesus

That night, some shepherds were in the fields nearby watching their sheep. 9 Then an angel of the Lord stood before them. The glory of the Lord was shining around them, and they became very frightened. 10 The angel said to them, "Do not be afraid. I am bringing you good news that will be a great joy to all the people. 11 Today your Savior was born in the town of David. He is Christ, the Lord. 12 This is how you will know him: You will find a baby wrapped in pieces of cloth and lying in a feeding box."

13 Then a very large group of angels from heaven joined the first angel, praising God and saying:

14 "Give glory to God in heaven,
and on earth let there be peace
among the people who
please God."

15 When the angels left them and went back to heaven, the shepherds said to each other, "Let's go to Bethlehem. Let's see this thing that has happened which the Lord has told us about."

16 So the shepherds went quickly and found Mary and Joseph and the baby, who was lying in a feeding box. 17 When they had seen him, they told what the angels had said about this child. 18 Everyone was amazed at what the shepherds said to them. 19 But Mary treasured these things and continued to think about them. 20 Then the shepherds went back to their sheep, praising God and thanking him for everything they had seen and heard. It had been just as the angel had told them.

21 When the baby was eight days old, he was circumcised and was named Jesus, the name given by the

angel before the baby began to grow inside Mary.

Jesus Is Presented in the Temple

When the time came for Mary and Joseph to do what the law of Moses taught about being made pure, they took Jesus to Jerusalem to present him to the Lord. 23 (It is written in the law of the Lord: "Every firstborn male shall be given to the Lord.") 24 Mary and Joseph also went to offer a sacrifice, as the law of the Lord says: "You must sacrifice two doves or two young pigeons."

Simeon Sees Jesus

In Jerusalem lived a man named Simeon who was a good man and godly. He was waiting for the time when God would take away Israel's sorrow, and the Holy Spirit was in him. 26 Simeon had been told by the Holy Spirit that he would not die before he saw the Christ promised by the Lord.

OLD TESTAMENT READING

The LORD, the LORD gives me
strength and makes me
sing.
He has saved me."
3 You will receive your salvation
with joy
as you would draw water from
a well.
4 At that time you will say,
"Praise the LORD and worship him.
Tell everyone what he has done
and how great he is.
5 Sing praise to the LORD, because
he has done great things."

Isaiah 12:2b–5a

INSIGHTS

In His holiness and love God could not wink at sin. He could not compromise either His justice or His mercy. Therefore, out of grace He sent His Son. . . . By God's mercy, He came in Christ to pay the full price, and at the cross, exposed His heart. God abhors, condemns, and judges sin, and yet by the power of the cross, He forgives sinners—people like you and me! . . .

. . . We have all gone over the line in breaking the Ten Commandments and Jesus' commandment to love. We've brought hurt, pain and suffering to ourselves and others by what we've done or said or refused to be. We've broken His heart. And even before we asked Him, He forgave us. He reconciled us. He exonerated us. We stutter out our yearning to be free in response to His cross, melted by His love, and healed by His forgiveness.

The same voice that cried, "Father forgive them," from Calvary, says to us with the commanding power of His cross-shaped heart, "The ransom has been paid for all time. And now in this propitious moment in your time it is a pardon for you. You are forgiven. You are free!"

Oh, the wonder of it all, indeed!

Lloyd Ogilvie

ACTION POINT

Think about all the things Jesus' birth represented to his parents, the shepherds, and Simeon. What does Jesus' coming to earth signify to you? Meditate on the wonder of it all. Thank him for his salvation.

WEEKEND

Called to Do the Father's Work

Luke 2:27–52

The Spirit led Simeon to the
Temple. When Mary and Joseph
brought the baby Jesus to the
Temple to do what the law said they
must do, 28 Simeon took the baby in
his arms and thanked God:

29 "Now, Lord, you can let me, your
servant,
die in peace as you said.
30 With my own eyes I have seen
your salvation,
31 which you prepared before all
people.
32 It is a light for the non-Jewish
people to see
and an honor for your people,
the Israelites."

33 Jesus' father and mother were
amazed at what Simeon had said
about him. 34 Then Simeon blessed
them and said to Mary, "God has
chosen this child to cause the fall
and rise of many in Israel. He will be
a sign from God that many people
will not accept 35 so that the thoughts
of many will be made known. And
the things that will happen will make
your heart sad, too."

Anna Sees Jesus

There was a prophetess, Anna, from
the family of Phanuel in the tribe of
Asher. Anna was very old. She had
once been married for seven years.
37 Then her husband died, and she
was a widow for eighty-four years.
Anna never left the Temple but worshiped God, going without food and
praying day and night. 38 Standing
there at that time, she thanked God
and spoke about Jesus to all who were
waiting for God to free Jerusalem.

Joseph and Mary Return Home

When Joseph and Mary had done
everything the law of the Lord commanded, they went home to
Nazareth, their own town in Galilee.
40 The little child grew and became
strong. He was filled with wisdom,
and God's goodness was upon him.

Jesus As a Boy

Every year Jesus' parents went to
Jerusalem for the Passover Feast.
42 When he was twelve years old,
they went to the feast as they always
did. 43 After the feast days were over,
they started home. The boy Jesus
stayed behind in Jerusalem, but his
parents did not know it. 44 Thinking
that Jesus was with them in the
group, they traveled for a whole day.
Then they began to look for him
among their family and friends.
45 When they did not find him, they
went back to Jerusalem to look for
him there. 46 After three days they
found Jesus sitting in the Temple
with the teachers, listening to them
and asking them questions. 47 All
who heard him were amazed at his
understanding and answers. 48 When
Jesus' parents saw him, they were
astonished. His mother said to him,
"Son, why did you do this to us? Your
father and I were very worried about
you and have been looking for you."

49 Jesus said to them, "Why were
you looking for me? Didn't you know
that I must be in my Father's
house?" 50 But they did not understand the meaning of what he said.

[51] Jesus went with them to Nazareth and was obedient to them. But his mother kept in her mind all that had happened. [52] Jesus became wiser and grew physically. People liked him, and he pleased God.

OLD TESTAMENT READING

Samuel Is Called to Do God's Work

When Samuel was old enough to eat, Hannah took him to the house of the LORD at Shiloh, along with a three-year-old bull, one-half bushel of flour, and a leather bag filled with wine. [25] After they had killed the bull for the sacrifice, Hannah brought Samuel to Eli. [26] She said to Eli, "As surely as you live, sir, I am the same woman who stood near you praying to the LORD. [27] I prayed for this child, and the LORD answered my prayer and gave him to me. [28] Now I give him back to the LORD. He will belong to the LORD all his life." And he worshiped the LORD there.

1 Samuel 1:24–28

INSIGHTS

Many people have the idea that God only calls preachers and missionaries, and the rest of us can do whatever we want to. But God has a calling for all of His children. . . .

. . . The people that God calls, the people God uses and chooses, His all-stars, are common ordinary people. . . .

. . . I thank God for the wise, noble, and mighty who love the Lord. I thank God for any athlete, movie star, or millionaire who will give his or her life to Christ. But God's work is going to be done primarily not through the superstar preachers, evangelists, or celebrities; God's work is going to be done through His ordinary everyday run-of-the-mill people. . . .

. . . God called a timid man with a stutter—a speech impediment—by the name of Moses and made him the greatest leader in the Old Testament. God called David, a little shepherd boy, right out of the pasture and made him the greatest king who ever ruled over Israel. . . . God's ways are above our ways, His thoughts are above our thoughts, and His calling confounds the wise. . . .

When I think of the weak I recall the life of Jonathan Edwards. He was one of the greatest revival preachers America or the world has ever known. . . .

He was an asthmatic. Whenever he would preach he would cough and hack and wheeze during most of the message. He was a very thin, frail man. He had horrible eyesight. . . .

. . . Jonathan Edwards' sermons, despite his disabilities, caused people to come writhing in anguish down the aisles wanting to get right with God. . . .

. . . The people that God uses and chooses, God's all-stars, are not people of ability; they are people of availability who have learned the secret of giving their praise to God. If you use your life for the glory of God, God will use your life for His glory.

James Merritt

ACTION POINT

Jesus knew he was called to do the Father's work. So did Samuel. What about you? Do you long for His clear call?

MONDAY

The Hope of the Coming Christ

Luke 3:1–22

The Preaching of John

3 It was the fifteenth year of the
rule of Tiberius Caesar. These
men were under Caesar: Pontius
Pilate, the ruler of Judea; Herod, the
ruler of Galilee; Philip, Herod's
brother, the ruler of Iturea and
Trachonitis; and Lysanias, the ruler
of Abilene. 2 Annas and Caiaphas
were the high priests. At this time,
the word of God came to John son
of Zechariah in the desert. 3 He went
all over the area around the Jordan
River preaching a baptism of
changed hearts and lives for the forgiveness of sins. 4 As it is written in
the book of Isaiah the prophet:

"This is a voice of one
who calls out in the desert:
'Prepare the way for the Lord.
Make the road straight for
him.
5 Every valley should be filled in,
and every mountain and hill
should be made flat.
Roads with turns should be made
straight,
and rough roads should be
made smooth.
6 And all people will know about
the salvation of God!'"

Isaiah 40:3-5

7 To the crowds of people who
came to be baptized by John, he said,
"You are all snakes! Who warned
you to run away from God's coming
punishment? 8 Do the things that
show you really have changed your
hearts and lives. Don't begin to say
to yourselves, 'Abraham is our father.' I tell you that God could make
children for Abraham from these
rocks. 9 The ax is now ready to cut
down the trees, and every tree that
does not produce good fruit will be
cut down and thrown into the fire."

10 The people asked John, "Then
what should we do?"

11 John answered, "If you have two
shirts, share with the person who
does not have one. If you have food,
share that also."

12 Even tax collectors came to
John to be baptized. They said to
him, "Teacher, what should we do?"

13 John said to them, "Don't take
more taxes from people than you
have been ordered to take."

14 The soldiers asked John, "What
about us? What should we do?"

John said to them, "Don't force
people to give you money, and don't
lie about them. Be satisfied with the
pay you get."

15 Since the people were hoping
for the Christ to come, they wondered if John might be the one.

16 John answered everyone, "I
baptize you with water, but there is
one coming who is greater than I
am. I am not good enough to untie
his sandals. He will baptize you with
the Holy Spirit and fire. 17 He will
come ready to clean the grain, separating the good grain from the chaff.
He will put the good part of the grain
into his barn, but he will burn the
chaff with a fire that cannot be put
out." 18 And John continued to preach
the Good News, saying many other
things to encourage the people.

19 But John spoke against Herod,
the governor, because of his sin with
Herodias, the wife of Herod's
brother, and because of the many

other evil things Herod did. [20]So
Herod did something even worse:
He put John in prison.

Jesus Is Baptized by John

When all the people were being baptized by John, Jesus also was baptized.
While Jesus was praying, heaven
opened [22]and the Holy Spirit came
down on him in the form of a dove.
Then a voice came from heaven, saying, "You are my Son, whom I love,
and I am very pleased with you."

OLD TESTAMENT READING

A voice says, "Cry out!"
Then I said, "What shall I cry out?"

"Say all people are like the grass,
and all their glory is like the flowers of the field.
8 The grass dies and the flowers fall,
but the word of our God will live forever."
9c Jerusalem, you have good news to tell.
Shout out loud the good news.
Shout it out and don't be afraid.
Say to the towns of Judah,
"Here is your God."
10 Look, the Lord God is coming with power
to rule all the people.

Isaiah 40:6, 8, 9c–10

INSIGHTS

Is it a waste to focus on the Lord's descent? Quite the contrary. It's biblical; it's the very thing Titus 2:13 says we ought to do.

When's the last time you—on your own—meditated on that fact? If you're like me it's been too long. People who are more practical than mystical, who are realistic rather than idealistic, tend to shove that stuff to times like funerals or near-death experiences. . . . Listen, this Bible of ours is full and running over with promises and encouragements directly related to the return of our Lord Christ. . . .

Critics have denied it. Cynics have laughed at it. Scholars have ignored it. Liberal theologians have explained it away (they call that "rethinking" it) and fanatics have perverted it. . . . But there it stands, solid as a stone, soon to be fulfilled, ready to offer us hope and encouragement amidst despair and unbelief.

"Okay, swell. But what do I do in the meantime?" I can hear a dozen or more pragmatists asking that question. First, it might be best for you to understand what you don't do. You don't sit around, listening for some bugle call. You don't keep staring up into the sky, looking for the rapture cloud. . . .

You do get your act together. You do live every day (as if it's your last) for His glory. You do work diligently on your job and in your home (as if He isn't coming for another ten years) for His Name's sake. You do shake salt out every chance you get . . . and do shine the light . . . and remain balanced, cheerful, winsome, and stable, anticipating His return day by day.

Charles Swindoll

APPLICATION

Do you feel the excitement of John's listeners? Do you await Christ's second coming with a yawn, or are you living each day as he wants you to?

TUESDAY

Jesus: The Promised King in David's Line

Luke 3:23–38

The Family History of Jesus

When Jesus began his ministry, he
was about thirty years old. People
thought that Jesus was Joseph's son.
Joseph was the son of Heli.
24 Heli was the son of Matthat.
Matthat was the son of Levi.
Levi was the son of Melki.
Melki was the son of Jannai.
Jannai was the son of Joseph.
25 Joseph was the son of Mattathias.
Mattathias was the son of Amos.
Amos was the son of Nahum.
Nahum was the son of Esli.
Esli was the son of Naggai.
26 Naggai was the son of Maath.
Maath was the son of Mattathias.
Mattathias was the son of Semein.
Semein was the son of Josech.
Josech was the son of Joda.
27 Joda was the son of Joanan.
Joanan was the son of Rhesa.
Rhesa was the son of Zerubbabel.
Zerubbabel was the grandson of Shealtiel.
Shealtiel was the son of Neri.
28 Neri was the son of Melchi.
Melchi was the son of Addi.
Addi was the son of Cosam.
Cosam was the son of Elmadam.
Elmadam was the son of Er.
29 Er was the son of Joshua.
Joshua was the son of Eliezer.
Eliezer was the son of Jorim.
Jorim was the son of Matthat.
Matthat was the son of Levi.
30 Levi was the son of Simeon.
Simeon was the son of Judah.
Judah was the son of Joseph.
Joseph was the son of Jonam.
Jonam was the son of Eliakim.
31 Eliakim was the son of Melea.
Melea was the son of Menna.
Menna was the son of Mattatha.
Mattatha was the son of Nathan.
Nathan was the son of David.
32 David was the son of Jesse.
Jesse was the son of Obed.
Obed was the son of Boaz.
Boaz was the son of Salmon.
Salmon was the son of Nahshon.
33 Nahshon was the son of Amminadab.
Amminadab was the son of Admin.
Admin was the son of Arni.
Arni was the son of Hezron.
Hezron was the son of Perez.
Perez was the son of Judah.
34 Judah was the son of Jacob.
Jacob was the son of Isaac.
Isaac was the son of Abraham.
Abraham was the son of Terah.
Terah was the son of Nahor.
35 Nahor was the son of Serug.
Serug was the son of Reu.
Reu was the son of Peleg.
Peleg was the son of Eber.
Eber was the son of Shelah.
36 Shelah was the son of Cainan.
Cainan was the son of Arphaxad.
Arphaxad was the son of Shem.
Shem was the son of Noah.
Noah was the son of Lamech.
37 Lamech was the son of Methuselah.
Methuselah was the son of Enoch.
Enoch was the son of Jared.
Jared was the son of Mahalalel.
Mahalalel was the son of Kenan.
38 Kenan was the son of Enosh.
Enosh was the son of Seth.
Seth was the son of Adam.
Adam was the son of God.

OLD TESTAMENT READING

A new branch will grow
from a stump of a tree;
so a new king will come
from the family of Jesse.
2The Spirit of the LORD will rest
upon that king.
The Spirit will give him
wisdom and understanding,
guidance and power.
The Spirit will teach him to
know and respect the LORD.
3This king will be glad to obey the
LORD.
He will not judge by the way things
look
or decide by what he hears.
4But he will judge the poor
honestly;
he will be fair in his decisions
for the poor people of the
land.
At his command evil people will
be punished,
and by his words the wicked
will be put to death.
5Goodness and fairness will give
him strength,
like a belt around his waist.

Isaiah 11:1–5

INSIGHTS

In coming to the kingdom-phase of Satan's antagonism, we believe that he was aware of Jacob's prophetic utterance in Genesis 49:10.

With the abandonment of Saul, the throne of Israel is transferred from Benjamin to Judah (1 Sam. 16). David, a man after God's own heart, is chosen and anointed king (1 Sam. 16:13; 2 Sam. 2:4; 5:2). And with such a change, there commences the desperate and determined attack of Satan upon "the seed royal," that is, the house of Judah, from which the Messiah must spring. . . .

Saul, the God-forsaken, Satan-possessed monarch (1 Sam. 16:14), tried his utmost to destroy the Lord's anointed one, and thus David is obliged to flee as a fugitive, hiding in caves and holes from his father-in-law. . . .

In the union of Jehoram and Athaliah, the daughter of Ahab, king of Israel, Satan continues his assault upon the house of Judah. . . .

At this critical moment, God's word appears to be at stake. Those of the royal seed are becoming fewer and fewer. In fact, the light was almost quenched, for Athaliah "arose and destroyed all the seed royal of the house of Judah" (2 Chron. 22:10). What followed?

Carefully he is hid and cared for while Athaliah reigns on in blissful ignorance until the day dawns when Joash is presented and crowned as king over Judah and Athaliah is slain (2 Kings 11:4–16; 2 Chron. 23:11, 15). Thus God, in a marvelous way, defeated the evil tactics of the devil, thereby fulfilling the promise of giving a light forever (2 Chron. 21:7).

Herbert Lockyer

PAUSE FOR REFLECTION

Although family history may not be very important to you, a king must be able to prove his royal heritage. What do these prophetic and genealogical verses tell you about the nature of Jesus' kingship?

WEDNESDAY

Jesus Claims to Be the One of Whom Isaiah Spoke

Luke 4:1–30

Jesus Is Tempted by the Devil

4 Jesus, filled with the Holy Spirit,
returned from the Jordan River.
The Spirit led Jesus into the desert
2 where the devil tempted Jesus for
forty days. Jesus ate nothing during
that time, and when those days were
ended, he was very hungry.
3 The devil said to Jesus, "If you
are the Son of God, tell this rock to
become bread."
4 Jesus answered, "It is written in
the Scriptures: 'A person does not
live by eating only bread.'"
5 Then the devil took Jesus and
showed him all the kingdoms of the
world in an instant. 6 The devil said
to Jesus, "I will give you all these
kingdoms and all their power and
glory. It has all been given to me, and
I can give it to anyone I wish. 7 If you
worship me, then it will all be yours."
8 Jesus answered, "It is written in
the Scriptures: 'You must worship the
Lord your God and serve only him.'"
9 Then the devil led Jesus to
Jerusalem and put him on a high
place of the Temple. He said to
Jesus, "If you are the Son of God,
jump down. 10 It is written in the
Scriptures:

'He has put his angels in charge
of you
to watch over you.' *Psalm 91:11*

11 It is also written:

'They will catch you in their hands
so that you will not hit your
foot on a rock.'" *Psalm 91:12*

12 Jesus answered, "But it also
says in the Scriptures: 'Do not test
the Lord your God.'"
13 After the devil had tempted
Jesus in every way, he left him to
wait until a better time.

Jesus Teaches the People

14 Jesus returned to Galilee in the
power of the Holy Spirit, and stories
about him spread all through the
area. 15 He began to teach in their synagogues, and everyone praised him.
16 Jesus traveled to Nazareth,
where he had grown up. On the Sabbath day he went to the synagogue,
as he always did, and stood up to
read. 17 The book of Isaiah the prophet
was given to him. He opened the
book and found the place where this
is written:

18 "The Lord has put his Spirit in me,
because he appointed me to
tell the Good News to the
poor.
He has sent me to tell the
captives they are free
and to tell the blind that they
can see again. *Isaiah 61:1*
God sent me to free those who
have been treated unfairly *Isaiah 58:6*
19 and to announce the time when
the Lord will show his
kindness." *Isaiah 61:2*

20 Jesus closed the book, gave it
back to the assistant, and sat down.
Everyone in the synagogue was
watching Jesus closely. 21 He began
to say to them, "While you heard
these words just now, they were
coming true!"
22 All the people spoke well of
Jesus and were amazed at the words
of grace he spoke. They asked, "Isn't
this Joseph's son?"

[23] Jesus said to them, "I know that you will tell me the old saying: 'Doctor, heal yourself.' You want to say, 'We heard about the things you did in Capernaum. Do those things here in your own town!'" [24] Then Jesus said, "I tell you the truth, a prophet is not accepted in his hometown. [25] But I tell you the truth, there were many widows in Israel during the time of Elijah. It did not rain in Israel for three and one-half years, and there was no food anywhere in the whole country. [26] But Elijah was sent to none of those widows, only to a widow in Zarephath, a town in Sidon. [27] And there were many with skin diseases living in Israel during the time of the prophet Elisha. But none of them were healed, only Naaman, who was from the country of Syria."

[28] When all the people in the synagogue heard these things, they became very angry. [29] They got up, forced Jesus out of town, and took him to the edge of the cliff on which the town was built. They planned to throw him off the edge, [30] but Jesus walked through the crowd and went on his way.

OLD TESTAMENT READING

The Lord God has put his Spirit
in me,
because the Lord has appointed me to tell the good
news to the poor.
He has sent me to comfort
those whose hearts are
broken,
to tell the captives they are free,
and to tell the prisoners they
are released.
2 He has sent me to announce the
time when the Lord will
show his kindness
and the time when our God
will punish evil people.
He has sent me to comfort all
those who are sad
3 and to help the sorrowing
people of Jerusalem.

Isaiah 61:1–3a

INSIGHTS

Jesus' words in the synagogue at Nazareth, spoken near the beginning of his public ministry, throb with hope for the poor. . . . Jesus informed his audience that this Scripture was now fulfilled in himself. The mission of the Incarnate One was to free the oppressed. . . .

Jesus' actual ministry corresponded precisely to the words of Luke 4. He spent most of his time not among the rich and powerful in Jerusalem, but among the poor in the cultural and economic backwater of Galilee. He healed the sick and blind. He fed the hungry. And he warned his followers in the strongest possible words that those who do not feed the hungry, clothe the naked, and visit the prisoners will experience eternal damnation (Matt. 25:31–46).

At the supreme moment of history when God took on human flesh, the God of Israel was still liberating the poor and oppressed and summoning his people to do the same.

Ronald Sider

PAUSE FOR REFLECTION

Why do you think Jesus so clearly proclaimed who he was in the synagogue at Nazareth? Why do you think he identified himself with these particular portions of Isaiah?

THURSDAY

Obedience Leads to Blessing and Faith

Luke 4:31—5:11

Jesus Forces Out an Evil Spirit

Jesus went to Capernaum, a city in
Galilee, and on the Sabbath day, he
taught the people. 32 They were
amazed at his teaching, because he
spoke with authority. 33 In the synagogue a man who had within him an
evil spirit shouted in a loud voice,
34 "Jesus of Nazareth! What do you
want with us? Did you come to destroy us? I know who you are—
God's Holy One!"

35 Jesus commanded the evil
spirit, "Be quiet! Come out of the
man!" The evil spirit threw the man
down to the ground before all the
people and then left the man without
hurting him.

36 The people were amazed and
said to each other, "What does this
mean? With authority and power he
commands evil spirits, and they
come out." 37 And so the news about
Jesus spread to every place in the
whole area.

Jesus Heals Many People

Jesus left the synagogue and went
to the home of Simon. Simon's
mother-in-law was sick with a high
fever, and they asked Jesus to help
her. 39 He came to her side and commanded the fever to leave. It left her,
and immediately she got up and began serving them.

40 When the sun went down, the
people brought those who were sick
to Jesus. Putting his hands on each
sick person, he healed every one of
them. 41 Demons came out of many
people, shouting, "You are the Son
of God." But Jesus commanded the
demons and would not allow them
to speak, because they knew Jesus
was the Christ.

42 At daybreak, Jesus went to a
lonely place, but the people looked
for him. When they found him, they
tried to keep him from leaving. 43 But
Jesus said to them, "I must preach
about God's kingdom to other towns,
too. This is why I was sent."

44 Then he kept on preaching in
the synagogues of Judea.

Jesus' First Followers

5 One day while Jesus was standing beside Lake Galilee, many
people were pressing all around him
to hear the word of God. 2 Jesus saw
two boats at the shore of the lake.
The fishermen had left them and
were washing their nets. 3 Jesus got
into one of the boats, the one that belonged to Simon, and asked him to
push off a little from the land. Then
Jesus sat down and continued to
teach the people from the boat.

4 When Jesus had finished speaking, he said to Simon, "Take the boat
into deep water, and put your nets
in the water to catch some fish."

5 Simon answered, "Master, we
worked hard all night trying to catch
fish, and we caught nothing. But you
say to put the nets in the water, so I
will." 6 When the fishermen did as
Jesus told them, they caught so many
fish that the nets began to break.
7 They called to their partners in the
other boat to come and help them.
They came and filled both boats so full
that they were almost sinking.

[8] When Simon Peter saw what
had happened, he bowed down before Jesus and said, "Go away from
me, Lord. I am a sinful man!" [9] He
and the other fishermen were
amazed at the many fish they
caught, as were [10] James and John,
the sons of Zebedee, Simon's partners.

Jesus said to Simon, "Don't be afraid. From now on you will fish for people." [11] When the men brought their boats to the shore, they left everything and followed Jesus.

OLD TESTAMENT READING

Elisha sent Naaman a messenger who said, "Go and wash in the Jordan River seven times. Then your skin will be healed, and you will be clean."

[11] Naaman became angry and left.
[13] Naaman's servants came near
and said to him, "My father, if the
prophet had told you to do some
great thing, wouldn't you have done
it? Doesn't it make more sense just
to do it? After all, he only told you,
'Wash, and you will be clean.'" [14] So
Naaman went down and dipped in
the Jordan seven times, just as
Elisha had said. Then his skin became new again, like the skin of a
child. And he was clean.

2 Kings 5:10–11a, 13–14

INSIGHTS

Trust and obey, for there's no other way
To be happy in Jesus, but to trust and obey."

All too often we glibly sing the words of this familiar Christian hymn without giving them much thought. These important words convey exactly what the Bible teaches. The secret of spiritual happiness and blessing is simply trusting and obeying the Lord. . . . The divine method for happiness and blessing is full trust in God and complete obedience to His Word. Lack of faith and partial obedience not only result in unhappiness and loss of blessing; they bring serious consequences in the life of the believer.

The Bible contains many passages that teach the trust-and-obey-for-happiness principle (see Psalm 119, for instance). In addition, many character studies from the Scriptures illustrate this same truth. Jacob is one such example. Jacob was a believer who had to learn over and over again throughout his life that halfway trust and obedience do not bring happiness and blessing. . . .

. . . God had stated in no uncertain terms His promises to Jacob, and yet Jacob had the audacity to hold back with an "if" type of faith and obedience. But let's not mock Jacob's faith and obedience before we examine our own. Can we say without reservation that we simply trust and obey, or must we confess that we selfishly bargain with God? . . .

. . . God does not expect us to question or change or compromise His commands; He expects us to simply trust Him and obey Him. That's the way to find spiritual blessing and happiness.

David Reid

PAUSE FOR REFLECTION

Did Naaman and Simon expect God to work the way he did? Do you think anything less than total obedience will accomplish God's work and blessing in your life?

FRIDAY

Jesus Often Slipped Away to Be Alone and Pray

Luke 5:12–35

Jesus Heals a Sick Man

When Jesus was in one of the towns,
there was a man covered with a skin
disease. When he saw Jesus, he
bowed before him and begged him,
"Lord, you can heal me if you will."
13 Jesus reached out his hand and
touched the man and said, "I will. Be
healed!" Immediately the disease
disappeared. 14 Then Jesus said,
"Don't tell anyone about this, but go
and show yourself to the priest and
offer a gift for your healing, as
Moses commanded. This will show
the people what I have done."
15 But the news about Jesus
spread even more. Many people
came to hear Jesus and to be healed
of their sicknesses, 16 but Jesus often
slipped away to be alone so he could
pray.

Jesus Heals a Paralyzed Man

One day as Jesus was teaching the
people, the Pharisees and teachers
of the law from every town in Galilee
and Judea and from Jerusalem were
there. The Lord was giving Jesus the
power to heal people. 18 Just then,
some men were carrying on a mat a
man who was paralyzed. They tried
to bring him in and put him down
before Jesus. 19 But because there
were so many people there, they
could not find a way in. So they went
up on the roof and lowered the man
on his mat through the ceiling into
the middle of the crowd right before
Jesus. 20 Seeing their faith, Jesus
said, "Friend, your sins are forgiven."
21 The Jewish teachers of the law
and the Pharisees thought to
themselves, "Who is this man who
is speaking as if he were God? Only
God can forgive sins."
22 But Jesus knew what they were
thinking and said, "Why are you
thinking these things? 23 Which is
easier: to say, 'Your sins are
forgiven,' or to say, 'Stand up and
walk'? 24 But I will prove to you that
the Son of Man has authority on
earth to forgive sins." So Jesus said
to the paralyzed man, "I tell you,
stand up, take your mat, and go
home."
25 At once the man stood up before them, picked up his mat, and
went home, praising God. 26 All the
people were fully amazed and began
to praise God. They were filled with
much respect and said, "Today we
have seen amazing things!"

Levi Follows Jesus

After this, Jesus went out and saw a
tax collector named Levi sitting in the
tax collector's booth. Jesus said to
him, "Follow me!" 28 So Levi got up, left
everything, and followed him.
29 Then Levi gave a big dinner for
Jesus at his house. Many tax
collectors and other people were
eating there, too. 30 But the Pharisees
and the men who taught the law for
the Pharisees began to complain to
Jesus' followers, "Why do you eat
and drink with tax collectors and sinners?"
31 Jesus answered them, "It is not
the healthy people who need a doctor, but the sick. 32 I have not come

to invite good people but sinners to
change their hearts and lives."

Jesus Answers a Question

They said to Jesus, "John's followers often give up eating for a certain time and pray, just as the Pharisees do. But your followers eat and drink all the time."
[34] Jesus said to them, "You cannot make the friends of the bridegroom give up eating while he is still with
them. [35] But the time will come when the bridegroom will be taken away from them, and then they will give up eating."

OLD TESTAMENT READING

LORD, I call to you with all my
heart.
Answer me, and I will keep
your demands.
146 I call to you.
Save me so I can obey your
rules.
147 I wake up early in the morning
and cry out.
I hope in your word.
148 I stay awake all night
so I can think about your
promises.
149 Listen to me because of your love;
LORD, give me life by your laws.
150 Those who love evil are near,
but they are far from your
teachings.
151 But, LORD, you are also near,
and all your commands are
true.

Psalm 119:145–151

INSIGHTS

Jesus needed solitude simply because he was human—the only fully human person who has ever lived. He sought solitude. . . .

He went apart to cure his loneliness. He needed the silence of eternity as a thirsting man in the desert needs water. And he essentially needed the silence of eternity which was interpreted by love. For he who was love incarnate had his own needs to love and be loved. His deepest need, and likewise ours, could be met only by God. Ultimately no human being, no matter how close or dear, can fully satisfy our need for love. Those who imagine they can end up devouring one another.

Jesus longed for time apart to bask and sunbathe in his Father's love, to soak in it and repose in it. No matter how drained he felt, it seems that this deep, silent communion refreshed him more than a good night's sleep. . . .

. . . Human love and friendship indeed enrich our lives and partly meet this need—but not entirely, for at the core of our being [is] . . . a lovelonging for God which will only be met by converting our loneliness into deep solitude, by fleeing the sweets and cordials that may give temporary satisfaction, and finding the real thing in him.

Margaret Magdalen

PAUSE FOR REFLECTION

It seems as if the psalmist thrived on his time with God, doesn't it? What is in your heart and on your lips when you slip away from life's demands to bask in the nearness of God's love? Isn't it about time you again slipped away to be refreshed by solitude with God?

WEEKEND

God Cares for Those Who Trust Him, but Will Judge the Wicked

Luke 5:36—6:23

Jesus told them this story: "No one
takes cloth off a new coat to cover a
hole in an old coat. Otherwise, he
ruins the new coat, and the cloth
from the new coat will not be the
same as the old cloth. 37 Also, no one
ever pours new wine into old leather
bags. Otherwise, the new wine will
break the bags, the wine will spill out,
and the leather bags will be ruined.
38 New wine must be put into new
leather bags. 39 No one after drinking
old wine wants new wine, because he
says, 'The old wine is better.'"

Jesus Is Lord over the Sabbath

6 One Sabbath day Jesus was walking through some fields of grain.
His followers picked the heads of
grain, rubbed them in their hands,
and ate them. 2 Some Pharisees said,
"Why do you do what is not lawful
on the Sabbath day?"
3 Jesus answered, "Have you not
read what David did when he and
those with him were hungry? 4 He
went into God's house and took and
ate the holy bread, which is lawful
only for priests to eat. And he gave
some to the people who were with
him." 5 Then Jesus said to the Pharisees, "The Son of Man is Lord of the
Sabbath day."

Jesus Heals a Man's Hand

On another Sabbath day Jesus went
into the synagogue and was teaching, and a man with a crippled right
hand was there. 7 The teachers of the
law and the Pharisees were watching closely to see if Jesus would heal
on the Sabbath day so they could
accuse him. 8 But he knew what they
were thinking, and he said to the
man with the crippled hand, "Stand
up here in the middle of everyone."
The man got up and stood there.
9 Then Jesus said to them, "I ask you,
which is lawful on the Sabbath day:
to do good or to do evil, to save a life
or to destroy it?" 10 Jesus looked
around at all of them and said to the
man, "Hold out your hand." The man
held out his hand, and it was healed.
11 But the Pharisees and the teachers of the law were very angry and
discussed with each other what they
could do to Jesus.

Jesus Chooses His Apostles

At that time Jesus went off to a
mountain to pray, and he spent the
night praying to God. 13 The next
morning, Jesus called his followers
to him and chose twelve of them,
whom he named apostles: 14 Simon
(Jesus named him Peter), his
brother Andrew, James, John, Philip,
Bartholomew, 15 Matthew, Thomas,
James son of Alphaeus, Simon
(called the Zealot), 16 Judas son of
James, and Judas Iscariot, who later
turned Jesus over to his enemies.

Jesus Teaches and Heals

Jesus and the apostles came down
from the mountain, and he stood on
level ground. A large group of his followers was there, as well as many
people from all around Judea, Jerusalem, and the seacoast cities of Tyre

and Sidon. [18]They all came to hear
Jesus teach and to be healed of their
sicknesses, and he healed those who
were troubled by evil spirits. [19] All the
people were trying to touch Jesus,
because power was coming from him
and healing them all.

[20]Jesus looked at his followers
and said,

"You people who are poor are
happy,
because the kingdom of God
belongs to you.
[21]You people who are now hungry
are happy,
because you will be satisfied.
You people who are now crying
are happy,
because you will laugh with
joy.

[22]"People will hate you, shut you
out, insult you, and say you are evil
because you follow the Son of Man.
But when they do, you will be happy.
[23]Be full of joy at that time, because
you have a great reward waiting for
you in heaven. Their ancestors did
the same things to the prophets."

OLD TESTAMENT READING

In a little while the wicked will
be no more.
You may look for them, but
they will be gone.
[11]People who are not proud will
inherit the land
and will enjoy complete peace.
[12]The wicked make evil plans
against good people.
They grind their teeth at them
in anger.
[13]But the Lord laughs at the wicked,
because he sees that their day
is coming.

Psalm 37:10–13

INSIGHTS

The representations of the Bible with regard to the final doom of the wicked are exceedingly striking. Spiritual truths are revealed by natural objects: e.g., the gates and walls of the New Jerusalem, to present the splendours and glories of the heavenly state. A spiritual telescope is put into our hands; we are permitted to point it towards the glorious city "whose builder and Maker is God"; we may survey its inner sanctuary, where the worshipping hosts praise God without ceasing. We see their flowing robes of white—the palms of victory in their hands—the beaming joy of their faces—the manifestations of ineffable bliss in their souls. . . .

Then we have the other side. The veil is lifted, and you come to the very verge of hell to see what is there. Whereas on the one hand all was glorious, on the other all is fearful, and full of horrors.

There is a bottomless pit. A deathless soul is cast therein; it sinks and sinks and sinks, going down that awful pit which knows no bottom, weeping and wailing as it descends, and you hear its groans as they echo and re-echo from the sides of that dread cavern of woe!

Charles Finney

PAUSE FOR REFLECTION

Study the contrasting images of reward and suffering on earth and in heaven for both the wicked and God's people. What do these images reveal to you about God's love and compassion? Thank God that he sees all and cares for those who love him.

MONDAY

Do Good to All—Show Mercy, as God Shows Mercy

Luke 6:24–45

But how terrible it will be for you
who are rich,
because you have had your
easy life.
25 How terrible it will be for you
who are full now,
because you will be hungry.
How terrible it will be for you
who are laughing now,
because you will be sad and cry.

26 "How terrible when everyone says only good things about you, because their ancestors said the same things about the false prophets.

Love Your Enemies

But I say to you who are listening, love your enemies. Do good to those who hate you, 28 bless those who curse you, pray for those who are cruel to you. 29 If anyone slaps you on one cheek, offer him the other cheek, too. If someone takes your coat, do not stop him from taking your shirt. 30 Give to everyone who asks you, and when someone takes something that is yours, don't ask for it back. 31 Do to others what you would want them to do to you. 32 If you love only the people who love you, what praise should you get? Even sinners love the people who love them. 33 If you do good only to those who do good to you, what praise should you get? Even sinners do that! 34 If you lend things to people, always hoping to get something back, what praise should you get? Even sinners lend to other sinners so that they can get back the same amount! 35 But love your enemies, do good to them, and lend to them without hoping to get anything back. Then you will have a great reward, and you will be children of the Most High God, because he is kind even to people who are ungrateful and full of sin. 36 Show mercy, just as your Father shows mercy.

Look at Yourselves

Don't judge other people, and you will not be judged. Don't accuse others of being guilty, and you will not be accused of being guilty. Forgive, and you will be forgiven. 38 Give, and you will receive. You will be given much. Pressed down, shaken together, and running over, it will spill into your lap. The way you give to others is the way God will give to you."

39 Jesus told them this story: "Can a blind person lead another blind person? No! Both of them will fall into a ditch. 40 A student is not better than the teacher, but the student who has been fully trained will be like the teacher.

41 "Why do you notice the little piece of dust in your friend's eye, but you don't notice the big piece of wood in your own eye? 42 How can you say to your friend, 'Friend, let me take that little piece of dust out of your eye' when you cannot see that big piece of wood in your own eye! You hypocrite! First, take the wood out of your own eye. Then you will see clearly to take the dust out of your friend's eye.

Two Kinds of Fruit

A good tree does not produce bad

fruit, nor does a bad tree produce good fruit. [44] Each tree is known by its own fruit. People don't gather figs from thornbushes, and they don't get grapes from bushes. [45] Good people bring good things out of the good they stored in their hearts. But evil people bring evil things out of the evil they stored in their hearts. People speak the things that are in their hearts."

OLD TESTAMENT READING

But this made Jonah very unhappy, and he became angry. [2] He prayed to the LORD, "When I was still in my own country this is what I said would happen, and that is why I quickly ran away to Tarshish. I knew that you are a God who is kind and shows mercy. You don't become angry quickly, and you have great love. I knew you would choose not to cause harm."

Jonah 4:1–2

INSIGHTS

Mercy is concern for people in need. It is ministry to the miserable. Offering help for those who hurt . . .

Those special servants of God who extend mercy to the miserable often do so with much encouragement because they identify with the sorrowing—they "get inside their skin." Rather than watching from a distance or keeping the needy safely at arm's length, they get in touch, involved, and offer assistance that alleviates some of the pain.

A large group of the collegians in our church in Fullerton, California, pile into our bus one weekend a month and travel together—not to a mountain resort or the beach for fun-n-games, but to a garbage dump in Tijuana, Mexico, where hundreds of poverty-stricken Mexican families live. Our young adults, under the encouraging leadership of Kenneth Kemp (one of our pastoral staff team members), bring apples and other foodstuff plus money they have collected to share with those in that miserable existence. . . .

What are they doing? They are showing mercy . . . . a ministry to others that is born out of the womb of identification. . . .

And what do they get in return? What does Christ promise? ". . . they shall receive mercy." Those who remain detached, distant, and disinterested in others will receive like treatment. But God promises that those who reach out and demonstrate mercy will, in turn, receive it. . . .

That is exactly what Jesus, our Savior, did for us when He came to earth. By becoming human. He got right inside our skin, literally. That made it possible for Him to see life through our eyes, feel the sting of our pain, and identify with the anguish of human need. He understands.

Charles Swindoll

ACTION POINT

Who is our model for mercy? Are any of his instructions in mercy difficult for you to practice? Pray that God will continue to reveal his mercy to you and enable you to be merciful—to those who suffer as well as to those who hate you.

TUESDAY

Build Your Life on a Solid Foundation

Luke 6:46—7:23

Two Kinds of People

Why do you call me, 'Lord, Lord,'
but do not do what I say? 47 I will
show you what everyone is like who
comes to me and hears my words
and obeys. 48 That person is like a
man building a house who dug deep
and laid the foundation on rock.
When the floods came, the water
tried to wash the house away, but it
could not shake it, because the
house was built well. 49 But the one
who hears my words and does not
obey is like a man who built his
house on the ground without a foundation. When the floods came, the
house quickly fell and was completely destroyed."

Jesus Heals a Soldier's Servant

7 When Jesus finished saying all
these things to the people, he
went to Capernaum. 2 There was an
army officer who had a servant who
was very important to him. The servant was so sick he was nearly dead.
3 When the officer heard about
Jesus, he sent some older Jewish
leaders to him to ask Jesus to come
and heal his servant. 4 The men went
to Jesus and begged him, saying,
"This officer is worthy of your help.
5 He loves our people, and he built
us a synagogue."
6 So Jesus went with the men. He
was getting near the officer's house
when the officer sent friends to say,
"Lord, don't trouble yourself, because I am not worthy to have you
come into my house. 7 That is why I
did not come to you myself. But you
only need to command it, and my
servant will be healed. 8 I, too, am a
man under the authority of others,
and I have soldiers under my command. I tell one soldier, 'Go,' and he
goes. I tell another soldier, 'Come,'
and he comes. I say to my servant,
'Do this,' and my servant does it."
9 When Jesus heard this, he was
amazed. Turning to the crowd that
was following him, he said, "I tell
you, this is the greatest faith I have
found anywhere, even in Israel."
10 Those who had been sent to
Jesus went back to the house where
they found the servant in good health.

Jesus Brings a Man Back to Life

Soon afterwards Jesus went to a
town called Nain, and his followers
and a large crowd traveled with him.
12 When he came near the town gate,
he saw a funeral. A mother, who was
a widow, had lost her only son. A
large crowd from the town was with
the mother while her son was being
carried out. 13 When the Lord saw
her, he felt very sorry for her and
said, "Don't cry." 14 He went up and
touched the coffin, and the people
who were carrying it stopped. Jesus
said, "Young man, I tell you, get up!"
15 And the son sat up and began to
talk. Then Jesus gave him back to
his mother.
16 All the people were amazed and
began praising God, saying, "A great
prophet has come to us! God has
come to help his people."
17 This news about Jesus spread
through all Judea and into all the
places around there.

John Asks a Question

John's followers told him about all
these things. He called for two of his
followers [19] and sent them to the
Lord to ask, "Are you the One who
is to come, or should we wait for
someone else?"
[20] When the men came to Jesus,
they said, "John the Baptist sent us
to you with this question: 'Are you
the One who is to come, or should
we wait for someone else?'"
[21] At that time, Jesus healed many
people of their sicknesses, diseases,
and evil spirits, and he gave sight to
many blind people. [22] Then Jesus answered John's followers, "Go tell
John what you saw and heard here.
The blind can see, the crippled can
walk, and people with skin diseases
are healed. The deaf can hear, the
dead are raised to life, and the Good
News is preached to the poor.
[23] Those who do not stumble in their
faith because of me are blessed!"

OLD TESTAMENT READING

The LORD lives!
May my Rock be praised.
Praise the God who saves me!

Psalm 18:46

INSIGHTS

Suppose it were possible for a man never to have seen any season but summer. Then suppose that this man was called upon to advise in the erection of a building. You can imagine his procedure; everything is to be light, because he never heard a high wind. Waterpipes may be exposed, for he never felt the severity of frost. The most flimsy roof will be sufficient, for he knows nothing of the great rains of winter and spring.

Tell such a man that the winds will become stormy, that the rivers will be chilled into ice, that his windows will be blinded with snow, and that floods will beat upon his roof. If he is a wise man, he will say, "I must not build for one season, but for all seasons. I must not build for fine days, but for days that will be tempestuous. I must, as far as possible, prepare for the most inclement and trying weather." That is simple common sense.

Why be less sensible in building a character than in building a house? We build our bricks for severity as well as for sunshine, so why build our character with less care? If in summer we think about the frost, why not in prosperity have some thought for adversity? If in July we prepare for December, why not in the flattering hour of exultation think of the judgment that is at once infallible and irresistible?

As he would be infinitely foolish who would build his house without thinking of the natural forces that will try its strength, so is he cursed with insanity who builds his character without thinking of the fire with which God will try every man's work.

Joseph Parker

ACTION POINT

On what are you building your life? Will your house stand firm against any storm? Write your own psalm that reminds you both of God's steadfast protection and your need to follow his ways.

WEDNESDAY

Be Sorry for Your Sin

Luke 7:24–50

*W*hen John's followers left, Jesus
began talking to the people about
John: "What did you go out into the
desert to see? A reed blown by the
wind? 25 What did you go out to see?
A man dressed in fine clothes? No,
people who have fine clothes and
much wealth live in kings' palaces.
26 But what did you go out to see? A
prophet? Yes, and I tell you, John is
more than a prophet. 27 This was
written about him:

'I will send my messenger ahead
of you,
who will prepare the way for
you.' *Malachi 3:1*

28 I tell you, John is greater than any
other person ever born, but even the
least important person in the kingdom of God is greater than John."

29 (When the people, including
the tax collectors, heard this, they all
agreed that God's teaching was
good, because they had been baptized by John. 30 But the Pharisees
and experts on the law refused to
accept God's plan for themselves;
they did not let John baptize them.)

31 Then Jesus said, "What shall I
say about the people of this time?
What are they like? 32 They are like
children sitting in the marketplace,
calling to one another and saying,

'We played music for you, but you
did not dance;
we sang a sad song, but you
did not cry.'

33 John the Baptist came and did not
eat bread or drink wine, and you say,
'He has a demon in him.' 34 The Son
of Man came eating and drinking,
and you say, 'Look at him! He eats
too much and drinks too much wine,
and he is a friend of tax collectors
and sinners!' 35 But wisdom is proved
to be right by what it does."

A Woman Washes Jesus' Feet

*O*ne of the Pharisees asked Jesus
to eat with him, so Jesus went into
the Pharisee's house and sat at the
table. 37 A sinful woman in the town
learned that Jesus was eating at the
Pharisee's house. So she brought an
alabaster jar of perfume 38 and stood
behind Jesus at his feet, crying. She
began to wash his feet with her tears,
and she dried them with her hair,
kissing them many times and rub-
bing them with the perfume. 39 When
the Pharisee who asked Jesus to
come to his house saw this, he
thought to himself, "If Jesus were a
prophet, he would know that the
woman touching him is a sinner!"

40 Jesus said to the Pharisee,
"Simon, I have something to say to
you."

Simon said, "Teacher, tell me."

41 Jesus said, "Two people owed
money to the same banker. One
owed five hundred coins and the
other owed fifty. 42 They had no
money to pay what they owed, but
the banker told both of them they
did not have to pay him. Which person will love the banker more?"

43 Simon, the Pharisee, answered,
"I think it would be the one who
owed him the most money."

Jesus said to Simon, "You are
right." 44 Then Jesus turned toward
the woman and said to Simon, "Do
you see this woman? When I came

into your house, you gave me no
water for my feet, but she washed
my feet with her tears and dried
them with her hair. 45 You gave me
no kiss of greeting, but she has been
kissing my feet since I came in.
46 You did not put oil on my head, but
she poured perfume on my feet. 47 I
tell you that her many sins are forgiven, so she showed great love. But
the person who is forgiven only a
little will love only a little."

48 Then Jesus said to her, "Your
sins are forgiven."

49 The people sitting at the table
began to say among themselves,
"Who is this who even forgives
sins?"

50 Jesus said to the woman, "Because you believed, you are saved
from your sins. Go in peace."

OLD TESTAMENT READING

You say, 'My teachings are right,
and I am clean in God's sight.'
5 I wish God would speak
and open his lips against you
6 and tell you the secrets of wisdom,
because wisdom has two sides.
Know this: God has even forgotten some of your sin."

Job 11:4–6

INSIGHTS

Before I can become wise, I must first realize that I am foolish. Before I can receive power, I must first confess that I am powerless. I must lament my sins before I can rejoice in a Savior. Mourning, in God's sequence, always comes before exultation. Blessed are those who mourn their unworthiness, their helplessness, and their inadequacy.

Isaiah, the mighty prophet of God, knew by experience that one must bow the knee in mourning before one can lift the voice in jubilation. When his sin appeared ugly and venomous in the bright light of God's holiness, he said: "Woe is me! for I am undone; because I am a man of unclean lips: for mine eyes have seen the King, the LORD of hosts" (Isaiah 6:5).

We cannot be satisfied with our goodness after beholding the holiness of God. But our mourning over our unworthiness and sinfulness should be of short duration, for God has said: "I, even I, am he that blotteth out thy transgressions for mine own sake, and will not remember thy sins" (Isaiah 43:25).

Isaiah had to experience the mourning inadequacy before he could realize the joy of forgiveness. . . .

In God's economy, a person must go down into the valley of grief before he or she can scale the heights of spiritual glory. One must become tired and weary of living without Christ before he or she can seek and find His fellowship. One must come to the end of "self" before one can really begin to live.

Billy Graham

ACTION POINT

Are you, like the Pharisees, ever tempted to brush your sins off as being of little consequence? Pray that you will truly mourn the burden of your sin and love God deeply because of his great forgiveness.

THURSDAY

Jesus Understands the Hearts of Spiritually Closed People

Luke 8:1–21

The Group with Jesus

8 After this, while Jesus was traveling through some cities and
small towns, he preached and told
the Good News about God's kingdom. The twelve apostles were with
him, 2 and also some women who
had been healed of sicknesses and
evil spirits: Mary, called Magdalene,
from whom seven demons had gone
out; 3 Joanna, the wife of Chuza (the
manager of Herod's house); Su-
sanna; and many others. These
women used their own money to
help Jesus and his apostles.

A Story About Planting Seed

When a great crowd was gathered,
and people were coming to Jesus
from every town, he told them this
story:
5 "A farmer went out to plant his
seed. While he was planting, some
seed fell by the road. People walked
on the seed, and the birds ate it up.
6 Some seed fell on rock, and when
it began to grow, it died because it
had no water. 7 Some seed fell among
thorny weeds, but the weeds grew
up with it and choked the good
plants. 8 And some seed fell on good
ground and grew and made a hundred times more."

As Jesus finished the story, he
called out, "You people who can hear
me, listen!"
9 Jesus' followers asked him what
this story meant.
10 Jesus said, "You have been chosen to know the secrets about the
kingdom of God. But I use stories to
speak to other people so that:

'They will look, but they may not
see.
They will listen, but they may
not understand.' *Isaiah 6:9*

11 "This is what the story means:
The seed is God's message. 12 The
seed that fell beside the road is like
the people who hear God's teaching,
but the devil comes and takes it away
from them so they cannot believe it
and be saved. 13 The seed that fell on
rock is like those who hear God's
teaching and accept it gladly, but they
don't allow the teaching to go deep
into their lives. They believe for a
while, but when trouble comes, they
give up. 14 The seed that fell among
the thorny weeds is like those who
hear God's teaching, but they let the
worries, riches, and pleasures of this
life keep them from growing and producing good fruit. 15 And the seed
that fell on the good ground is like
those who hear God's teaching with
good, honest hearts and obey it and
patiently produce good fruit.

Use What You Have

No one after lighting a lamp covers
it with a bowl or hides it under a bed.
Instead, the person puts it on a
lampstand so those who come in will
see the light. 17 Everything that is
hidden will become clear, and every
secret thing will be made known.
18 So be careful how you listen.
Those who have understanding will
be given more. But those who do not
have understanding, even what they

think they have will be taken away from them."

Jesus' True Family

Jesus' mother and brothers came to see him, but there was such a crowd they could not get to him. [20] Someone said to Jesus, "Your mother and your brothers are standing outside, wanting to see you."

[21] Jesus answered them, "My mother and my brothers are those who listen to God's teaching and obey it!"

OLD TESTAMENT READING

My people, listen to my teaching;
 listen to what I say.
[2] I will speak using stories;
 I will tell secret things from
 long ago.
[3] We have heard them and known
 them
 by what our ancestors have
 told us.
[4] We will not keep them from our
 children;
 we will tell those who come later
 about the praises of the LORD.
We will tell about his power
 and the miracles he has done.

Psalm 78:1–4

INSIGHTS

Not all of Christ's parables are explained. In fact, most are not. But this one is. . . .

The first type of soil represents the hard heart. . . . What is it that makes the human heart hard? Sin hardens the heart, and the heart that is hardened sins even more.

. . . That type of person is described in the first chapter of Romans. He or she begins by suppressing the truth about God that may be known from nature (vv. 18–20), plunges inevitably into spiritual ignorance and moral degradation (vv. 21–31), and eventually comes not only to practice the sins of the heathen but to approve them as well (v. 32). Here we see both halves of the circle; sin leads to a rejection of God and God's truth, and the rejection of God's truth leads to even greater sin. What is it that leads such a person to reject the truth of God in the first place? According to Paul, it is a determined opposition to the nature of God Himself, which the apostle describes as human "godlessness and wickedness" (Rom. 1:18).

So rather than repent of sin and turn for mercy to a God who is altogether sovereign, holy, knowing, and unchangeable, men and women suppress what knowledge they have and refuse to seek out that additional knowledge that could be the salvation of their souls. . . .

. . . When Jesus came preaching the kingdom of God, He came preaching God's right to rule over the minds and hearts of all people. But that is precisely what the people involved did not want. . . .

So it is also today. That is probably the greatest reason for the rejection of the gospel of God's grace in Jesus Christ.

James Boice

APPLICATION

Why do you think Jesus twice warns his hearers to listen to his teaching carefully? What message do you think Jesus wants you to hear? What difference do his words make in your heart and life?

FRIDAY

God Meets Us in Our Suffering

Luke 8:22–48

Jesus Calms a Storm

One day Jesus and his followers got into a boat, and he said to them, "Let's go across the lake." And so they started across. 23 While they were sailing, Jesus fell asleep. A very strong wind blew up on the lake, causing the boat to fill with water, and they were in danger.

24 The followers went to Jesus and woke him, saying, "Master! Master! We will drown!"

Jesus got up and gave a command to the wind and the waves. They stopped, and it became calm. 25 Jesus said to his followers, "Where is your faith?"

The followers were afraid and amazed and said to each other, "Who is this that commands even the wind and the water, and they obey him?"

A Man with Demons Inside Him

Jesus and his followers sailed across the lake from Galilee to the area of the Gerasene people. 27 When Jesus got out on the land, a man from the town who had demons inside him came to Jesus. For a long time he had worn no clothes and had lived in the burial caves, not in a house. 28 When he saw Jesus, he cried out and fell down before him. He said with a loud voice, "What do you want with me, Jesus, Son of the Most High God? I beg you, don't torture me!" 29 He said this because Jesus was commanding the evil spirit to come out of the man. Many times it had taken hold of him. Though he had been kept under guard and chained hand and foot, he had broken his chains and had been forced by the demon out into a lonely place.

30 Jesus asked him, "What is your name?"

He answered, "Legion," because many demons were in him. 31 The demons begged Jesus not to send them into eternal darkness. 32 A large herd of pigs was feeding on a hill, and the demons begged Jesus to allow them to go into the pigs. So Jesus allowed them to do this. 33 When the demons came out of the man, they went into the pigs, and the herd ran down the hill into the lake and was drowned.

34 When the herdsmen saw what had happened, they ran away and told about this in the town and the countryside. 35 And people went to see what had happened. When they came to Jesus, they found the man sitting at Jesus' feet, clothed and in his right mind, because the demons were gone. But the people were frightened. 36 The people who saw this happen told the others how Jesus had made the man well. 37 All the people of the Gerasene country asked Jesus to leave, because they were all very afraid. So Jesus got into the boat and went back to Galilee.

38 The man whom Jesus had healed begged to go with him, but Jesus sent him away, saying, 39 "Go back home and tell people how much God has done for you." So the man went all over town telling how much Jesus had done for him.

Jesus Gives Life to a Dead Girl and Heals a Sick Woman

When Jesus got back to Galilee, a
crowd welcomed him, because everyone was waiting for him. 41 A man
named Jairus, a leader of the synagogue, came to Jesus and fell at his
feet, begging him to come to his
house. 42 Jairus' only daughter, about
twelve years old, was dying.

While Jesus was on his way to
Jairus' house, the people were crowding all around him. 43 A woman was in
the crowd who had been bleeding for
twelve years, but no one was able to
heal her. 44 She came up behind Jesus
and touched the edge of his coat, and
instantly her bleeding stopped. 45 Then
Jesus said, "Who touched me?"

When all the people said they had
not touched him, Peter said, "Master, the people are all around you and
are pushing against you."

46 But Jesus said, "Someone did
touch me, because I felt power go out
from me." 47 When the woman saw she
could not hide, she came forward,
shaking, and fell down before Jesus.
While all the people listened, she told
why she had touched him and how she
had been instantly healed. 48 Jesus said
to her, "Dear woman, you are made well
because you believed. Go in peace."

OLD TESTAMENT READING

The LORD defends those who suffer;
he defends them in times of trouble.

Psalm 9:9

INSIGHTS

The image Jesus left with the world, the cross, . . . is proof that God cares about our suffering and pain. He died of it. . . .

. . . Jesus, who had said He could call down angels at any moment and rescue Himself from the horror, chose not to—because of us. For God so loved us, that He sent His only Son to die for us.

And thus the cross, an eternal stumbling block to some, became the cornerstone of our faith. . . .

By taking it on Himself, Jesus in a sense dignified pain. Of all the kinds of lives He could have lived, He chose a suffering one. . . . Even though Jesus died, His death became the great victory of history, pulling man and God together. God made a supreme good out of that awful day.

Jesus' followers are not insulated from the tragedies of this world, just as He was not. God has never promised that tornados will skip our houses on the way to our pagan neighbors'. Microbes do not flee from Christian bodies. Rather, Peter could say to suffering Christians, "This suffering is all part of the work God has given you. Christ, who suffered for you, is your example. Follow in his steps" (1 Peter 2:21 LB).

Philip Yancey

PAUSE FOR REFLECTION

These verses show Jesus surrounded by suffering. How did he respond? How much does he care about your suffering? Thank him that he not only relieves our suffering, but took our greatest suffering upon himself on the cross.

WEEKEND

God Is in Control

Luke 8:49—9:17

While Jesus was still speaking,
someone came from the house of the
synagogue leader and said to him,
"Your daughter is dead. Don't
bother the teacher anymore."
50 When Jesus heard this, he said
to Jairus, "Don't be afraid. Just believe, and your daughter will be
well."
51 When Jesus went to the house,
he let only Peter, John, James, and
the girl's father and mother go inside
with him. 52 All the people were crying and feeling sad because the girl
was dead, but Jesus said, "Stop crying. She is not dead, only asleep."
53 The people laughed at Jesus because they knew the girl was dead.
54 But Jesus took hold of her hand
and called to her, "My child, stand
up!" 55 Her spirit came back into her,
and she stood up at once. Then Jesus
ordered that she be given something
to eat. 56 The girl's parents were
amazed, but Jesus told them not to
tell anyone what had happened

Jesus Sends Out the Apostles

9 Jesus called the twelve apostles
together and gave them power
and authority over all demons and
the ability to heal sicknesses. 2 He
sent the apostles out to tell about
God's kingdom and to heal the sick.
3 He said to them, "Take nothing for
your trip, neither a walking stick,
bag, bread, money, or extra clothes.
4 When you enter a house, stay there
until it is time to leave. 5 If people do
not welcome you, shake the dust off
of your feet as you leave the town,
as a warning to them."
6 So the apostles went out and
traveled through all the towns,
preaching the Good News and healing people everywhere.

Herod Is Confused About Jesus

Herod, the governor, heard about
all the things that were happening
and was confused, because some
people said, "John the Baptist has
risen from the dead." 8 Others said,
"Elijah has come to us." And still others said, "One of the prophets who
lived long ago has risen from the
dead." 9 Herod said, "I cut off John's
head, so who is this man I hear such
things about?" And Herod kept trying to see Jesus.

More than Five Thousand Fed

When the apostles returned, they
told Jesus everything they had done.
Then Jesus took them with him to a
town called Bethsaida where they
could be alone together. 11 But the
people learned where Jesus went
and followed him. He welcomed
them and talked with them about
God's kingdom and healed those
who needed to be healed.
12 Late in the afternoon, the
twelve apostles came to Jesus and
said, "Send the people away. They
need to go to the towns and countryside around here and find places
to sleep and something to eat, because no one lives in this place."
13 But Jesus said to them, "You
give them something to eat."
They said, "We have only five

loaves of bread and two fish, unless we go buy food for all these people."
14 (There were about five thousand men there.)

Jesus said to his followers, "Tell the people to sit in groups of about fifty people."
15 So the followers did this, and all
the people sat down. 16 Then Jesus
took the five loaves of bread and two fish, and looking up to heaven, he thanked God for the food. Then he divided the food and gave it to the followers to give to the people.
17 They all ate and were satisfied, and
what was left over was gathered up, filling twelve baskets.

OLD TESTAMENT READING

*B*ut ask the animals, and they
 will teach you,
 or ask the birds of the air, and
 they will tell you.
8 Speak to the earth, and it will
 teach you,
 or let the fish of the sea tell you.
9 Every one of these knows
 that the hand of the LORD has
 done this.
10 The life of every creature
 and the breath of all people are
 in God's hand."

Job 12:7–10

INSIGHTS

No two days were ever exactly the same on my bit of beach. Part of its great appeal lay in the ever-changing appearance of its shoreline.

The subtle play of sunlight and shadow on the cliff faces altered their contours. Some mornings the rugged rocks seemed softened by the muted shades of the rising sun. They glowed warm, golden, wrapped in sunshine and serenity.

Other days the same rock buttresses stood gray and forbidding in the fog and mist that swirled in off the sea. The shoreline looked almost black, dark with dampness, soaked with sea spray.

Always, always, always the ocean is at work on the land. Summer and winter, spring and autumn the changing tides rise and ebb, shaping the character of the coast. Their force is utterly relentless—their power immeasurable—their titanic thrust untamed.

Great mysteries surround the majestic, awesome action of the tides. With incredible precision they move billions of tons of water from surface to surface upon the sea. They are the reflection of gigantic energy within the cosmos that knows no rest, that never slumbers, that never sleeps.

In the same overshadowing way, our Father watches over His children, quietly overseeing the events of their lives that they might accomplish His purposes for Him.

W. Phillip Keller

ACTION POINT

What do these readings show that God controls? Is there anything more for him to control? What experience in your life or image from nature reminds you that God is in control? Think of it often, and praise God for his great sovereignty!

MONDAY

God Is a Patient Teacher

Luke 9:18–43a

Jesus Is the Christ

One time when Jesus was praying alone, his followers were with him, and he asked them, "Who do the people say I am?"

19 They answered, "Some say you are John the Baptist. Others say you are Elijah. And others say you are one of the prophets from long ago who has come back to life."

20 Then Jesus asked, "But who do you say I am?"

Peter answered, "You are the Christ from God."

21 Jesus warned them not to tell
anyone, saying, 22 "The Son of Man must suffer many things. He will be rejected by the older Jewish leaders, the leading priests, and the teachers of the law. He will be killed and after three days will be raised from the dead."

23 Jesus said to all of them, "If people want to follow me, they must give up the things they want. They must be willing to give up their lives
daily to follow me. 24 Those who want to save their lives will give up true life. But those who give up their lives
for me will have true life. 25 It is worth nothing for them to have the whole world if they themselves are
destroyed or lost. 26 If people are ashamed of me and my teaching, then the Son of Man will be ashamed of them when he comes in his glory and with the glory of the Father and
the holy angels. 27 I tell you the truth, some people standing here will see the kingdom of God before they die."

Jesus Talks with Moses and Elijah

About eight days after Jesus said these things, he took Peter, John, and James and went up on a mountain to pray.
29 While Jesus was praying, the appearance of his face changed, and his clothes became shining white.
30 Then two men, Moses and Elijah, were talking with Jesus.
31 They appeared in heavenly glory, talking about his departure which he would soon bring about in Jerusalem.
32 Peter and the others were very sleepy, but when they awoke fully, they saw the glory of Jesus and the two men standing with him.
33 When Moses and Elijah were about to leave, Peter said to Jesus, "Master, it is good that we are here. Let us make three tents—one for you, one for Moses, and one for Elijah." (Peter did not know what he was talking about.)

34 While he was saying these things, a cloud came and covered them, and they became afraid as the cloud covered them.
35 A voice came from the cloud, saying, "This is my Son, whom I have chosen. Listen to him!"

36 When the voice finished speaking, only Jesus was there. Peter, John, and James said nothing and told no one at that time what they had seen.

Jesus Heals a Sick Boy

The next day, when they came down from the mountain, a large crowd met Jesus.
38 A man in the

crowd shouted to him, "Teacher, please come and look at my son, because he is my only child.
39 An evil spirit seizes my son, and suddenly he screams. It causes him to lose control of himself and foam at the mouth. The evil spirit keeps on hurting him and almost never leaves him.
40 I begged your followers to force the evil spirit out, but they could not do it."
41 Jesus answered, "You people have no faith, and your lives are all wrong. How long must I stay with you and put up with you? Bring your son here."
42 While the boy was coming, the demon threw him on the ground and made him lose control of himself. But Jesus gave a strong command to the evil spirit and healed the boy and gave him back to his father.
43 All the people were amazed at the great power of God.

OLD TESTAMENT READING

You were patient with them for
many years
and warned them by your
Spirit through the prophets,
but they did not pay attention.
So you handed them over to
other countries.
31 But because your mercy is great,
you did not kill them all or
leave them.
You are a kind and merciful
God."

Nehemiah 9:30–31

INSIGHTS

In Judaism it was the custom for the pupil to select the rabbi of his choice and attach himself to him for instruction. Thus Paul sat "at the feet of Gamaliel" (Acts 22:3, KJV). But here it was Jesus and not the disciples who took the initiative. "When day came, He called His disciples to Him; and chose twelve of them" (Luke 6:13). . . . He called them personally and bound them to Him with bonds of affection that stood the test of time. Thus He chose to invest His life and channel it into that little group of men. . . .

. . . They were not theologians or political leaders—just ordinary men who became extraordinary under the molding hand of the Master Potter. That makes His selection of them the more wonderful. . . .

Their imperfections were painfully apparent, but those did not debar them from His fellowship and friendship. If God required perfection before He admitted us into the circle of His fellowship, who would qualify? Quirks of temperament did not disqualify them, or Peter with his volatile nature would not have been counted in. Nor would James and John with their selfish ambition and callous racism. Thomas's disbelief would have placed him outside the circle. But Jesus welcomed them all into the circle of His love and intimacy.

J. Oswald Sanders

PAUSE FOR REFLECTION

Chronicle your own spiritual journey in a way similar to Nehemiah's account of God's dealings with the children of Israel (9:19–31). In what ways has God stood beside you as a patient, wise, and ever-merciful teacher? Thank him for claiming you as his own.

TUESDAY

God Seeks Those Who Follow Him Faithfully

Luke 9:43b—10:7

Jesus Talks About His Death

While everyone was wondering about all that Jesus did, he said to his followers, 44 "Don't forget what I tell you now: The Son of Man will be handed over to people." 45 But the followers did not understand what this meant; the meaning was hidden from them so they could not understand. But they were afraid to ask Jesus about it.

Who Is the Greatest?

Jesus' followers began to have an argument about which one of them was the greatest. 47 Jesus knew what they were thinking, so he took a little child and stood the child beside him. 48 Then Jesus said, "Whoever accepts this little child in my name accepts me. And whoever accepts me accepts the One who sent me, because whoever is least among you all is really the greatest."

Anyone Not Against Us Is for Us

John answered, "Master, we saw someone using your name to force demons out of people. We told him to stop, because he does not belong to our group."

50 But Jesus said to him, "Don't stop him, because whoever is not against you is for you."

A Town Rejects Jesus

When the time was coming near for Jesus to depart, he was determined to go to Jerusalem. 52 He sent some men ahead of him, who went into a town in Samaria to make everything ready for him. 53 But the people there would not welcome him, because he was set on going to Jerusalem. 54 When James and John, followers of Jesus, saw this, they said, "Lord, do you want us to call fire down from heaven and destroy those people?"

55 But Jesus turned and scolded them. 56 Then they went to another town.

Following Jesus

As they were going along the road, someone said to Jesus, "I will follow you any place you go."

58 Jesus said to them, "The foxes have holes to live in, and the birds have nests, but the Son of Man has no place to rest his head."

59 Jesus said to another man, "Follow me!"

But he said, "Lord, first let me go and bury my father."

60 But Jesus said to him, "Let the people who are dead bury their own dead. You must go and tell about the kingdom of God."

61 Another man said, "I will follow you, Lord, but first let me go and say good-bye to my family."

62 Jesus said, "Anyone who begins to plow a field but keeps looking back is of no use in the kingdom of God."

Jesus Sends Out the Seventy-Two

10 After this, the Lord chose seventy-two others and sent them out in pairs ahead of him into every town and place where he planned to go. 2 He said to them, "There are a

great many people to harvest, but there are only a few workers. So pray to God, who owns the harvest, that he will send more workers to help gather his harvest. [3] Go now, but listen! I am sending you out like sheep among wolves. [4] Don't carry a purse, a bag, or sandals, and don't waste time talking with people on the road. [5] Before you go into a house, say, 'Peace be with this house.' [6] If peaceful people live there, your blessing of peace will stay with them, but if not, then your blessing will come back to you. [7] Stay in the peaceful house, eating and drinking what the people there give you. A worker should be given his pay. Don't move from house to house."

OLD TESTAMENT READING

At that time Hanani the seer came to Asa king of Judah and said to him, "You depended on the king of Aram to help you and not on the LORD your God. So the king of Aram's army escaped from you. [8] The Cushites and Libyans had a large and powerful army and many chariots and horsemen. But you depended on the LORD to help you, so he handed them over to you. [9] The LORD searches all the earth for people who have given themselves completely to him. He wants to make them strong."

2 Chronicles 16:7–9b

INSIGHTS

When you begin to pray, your life can take on all kinds of perils and problems that you never had before. Think about it. As far as we know, Abraham was living a comfortable, trouble-free life until he began to pray. It was through prayer that he heard God's message to leave home, move out, hit the road for an unknown destination, and start a journey of indeterminate length. His life became exceedingly difficult and dangerous. . . .

Prayer was the launching pad for Moses as well. He was quietly tending sheep in the Midian hills, leading a settled life with his wife and sons and his father-in-law. Things changed when he started to pray. It started dramatically enough at a burning bush, where he heard God speak to him and entrust him with an impossible task—that of leading the Israelites out of Egypt. From one perspective, that was the last really comfortable day of Moses' life. . . .

Peter, James, John, and Andrew were comfortable, middle-class businessmen, settled and respected in their community, until their dialog with Jesus began. As they responded to his invitation to, "Follow me," all of that ended. They embarked on three years of intense ministry and then carried out the commission to "go and make disciples of all nations" (Matt. 28:19) in the face of unimaginable adversity and persecution. . . .

That is the peril of prayer. . . . As we begin to talk to God and hear him speak to us, life may never be the same.

Bruce Larson

APPLICATION

When Jesus walked on earth, he literally called his disciples to follow him. How does he call people when he isn't living on earth? Is God calling you, through your prayers, to break out into new territory, to follow him more faithfully?

WEDNESDAY

God Gives His Wisdom and Power to His Servants

Luke 10:8–29

If you go into a town and the people
welcome you, eat what they give
you. 9 Heal the sick who live there,
and tell them, 'The kingdom of God
is near you.' 10 But if you go into a
town, and the people don't welcome
you, then go into the streets and say,
11 'Even the dirt from your town that
sticks to our feet we wipe off against
you. But remember that the kingdom of God is near.' 12 I tell you, on
the Judgment Day it will be better
for the people of Sodom than for the
people of that town.

Jesus Warns Unbelievers

How terrible for you, Korazin! How
terrible for you, Bethsaida! If the
miracles I did in you had happened
in Tyre and Sidon, those people
would have changed their lives long
ago. They would have worn rough
cloth and put ashes on themselves
to show they had changed. 14 But on
the Judgment Day it will be better
for Tyre and Sidon than for you.
15 And you, Capernaum, will you be
lifted up to heaven? No! You will be
thrown down to the depths!

16 "Whoever listens to you listens
to me, and whoever refuses to accept
you refuses to accept me. And whoever refuses to accept me refuses to
accept the One who sent me."

Satan Falls

When the seventy-two came back,
they were very happy and said,
"Lord, even the demons obeyed us
when we used your name!"

18 Jesus said, "I saw Satan fall like
lightning from heaven. 19 Listen, I
have given you power to walk on
snakes and scorpions, power that is
greater than the enemy has. So nothing will hurt you. 20 But you should
not be happy because the spirits
obey you but because your names
are written in heaven."

Jesus Prays to the Father

Then Jesus rejoiced in the Holy
Spirit and said, "I praise you, Father,
Lord of heaven and earth, because
you have hidden these things from
the people who are wise and smart.
But you have shown them to those
who are like little children. Yes, Father, this is what you really wanted.

22 "My Father has given me all
things. No one knows who the Son
is, except the Father. And no one
knows who the Father is, except the
Son and those whom the Son
chooses to tell."

23 Then Jesus turned to his followers and said privately, "You are
blessed to see what you now see. 24 I
tell you, many prophets and kings
wanted to see what you now see, but
they did not, and they wanted to hear
what you now hear, but they did
not."

The Good Samaritan

Then an expert on the law stood up
to test Jesus, saying, "Teacher, what
must I do to get life forever?"

26 Jesus said, "What is written in
the law? What do you read there?"

27 The man answered, "Love the
Lord your God with all your heart,

all your soul, all your strength, and all your mind." Also, "Love your neighbor as you love yourself."
[28] Jesus said to him, "Your answer is right. Do this and you will live."
[29] But the man, wanting to show the importance of his question, said to Jesus, "And who is my neighbor?"

OLD TESTAMENT READING

God gave Solomon great wisdom so he could understand many things. His wisdom was as hard to measure as the grains of sand on the seashore.
[30] His wisdom was greater than any wisdom of the East, or any wisdom in Egypt.
[31] He was wiser than anyone on earth. He was even wiser than Ethan the Ezrahite, as well as Heman, Calcol, and Darda—the three sons of Mahol. King Solomon became famous in all the surrounding countries.
[32] During his life he spoke three thousand wise sayings and also wrote one thousand five songs.
[33] He taught about many kinds of plants—everything from the great cedar trees of Lebanon to the weeds that grow out of the walls. He also taught about animals, birds, crawling things, and fish.
[34] People from all nations came to listen to King Solomon's wisdom. The kings of all nations sent them to him, because they had heard of Solomon's wisdom.

1 Kings 4:29–34

INSIGHTS

Too many Christians do not believe Christ's promise that He would endue the Church with spiritual power; they doubt that His promise is to every believer. Consequently, they have no faith to lay hold of Christ's power. If His promise does not belong to all, how can they know to whom it does belong? Of course, with this limited understanding they cannot lay hold of the promise by faith.

Another lack in Christians is persistence in waiting upon God for that which He has promised to us in the Scriptures. People give up before they have prevailed, and hence, the enduement of spiritual power is not received.

Of great concern also is the extent to which the Church has practically lost sight of the necessity of the enduement of spiritual power. Much is said about our dependence upon the Holy Spirit by almost everybody, but how little is this dependence realized. Christians and even ministers go to work without any spiritual power. I mourn to be obliged to say that the ranks of the ministry seem to be filling up with those who do not possess spiritual power. May the Lord have mercy upon us! Will this last remark be thought uncharitable? If so, let the current state of the Church and her success in evangelism be heard on this subject. Surely, something is wrong.

Charles Finney

APPLICATION

What is the source of the believer's wisdom and power? What is the believer's true reason for happiness? Take a look at your life. In what do you find happiness? Is spiritual power evident in your life? Pray that God's spirit will be alive in you.

THURSDAY

It Is Good to Show Kindness to Others

Luke 10:30—11:13

Jesus answered, "As a man was going down from Jerusalem to Jericho,
some robbers attacked him. They
tore off his clothes, beat him, and left
him lying there, almost dead. 31 It
happened that a Jewish priest was
going down that road. When he saw
the man, he walked by on the other
side. 32 Next, a Levite came there,
and after he went over and looked at
the man, he walked by on the other
side of the road. 33 Then a Samaritan
traveling down the road came to
where the hurt man was. When he
saw the man, he felt very sorry for
him. 34 The Samaritan went to him,
poured olive oil and wine on his
wounds, and bandaged them. Then
he put the hurt man on his own donkey and took him to an inn where he
cared for him. 35 The next day, the
Samaritan brought out two coins,
gave them to the innkeeper, and
said, 'Take care of this man. If you
spend more money on him, I will pay
it back to you when I come again.'"
36 Then Jesus said, "Which one of
these three men do you think was a
neighbor to the man who was attacked by the robbers?"
37 The expert on the law answered,
"The one who showed him mercy."
Jesus said to him, "Then go and
do what he did."

Mary and Martha

While Jesus and his followers were
traveling, Jesus went into a town. A
woman named Martha let Jesus stay
at her house. 39 Martha had a sister
named Mary, who was sitting at
Jesus' feet and listening to him
teach. 40 But Martha was busy with
all the work to be done. She went in
and said, "Lord, don't you care that
my sister has left me alone to do all
the work? Tell her to help me."
41 But the Lord answered her,
"Martha, Martha, you are worried
and upset about many things. 42 Only
one thing is important. Mary has
chosen the better thing, and it will
never be taken away from her."

Jesus Teaches About Prayer

11 One time Jesus was praying in
a certain place. When he finished, one of his followers said to
him, "Lord, teach us to pray as John
taught his followers."
2 Jesus said to them, "When you
pray, say:
'Father, may your name always be
kept holy.
May your kingdom come.
3 Give us the food we need for each
day.
4 Forgive us for our sins,
because we forgive everyone
who has done wrong to us.
And do not cause us to be
tempted.'"

Continue to Ask

Then Jesus said to them, "Suppose
one of you went to your friend's
house at midnight and said to him,
'Friend, loan me three loaves of
bread. 6 A friend of mine has come
into town to visit me, but I have nothing for him to eat.' 7 Your friend inside the house answers, 'Don't
bother me! The door is already

locked, and my children and I are in bed. I cannot get up and give you anything.' [8] I tell you, if friendship is not enough to make him get up to give you the bread, your boldness will make him get up and give you whatever you need. [9] So I tell you, ask, and God will give to you. Search, and you will find. Knock, and the door will open for you. [10] Yes, everyone who asks will receive. The one who searches will find. And everyone who knocks will have the door opened. [11] If your children ask for a fish, which of you would give them a snake instead? [12] Or, if your children ask for an egg, would you give them a scorpion? [13] Even though you are bad, you know how to give good things to your children. How much more your heavenly Father will give the Holy Spirit to those who ask him!"

OLD TESTAMENT READING

Whenever you are able,
do good to people who need help.
[28] If you have what your neighbor asks for,
don't say, "Come back later.
I will give it to you tomorrow."

Proverbs 3:27–28

INSIGHTS

Kindness is a sincere desire for the happiness of others; goodness is the activity calculated to advance that happiness. . . .

. . . The New Testament has much to say about the kindness of God. The first mention is in Luke 6: Jesus says that God "is kind to the ungrateful and wicked." Next we find that God's kindness leads sinners toward repentance (Romans 2:4). In Ephesians 2:7, in the context of our utter lostness and sin, Paul speaks of the incomparable riches of God's grace, expressed in his kindness to us in Christ Jesus. . . .

What lesson can we draw from these accounts of the kindness of God? He is kind to all men—the ungrateful, the wicked, the utterly lost and hopeless, the rebellious—without distinction. . . .

Our natural inclination is to show kindness only to those for whom we have some natural affinity—family, friends, likable neighbors. But God shows kindness to those who are most despicable—the ungrateful and wicked. Have you ever tried to be kind to someone who was ungrateful? Unless God's grace was working in your heart in a significant way, your reaction to his ingratitude may well have been, "I'll never do anything for him again!" But God doesn't turn his back on the ungrateful. . . .

We need to develop a kind disposition, to be sensitive to others and truly desire their happiness. But sensitivity alone is not enough: the grace of goodness impels us to take action to meet those needs.

Jerry Bridges

ACTION POINT

Think about contemporary parallels to the story of the good Samaritan that show what it means for you to do good to anyone who needs help even when it is inconvenient or unpleasant. Diligently pray that you will seek ways to express God's kindness.

FRIDAY

Focus Your Eyes on the Things of God

Luke 11:14–36

Jesus' Power Is from God

One time Jesus was sending out a
demon that could not talk. When the
demon came out, the man who had
been unable to speak, then spoke. The
people were amazed. 15 But some of
them said, "Jesus uses the power of
Beelzebul, the ruler of demons, to
force demons out of people."
16 Other people, wanting to test
Jesus, asked him to give them a sign
from heaven. 17 But knowing their
thoughts, he said to them, "Every
kingdom that is divided against itself
will be destroyed. And a family that
is divided against itself will not continue. 18 So if Satan is divided against
himself, his kingdom will not continue. You say that I use the power
of Beelzebul to force out demons.
19 But if I use the power of Beelzebul
to force out demons, what power do
your people use to force demons
out? So they will be your judges.
20 But if I use the power of God to
force out demons, then the kingdom
of God has come to you.
21 "When a strong person with
many weapons guards his own
house, his possessions are safe.
22 But when someone stronger
comes and defeats him, the stronger
one will take away the weapons the
first man trusted and will give away
the possessions.
23 "Anyone who is not with me is
against me, and anyone who does not
work with me is working against me.

The Empty Person

When an evil spirit comes out of a
person, it travels through dry places,
looking for a place to rest. But when
it finds no place, it says, 'I will go
back to the house I left.' 25 And when
it comes back, it finds that house
swept clean and made neat. 26 Then
the evil spirit goes out and brings
seven other spirits more evil than it
is, and they go in and live there. So
the person has even more trouble
than before."

People Who Are Truly Happy

As Jesus was saying these things,
a woman in the crowd called out to
Jesus, "Happy is the mother who
gave birth to you and nursed you."
28 But Jesus said, "No, happy are
those who hear the teaching of God
and obey it."

The People Want a Miracle

As the crowd grew larger, Jesus
said, "The people who live today are
evil. They want to see a miracle for
a sign, but no sign will be given
them, except the sign of Jonah. 30 As
Jonah was a sign for those people
who lived in Nineveh, the Son of
Man will be a sign for the people of
this time. 31 On the Judgment Day
the Queen of the South will stand up
with the people who live now. She
will show they are guilty, because
she came from far away to listen to
Solomon's wise teaching. And I tell
you that someone greater than
Solomon is here. 32 On the Judgment
Day the people of Nineveh will stand

up with the people who live now, and
they will show that you are guilty.
When Jonah preached to them, they
were sorry and changed their lives.
And I tell you that someone greater
than Jonah is here.

Be a Light for the World

No one lights a lamp and puts it in
a secret place or under a bowl, but on
a lampstand so the people who come
in can see. 34 Your eye is a light for
the body. When your eyes are good,
your whole body will be full of light.
But when your eyes are evil, your
whole body will be full of darkness.
35 So be careful not to let the light in
you become darkness. 36 If your
whole body is full of light, and none
of it is dark, then you will shine bright,
as when a lamp shines on you."

OLD TESTAMENT READING

Keep your eyes focused on what
    is right,
  and look straight ahead to
    what is good.
26 Be careful what you do,
  and always do what is right.
27 Don't turn off the road of good-
    ness;
  keep away from evil paths.

Proverbs 4:25–27

INSIGHTS

The nature of the Christian life is Christ's life taking hold upon all the inner life of a man, changing, dominating, pulsating. It is seen therefore, and I do not think we can be too careful in emphasizing this, that Christian life is neither human imitation of Christ, nor correct intellectual positions concerning Christ. Neither is it a cult, or a system of thought. I may attempt to imitate Christ sincerely through long years, and yet never be a Christian. I may hold absolutely correct intellectual views concerning Christ as a person, and His power, and yet never be a Christian. It is possible for me to admire Him, and attempt with all the power of my life to imitate Him, and yet never realize Him. It is quite possible for a person to believe most sincerely in His Deity, and in the fact of His atoning work, and moreover, in the necessity for regeneration, and yet never be submitted to His Lordship, never to have personal share in the work of His atonement, never to be born again.

Nothing short of the coming into life of the individual of Christ Himself constitutes a Christian. If Jesus Christ is external to your life there will be times when the world will not see Him and hear Him, and will not know you belong to Him. But if Christ be in you, living, reigning there absolutely, and you are obeying Him, there never will be a moment when the truth will not be evident. You cannot hide Christ if once He comes within. If the light is there, it simply must shine.

G. Campbell Morgan

APPLICATION

What happens when a person focuses his or her eyes on the good things of God? Is your body filled with the light of Christ? What practical reminder will help you keep your eyes focused on God?

WEEKEND

Trust God; Don't Fear People

Luke 11:37—12:7

Jesus Accuses the Pharisees

After Jesus had finished speaking,
a Pharisee asked Jesus to eat with
him. So Jesus went in and sat at the
table. 38 But the Pharisee was surprised when he saw that Jesus did
not wash his hands before the meal.
39 The Lord said to him, "You Pharisees clean the outside of the cup and
the dish, but inside you are full of
greed and evil. 40 You foolish people!
The same one who made what is
outside also made what is inside.
41 So give what is in your dishes to
the poor, and then you will be fully
clean. 42 How terrible for you Pharisees! You give God one-tenth of even
your mint, your rue, and every other
plant in your garden. But you fail to
be fair to others and to love God.
These are the things you should do
while continuing to do those other
things. 43 How terrible for you Pharisees, because you love to have the
most important seats in the synagogues, and you love to be greeted
with respect in the marketplaces.
44 How terrible for you, because you
are like hidden graves, which people
walk on without knowing."

Jesus Talks to Experts on the Law

One of the experts on the law said
to Jesus, "Teacher, when you say
these things, you are insulting us,
too."
46 Jesus answered, "How terrible
for you, you experts on the law! You
make strict rules that are very hard
for people to obey, but you yourselves don't even try to follow those
rules. 47 How terrible for you, because you build tombs for the prophets whom your ancestors killed!
48 And now you show that you approve of what your ancestors did.
They killed the prophets, and you
build tombs for them! 49 This is why
in his wisdom God said, 'I will send
prophets and apostles to them. They
will kill some, and they will treat others cruelly.' 50 So you who live now
will be punished for the deaths of all
the prophets who were killed since
the beginning of the world—51 from
the killing of Abel to the killing of
Zechariah, who died between the altar and the Temple. Yes, I tell you
that you who are alive now will be
punished for them all.
52 "How terrible for you, you experts on the law. You have taken away
the key to learning about God. You
yourselves would not learn, and you
stopped others from learning, too."
53 When Jesus left, the teachers of
the law and the Pharisees began to
give him trouble, asking him questions about many things, 54 trying to
catch him saying something wrong.

Don't Be Like the Pharisees

12 So many thousands of people
had gathered that they were
stepping on each other. Jesus spoke
first to his followers, saying, "Beware
of the yeast of the Pharisees, because they are hypocrites. 2 Everything that is hidden will be shown,
and everything that is secret will be
made known. 3 What you have said
in the dark will be heard in the light,

and what you have whispered in an inner room will be shouted from the housetops.

4 "I tell you, my friends, don't be afraid of people who can kill the body but after that can do nothing more to hurt you. 5 I will show you the one to fear. Fear the one who has the power to kill you and also to throw you into hell. Yes, this is the one you should fear.

6 "Five sparrows are sold for only two pennies, and God does not forget any of them. 7 But God even knows how many hairs you have on your head. Don't be afraid. You are worth much more than many sparrows."

OLD TESTAMENT READING

The LORD says, "I am the one
who comforts you.
So why should you be afraid of
people, who die?
Why should you fear people
who die like the grass?
13 Have you forgotten the LORD who
made you,
who stretched out the skies
and made the earth?"

Isaiah 51:12–13a

INSIGHTS

Many of us have lost the fear of the Lord. We have forgotten our deep awe for the character of God, His holiness, His eternality, His sovereignty over all the affairs of men. We let Him get smaller. We let our impression of ourselves get bigger. We see ourselves as larger in intellect and capabilities, as more technologically advanced and more scientific. As we prosper, we don't need God as we once did.

What is the fear of the Lord? And how can we get it into our lives? The fear of the Lord is to love what God loves and to hate what God hates. The fear of the Lord is both positive and negative. . . .

The positive is to love what God loves—wisdom. God loves wisdom. The fear of the Lord is to love wisdom. "My son, if you accept my words and store up my commands within you, turning your ear to wisdom and applying your heart to understanding . . . then you will understand the fear of the Lord and find the knowledge of God. For the Lord gives wisdom." (Proverbs 2:1–2, 5–6). . . .

The negative is to hate what God hates—evil. God hates evil. "To fear the Lord is to hate evil." (Proverbs 8:13). "Through the fear of the Lord a man avoids evil" (Proverbs 16:6). "To shun evil is understanding" (Job 28:28). The person who would understand the fear of the Lord will hate what God hates. God hates evil, so he will hate evil. . . .

The person gripped by godly fear cannot tolerate evil because God does not tolerate evil. He hates evil with the intensity that God hates evil, or at least he tries to. He is a reformer, not a recluse. His hatred of evil sanctions him no occasion to tolerate.

Patrick Morley

PAUSE FOR REFLECTION

What kind of fear of God did Jesus tell the Pharisees and teachers of the law they should have? In your own words, describe the two kinds of fear that those who trust the Lord should have.

MONDAY

Where Is Your Treasure?

Luke 12:8–34

Don't Be Ashamed of Jesus

I tell you, all those who stand before others and say they believe in me, I, the Son of Man, will say before the angels of God that they belong to me. 9 But all who stand before others and say they do not believe in me, I will say before the angels of God that they do not belong to me.

10 "Anyone who speaks against the Son of Man can be forgiven, but anyone who speaks against the Holy Spirit will not be forgiven.

11 "When you are brought into the synagogues before the leaders and other powerful people, don't worry about how to defend yourself or what to say. 12 At that time the Holy Spirit will teach you what you must say."

Jesus Warns Against Selfishness

Someone in the crowd said to Jesus, "Teacher, tell my brother to divide with me the property our father left us."

14 But Jesus said to him, "Who said I should judge or decide between you?" 15 Then Jesus said to them, "Be careful and guard against all kinds of greed. Life is not measured by how much one owns."

16 Then Jesus told this story: "There was a rich man who had some land, which grew a good crop. 17 He thought to himself, 'What will I do? I have no place to keep all my crops.' 18 Then he said, 'This is what I will do: I will tear down my barns and build bigger ones, and there I will store all my grain and other goods. 19 Then I can say to myself, "I have enough good things stored to last for many years. Rest, eat, drink, and enjoy life!"'

20 "But God said to him, 'Foolish man! Tonight your life will be taken from you. So who will get those things you have prepared for yourself?'

21 "This is how it will be for those who store up things for themselves and are not rich toward God."

Don't Worry

Jesus said to his followers, "So I tell you, don't worry about the food you need to live, or about the clothes you need for your body. 23 Life is more than food, and the body is more than clothes. 24 Look at the birds. They don't plant or harvest, they don't have storerooms or barns, but God feeds them. And you are worth much more than birds. 25 You cannot add any time to your life by worrying about it. 26 If you cannot do even the little things, then why worry about the big things? 27 Consider how the lilies grow; they don't work or make clothes for themselves. But I tell you that even Solomon with his riches was not dressed as beautifully as one of these flowers. 28 God clothes the grass in the field, which is alive today but tomorrow is thrown into the fire. So how much more will God clothe you? Don't have so little faith! 29 Don't always think about what you will eat or what you will drink, and don't keep worrying. 30 All the people in the world are trying to get these things, and your Father knows you need them. 31 But seek God's kingdom, and all the other things you need will be given to you.

Don't Trust in Money

Don't fear, little flock, because your Father wants to give you the kingdom. 33 Sell your possessions and give to the poor. Get for yourselves purses that will not wear out, the treasure in heaven that never runs out, where thieves can't steal and moths can't destroy. 34 Your heart will be where your treasure is."

OLD TESTAMENT READING

Whoever loves money
 will never have enough money;
Whoever loves wealth
 will not be satisfied with it.
 This is also useless.
11 The more wealth people have,
 the more friends they have to
 help spend it.
So what do people really gain?
 They gain nothing except to
 look at their riches.

Ecclesiastes 5:10–11

INSIGHTS

Constantly the Bible deals decisively with the inner spirit of slavery that an idolatrous attachment to wealth brings. "If riches increase, set not your heart on them," counsels the psalmist (Ps. 62:10). . . .

. . . Jesus . . . saw the grip that wealth can have on a person. He knew that "where your treasure is, there will your heart be also," which is precisely why he commanded his followers: "Do not lay up for yourselves treasures on earth" (Matt. 6:21, 19). He is not saying that the heart should or should not be where the treasure is. He is stating the plain fact that wherever you find the treasure, you will find the heart.

He exhorted the rich young ruler not just to have an inner attitude of detachment from his possessions, but literally to get rid of his possessions if he wanted the kingdom of God (Matt. 19:16–22). . . . He counseled people who came seeking God, "Sell your possessions, and give alms; provide yourselves with purses that do not grow old, with a treasure in the heavens that does not fail . . ." (Luke 12:33). He told the parable of the rich farmer whose life centered in hoarding—we would call him prudent; Jesus called him a fool (Luke 12:16–21). He states that if we really want the kingdom of God we must, like a merchant in search of fine pearls, be willing to sell everything we have to get it (Matt. 13:45, 46). He calls all who would follow him to a joyful life of carefree unconcern for possessions: "Give to every one who begs from you; and of him who takes away your goods do not ask them again" (Luke 6:30).

Richard Foster

PAUSE FOR REFLECTION

What things does God say are important in life? What causes people to be greedy? What necessities are we to trust God to provide? Why is it important for those who follow Christ to guard against greed?

TUESDAY

Live a Godly Life While You Wait for Christ's Return

Luke 12:35–56

Always Be Ready

*B*e dressed, ready for service, and have your lamps shining. 36 Be like servants who are waiting for their master to come home from a wedding party. When he comes and knocks, the servants immediately open the door for him. 37 They will be blessed when their master comes home, because he sees that they were watching for him. I tell you the truth, the master will dress himself to serve and tell the servants to sit at the table, and he will serve them. 38 Those servants will be happy when he comes in and finds them still waiting, even if it is midnight or later.

39 "Remember this: If the owner of the house knew what time a thief was coming, he would not allow the thief to enter his house. 40 So you also must be ready, because the Son of Man will come at a time when you don't expect him!"

Who Is the Trusted Servant?

*P*eter said, "Lord, did you tell this story to us or to all people?"

42 The Lord said, "Who is the wise and trusted servant that the master trusts to give the other servants their food at the right time? 43 When the master comes and finds the servant doing his work, the servant will be blessed. 44 I tell you the truth, the master will choose that servant to take care of everything he owns. 45 But suppose the servant thinks to himself, 'My master will not come back soon,' and he begins to beat the other servants, men and women, and to eat and drink and get drunk. 46 The master will come when that servant is not ready and is not expecting him. Then the master will cut him in pieces and send him away to be with the others who don't obey.

47 "The servant who knows what his master wants but is not ready, or who does not do what the master wants, will be beaten with many blows! 48 But the servant who does not know what his master wants and does things that should be punished will be beaten with few blows. From everyone who has been given much, much will be demanded. And from the one trusted with much, much more will be expected.

Jesus Causes Division

I came to set fire to the world, and I wish it were already burning! 50 I have a baptism to suffer through, and I feel very troubled until it is over. 51 Do you think I came to give peace to the earth? No, I tell you, I came to divide it. 52 From now on, a family with five people will be divided, three against two, and two against three. 53 They will be divided: father against son and son against father, mother against daughter and daughter against mother, mother-in-law against daughter-in-law and daughter-in-law against mother-in-law."

Understanding the Times

*T*hen Jesus said to the people, "When you see clouds coming up in

the west, you say, 'It's going to rain,'
and it happens. 55 When you feel the
wind begin to blow from the south,
you say, 'It will be a hot day,' and it
happens. 56 Hypocrites! You know
how to understand the appearance
of the earth and sky. Why don't you
understand what is happening now?"

OLD TESTAMENT READING

The earth belongs to the LORD,
and everything in it—
the world and all its people.
2 He built it on the waters
and set it on the rivers.

3 Who may go up on the mountain
of the LORD?
Who may stand in his holy
Temple?
4 Only those with clean hands and
pure hearts,
who have not worshiped idols,
who have not made promises
in the name of a false god.
5 They will receive a blessing from
the LORD;
the God who saves them will
declare them right.
6 They try to follow God;
they look to the God of Jacob
for help. *Selah*

Psalm 24:1–6

INSIGHTS

The last message the risen Christ gave his people was the promise of his soon return. Couple this with Paul's admonition to the Thessalonian Christians and you get a good rule for life: Live both expectantly and patiently, and you will be fulfilling the Lord's will until he returns.

What are some of the blessings awaiting the believer when Jesus Christ comes back? First of all, the faithful ones can confidently expect to be rewarded for their faithfulness. . . .

There is also a clear-cut promise of reward to the obedient Christian. . . .

But in addition to waiting expectantly, we are also admonished to wait patiently, to "occupy 'til he comes." And while we are waiting, we are to be yielded to the "love of God" operative in our lives. If the love of God flows through us, we will find ourselves sharing that love with those around us, for God is love, and that love is bigger than its container, the Christian, so it must overflow. Those around us long for love, for our world is full of hate, Satan's legacy since the Garden of Eden episode. Let us as Christians share God's love as we await the return of his Son from heaven.

Al Bryant

PAUSE FOR REFLECTION

What warnings does Jesus give to servants who are not ready for his return? What does he promise to those who are ready? What must your life be like in order to obey Jesus' words, "Be dressed, ready for service, and have your lamps shining"?

WEDNESDAY

Produce Good Fruit or Be Destroyed

Luke 12:57—13:21

Settle Your Problems

Why can't you decide for yourselves what is right? [58] If your enemy is taking you to court, try hard to settle it on the way. If you don't, your enemy might take you to the judge, and the judge might turn you over to the officer, and the officer might throw you into jail. [59] I tell you, you will not get out of there until you have paid everything you owe."

Change Your Hearts

13 At that time some people were there who told Jesus that Pilate had killed some people from Galilee while they were worshiping. He mixed their blood with the blood of the animals they were sacrificing to God. [2] Jesus answered, "Do you think this happened to them because they were more sinful than all others from Galilee? [3] No, I tell you. But unless you change your hearts and lives, you will be destroyed as they were! [4] What about those eighteen people who died when the tower of Siloam fell on them? Do you think they were more sinful than all the others who live in Jerusalem? [5] No, I tell you. But unless you change your hearts and lives, you will all be destroyed too!"

The Useless Tree

Jesus told this story: "A man had a fig tree planted in his vineyard. He came looking for some fruit on the tree, but he found none. [7] So the man said to his gardener, 'I have been looking for fruit on this tree for three years, but I never find any. Cut it down. Why should it waste the ground?' [8] But the servant answered, 'Master, let the tree have one more year to produce fruit. Let me dig up the dirt around it and put on some fertilizer. [9] If the tree produces fruit next year, good. But if not, you can cut it down.'"

Jesus Heals on the Sabbath

Jesus was teaching in one of the synagogues on the Sabbath day. [11] A woman was there who, for eighteen years, had an evil spirit in her that made her crippled. Her back was always bent; she could not stand up straight. [12] When Jesus saw her, he called her over and said, "Woman, you are free from your sickness." [13] Jesus put his hands on her, and immediately she was able to stand up straight and began praising God.

[14] The synagogue leader was angry because Jesus healed on the Sabbath day. He said to the people, "There are six days when one has to work. So come to be healed on one of those days, and not on the Sabbath day."

[15] The Lord answered, "You hypocrites! Doesn't each of you untie your work animals and lead them to drink water every day—even on the Sabbath day? [16] This woman that I healed, a daughter of Abraham, has been held by Satan for eighteen years. Surely it is not wrong for her to be freed from her sickness on a Sabbath day!" [17] When Jesus said this, all of those who were criticizing him were ashamed, but the

entire crowd rejoiced at all the wonderful things Jesus was doing.

Stories of Mustard Seed and Yeast

Then Jesus said, "What is God's kingdom like? What can I compare it with? 19 It is like a mustard seed that a man plants in his garden. The seed grows and becomes a tree, and the wild birds build nests in its branches."

20 Jesus said again, "What can I
compare God's kingdom with? 21 It
is like yeast that a woman took and hid in a large tub of flour until it made all the dough rise."

OLD TESTAMENT READING

The vineyard belonging to the
LORD All-Powerful
is the nation of Israel;
the garden that he loves
is the people of Judah.
He looked for justice, but there
was only killing.
He hoped for right living, but
there were only cries of
pain.

15 So the common people and the
great people will be brought
down;
those who are proud will be
humbled.
16 The LORD All-Powerful will
receive glory by judging
fairly;
the holy God will show himself
holy by doing what is right.

Isaiah 5:7, 15–16

INSIGHTS

We all know what fruit is. The produce of the branch, by which men are refreshed and nourished. The fruit is not for the branch, but for those who come to carry it away. As soon as the fruit is ripe, the branch gives it off, to commence afresh its work of beneficence, and anew prepare its fruit for another season. A fruit-bearing tree lives not for itself, but wholly for those to whom its fruit brings refreshment and life. And so the branch exists only and entirely for the sake of the fruit. To make glad the heart of the husbandman is its object, its safety, and its glory.

Beautiful image of the believer, abiding in Christ! He not only grows in strength, the union with the vine becoming ever surer and firmer, he also bears fruit, yea, much fruit. He has the power to offer that to others of which they can eat and live. Amid all who surround him he becomes like a tree of life, of which they can taste and be refreshed. He is in his circle a centre of life and of blessing, and that simply because he abides in Christ, and receives from Him the Spirit and the life of which he can impart to others. Learn thus, if you would bless others, to abide in Christ, and that if you do abide, you shall surely bless.

Andrew Murray

APPLICATION

What result did Christ's healing work have on the people? Does he expect anything less from those who follow him? What does he do to nurture his people so they will bear good fruit? What does he promise if they don't? Are you bearing the fruit Christ has prepared you to bear?

THURSDAY

Pride Leads to Dishonor

Luke 13:22—14:14

The Narrow Door

Jesus was teaching in every town and
village as he traveled toward Jerusalem. 23 Someone said to Jesus, "Lord,
will only a few people be saved?"
Jesus said, 24 "Try hard to enter
through the narrow door, because
many people will try to enter there,
but they will not be able. 25 When the
owner of the house gets up and closes
the door, you can stand outside and
knock on the door and say, 'Sir, open
the door for us.' But he will answer, 'I
don't know you or where you come
from.' 26 Then you will say, 'We ate and
drank with you, and you taught in the
streets of our town.' 27 But he will say
to you, 'I don't know you or where you
come from. Go away from me, all you
who do evil!' 28 You will cry and grind
your teeth with pain when you see
Abraham, Isaac, Jacob, and all the
prophets in God's kingdom, but you
yourselves thrown outside. 29 People
will come from the east, west, north,
and south and will sit down at the table
in the kingdom of God. 30 There are
those who have the lowest place in life
now who will have the highest place
in the future. And there are those who
have the highest place now who will
have the lowest place in the future."

Jesus Will Die in Jerusalem

At that time some Pharisees came
to Jesus and said, "Go away from here!
Herod wants to kill you!"
32 Jesus said to them, "Go tell that
fox Herod, 'Today and tomorrow I
am forcing demons out and healing
people. Then, on the third day, I will
reach my goal.' 33 Yet I must be on
my way today and tomorrow and the
next day. Surely it cannot be right for
a prophet to be killed anywhere except in Jerusalem.
34 "Jerusalem, Jerusalem! You kill
the prophets and stone to death
those who are sent to you. Many
times I wanted to gather your people
as a hen gathers her chicks under
her wings, but you would not let me.
35 Now your house is left completely
empty. I tell you, you will not see me
until that time when you will say,
'God bless the One who comes in
the name of the Lord.'"

Healing on the Sabbath

14 On a Sabbath day, when Jesus
went to eat at the home of a leading
Pharisee, the people were watching
Jesus very closely. 2 And in front of
him was a man with dropsy. 3 Jesus
said to the Pharisees and experts on
the law, "Is it right or wrong to heal
on the Sabbath day?" 4 But they would
not answer his question. So Jesus took
the man, healed him, and sent him
away. 5 Jesus said to the Pharisees and
teachers of the law, "If your child or
ox falls into a well on the Sabbath day,
will you not pull him out quickly?"
6 And they could not answer him.

Don't Make Yourself Important

When Jesus noticed that some of
the guests were choosing the best
places to sit, he told this story:
8 "When someone invites you to a
wedding feast, don't take the most
important seat, because someone
more important than you may have

been invited. 9 The host, who invited both of you, will come to you and say, 'Give this person your seat.' Then you will be embarrassed and will have to move to the last place. 10 So when you are invited, go sit in a seat that is not important. When the host comes to you, he may say, 'Friend, move up here to a more important place.' Then all the other guests will respect you. 11 All who make themselves great will be made humble, but those who make themselves humble will be made great."

You Will Be Rewarded

Then Jesus said to the man who had invited him, "When you give a lunch or a dinner, don't invite only your friends, your family, your other relatives, and your rich neighbors. At another time they will invite you to eat with them, and you will be repaid. 13 Instead, when you give a feast, invite the poor, the crippled, the lame, and the blind. 14 Then you will be blessed, because they have nothing and cannot pay you back. But you will be repaid when the good people rise from the dead."

OLD TESTAMENT READING

Proud people will be ruined,
but the humble will be honored.
Proverbs 18:12

The LORD laughs at those who
laugh at him,
but he gives grace to those
who are not proud.
Proverbs 3:34

INSIGHTS

God does not denigrate pride in its positive sense. The Bible has a hundred ways to illustrate the quiet feeling of competence that lies behind one's ability to do what he knows he has to do and can do. The apostle Paul's ministry was grounded on the assurance that Christ would help him finish what he had started. If that is what is meant by pride, we should certainly cultivate it and thank God for it. . . .

Pride in the dictionary sense of conceited and overbearing behavior . . . brings out the worst in antisocial relationships. Such pride is not the answer to the human problem; it is the human problem. . . . All of the major transgressions to inflict woe upon the human race—fear, greed, avarice, cruelty, lust, unbelief—can be traced to runaway pride. . . .

As to whether or not our pride is sin, the answer ultimately rests with each of us. The Christian knows the condition of his own heart. He measures it by the Word of God. Is he at peace? Is his conscience clear? Is he filled with the Spirit? . . . Then his personal life should reflect the modest, open, worshipful, loving stance of a humble creature of God who has been in the presence of his Creator.

Sherwood Wirt

PAUSE FOR REFLECTION

Why do you think Jesus spoke out against the seemingly mild form of pride he saw at the Pharisee's dinner? Why does God so detest pride? Why is humility necessary in the lives of those who belong to God? How does God honor humility?

FRIDAY

Count the Cost of Serving Christ

Luke 14:15—15:10

A Story About a Big Banquet

One of those at the table with Jesus heard these things and said to him, "Happy are the people who will share in the meal in God's kingdom."

[16] Jesus said to him, "A man gave a big banquet and invited many people. [17] When it was time to eat, the man sent his servant to tell the guests, 'Come. Everything is ready.'

[18] "But all the guests made excuses. The first one said, 'I have just bought a field, and I must go look at it. Please excuse me.' [19] Another said, 'I have just bought five pairs of oxen; I must go and try them. Please excuse me.' [20] A third person said, 'I just got married; I can't come.' [21] So the servant returned and told his master what had happened. Then the master became angry and said, 'Go at once into the streets and alleys of the town, and bring in the poor, the crippled, the blind, and the lame.' [22] Later the servant said to him, 'Master, I did what you commanded, but we still have room.' [23] The master said to the servant, 'Go out to the roads and country lanes, and urge the people there to come so my house will be full. [24] I tell you, none of those whom I invited first will eat with me.'"

The Cost of Being Jesus' Follower

Large crowds were traveling with Jesus, and he turned and said to them, [26] "If anyone comes to me but loves his father, mother, wife, children, brothers, or sisters—or even life—more than me, he cannot be my follower. [27] Whoever is not willing to carry the cross and follow me cannot be my follower. [28] If you want to build a tower, you first sit down and decide how much it will cost, to see if you have enough money to finish the job. [29] If you don't, you might lay the foundation, but you would not be able to finish. Then all who would see it would make fun of you, [30] saying, 'This person began to build but was not able to finish.'

[31] "If a king is going to fight another king, first he will sit down and plan. He will decide if he and his ten thousand soldiers can defeat the other king who has twenty thousand soldiers. [32] If he can't, then while the other king is still far away, he will send some people to speak to him and ask for peace. [33] In the same way, you must give up everything you have to be my follower.

Don't Lose Your Influence

Salt is good, but if it loses its salty taste, you cannot make it salty again. [35] It is no good for the soil or for manure; it is thrown away.

"You people who can hear me, listen."

A Lost Sheep, A Lost Coin

15 The tax collectors and sinners all came to listen to Jesus. [2] But the Pharisees and the teachers of the law began to complain: "Look, this man welcomes sinners and even eats with them."

[3] Then Jesus told them this story: [4] "Suppose one of you has a hundred

sheep but loses one of them. Then
he will leave the other ninety-nine
sheep in the open field and go out
and look for the lost sheep until he
finds it. 5 And when he finds it, he
happily puts it on his shoulders 6 and
goes home. He calls to his friends
and neighbors and says, 'Be happy
with me because I found my lost
sheep.' 7 In the same way, I tell you
there is more joy in heaven over one
sinner who changes his heart and
life, than over ninety-nine good
people who don't need to change.
8 "Suppose a woman has ten silver
coins, but loses one. She will light a
lamp, sweep the house, and look
carefully for the coin until she finds
it. 9 And when she finds it, she will
call her friends and neighbors and
say, 'Be happy with me because I
have found the coin that I lost.' 10 In
the same way, there is joy in the
presence of the angels of God when
one sinner changes his heart and
life."

OLD TESTAMENT READING

Shadrach, Meshach, and Abednego
answered the king, saying, "Nebuchadnezzar, we do not need to defend ourselves to you. 17 If you throw
us into the blazing furnace, the God
we serve is able to save us from the
furnace. He will save us from your
power, O king. 18 But even if God
does not save us, we want you, O
king, to know this: We will not serve
your gods or worship the gold statue
you have set up."

Daniel 3:16–18

INSIGHTS

When Christ said time after time that one must "deny himself and take up his cross and follow me" He was indicating that it is not easy to be His true follower. The apostle Paul warned, "Everyone who wants to live a godly life in Christ Jesus will be persecuted" (2 Timothy 3:12). He offers no cheap grace, no easy life. As someone has said, "Salvation is free but not cheap. . . ."

The Christian faith brings its own "blood, sweat and tears" to those who would follow Jesus Christ. Christ calls us to discipleship. When we come to Him, He takes away one set of burdens—the burden of sin, the burden of guilt, the burden of separation from God, the burden of hopelessness. But He also calls upon us to "Take my yoke upon you and learn from me" (Matthew 11:29). It is not a yoke that is too heavy for us to bear, for Christ bears it with us: "For my yoke is easy and my burden is light" (Matthew 11:30). Nevertheless, Christ calls us to follow Him, regardless of the cost, and He has never promised that our path will always be smooth. . . .

But in the midst of the suffering, trials and temptations, He will provide His peace, joy and fellowship. . . . In the midst of every situation of life He can give an inner calm and strength that you could never imagine apart from Him.

Billy Graham

APPLICATION

What price were Shadrach, Meshach, and Abednego willing to pay to serve God? What might it cost you to serve Christ, given your family or social setting? Are you willing to pay that price?

WEEKEND

God Welcomes All Who Come to Him

Luke 15:11—16:8

The Son Who Left Home

Then Jesus said, "A man had two sons. 12 The younger son said to his father, 'Give me my share of the property.' So the father divided the property between his two sons. 13 Then the younger son gathered up all that was his and traveled far away to another country. There he wasted his money in foolish living. 14 After he had spent everything, a time came when there was no food anywhere in the country, and the son was poor and hungry. 15 So he got a job with one of the citizens there who sent the son into the fields to feed pigs. 16 The son was so hungry that he wanted to eat the pods the pigs were eating, but no one gave him anything. 17 When he realized what he was doing, he thought, 'All of my father's servants have plenty of food. But I am here, almost dying with hunger. 18 I will leave and return to my father and say to him, "Father, I have sinned against God and have done wrong to you. 19 I am no longer worthy to be called your son, but let me be like one of your servants."' 20 So the son left and went to his father.

"While the son was still a long way off, his father saw him and felt sorry for his son. So the father ran to him and hugged and kissed him. 21 The son said, 'Father, I have sinned against God and have done wrong to you. I am no longer worthy to be called your son.' 22 But the father said to his servants, 'Hurry! Bring the best clothes and put them on him. Also, put a ring on his finger and sandals on his feet. 23 And get our fat calf and kill it so we can have a feast and celebrate. 24 My son was dead, but now he is alive again! He was lost, but now he is found!' So they began to celebrate.

25 "The older son was in the field, and as he came closer to the house, he heard the sound of music and dancing. 26 So he called to one of the servants and asked what all this meant. 27 The servant said, 'Your brother has come back, and your father killed the fat calf, because your brother came home safely.' 28 The older son was angry and would not go in to the feast. So his father went out and begged him to come in. 29 But the older son said to his father, 'I have served you like a slave for many years and have always obeyed your commands. But you never gave me even a young goat to have at a feast with my friends. 30 But your other son, who wasted all your money on prostitutes, comes home, and you kill the fat calf for him!' 31 The father said to him, 'Son, you are always with me, and all that I have is yours. 32 We had to celebrate and be happy because your brother was dead, but now he is alive. He was lost, but now he is found.'"

True Wealth

16 Jesus also said to his followers, "Once there was a rich man who had a manager to take care of his business. This manager was accused of cheating him. 2 So he called the manager in and said to him, 'What is this I hear about you? Give me a report of what you have done with my money, because you can't be my manager any longer.' 3 The

manager thought to himself, 'What will I do since my master is taking my job away from me? I am not strong enough to dig ditches, and I am ashamed to beg. [4] I know what I'll do so that when I lose my job people will welcome me into their homes.'

[5] "So the manager called in everyone who owed the master any money. He asked the first one, 'How much do you owe?' [6] He answered, 'Eight hundred gallons of olive oil.' The manager said to him, 'Take your bill, sit down quickly, and write four hundred gallons.' [7] Then the manager asked another one, 'How much do you owe?' He answered, 'One thousand bushels of wheat.' Then the manager said to him, 'Take your bill and write eight hundred bushels.' [8] So, the master praised the dishonest manager for being smart. Yes, worldly people are smarter with their own kind than spiritual people are."

OLD TESTAMENT READING

For example, they may return what somebody gave them as a promise to repay a loan, or pay back what they stole. If they live by the rules that give life and do not sin, then they will surely live, and they will not die."

Ezekiel 33:15

INSIGHTS

Repentance is a rather dramatic word. It refers to the act of traveling in one direction and then suddenly changing to go the opposite way. Both John the Baptizer and Jesus used repentance as the centerpoint of their teaching because they were talking to a generation of people whose personal worlds were terribly broken. Yet the people would not face up to the changes necessary to make their worlds come back together again. Stubborn people do not repent very easily, and those people were stubborn.

Repentance is activated, first, in the act of confession: the candid acknowledgment before God, and perhaps to others, that one has sinned and is in need of forgiveness. Both by example and by teaching, the Scriptures place a high priority on confessing, for in so doing, one actually reveals the secrets of the heart. And until the heart is voluntarily opened up, the process of rebuilding a broken world cannot begin. . . .

. . . Restoration looks to the damage done in a broken-world experience and asks how it can be repaired. Broken relationships must be examined and, if possible, glued back together again. Forgiveness must be requested and granted, and that requires people to come together and offer mercy and grace to one another. These are not simple or easy things to give . . .

But restoration is one of the unique acts of the Christian community. In the final analysis, it cannot be demanded or even earned by the broken-world person; it must be freely given as God once freely gave grace to whoever wished to receive it.

Gordon MacDonald

PAUSE FOR REFLECTION

What does God want every person to do? What does he promise to those who confess and reject their sins? Is repentance a one-time or ongoing action? How freely do you extend mercy to restore repentant sinners?

MONDAY

God Knows Our Hearts

Luke 16:9—17:4

I tell you, make friends for yourselves using worldly riches so that
when those riches are gone, you will
be welcomed in those homes that
continue forever. 10 Whoever can be
trusted with a little can also be
trusted with a lot, and whoever is
dishonest with a little is dishonest
with a lot. 11 If you cannot be trusted
with worldly riches, then who will
trust you with true riches? 12 And if
you cannot be trusted with things
that belong to someone else, who
will give you things of your own?

13 "No servant can serve two masters. The servant will hate one master and love the other, or will follow
one master and refuse to follow the
other. You cannot serve both God
and worldly riches."

God's Law Cannot Be Changed

The Pharisees, who loved money,
were listening to all these things and
made fun of Jesus. 15 He said to them,
"You make yourselves look good in
front of people, but God knows what
is really in your hearts. What is important to people is hateful in God's
sight.

16 "The law of Moses and the writings of the prophets were preached
until John came. Since then the
Good News about the kingdom of
God is being told, and everyone tries
to enter it by force. 17 It would be
easier for heaven and earth to pass
away than for the smallest part of a
letter in the law to be changed.

Divorce and Remarriage

If a man divorces his wife and marries another woman, he is guilty of
adultery, and the man who marries
a divorced woman is also guilty of
adultery."

The Rich Man and Lazarus

Jesus said, "There was a rich man
who always dressed in the finest
clothes and lived in luxury every
day. 20 And a very poor man named
Lazarus, whose body was covered
with sores, was laid at the rich man's
gate. 21 He wanted to eat only the
small pieces of food that fell from the
rich man's table. And the dogs would
come and lick his sores. 22 Later,
Lazarus died, and the angels carried
him to the arms of Abraham. The
rich man died, too, and was buried.
23 In the place of the dead, he was in
much pain. The rich man saw
Abraham far away with Lazarus at
his side. 24 He called, 'Father
Abraham, have mercy on me! Send
Lazarus to dip his finger in water and
cool my tongue, because I am suffering in this fire!' 25 But Abraham
said, 'Child, remember when you
were alive you had the good things
in life, but bad things happened to
Lazarus. Now he is comforted here,
and you are suffering. 26 Besides,
there is a big pit between you and
us, so no one can cross over to you,
and no one can leave there and come
here.' 27 The rich man said, 'Father,
then please send Lazarus to my
father's house. 28 I have five brothers,
and Lazarus could warn them so that
they will not come to this place of
pain.' 29 But Abraham said, 'They
have the law of Moses and the writings of the prophets; let them learn

from them.' 30 The rich man said,
'No, father Abraham! If someone
goes to them from the dead, they
would believe and change their
hearts and lives.' 31 But Abraham
said to him, 'If they will not listen to
Moses and the prophets, they will
not listen to someone who comes
back from the dead.'"

Sin and Forgiveness

17 Jesus said to his followers,
"Things that cause people to
sin will happen, but how terrible for
the person who causes them to happen! 2 It would be better for you to
be thrown into the sea with a large
stone around your neck than to
cause one of these little ones to sin.
3 So be careful!
"If another follower sins, warn him,
and if he is sorry and stops sinning,
forgive him. 4 If he sins against you
seven times in one day and says that
he is sorry each time, forgive him."

OLD TESTAMENT READING

God, examine me and know my
heart;
test me and know my nervous
thoughts.
24 See if there is any bad thing in
me.
Lead me on the road to
everlasting life.

Psalm 139:23–24

INSIGHTS

Making good judgments in this world is sometimes a hit-and-miss proposition. Often we fail. In baseball, a hitter is constantly trying to guess what the pitcher will throw next. In football, a defensive coach tries to predict where the offense will run next. Basketball coaches continually try to outmaneuver each other. Sometimes they are right, and sometimes they are wrong. We fail because we seldom have all the facts. We have no idea what the other person is thinking. We're looking for a fast ball, and the pitcher throws a curve ball, or we're looking for a pass and they run! . . . We don't know all the facts, we don't know the future, and sometimes we don't even react properly when we do know! But with God, life is not a guessing game. His judgments are sure, because He knows all the facts. God knows everything about us. He knows our thoughts before we think them (Psalm 139:1–6). No one can escape His sight (Psalm 139:7–12). He even judges the thoughts and intentions of our hearts (Hebrews 4:12–13). God's judgment is always perfect, because He knows all the facts. Those who think they are getting away with something may escape our notice, but they will never escape the notice of God. The eyes of the Lord are in every place, watching the evil and the good (Proverbs 15:3). Take comfort, righteous ones, for goodness will be vindicated and evil will be punished!

Elliot Johnson / Al Schierbaum

ACTION POINT

What feelings do you have when you realize that God knows what is in your heart and that he knows it even better than you do? Pray that God's knowledge of you will lead you closer to him. Take comfort that he not only knows you, but loves you! Praise him for his amazing knowledge!

TUESDAY

When God's Judgment Comes, There Will Be No Turning Back

Luke 17:5–37

How Big Is Your Faith?

The apostles said to the Lord, "Give us more faith!"

6 The Lord said, "If your faith were the size of a mustard seed, you could say to this mulberry tree, 'Dig yourself up and plant yourself in the sea,' and it would obey you.

Be Good Servants

Suppose one of you has a servant who has been plowing the ground or caring for the sheep. When the servant comes in from working in the field, would you say, 'Come in and sit down to eat'? 8 No, you would say to him, 'Prepare something for me to eat. Then get yourself ready and serve me. After I finish eating and drinking, you can eat.' 9 The servant does not get any special thanks for doing what his master commanded. 10 It is the same with you. When you have done everything you are told to do, you should say, 'We are unworthy servants; we have only done the work we should do.'"

Be Thankful

While Jesus was on his way to Jerusalem, he was going through the area between Samaria and Galilee. 12 As he came into a small town, ten men who had a skin disease met him there. They did not come close to Jesus 13 but called to him, "Jesus! Master! Have mercy on us!"

14 When Jesus saw the men, he said, "Go and show yourselves to the priests."

As the ten men were going, they were healed. 15 When one of them saw that he was healed, he went back to Jesus, praising God in a loud voice. 16 Then he bowed down at Jesus' feet and thanked him. (And this man was a Samaritan.) 17 Jesus said, "Weren't ten men healed? Where are the other nine? 18 Is this Samaritan the only one who came back to thank God?" 19 Then Jesus said to him, "Stand up and go on your way. You were healed because you believed."

God's Kingdom Is Within You

Some of the Pharisees asked Jesus, "When will the kingdom of God come?"

Jesus answered, "God's kingdom is coming, but not in a way that you will be able to see with your eyes. 21 People will not say, 'Look, here it is!' or, 'There it is!' because God's kingdom is within you."

22 Then Jesus said to his followers, "The time will come when you will want very much to see one of the days of the Son of Man. But you will not see it. 23 People will say to you, 'Look, there he is!' or, 'Look, here he is!' Stay where you are; don't go away and search.

When Jesus Comes Again

When the Son of Man comes again, he will shine like lightning, which flashes across the sky and lights it up from one side to the other. 25 But first he must suffer many things and be

rejected by the people of this time.
26 When the Son of Man comes again,
it will be as it was when Noah lived.
27 People were eating, drinking, marrying, and giving their children to be
married until the day Noah entered
the boat. Then the flood came and
killed them all. 28 It will be the same
as during the time of Lot. People were
eating, drinking, buying, selling, planting, and building. 29 But the day Lot left
Sodom, fire and sulfur rained down
from the sky and killed them all.
30 This is how it will be when the Son
of Man comes again.

31 "On that day, a person who is on
the roof and whose belongings are
in the house should not go inside to
get them. A person who is in the field
should not go back home. 32 Remember Lot's wife. 33 Those who try to
keep their lives will lose them. But
those who give up their lives will
save them. 34 I tell you, on that night
two people will be sleeping in one
bed; one will be taken and the other
will be left. 35 There will be two
women grinding grain together; one
will be taken, and the other will be
left. 36 Two people will be in the field.
One will be taken, and the other will
be left."

37 The followers asked Jesus,
"Where will this be, Lord?"

Jesus answered, "Where there is a dead body, there the vultures will gather."

OLD TESTAMENT READING

The two men said to Lot, "Do you have any other relatives in this city? Do you have any sons-in-law, sons, daughters, or any other relatives? If
you do, tell them to leave now, 13 be-
cause we are about to destroy this city. The LORD has heard of all the evil that is here, so he has sent us to destroy it."

Genesis 19:12–13

INSIGHTS

In John's vision . . . you will get a feeling for the absolute horror of this final judgment for those who do not believe. Picture it. Carefully the Lamb opens the sixth seal (Revelation 6:12–17). Suddenly, chaos grips the universe. An earthquake shakes the entire world, no Richter scale could measure its fury. There is a complete eclipse of the sun. . . .

The world is trembling with terror. The great cities collapse. John sees kings, princes, generals; the rich, the mighty, slave and free—every human being left on the earth running to escape the horror of God's final judgment. They flee to mountain caves. They cower behind rocks and boulders. But there is no escape. Desperately they cry out, "Hide us from the face of him who sits on the throne and from the wrath of the Lamb! For the great day of their wrath has come, and who can stand?" (Revelation 6:16, 17).

There will be a day of reckoning when God closes His books on time and judges every creature, living and dead.

Billy Graham

APPLICATION

When God decides it's time for judgment, is there any room for doubt about what he is doing? Will there be any doubt about his coming judgment? How does Jesus' warning about his coming judgment affect your everyday life?

WEDNESDAY

Trust in God, Not in Pride or Riches

Luke 18:1–25

God Will Answer His People

18 Then Jesus used this story to
teach his followers that they
should always pray and never lose
hope. 2 "In a certain town there was
a judge who did not respect God or
care about people. 3 In that same
town there was a widow who kept
coming to this judge, saying, 'Give
me my rights against my enemy.'
4 For a while the judge refused to
help her. But afterwards, he thought
to himself, 'Even though I don't respect God or care about people, 5 I
will see that she gets her rights. Otherwise she will continue to bother
me until I am worn out.'"
6 The Lord said, "Listen to what
the unfair judge said. 7 God will always give what is right to his people
who cry to him night and day, and
he will not be slow to answer them.
8 I tell you, God will help his people
quickly. But when the Son of Man
comes again, will he find those on
earth who believe in him?"

Being Right with God

Jesus told this story to some people
who thought they were very good
and looked down on everyone else:
10 "A Pharisee and a tax collector
both went to the Temple to pray.
11 The Pharisee stood alone and
prayed, 'God, I thank you that I am
not like other people who steal,
cheat, or take part in adultery, or
even like this tax collector. 12 I give
up eating twice a week, and I give
one-tenth of everything I get!'
13 "The tax collector, standing at
a distance, would not even look up
to heaven. But he beat on his chest
because he was so sad. He said,
'God, have mercy on me, a sinner.'
14 I tell you, when this man went
home, he was right with God, but the
Pharisee was not. All who make
themselves great will be made
humble, but all who make themselves humble will be made great."

Who Will Enter God's Kingdom?

Some people brought even their babies to Jesus so he could touch them.
When the followers saw this, they told
them to stop. 16 But Jesus called for the
children, saying, "Let the little children come to me. Don't stop them,
because the kingdom of God belongs
to people who are like these children.
17 I tell you the truth, you must accept
the kingdom of God as if you were a
child, or you will never enter it."

A Rich Man's Question

A certain leader asked Jesus,
"Good Teacher, what must I do to
have life forever?"
19 Jesus said to him, "Why do you
call me good? Only God is good. 20 You
know the commands: 'You must not
be guilty of adultery. You must not
murder anyone. You must not steal.
You must not tell lies about your neighbor. Honor your father and mother.'"
21 But the leader said, "I have
obeyed all these commands since I
was a boy."
22 When Jesus heard this, he said

to him, "There is still one more thing you need to do. Sell everything you have and give it to the poor, and you will have treasure in heaven. Then come and follow me." 23 But when the man heard this, he became very sad, because he was very rich.
24 Jesus looked at him and said, "It is very hard for rich people to enter the kingdom of God. 25 It is easier for a camel to go through the eye of a needle than for a rich person to enter the kingdom of God."

OLD TESTAMENT READING

This is what the LORD says:
"The wise must not brag about
their wisdom.
The strong must not brag
about their strength.
The rich must not brag about
their money.
24 But if someone wants to brag, let
him brag
that he understands and knows
me."

Jeremiah 9:23–24a

INSIGHTS

To receive what we have as a gift from God is the first inner attitude of simplicity. We work but we know that it is not our work that gives us what we have. We live by grace even when it comes to "daily bread." We are dependent upon God for the simplest elements of life: air, water, sun. What we have is not the result of our labor, but of the gracious care of God. When we are tempted to think that what we own is the result of our personal efforts, it takes only a little drought or a small accident to show us once again how utterly dependent we are for everything.

To know that it is God's business, and not ours, to care for what we have is the second inner attitude of simplicity. God is able to protect what we possess. We can trust him. . . . Obviously, these matters are not restricted to possessions but include such things as our reputation and our employment. Simplicity means the freedom to trust God for these (and all) things.

To have our goods available to others marks the third inner attitude of simplicity. If our goods are not available to the community when it is clearly right and good, then they are stolen goods. . . . We cling to our possessions rather than sharing them because we are anxious about tomorrow. But if we truly believe that God is who Jesus says he is, then we do not need to be afraid. When we come to see God as the almighty Creator and our loving Father, we can share because we know that he will care for us. . . .

When we are seeking first the kingdom of God, these three attitudes will characterize our lives. Taken together they define what Jesus means by "do not be anxious." They comprise the inner reality of Christian simplicity.

Richard Foster

APPLICATION

Can we truly achieve anything for ourselves? What is the next step for you to take in trusting God?

THURSDAY

When God Changes Our Hearts, Our Actions Change, Too

Luke 18:26—19:10

Who Can Be Saved?

When the people heard this, they
asked, "Then who can be saved?"
27 Jesus answered, "God can do
things that are not possible for
people to do."
28 Peter said, "Look, we have left
everything and followed you."
29 Jesus said, "I tell you the truth,
all those who have left houses,
wives, brothers, parents, or children
for the kingdom of God 30 will get
much more in this life. And in the
age that is coming, they will have life
forever."

Jesus Will Rise from the Dead

Then Jesus took the twelve apostles
aside and said to them, "We are going to Jerusalem. Everything the
prophets wrote about the Son of
Man will happen. 32 He will be turned
over to those who are not Jews. They
will laugh at him, insult him, spit on
him, 33 beat him with whips, and kill
him. But on the third day, he will rise
to life again." 34 The apostles did not
understand this; the meaning was
hidden from them, and they did not
realize what was said.

Jesus Heals a Blind Man

As Jesus came near the city of Jericho, a blind man was sitting beside
the road, begging. 36 When he heard
the people coming down the road, he
asked, "What is happening?"
37 They told him, "Jesus, from
Nazareth, is going by."
38 The blind man cried out, "Jesus,
Son of David, have mercy on me!"
39 The people leading the group
warned the blind man to be quiet. But
the blind man shouted even more,
"Son of David, have mercy on me!"
40 Jesus stopped and ordered the
blind man to be brought to him. When
he came near, Jesus asked him,
41 "What do you want me to do for you?"
He said, "Lord, I want to see."
42 Jesus said to him, "Then see. You
are healed because you believed."
43 At once the man was able to see,
and he followed Jesus, thanking
God. All the people who saw this
praised God.

Zacchaeus Meets Jesus

19 Jesus was going through the
city of Jericho. 2 A man was
there named Zacchaeus, who was a
very important tax collector, and he
was wealthy. 3 He wanted to see who
Jesus was, but he was not able because he was too short to see above
the crowd. 4 He ran ahead to a place
where Jesus would come, and he
climbed a sycamore tree so he could
see him. 5 When Jesus came to that
place, he looked up and said to him,
"Zacchaeus, hurry and come down!
I must stay at your house today."
6 Zacchaeus came down quickly
and welcomed him gladly. 7 All the
people saw this and began to complain, "Jesus is staying with a sinner!"
8 But Zacchaeus stood and said to
the Lord, "I will give half of my possessions to the poor. And if I have
cheated anyone, I will pay back four
times more."

[9] Jesus said to him, "Salvation has come to this house today, because this man also belongs to the family of Abraham. [10] The Son of Man came to find lost people and save them."

OLD TESTAMENT READING

After Jonah had entered the city and walked for one day, he preached to the people, saying, "After forty days, Nineveh will be destroyed!"

[5] The people of Nineveh believed God. They announced that they would stop eating for a while, and they put on rough cloth to show their sadness. All the people in the city did this, from the most important to the least important.

[10] When God saw what the people did, that they stopped doing evil, he changed his mind and did not do what he had warned. He did not punish them.

Jonah 3:4–5, 10

When the Passover celebration was finished, all the Israelites in Jerusalem went out to the towns of Judah. There they smashed the stone pillars used to worship gods. They cut down the Asherah idols and destroyed the altars and places for worshiping gods in all of Judah, Benjamin, Ephraim, and Manasseh. After they had destroyed all of them, the Israelites returned to their own towns and homes.

2 Chronicles 31:1

INSIGHTS

True repentance occurs when we begin to see sin from God's point of view—when we see the way our sin has broken his heart. Perhaps the idea that God's heart can be broken by our sin is new to you. In Genesis 6:5–6 we are told, "Then the LORD saw that the wickedness of man was great on the earth, and that every intent of the thoughts of his heart was only evil continually. And the LORD was sorry that he had made man on the earth, and he was grieved in his heart" (NASB). God was so disappointed with what he saw that there was a grief or sorrow in his heart.

Jesus also was brokenhearted as he wept over Jerusalem. "O Jerusalem, Jerusalem, you who kill the prophets and stone those sent to you, how often I have longed to gather your children together, as a hen gathers her chicks under her wings, but you were not willing!" (Lk 13:34). God's heart aches over our sin. It alienates us from him and from our fellow believers.

If we want to have victory over sin and turn our lives wholeheartedly over to God, then we must see our sin from God's perspective. No sermon on hell can ever change a person's heart like seeing the grief sin has brought to the heart of the One who created us. We must ask God to show us what our sin does to him. As we do this and begin to understand his great love for us, despite how much we have hurt and grieved his heart, turning away from that sin is the natural thing to do. This is the test of our sincerity and of the level of our desperation to be right with God.

Floyd McClung

ACTION POINT

Do you think the people mentioned in these passages recognized that their sin grieved God? What in your life grieves God?

FRIDAY

God Will Reward the Righteous and Punish Those Who Don't Serve Him

Luke 19:11–40

A Story About Three Servants

As the people were listening to this, Jesus told them a story because he was near Jerusalem and they thought God's kingdom would appear immediately. 12 He said: "A very important man went to a country far away to be made a king and then to return home. 13 So he called ten of his servants and gave a coin to each servant. He said, 'Do business with this money until I get back.' 14 But the people in the kingdom hated the man. So they sent a group to follow him and say, 'We don't want this man to be our king.'

15 "But the man became king. When he returned home, he said, 'Call those servants who have my money so I can know how much they earned with it.'

16 "The first servant came and said, 'Sir, I earned ten coins with the one you gave me.' 17 The king said to the servant, 'Excellent! You are a good servant. Since I can trust you with small things, I will let you rule over ten of my cities.'

18 "The second servant said, 'Sir, I earned five coins with your one.' 19 The king said to this servant, 'You can rule over five cities.'

20 "Then another servant came in and said to the king, 'Sir, here is your coin which I wrapped in a piece of cloth and hid. 21 I was afraid of you, because you are a hard man. You even take money that you didn't earn and gather food that you didn't plant.' 22 Then the king said to the servant, 'I will condemn you by your own words, you evil servant. You knew that I am a hard man, taking money that I didn't earn and gathering food that I didn't plant. 23 Why then didn't you put my money in the bank? Then when I came back, my money would have earned some interest.'

24 "The king said to the men who were standing by, 'Take the coin away from this servant and give it to the servant who earned ten coins.' 25 They said, 'But sir, that servant already has ten coins.' 26 The king said, 'Those who have will be given more, but those who do not have anything will have everything taken away from them. 27 Now where are my enemies who didn't want me to be king? Bring them here and kill them before me.'"

Jesus Enters Jerusalem as a King

After Jesus said this, he went on toward Jerusalem. 29 As Jesus came near Bethphage and Bethany, towns near the hill called the Mount of Olives, he sent out two of his followers. 30 He said, "Go to the town you can see there. When you enter it, you will find a colt tied there, which no one has ever ridden. Untie it and bring it here to me. 31 If anyone asks you why you are untying it, say that the Master needs it."

32 The two followers went into town and found the colt just as Jesus had told them. 33 As they were untying it, its owners came out and asked the followers, "Why are you untying our colt?"

34 The followers answered, "The Master needs it." 35 So they brought it

to Jesus, threw their coats on the colt's
back, and put Jesus on it. 36 As Jesus
rode toward Jerusalem, others spread
their coats on the road before him.
37 As he was coming close to
Jerusalem, on the way down the
Mount of Olives, the whole crowd of
followers began joyfully shouting
praise to God for all the miracles
they had seen. 38 They said,

"God bless the king who comes
in the name of the Lord!

Psalm 118:26

There is peace in heaven and
glory to God!"

39 Some of the Pharisees in the
crowd said to Jesus, "Teacher, tell
your followers not to say these
things."
40 But Jesus answered, "I tell you,
if my followers didn't say these
things, then the stones would cry
out."

OLD TESTAMENT READING

People will be rewarded for what
they say,
and they will also be rewarded
for what they do.

Proverbs 12:14

Tell those who do what is right
that things will go well for
them,
because they will receive a
reward for what they do.
11 But how terrible it will be for the
wicked!
They will be punished for all
the wrong they have done.

Isaiah 3:10–11

INSIGHTS

How does free forgiveness and justification by faith square with judgment according to works? The answer seems to be as follows. First, the gift of justification certainly shields believers from being condemned and banished from God's presence as sinners. This appears from the vision of judgment in Revelation 20:11–15, where alongside 'the books' recording each man's work 'the book of life' is opened, and those whose names are written there are not 'cast into the lake of fire' as the rest of men are. But, second, the gift of justification does not at all shield believers from being assessed as Christians, and from forfeiting good which others will enjoy if it turns out that as Christians they have been slack, mischievous and destructive. This appears from Paul's warning to the Corinthians to be careful what life-style they build on Christ, the one foundation. 'If any man builds upon this foundation . . . If any man's work abide . . . he shall receive a reward. If any man's work shall be burned, he shall suffer loss: but he himself shall be saved; yet so as by fire' (1 Corinthians 3:12–15). 'Reward' and 'loss' signify an enriched or impoverished relationship with God, though in what ways it is beyond our present power to know.

J. I. Packer

APPLICATION

For what does God punish or reward people? What do you think God expects his servants to do while they wait for his return? What kind of servant do you want to be for your Lord? How can you be a better one?

WEEKEND

God Punishes Sin

Luke 19:41—20:19

Jesus Cries for Jerusalem

As Jesus came near Jerusalem, he
saw the city and cried for it, 42 saying, "I wish you knew today what
would bring you peace. But now it
is hidden from you. 43 The time is
coming when your enemies will
build a wall around you and will hold
you in on all sides. 44 They will destroy you and all your people, and
not one stone will be left on another.
All this will happen because you did
not recognize the time when God
came to save you."

Jesus Goes to the Temple

Jesus went into the Temple and began to throw out the people who
were selling things there. 46 He said,
"It is written in the Scriptures, 'My
Temple will be a house for prayer.'
But you have changed it into a 'hideout for robbers'!"

47 Jesus taught in the Temple every day. The leading priests, the experts on the law, and some of the
leaders of the people wanted to kill
Jesus. 48 But they did not know how
they could do it, because all the
people were listening closely to him.

Jewish Leaders Question Jesus

20 One day Jesus was in the
Temple, teaching the people
and telling them the Good News. The
leading priests, teachers of the law,
and older Jewish leaders came up to
talk with him, 2 saying, "Tell us what
authority you have to do these things?
Who gave you this authority?"

3 Jesus answered, "I will also ask
you a question. Tell me: 4 When John
baptized people, was that authority
from God or just from other people?"

5 They argued about this, saying,
"If we answer, 'John's baptism was
from God,' Jesus will say, 'Then why
did you not believe him?' 6 But if we
say, 'It was from other people,' all the
people will stone us to death, because they believe John was a
prophet." 7 So they answered that
they didn't know where it came
from.

8 Jesus said to them, "Then I
won't tell you what authority I have
to do these things."

A Story About God's Son

Then Jesus told the people this
story: "A man planted a vineyard and
leased it to some farmers. Then he
went away for a long time. 10 When
it was time for the grapes to be
picked, he sent a servant to the farmers to get some of the grapes. But
they beat the servant and sent him
away empty-handed. 11 Then he sent
another servant. They beat this servant also, and showed no respect for
him, and sent him away empty-
handed. 12 So the man sent a third
servant. The farmers wounded him
and threw him out. 13 The owner of
the vineyard said, 'What will I do
now? I will send my son whom I love.
Maybe they will respect him.' 14 But
when the farmers saw the son, they
said to each other, 'This son will inherit the vineyard. If we kill him, it
will be ours.' 15 So the farmers threw
the son out of the vineyard and killed
him.

"What will the owner of this vineyard do to them? 16 He will come and kill those farmers and will give the vineyard to other farmers."

When the people heard this story, they said, "Let this never happen!"

17 But Jesus looked at them and said,

"Then what does this verse mean:

'The stone that the builders
rejected became the
cornerstone'? *Psalm 118:22*

18 Everyone who falls on that stone will be broken, and the person on whom it falls, that person will be crushed!"

19 The teachers of the law and the leading priests wanted to arrest Jesus at once, because they knew the story was about them. But they were afraid of what the people would do.

OLD TESTAMENT READING

Jerusalem, your rulers are like
those of Sodom,
and your people are like those
of Gomorrah.
Hear the word of the LORD;
listen to the teaching of our God!
15b Even if you say many prayers,
I will not listen to you,
because your hands are full of
blood.
16 Wash yourselves and make
yourselves clean.
Stop doing the evil things I see
you do.
Stop doing wrong.

Isaiah 1:10, 15b–16

INSIGHTS

Jesus did not come to change Israel's politics, He came to change men's hearts. When He rode into Jerusalem, Jesus presented Himself as a humble king, not a violent conqueror. Led by the spiritually blind rulers, the nation rejected Him and said, "We have no king but Caesar!"

What were the consequences of this rebellion? In a few years, Jerusalem was reduced to shambles by the Roman armies and the temple was destroyed. The Jewish nation was dispersed across the face of the earth to wander "many days, without a king, and without a prince" (Hosea 3:4).

But there is a much wider application. When the Lord returns, He will have to punish those who will not bow before Him and submit to His will. . . .

Sad to say, most of the people in our world want nothing to do with Jesus Christ. "There is none that understandeth, there is none that seeketh after God" (Rom. 3:11). But God is seeking after men! "For the Son of man is come to seek and to save that which was lost." . . .

When the Lord returns, it will mean reward for the faithful, loss of reward for the unfaithful, and terrible judgment for the unbelieving, rebellious people who rejected Him. . . (2 Thes. 1:8–9).

Warren Wiersbe

APPLICATION

Jerusalem is identified in Scripture as God's holy city. For what reasons did Jesus weep over it? In a broader sense, what does this scene reveal about how Jesus views sin? Does Jesus weep or rejoice over the condition of your heart?

MONDAY

Jesus Warns Against False Religious Leaders

Luke 20:20–47

Is It Right to Pay Taxes or Not?

So they watched Jesus and sent some spies who acted as if they were sincere. They wanted to trap Jesus in saying something wrong so they could hand him over to the authority and power of the governor. 21 So the spies asked Jesus, "Teacher, we know that what you say and teach is true. You pay no attention to who people are, and you always teach the truth about God's way. 22 Tell us, is it right for us to pay taxes to Caesar or not?"

23 But Jesus, knowing they were trying to trick him, said, 24 "Show me a coin. Whose image and name are on it?"

They said, "Caesar's."

25 Jesus said to them, "Then give to Caesar the things that are Caesar's, and give to God the things that are God's."

26 So they were not able to trap Jesus in anything he said in the presence of the people. And being amazed at his answer, they became silent.

Some Sadducees Try to Trick Jesus

Some Sadducees, who believed people would not rise from the dead, came to Jesus. 28 They asked, "Teacher, Moses wrote that if a man's brother dies and leaves a wife but no children, then that man must marry the widow and have children for his brother. 29 Once there were seven brothers. The first brother married and died, but had no children. 30 Then the second brother married the widow, and he died. 31 And the third brother married the widow, and he died. The same thing happened with all seven brothers; they died and had no children. 32 Finally, the woman died also. 33 Since all seven brothers had married her, whose wife will she be when people rise from the dead?"

34 Jesus said to them, "On earth, people marry and are given to someone to marry. 35 But those who will be worthy to be raised from the dead and live again will not marry, nor will they be given to someone to marry. 36 In that life they are like angels and cannot die. They are children of God, because they have been raised from the dead. 37 Even Moses clearly showed that the dead are raised to life. When he wrote about the burning bush, he said that the Lord is 'the God of Abraham, the God of Isaac, and the God of Jacob.' 38 God is the God of the living, not the dead, because all people are alive to him."

39 Some of the teachers of the law said, "Teacher, your answer was good." 40 No one was brave enough to ask him another question.

Is the Christ the Son of David?

Then Jesus said, "Why do people say that the Christ is the Son of David? 42 In the book of Psalms, David himself says:

'The Lord said to my Lord:
  Sit by me at my right side,
43 until I put your enemies under
    your control.' *Psalm 110:1*

44 David calls the Christ 'Lord,' so how can the Christ be his son?"

Jesus Accuses Some Leaders

While all the people were listening,
Jesus said to his followers, [46]"Beware
of the teachers of the law. They like
to walk around wearing fancy clothes,
and they love for people to greet
them with respect in the marketplaces. They love to have the most
important seats in the synagogues
and at feasts. [47]But they cheat widows and steal their houses and then
try to make themselves look good by
saying long prayers. They will receive a greater punishment."

OLD TESTAMENT READING

How terrible it will be for people
who plan wickedness,
who lie on their beds and make
evil plans.
When the morning light comes,
they do what they planned,
because they have the power
to do so.
[2]They want fields, so they take
them;
they want houses, so they take
them away.
They cheat people to get their
houses;
they rob them even of their
property.

[3]That is why the LORD says:
"Look, I am planning trouble
against such people,
and you won't be able to save
yourselves.
You will no longer walk proudly,
because it will be a terrible time."

Micah 2:1–3

INSIGHTS

Not long ago a discerning man said that his minister preaches against sin, but he does not tell what sin is. He preaches against sin in general, but never against any particular sin. He denounces it in the aggregate, but never meddles with it in detail as it exists among his people. . . .

Do you see the importance of praying continually for a quick and tender and powerful conscience? Do you see the importance of great watchfulness lest we should abuse and seduce our conscience by indulgence in sin? Do you see the great importance of faithful dealings with the consciences all around you, so as to keep your own and their consciences fully awake and as quick and sensitive as the apple of the eye? . . .

It is impossible for me to understand how some could really be in love with the law of God, earnestly and honestly engaged in supporting it in all the length and breadth of its claims, and yet indulge in so many forms of violating it with so little compunction or misgiving. Is there not, my beloved brethren, some delusion in this?

Charles Finney

ACTION POINT

What are the leaders of God's people responsible to do? What does God promise to spiritual leaders who plan wickedness? Pray that God will open your eyes and protect you from the blinding influence of false spiritual leaders.

TUESDAY

God Gives His People Words to Say

Luke 21:1–28

True Giving

21 As Jesus looked up, he saw some rich people putting their gifts into the Temple money box. 2 Then he saw a poor widow putting two small copper coins into the box. 3 He said, "I tell you the truth, this poor widow gave more than all those rich people. 4 They gave only what they did not need. This woman is very poor, but she gave all she had to live on."

The Temple Will Be Destroyed

Some people were talking about the Temple and how it was decorated with beautiful stones and gifts offered to God.

But Jesus said, 6 "As for these things you are looking at, the time will come when not one stone will be left on another. Every stone will be thrown down."

7 They asked Jesus, "Teacher, when will these things happen? What will be the sign that they are about to take place?"

8 Jesus said, "Be careful so you are not fooled. Many people will come in my name, saying, 'I am the One' and, 'The time has come!' But don't follow them. 9 When you hear about wars and riots, don't be afraid, because these things must happen first, but the end will come later."

10 Then he said to them, "Nations will fight against other nations, and kingdoms against other kingdoms. 11 In various places there will be great earthquakes, sicknesses, and a lack of food. Fearful events and great signs will come from heaven.

12 "But before all these things happen, people will arrest you and treat you cruelly. They will judge you in their synagogues and put you in jail and force you to stand before kings and governors, because you follow me. 13 But this will give you an opportunity to tell about me. 14 Make up your minds not to worry ahead of time about what you will say. 15 I will give you the wisdom to say things that none of your enemies will be able to stand against or prove wrong. 16 Even your parents, brothers, relatives, and friends will turn against you, and they will kill some of you. 17 All people will hate you because you follow me. 18 But none of these things can really harm you. 19 By continuing to have faith you will save your lives.

Jerusalem Will Be Destroyed

When you see armies all around Jerusalem, you will know it will soon be destroyed. 21 At that time, the people in Judea should run away to the mountains. The people in Jerusalem must get out, and those who are near the city should not go in. 22 These are the days of punishment to bring about all that is written in the Scriptures. 23 How terrible it will be for women who are pregnant or have nursing babies! Great trouble will come upon this land, and God will be angry with these people. 24 They will be killed by the sword and taken as prisoners to all nations. Jerusalem will be crushed by non-Jewish people until their time is over.

Don't Fear

There will be signs in the sun,
moon, and stars. On earth, nations
will be afraid and confused because
of the roar and fury of the sea.
26 People will be so afraid they will
faint, wondering what is happening
to the world, because the powers of
the heavens will be shaken. 27 Then
people will see the Son of Man coming in a cloud with power and great
glory. 28 When these things begin to
happen, look up and hold your heads
high, because the time when God
will free you is near!"

OLD TESTAMENT READING

But Moses said to the LORD,
"Please, Lord, I have never been a
skilled speaker. Even now, after talking to you, I cannot speak well. I
speak slowly and can't find the best
words."
11 Then the LORD said to him,
"Who made a person's mouth? And
who makes someone deaf or not able
to speak? Or who gives a person
sight or blindness? It is I, the LORD."
14 The LORD became angry with
Moses and said, "Your brother
Aaron, from the family of Levi, is a
skilled speaker. He is already coming to meet you, and he will be happy
when he sees you. 15 You will speak
to Aaron and tell him what to say. I
will help both of you to speak and
will teach you what to do."

Exodus 4:10–11, 14–15

INSIGHTS

What in the world will I say?"

At some time in life we're all confronted with this challenge. . . .

In today's passage Jesus is talking about our concern over what to say when we are faced with giving testimony about Him in a setting which is hostile to the Christian faith. He assures us that the Holy Spirit will give us the thoughts, the words, and the courage which we so often lack. . . . There may be times when you are concerned about sharing your faith in Christ with someone or when you are challenged in your faith by other people. Rely upon the fact that God is the source of your thoughts and words at those times. Dr. Lloyd Ogilvie says:

> *Our only task is to open our minds in calm expectation of wisdom beyond our own capacity. We were never meant to be adequate on our own. It is when we think we are adequate that we get into trouble. A Christian is not one who works for the Lord but one in whom and through whom the Lord works. We are not to speak for God but to yield our tongues to express the thoughts the Lord has implanted.*

What can we draw from these words? Listen to the Lord before you speak and, after you have heard Him, speak with confidence and concern.

H. Norman Wright

ACTION POINT

What did God promise to do for both Moses and Aaron? Have you ever been (or are you) worried about what to say? Pray for a willing spirit that God can use; then trust him to give his message through you!

WEDNESDAY

Focus Your Eyes on God; Be Ready for His Coming

Luke 21:29—22:20

Jesus' Words Will Live Forever

Then Jesus told this story: "Look at the fig tree and all the other trees. 30 When their leaves appear, you know that summer is near. 31 In the same way, when you see these things happening, you will know that God's kingdom is near.

32 "I tell you the truth, all these things will happen while the people of this time are still living. 33 Earth and sky will be destroyed, but the words I have spoken will never be destroyed.

Be Ready All the Time

Be careful not to spend your time feasting, drinking, or worrying about worldly things. If you do, that day might come on you suddenly, 35 like a trap on all people on earth. 36 So be ready all the time. Pray that you will be strong enough to escape all these things that will happen and that you will be able to stand before the Son of Man."

37 During the day, Jesus taught the people in the Temple, and at night he went out of the city and stayed on the Mount of Olives. 38 Every morning all the people got up early to go to the Temple to listen to him.

Judas Becomes an Enemy of Jesus

22 It was almost time for the Feast of Unleavened Bread, called the Passover Feast. 2 The leading priests and teachers of the law were trying to find a way to kill Jesus, because they were afraid of the people.

3 Satan entered Judas Iscariot, one of Jesus' twelve apostles. 4 Judas went to the leading priests and some of the soldiers who guarded the Temple and talked to them about a way to hand Jesus over to them. 5 They were pleased and agreed to give Judas money. 6 He agreed and watched for the best time to hand Jesus over to them when he was away from the crowd.

Jesus Eats the Passover Meal

The Day of Unleavened Bread came when the Passover lambs had to be sacrificed. 8 Jesus said to Peter and John, "Go and prepare the Passover meal for us to eat."

9 They asked, "Where do you want us to prepare it?" 10 Jesus said to them, "After you go into the city, a man carrying a jar of water will meet you. Follow him into the house that he enters, 11 and tell the owner of the house, 'The Teacher says: Where is the guest room in which I may eat the Passover meal with my followers?' 12 Then he will show you a large, furnished room upstairs. Prepare the Passover meal there."

13 So Peter and John left and found everything as Jesus had said. And they prepared the Passover meal.

The Lord's Supper

When the time came, Jesus and the apostles were sitting at the table. 15 He said to them, "I wanted very much to eat this Passover meal with you before I suffer. 16 I will not eat another Passover meal until it is given its true meaning in the kingdom of God."

[17] Then Jesus took a cup, gave thanks, and said, "Take this cup and share it among yourselves. [18] I will not drink again from the fruit of the vine until God's kingdom comes."

[19] Then Jesus took some bread, gave thanks, broke it, and gave it to the apostles, saying, "This is my body, which I am giving for you. Do this to remember me." [20] In the same way, after supper, Jesus took the cup and said, "This cup is the new agreement that God makes with his people. This new agreement begins with my blood which is poured out for you."

OLD TESTAMENT READING

LORD, you are my share in life;
I have promised to obey your words.
58 I prayed to you with all my heart.
Have mercy on me as you have promised.
59 I thought about my life,
and I decided to follow your rules.
60 I hurried and did not wait
to obey your commands.

Psalm 119:57–60

INSIGHTS

The coming of God's Son is the real hope of the believers. . . . The early Christians constantly looked forward to it. The Church in its first love waited for its Lord. How often too Jesus Himself and His apostles admonished us to wait for His coming and to hasten to meet Him! The return of the Lord is not a theme with which certain specialists occupy themselves, but it is the great theme of Scripture and it must also become ours. We are all deeply aware of the fact that our congregations need a spiritual renewal. "How can this take place?" I asked a missionary. "When the hope of the Lord's return becomes living in our congregations," he answered. . . .

Think of a congregation of three hundred in which there were thirty who really were waiting for the Lord. What holiness and what light these could give to a congregation! John says, "Everyone that hath this hope set on him purifieth himself even as he is pure." He that does not have this hope, does not cleanse himself. Those who are really waiting need not be exhorted to cleanse themselves; they do it without outward prompting. They do not need to be urged to press forward, to deny themselves, to humble themselves; they just naturally strive to be like the Lamb. . . . As long as we do not have this Hope, we are really without hope; and the state of such persons is known to us all. . . .

Hitherto many of us have been like the brother who once said: "For many years I have known that I was converted, but I did not know for what purpose. I have long known that I was sealed with the Holy Spirit, but not to what end. But I understood it when I Thess. 1:9–10 and Eph. 4:30 became clear to me: we are converted to serve the true and living God, and to wait for His Son from Heaven."

G. Steinberger

ACTION POINT

What must we do to be ready for Jesus return? Will you pray daily to be ready?

THURSDAY

Jesus Sought the Will of the Father

Luke 22:21–53

Who Will Turn Against Jesus?

But one of you will turn against me, and his hand is with mine on the table. 22 What God has planned for the Son of Man will happen, but how terrible it will be for that one who turns against the Son of Man."

23 Then the apostles asked each other which one of them would do that.

Be Like a Servant

The apostles also began to argue about which one of them was the most important. 25 But Jesus said to them, "The kings of the non-Jewish people rule over them, and those who have authority over others like to be called 'friends of the people.' 26 But you must not be like that. Instead, the greatest among you should be like the youngest, and the leader should be like the servant. 27 Who is more important: the one sitting at the table or the one serving? You think the one at the table is more important, but I am like a servant among you.

28 "You have stayed with me through my struggles. 29 Just as my Father has given me a kingdom, I also give you a kingdom 30 so you may eat and drink at my table in my kingdom. And you will sit on thrones, judging the twelve tribes of Israel.

Don't Lose Your Faith!

Simon, Simon, Satan has asked to test all of you as a farmer sifts his wheat. 32 I have prayed that you will not lose your faith! Help your brothers be stronger when you come back to me."

33 But Peter said to Jesus, "Lord, I am ready to go with you to prison and even to die with you!"

34 But Jesus said, "Peter, before the rooster crows this day, you will say three times that you don't know me."

Be Ready for Trouble

Then Jesus said to the apostles, "When I sent you out without a purse, a bag, or sandals, did you need anything?"

They said, "No."

36 He said to them, "But now if you have a purse or a bag, carry that with you. If you don't have a sword, sell your coat and buy one. 37 The Scripture says, 'He was treated like a criminal,' and I tell you this scripture must have its full meaning. It was written about me, and it is happening now."

38 His followers said, "Look, Lord, here are two swords."

He said to them, "That is enough."

Jesus Prays Alone

Jesus left the city and went to the Mount of Olives, as he often did, and his followers went with him. 40 When he reached the place, he said to them, "Pray for strength against temptation."

41 Then Jesus went about a stone's throw away from them. He kneeled down and prayed, 42 "Father, if you are willing, take away this cup of suffering. But do what you want, not what I want." 43 Then an angel from heaven appeared to him to strengthen him. 44 Being full of pain, Jesus prayed even harder. His sweat

was like drops of blood falling to the
ground. 45 When he finished praying,
he went to his followers and found
them asleep because of their sadness. 46 Jesus said to them, "Why are
you sleeping? Get up and pray for
strength against temptation."

Jesus Is Arrested

While Jesus was speaking, a crowd
came up, and Judas, one of the twelve
apostles, was leading them. He came
close to Jesus so he could kiss him.
48 But Jesus said to him, "Judas,
are you using the kiss to give the Son
of Man to his enemies?"
49 When those who were standing
around him saw what was happening, they said, "Lord, should we
strike them with our swords?" 50 And
one of them struck the servant of the
high priest and cut off his right ear.
51 Jesus said, "Stop! No more of
this." Then he touched the servant's
ear and healed him.
52 Those who came to arrest Jesus
were the leading priests, the soldiers
who guarded the Temple, and the
older Jewish leaders. Jesus said to
them, "You came out here with
swords and clubs as though I were a
criminal. 53 I was with you every day
in the Temple, and you didn't arrest
me there. But this is your time—the
time when darkness rules."

OLD TESTAMENT READING

LORD, save me from my en-
emies;
I hide in you.
10 Teach me to do what you want,
because you are my God.
Let your good Spirit
lead me on level ground.

Psalm 143:9–10

INSIGHTS

I seek at the beginning to get my heart in such a state that it has no will of its own in regard to a given matter. Nine tenths of the trouble with people generally is just here. Nine tenths of the difficulties are overcome when our hearts are ready to do the Lord's will, whatever it may be. When one is truly in this state, it is usually but a little way to the knowledge of what His will is.

Having done this, I do not leave the result to feeling or simple impression. If so, I make myself liable to great delusions.

I seek the will of the Spirit of God through, or in connection with, the Word of God. The Spirit and the Word must be combined. If I look to the Spirit alone without the Word, I lay myself open to great delusions also. If the Holy Spirit guides us at all, He will do it according to the Scriptures and never contrary to them.

Next I take into account providential circumstances. These often plainly indicate God's will in connection with His Word and Spirit.

I ask God in prayer to reveal His will to me aright.

Thus through prayer to God, the study of the Word, and reflection, I come to a deliberate judgment according to the best of my ability and knowledge; and if my mind is thus at peace, and continues so after two or three more petitions, I proceed accordingly.

George Müller

PAUSE FOR REFLECTION

What did Jesus do to know God's will? What do you do to discover God's will?

FRIDAY

Deceit Leads to Great Pain

Luke 22:54—23:12

Peter Says He Doesn't Know Jesus

They arrested Jesus, and led him
away, and brought him into the
house of the high priest. Peter followed far behind them. 55 After the
soldiers started a fire in the middle
of the courtyard and sat together,
Peter sat with them. 56 A servant girl
saw Peter sitting there in the fire-
light, and looking closely at him,
she said, "This man was also with
him."

57 But Peter said this was not true;
he said, "Woman, I don't know him."

58 A short time later, another person saw Peter and said, "You are also
one of them."

But Peter said, "Man, I am not!"

59 About an hour later, another
man insisted, "Certainly this man
was with him, because he is from
Galilee, too."

60 But Peter said, "Man, I don't
know what you are talking about!"

At once, while Peter was still
speaking, a rooster crowed. 61 Then
the Lord turned and looked straight
at Peter. And Peter remembered
what the Lord had said: "Before the
rooster crows this day, you will say
three times that you don't know me."
62 Then Peter went outside and cried
painfully.

The People Make Fun of Jesus

The men who were guarding Jesus
began making fun of him and beating him.
64 They blindfolded him and said,
"Prove that you are a prophet, and
tell us who hit you." 65 They said
many cruel things to Jesus.

Jesus Before the Leaders

When day came, the council of the
older leaders of the people, both the
leading priests and the teachers of
the law, came together and led Jesus
to their highest court. 67 They said,
"If you are the Christ, tell us."

Jesus said to them, "If I tell you,
you will not believe me. 68 And if I
ask you, you will not answer. 69 But
from now on, the Son of Man will
sit at the right hand of the powerful God."

70 They all said, "Then are you the
Son of God?"

Jesus said to them, "You say that
I am."

71 They said, "Why do we need
witnesses now? We ourselves heard
him say this."

Pilate Questions Jesus

23 Then the whole group stood up
and led Jesus to Pilate. 2 They
began to accuse Jesus, saying, "We
caught this man telling things that
mislead our people. He says that we
should not pay taxes to Caesar, and
he calls himself the Christ, a king."

3 Pilate asked Jesus, "Are you the
king of the Jews?"

Jesus answered, "Those are your
words."

4 Pilate said to the leading priests
and the people, "I find nothing
against this man."

5 They were insisting, saying, "But
Jesus makes trouble with the people,
teaching all around Judea. He began
in Galilee, and now he is here."

Pilate Sends Jesus to Herod

Pilate heard this and asked if Jesus
was from Galilee. [7] Since Jesus was
under Herod's authority, Pilate sent
Jesus to Herod, who was in Jerusalem at that time. [8] When Herod saw
Jesus, he was very glad, because he
had heard about Jesus and had
wanted to meet him for a long time.
He was hoping to see Jesus work a
miracle. [9] Herod asked Jesus many
questions, but Jesus said nothing.
[10] The leading priests and teachers of
the law were standing there,
strongly accusing Jesus. [11] After
Herod and his soldiers had made fun
of Jesus, they dressed him in a
kingly robe and sent him back to
Pilate. [12] In the past, Pilate and Herod
had always been enemies, but on
that day they became friends.

OLD TESTAMENT READING

But Isaac said, "Your brother came
and tricked me. He has taken your
blessing."

[36] Esau said, "Jacob is the right
name for him. He has tricked me
these two times. He took away my
share of everything you own, and
now he has taken away my blessing." Then Esau asked, "Haven't you
saved a blessing for me?"

[37] Isaac answered, "I gave Jacob
the power to be master over you, and
all his brothers will be his servants.
And I kept him strong with grain and
wine. There is nothing left to give
you, my son."

[41] After that Esau hated Jacob because of the blessing from Isaac. He
thought to himself, "My father will
soon die, and I will be sad for him.
Then I will kill Jacob."

Genesis 27:35–37, 41

INSIGHTS

For the Old Testament Jew, truth was a sacred matter. Truth involved a proper understanding of reality, but it also involved much more than that. For the Jew truth also had a personal dimension, an emotional dimension, and an ethical dimension.

Truth is personal—it is a special part of any close human relationship. Trust is a by-product of truth, and personal relationships are built upon trust. I trust people who demonstrate that they are truthful. I do not trust people who show themselves to be habitual liars.

Broken truth hurts. Satan, "the father of lies," loves to attack and distort truth. The Scripture says that Satan was a liar from the beginning. It is painful for anybody to invest his heart in a lie. A broken truth often means a broken heart.

This is the problem with lies. We do invest our hearts in the promises people make and the stories they tell us. When the promises are not kept and the stories prove to be false, we are hurt. We are disillusioned. We sometimes grow bitter. Trust is a fragile commodity and is as precious as it is delicate. Deep levels of trust take years to develop. Yet, such trust can be smashed to pieces in seconds.

R. C. Sproul

PAUSE FOR REFLECTION

How did deceit in Isaac's family change the family relationships? When Peter lied about knowing Jesus, how did he feel? How did his relationship with Jesus change? Thank Jesus that his trust never fails!

WEEKEND

God Always Welcomes Repentant Sinners

Luke 23:13–43

Jesus Must Die

Pilate called the people together with the leading priests and the Jewish leaders. 14 He said to them, "You brought this man to me, saying he makes trouble among the people. But I have questioned him before you all, and I have not found him guilty of what you say. 15 Also, Herod found nothing wrong with him; he sent him back to us. Look, he has done nothing for which he should die. 16 So, after I punish him, I will let him go free." 17 Every year at the Passover Feast, Pilate had to release one prisoner to the people.

18 But the people shouted together, "Take this man away! Let Barabbas go free!" 19 (Barabbas was a man who was in prison for his part in a riot in the city and for murder.)

20 Pilate wanted to let Jesus go free and told this to the crowd. 21 But they shouted again, "Crucify him! Crucify him!"

22 A third time Pilate said to them, "Why? What wrong has he done? I can find no reason to kill him. So I will have him punished and set him free."

23 But they continued to shout, demanding that Jesus be crucified. Their yelling became so loud that 24 Pilate decided to give them what they wanted. 25 He set free the man who was in jail for rioting and murder, and he handed Jesus over to them to do with him as they wished.

Jesus Is Crucified

As they led Jesus away, Simon, a man from Cyrene, was coming in from the fields. They forced him to carry Jesus' cross and to walk behind him.

27 A large crowd of people was following Jesus, including some women who were sad and crying for him. 28 But Jesus turned and said to them, "Women of Jerusalem, don't cry for me. Cry for yourselves and for your children. 29 The time is coming when people will say, 'Happy are the women who cannot have children and who have no babies to nurse.' 30 Then people will say to the mountains, 'Fall on us!' And they will say to the hills, 'Cover us!' 31 If they act like this now when life is good, what will happen when bad times come?"

32 There were also two criminals led out with Jesus to be put to death. 33 When they came to a place called the Skull, the soldiers crucified Jesus and the criminals—one on his right and the other on his left. 34 Jesus said, "Father, forgive them, because they don't know what they are doing."

The soldiers threw lots to decide who would get his clothes. 35 The people stood there watching. And the leaders made fun of Jesus, saying, "He saved others. Let him save himself if he is God's Chosen One, the Christ."

36 The soldiers also made fun of him, coming to Jesus and offering him some vinegar. 37 They said, "If you are the king of the Jews, save yourself!" 38 At the top of the cross these words were written: THIS IS THE KING OF THE JEWS.

39 One of the criminals on a cross

began to shout insults at Jesus: "Aren't you the Christ? Then save yourself and us."

40 But the other criminal stopped him and said, "You should fear God! You are getting the same punishment he is. 41 We are punished justly, getting what we deserve for what we did. But this man has done nothing wrong." 42 Then he said, "Jesus, remember me when you come into your kingdom."

43 Jesus said to him, "I tell you the truth, today you will be with me in paradise."

OLD TESTAMENT READING

This is what the Lord GOD, the Holy One of Israel, says:

"If you come back to me and trust
 me, you will be saved.
If you will be calm and trust
 me, you will be strong."
But you don't want to do that.
18 The LORD wants to show his
 mercy to you.
He wants to rise and comfort
 you.
The LORD is a fair God,
 and everyone who waits for his
 help will be happy.

Isaiah 30:15, 18

INSIGHTS

The prisoners in the Montinlupa Prison who gathered for a large assembly were astonished to see a woman in her seventies make her way up the steps of the platform to address them. What would an old woman have to say to them? . . .

. . . She told how she and her family had hidden Jews from the Nazis during World War II and how German police, because of a tip from two of her fellow citizens, had pounded on their door one frigid February day in 1944 with warrants for their arrest. The speaker was Corrie ten Boom. . . .

After the war was over, the two Dutchmen who had betrayed her family were taken into custody and put on trial. . . . "My sister Nollie," Corrie told her audience, "heard of the trial of these two men who told the Gestapo about us, and she wrote a letter to both of them. . . . She told them that we had forgiven them and that we could do this because of Jesus, who is in our hearts."

Both men responded. One wrote: "I have received Jesus as my Savior. When you can give such ability to forgive to people like Corrie ten Boom and her sister, then there is hope for me. I brought my sins to Him." The other letter gave an opposite viewpoint: "I know what I have done to your family, that I have caused the death of several of you who have saved Jews, and above that I have helped to kill many hundreds of Jewish people. The only thing I regret is that I have not been able to kill more of your kind." Corrie went on to challenge the prisoners that every one of them—even as those criminals who had been on the cross—could accept or reject Christ and his forgiveness.

Ruth Tucker

APPLICATION

How much evil will God forgive? What does he require to receive forgiveness? Are you willing to turn away from a life of sin and trust God for your salvation?

MONDAY

The Resurrected Christ Saves His People

Luke 23:44—24:12

Jesus Dies

It was about noon, and the whole
land became dark until three o'clock
in the afternoon, 45 because the sun
did not shine. The curtain in the
Temple was torn in two. 46 Jesus
cried out in a loud voice, "Father, I
give you my life." After Jesus said
this, he died.

47 When the army officer there
saw what happened, he praised God,
saying, "Surely this was a good
man!"

48 When all the people who had
gathered there to watch saw what
happened, they returned home,
beating their chests because they
were so sad. 49 But those who were
close friends of Jesus, including the
women who had followed him from
Galilee, stood at a distance and
watched.

Joseph Takes Jesus' Body

There was a good and religious
man named Joseph who was a member of the Jewish council. 51 But he
had not agreed to the other leaders'
plans and actions against Jesus. He
was from the Jewish town of
Arimathea and was waiting for the
kingdom of God to come. 52 Joseph
went to Pilate to ask for the body of
Jesus. 53 He took the body down from
the cross, wrapped it in cloth, and
put it in a tomb that was cut out of a
wall of rock. This tomb had never
been used before. 54 This was late on
Preparation Day, and when the sun
went down, the Sabbath day would
begin.

55 The women who had come
from Galilee with Jesus followed Joseph and saw the tomb and how
Jesus' body was laid. 56 Then the
women left to prepare spices and
perfumes.

On the Sabbath day they rested,
as the law of Moses commanded.

Jesus Rises from the Dead

24 Very early on the first day of
the week, at dawn, the women
came to the tomb, bringing the
spices they had prepared. 2 They
found the stone rolled away from the
entrance of the tomb, 3 but when
they went in, they did not find the
body of the Lord Jesus. 4 While they
were wondering about this, two men
in shining clothes suddenly stood
beside them. 5 The women were
very afraid; they bowed their heads
to the ground. The men said to
them, "Why are you looking for a living person in this place for the dead?
6 He is not here; he has risen from
the dead. Do you remember what he
told you in Galilee? 7 He said the Son
of Man must be handed over to sinful people, be crucified, and rise
from the dead on the third day."
8 Then the women remembered
what Jesus had said.

9 The women left the tomb and
told all these things to the eleven
apostles and the other followers. 10 It
was Mary Magdalene, Joanna, Mary
the mother of James, and some
other women who told the apostles
everything that had happened at the
tomb. 11 But they did not believe the
women, because it sounded like non-

sense. 12 But Peter got up and ran to
the tomb. Bending down and looking in, he saw only the cloth that Jesus' body had been wrapped in. Peter went away to his home, wondering about what had happened.

OLD TESTAMENT READING

Here is my servant, the one I support.
He is the one I chose, and I am pleased with him.
I have put my Spirit upon him,
and he will bring justice to all nations.
2 He will not cry out or yell
or speak loudly in the streets.
3 He will not break a crushed blade of grass
or put out even a weak flame.
He will truly bring justice;
4 he will not lose hope or give up
until he brings justice to the world.
And people far away will trust his teachings."

6 The LORD says, "I, the LORD,
called you to do right,
and I will hold your hand
and protect you.
You will be the sign of my agreement with the people,
a light to shine for all people.
7 You will help the blind to see.
You will free those who are in prison."

Isaiah 42:1–4, 6–7b

INSIGHTS

Never underestimate the power of a seed.

God didn't. When his kingdom was ravaged and his people had forgotten his name, he planted his seed. When the soil of the human heart had grown crusty, he planted his seed. When religion had become a ritual and the temple a trading post, he planted his seed.

Want to see a miracle? Watch him as he places the seed of his own self in the fertile womb of a Jewish girl.

Up it grew, "like a tender green shoot, sprouting from a root in dry and sterile ground." The seed spent a lifetime pushing back the stones that tried to keep it underground. The seed made a ministry out of shoving away the rocks that cluttered his father's soil.

The stones of legalism that burdened backs.

The stones of oppression that broke bones.

The stones of prejudice that fenced out the needy.

But it was the final stone that proved to be the supreme test of the seed. The stone of death—rolled by humans and sealed by Satan in front of the tomb. For a moment it appeared the seed would be stuck in the earth. For a moment, it looked like this rock was too big to be budged.

But then, somewhere in the heart of the earth, the seed of God stirred, shoved, and sprouted. The ground trembled, and the rock of the tomb tumbled. And the flower of Easter blossomed.

Never underestimate the power of a seed.

Max Lucado

PAUSE FOR REFLECTION

What warnings did Jesus' followers have that he would die and rise again? When you ponder Christ's awesome salvation, do you, like Peter, take time alone to take it all in?

TUESDAY

Jesus Sends His Witnesses to All Nations

Luke 24:13–53

Jesus on the Road to Emmaus

That same day two of Jesus' followers were going to a town named
Emmaus, about seven miles from
Jerusalem. 14 They were talking
about everything that had happened.
15 While they were talking and dis-
cussing, Jesus himself came near
and began walking with them, 16 but
they were kept from recognizing
him. 17 Then he said, "What are
these things you are talking about
while you walk?"

The two followers stopped, looking very sad. 18 The one named
Cleopas answered, "Are you the only
visitor in Jerusalem who does not
know what just happened there?"

19 Jesus said to them, "What are
you talking about?"

They said, "About Jesus of
Nazareth. He was a prophet who
said and did many powerful things
before God and all the people. 20 Our
leaders and the leading priests
handed him over to be sentenced to
death, and they crucified him. 21 But
we were hoping that he would free
Israel. Besides this, it is now the
third day since this happened. 22 And
today some women among us
amazed us. Early this morning they
went to the tomb, 23 but they did not
find his body there. They came and
told us that they had seen a vision
of angels who said that Jesus was
alive! 24 So some of our group went
to the tomb, too. They found it just
as the women said, but they did not
see Jesus."

25 Then Jesus said to them, "You
are foolish and slow to believe everything the prophets said. 26 They said
that the Christ must suffer these
things before he enters his glory."
27 Then starting with what Moses
and all the prophets had said about
him, Jesus began to explain everything that had been written about
himself in the Scriptures.

28 They came near the town of
Emmaus, and Jesus acted as if he
were going farther. 29 But they
begged him, "Stay with us, because
it is late; it is almost night." So he
went in to stay with them.

30 When Jesus was at the table
with them, he took some bread, gave
thanks, divided it, and gave it to
them. 31 And then, they were allowed
to recognize Jesus. But when they
saw who he was, he disappeared.
32 They said to each other, "It felt like
a fire burning in us when Jesus
talked to us on the road and explained the Scriptures to us."

33 So the two followers got up at
once and went back to Jerusalem.
There they found the eleven apostles
and others gathered. 34 They were
saying, "The Lord really has risen
from the dead! He showed himself
to Simon."

35 Then the two followers told
what had happened on the road and
how they recognized Jesus when he
divided the bread.

Jesus Appears to His Followers

While the two followers were telling this, Jesus himself stood right in
the middle of them and said, "Peace
be with you."

37 They were fearful and terrified

and thought they were seeing a
ghost. 38 But Jesus said, "Why are
you troubled? Why do you doubt
what you see? 39 Look at my hands
and my feet. It is I myself! Touch me
and see, because a ghost does not
have a living body as you see I have."
40 After Jesus said this, he showed
them his hands and feet. 41 While they
still could not believe it because they
were amazed and happy, Jesus said to
them, "Do you have any food here?"
42 They gave him a piece of broiled
fish. 43 While the followers watched,
Jesus took the fish and ate it.

44 He said to them, "Remember
when I was with you before? I said
that everything written about me
must happen—everything in the law
of Moses, the books of the prophets,
and the Psalms."

45 Then Jesus opened their minds
so they could understand the Scriptures. 46 He said to them, "It is written that the Christ would suffer and
rise from the dead on the third day
47 and that a change of hearts and
lives and forgiveness of sins would
be preached in his name to all nations, starting at Jerusalem. 48 You
are witnesses of these things. 49 I will
send you what my Father has promised, but you must stay in Jerusalem
until you have received that power
from heaven."

Jesus Goes Back to Heaven

Jesus led his followers as far as
Bethany, and he raised his hands
and blessed them. 51 While he was
blessing them, he was separated
from them and carried into heaven.
52 They worshiped him and returned
to Jerusalem very happy. 53 They
stayed in the Temple all the time,
praising God.

OLD TESTAMENT READING

Jerusalem, you have good news
to tell.
Go up on a high mountain.
Jerusalem, you have good news
to tell.
Shout out loud the good news.
Shout it out and don't be afraid.
Say to the towns of Judah,
"Here is your God."
10 Look, the Lord GOD is coming
with power
to rule all the people.

Isaiah 40:9–10a

INSIGHTS

Everyone has the great responsibility to win as many people as possible to Christ. This is the great privilege and the great duty of all disciples of Christ. . .

I fear I must say that the great mass of people professing to be believers seem never to have been impressed with this truth. The work of saving souls is something they feel they can leave to ministers.

Many believers suppose it belongs only to those who are called to preach the gospel as a life work. They fail to realize that all are called to preach the gospel, that the whole life of every believer is to be a proclamation of the glad tidings.

Charles Finney

ACTION POINT

Write, in your own words, the essential message of salvation that Jesus wants his followers to proclaim. To whom does he want you to deliver that message? Will you?

WEDNESDAY

Christ: The True Light of the World

John 1:1–28

Christ Comes to the World

1 In the beginning there was the Word. The Word was with God, and the Word was God. [2] He was with God in the beginning. [3] All things were made by him, and nothing was made without him. [4] In him there was life, and that life was the light of all people. [5] The Light shines in the darkness, and the darkness has not overpowered it.

[6] There was a man named John who was sent by God. [7] He came to tell people the truth about the Light so that through him all people could hear about the Light and believe. [8] John was not the Light, but he came to tell people the truth about the Light. [9] The true Light that gives light to all was coming into the world!

[10] The Word was in the world, and the world was made by him, but the world did not know him. [11] He came to the world that was his own, but his own people did not accept him. [12] But to all who did accept him and believe in him he gave the right to become children of God. [13] They did not become his children in any human way—by any human parents or human desire. They were born of God.

[14] The Word became a human and lived among us. We saw his glory—the glory that belongs to the only Son of the Father—and he was full of grace and truth. [15] John tells the truth about him and cries out, saying, "This is the One I told you about: 'The One who comes after me is greater than I am, because he was living before me.'"

[16] Because he was full of grace and truth, from him we all received one gift after another. [17] The law was given through Moses, but grace and truth came through Jesus Christ. [18] No one has ever seen God. But God the only Son is very close to the Father, and he has shown us what God is like.

John Tells People About Jesus

*H*ere is the truth John told when the Jews in Jerusalem sent priests and Levites to ask him, "Who are you?"

[20] John spoke freely and did not refuse to answer. He said, "I am not the Christ."

[21] So they asked him, "Then who are you? Are you Elijah?"

He answered, "No, I am not."

"Are you the Prophet?" they asked.

He answered, "No."

[22] Then they said, "Who are you? Give us an answer to tell those who sent us. What do you say about yourself?"

[23] John told them in the words of the prophet Isaiah:

"I am the voice of one
calling out in the desert:
'Make the road straight for the
Lord.'" *Isaiah 40:3*

[24] Some Pharisees who had been sent asked John: [25] "If you are not the Christ or Elijah or the Prophet, why do you baptize people?"

[26] John answered, "I baptize with water, but there is one here with you

that you don't know about. 27 He is
the One who comes after me. I am
not good enough to untie the strings
of his sandals."
28 This all happened at Bethany on
the other side of the Jordan River,
where John was baptizing people.

OLD TESTAMENT READING

Before those people lived in
  darkness,
  but now they have seen a great
    light.
They lived in a dark land,
  but a light has shined on them.
6 A child has been born to us;
  God has given a son to us.
  He will be responsible for
    leading the people.
His name will be Wonderful
    Counselor, Powerful God,
  Father Who Lives Forever,
    Prince of Peace.

Isaiah 9:2, 6

INSIGHTS

Thanks to the great mercy and marvel of the Incarnation, the cosmic scene is resolved into a human drama. God reaches down to relate himself to man, and man reaches up to relate himself to God. Time looks into eternity and eternity into time, making now always and always now. Everything is transformed by this sublime drama of the Incarnation, God's special parable for fallen man in a fallen world. The way opens before us that was charted in the birth, ministry, death, and resurrection of Jesus Christ, a way that successive generations of believers have striven to follow. They have derived therefrom the moral, spiritual, and intellectual creativity out of which has come everything truly great in our art, our literature, our music. . . .

. . . Whatever may happen, however seemingly inimical to it may be the world's going and those who preside over the world's affairs, the truth of the Incarnation remains intact and inviolate. . . .

. . . Christ shows what life really is, and what our true destiny is. We escape from the cave. We emerge from the darkness and instead of shadows we have all around us the glory of God's creation. Instead of darkness we have light; instead of despair, hope; instead of time and the clocks ticking inexorably on, eternity, which never began and never ends and yet is sublimely now. . . . By identifying ourselves with Christ, by absorbing ourselves in his teaching, by living out the drama of his life with him, including especially the passion, that powerhouse of love and creativity—by living with, by, and in him, we can be reborn to become new men and women in a new world.

Malcolm Muggeridge

PAUSE FOR REFLECTION

In what ways would you say Christ's coming to earth enlightened the world? What did Christ's coming reveal? What difference does being reborn of God—becoming one of his children—make in your life?

THURSDAY

Jesus Comes as the Lamb of God

John 1:29–51

The next day John saw Jesus coming toward him. John said, "Look,
the Lamb of God, who takes away
the sin of the world! 30 This is the
One I was talking about when I said,
'A man will come after me, but he is
greater than I am, because he was
living before me.' 31 Even I did not
know who he was, although I came
baptizing with water so that the
people of Israel would know who he
is."
32–33 Then John said, "I saw the
Spirit come down from heaven in the
form of a dove and rest on him. Until then I did not know who the
Christ was. But the God who sent
me to baptize with water told me,
'You will see the Spirit come down
and rest on a man; he is the One who
will baptize with the Holy Spirit.' 34 I
have seen this happen, and I tell you
the truth: This man is the Son of
God."

The First Followers of Jesus

The next day John was there again
with two of his followers. 36 When he
saw Jesus walking by, he said, "Look,
the Lamb of God!"
37 The two followers heard John
say this, so they followed Jesus.
38 When Jesus turned and saw them
following him, he asked, "What are
you looking for?"
They said, "Rabbi, where are you
staying?" ("Rabbi" means "Teacher.")
39 He answered, "Come and see."
So the two men went with Jesus and
saw where he was staying and
stayed there with him that day. It was
about four o'clock in the afternoon.
40 One of the two men who followed Jesus after they heard John
speak about him was Andrew, Simon
Peter's brother. 41 The first thing
Andrew did was to find his brother
Simon and say to him, "We have
found the Messiah." ("Messiah"
means "Christ.")
42 Then Andrew took Simon to
Jesus. Jesus looked at him and said,
"You are Simon son of John. You will
be called Cephas." ("Cephas" means
"Peter.")
43 The next day Jesus decided to
go to Galilee. He found Philip and
said to him, "Follow me." 44 Philip
was from the town of Bethsaida,
where Andrew and Peter lived.
45 Philip found Nathanael and told
him, "We have found the man that
Moses wrote about in the law, and
the prophets also wrote about him.
He is Jesus, the son of Joseph, from
Nazareth."
46 But Nathanael said to Philip,
"Can anything good come from
Nazareth?"
Philip answered, "Come and see."
47 As Jesus saw Nathanael coming
toward him, he said, "Here is truly
an Israelite. There is nothing false in
him."
48 Nathanael asked, "How do you
know me?"
Jesus answered, "I saw you when
you were under the fig tree, before
Philip told you about me."
49 Then Nathanael said to Jesus,
"Teacher, you are the Son of God;
you are the King of Israel."
50 Jesus said to Nathanael, "Do

you believe simply because I told
you I saw you under the fig tree? You
will see greater things than that."
51 And Jesus said to them, "I tell you
the truth, you will all see heaven
open and 'angels of God going up
and coming down' on the Son of
Man."

OLD TESTAMENT READING

We all have wandered away like sheep;
each of us has gone his own way.
But the LORD has put on him the punishment
for all the evil we have done.

7 He was beaten down and punished,
but he didn't say a word.
He was like a lamb being led to be killed.
He was quiet, as a sheep is quiet while its wool is being cut;
he never opened his mouth.
8 Men took him away roughly and unfairly.
He died without children to continue his family.
He was put to death;
he was punished for the sins of my people.

Isaiah 53:6–8

INSIGHTS

It was never meant
to burst from the body
so fiercely, to pour
unchannelled from
the five wounds
and the unbandaged brow,
drowning the dark wood,
staining the stones
and the gravel below,
clotting in the air
dark with God's absence.

It was created for
a closed system—
the unbroken
rhythms of human blood
binding the body
of God, circulating
hot, brilliant,
saline, without
interruption
between heart, lungs
and all cells.

But because he
was once emptied
I am each day refilled;
my spirit-arteries
pulse with the vital red
of love; poured out,
it is his life
that now pumps through
my own heart's core.
He bled, and died, and I
have been transfused.

Luci Shaw

PAUSE FOR REFLECTION

What an awesome thing to be saved by the Lamb of God! How well do you know the Lamb of God? As certainly as John, Andrew, and Philip did? Or are you a bit skeptical, as Nathanael was? Reread the Isaiah passage and pray for a renewed knowledge of the Lamb of God—in your mind and in your heart.

FRIDAY

Jesus Shows His Love for God's Temple and His Hatred of Sin

John 2:1–25

The Wedding at Cana

2 Two days later there was a wedding in the town of Cana in Galilee. Jesus' mother was there, 2 and Jesus and his followers were also invited to the wedding. 3 When all the wine was gone, Jesus' mother said to him, "They have no more wine."

4 Jesus answered, "Dear woman, why come to me? My time has not yet come."

5 His mother said to the servants, "Do whatever he tells you to do."

6 In that place there were six stone water jars that the Jews used in their washing ceremony. Each jar held about twenty or thirty gallons.

7 Jesus said to the servants, "Fill the jars with water." So they filled the jars to the top.

8 Then he said to them, "Now take some out and give it to the master of the feast."

So they took the water to the master. 9 When he tasted it, the water had become wine. He did not know where the wine came from, but the servants who had brought the water knew. The master of the wedding called the bridegroom 10 and said to him, "People always serve the best wine first. Later, after the guests have been drinking awhile, they serve the cheaper wine. But you have saved the best wine till now."

11 So in Cana of Galilee Jesus did his first miracle. There he showed his glory, and his followers believed in him.

Jesus in the Temple

After this, Jesus went to the town of Capernaum with his mother, brothers, and followers. They stayed there for just a few days. 13 When it was almost time for the Jewish Passover Feast, Jesus went to Jerusalem. 14 In the Temple he found people selling cattle, sheep, and doves. He saw others sitting at tables, exchanging different kinds of money. 15 Jesus made a whip out of cords and forced all of them, both the sheep and cattle, to leave the Temple. He turned over the tables and scattered the money of those who were exchanging it. 16 Then he said to those who were selling pigeons, "Take these things out of here! Don't make my Father's house a place for buying and selling!"

17 When this happened, the followers remembered what was written in the Scriptures: "My strong love for your Temple completely controls me."

18 The Jews said to Jesus, "Show us a miracle to prove you have the right to do these things."

19 Jesus answered them, "Destroy this temple, and I will build it again in three days."

20 The Jews answered, "It took forty-six years to build this Temple! Do you really believe you can build it again in three days?"

21 (But the temple Jesus meant was his own body. 22 After Jesus was raised from the dead, his followers remembered that Jesus had said this. Then they believed the Scrip-

ture and the words Jesus had said.)
[23] When Jesus was in Jerusalem
for the Passover Feast, many people
believed in him because they saw
the miracles he did. [24] But Jesus did
not trust himself to them because he
knew them all. [25] He did not need
anyone to tell him about people, because he knew what was in people's
minds.

OLD TESTAMENT READING

I will look for trustworthy people
so I can live with them in the
land.
Only those who live innocent
lives
will be my servants.
[7] No one who is dishonest will live
in my house;
no liars will stay around me.
[8] Every morning I will destroy the
wicked in the land.
I will rid the LORD's city of
people who do evil.

Psalm 101:6–8

INSIGHTS

In Cana Jesus manifested His power as the Creator. Now He came to manifest His authority as the Messiah, the Son of God. Not only did He drive the sheep and oxen out of the temple, but He whipped the merchants out of the place. These Jews knew that He was right. The law and their consciences were witnesses against them. Christ was filled with righteous indignation in His zeal for His Father's house.

Christ cleansed the temple by crying, "Make not my Father's house an house of merchandise." Mark that He calls the temple "My Father's house." Christ was claiming a unique relationship with the Living God. . . .

When Christ drove the merchandisers out of the temple, they experienced something of the terror of the Lord. In the future men will cry to the mountains and rocks to hide them "from the face of him that sitteth on the throne, and from the wrath of the Lamb: For the great day of his wrath is come; and who shall be able to stand?" (Revelation 6:16–17).

Sometimes we forget that He is a righteous God and that every one of us must one day stand in His presence and give an account to Him. "It is a fearful thing to fall into the hands of the living God" (Hebrews 10:31). . . .

. . . Christ cleansed the temple when men sinned and made it unclean. Similarly, the Lord has a right to cleanse us when we sin. It is much better for us to willingly confess our sins so that He may forgive and cleanse us. And He is willing and ready to do just that. How wonderful it is to know that the blood of Jesus Christ, God's Son, cleanseth us from all sin (1 John 1:7).

John G. Mitchell

ACTION POINT

What was revealed by the Jews' demand that Jesus prove he had the right to cleanse God's temple? In what ways do you demand that Jesus prove his right to purge the sin from your heart (which is also his temple)? Ask for his forgiveness.

WEEKEND

God's Love Caused Him to Send Salvation Through His Son

John 3:1–30

Nicodemus Comes to Jesus

3 There was a man named
Nicodemus who was one of the
Pharisees and an important Jewish
leader. 2 One night Nicodemus came
to Jesus and said, "Teacher, we know
you are a teacher sent from God, because no one can do the miracles
you do unless God is with him."
3 Jesus answered, "I tell you the
truth, unless one is born again, he
cannot be in God's kingdom."
4 Nicodemus said, "But if a person
is already old, how can he be born
again? He cannot enter his mother's
body again. So how can a person be
born a second time?"
5 But Jesus answered, "I tell you
the truth, unless one is born from
water and the Spirit, he cannot enter God's kingdom. 6 Human life
comes from human parents, but
spiritual life comes from the Spirit.
7 Don't be surprised when I tell you,
'You must all be born again.' 8 The
wind blows where it wants to and
you hear the sound of it, but you
don't know where the wind comes
from or where it is going. It is the
same with every person who is born
from the Spirit."
9 Nicodemus asked, "How can
this happen?"
10 Jesus said, "You are an important teacher in Israel, and you don't
understand these things? 11 I tell you
the truth, we talk about what we
know, and we tell about what we
have seen, but you don't accept what
we tell you. 12 I have told you about
things here on earth, and you do not
believe me. So you will not believe
me if I tell you about things of
heaven. 13 The only one who has ever
gone up to heaven is the One who
came down from heaven—the Son
of Man.
14 "Just as Moses lifted up the
snake in the desert, the Son of Man
must also be lifted up. 15 So that everyone who believes can have eternal life in him.
16 "God loved the world so much
that he gave his one and only Son
so that whoever believes in him may
not be lost, but have eternal life.
17 God did not send his Son into the
world to judge the guilty, but to save
the world through him. 18 People
who believe in God's Son are not
judged guilty. Those who do not believe have already been judged
guilty, because they have not believed in God's one and only Son.
19 They are judged by this fact: The
Light has come into the world, but
they did not want light. They wanted
darkness, because they were doing
evil things. 20 All who do evil hate the
light and will not come to the light,
because it will show all the evil
things they do. 21 But those who follow the true way come to the light,
and it shows that the things they do
were done through God."

Jesus and John the Baptist

After this, Jesus and his followers
went into the area of Judea, where
he stayed with his followers and baptized people. 23 John was also baptiz-

ing in Aenon, near Salim, because
there was plenty of water there.
People were going there to be baptized. 24 (This was before John was
put into prison.)
25 Some of John's followers had an
argument with a Jew about religious
washing. 26 So they came to John and
said, "Teacher, remember the man
who was with you on the other side
of the Jordan River, the one you
spoke about so much? He is baptizing, and everyone is going to him."
27 John answered, "A man can get
only what God gives him. 28 You
yourselves heard me say, 'I am not
the Christ, but I am the one sent to
prepare the way for him.' 29 The
bride belongs only to the bridegroom. But the friend who helps the
bridegroom stands by and listens to
him. He is thrilled that he gets to
hear the bridegroom's voice. In the
same way, I am really happy. 30 He
must become greater, and I must
become less important."

OLD TESTAMENT READING

The LORD looked and could not
find any justice,
and he was displeased.
16 He could not find anyone to help
the people,
and he was surprised that
there was no one to help.
So he used his own power to save
the people;
his own goodness gave him
strength.
17 He covered himself with goodness like armor.
He put the helmet of salvation
on his head.
He put on the clothes of punishment
and wrapped himself in the
coat of his strong love.

Isaiah 59:15b–17

INSIGHTS

God loves us, not only as a host of human beings who are living on the earth at this time, but as individuals whom He knows by name. He has a personal interest in each one. He has a perfect plan for every detail in the life of each individual. He is not willing that any should perish, but wants all mankind to be saved and come to the knowledge of the truth (1 Timothy 2:4).

The greatest and most profound expression of God's love for us is in the death of Christ on the cross. Men rejected the Lord Jesus Christ as God's Son, falsely accused Him, condemned Him to death, beat Him, crowned Him with thorns, spit on Him, made sport of Him, crucified Him with thieves, and ridiculed Him. While they were doing this, He forgave them and paid the penalty of their sin by dying for them.

This speaks most powerfully of the extent of God's unchanging, everlasting love. There is no greater expression of love than for a man to lay down his life for his friends.

Lucille Sollenberger

ACTION POINT

What motivated God to use his own power, to send his own son, to save us? Why do some reject God's salvation? Reread Isaiah 59:15b–17 and as you do, ask God for his forgiveness of your wrongs and praise him for offering himself to save you.

MONDAY

Jesus Gives Living Water

John 3:31—4:26

The One Who Comes from Heaven

The One who comes from above is
greater than all. The one who is from
the earth belongs to the earth and
talks about things on the earth. But
the One who comes from heaven is
greater than all. 32 He tells what he has
seen and heard, but no one accepts
what he says. 33 Whoever accepts what
he says has proven that God is true.
34 The One whom God sent speaks the
words of God, because God gives him
the Spirit fully. 35 The Father loves the
Son and has given him power over
everything. 36 Those who believe in
the Son have eternal life, but those
who do not obey the Son will never
have life. God's anger stays on them."

Jesus and a Samaritan Woman

4 The Pharisees heard that Jesus
was making and baptizing more
followers than John, 2 although Jesus
himself did not baptize people, but
his followers did. 3 Jesus knew that
the Pharisees had heard about him,
so he left Judea and went back to Galilee. 4 But on the way he had to go
through the country of Samaria.

5 In Samaria Jesus came to the
town called Sychar, which is near the
field Jacob gave to his son Joseph.
6 Jacob's well was there. Jesus was
tired from his long trip, so he sat
down beside the well. It was about
twelve o'clock noon. 7 When a Samaritan woman came to the well to
get some water, Jesus said to her,
"Please give me a drink." 8 (This happened while Jesus' followers were in
town buying some food.)

9 The woman said, "I am surprised
that you ask me for a drink, since
you are a Jewish man and I am a Samaritan woman." (Jewish people are
not friends with Samaritans.)

10 Jesus said, "If you only knew the
free gift of God and who it is that is
asking you for water, you would have
asked him, and he would have given
you living water."

11 The woman said, "Sir, where
will you get this living water? The
well is very deep, and you have nothing to get water with. 12 Are you
greater than Jacob, our father, who
gave us this well and drank from it
himself along with his sons and
flocks?"

13 Jesus answered, "Everyone
who drinks this water will be thirsty
again, 14 but whoever drinks the water I give will never be thirsty. The
water I give will become a spring of
water gushing up inside that person,
giving eternal life."

15 The woman said to him, "Sir,
give me this water so I will never be
thirsty again and will not have to
come back here to get more water."

16 Jesus told her, "Go get your husband and come back here."

17 The woman answered, "I have
no husband."

Jesus said to her, "You are right
to say you have no husband. 18 Really
you have had five husbands, and the
man you live with now is not your
husband. You told the truth."

19 The woman said, "Sir, I can see
that you are a prophet. 20 Our ancestors worshiped on this mountain, but
you Jews say that Jerusalem is the

place where people must worship."
21 Jesus said, "Believe me, woman.
The time is coming when neither in
Jerusalem nor on this mountain will
you actually worship the Father.
22 You Samaritans worship something you don't understand. We understand what we worship, because
salvation comes from the Jews.
23 The time is coming when the true
worshipers will worship the Father
in spirit and truth, and that time is
here already. You see, the Father too
is actively seeking such people to
worship him. 24 God is spirit, and
those who worship him must worship in spirit and truth."
25 The woman said, "I know that
the Messiah is coming." (Messiah is
the One called Christ.) "When the
Messiah comes, he will explain everything to us."
26 Then Jesus said, "I am he—I,
the one talking to you."

OLD TESTAMENT READING

Skies, be shocked at the things
that have happened
and shake with great fear!"
says the LORD.
13 "My people have done two evils:
They have turned away from me,
the spring of living water.
And they have dug their own
wells,
which are broken wells that
cannot hold water.
18 It did not help to go to Egypt
and drink from the Shihor
River.
It did not help to go to Assyria
and drink from the Euphrates
River.
19 Your evil will bring punishment to
you,
and the wrong you have done
will teach you a lesson.
Think about it and understand
that it is a terrible evil to
turn away from the LORD
your God.
It is wrong not to fear me,"
says the Lord GOD All-Powerful.

Jeremiah 2:12–13, 18–19

INSIGHTS

The flow of life surging and pulsing through me to refresh this weary old world must be from God Himself. It must be the continuous outpouring of His Presence by His Spirit which touches and transforms all around me. Any person naive enough, arrogant enough, stupid enough to believe that it is his or her own charm, charisma, or capabilities that change and enliven others, lives in utter self-delusion.

One of the terrible tragedies of human behavior is for people to turn to other human beings in an effort to find sustenance for their spirits. They are always deluded, ever disappointed. Our spirits can only find life in the Living Spirit of the Living Lord. Our eternal quest for life-giving water can only be quenched by the eternal life of God Himself coming to us through the hidden springs of His own person who indwells those who are open channels for His life.

W. Phillip Keller

PAUSE FOR REFLECTION

What do those who drink of Jesus' living water receive? How does one receive living water? What is the source of your sustenance?

TUESDAY

When People Believe, God Does Great Things

John 4:27–54

Just then his followers came back
from town and were surprised to see
him talking with a woman. But none
of them asked, "What do you want?"
or "Why are you talking with her?"
28 Then the woman left her water
jar and went back to town. She said
to the people, 29 "Come and see a
man who told me everything I ever
did. Do you think he might be the
Christ?" 30 So the people left the town
and went to see Jesus.
31 Meanwhile, his followers were
begging him, "Teacher, eat something."
32 But Jesus answered, "I have food
to eat that you know nothing about."
33 So the followers asked themselves, "Did somebody already bring
him food?"
34 Jesus said, "My food is to do
what the One who sent me wants me
to do and to finish his work. 35 You
have a saying, 'Four more months till
harvest.' But I tell you, open your
eyes and look at the fields ready for
harvest now. 36 Already, the one who
harvests is being paid and is gathering crops for eternal life. So the one
who plants and the one who harvests
celebrate at the same time. 37 Here
the saying is true, 'One person plants,
and another harvests.' 38 I sent you to
harvest a crop that you did not work
on. Others did the work, and you get
to finish up their work."
39 Many of the Samaritans in that
town believed in Jesus because of
what the woman said: "He told me
everything I ever did." 40 When the
Samaritans came to Jesus, they
begged him to stay with them, so he
stayed there two more days. 41 And
many more believed because of the
things he said.
42 They said to the woman, "First
we believed in Jesus because of your
speech, but now we believe because
we heard him ourselves. We know
that this man really is the Savior of
the world."

Jesus Heals an Officer's Son

Two days later, Jesus left and went
to Galilee. 44 (Jesus had said before
that a prophet is not respected in his
own country.) 45 When Jesus arrived
in Galilee, the people there welcomed him. They had seen all the
things he did at the Passover Feast
in Jerusalem, because they had been
there, too.
46 Jesus went again to visit Cana
in Galilee where he had changed the
water into wine. One of the king's
important officers lived in the city of
Capernaum, and his son was sick.
47 When he heard that Jesus had
come from Judea to Galilee, he went
to Jesus and begged him to come to
Capernaum and heal his son, because his son was almost dead.
48 Jesus said to him, "You people
must see signs and miracles before
you will believe in me."
49 The officer said, "Sir, come before my child dies."
50 Jesus answered, "Go. Your son
will live."
The man believed what Jesus told
him and went home. 51 On the way
the man's servants came and met
him and told him, "Your son is alive."
52 The man asked, "What time did
my son begin to get well?"

They answered, "Yesterday at one o'clock the fever left him."

53 The father knew that one o'clock was the exact time that Jesus had said, "Your son will live." So the man and all the people who lived in his house believed in Jesus.

54 That was the second miracle Jesus did after coming from Judea to Galilee.

OLD TESTAMENT READING

Jehoshaphat's army went out into the Desert of Tekoa early in the morning. As they were starting out, Jehoshaphat stood and said, "Listen to me, people of Judah and Jerusalem. Have faith in the LORD your God, and you will stand strong. Have faith in his prophets, and you will succeed." 21 Jehoshaphat listened to the people's advice. Then he chose men to be singers to the LORD, to praise him because he is holy and wonderful. As they marched in front of the army, they said,

"Thank the LORD,
because his love continues
forever."

22 As they began to sing and praise God, the LORD set ambushes for the people of Ammon, Moab, and Edom who had come to attack Judah. And they were defeated.

2 Chronicles 20:20–22

INSIGHTS

As Joshua 3 opens, the Israelites are camped on the bank of the Jordan River. . . . They are in sight of the Promised Land, Canaan, but they have an enormous problem: a river is right in their path, and there's no convenient way around it. To make matters worse, it is flood season, and any usual fording places are impassable. The waters are deep and turbulent and menacing.

God could easily make the river subside right before their eyes. He could throw a wide bridge across it. But he doesn't. Instead, he gives Joshua some strange orders that he passes on. . . .

. . . Joshua commands the priests to pick up the ark and go stand in the river. . . .

In spite of the problems, the priests had faith enough to obey, and this is what happened: "As soon as the priests who carried the ark reached the Jordan and their feet touched the water's edge, the water from upstream stopped flowing. . . . The priests who carried the ark of the covenant of the LORD stood firm on dry ground in the middle of the Jordan, while all Israel passed by until the whole nation had completed the crossing on dry ground" (Josh 3:15–17).

God didn't give the priests absolute proof or even overwhelming evidence that the waters would part. He did nothing until they put their feet in the water, taking the first step of commitment and obedience. Only then did he stop the flow of the river. In the same way, mountain-moving faith will be given to us as we step out and follow the Lord's direction.

Bill Hybels

PAUSE FOR REFLECTION

Whoever heard of an army singing its way into battle? A flooding river that stopped instantly? An adulterous woman bringing others to Christ? For what do you believe God?

WEDNESDAY

God Gives Eternal Life to Those Who Believe

John 5:1–29

Jesus Heals a Man at a Pool

5 Later Jesus went to Jerusalem for
a special Jewish feast. 2 In Jerusalem there is a pool with five covered
porches, which is called Bethzatha
in the Jewish language. This pool is
near the Sheep Gate. 3 Many sick
people were lying on the porches
beside the pool. Some were blind,
some were crippled, and some were
paralyzed and they waited for the
water to move. 4 Sometimes an angel
of the Lord came down to the pool
and stirred up the water. After the
angel did this, the first person to go
into the pool was healed from any
sickness he had. 5 A man was lying
there who had been sick for thirty-
eight years. 6 When Jesus saw the
man and knew that he had been sick
for such a long time, Jesus asked
him, "Do you want to be well?"
7 The sick man answered, "Sir,
there is no one to help me get into the
pool when the water starts moving.
While I am coming to the water, someone else always gets in before me."
8 Then Jesus said, "Stand up. Pick
up your mat and walk." 9 And immediately the man was well; he picked
up his mat and began to walk.
The day this happened was a Sabbath day. 10 So the Jews said to the
man who had been healed, "Today
is the Sabbath. It is against our law
for you to carry your mat on the Sabbath day."
11 But he answered, "The man
who made me well told me, 'Pick up
your mat and walk.'"
12 Then they asked him, "Who is
the man who told you to pick up your
mat and walk?"
13 But the man who had been
healed did not know who it was, because there were many people in
that place, and Jesus had left.
14 Later, Jesus found the man at
the Temple and said to him, "See,
you are well now. Stop sinning so
that something worse does not happen to you."
15 Then the man left and told the
Jews that Jesus was the one who had
made him well.
16 Because Jesus was doing this
on the Sabbath day, the Jews began
to persecute him. 17 But Jesus said to
them, "My Father never stops working, and so I keep working, too."
18 This made the Jews try still
harder to kill him. They said, "First
Jesus was breaking the law about the
Sabbath day. Now he says that God
is his own Father, making himself
equal with God!"

Jesus Has God's Authority

But Jesus said, "I tell you the truth,
the Son can do nothing alone. The
Son does only what he sees the Father doing, because the Son does
whatever the Father does. 20 The Father loves the Son and shows the
Son all the things he himself does.
But the Father will show the Son
even greater things than this so that
you can all be amazed. 21 Just as the
Father raises the dead and gives
them life, so also the Son gives life
to those he wants to. 22 In fact, the
Father judges no one, but he has
given the Son power to do all the
judging 23 so that all people will

honor the Son as much as they
honor the Father. Anyone who does
not honor the Son does not honor
the Father who sent him.
24 "I tell you the truth, whoever
hears what I say and believes in the
One who sent me has eternal life. That
person will not be judged guilty but
has already left death and entered life.
25 I tell you the truth, the time is coming and is already here when the dead
will hear the voice of the Son of God,
and those who hear will have life.
26 Life comes from the Father himself,
and he has allowed the Son to have
life in himself as well. 27 And the Father has given the Son the power to
judge, because he is the Son of Man.
28 Don't be surprised at this: A time is
coming when all who are dead and in
their graves will hear his voice. 29 Then
they will come out of their graves.
Those who did good will rise and have
life forever, but those who did evil will
rise to be judged guilty."

OLD TESTAMENT READING

Evil will kill the wicked;
those who hate good people
will be judged guilty.
22 But the LORD saves his servants'
lives;
no one who trusts him will be
judged guilty.

Psalm 34:21–22

The LORD is my light and the one
who saves me.
I fear no one.
The LORD protects my life;
I am afraid of no one.

Psalm 27:1

INSIGHTS

The New Testament teaching is not that everyone has eternal life, but that those who come to God through Jesus Christ are given eternal life as a gift. Many passages contain this teaching; it is not found in only one or two texts. The new birth, being "born of the Spirit," is to have the life of God given to us. Not all are born of the Spirit. The Scripture rejects the idea that everybody has a spark of deity within. In fact, the Bible says that man, in his natural condition, is "dead to God" and that rebirth, an action of the Holy Spirit, is required to plant the life of God.

That "the gift of God is eternal life" doesn't mean that our lives just go on and on and on. It means that we share in the divine nature of God, which is itself eternal. It is His life, then, that is lived in our bodies. That's what's meant by eternal life. We don't begin eternal life when we die; we begin it while we still live. Eternity begins with belief in Christ. . . .

. . . Eternal life comes to those who believe in the Son of Man, who has been lifted up on the cross—that act of obedience to the Father, His death, that brought salvation to all who believe in Him. It belongs to those who will share in the resurrection victory of Jesus Christ over death.

Terry Fullam

APPLICATION

In the Old Testament, God is clearly recognized as the source and giver of life. What claims does Jesus make regarding his ability to give eternal life? Have you accepted Jesus' daring offer of eternal life?

THURSDAY

People Choose Whether or Not to Believe in Christ

John 5:30—6:15

Jesus Is God's Son

I can do nothing alone. I judge only
the way I am told, so my judgment is
fair. I don't try to please myself, but I
try to please the One who sent me.
31 "If only I tell people about myself, what I say is not true. 32 But
there is another who tells about me,
and I know that the things he says
about me are true.
33 "You have sent people to John,
and he has told you the truth. 34 It is
not that I accept such human telling;
I tell you this so you can be saved.
35 John was like a burning and shining lamp, and you were happy to enjoy his light for a while.
36 "But I have a proof about myself
that is greater than that of John. The
things I do, which are the things my
Father gave me to do, prove that the
Father sent me. 37 And the Father
himself who sent me has given proof
about me. You have never heard his
voice or seen what he looks like.
38 His teaching does not live in you,
because you don't believe in the One
the Father sent. 39 You carefully
study the Scriptures because you
think they give you eternal life. They
do in fact tell about me, 40 but you
refuse to come to me to have that
life.
41 "I don't need praise from
people. 42 But I know you—I know
that you don't have God's love in
you. 43 I have come from my Father
and speak for him, but you don't accept me. But when another person
comes, speaking only for himself,
you will accept him. 44 You try to get
praise from each other, but you do
not try to get the praise that comes
from the only God. So how can you
believe? 45 Don't think that I will
stand before the Father and say you
are wrong. The one who says you
are wrong is Moses, the one you
hoped would save you. 46 If you really believed Moses, you would believe me, because Moses wrote
about me. 47 But if you don't believe
what Moses wrote, how can you believe what I say?"

More than Five Thousand Fed

6 After this, Jesus went across
Lake Galilee (or, Lake Tiberias).
2 Many people followed him because
they saw the miracles he did to heal
the sick. 3 Jesus went up on a hill and
sat down there with his followers. 4 It
was almost the time for the Jewish
Passover Feast.
5 When Jesus looked up and saw
a large crowd coming toward him,
he said to Philip, "Where can we buy
enough bread for all these people to
eat?" 6 (Jesus asked Philip this question to test him, because Jesus already knew what he planned to do.)
7 Philip answered, "We would all
have to work a month to buy enough
bread for each person to have only
a little piece."
8 Another one of his followers, Andrew, Simon Peter's brother, said,
9 "Here is a boy with five loaves of
barley bread and two little fish, but
that is not enough for so many
people."
10 Jesus said, "Tell the people to
sit down." This was a very grassy
place, and about five thousand men

sat down there. [11]Then Jesus took the loaves of bread, thanked God for them, and gave them to the people who were sitting there. He did the same with the fish, giving as much as the people wanted.

[12]When they had all had enough to eat, Jesus said to his followers, "Gather the leftover pieces of fish and bread so that nothing is wasted."
[13]So they gathered up the pieces and filled twelve baskets with the pieces left from the five barley loaves.

[14]When the people saw this miracle that Jesus did, they said, "He must truly be the Prophet who is coming into the world."

[15]Jesus knew that the people planned to come and take him by force and make him their king, so he left and went into the hills alone.

OLD TESTAMENT READING

Judah is like a young lion.
You have returned from killing, my son.
Like a lion, he stretches out and lies down to rest,
and no one is brave enough to wake him.
[10]Kings will come from Judah's family;
someone from Judah will always be on the throne.
Judah will rule until Shiloh comes,
and the nations will obey him."

Genesis 49:9–10

INSIGHTS

What God did makes sense. It makes sense that Jesus would be our sacrifice because a sacrifice was needed to justify man's presence before God. It makes sense that God would use the Old Law to tutor Israel on their need for grace. It makes sense that Jesus would be our High Priest. What God did makes sense. It can be taught, charted, and put in books on systematic theology.

However, why God did it is absolutely absurd. When one leaves the method and examines the motive, the carefully stacked blocks of logic begin to tumble. That type of love isn't logical; it can't be neatly outlined in a sermon or explained in a term paper. . . .

Even after generations of people had spit in his face, he still loved them. After a nation of chosen ones had stripped him naked and ripped his incarnated flesh, he still died for them. And even today, after billions have chosen to prostitute themselves before pimps of power, fame, and wealth, he still waits for them.

It is inexplicable. It doesn't have a drop of logic nor a thread of rationality. . . .

Bloodstained royalty. A God with tears. A creator with a heart. God became earth's mockery to save his children.

How absurd to think that such nobility would go to such poverty to share such a treasure with such thankless souls.

But he did.

In fact, the only thing more absurd than the gift is our stubborn unwillingness to receive it.

Max Lucado

APPLICATION

What evidence from his life and from the Scriptures proves that Jesus was who he said he was? Why didn't most Jews believe Jesus? Do you believe and trust him?

FRIDAY

Believe in the God of Miracles

John 6:16–40

Jesus Walks on the Water

That evening Jesus' followers went down to Lake Galilee. 17 It was dark now, and Jesus had not yet come to them. The followers got into a boat and started across the lake to Capernaum. 18 By now a strong wind was blowing, and the waves on the lake were getting bigger. 19 When they had rowed the boat about three or four miles, they saw Jesus walking on the water, coming toward the boat. The followers were afraid, 20 but Jesus said to them, "It is I. Do not be afraid." 21 Then they were glad to take him into the boat. At once the boat came to land at the place where they wanted to go.

The People Seek Jesus

The next day the people who had stayed on the other side of the lake knew that Jesus had not gone in the boat with his followers but that they had left without him. And they knew that only one boat had been there. 23 But then some boats came from Tiberias and landed near the place where the people had eaten the bread after the Lord had given thanks. 24 When the people saw that Jesus and his followers were not there now, they got into boats and went to Capernaum to find Jesus.

Jesus, the Bread of Life

When the people found Jesus on the other side of the lake, they asked him, "Teacher, when did you come here?"

26 Jesus answered, "I tell you the truth, you aren't looking for me because you saw me do miracles. You are looking for me because you ate the bread and were satisfied. 27 Don't work for the food that spoils. Work for the food that stays good always and gives eternal life. The Son of Man will give you this food, because on him God the Father has put his power."

28 The people asked Jesus, "What are the things God wants us to do?"

29 Jesus answered, "The work God wants you to do is this: Believe the One he sent."

30 So the people asked, "What miracle will you do? If we see a miracle, we will believe you. What will you do? 31 Our fathers ate the manna in the desert. This is written in the Scriptures: 'He gave them bread from heaven to eat.'"

32 Jesus said, "I tell you the truth, it was not Moses who gave you bread from heaven; it is my Father who is giving you the true bread from heaven. 33 God's bread is the One who comes down from heaven and gives life to the world."

34 The people said, "Sir, give us this bread always."

35 Then Jesus said, "I am the bread that gives life. Whoever comes to me will never be hungry, and whoever believes in me will never be thirsty. 36 But as I told you before, you have seen me and still don't believe. 37 The Father gives me my people. Every one of them will come to me, and I will always accept them. 38 I came down from heaven to do what God wants me to do, not what I want to do. 39 Here is what the One

who sent me wants me to do: I must not lose even one whom God gave me, but I must raise them all on the
last day. 40 Those who see the Son and believe in him have eternal life, and I will raise them on the last day. This is what my Father wants."

OLD TESTAMENT READING

Give thanks to the LORD and
pray to him.
Tell the nations what he has
done.
9 Sing to him; sing praises to him.
Tell about all his miracles.
10 Be glad that you are his;
let those who seek the LORD be
happy.
11 Depend on the LORD and his
strength;
always go to him for help.
12 Remember the miracles he has
done,
his wonders, and his decisions.

1 Chronicles 16:8–12

INSIGHTS

Mom, I need new shoes," Nicky announced as he burst through the door after school. "Miss Bell says it's dangerous to run in gym with my toe sticking out."

I looked down at my son's blue tennies. Hadn't I just bought them last month? But the protruding toe, a slit along the side, and tattered laces told me he'd had them longer. "You're right, Nicky. It's time for some new tennies, but you'll have to wait until our next paycheck. . . ."

"But, Mother," Nicky protested, "I can't wear these shoes for gym anymore. Miss Bell said!"

I launched into an elaborate discourse on budgeting principles. "So you see, Nicky," I concluded, "that's how Mommy and Daddy spend money. Tennis shoes are not in the budget this time; next time they will be."

"Then I'll pray about my shoes," Nicky announced. "I'll tell God I need the money by tomorrow." . . .

. . . When he left for school the next morning, new tennis shoes were still uppermost on his mind. "Can we buy my shoes tonight? You'll get the money today, because I prayed about it."

"We'll see, Nicky," I replied as I kissed him good-bye. There wasn't time to explain just then.

But the need to explain didn't come; Nicky's answer came instead. "This is long overdue . . . sorry for the oversight," said the note I received in the mail that afternoon. The enclosed check, payment for an article I'd written long ago and forgotten, was more than enough to pay for Nicky's new shoes.

After school, Nicky's blue eyes danced. "See, Mom I told you it would come. Now can we buy my shoes?"

Today Nicky wears new blue-and-gold tennis shoes—poignant reminders of a child's simple trust and of my need to continually relearn what faith is all about.

Ruth Senter

ACTION POINT

What is your psalm of praise to the God of miracles? What wonders has he done for you? Praise him with joy! Believe him and seek after the food that gives eternal life.

WEEKEND

When Difficulties Come, Some Want to Reject God

John 6:41–71

The Jews began to complain about Jesus because he said, "I am the bread that comes down from heaven." 42 They said, "This is Jesus, the son of Joseph. We know his father and mother. How can he say, 'I came down from heaven'?"

43 But Jesus answered, "Stop complaining to each other. 44 The Father is the One who sent me. No one can come to me unless the Father draws him to me, and I will raise that person up on the last day. 45 It is written in the prophets, 'They will all be taught by God.' Everyone who listens to the Father and learns from him comes to me. 46 No one has seen the Father except the One who is from God; only he has seen the Father. 47 I tell you the truth, whoever believes has eternal life. 48 I am the bread that gives life. 49 Your ancestors ate the manna in the desert, but still they died. 50 Here is the bread that comes down from heaven. Anyone who eats this bread will never die. 51 I am the living bread that came down from heaven. Anyone who eats this bread will live forever. This bread is my flesh, which I will give up so that the world may have life."

52 Then the Jews began to argue among themselves, saying, "How can this man give us his flesh to eat?"

53 Jesus said, "I tell you the truth, you must eat the flesh of the Son of Man and drink his blood. Otherwise, you won't have real life in you. 54 Those who eat my flesh and drink my blood have eternal life, and I will raise them up on the last day. 55 My flesh is true food, and my blood is true drink. 56 Those who eat my flesh and drink my blood live in me, and I live in them. 57 The living Father sent me, and I live because of the Father. So whoever eats me will live because of me. 58 I am not like the bread your ancestors ate. They ate that bread and still died. I am the bread that came down from heaven, and whoever eats this bread will live forever." 59 Jesus said all these things while he was teaching in the synagogue in Capernaum.

The Words of Eternal Life

When the followers of Jesus heard this, many of them said, "This teaching is hard. Who can accept it?"

61 Knowing that his followers were complaining about this, Jesus said, "Does this teaching bother you? 62 Then will it also bother you to see the Son of Man going back to the place where he came from? 63 It is the Spirit that gives life. The flesh doesn't give life. The words I told you are spirit, and they give life. 64 But some of you don't believe." (Jesus knew from the beginning who did not believe and who would turn against him.) 65 Jesus said, "That is the reason I said, 'If the Father does not bring a person to me, that one cannot come.'"

66 After Jesus said this, many of his followers left him and stopped following him.

67 Jesus asked the twelve followers, "Do you want to leave, too?"

68 Simon Peter answered him, "Lord, where would we go? You have

the words that give eternal life. [69] We
believe and know that you are the
Holy One from God."

[70] Then Jesus answered, "I chose
all twelve of you, but one of you is a
devil."

[71] Jesus was talking about Judas,
the son of Simon Iscariot. Judas was
one of the twelve, but later he was
going to turn against Jesus.

OLD TESTAMENT READING

That night all the people in the
camp began crying loudly. [2] All the
Israelites complained against Moses
and Aaron, and all the people said to
them, "We wish we had died in
Egypt or in this desert. [3] Why is the
LORD bringing us to this land to be
killed with swords? Our wives and
children will be taken away. We
would be better off going back to
Egypt." [4] They said to each other,
"Let's choose a leader and go back
to Egypt."

Numbers 14:1–4

INSIGHTS

As God's children, through having accepted Christ's work for us, accusations are definitely always off limits. As we stand before the Creator of the universe, the all-wise, perfectly holy, mighty God, who made us in His image, who upholds the universe, who understands all things, who has shown His compassion in providing a way for us to come to Him through the Messiah, the Lamb . . . how dare we shake our fist in His face? How dare we question God and say, "Why did you do this to me?" . . .

. . . We can be angry at a person when we are caught in the awful results of cause-and-effect history following the Fall, or following attacks of Satan, or following human choices of one kind or another—but that person is never God. We may not understand our tragic situation. We may not feel we can face life after a terrible shock. We may not feel that we know how to cope in the midst of a war, or avalanche, or earthquake, or famine. But it is always off limits to blame God. We are not to run away from God, shaking our fist at Him and screaming. We are to run to Him when we are shaking with grief or trembling with fear.

He is our refuge and strength; a very present help in trouble. Our help is to come from Him as we run into the shelter of His arms, away from the noise of the battle, or the storm. He has promised us comfort, and we need to climb on His lap as a weeping, hurt child, not to kick at Him.

Edith Schaeffer

PAUSE FOR REFLECTION

What difficulties or lack of understanding in life have tempted you to turn away from God? Did you reject or run toward God? What gives you confidence that Jesus is the "Holy One from God," the one on whom you can believe, the one you can run to for shelter?

MONDAY

The World Hates Those Who Expose Evil

John 7:1–31

Jesus' Brothers Don't Believe

7 After this, Jesus traveled around
Galilee. He did not want to travel
in Judea, because the Jews there
wanted to kill him. 2 It was time for
the Jewish Feast of Shelters. 3 So
Jesus' brothers said to him, "You
should leave here and go to Judea
so your followers there can see the
miracles you do. 4 Anyone who wants
to be well known does not hide what
he does. If you are doing these
things, show yourself to the world."
5 (Even Jesus' brothers did not believe in him.)

6 Jesus said to his brothers, "The
right time for me has not yet come,
but any time is right for you. 7 The
world cannot hate you, but it hates
me, because I tell it the evil things it
does. 8 So you go to the feast. I will
not go yet to this feast, because the
right time for me has not yet come."
9 After saying this, Jesus stayed in
Galilee.

10 But after Jesus' brothers had
gone to the feast, Jesus went also.
But he did not let people see him.
11 At the feast the Jews were looking
for him and saying, "Where is that
man?"

12 Within the large crowd there,
many people were whispering to
each other about Jesus. Some said,
"He is a good man."

Others said, "No, he fools the
people." 13 But no one was brave
enough to talk about Jesus openly,
because they were afraid of the Jews.

Jesus Teaches at the Feast

When the feast was about half over,
Jesus went to the Temple and began
to teach. 15 The Jews were amazed
and said, "This man has never studied in school. How did he learn so
much?"

16 Jesus answered, "The things I
teach are not my own, but they come
from him who sent me. 17 If people
choose to do what God wants, they
will know that my teaching comes
from God and not from me. 18 Those
who teach their own ideas are trying to get honor for themselves. But
those who try to bring honor to the
one who sent him speak the truth,
and there is nothing false in them.
19 Moses gave you the law, but none
of you obeys that law. Why are you
trying to kill me?"

20 The people answered, "A demon has come into you. We are not
trying to kill you."

21 Jesus said to them, "I did one
miracle, and you are all amazed.
22 Moses gave you the law about circumcision. (But really Moses did not
give you circumcision; it came from
our ancestors.) And yet you circumcise a baby on a Sabbath day. 23 If a
baby can be circumcised on a Sabbath day to obey the law of Moses,
why are you angry at me for healing a person's whole body on the
Sabbath day? 24 Stop judging by the
way things look, but judge by what
is really right."

Is Jesus the Christ?

Then some of the people who lived
in Jerusalem said, "This is the man
they are trying to kill. 26 But he is

teaching where everyone can see and hear him, and no one is trying to stop him. Maybe the leaders have decided he really is the Christ. [27] But we know where this man is from. And when the real Christ comes, no one will know where he comes from."

[28] Jesus, teaching in the Temple, cried out, "Yes, you know me, and you know where I am from. But I have not come by my own authority. I was sent by the One who is true, whom you don't know. [29] But I know him, because I am from him, and he sent me."

[30] When Jesus said this, the people tried to take him. But no one was able to touch him, because it was not yet the right time. [31] But many of the people believed in Jesus. They said, "When the Christ comes, will he do more miracles than this man has done?"

OLD TESTAMENT READING

But Jehoshaphat asked, "Isn't there a prophet of the LORD here? Let's ask him what we should do."

[8] Then King Ahab said to Jehoshaphat, "There is one other prophet. We could ask the LORD through him, but I hate him. He never prophesies anything good about me, but something bad. He is Micaiah son of Imlah."

1 Kings 22:7–8

INSIGHTS

A few years ago one of the leading golfers on the professional tour was invited to play in a foursome with Gerald Ford, then president of the United States, Jack Nicklaus, and Billy Graham. . . .

After the round of golf was finished, one of the other pros came up to the golfer and asked, "Hey, what was it like playing with the president and with Billy Graham?"

The pro unleashed a torrent of cursing, and in a disgusted manner said, "I don't need Billy Graham stuffing religion down my throat." With that he turned on his heel and stormed off, heading for the practice tee. . . .

Astonishing. Billy Graham had said not a word about God, Jesus, or religion, yet the pro had stormed away after the game accusing Billy of trying to ram religion down his throat. How can we explain this? It's really not difficult. Billy Graham didn't have to say a word; he didn't have to give a single sideward glance to make the pro feel uncomfortable. Billy Graham is so identified with religion, so associated with the things of God, that his very presence is enough to smother the wicked man who flees when no man pursues. . . .

. . . The greater the holiness the greater the human hostility toward it. It seems insane. No man was ever more loving than Jesus Christ. Yet even His love provoked men to anger. His love was a perfect love, a transcendent and holy love, but His very love brought trauma to people. This kind of love is so majestic we can't stand it.

R. C. Sproul

PAUSE FOR REFLECTION

For what reasons did the leaders of the Jews hate Jesus? Is your life holy enough to incur the wrath of the unrighteous?

TUESDAY

Everyone Has Sinned

John 7:32—8:11

The Leaders Try to Arrest Jesus

The Pharisees heard the crowd
whispering these things about Jesus.
So the leading priests and the Pharisees sent some Temple guards to arrest him. 33 Jesus said, "I will be with
you a little while longer. Then I will
go back to the One who sent me.
34 You will look for me, but you will
not find me. And you cannot come
where I am."

35 The Jews said to each other,
"Where will this man go so we cannot find him? Will he go to the Greek
cities where our people live and teach
the Greek people there? 36 What did
he mean when he said, 'You will look
for me, but you will not find me,' and
'You cannot come where I am'?"

Jesus Talks About the Spirit

On the last and most important day
of the feast Jesus stood up and said
in a loud voice, "Let anyone who is
thirsty come to me and drink. 38 If
anyone believes in me, rivers of living water will flow out from that
person's heart, as the Scripture
says." 39 Jesus was talking about the
Holy Spirit. The Spirit had not yet
been given, because Jesus had not
yet been raised to glory. But later,
those who believed in Jesus would
receive the Spirit.

The People Argue About Jesus

When the people heard Jesus'
words, some of them said, "This
man really is the Prophet."

41 Others said, "He is the Christ."

Still others said, "The Christ will
not come from Galilee. 42 The Scripture says that the Christ will come
from David's family and from
Bethlehem, the town where David
lived." 43 So the people did not agree
with each other about Jesus. 44 Some
of them wanted to arrest him, but no
one was able to touch him.

Some Leaders Won't Believe

The Temple guards went back to
the leading priests and the Pharisees, who asked, "Why didn't you
bring Jesus?"

46 The guards answered, "The
words he says are greater than the
words of any other person who has
ever spoken!"

47 The Pharisees answered, "So
Jesus has fooled you also! 48 Have
any of the leaders or the Pharisees
believed in him? No! 49 But these
people, who know nothing about the
law, are under God's curse."

50 Nicodemus, who had gone to
see Jesus before, was in that group.
He said, 51 "Our law does not judge
a man without hearing him and
knowing what he has done."

52 They answered, "Are you from
Galilee, too? Study the Scriptures,
and you will learn that no prophet
comes from Galilee."

53 And everyone left and went
home.

The Woman Caught in Adultery

8 Jesus went to the Mount of Olives.
2 But early in the morning he
went back to the Temple, and all the
people came to him, and he sat and

taught them. [3]The teachers of the
law and the Pharisees brought a
woman who had been caught in
adultery. They forced her to stand
before the people. [4]They said to
Jesus, "Teacher, this woman was
caught having sexual relations with
a man who is not her husband. [5]The
law of Moses commands that we
stone to death every woman who
does this. What do you say we
should do?" [6]They were asking this
to trick Jesus so that they could have
some charge against him.

But Jesus bent over and started
writing on the ground with his finger. [7]When they continued to ask
Jesus their question, he raised up
and said, "Anyone here who has
never sinned can throw the first
stone at her." [8]Then Jesus bent over
again and wrote on the ground.

[9]Those who heard Jesus began to
leave one by one, first the older men
and then the others. Jesus was left
there alone with the woman standing before him. [10]Jesus raised up
again and asked her, "Woman,
where are they? Has no one judged
you guilty?"

[11]She answered, "No one, sir."

Then Jesus said, "I also don't judge you guilty. You may go now, but don't sin anymore."

OLD TESTAMENT READING

> No one can say, "I am innocent;
> I have never done anything
> wrong."
>
> *Proverbs 20:9*

INSIGHTS

The same sin that Adam introduced has polluted the entire human race. No one is immune to the sin disease. And no human accomplishment can erase the internal stain that separates us from God. Because Adam sinned, all have sinned. This leads to one conclusion: We all need help. We need forgiveness. We need a Savior.

So . . . how do we get out of this mess? Read the next two verses slowly and carefully.

> *So then as through one transgression there resulted condemnation to all men, even so through one act of righteousness there resulted justification of life to all men. For as through the one man's disobedience the many were made sinners, even so through the obedience of the One the many will be made righteous. (Rom. 5:18–19)*

Wonderful! Marvelous reassurance!

"You're telling me, Chuck, that by simply believing in Jesus Christ I can have eternal life with God, my sins forgiven, a destiny secure in heaven, all of this and much more without my working for that?" Yes, that is precisely what Scripture teaches. I remind you, it is called grace. It's what the Protestant Reformation was all about. Salvation is offered by divine grace, not by human works.

Charles Swindoll

PAUSE FOR REFLECTION

List the ways Scripture readings show that every person has sinned. What did Jesus say to the woman caught in adultery? Is it different than what he says to you? How have you responded?

WEDNESDAY

Jesus' Relationship with His Father

John 8:12–41

Jesus Is the Light of the World

Later, Jesus talked to the people
again, saying, "I am the light of the
world. The person who follows me
will never live in darkness but will
have the light that gives life."
13 The Pharisees said to Jesus,
"When you talk about yourself, you
are the only one to say these things
are true. We cannot accept what you
say."
14 Jesus answered, "Yes, I am saying these things about myself, but
they are true. I know where I came
from and where I am going. But you
don't know where I came from or
where I am going. 15 You judge by human standards. I am not judging anyone. 16 But when I do judge, my judging is true, because I am not alone.
The Father who sent me is with me.
17 Your own law says that when two
witnesses say the same thing, you
must accept what they say. 18 I am
one of the witnesses who speaks
about myself, and the Father who
sent me is the other witness."
19 They asked, "Where is your father?"
Jesus answered, "You don't know
me or my Father. If you knew me,
you would know my Father, too."
20 Jesus said these things while he
was teaching in the Temple, near
where the money is kept. But no one
arrested him, because the right time
for him had not yet come.

The People Misunderstand Jesus

Again, Jesus said to the people, "I
will leave you, and you will look for
me, but you will die in your sins. You
cannot come where I am going."
22 So the Jews asked, "Will Jesus
kill himself? Is that why he said, 'You
cannot come where I am going'?"
23 Jesus said, "You people are
from here below, but I am from
above. You belong to this world, but
I don't belong to this world. 24 So I
told you that you would die in your
sins. Yes, you will die in your sins if
you don't believe that I am he."
25 They asked, "Then who are
you?"
Jesus answered, "I am what I have
told you from the beginning. 26 I have
many things to say and decide about
you. But I tell people only the things
I have heard from the One who sent
me, and he speaks the truth."
27 The people did not understand
that he was talking to them about
the Father. 28 So Jesus said to them,
"When you lift up the Son of Man,
you will know that I am he. You will
know that these things I do are not
by my own authority but that I say
only what the Father has taught
me. 29 The One who sent me is with
me. I always do what is pleasing to
him, so he has not left me alone."
30 While Jesus was saying these
things, many people believed in
him.

Freedom from Sin

So Jesus said to the Jews who believed in him, "If you continue to obey
my teaching, you are truly my followers. 32 Then you will know the truth,
and the truth will make you free."

33 They answered, "We are
Abraham's children, and we have
never been anyone's slaves. So why
do you say we will be free?"
34 Jesus answered, "I tell you the
truth, everyone who lives in sin is a
slave to sin. 35 A slave does not stay
with a family forever, but a son belongs to the family forever. 36 So if the
Son makes you free, you will be truly
free. 37 I know you are Abraham's children, but you want to kill me because
you don't accept my teaching. 38 I am
telling you what my Father has shown
me, but you do what your father has
told you."
39 They answered, "Our father is
Abraham."
Jesus said, "If you were really
Abraham's children, you would do
the things Abraham did. 40 I am a
man who has told you the truth
which I heard from God, but you are
trying to kill me. Abraham did nothing like that. 41 So you are doing the
things your own father did."
But they said, "We are not like
children who never knew who their
father was. God is our Father; he is
the only Father we have."

OLD TESTAMENT READING

So, kings, be wise;
rulers, learn this lesson.
11 Obey the LORD with great fear.
Be happy, but tremble.
12 Show that you are loyal to his
son,
or you will be destroyed by his
anger,
because he can quickly become
angry.
But happy are those who trust
him for protection.

Psalm 2:10–12

INSIGHTS

Think first of the origin of that life of Christ in the Father. They were ONE—*one in life and one in love. In this His abiding in the Father had its root. Though dwelling here on earth, He knew that He was one with the Father; that the Father's life was in Him, and His love on Him. . . .*

. . . The Son is not afraid of losing aught by giving up all to the Father, for He knows that the Father loves Him, and can have no interest apart from that of the beloved Son. He knows that as complete as is the dependence on His part is the communication on the part of the Father of all He possesses. Hence when He had said, "The Son can do nothing of Himself, except he see the Father do it," He adds at once, "Whatsoever things the Father doeth, them also doeth the Son likewise: for the Father loveth the Son, and showeth Him all things that Himself doeth." . . .

. . . Christ was the revelation of the Father on earth. He could not be this if there were not the most perfect unity, the most complete communication of all the Father had to the Son. He could be it because the Father loved Him, and He abode in that love.

Andrew Murray

PAUSE FOR REFLECTION

How many different ways in this passage did Jesus tell the people he was the Son of God? How does God say the people of earth are to treat his son? What convinced you that Jesus is God's son?

THURSDAY

What Does It Mean to Honor God?

John 8:42—9:12

Jesus said to them, "If God were really your Father, you would love me,
because I came from God and now I
am here. I did not come by my own
authority; God sent me. 43 You don't
understand what I say, because you
cannot accept my teaching. 44 You
belong to your father the devil, and
you want to do what he wants. He
was a murderer from the beginning
and was against the truth, because
there is no truth in him. When he
tells a lie, he shows what he is really
like, because he is a liar and the father of lies. 45 But because I speak
the truth, you don't believe me.
46 Can any of you prove that I am
guilty of sin? If I am telling the truth,
why don't you believe me? 47 The
person who belongs to God accepts
what God says. But you don't accept
what God says, because you don't
belong to God."

Jesus Is Greater than Abraham

The Jews answered, "We say you
are a Samaritan and have a demon
in you. Are we not right?"

49 Jesus answered, "I have no demon in me. I give honor to my Father, but you dishonor me. 50 I am not
trying to get honor for myself. There
is One who wants this honor for me,
and he is the judge. 51 I tell you the
truth, whoever obeys my teaching
will never die."

52 The Jews said to Jesus, "Now
we know that you have a demon in
you! Even Abraham and the prophets died. But you say, 'Whoever
obeys my teaching will never die.'
53 Do you think you are greater than
our father Abraham, who died? And
the prophets died, too. Who do you
think you are?"

54 Jesus answered, "If I give honor
to myself, that honor is worth nothing. The One who gives me honor
is my Father, and you say he is your
God. 55 You don't really know him,
but I know him. If I said I did not
know him, I would be a liar like you.
But I do know him, and I obey what
he says. 56 Your father Abraham was
very happy that he would see my
day. He saw that day and was glad."

57 The Jews said to him, "You have
never seen Abraham! You are not
even fifty years old."

58 Jesus answered, "I tell you the
truth, before Abraham was even
born, I am!" 59 When Jesus said this,
the people picked up stones to throw
at him. But Jesus hid himself, and
then he left the Temple.

Jesus Heals a Man Born Blind

9 As Jesus was walking along, he
saw a man who had been born
blind. 2 His followers asked him,
"Teacher, whose sin caused this
man to be born blind—his own sin
or his parents' sin?"

3 Jesus answered, "It is not this
man's sin or his parents' sin that
made him be blind. This man was
born blind so that God's power could
be shown in him. 4 While it is day-
time, we must continue doing the
work of the One who sent me. Night
is coming, when no one can work.
5 While I am in the world, I am the
light of the world."

6 After Jesus said this, he spit on the

ground and made some mud with it and put the mud on the man's eyes.
7 Then he told the man, "Go and wash in the Pool of Siloam." (Siloam means Sent.) So the man went, washed, and came back seeing.
8 The neighbors and some people who had earlier seen this man begging said, "Isn't this the same man who used to sit and beg?"
9 Some said, "He is the one," but others said, "No, he only looks like him."

The man himself said, "I am the man."
10 They asked, "How did you get your sight?"
11 He answered, "The man named Jesus made some mud and put it on my eyes. Then he told me to go to Siloam and wash. So I went and washed, and then I could see."
12 They asked him, "Where is this man?"

"I don't know," he answered.

OLD TESTAMENT READING

The LORD said to Moses, 11 "Phinehas son of Eleazar, the son of Aaron, the priest, has saved the Israelites from my anger. He hates sin as much as I do. Since he tried to save my honor among them, I will not kill them. 12 So tell Phinehas that I am making my peace agreement with him."

Numbers 25:10–12

INSIGHTS

Jesus glorified God by giving himself for the work of His redeeming love. God's glory is His holiness, and God's holiness is His redeeming love—love that triumphs over sin by conquering the sin and rescuing the sinner. Jesus not only told of the Father being the righteous One, whose condemnation must rest on sin, and the loving One, who saves everyone who turns from his sin, but He gave himself to be a sacrifice to that righteousness, a servant to that love, even unto death. It was not only in acts of obedience or words of confession that He glorified God, but in giving himself to magnify the holiness of God, to vindicate at once His law and His love by His atonement. He gave himself, His whole life and being, to show how the Father loved, how the Father must condemn the sin, and yet would save the sinner. He counted nothing too great a sacrifice. He lived and died only that the glory of the Father, the glory of His holiness, of His redeeming love, might break through the dark veil of sin and flesh, and shine into the hearts of the children. . . .

If we want to know the way, let us again study Jesus. He obeyed the Father. Let simple obedience mark our whole life. Let humble, childlike waiting for direction, a Christlike dependence on the Father's showing us His way, be our daily attitude. Let everything be done to the Lord, according to His will, for His glory, in direct relationship to himself. Let God's glory shine out in the holiness of our life.

Andrew Murray

ACTION POINT

What brings honor to God? How did Jesus honor God? How do you think God wants you to honor him? Are you willing to honor him with a holy life?

FRIDAY

Jesus Opens the Eyes of Those Who Believe

John 9:13–41

Pharisees Question the Healing

Then the people took to the Pharisees the man who had been blind.
14 The day Jesus had made mud and
healed his eyes was a Sabbath day.
15 So now the Pharisees asked the
man, "How did you get your sight?"
He answered, "He put mud on my
eyes, I washed, and now I see."
16 So some of the Pharisees were
saying, "This man does not keep the
Sabbath day, so he is not from God."
But others said, "A man who is a
sinner can't do miracles like these."
So they could not agree with each
other.
17 They asked the man again,
"What do you say about him since it
was your eyes he opened?"
The man answered, "He is a
prophet."
18 The Jews did not believe that he
had been blind and could now see
again. So they sent for the man's parents 19 and asked them, "Is this your
son who you say was born blind?
Then how does he now see?"
20 His parents answered, "We know
that this is our son and that he was
born blind. 21 But we don't know how
he can now see. We don't know who
opened his eyes. Ask him. He is old
enough to speak for himself." 22 His
parents said this because they were
afraid of the Jews, who had already
decided that anyone who said Jesus
was the Christ would be put out of the
synagogue. 23 That is why his parents
said, "He is old enough. Ask him."
24 So for the second time, they
called the man who had been blind.
They said, "You should give God the
glory by telling the truth. We know
that this man is a sinner."
25 He answered, "I don't know if
he is a sinner. One thing I do know:
I was blind, and now I see."
26 They asked, "What did he do to
you? How did he make you see
again?"
27 He answered, "I already told
you, and you didn't listen. Why do
you want to hear it again? Do you
want to become his followers, too?"
28 Then they insulted him and
said, "You are his follower, but we
are followers of Moses. 29 We know
that God spoke to Moses, but we
don't even know where this man
comes from."
30 The man answered, "This is a
very strange thing. You don't know
where he comes from, and yet he
opened my eyes. 31 We all know that
God does not listen to sinners, but
he listens to anyone who worships
and obeys him. 32 Nobody has ever
heard of anyone giving sight to a
man born blind. 33 If this man were
not from God, he could do nothing."
34 They answered, "You were
born full of sin! Are you trying to
teach us?" And they threw him out.

Spiritual Blindness

When Jesus heard that they had
thrown him out, Jesus found him
and said, "Do you believe in the Son
of Man?"
36 He asked, "Who is the Son of
Man, sir, so that I can believe in him?"
37 Jesus said to him, "You have

seen him. The Son of Man is the one talking with you."

38 He said, "Lord, I believe!" Then the man worshiped Jesus.

39 Jesus said, "I came into this world so that the world could be judged. I came so that the blind would see and so that those who see will become blind."

40 Some of the Pharisees who were nearby heard Jesus say this and asked, "Are you saying we are blind, too?"

41 Jesus said, "If you were blind, you would not be guilty of sin. But since you keep saying you see, your guilt remains."

OLD TESTAMENT READING

Do good to me, your servant, so
I can live,
so I can obey your word.
18 Open my eyes to see
the miracles in your teachings.
19 I am a stranger on earth.
Do not hide your commands
from me.
20 I wear myself out with desire
for your laws all the time.
21 You scold proud people;
those who ignore your commands are cursed.
22 Don't let me be insulted and
hated
because I keep your rules.
23 Even if princes speak against me,
I, your servant, will think about
your demands.
24 Your rules give me pleasure;
they give me good advice.

Psalm 119:17–24

INSIGHTS

The Lord loves to do things differently. At least four times He opened blind eyes, and He does it a different way each time, depending on the personality and the circumstances.

The Lord deals with each of us, not en masse, but as individuals. Each of us is a special object of the grace and care and faithfulness of God. If you were the only one on the face of the earth, He would still take care of you. This is demonstrated here. He made clay and put it on the man's eyes. And this calls for two things from the man: faith and obedience. The moment he obeyed, he had deliverance. Deliverance comes from obedience.

. . . To follow Him means not to walk in darkness. Here is a man who has never seen the light of day, or seen a tree or a flower, or seen his mother. He has never seen anything. He has always lived in the dark. How glad I am the Savior is the light of the world and can come into any darkened heart that wants to know God. The moment your heart is open to Him, the light shines in.

John G. Mitchell

APPLICATION

What words of faith and wisdom did the blind man speak to the Jewish leaders? Why do you think Jesus looked for him after he was thrown out of the temple? Pray that you will see how much Jesus wants you to believe and trust him.

WEEKEND

Jesus Is Our Caring Shepherd

John 10:1–33

The Shepherd and His Sheep

10 Jesus said, "I tell you the truth, the person who does not enter the sheepfold by the door, but climbs in some other way, is a thief and a robber. 2 The one who enters by the door is the shepherd of the sheep. 3 The one who guards the door opens it for him. And the sheep listen to the voice of the shepherd. He calls his own sheep by name and leads them out. 4 When he brings all his sheep out, he goes ahead of them, and they follow him because they know his voice. 5 But they will never follow a stranger. They will run away from him because they don't know his voice." 6 Jesus told the people this story, but they did not understand what it meant.

Jesus Is the Good Shepherd

So Jesus said again, "I tell you the truth, I am the door for the sheep. 8 All the people who came before me were thieves and robbers. The sheep did not listen to them. 9 I am the door, and the person who enters through me will be saved and will be able to come in and go out and find pasture. 10 A thief comes to steal and kill and destroy, but I came to give life—life in all its fullness.

11 "I am the good shepherd. The good shepherd gives his life for the sheep. 12 The worker who is paid to keep the sheep is different from the shepherd who owns them. When the worker sees a wolf coming, he runs away and leaves the sheep alone. Then the wolf attacks the sheep and scatters them. 13 The man runs away because he is only a paid worker and does not really care about the sheep.

14–15 "I am the good shepherd. I know my sheep, as the Father knows me. And my sheep know me, as I know the Father. I give my life for the sheep. 16 I have other sheep that are not in this flock, and I must bring them also. They will listen to my voice, and there will be one flock and one shepherd. 17 The Father loves me because I give my life so that I can take it back again. 18 No one takes it away from me; I give my own life freely. I have the right to give my life, and I have the right to take it back. This is what my Father commanded me to do."

19 Again the Jews did not agree with each other because of these words of Jesus. 20 Many of them said, "A demon has come into him and made him crazy. Why listen to him?"

21 But others said, "A man who is crazy with a demon does not say things like this. Can a demon open the eyes of the blind?"

Jesus Is Rejected

The time came for the Feast of Dedication at Jerusalem. It was winter, 23 and Jesus was walking in the Temple in Solomon's Porch. 24 The Jews gathered around him and said, "How long will you make us wonder about you? If you are the Christ, tell us plainly."

25 Jesus answered, "I told you already, but you did not believe. The

miracles I do in my Father's name
show who I am. [26] But you don't believe, because you are not my sheep.
[27] My sheep listen to my voice; I
know them, and they follow me. [28] I
give them eternal life, and they will
never die, and no one can steal them
out of my hand. [29] My Father gave
my sheep to me. He is greater than
all, and no person can steal my sheep
out of my Father's hand. [30] The Father and I are one."

[31] Again the Jews picked up stones
to kill Jesus. [32] But he said to them,
"I have done many good works from
the Father. Which of these good
works are you killing me for?"

[33] The Jews answered, "We are not
killing you because of any good work
you did, but because you speak
against God. You are only a human,
but you say you are the same as God!"

OLD TESTAMENT READING

He takes care of his people like
  a shepherd.
 He gathers them like lambs in
  his arms
 and carries them close to him.
He gently leads the mothers of
  the lambs.

Isaiah 40:11

INSIGHTS

Do you need guidance as to your path? Look unto Jesus; it is always possible to discern His form, though partially veiled in mist; and when it is lost, be sure to stand still until He comes back to find and re-establish the blessed connection. . . . Do not get anxious or flurried. Put the government of your life upon His shoulder, and leave Him to execute His plan.

Sometimes He guides us to the rest of the green pastures, and the quiet of the still waters. In other words, we are left through happy months and years to fulfil the ordinary commonplaces of life, content to fill a little space, and receiving great increments of spiritual force for future service. At other times, we are guided from the lowland pastures up into the hills. The way is sunny, above us the precipitous cliffs, beneath the dark turbid stream; but this is well; we would not always be lying the pastures or walking softly by the waters. It is good to climb the heights with their far view and bracing air.

In the late afternoon the Shepherd may lead his flock back into the valleys, through the dark woods, where the branches meet overhead and the wild beast lurks in ambush, but we know that in one hand He has the rod or club, with which to belabour anything that may attack; and in the other the crook to drag us out of the hole. He would not lead us into the dark valley which He had not explored, and whose perils He was not prepared to overcome. Darkness, sorrow, or death do not prove that we have missed His guidance, or have taken the wrong path, but rather that He accounts us able to bear the trial by faith in Himself.

F. B. Meyer

PAUSE FOR REFLECTION

What does Jesus promise to give his sheep who follow him? Study the qualities of the good shepherd that Jesus describes and think about the ways Jesus has been your shepherd. Praise him for his goodness!

MONDAY

Trust in God to Protect and Care for You

John 10:34—11:27

Jesus answered, "It is written in your law that God said, 'I said, you are gods.' 35 This Scripture called those people gods who received God's message, and Scripture is always true. 36 So why do you say that I speak against God because I said, 'I am God's Son'? I am the one God chose and sent into the world. 37 If I don't do what my Father does, then don't believe me. 38 But if I do what my Father does, even though you don't believe in me, believe what I do. Then you will know and understand that the Father is in me and I am in the Father."

39 They tried to take Jesus again, but he escaped from them.

40 Then he went back across the Jordan River to the place where John had first baptized. Jesus stayed there, 41 and many people came to him and said, "John never did a miracle, but everything John said about this man is true." 42 And in that place many believed in Jesus.

The Death of Lazarus

11 A man named Lazarus was sick. He lived in the town of Bethany, where Mary and her sister Martha lived. 2 Mary was the woman who later put perfume on the Lord and wiped his feet with her hair. Mary's brother was Lazarus, the man who was now sick. 3 So Mary and Martha sent someone to tell Jesus, "Lord, the one you love is sick."

4 When Jesus heard this, he said, "This sickness will not end in death. It is for the glory of God, to bring glory to the Son of God." 5 Jesus loved Martha and her sister and Lazarus. 6 But when he heard that Lazarus was sick, he stayed where he was for two more days. 7 Then Jesus said to his followers, "Let's go back to Judea."

8 The followers said, "But Teacher, the Jews there tried to stone you to death only a short time ago. Now you want to go back there?"

9 Jesus answered, "Are there not twelve hours in the day? If anyone walks in the daylight, he will not stumble, because he can see by this world's light. 10 But if anyone walks at night, he stumbles because there is no light to help him see."

11 After Jesus said this, he added, "Our friend Lazarus has fallen asleep, but I am going there to wake him."

12 The followers said, "But Lord, if he is only asleep, he will be all right."

13 Jesus meant that Lazarus was dead, but his followers thought he meant Lazarus was really sleeping. 14 So then Jesus said plainly, "Lazarus is dead. 15 And I am glad for your sakes I was not there so that you may believe. But let's go to him now."

16 Then Thomas (the one called Didymus) said to the other followers, "Let us also go so that we can die with him."

Jesus in Bethany

When Jesus arrived, he learned that Lazarus had already been dead and in the tomb for four days. 18 Bethany was about two miles from Jerusalem. 19 Many of the Jews had

come there to comfort Martha and
Mary about their brother.
20 When Martha heard that Jesus
was coming, she went out to meet
him, but Mary stayed home. 21 Martha
said to Jesus, "Lord, if you had been
here, my brother would not have died.
22 But I know that even now God will
give you anything you ask."
23 Jesus said, "Your brother will
rise and live again."
24 Martha answered, "I know that
he will rise and live again in the resurrection on the last day."
25 Jesus said to her, "I am the resurrection and the life. Those who
believe in me will have life even if
they die. 26 And everyone who lives
and believes in me will never die.
Martha, do you believe this?"
27 Martha answered, "Yes, Lord. I
believe that you are the Christ, the
Son of God, the One coming to the
world."

OLD TESTAMENT READING

I waited patiently for the LORD.
He turned to me and heard my cry.
2 He lifted me out of the pit of destruction,
out of the sticky mud.
He stood me on a rock
and made my feet steady.
3 He put a new song in my mouth,
a song of praise to our God.
Many people will see this and worship him.
Then they will trust the LORD.

Psalm 40:1–3

INSIGHTS

A pair of scientists and botanists were exploring in the Alps for some special kinds of flowers. One day they spied through their field glass a flower of rare beauty. But it was in a ravine with perpendicular cliffs on both sides. Someone must be lowered over the cliff to get it.

A native boy was watching. They said to him, "We will give you five pounds if you will let us lower you into the valley to get the flower." The boy looked into the valley and said, "Just a moment. I'll be back." He soon returned with a man. "I'll go over the cliff," he said, "and get the flower for you if this man holds the rope. He's my dad." Have we learned to trust the Lord as this little boy did his father?

Sometimes we find ourselves putting our confidence in man and what we think he can do for us. But man can let us down. Man can disappoint us. Not so the Lord. Needs may be pressing in but we can look up, trusting an all-wise, all-loving God to do all for our good and His glory.

We can trust the rope of our circumstances to Him. Man may become weary and let the rope drop; or he may be distracted or become impatient. But God never wearies of holding the rope. We can confidently leave it in His strong hand.

Millie Stamm

PAUSE FOR REFLECTION

How long had Lazarus been dead before Jesus reached out and saved him? Doesn't that stretch your ability to trust in his protection? Can you, like the psalmist, confidently praise God for his protection?

TUESDAY

God Honors Our Faith

John 11:28–57

Jesus Cries

After Martha said this, she went
back and talked to her sister Mary
alone. Martha said, "The Teacher is
here and he is asking for you."
29 When Mary heard this, she got
up quickly and went to Jesus. 30 Jesus
had not yet come into the town
but was still at the place where
Martha had met him. 31 The Jews
were with Mary in the house, comforting her. When they saw her
stand and leave quickly, they followed her, thinking she was going
to the tomb to cry there. 32 But Mary
went to the place where Jesus was.
When she saw him, she fell at his
feet and said, "Lord, if you had been
here, my brother would not have
died."

33 When Jesus saw Mary crying
and the Jews who came with her also
crying, he was upset and was deeply
troubled. 34 He asked, "Where did
you bury him?"

"Come and see, Lord," they said.

35 Jesus cried.

36 So the Jews said, "See how
much he loved him."

37 But some of them said, "If Jesus
opened the eyes of the blind man, why
couldn't he keep Lazarus from dying?"

Jesus Raises Lazarus

Again feeling very upset, Jesus
came to the tomb. It was a cave with
a large stone covering the entrance.
39 Jesus said, "Move the stone away."

Martha, the sister of the dead
man, said, "But, Lord, it has been four
days since he died. There will be a
bad smell."

40 Then Jesus said to her, "Didn't I
tell you that if you believed you would
see the glory of God?"

41 So they moved the stone away
from the entrance. Then Jesus
looked up and said, "Father, I thank
you that you heard me. 42 I know that
you always hear me, but I said these
things because of the people here
around me. I want them to believe
that you sent me." 43 After Jesus said
this, he cried out in a loud voice,
"Lazarus, come out!" 44 The dead
man came out, his hands and feet
wrapped with pieces of cloth, and a
cloth around his face.

Jesus said to them, "Take the
cloth off of him and let him go."

The Plan to Kill Jesus

Many of the Jews, who had come
to visit Mary and saw what Jesus did,
believed in him. 46 But some of them
went to the Pharisees and told them
what Jesus had done. 47 Then the
leading priests and Pharisees called
a meeting of the Jewish council.
They asked, "What should we do?
This man is doing many miracles.
48 If we let him continue doing these
things, everyone will believe in him.
Then the Romans will come and take
away our Temple and our nation."

49 One of the men there was
Caiaphas, the high priest that year. He
said, "You people know nothing! 50 You
don't realize that it is better for one
man to die for the people than for the
whole nation to be destroyed."

51 Caiaphas did not think of this
himself. As high priest that year, he
was really prophesying that Jesus
would die for the Jewish nation 52 and

for God's scattered children to bring them all together and make them one.
[53]That day they started planning to kill Jesus. [54]So Jesus no longer traveled openly among the Jews. He left there and went to a place near the desert, to a town called Ephraim and stayed there with his followers.
[55]It was almost time for the Jewish Passover Feast. Many from the country went up to Jerusalem before the Passover to do the special things to make themselves pure. [56]The people looked for Jesus and stood in the Temple asking each other, "Is he coming to the Feast? What do you think?" [57]But the leading priests and the Pharisees had given orders that if anyone knew where Jesus was, he must tell them. Then they could arrest him.

OLD TESTAMENT READING

Elijah lay on top of the boy three times. He prayed to the LORD, "Lord my God, let this boy live again!"
[22]The LORD answered Elijah's prayer; the boy began breathing again and was alive.
[24]"Now I know you really are a man from God," the woman said to Elijah. "I know that the LORD truly speaks through you!"

1 Kings 17:21–22, 24

INSIGHTS

Faith is man's response to God's initiative. . . .

To realize that faith is your response to something God does or says, will take pressure off you and enable you to adopt a more constructive attitude to it. Do not look inside yourself and ask, "How much faith do I have?" Look to God and ask, "What is he saying to me? What would he have me do?" When Jesus praised the great faith of different men and women in the Gospels, he was not praising a mystical inner state. He was usually commenting on a concrete action by which someone responded to him. . . .

Once you understand this you will also begin to see why the amount of faith you have is a less crucial issue than you might have thought. The saying of Jesus about the grain of mustard seed begins to make sense. . . .

How much faith did Martha need to get Lazarus back from the dead? Precious little (Jn. 11:38–40). If we are to go by mystical inner states, every evidence points to Martha having no faith at all. No, what she needed (and what she had) was enough faith to give orders for the tombstone to be moved, in spite of the doubts she felt. And Lazarus was raised from the dead. . . .

Faith then is your decision to respond to God's Word. The decision may either manifest itself in some outward action or else in what we might call an "interior action"—like the committing of your eternal destiny into the hands of Christ. In time the decision grows into an attitude, an attitude of always being ready to respond positively to God's Word.

John White

PAUSE FOR REFLECTION

When Jesus came to them, did Mary and Martha believe he had come to raise Lazarus from the dead? What faith did they have in Jesus? Is your faith in Jesus enough for him to accomplish his purposes?

WEDNESDAY

Evil People Have Always Conspired Against the Righteous and Innocent

John 12:1–26

Jesus with Friends in Bethany

12 Six days before the Passover Feast, Jesus went to Bethany, where Lazarus lived. (Lazarus is the man Jesus raised from the dead.) 2 There they had a dinner for Jesus. Martha served the food, and Lazarus was one of the people eating with Jesus. 3 Mary brought in a pint of very expensive perfume made from pure nard. She poured the perfume on Jesus' feet, and then she wiped his feet with her hair. And the sweet smell from the perfume filled the whole house.

4 Judas Iscariot, one of Jesus' followers who would later turn against him, was there. Judas said, 5 "This perfume was worth three hundred coins. Why wasn't it sold and the money given to the poor?" 6 But Judas did not really care about the poor; he said this because he was a thief. He was the one who kept the money box, and he often stole from it.

7 Jesus answered, "Leave her alone. It was right for her to save this perfume for today, the day for me to be prepared for burial. 8 You will always have the poor with you, but you will not always have me."

The Plot Against Lazarus

A large crowd of Jews heard that Jesus was in Bethany. So they went there to see not only Jesus but Lazarus, whom Jesus raised from the dead. 10 So the leading priests made plans to kill Lazarus, too. 11 Because of Lazarus many of the Jews were leaving them and believing in Jesus.

Jesus Enters Jerusalem

The next day a great crowd who had come to Jerusalem for the Passover Feast heard that Jesus was coming there. 13 So they took branches of palm trees and went out to meet Jesus, shouting,

"Praise God!
God bless the One who comes in
the name of the Lord!
God bless the King of Israel!"

Psalm 118:25-26

14 Jesus found a colt and sat on it. This was as the Scripture says,

15 "Don't be afraid, people of
Jerusalem!
Your king is coming,
sitting on the colt of a donkey."

Zechariah 9:9

16 The followers of Jesus did not understand this at first. But after Jesus was raised to glory, they remembered that this had been written about him and that they had done these things to him.

People Tell About Jesus

There had been many people with Jesus when he raised Lazarus from the dead and told him to come out of the tomb. Now they were telling others about what Jesus did. 18 Many people went out to meet Jesus, because they had heard about this miracle. 19 So the Pharisees said to each other, "You can see that nothing is going right for us. Look!

The whole world is following him."

Jesus Talks About His Death

There were some Greek people,
too, who came to Jerusalem to worship at the Passover Feast. 21 They
went to Philip, who was from
Bethsaida in Galilee, and said, "Sir,
we would like to see Jesus." 22 Philip
told Andrew, and then Andrew and
Philip told Jesus.

23 Jesus said to them, "The time
has come for the Son of Man to receive his glory. 24 I tell you the truth,
a grain of wheat must fall to the
ground and die to make many seeds.
But if it never dies, it remains only a
single seed. 25 Those who love their
lives will lose them, but those who
hate their lives in this world will keep
true life forever. 26 Whoever serves
me must follow me. Then my servant will be with me everywhere I
am. My Father will honor anyone
who serves me."

OLD TESTAMENT READING

LORD, rise up and punish the
wicked.
Don't forget those who need help.
13 Why do wicked people hate God?
They say to themselves, "God
won't punish us."
14 LORD, surely you see these cruel
and evil things;
look at them and do something.
People in trouble look to you for
help.
You are the one who helps the
orphans.
15 Break the power of wicked people.
Punish them for the evil they
have done.

Psalm 10:12–15

INSIGHTS

Charles Haddon Spurgeon remains one of the most colorful and gifted preachers in the history of the church. . . . The new Tabernacle was filled to overflowing every Lord's Day as people came miles by horse and buggy to hear the gifted man handle the Word of God. They were challenged, encouraged, exhorted, fed, and built up in the Christian faith. He was truly a phenomenon. As a result, he became the object of great criticism by the press, by other pastors, by influential people in London, and by petty parishioners. . . .

I am told that his wife, seeing the results of those verbal blows on her husband, decided to assist him in getting back on his feet and regaining his powerful stature in the pulpit. She found in her Bible Matthew 5:10–12—and she printed in beautiful old English the words of this passage on a large sheet of paper. Then she tacked that sheet to the ceiling of their bedroom, directly above Charles' side of the bed! . . . . . . Servants, that statement will help us call a halt to the next pity party we are tempted to throw for ourselves. We are not alone. It has been going on for centuries.

Charles Swindoll

PAUSE FOR REFLECTION

Why did the religious leaders of the day hate Jesus and Lazarus? From whom does persecution come in your life? What portion of Scripture encourages and comforts you during such times?

THURSDAY

Some Who See God's Work Still Do Not Believe

John 12:27—13:5

*N*ow I am very troubled. Should I
say, 'Father, save me from this time'?
No, I came to this time so I could suffer.
28 Father, bring glory to your name!"
Then a voice came from heaven,
"I have brought glory to it, and I will
do it again."
29 The crowd standing there, who
heard the voice, said it was thunder.
But others said, "An angel has
spoken to him."
30 Jesus said, "That voice was for
your sake, not mine. 31 Now is the
time for the world to be judged; now
the ruler of this world will be thrown
down. 32 If I am lifted up from the
earth, I will draw all people toward
me." 33 Jesus said this to show how
he would die.
34 The crowd said, "We have
heard from the law that the Christ
will live forever. So why do you say,
'The Son of Man must be lifted up'?
Who is this 'Son of Man'?"
35 Then Jesus said, "The light will
be with you for a little longer, so walk
while you have the light. Then the
darkness will not catch you. If you
walk in the darkness, you will not
know where you are going. 36 Believe
in the light while you still have it so
that you will become children of
light." When Jesus had said this, he
left and hid himself from them.

Some Won't Believe in Jesus

*T*hough Jesus had done many
miracles in front of the people, they
still did not believe in him. 38 This
was to bring about what Isaiah the
prophet had said:

"Lord, who believed what we told
them?
Who saw the Lord's power in
this?" *Isaiah 53:1*

39 This is why the people could not
believe: Isaiah also had said,
40 "He has blinded their eyes,
and he has closed their minds.
Otherwise they would see with
their eyes
and understand in their minds
and come back to me and be
healed." *Isaiah 6:10*

41 Isaiah said this because he saw
Jesus' glory and spoke about him.
42 But many believed in Jesus,
even many of the leaders. But because of the Pharisees, they did not
say they believed in him for fear they
would be put out of the synagogue.
43 They loved praise from people
more than praise from God.
44 Then Jesus cried out, "Whoever
believes in me is really believing in
the One who sent me. 45 Whoever
sees me sees the One who sent me.
46 I have come as light into the world
so that whoever believes in me
would not stay in darkness.
47 "Anyone who hears my words
and does not obey them, I do not
judge, because I did not come to
judge the world, but to save the
world. 48 There is a judge for those
who refuse to believe in me and do
not accept my words. The word I
have taught will be their judge on the
last day. 49 The things I taught were
not from myself. The Father who
sent me told me what to say and
what to teach. 50 And I know that
eternal life comes from what the Father commands. So whatever I say
is what the Father told me to say."

Jesus Washes His Followers' Feet

13 It was almost time for the Jewish Passover Feast. Jesus
knew that it was time for him to leave
this world and go back to the Father.
He had always loved those who were
his own in the world, and he loved
them all the way to the end.
2 Jesus and his followers were at
the evening meal. The devil had already persuaded Judas Iscariot, the
son of Simon, to turn against Jesus.
3 Jesus knew that the Father had
given him power over everything
and that he had come from God and
was going back to God. 4 So during
the meal Jesus stood up and took off
his outer clothing. Taking a towel, he
wrapped it around his waist. 5 Then
he poured water into a bowl and began to wash the followers' feet, dry-
ing them with the towel that was
wrapped around him.

OLD TESTAMENT READING

Moses heard every family crying
as they stood in the entrances of
their tents. Then the LORD became
very angry, and Moses got upset.
11 He asked the LORD, "Why have you
brought me, your servant, this
trouble? What have I done wrong
that you made me responsible for all
these people? 13b They keep crying to
me, 'We want meat!' 14 I can't take
care of all these people alone. It is
too much for me. 15 If you are going
to continue doing this to me, then
kill me now. If you care about me,
put me to death, and then I won't
have any more troubles."
16 The LORD said to Moses, . . .
18 "Tell the people this: 'Make yourselves holy for tomorrow, and you
will eat meat. You cried to the LORD,
"We want meat! We were better off
in Egypt!" So now the LORD will give
you meat to eat.'"
21 Moses said, "LORD, here are six
hundred thousand people standing
around me, and you say, 'I will give
them enough meat to eat for a
month!' 22 If we killed all the flocks
and herds, that would not be
enough. If we caught all the fish in
the sea, that would not be enough."
23 But the LORD said to Moses, "Do
you think I'm weak? Now you will
see if I can do what I say."

Numbers 11:10–11, 13b–16a, 18, 21–23

INSIGHTS

The late Dr. Heugh, of Glasgow, a short time before he breathed his last, said, "There is nothing I feel more than the criminality of not trusting Christ without doubt—without doubt. Oh, to think what Christ is, what he did, and whom he did it for, and then not to believe him, not to trust him! There is no wickedness like the wickedness of unbelief!"

Charles Spurgeon

PAUSE FOR REFLECTION

Does it surprise you that Moses, even after all the miracles he had seen (and been a part of), still struggled with unbelief? Why is it important for us to believe Jesus? In what ways do you find it difficult to trust and believe Jesus? What "miracles" have you seen that ought to strengthen your belief?

FRIDAY

Jesus Gives a New Commandment to His People

John 13:6–35

Jesus came to Simon Peter, who said
to him, "Lord, are you going to wash
my feet?"
7 Jesus answered, "You don't understand now what I am doing, but
you will understand later."
8 Peter said, "No, you will never
wash my feet."
Jesus answered, "If I don't wash
your feet, you are not one of my
people."
9 Simon Peter answered, "Lord,
then wash not only my feet, but wash
my hands and my head, too!"
10 Jesus said, "After a person has
had a bath, his whole body is clean.
He needs only to wash his feet. And
you men are clean, but not all of
you." 11 Jesus knew who would turn
against him, and that is why he said,
"Not all of you are clean."
12 When he had finished washing
their feet, he put on his clothes and
sat down again. He asked, "Do you
understand what I have just done for
you? 13 You call me 'Teacher' and
'Lord,' and you are right, because
that is what I am. 14 If I, your Lord
and Teacher, have washed your feet,
you also should wash each other's
feet. 15 I did this as an example so
that you should do as I have done
for you. 16 I tell you the truth, a servant is not greater than his master.
A messenger is not greater than the
one who sent him. 17 If you know
these things, you will be happy if you
do them.
18 "I am not talking about all of
you. I know those I have chosen. But
this is to bring about what the Scripture said: 'The man who ate at my
table has turned against me.' 19 I am
telling you this now before it happens so that when it happens, you
will believe that I am he. 20 I tell you
the truth, whoever accepts anyone I
send also accepts me. And whoever
accepts me also accepts the One
who sent me."

Jesus Talks About His Death

After Jesus said this, he was very
troubled. He said openly, "I tell you
the truth, one of you will turn against
me."
22 The followers all looked at each
other, because they did not know
whom Jesus was talking about.
23 One of the followers sitting next to
Jesus was the follower Jesus loved.
24 Simon Peter motioned to him to
ask Jesus whom he was talking
about.
25 That follower leaned closer to
Jesus and asked, "Lord, who is it?"
26 Jesus answered, "I will dip this
bread into the dish. The man I give
it to is the man who will turn against
me." So Jesus took a piece of bread,
dipped it, and gave it to Judas
Iscariot, the son of Simon. 27 As soon
as Judas took the bread, Satan entered him. Jesus said to him, "The
thing that you will do—do it quickly."
28 No one at the table understood
why Jesus said this to Judas. 29 Since
he was the one who kept the money
box, some of the followers thought
Jesus was telling him to buy what
was needed for the feast or to give
something to the poor.
30 Judas took the bread Jesus gave
him and immediately went out. It
was night.

31 When Judas was gone, Jesus
said, "Now the Son of Man receives
his glory, and God receives glory
through him. 32 If God receives glory
through him, then God will give
glory to the Son through himself.
And God will give him glory
quickly."
33 Jesus said, "My children, I will
be with you only a little longer. You
will look for me, and what I told the
Jews, I tell you now: Where I am going you cannot come.
34 "I give you a new command:
Love each other. You must love each
other as I have loved you. 35 All
people will know that you are my followers if you love each other."

OLD TESTAMENT READING

You must not have any other gods
except me.
5 "You must not worship or serve
any idol.
7 "You must not use the name of
the LORD your God thoughtlessly.
8 "Remember to keep the Sabbath
holy.
12 "Honor your father and your
mother.
13 "You must not murder anyone.
14 "You must not be guilty of adultery.
15 "You must not steal.
16 "You must not tell lies about
your neighbor.
17 "You must not want to take your
neighbor's house."

Exodus 20:3, 5a, 7a, 8, 12a, 13–17a

INSIGHTS

With the resurrection of the Lord Jesus and the day of Pentecost came a breath of heavenly love. Those who received Jesus, the incarnation of love, into their lives and who chose to obey His command began to love one another. The pagan world looked on in amazement and said of the believers, "How they love one another!"

Within a few years following this command to love one another, the gospel had spread like a prairie fire throughout the known world. The miracle of God's love, His supernatural agape, had captivated multitudes throughout the decadent, wicked Roman Empire.

Tragically, today one seldom hears "How they love one another!" about Christians. Instead there is far too much suspicion, jealousy, criticism and conflict between Christians, churches and denominations. The unbelieving world often laughs at our publicized conflicts.

But those individuals who do demonstrate this supernatural love are usually warmly received by nonbelievers as well as believers. The churches that obey our Lord's command to "love one another" usually are filled to overflowing and are making a great impact for good and for the glory of God. They represent a highly desirable alternative to secular society.

How does one love supernaturally? By faith. God's Word commands us to love (John 13:34, 35). God's Word promises that He will enable us to do what He commands us to do (1 John 5:14, 15).

Bill Bright

APPLICATION

As Jesus prepared to leave his disciples, what one command did he give them? How can you more fully follow this command?

WEEKEND

Our Obedience Demonstrates Our Love for God

John 13:36—14:26

Peter Will Say He Doesn't Know Jesus

Simon Peter asked Jesus, "Lord,
where are you going?"

Jesus answered, "Where I am
going you cannot follow now, but you
will follow later."

37 Peter asked, "Lord, why can't I
follow you now? I am ready to die for
you!"

38 Jesus answered, "Are you ready
to die for me? I tell you the truth, before the rooster crows, you will say
three times that you don't know me."

Jesus Comforts His Followers

14 Jesus said, "Don't let your
hearts be troubled. Trust in
God, and trust in me. 2 There are
many rooms in my Father's house; I
would not tell you this if it were not
true. I am going there to prepare a
place for you. 3 After I go and prepare
a place for you, I will come back and
take you to be with me so that you
may be where I am. 4 You know the
way to the place where I am going."

5 Thomas said to Jesus, "Lord, we
don't know where you are going. So
how can we know the way?"

6 Jesus answered, "I am the way,
and the truth, and the life. The only
way to the Father is through me. 7 If
you really knew me, you would know
my Father, too. But now you do
know him, and you have seen him."

8 Philip said to him, "Lord, show
us the Father. That is all we need."

9 Jesus answered, "I have been with
you a long time now. Do you still not
know me, Philip? Whoever has seen
me has seen the Father. So why do
you say, 'Show us the Father'? 10 Don't
you believe that I am in the Father and
the Father is in me? The words I say
to you don't come from me, but the
Father lives in me and does his own
work. 11 Believe me when I say that I
am in the Father and the Father is in
me. Or believe because of the
miracles I have done. 12 I tell you the
truth, whoever believes in me will do
the same things that I do. Those who
believe will do even greater things
than these, because I am going to the
Father. 13 And if you ask for anything
in my name, I will do it for you so that
the Father's glory will be shown
through the Son. 14 If you ask me for
anything in my name, I will do it.

The Promise of the Holy Spirit

If you love me, you will obey my
commands. 16 I will ask the Father,
and he will give you another Helper
to be with you forever— 17 the Spirit
of truth. The world cannot accept
him, because it does not see him or
know him. But you know him, because he lives with you and he will
be in you.

18 "I will not leave you all alone like
orphans; I will come back to you.
19 In a little while the world will not
see me anymore, but you will see
me. Because I live, you will live, too.
20 On that day you will know that I
am in my Father, and that you are in
me and I am in you. 21 Those who
know my commands and obey them
are the ones who love me, and my

Father will love those who love me. I will love them and will show myself to them."

22 Then Judas (not Judas Iscariot) said, "But, Lord, why do you plan to show yourself to us and not to the rest of the world?"

23 Jesus answered, "If people love me, they will obey my teaching. My Father will love them, and we will come to them and make our home with them. 24 Those who do not love me do not obey my teaching. This teaching that you hear is not really mine; it is from my Father, who sent me.

25 "I have told you all these things while I am with you. 26 But the Helper will teach you everything and will cause you to remember all that I told you. This Helper is the Holy Spirit whom the Father will send in my name."

OLD TESTAMENT READING

If you carefully obey the commands I am giving you today and love the LORD your God and serve him with your whole being, 14 then he will send rain on your land at the right time, in the fall and spring, and you will be able to gather your grain, new wine, and oil.

Deuteronomy 11:13–14

INSIGHTS

The Master has revealed Himself to you, and is calling for your complete surrender, and you shrink and hesitate. A measure of surrender you are willing to make, and think indeed it is fit and proper that you should. But an utter abandonment, without any reserves, seems to you too much to be asked for. You are afraid of it. It involves too much, you think, and is too great a risk. . . .

. . . Your Lord says, "He that hath my commandments, and keepeth them, he it is that loveth me; and he that loveth me shall be loved of my Father, and I will love him, and will manifest myself to him. . . ."

He loves you with more than the love of friendship. . . . He has given you all, and He asks for all in return. The slightest reserve will grieve Him to the heart. He spared not Himself, and how can you spare yourself? . . .

Oh, be generous in your self-surrender! Meet His measureless devotion for you with a measureless devotion to Him. . . . Whatever there is of you, let Him have it all. Give up forever everything that is separate from Him. . . .

. . . The obligations of love will be to you its sweetest privileges; and the right you have acquired to lavish the uttermost wealth of abandonment of all that you have upon your Lord will seem to lift you into a region of unspeakable glory. The perfect happiness of perfect obedience will dawn upon your soul, and you will begin to know something of what Jesus meant when He said, "I delight to do thy will, O my God."

Hannah Whitall Smith

PAUSE FOR REFLECTION

Why do you obey God? Out of obligation? Because it is the "right" thing to do? God wants us to obey him simply because we love him! Pray for such a love-filled heart that obedience will be a delight!

MONDAY

Serving God Brings Joy

John 14:27—15:27

I leave you peace; my peace I give
you. I do not give it to you as the
world does. So don't let your hearts
be troubled or afraid. 28 You heard
me say to you, 'I am going, but I am
coming back to you.' If you loved me,
you should be happy that I am going back to the Father, because he
is greater than I am. 29 I have told you
this now, before it happens, so that
when it happens, you will believe. 30 I
will not talk with you much longer,
because the ruler of this world is
coming. He has no power over me,
31 but the world must know that I
love the Father, so I do exactly what
the Father told me to do.

"Come now, let us go.

Jesus Is Like a Vine

15 "I am the true vine; my Father
is the gardener. 2 He cuts off
every branch of mine that does not
produce fruit. And he trims and
cleans every branch that produces
fruit so that it will produce even
more fruit. 3 You are already clean
because of the words I have spoken
to you. 4 Remain in me, and I will remain in you. A branch cannot produce fruit alone but must remain in
the vine. In the same way, you cannot produce fruit alone but must remain in me.

5 "I am the vine, and you are the
branches. If any remain in me and I
remain in them, they produce much
fruit. But without me they can do nothing. 6 If any do not remain in me, they
are like a branch that is thrown away
and then dies. People pick up dead
branches, throw them into the fire,
and burn them. 7 If you remain in me
and follow my teachings, you can ask
anything you want, and it will be given
to you. 8 You should produce much
fruit and show that you are my followers, which brings glory to my Father.
9 I loved you as the Father loved me.
Now remain in my love. 10 I have
obeyed my Father's commands, and
I remain in his love. In the same way,
if you obey my commands, you will
remain in my love. 11 I have told you
these things so that you can have the
same joy I have and so that your joy
will be the fullest possible joy.

12 "This is my command: Love
each other as I have loved you. 13 The
greatest love a person can show is
to die for his friends. 14 You are my
friends if you do what I command
you. 15 I no longer call you servants,
because a servant does not know
what his master is doing. But I call
you friends, because I have made
known to you everything I heard
from my Father. 16 You did not
choose me; I chose you. And I gave
you this work: to go and produce
fruit, fruit that will last. Then the
Father will give you anything you
ask for in my name. 17 This is my
command: Love each other.

Jesus Warns His Followers

*I*f the world hates you, remember
that it hated me first. 19 If you belonged to the world, it would love
you as it loves its own. But I have
chosen you out of the world, so you
don't belong to it. That is why the
world hates you. 20 Remember what
I told you: A servant is not greater
than his master. If people did wrong

to me, they will do wrong to you, too.
And if they obeyed my teaching,
they will obey yours, too. 21 They will
do all this to you on account of me,
because they do not know the One
who sent me. 22 If I had not come and
spoken to them, they would not be
guilty of sin, but now they have no
excuse for their sin. 23 Whoever
hates me also hates my Father. 24 I
did works among them that no one
else has ever done. If I had not done
these works, they would not be
guilty of sin. But now they have seen
what I have done, and yet they have
hated both me and my Father. 25 But
this happened so that what is written in their law would be true: 'They
hated me for no reason.'

26 "I will send you the Helper from
the Father; he is the Spirit of truth
who comes from the Father. When
he comes, he will tell about me,
27 and you also must tell people about
me, because you have been with me
from the beginning."

OLD TESTAMENT READING

Create in me a pure heart, God,
and make my spirit right again.
11 Do not send me away from you
or take your Holy Spirit away
from me.
12 Give me back the joy of your
salvation.
Keep me strong by giving me a
willing spirit.
13 Then I will teach your ways to
those who do wrong,
and sinners will turn back to
you.

Psalm 51:10–13

INSIGHTS

If anyone asks the question, "How can I be a happy Christian?" our Lord's answer is very simple: . . . "You cannot have My joy without My life. Abide in Me, and let Me abide in you, and My joy will be in you." . . .

. . . There is no joy like love. There is no joy but love. Christ had just spoken of the Father's love and His own abiding in it, and of His having loved us with that same love. His joy is nothing but the joy of love, of being loved and of loving. It was the joy of receiving His Father's love and abiding in it, and then the joy of passing on that love and pouring it out on sinners. It is this joy He wants us to share: the joy of being loved of the Father and of Him; the joy of in our turn loving and living for those around us. . . .

. . . How sad that we should so need to be reminded that as God alone is the fountain of all joy, "God our exceeding joy," the only way to be perfectly happy is to have as much of God, as much of His will and fellowship, as possible! Religion is meant to be in everyday life a thing of unspeakable joy. And why do so many complain that it is not so? Because they do not believe that there is no joy like the joy of abiding in Christ and in His love, and being branches through whom He can pour out His love on a dying world.

Andrew Murray

PAUSE FOR REFLECTION

In what ways do you think the peace that Jesus promises (John 14:27) differs from the world's peace? What does Jesus say about the relationship between love, joy, and obedience to God?

TUESDAY

God Cares for Those Who Serve Him

John 16:1–28

16 "I have told you these things
to keep you from giving up.
2 People will put you out of their
synagogues. Yes, the time is coming
when those who kill you will think
they are offering service to God.
3 They will do this because they have
not known the Father and they have
not known me. 4 I have told you
these things now so that when the
time comes you will remember that
I warned you.

The Work of the Holy Spirit

I did not tell you these things at the
beginning, because I was with you
then. 5 Now I am going back to the
One who sent me. But none of you
asks me, 'Where are you going?'
6 Your hearts are filled with sadness
because I have told you these things.
7 But I tell you the truth, it is better
for you that I go away. When I go
away, I will send the Helper to you.
If I do not go away, the Helper will
not come. 8 When the Helper comes,
he will prove to the people of the
world the truth about sin, about being right with God, and about judgment. 9 He will prove to them that sin
is not believing in me. 10 He will
prove to them that being right with
God comes from my going to the
Father and not being seen anymore.
11 And the Helper will prove to them
that judgment happened when the
ruler of this world was judged.

12 "I have many more things to say
to you, but they are too much for you
now. 13 But when the Spirit of truth
comes, he will lead you into all truth.
He will not speak his own words, but
he will speak only what he hears,
and he will tell you what is to come.
14 The Spirit of truth will bring glory
to me, because he will take what I
have to say and tell it to you. 15 All
that the Father has is mine. That is
why I said that the Spirit will take
what I have to say and tell it to you.

Sadness Will Become Happiness

After a little while you will not see
me, and then after a little while you
will see me again."

17 Some of the followers said to
each other, "What does Jesus mean
when he says, 'After a little while you
will not see me, and then after a little
while you will see me again'? And
what does he mean when he says,
'Because I am going to the Father'?"
18 They also asked, "What does he
mean by 'a little while'? We don't
understand what he is saying."

19 Jesus saw that the followers
wanted to ask him about this, so he
said to them, "Are you asking each
other what I meant when I said, 'After
a little while you will not see me, and
then after a little while you will see me
again'? 20 I tell you the truth, you will
cry and be sad, but the world will be
happy. You will be sad, but your sadness will become joy. 21 When a
woman gives birth to a baby, she has
pain, because her time has come. But
when her baby is born, she forgets the
pain, because she is so happy that a
child has been born into the world. 22 It
is the same with you. Now you are
sad, but I will see you again and you
will be happy, and no one will take
away your joy. 23 In that day you will

not ask me for anything. I tell you the
truth, my Father will give you anything you ask for in my name. [24] Until now you have not asked for anything in my name. Ask and you will
receive, so that your joy will be the
fullest possible joy.

Victory over the World

I have told you these things, using
stories that hide the meaning. But
the time will come when I will not
use stories like that to tell you
things; I will speak to you in plain
words about the Father. [26] In that day
you will ask the Father for things in
my name. I mean, I will not need to
ask the Father for you. [27] The Father
himself loves you. He loves you because you loved me and believed
that I came from God. [28] I came from
the Father into the world. Now I am
leaving the world and going back to
the Father."

OLD TESTAMENT READING

Trust the LORD and do good.
  Live in the land and feed on
    truth.
[4] Enjoy serving the LORD,
  and he will give you what you
    want.
[5] Depend on the LORD;
  trust him, and he will take care
    of you.
[6] Then your goodness will shine
    like the sun,
  and your fairness like the
    noonday sun.

Psalm 37:3–6

INSIGHTS

You walk your daughter down the aisle. "When did she grow up?"

You wake up in an emergency room to the beeping of a machine and find wires suction-cupped to your chest.

Be the event pleasant or painful, the result is the same. Reality breaks through the papier-mâché mask and screams at you like a Marine drill sergeant. "You are getting old! You are going to die! You can't be someone you are not!". . .

Jesus does his best work at such moments. Just when the truth about life sinks in, his truth starts to surface. He takes us by the hand and dares us not to sweep the facts under the rug but to confront them with him at our side.

Aging? A necessary process to pass on to a better world.

Death? Merely a brief passage, a tunnel.

Self? Designed and created for a purpose, purchased by God himself.

There, was that so bad? . . .

The next time you find yourself alone in a dark alley facing the undeniables of life, don't cover them with a blanket, or ignore them with a nervous grin. Don't turn up the TV and pretend they aren't there. Instead, stand still, whisper his name, and listen. He is nearer than you think.

Max Lucado

PAUSE FOR REFLECTION

Who did Jesus promise to send to his followers? What would he do for them? Why does God love Jesus' followers? What does God do for those he loves? How is he comforting and caring for you today?

WEDNESDAY

God Protects Those Who Follow Him

John 16:29—17:20

Then the followers of Jesus said, "You are speaking clearly to us now and are not using stories that are hard to understand. 30 We can see now that you know all things. You can answer a person's question even before it is asked. This makes us believe you came from God."

31 Jesus answered, "So now you believe? 32 Listen to me; a time is coming when you will be scattered, each to his own home. That time is now here. You will leave me alone, but I am never really alone, because the Father is with me.

33 "I told you these things so that you can have peace in me. In this world you will have trouble, but be brave! I have defeated the world."

Jesus Prays for His Followers

17 After Jesus said these things, he looked toward heaven and prayed, "Father, the time has come. Give glory to your Son so that the Son can give glory to you. 2 You gave the Son power over all people so that the Son could give eternal life to all those you gave him. 3 And this is eternal life: that people know you, the only true God, and that they know Jesus Christ, the One you sent. 4 Having finished the work you gave me to do, I brought you glory on earth. 5 And now, Father, give me glory with you; give me the glory I had with you before the world was made.

6 "I showed what you are like to those you gave me from the world. They belonged to you, and you gave them to me, and they have obeyed your teaching. 7 Now they know that everything you gave me comes from you. 8 I gave them the teachings you gave me, and they accepted them. They knew that I truly came from you, and they believed that you sent me. 9 I am praying for them. I am not praying for people in the world but for those you gave me, because they are yours. 10 All I have is yours, and all you have is mine. And my glory is shown through them. 11 I am coming to you; I will not stay in the world any longer. But they are still in the world. Holy Father, keep them safe by the power of your name, the name you gave me, so that they will be one, just as you and I are one. 12 While I was with them, I kept them safe by the power of your name, the name you gave me. I protected them, and only one of them, the one worthy of destruction, was lost so that the Scripture would come true.

13 "I am coming to you now. But I pray these things while I am still in the world so that these followers can have all of my joy in them. 14 I have given them your teaching. And the world has hated them, because they don't belong to the world, just as I don't belong to the world. 15 I am not asking you to take them out of the world but to keep them safe from the Evil One. 16 They don't belong to the world, just as I don't belong to the world. 17 Make them ready for your service through your truth; your teaching is truth. 18 I have sent them into the world, just as you sent me into the world. 19 For their sake, I am making myself ready to serve so that they can be ready for their service of the truth.

[20]"I pray for these followers, but I am also praying for all those who will believe in me because of their teaching."

OLD TESTAMENT READING

Those who go to God Most High
for safety
will be protected by the
Almighty.
[2]I will say to the LORD, "You are
my place of safety and
protection.
You are my God and I trust
you."

[3]God will save you from hidden
traps
and from deadly diseases.
[4]He will cover you with his
feathers,
and under his wings you can
hide.
His truth will be your shield
and protection.
[5]You will not fear any danger by
night
or an arrow during the day.
[6]You will not be afraid of diseases
that come in the dark
or sickness that strikes at noon.
[7]At your side one thousand people
may die,
or even ten thousand right
beside you,
but you will not be hurt.
[8]You will only watch
and see the wicked punished.

Psalm 91:1–8

INSIGHTS

Someone has said that Psalm 91 is an expanded commentary on the great cry of the apostle Paul: "If God is for us, who can be against us?" (Rom. 8:31). What is the message of the Psalm? . . .

. . . God promises us shelter, covering, and comprehensive protection based on His very nature. Those who claim the promise and dwell in the shelter of the Most High will rest in the shadow of the Almighty. God offers us security, says the psalmist, by providing secret shelter. . . .

. . . Almighty God is saying, in effect, "When you dwell in My most secret place, I promise to be your divine host with the sacred responsibility of covering and caring for you." When we deposit our trust in Him, then He guarantees He will give us His sheltering protection against all that harms us—until our duty is done and our race is finished in His service.

We will still go through trials. That is part of life. But . . . if we are "dwelling" in communion with God, if we are accepting the shelter only He can give, then we will be safe until our work for the Lord is over, until our time on this earth is done. . . .

Our security does not rest in our weak, feeble, timid, fragile, finite humanity—not for a moment. Our security is in clinging to a God who takes care of those who take the conscious step of faith to believe.

Joel Gregory

PAUSE FOR REFLECTION

Why did Jesus pray for protection for all of his followers? What kind of protection did Jesus want for his followers? What assurances does Psalm 91 give to you? As you read Jesus' prayer, do you feel his personal love and care for you? Thank him.

THURSDAY

The Unity of All Believers

John 17:21—18:18

Father, I pray that they can be one. As you are in me and I am in you, I pray that they can also be one in us. Then the world will believe that you sent me. 22 I have given these people the glory that you gave me so that they can be one, just as you and I are one. 23 I will be in them and you will be in me so that they will be completely one. Then the world will know that you sent me and that you loved them just as much as you loved me.

24 "Father, I want these people that you gave me to be with me where I am. I want them to see my glory, which you gave me because you loved me before the world was made. 25 Father, you are the One who is good. The world does not know you, but I know you, and these people know you sent me. 26 I showed them what you are like, and I will show them again. Then they will have the same love that you have for me, and I will live in them."

Jesus Is Arrested

18 When Jesus finished praying, he went with his followers across the Kidron Valley. On the other side there was a garden, and Jesus and his followers went into it.

2 Judas knew where this place was, because Jesus met there often with his followers. Judas was the one who turned against Jesus. 3 So Judas came there with a group of soldiers and some guards from the leading priests and the Pharisees. They were carrying torches, lanterns, and weapons.

4 Knowing everything that would happen to him, Jesus went out and asked, "Who is it you are looking for?"

5 They answered, "Jesus from Nazareth."

"I am he," Jesus said. (Judas, the one who turned against Jesus, was standing there with them.) 6 When Jesus said, "I am he," they moved back and fell to the ground.

7 Jesus asked them again, "Who is it you are looking for?"

They said, "Jesus of Nazareth."

8 "I told you that I am he," Jesus said. "So if you are looking for me, let the others go." 9 This happened so that the words Jesus said before would come true: "I have not lost any of the ones you gave me."

10 Simon Peter, who had a sword, pulled it out and struck the servant of the high priest, cutting off his right ear. (The servant's name was Malchus.) 11 Jesus said to Peter, "Put your sword back. Shouldn't I drink the cup the Father gave me?"

Jesus Is Brought Before Annas

Then the soldiers with their commander and the Jewish guards arrested Jesus. They tied him 13 and led him first to Annas, the father-in-law of Caiaphas, the high priest that year. 14 Caiaphas was the one who told the Jews that it would be better if one man died for all the people.

Peter Says He Doesn't Know Jesus

Simon Peter and another one of Jesus' followers went along after

Jesus. This follower knew the high
priest, so he went with Jesus into the
high priest's courtyard. 16 But Peter
waited outside near the door. The
follower who knew the high priest
came back outside, spoke to the girl
at the door, and brought Peter inside. 17 The girl at the door said to
Peter, "Aren't you also one of that
man's followers?"

Peter answered, "No, I am not!"

18 It was cold, so the servants and
guards had built a fire and were
standing around it, warming themselves. Peter also was standing with
them, warming himself.

OLD TESTAMENT READING

It is good and pleasant
when God's people live
together in peace!
2 It is like perfumed oil poured on
the priest's head
and running down his beard.
It ran down Aaron's beard
and on to the collar of his
robes.
3 It is like the dew of Mount
Hermon
falling on the hills of Jerusalem.
There the LORD gives his blessing
of life forever.

Psalm 133:1–3

INSIGHTS

Our God is a God of unity. It is against His nature to work in the midst of division. That is why in His high priestly prayer (John 17) Jesus repeatedly prayed that "they may be one, just as We are one." Jesus knew that Satan would try to destroy the church through disunity. Thus, He earnestly prayed that the church would be a unified body through which God could accomplish His work.

God's insistence on unity is why so much of the New Testament gives instruction for maintaining the unity of the church. For example, 1 Corinthians 14:40 instructs the church to do all things properly and in order. Ephesians 4:3 exhorts believers to be "diligent to preserve the unity of the Spirit in the bond of peace." . . .

Satan recognizes the power of God's people. He knows that we are the only ones in the world who can keep him from messing up God's plan. So he is desperate to stop us. That is why the church is always under attack from Satan. He wants to get choir folks fighting each other. He wants to get church leaders fighting each other. He wants to get members fighting each other. He wants husbands and wives to be fighting each other. If he succeeds, God's people become ineffective.

As God's people, we must overcome disunity before we can fight any other battles. When we see disunity, we should not join Satan's side and keep it going. We should stop, recognize the source, and act under God's authority to restore our unity so He can continue His work through us.

Anthony Evans

ACTION POINT

Why does Jesus want his followers to be one? In what ways does disunity limit God's work through your life? Prayerfully read Psalm 133 and begin working for the unity that is such a precious blessing to God.

FRIDAY

God Is Truth

John 18:19—19:3

The High Priest Questions Jesus

The high priest asked Jesus questions about his followers and his teaching. [20] Jesus answered, "I have spoken openly to everyone. I have always taught in synagogues and in the Temple, where all the Jews come together. I never said anything in secret. [21] So why do you question me? Ask the people who heard my teaching. They know what I said."

[22] When Jesus said this, one of the guards standing there hit him. The guard said, "Is that the way you answer the high priest?"

[23] Jesus answered him, "If I said something wrong, then show what it was. But if what I said is true, why do you hit me?"

[24] Then Annas sent Jesus, who was still tied, to Caiaphas the high priest.

Peter Again Denies He Knows Jesus

As Simon Peter was standing and warming himself, they said to him, "Aren't you one of that man's followers?"

Peter said it was not true; he said, "No, I am not."

[26] One of the servants of the high priest was there. This servant was a relative of the man whose ear Peter had cut off. The servant said, "Didn't I see you with him in the garden?"

[27] Again Peter said it wasn't true. At once a rooster crowed.

Jesus Is Brought Before Pilate

Early in the morning they led Jesus from Caiaphas's house to the Roman governor's palace. They would not go inside the palace, because they did not want to make themselves unclean; they wanted to eat the Passover meal. [29] So Pilate went outside to them and asked, "What charges do you bring against this man?"

[30] They answered, "If he were not a criminal, we wouldn't have brought him to you."

[31] Pilate said to them, "Take him yourselves and judge him by your own law."

"But we are not allowed to put anyone to death," the Jews answered. [32] (This happened so that what Jesus said about how he would die would come true.)

[33] Then Pilate went back inside the palace and called Jesus to him and asked, "Are you the king of the Jews?"

[34] Jesus said, "Is that your own question, or did others tell you about me?"

[35] Pilate answered, "I am not Jewish. It was your own people and their leading priests who handed you over to me. What have you done wrong?"

[36] Jesus answered, "My kingdom does not belong to this world. If it belonged to this world, my servants would fight so that I would not be given over to the Jews. But my kingdom is from another place."

[37] Pilate said, "So you are a king!"

Jesus answered, "You are the one saying I am a king. This is why I was born and came into the world: to tell people the truth. And everyone who belongs to the truth listens to me."

[38] Pilate said, "What is truth?" After he said this, he went out to the Jews again and said to them, "I find nothing against this man. [39] But it is your custom that I free one prisoner to you at Passover time. Do you want me to free the 'king of the Jews'?"

[40] They shouted back, "No, not him! Let Barabbas go free!" (Barabbas was a robber.)

19 Then Pilate ordered that Jesus be taken away and whipped. [2] The soldiers made a crown from some thorny branches and put it on Jesus' head and put a purple robe around him. [3] Then they came to him many times and said, "Hail, King of the Jews!" and hit him in the face.

OLD TESTAMENT READING

All you nations, praise the LORD.
All you people, praise him
[2] because the LORD loves us very much,
and his truth is everlasting.
Praise the LORD!

Psalm 117:1–2

LORD, you do what is right,
and your laws are fair.
[138] The rules you commanded are right
and completely trustworthy.
[139] I am so upset I am worn out,
because my enemies have forgotten your words.
[140] Your promises are proven,
so I, your servant, love them.
[141] I am unimportant and hated,
but I have not forgotten your orders.
[142] Your goodness continues forever,
and your teachings are true.

Psalm 119:137–142

INSIGHTS

What is truth? I have often wondered how Pilate asked this question. What was his tone of voice? What kind of expression did he have on his face? Was the question raised in jest? Was it cynical? Was Pilate pensive for a moment? We don't really know. If Pilate was momentarily concerned for truth, his mood soon gave way to a spirit of expediency. If he cared about knowing the truth, he certainly didn't care much about doing the truth. . . .

To declare that Jesus was without fault and then minutes later to turn Him over to a barbarous mob was to slaughter the truth. Pilate judged the Truth. He sentenced the Truth. He scourged the Truth. He mocked the Truth. He crucified the Truth.

The irony is that at the very moment he asked his question "What is truth?" he was staring at the pure incarnation of Truth. The One who is the Truth had just said to him, "Everyone who is of the truth hears My voice."

Pilate missed that voice. The words bounced off his ears. He was not "of the truth."

R. C. Sproul

APPLICATION

How ironic that Pilate was so close to the God of truth, yet failed to understand truth. What claims to truth does God make? Does he make his truth available to people? How? Pray that you will draw close to God and trust his truth.

WEEKEND

All Power on Earth Is Given by God

John 19:4–27

Again Pilate came out and said to them, "Look, I am bringing Jesus out to you. I want you to know that I find nothing against him." [5]So Jesus came out, wearing the crown of thorns and the purple robe. Pilate said to them, "Here is the man!"

[6]When the leading priests and the guards saw Jesus, they shouted, "Crucify him! Crucify him!"

But Pilate answered, "Crucify him yourselves, because I find nothing against him."

[7]The Jews answered, "We have a law that says he should die, because he said he is the Son of God."

[8]When Pilate heard this, he was even more afraid. [9]He went back inside the palace and asked Jesus, "Where do you come from?" But Jesus did not answer him. [10]Pilate said, "You refuse to speak to me? Don't you know I have power to set you free and power to have you crucified?"

[11]Jesus answered, "The only power you have over me is the power given to you by God. The man who turned me in to you is guilty of a greater sin."

[12]After this, Pilate tried to let Jesus go. But the Jews cried out, "Anyone who makes himself king is against Caesar. If you let this man go, you are no friend of Caesar."

[13]When Pilate heard what they were saying, he brought Jesus out and sat down on the judge's seat at the place called The Stone Pavement. (In the Jewish language the name is Gabbatha.) [14]It was about noon on Preparation Day of Passover week. Pilate said to the Jews, "Here is your king!"

[15]They shouted, "Take him away! Take him away! Crucify him!"

Pilate asked them, "Do you want me to crucify your king?"

The leading priests answered, "The only king we have is Caesar."

[16]So Pilate handed Jesus over to them to be crucified.

Jesus Is Crucified

The soldiers took charge of Jesus. [17]Carrying his own cross, Jesus went out to a place called The Place of the Skull, which in the Jewish language is called Golgotha. [18]There they crucified Jesus. They also crucified two other men, one on each side, with Jesus in the middle. [19]Pilate wrote a sign and put it on the cross. It read: JESUS OF NAZARETH, THE KING OF THE JEWS. [20]The sign was written in the Jewish language, in Latin, and in Greek. Many of the Jews read the sign, because the place where Jesus was crucified was near the city. [21]The leading Jewish priests said to Pilate, "Don't write, 'The King of the Jews.' But write, 'This man said, "I am the King of the Jews."'"

[22]Pilate answered, "What I have written, I have written."

[23]After the soldiers crucified Jesus, they took his clothes and divided them into four parts, with each soldier getting one part. They also took his long shirt, which was all one piece of cloth, woven from top to bottom. [24]So the soldiers said to each other, "We should not tear this

into parts. Let's throw lots to see who will get it." This happened so that this Scripture would come true:

"They divided my clothes among
them,
and they threw lots for my
clothing." *Psalm 22:18*

So the soldiers did this.

25 Standing near his cross were
Jesus' mother, his mother's sister,
Mary the wife of Clopas, and Mary
Magdalene. 26 When Jesus saw his
mother and the follower he loved
standing nearby, he said to his
mother, "Dear woman, here is your
son." 27 Then he said to the follower,
"Here is your mother." From that
time on, the follower took her to live
in his home.

OLD TESTAMENT READING

Tell them to give this message to their masters: 'The LORD All-Powerful, the God of Israel, says: "Tell
your masters: 5 I made the earth, its
people, and all its animals with my
great power and strength. I can give
the earth to anyone I want. 6 Now I
have given all these lands to
Nebuchadnezzar king of Babylon,
my servant. I will make even the wild
animals obey him. 7 All nations will
serve Nebuchadnezzar and his son and grandson. Then the time will come for Babylon to be defeated, and many nations and great kings will make Babylon their servant."'"

Jeremiah 27:4–7

INSIGHTS

Our sovereign Lord . . . exerts control over His entire universe from beginning to end! His sovereignty means that He either causes or He allows all things to happen that do happen. He is absolutely independent, subject to no one, and influenced by no one. Despite the suffering, violence, and filth of this world, God remains in control—whether or not we acknowledge him. Before time began, God was in control. He has ruled over all creation ever since He created heaven and earth. . . .

The Israelites must have wondered whether God was in control, as they spent four hundred years of bondage in Egypt. Driven day after day by cruel taskmasters, they surely asked, "If there is a God, where is He?" . . . They probably reasoned that either there is no God, or that God did not have the power to stop the madness. But what happened? The sovereign God who controls every circumstance led Israel out of Egypt with mighty demonstrations of His power! Israel never forgot His deliverance. The entire world was shaken! Nations trembled at the prospect of confronting God's people.

Elliot Johnson / Al Schierbaum

PAUSE FOR REFLECTION

Who holds the only real power there is? Why does God give power to certain people for a time? What happens to those who think their power is their own? Submit your heart to his power today!

MONDAY

Rejoice! Jesus Has Risen

John 19:28—20:9

Jesus Dies

After this, Jesus knew that everything had been done. So that the
Scripture would come true, he said,
"I am thirsty." 29 There was a jar full
of vinegar there, so the soldiers
soaked a sponge in it, put the sponge
on a branch of a hyssop plant, and
lifted it to Jesus' mouth. 30 When
Jesus tasted the vinegar, he said, "It
is finished." Then he bowed his head
and died.

31 This day was Preparation Day,
and the next day was a special Sabbath day. Since the Jews did not want
the bodies to stay on the cross on the
Sabbath day, they asked Pilate to order that the legs of the men be broken and the bodies be taken away.
32 So the soldiers came and broke the
legs of the first man on the cross beside Jesus. Then they broke the legs
of the man on the other cross beside
Jesus. 33 But when the soldiers came
to Jesus and saw that he was already
dead, they did not break his legs.
34 But one of the soldiers stuck his
spear into Jesus' side, and at once
blood and water came out. 35 (The one
who saw this happen is the one who
told us this, and whatever he says is
true. And he knows that he tells the
truth, and he tells it so that you might
believe.) 36 These things happened to
make the Scripture come true: "Not
one of his bones will be broken."
37 And another Scripture says, "They
will look at the one they stabbed."

Jesus Is Buried

Later, Joseph from Arimathea
asked Pilate if he could take the
body of Jesus. (Joseph was a secret
follower of Jesus, because he was
afraid of the Jews.) Pilate gave his
permission, so Joseph came and
took Jesus' body away. 39 Nicodemus,
who earlier had come to Jesus at
night, went with Joseph. He brought
about seventy-five pounds of myrrh
and aloes. 40 These two men took
Jesus' body and wrapped it with the
spices in pieces of linen cloth, which
is how the Jewish people bury the
dead. 41 In the place where Jesus was
crucified, there was a garden. In the
garden was a new tomb that had
never been used before. 42 The men
laid Jesus in that tomb because it
was nearby, and the Jews were preparing to start their Sabbath day.

Jesus' Tomb Is Empty

20 Early on the first day of the
week, Mary Magdalene went
to the tomb while it was still dark.
When she saw that the large stone
had been moved away from the
tomb, 2 she ran to Simon Peter and
the follower whom Jesus loved.
Mary said, "They have taken the
Lord out of the tomb, and we don't
know where they have put him."

3 So Peter and the other follower
started for the tomb. 4 They were
both running, but the other follower
ran faster than Peter and reached
the tomb first. 5 He bent down and
looked in and saw the strips of linen
cloth lying there, but he did not go
in. 6 Then following him, Simon Peter arrived and went into the tomb
and saw the strips of linen lying

there. 7 He also saw the cloth that
had been around Jesus' head, which
was folded up and laid in a different
place from the strips of linen. 8 Then
the other follower, who had reached
the tomb first, also went in. He saw
and believed. 9 (They did not yet understand from the Scriptures that
Jesus must rise from the dead.)

OLD TESTAMENT READING

Clap your hands, all you people.
  Shout to God with joy.
2 The LORD Most High is wonderful.
  He is the great King over all
    the earth!
3 He defeated nations for us
  and put them under our
    control.
4 He chose the land we would
    inherit.
  We are the children of Jacob,
    whom he loved. *Selah*

5 God has risen with a shout of joy;
  the LORD has risen as the
    trumpets sounded.
6 Sing praises to God. Sing praises.
  Sing praises to our King. Sing
    praises.
7 God is King of all the earth,
  so sing a song of praise to him.
8 God is King over the nations.
  God sits on his holy throne.
9 The leaders of the nations meet
  with the people of the God of
    Abraham,
because the leaders of the earth
    belong to God.
  He is supreme.

Psalm 47:1–9

I know that my Defender lives,
  and in the end he will stand
    upon the earth.
26 Even after my skin has been
    destroyed,
  in my flesh I will see God.
27 I will see him myself;
  I will see him with my very
    own eyes.
  How my heart wants that to
    happen!

Job 19:25–27

INSIGHTS

Christ is risen:
  The world below lies desolate.
Christ is risen:
  The spirits of evil are fallen.
Christ is risen:
  The angels of God are rejoicing.
Christ is risen:
  The tombs of the dead are
    empty.
Christ is risen indeed from the
    dead,
  The first of the sleepers.
Glory and power are his forever
    and ever.
  Amen.

Hippolytus of Rome

ACTION POINT

When Mary revealed the stunning news that Jesus was no longer in the tomb, the disciples took off running to see it for themselves! Does the realization that Jesus is truly alive set your heart racing? Ask God to renew your excitement and joy in Jesus' resurrection.

TUESDAY

Thomas Wasn't Alone in His Unbelief

John 20:10—21:3

Jesus Appears to Mary Magdalene

Then the followers went back home.
11 But Mary stood outside the tomb,
crying. As she was crying, she bent
down and looked inside the tomb.
12 She saw two angels dressed in white,
sitting where Jesus' body had been,
one at the head and one at the feet.
13 They asked her, "Woman, why
are you crying?"
She answered, "They have taken
away my Lord, and I don't know
where they have put him." 14 When
Mary said this, she turned around
and saw Jesus standing there, but
she did not know it was Jesus.
15 Jesus asked her, "Woman, why
are you crying? Whom are you looking for?"
Thinking he was the gardener,
she said to him, "Did you take him
away, sir? Tell me where you put
him, and I will get him."
16 Jesus said to her, "Mary."
Mary turned toward Jesus and
said in the Jewish language,
"Rabboni." (This means Teacher.)
17 Jesus said to her, "Don't hold on
to me, because I have not yet gone
up to the Father. But go to my brothers and tell them, 'I am going back
to my Father and your Father, to my
God and your God.'"
18 Mary Magdalene went and said
to the followers, "I saw the Lord!"
And she told them what Jesus had
said to her.

Jesus Appears to His Followers

When it was evening on the first
day of the week, the followers were
together. The doors were locked, because they were afraid of the Jews.
Then Jesus came and stood right in
the middle of them and said, "Peace
be with you." 20 After he said this, he
showed them his hands and his side.
The followers were thrilled when
they saw the Lord.
21 Then Jesus said again, "Peace
be with you. As the Father sent me,
I now send you." 22 After he said this,
he breathed on them and said, "Receive the Holy Spirit. 23 If you forgive
anyone his sins, they are forgiven.
If you don't forgive them, they are
not forgiven."

Jesus Appears to Thomas

Thomas (called Didymus), who was
one of the twelve, was not with them
when Jesus came. 25 The other followers kept telling Thomas, "We saw
the Lord."
But Thomas said, "I will not believe it until I see the nail marks in
his hands and put my finger where
the nails were and put my hand into
his side."
26 A week later the followers were
in the house again, and Thomas was
with them. The doors were locked,
but Jesus came in and stood right in
the middle of them. He said, "Peace
be with you." 27 Then he said to Thomas, "Put your finger here, and look
at my hands. Put your hand here in
my side. Stop being an unbeliever
and believe."
28 Thomas said to him, "My Lord
and my God!"
29 Then Jesus told him, "You be-

lieve because you see me. Those
who believe without seeing me will
be truly happy."

Why John Wrote This Book

Jesus did many other miracles in the
presence of his followers that are not
written in this book. 31 But these are
written so that you may believe that
Jesus is the Christ, the Son of God.
Then, by believing, you may have life
through his name.

Jesus Appears to Seven Followers

21 Later, Jesus showed himself
to his followers again—this
time at Lake Galilee. This is how he
showed himself: 2 Some of the followers were together: Simon Peter, Thomas (called Didymus), Nathanael
from Cana in Galilee, the two sons
of Zebedee, and two other followers.
3 Simon Peter said, "I am going out
to fish."

The others said, "We will go with
you." So they went out and got into
the boat. They fished that night but
caught nothing.

OLD TESTAMENT READING

Then Gideon said to God, "You said
you would help me save Israel. 37 I
will put some wool on the threshing
floor. If there is dew only on the wool
but all of the ground is dry, then I
will know that you will use me to
save Israel, as you said." 38 And that
is just what happened. When Gideon
got up early the next morning and
squeezed the wool, he got a full bowl
of water from it.

39 Then Gideon said to God, "Don't
be angry with me if I ask just one more
thing. Please let me make one more
test. Let only the wool be dry while the
ground around it gets wet with dew."
40 That night God did that very thing.
Just the wool was dry, but the ground
around it was wet with dew.

Judges 6:36–40

INSIGHTS

Give your whole being to God without holding back and without doubting. He will prove himself to you, and work in you that which is pleasing in His sight through Jesus Christ. Keep His ways as you know them in the Word. Keep His ways, as nature teaches them, in always doing what appears right. Keep His ways as providence points them out. Keep His ways as the Holy Spirit suggests. Do not think of waiting on God while you say you are not willing to walk in His path. However weak you feel, only be willing, and he who has worked to will, will work to do by His power. . . .

. . . So come with every temptation you feel in yourself, every memory of unwillingness, unwatchfulness, unfaithfulness, and all that causes your unceasing self-condemnation. Put your powerlessness in God's almighty power, and find in waiting on God your deliverance.

Andrew Murray

ACTION POINT

How does God treat those who doubt? What did he do for Gideon, for Mary, for Thomas? What was their response? Do you struggle with unbelief? Ask God to prove himself to you; his answer will overwhelm you!

WEDNESDAY

God's People Need a Shepherd

John 21:4–25

Early the next morning Jesus stood
on the shore, but the followers did
not know it was Jesus. 5 Then he said
to them, "Friends, did you catch any
fish?"
They answered, "No."
6 He said, "Throw your net on the
right side of the boat, and you will
find some." So they did, and they
caught so many fish they could not
pull the net back into the boat.
7 The follower whom Jesus loved
said to Peter, "It is the Lord!" When
Peter heard him say this, he
wrapped his coat around himself.
(Peter had taken his clothes off.)
Then he jumped into the water. 8 The
other followers went to shore in the
boat, dragging the net full of fish.
They were not very far from shore,
only about a hundred yards. 9 When
the followers stepped out of the boat
and onto the shore, they saw a fire
of hot coals. There were fish on the
fire, and there was bread.
10 Then Jesus said, "Bring some of
the fish you just caught."
11 Simon Peter went into the boat
and pulled the net to the shore. It
was full of big fish, one hundred fifty-
three in all, but even though there
were so many, the net did not tear.
12 Jesus said to them, "Come and
eat." None of the followers dared ask
him, "Who are you?" because they
knew it was the Lord. 13 Jesus came
and took the bread and gave it to
them, along with the fish.
14 This was now the third time
Jesus showed himself to his followers
after he was raised from the dead.

Jesus Talks to Peter

When they finished eating, Jesus
said to Simon Peter, "Simon son of
John do you love me more than
these?"
He answered, "Yes, Lord, you
know that I love you."
Jesus said, "Feed my lambs."
16 Again Jesus said, "Simon son of
John do you love me?"
He answered, "Yes, Lord, you
know that I love you."
Jesus said, "Take care of my
sheep."
17 A third time he said, "Simon son
of John do you love me?"
Peter was hurt because Jesus
asked him the third time, "Do you
love me?" Peter said, "Lord, you
know everything; you know that I
love you!"
He said to him, "Feed my sheep.
18 I tell you the truth, when you were
younger, you tied your own belt and
went where you wanted. But when
you are old, you will put out your
hands and someone else will tie you
and take you where you don't want
to go." 19 (Jesus said this to show
how Peter would die to give glory to
God.) Then Jesus said to Peter, "Follow me!"
20 Peter turned and saw that the
follower Jesus loved was walking
behind them. (This was the follower
who had leaned against Jesus at the
supper and had said, "Lord, who will
turn against you?") 21 When Peter
saw him behind them, he asked
Jesus, "Lord, what about him?"
22 Jesus answered, "If I want him

to live until I come back, that is not your business. You follow me."

[23] So a story spread among the followers that this one would not die. But Jesus did not say he would not die. He only said, "If I want him to live until I come back, that is not your business."

[24] That follower is the one who is telling these things and who has now written them down. We know that what he says is true.

[25] There are many other things Jesus did. If every one of them were written down, I suppose the whole world would not be big enough for all the books that would be written.

OLD TESTAMENT READING

Moses said to the LORD, [16] "The LORD is the God of the spirits of all people. May he choose a leader for these people, [17] who will go in and out before them. He must lead them out like sheep and bring them in; the LORD's people must not be like sheep without a shepherd."

Numbers 27:15–17

Then they will know that I, the LORD their God, am with them. The nation of Israel will know that they are my people, says the Lord GOD. [31] You, my human sheep, are the sheep I care for, and I am your God, says the Lord GOD.'"

Ezekiel 34:30–31

INSIGHTS

The shepherd is at the very center of the life of the sheep. He provides for their every need, satisfying them completely.

Sheep will not lie down if they have cause to be fearful. They are easily frightened. However, as soon as the shepherd appears and moves in the midst of the restless flock, they become quiet.

. . . Our Good Shepherd appears, saying, "Fear THOU not; for I am with thee" (Isa. 41:10). His presence in the midst of our need removes fear and gives rest.

Sheep will not lie down if they are hungry. The shepherd searches for the best pasture land available for his sheep. Our Good Shepherd knows we need to be well nourished for inner satisfaction. He provides nourishment for us from the green pastures of His Word. Nourished by it, we can lie down in quiet contentment.

Occasionally He has to MAKE us lie down. It may take illness, loneliness, heartache, or sorrow to accomplish this.

Not only does the shepherd lead his sheep in the green meadows of nourishment and rest, but beside the still waters. We are refreshed at the waters of quietness. . . .

Our Good Shepherd loves to see His sheep contented and relaxed, refreshed and satisfied with Him.

Millie Stamm

PAUSE FOR REFLECTION

Why is it important that God's people be led by a shepherd? How will a good shepherd lead the Lord's sheep? What relationship do you see between loving Jesus and caring for his sheep?

THURSDAY

Tell All the Nations that Jesus Will Return!

Acts 1:1–26

Luke Writes Another Book

1 To Theophilus.

The first book I wrote was about everything Jesus began to do and teach 2 until the day he was taken up into heaven. Before this, with the help of the Holy Spirit, Jesus told the apostles he had chosen what they should do. 3 After his death, he showed himself to them and proved in many ways that he was alive. The apostles saw Jesus during the forty days after he was raised from the dead, and he spoke to them about the kingdom of God. 4 Once when he was eating with them, he told them not to leave Jerusalem. He said, "Wait here to receive the promise from the Father which I told you about. 5 John baptized people with water, but in a few days you will be baptized with the Holy Spirit."

Jesus Is Taken Up Into Heaven

When the apostles were all together, they asked Jesus, "Lord, are you now going to give the kingdom back to Israel?"

7 Jesus said to them, "The Father is the only One who has the authority to decide dates and times. These things are not for you to know. 8 But when the Holy Spirit comes to you, you will receive power. You will be my witnesses—in Jerusalem, in all of Judea, in Samaria, and in every part of the world."

9 After he said this, as they were watching, he was lifted up, and a cloud hid him from their sight. 10 As he was going, they were looking into the sky. Suddenly, two men wearing white clothes stood beside them. 11 They said, "Men of Galilee, why are you standing here looking into the sky? Jesus, whom you saw taken up from you into heaven, will come back in the same way you saw him go."

A New Apostle Is Chosen

Then they went back to Jerusalem from the Mount of Olives. (This mountain is about half a mile from Jerusalem.) 13 When they entered the city, they went to the upstairs room where they were staying. Peter, John, James, Andrew, Philip, Thomas, Bartholomew, Matthew, James son of Alphaeus, Simon (known as the Zealot), and Judas son of James were there. 14 They all continued praying together with some women, including Mary the mother of Jesus, and Jesus' brothers.

15 During this time there was a meeting of the believers (about one hundred twenty of them). Peter stood up and said, 16-17 "Brothers and sisters, in the Scriptures the Holy Spirit said through David something that must happen involving Judas. He was one of our own group and served together with us. He led those who arrested Jesus." 18 (Judas bought a field with the money he got for his evil act. But he fell to his death, his body burst open, and all his intestines poured out. 19 Everyone in Jerusalem learned about this so they named this place Akeldama. In their language Akeldama means

"Field of Blood.") [20] "In the Book of
Psalms," Peter said, "this is written:

'May his place be empty;
leave no one to live in it.'

Psalm 69:25

And it is also written:

'Let another man replace him as
leader.' *Psalm 109:8*

[21-22] "So now a man must become
a witness with us of Jesus' being raised from the dead. He must be one of the men who were part of our group during all the time the Lord Jesus was among us—from the time John was baptizing people until the day Jesus was taken up from us to heaven."

[23] They put the names of two men
before the group. One was Joseph Barsabbas, who was also called Justus. The other was Matthias.
[24-25] The apostles prayed, "Lord, you
know the thoughts of everyone. Show us which one of these two you have chosen to do this work. Show us who should be an apostle in place of Judas, who turned away and went
where he belongs." [26] Then they
used lots to choose between them, and the lots showed that Matthias was the one. So he became an apostle with the other eleven.

OLD TESTAMENT READING

Let the fields and everything in
them rejoice.
Then all the trees of the forest
will sing for joy
13 before the LORD, because he is
coming.
He is coming to judge the world;
he will judge the world with
fairness
and the peoples with truth.

Psalm 96:12–13

INSIGHTS

All true Christians believe that Jesus Christ is coming again. They may differ in their views of when certain promised events will occur, but they all agree that He is returning as He promised. Furthermore, all Christians agree that this faith in future glory ought to motivate the church. . . .

Because we do not know the day or the hour of our Lord's return, we must constantly be ready. The believer who starts to neglect the "blessed hope" (Titus 2:13) will gradually develop a cold heart, a worldly attitude, and an unfaithful life (Luke 12:35–48). . . .

Not only should this expectant attitude make a difference in our conduct, but it should also make a difference in our witness. . . .

Since this is the day of salvation, we must be diligent to do all we can to win the lost. . . . We must understand what the Bible teaches about God's program for this present age, and we must be motivated by a love for the lost (2 Cor. 5:14) and a desire to be pleasing to Him when He returns.

Warren Wiersbe

ACTION POINT

What were Jesus' last words to his apostles? After he went up into heaven, what did God's messengers promise them? Praise God that his people still take his message into every part of the world!

FRIDAY

God's Spirit Fills His People

Acts 2:1–28

The Coming of the Holy Spirit

2 When the day of Pentecost came,
they were all together in one place.
2 Suddenly a noise like a strong,
blowing wind came from heaven and
filled the whole house where they
were sitting. 3 They saw something
like flames of fire that were separated
and stood over each person there.
4 They were all filled with the Holy
Spirit, and they began to speak different languages by the power the
Holy Spirit was giving them.

5 There were some religious Jews
staying in Jerusalem who were from
every country in the world. 6 When
they heard this noise, a crowd came
together. They were all surprised, because each one heard them speaking
in his own language. 7 They were completely amazed at this. They said,
"Look! Aren't all these people that we
hear speaking from Galilee? 8 Then
how is it possible that we each hear
them in our own languages? We are
from different places: 9 Parthia, Me-
dia, Elam, Mesopotamia, Judea,
Cappadocia, Pontus, Asia, 10 Phrygia,
Pamphylia, Egypt, the areas of Libya
near Cyrene, Rome 11 (both Jews and
those who had become Jews), Crete,
and Arabia. But we hear them telling
in our own languages about the great
things God has done!" 12 They were all
amazed and confused, asking each
other, "What does this mean?"

13 But others were making fun of
them, saying, "They have had too
much wine."

Peter Speaks to the People

But Peter stood up with the eleven
apostles, and in a loud voice he
spoke to the crowd: "My fellow Jews,
and all of you who are in Jerusalem,
listen to me. Pay attention to what I
have to say. 15 These people are not
drunk, as you think; it is only nine
o'clock in the morning! 16 But Joel
the prophet wrote about what is happening here today:

17 'God says: In the last days
I will pour out my Spirit on all
kinds of people.
Your sons and daughters will
prophesy.
Your young men will see visions,
and your old men will dream
dreams.
18 At that time I will pour out my
Spirit
also on my male slaves and
female slaves,
and they will prophesy.
19 I will show miracles
in the sky and on the earth:
blood, fire, and thick smoke.
20 The sun will become dark,
the moon red as blood,
before the overwhelming and
glorious day of the Lord will
come.
21 Then anyone who calls on the Lord
will be saved.' *Joel 2:28-32*

22 "People of Israel, listen to these
words: Jesus from Nazareth was a
very special man. God clearly
showed this to you by the miracles,
wonders, and signs he did through
Jesus. You all know this, because it
happened right here among you.
23 Jesus was given to you, and with
the help of those who don't know the
law, you put him to death by nailing
him to a cross. But this was God's

plan which he had made long ago;
he knew all this would happen.
24 God raised Jesus from the dead
and set him free from the pain of
death, because death could not hold
him. 25 For David said this about him:

'I keep the Lord before me
always.
Because he is close by my
side,
I will not be hurt.
26 So I am glad, and I rejoice.
Even my body has hope,
27 because you will not leave me in
the grave.
You will not let your Holy One
rot.
28 You will teach me how to live a
holy life.
Being with you will fill me with
joy.'" *Psalm 16: 8-11*

OLD TESTAMENT READING

The LORD says, "People of Jacob,
you are my servants. Listen
to me!
People of Israel, I chose you."
2 This is what the LORD says, who
made you,
who formed you in your
mother's body,
who will help you:
"People of Jacob, my servants,
don't be afraid.
Israel, I chose you.
3 I will pour out water for the
thirsty land
and make streams flow on dry
land.
I will pour out my Spirit into your
children
and my blessing on your
descendants." *Isaiah 44:1–3*

INSIGHTS

One day while I was sailing, the wind went down and the sea became calm and flat. There was nothing to do but sit in irons and wait for the wind. "Irons" is a sailing term for a windless time of drifting. While waiting for the wind, I drifted past another sailboat that was floating aimlessly. The people on board the craft waved and made a flat of the hand gesture of complaint about the lack of wind. One man stood by the sails and blew on them.

I thought about that for a long time afterward. How like many Christians and far too many churches. Human breath blowing on the sails—no wonder we make so little progress!

The Spirit of God in Hebrew is ruach, meaning "breath" and "wind." At Pentecost the power of the Holy Spirit was like a mighty wind. The Spirit filled the disciples and got them moving again. What we need is a mighty wind—a fresh, bracing wind of a new Pentecost. . . .

. . . So stop blowing your own breath into the sails of your life or your church. Ask for a fresh wind to fill the sails. Without the Holy Spirit, we'll drift in irons and be lost at sea. . . .

Lloyd Ogilvie

ACTION POINT

What did God's Spirit enable the believers to do? For what purpose? Has your life been renewed by God's Spirit? Pray that God's Spirit will fill you, direct you, and enable you to complete God's work in your life!

WEEKEND

Change Your Hearts, and God Will Forgive

Acts 2:29—3:10

Brothers and sisters, I can tell you truly that David, our ancestor, died and was buried. His grave is still here with us today. [30] He was a prophet and knew God had promised him that he would make a person from David's family a king just as he was. [31] Knowing this before it happened, David talked about the Christ rising from the dead. He said:

'He was not left in the grave.
His body did not rot.'

[32] So Jesus is the One whom God raised from the dead. And we are all witnesses to this. [33] Jesus was lifted up to heaven and is now at God's right side. The Father has given the Holy Spirit to Jesus as he promised. So Jesus has poured out that Spirit, and this is what you now see and hear. [34] David was not the one who was lifted up to heaven, but he said:

'The Lord said to my Lord,
"Sit by me at my right side,
35 until I put your enemies under
your control."' *Psalm 110:1*

[36] "So, all the people of Israel should know this truly: God has made Jesus—the man you nailed to the cross—both Lord and Christ."

[37] When the people heard this, they felt guilty and asked Peter and the other apostles, "What shall we do?"

[38] Peter said to them, "Change your hearts and lives and be baptized, each one of you, in the name of Jesus Christ for the forgiveness of your sins. And you will receive the gift of the Holy Spirit. [39] This promise is for you, for your children, and for all who are far away. It is for everyone the Lord our God calls to himself."

[40] Peter warned them with many other words. He begged them, "Save yourselves from the evil of today's people!" [41] Then those people who accepted what Peter said were baptized. About three thousand people were added to the number of believers that day. [42] They spent their time learning the apostles' teaching, sharing, breaking bread, and praying together.

The Believers Share

The apostles were doing many miracles and signs, and everyone felt great respect for God. [44] All the believers were together and shared everything. [45] They would sell their land and the things they owned and then divide the money and give it to anyone who needed it. [46] The believers met together in the Temple every day. They ate together in their homes, happy to share their food with joyful hearts. [47] They praised God and were liked by all the people. Every day the Lord added those who were being saved to the group of believers.

Peter Heals a Crippled Man

3 One day Peter and John went to the Temple at three o'clock, the time set each day for the afternoon prayer service. [2] There, at the Temple gate called Beautiful Gate, was a man who had been crippled all his life. Every day he was carried to this gate to beg for money from the people going into the Temple. [3] The man saw Peter and John going into the Temple and asked them for

money. 4 Peter and John looked
straight at him and said, "Look at
us!" 5 The man looked at them, thinking they were going to give him
some money. 6 But Peter said, "I
don't have any silver or gold, but I
do have something else I can give
you. By the power of Jesus Christ
from Nazareth, stand up and walk!"
7 Then Peter took the man's right
hand and lifted him up. Immediately
the man's feet and ankles became
strong. 8 He jumped up, stood on his
feet, and began to walk. He went into
the Temple with them, walking and
jumping and praising God. 9-10 All the
people recognized him as the
crippled man who always sat by the
Beautiful Gate begging for money.
Now they saw this same man walking and praising God, and they were
amazed. They wondered how this
could happen.

OLD TESTAMENT READING

Come, let's go back to the LORD.
He has hurt us, but he will heal us.
He has wounded us, but he will bandage our wounds.
2 In two days he will put new life in us;
on the third day he will raise us up
so that we may live in his presence 3 and know him.
Let's try to learn about the LORD;
he will come to us as surely as the dawn comes."

Hosea 6:1–3b

INSIGHTS

Are you running on empty because of sin in your life that you think is well hidden? God sees and knows all about it. He wants you to face it, name it, confess it, turn from it, and, where you can, put things right. Self-flagellation will not make any lasting difference. Listen to David: "You do not delight in sacrifice, or I would bring it; you do not take pleasure in burnt offerings. The sacrifices of God are a broken spirit; a broken and contrite heart, O God, you will not despise" (Ps. 51:16–17).

God looks for brokenness of spirit—for a contrite, humble heart that, quickened by the Holy Spirit, teaches us to regard our sin as He does. We learn to pray, in the words of the old hymn:

Throw light into the darkened cells,
Where passion reigns within;
Quicken my conscience till it feels
The loathsomeness of sin.

And when we have seen our sin for what it is and rejected it, God will help us to have the right spirit in our hearts. Then we will be able to add:

Thus prostrate I shall learn of Thee,
What now I feebly prove,
That God alone in Christ can be
Unutterable love.

Jill Briscoe

ACTION POINT

How did Peter's audience respond when they learned the truth about Christ? What did he tell them to do? Do your sins make you sick at heart? Then there is hope for you! Peter's message applies to you as well. Do what he says!

MONDAY

Jesus Is the Only Way to Salvation

Acts 3:11—4:12

Peter Speaks to the People

While the man was holding on to
Peter and John, all the people were
amazed and ran to them at
Solomon's Porch. 12 When Peter saw
this, he said to them, "People of Israel, why are you surprised? You are
looking at us as if it were our own
power or goodness that made this
man walk. 13 The God of Abraham,
Isaac, and Jacob, the God of our ancestors, gave glory to Jesus, his servant. But you handed him over to be
killed. Pilate decided to let him go
free, but you told Pilate you did not
want Jesus. 14 You did not want the
One who is holy and good but asked
Pilate to give you a murderer instead.
15 And so you killed the One who gives
life, but God raised him from the dead.
We are witnesses to this. 16 It was faith
in Jesus that made this crippled man
well. You can see this man, and you
know him. He was made completely
well because of trust in Jesus, and
you all saw it happen!

17 "Brothers and sisters, I know
you did those things to Jesus because neither you nor your leaders
understood what you were doing.
18 God said through the prophets
that his Christ would suffer and die.
And now God has made these things
come true in this way. 19 So you must
change your hearts and lives! Come
back to God, and he will forgive your
sins. Then the Lord will send the
time of rest. 20 And he will send
Jesus, the One he chose to be the
Christ. 21 But Jesus must stay in
heaven until the time comes when
all things will be made right again.
God told about this time long ago
when he spoke through his holy
prophets. 22 Moses said, 'The Lord
your God will give you a prophet like
me, who is one of your own people.
You must listen to everything he
tells you. 23 Anyone who does not listen to that prophet will die, cut off
from God's people.' 24 Samuel, and all
the other prophets who spoke for
God after Samuel, told about this
time now. 25 You are descendants of
the prophets. You have received the
agreement God made with your ancestors. He said to your father
Abraham, 'Through your descendants all the nations on the earth will
be blessed.' 26 God has raised up his
servant Jesus and sent him to you
first to bless you by turning each of
you away from doing evil."

Peter and John at the Council

4 While Peter and John were
speaking to the people, Jewish
priests, the captain of the soldiers
that guarded the Temple, and
Sadducees came up to them. 2 They
were upset because the two apostles
were teaching the people and were
preaching that people will rise from
the dead through the power of Jesus.
3 The Jewish leaders grabbed Peter
and John and put them in jail. Since
it was already night, they kept them
in jail until the next day. 4 But many
of those who had heard Peter and
John preach believed the things they
said. There were now about five thousand in the group of believers.

5 The next day the Jewish rulers, the
older Jewish leaders, and the teachers

of the law met in Jerusalem. [6] Annas
the high priest, Caiaphas, John, and
Alexander were there, as well as everyone from the high priest's family. [7] They made Peter and John
stand before them and then asked
them, "By what power or authority
did you do this?"

[8] Then Peter, filled with the Holy
Spirit, said to them, "Rulers of the
people and you older leaders, [9] are
you questioning us about a good
thing that was done to a crippled man?
Are you asking us who made him
well? [10] We want all of you and all the
Jewish people to know that this man
was made well by the power of Jesus
Christ from Nazareth. You crucified
him, but God raised him from the
dead. This man was crippled, but he
is now well and able to stand here
before you because of the power of
Jesus. [11] Jesus is

'the stone that you builders
rejected,
which has become the cornerstone.' *Psalm 118:22*

[12] Jesus is the only One who can save
people. His name is the only power
in the world that has been given to
save people. We must be saved
through him."

OLD TESTAMENT READING

Because of these things, this is what the Lord God says:

"I will put a stone in the ground in
Jerusalem,
a tested stone.
Everything will be built on this
important and precious
rock.
Anyone who trusts in it will
never be disappointed.
[17] I will use justice as a measuring
line
and goodness as the standard.
The lies you hide behind will be
destroyed as if by hail.
They will be washed away as if
in a flood."

Isaiah 28:16–17

INSIGHTS

I am the way and the truth and the life. No one comes to the Father except through me" (John 14:6). . . .

. . . Jesus did not merely show the way to God; He said, "I am the way." He did not claim merely to know the truth; He said, "I am the truth." He did not merely point to the abundant life; He said, "I am the life." Therefore, within Christianity if there is no Christ, there is no way to God, no truth about God, and no vitality.

How could Jesus make such claims? If He was only a man, His claims are preposterous. But if He is who He said He is, and if He did what He said He would do, His claims make sense. Jesus claimed to be God and to have come to earth to die for our own sin. We deserve to die for our own sin, but Jesus died in our place. He who was sinless accepted the guilt of our sin and died for us. No one else could do it, but He could and did. Thus, He literally became the door by which sinful men and women can approach the Father.

James Boice

APPLICATION

Who is the rock on whom God's salvation is built? What is the way of salvation? Why does no other way of salvation exist?

TUESDAY

Christ's Witnesses Have Nothing to Fear

Acts 4:13–37

The Jewish leaders saw that Peter
and John were not afraid to speak,
and they understood that these men
had no special training or education.
So they were amazed. Then they realized that Peter and John had been
with Jesus. 14 Because they saw the
healed man standing there beside
the two apostles, they could say
nothing against them. 15 After the
Jewish leaders ordered them to
leave the meeting, they began to talk
to each other. 16 They said, "What
shall we do with these men? Everyone in Jerusalem knows they have
done a great miracle, and we cannot
say it is not true. 17 But to keep it
from spreading among the people,
we must warn them not to talk to
people anymore using that name."

18 So they called Peter and John in
again and told them not to speak or to
teach at all in the name of Jesus. 19 But
Peter and John answered them, "You
decide what God would want. Should
we obey you or God? 20 We cannot
keep quiet. We must speak about what
we have seen and heard." 21 The Jewish leaders warned the apostles again
and let them go free. They could not
find a way to punish them, because all
the people were praising God for what
had been done. 22 The man who received the miracle of healing was
more than forty years old.

The Believers Pray

After Peter and John left the meeting of Jewish leaders, they went to
their own group and told them everything the leading priests and the
older Jewish leaders had said to
them. 24 When the believers heard
this, they prayed to God together,
"Lord, you are the One who made
the sky, the earth, the sea, and everything in them. 25 By the Holy
Spirit, through our father David your
servant, you said:

'Why are the nations so angry?
Why are the people making
useless plans?
26 The kings of the earth prepare to
fight,
and their leaders make plans
together
against the Lord
and his Christ.' *Psalm 2:1-2*

27 These things really happened
when Herod, Pontius Pilate, those
who are not Jews, and the Jewish
people all came together against
Jesus here in Jerusalem. Jesus is
your holy servant, the One you
made to be the Christ. 28 These
people made your plan happen because of your power and your will.
29 And now, Lord, listen to their
threats. Lord, help us, your servants,
to speak your word without fear.
30 Help us to be brave by showing us
your power to heal. Give proofs and
make miracles happen by the power
of Jesus, your holy servant."

31 After they had prayed, the place
where they were meeting was
shaken. They were all filled with the
Holy Spirit, and they spoke God's
word without fear.

The Believers Share

The group of believers were united
in their hearts and spirit. All those
in the group acted as though their

private property belonged to everyone in the group. In fact, they shared
everything. 33 With great power the
apostles were telling people that the
Lord Jesus was truly raised from the
dead. And God blessed all the believers very much. 34 No one in the
group needed anything. From time
to time those who owned fields or
houses sold them, brought the
money, 35 and gave it to the apostles.
Then the money was given to anyone who needed it.
36 One of the believers was named
Joseph, a Levite born in Cyprus. The
apostles called him Barnabas (which
means "one who encourages"). 37 Joseph owned a field, sold it, brought
the money, and gave it to the
apostles.

OLD TESTAMENT READING

Because you are precious to me,
 because I give you honor and
  love you,
I will give other people in your
  place;
 I will give other nations to save
  your life.
5 Don't be afraid, because I am
  with you.
 I will bring your children from
  the east
 and gather you from the west.
6 I will tell the north: Give my
  people to me.
 I will tell the south: Don't keep
  my people in prison.
Bring my sons from far away
 and my daughters from
  faraway places.
7 Bring to me all the people who are
  mine,
 whom I made for my glory,
 whom I formed and made."

Isaiah 43:4–7

INSIGHTS

If we are Christians, we have all been delivered to be deliverers! The Word of God commands us to tell people they are in bondage to sin and that God would love to set them free from that taskmaster. . . .

Sometimes this is disappointing work. The people we go to may not want us to deliver them. Moses knew that particular scenario (Exod. 2:13–14). Or it can even be dangerous work. We may not be in danger of losing our life . . . but we may be in danger of losing our popularity, our friends, or in some extreme cases, even our job. Yes, a delivering work can be a disappointing work and even a dangerous work. But it is above all, a directed work, and that's what helps. To have a sense of God's direction when we are disappointed or in danger is a huge boost to our morale. The inner thrill that God has invited us to cooperate with Him takes the worry out of the work. People work is His work, and He will show us what to do, and even how to do it.

Jill Briscoe

PAUSE FOR REFLECTION

Notice how, in these readings, the recitation of one's spiritual heritage served as encouragement to be God's fearless witness. How does your spiritual heritage encourage you to bravely proclaim God's truth?

WEDNESDAY

Give to God What Is His

Acts 5:1–26

Ananias and Sapphira Die

5 But a man named Ananias and
his wife Sapphira sold some land.
2 He kept back part of the money for
himself; his wife knew about this and
agreed to it. But he brought the rest
of the money and gave it to the
apostles. 3 Peter said, "Ananias, why
did you let Satan rule your thoughts
to lie to the Holy Spirit and to keep
for yourself part of the money you
received for the land? 4 Before you
sold the land, it belonged to you. And
even after you sold it, you could have
used the money any way you
wanted. Why did you think of doing
this? You lied to God, not to us!"
5-6 When Ananias heard this, he fell
down and died. Some young men
came in, wrapped up his body, carried it out, and buried it. And everyone who heard about this was filled
with fear.

7 About three hours later his wife
came in, but she did not know what
had happened. 8 Peter said to her,
"Tell me, was the money you got for
your field this much?"

Sapphira answered, "Yes, that
was the price."

9 Peter said to her, "Why did you
and your husband agree to test the
Spirit of the Lord? Look! The men
who buried your husband are at the
door, and they will carry you out."
10 At that moment Sapphira fell down
by his feet and died. When the
young men came in and saw that she
was dead, they carried her out and
buried her beside her husband.
11 The whole church and all the others who heard about these things
were filled with fear.

The Apostles Heal Many

The apostles did many signs and
miracles among the people. And
they would all meet together on
Solomon's Porch. 13 None of the others dared to join them, but all the
people respected them. 14 More and
more men and women believed in
the Lord and were added to the
group of believers. 15 The people
placed their sick on beds and mats
in the streets, hoping that when Peter passed by at least his shadow
might fall on them. 16 Crowds came
from all the towns around Jerusalem, bringing their sick and those
who were bothered by evil spirits,
and all of them were healed.

Leaders Try to Stop the Apostles

The high priest and all his friends
(a group called the Sadducees) became very jealous. 18 They took the
apostles and put them in jail. 19 But
during the night, an angel of the
Lord opened the doors of the jail and
led the apostles outside. The angel
said, 20 "Go stand in the Temple and
tell the people everything about this
new life." 21 When the apostles heard
this, they obeyed and went into the
Temple early in the morning and
continued teaching.

When the high priest and his
friends arrived, they called a meeting of the Jewish leaders and all the
important older Jewish men. They
sent some men to the jail to bring the
apostles to them. 22 But, upon arriv-
ing, the officers could not find the

apostles. So they went back and reported to the Jewish leaders. 23 They
said, "The jail was closed and
locked, and the guards were standing at the doors. But when we
opened the doors, the jail was
empty!" 24 Hearing this, the captain
of the Temple guards and the leading priests were confused and wondered what was happening.
25 Then someone came and told
them, "Listen! The men you put in
jail are standing in the Temple teaching the people." 26 Then the captain
and his men went out and brought
the apostles back. But the soldiers
did not use force, because they were
afraid the people would stone them
to death.

OLD TESTAMENT READING

Achan answered, "It is true! I have
sinned against the LORD, the God of
Israel. This is what I did: 21 Among
the things I saw a beautiful coat from
Babylonia and about five pounds of
silver and more than one and one-
fourth pounds of gold. I wanted
these things very much for myself,
so I took them. You will find them
buried in the ground under my tent,
with the silver underneath."
24 Then Joshua and all the people
led Achan son of Zerah to the Valley
of Trouble. They also took the silver,
the coat, the gold, Achan's sons,
daughters, cattle, donkeys, sheep,
tent, and everything he owned.
25 Joshua said, "I don't know why you
caused so much trouble for us, but
now the LORD will bring trouble to
you." Then all the people threw
stones at Achan and his family until
they died. Then the people burned
them.

Joshua 7:20–21, 24–25

INSIGHTS

When I have made it, I'll have time for . . ." How was that again?

"I want to make a lot of money for God. I must make money now so I can give money later." What was that again?

A farmer was explaining to a minister, "Well, if I'd get enough, I'd give half to the Lord."

"If you had two thousand acres of oil wells," asked the preacher, "would you give revenues from one thousand acres to the Lord?"

"Why, sure," the farmer gloated. "Anyone could live off a thousand acres of oil."

"If you had two hogs, would you give one to the Lord?" queried the minister.

At that, the farmer complained, "That's not fair. You know I have two pigs!"

We don't suddenly, someday, have an abundance of time and money to give. We begin with the little pieces. We are in training now, learning bit by bit to manage money, power, time, relationships and temptation. Then maybe someday we will find ourselves competent to manage life on a grander scale.

Lynn Anderson

PAUSE FOR REFLECTION

What was Ananias and Sapphira's sin against God? Achan's sin? Are you waiting to acquire enough to satisfy yourself before you give to God? What do you have now that you give to him?

THURSDAY

God's Will Can't Be Thwarted

Acts 5:27—6:7

The soldiers brought the apostles to the meeting and made them stand before the Jewish leaders. The high priest questioned them, 28 saying, "We gave you strict orders not to continue teaching in that name. But look, you have filled Jerusalem with your teaching and are trying to make us responsible for this man's death."

29 Peter and the other apostles answered, "We must obey God, not human authority! 30 You killed Jesus by hanging him on a cross. But God, the God of our ancestors, raised Jesus up from the dead! 31 Jesus is the One whom God raised to be on his right side, as Leader and Savior. Through him, all Jewish people could change their hearts and lives and have their sins forgiven. 32 We saw all these things happen. The Holy Spirit, whom God has given to all who obey him, also proves these things are true."

33 When the Jewish leaders heard this, they became angry and wanted to kill them. 34 But a Pharisee named Gamaliel stood up in the meeting. He was a teacher of the law, and all the people respected him. He ordered the apostles to leave the meeting for a little while. 35 Then he said, "People of Israel, be careful what you are planning to do to these men. 36 Remember when Theudas appeared? He said he was a great man, and about four hundred men joined him. But he was killed, and all his followers were scattered; they were able to do nothing. 37 Later, a man named Judas came from Galilee at the time of the registration. He also led a group of followers and was killed, and all his followers were scattered. 38 And so now I tell you: Stay away from these men, and leave them alone. If their plan comes from human authority, it will fail. 39 But if it is from God, you will not be able to stop them. You might even be fighting against God himself!"

The Jewish leaders agreed with what Gamaliel said. 40 They called the apostles in, beat them, and told them not to speak in the name of Jesus again. Then they let them go free. 41 The apostles left the meeting full of joy because they were given the honor of suffering disgrace for Jesus. 42 Every day in the Temple and in people's homes they continued teaching the people and telling the Good News—that Jesus is the Christ.

Seven Leaders Are Chosen

6 The number of followers was growing. But during this same time, the Greek-speaking followers had an argument with the other Jewish followers. The Greek-speaking widows were not getting their share of the food that was given out every day. 2 The twelve apostles called the whole group of followers together and said, "It is not right for us to stop our work of teaching God's word in order to serve tables. 3 So, brothers and sisters, choose seven of your own men who are good, full of the Spirit and full of wisdom. We will put them in charge of this work. 4 Then we can continue to pray and to teach the word of God."

5 The whole group liked the idea, so they chose these seven men: Stephen (a man with great faith and

full of the Holy Spirit), Philip,
Procorus, Nicanor, Timon, Par-
menas, and Nicolas (a man from
Antioch who had become a Jew).
6 Then they put these men before the
apostles, who prayed and laid their
hands on them.
7 The word of God was continuing
to spread. The group of followers in
Jerusalem increased, and a great
number of the Jewish priests believed and obeyed.

OLD TESTAMENT READING

Remember this, and do not
forget it!
Think about these things, you
who turn against God.
9 Remember what happened long
ago.
Remember that I am God, and
there is no other God.
I am God, and there is no one
like me.
10 From the beginning I told you
what would happen in the end.
A long time ago I told you
things that have not yet
happened.
When I plan something, it
happens.
What I want to do, I will do.
11 I am calling a man from the east
to carry out my plan;
he will come like a hawk from
a country far away.
I will make what I have said come
true;
I will do what I have planned."

Isaiah 46:8–11

INSIGHTS

The Lord's thoughts are all working toward "an expected end." . . . God is working with a motive. All things are working together for one object: the good of those who love God. We see only the beginning; God sees the end from the beginning. He knows every letter of the Book of Providence; He sees not only what He is doing, but what will come of what He is doing.

As to our present pain and grief, God sees not these things exclusively, but He sees the future joy and usefulness which will come of them. He regards not only the tearing up of the soil with the plow, but the clothing of that soil with the golden harvest. He sees the after consequences of affliction, and He accounts those painful incidents to be blessed which lead up to so much of happiness. Let us comfort ourselves with this. . . .

You have never seen the Great Artist's masterpiece; you have seen the rough marble, you have marked the chippings that fall on the ground; you have felt the edge of His chisel, you know the weight of His hammer, and you are full of the memory of these things; but oh, could you see that glorious image as it will be when He has put the finishing stroke to it, you would then understand the chisel, and the hammer, and the Worker better than you now do!

Charles Spurgeon

APPLICATION

Did Gamaliel speak to the Jews with true wisdom? What do you learn about God's sovereign will in these readings? Pray to remember that God is working toward "an expected end" and to understand that what happens in your life is part of his work.

FRIDAY

Tell the Nations What God Has Done

Acts 6:8—7:16

Stephen Is Accused

Stephen was richly blessed by God who gave him the power to do great miracles and signs among the people. 9 But some Jewish people were against him. They belonged to the synagogue of Free Men (as it was called), which included Jewish people from Cyrene, Alexandria, Cilicia, and Asia. They all came and argued with Stephen.

10 But the Spirit was helping him to speak with wisdom, and his words were so strong that they could not argue with him. 11 So they secretly urged some men to say, "We heard Stephen speak against Moses and against God."

12 This upset the people, the older Jewish leaders, and the teachers of the law. They came and grabbed Stephen and brought him to a meeting of the Jewish leaders. 13 They brought in some people to tell lies about Stephen, saying, "This man is always speaking against this holy place and the law of Moses. 14 We heard him say that Jesus from Nazareth will destroy this place and that Jesus will change the customs Moses gave us." 15 All the people in the meeting were watching Stephen closely and saw that his face looked like the face of an angel.

Stephen's Speech

7 The high priest said to Stephen, "Are these things true?"

2 Stephen answered, "Brothers and fathers, listen to me. Our glorious God appeared to Abraham, our ancestor, in Mesopotamia before he lived in Haran. 3 God said to Abraham, 'Leave your country and your relatives, and go to the land I will show you.' 4 So Abraham left the country of Chaldea and went to live in Haran. After Abraham's father died, God sent him to this place where you now live. 5 God did not give Abraham any of this land, not even a foot of it. But God promised that he would give this land to him and his descendants, even before Abraham had a child. 6 This is what God said to him: 'Your descendants will be strangers in a land they don't own. The people there will make them slaves and will mistreat them for four hundred years. 7 But I will punish the nation where they are slaves. Then your descendants will leave that land and will worship me in this place.' 8 God made an agreement with Abraham, the sign of which was circumcision. And so when Abraham had his son Isaac, Abraham circumcised him when he was eight days old. Isaac also circumcised his son Jacob, and Jacob did the same for his sons, the twelve ancestors of our people.

9 "Jacob's sons became jealous of Joseph and sold him to be a slave in Egypt. But God was with him 10 and saved him from all his troubles. The king of Egypt liked Joseph and respected him because of the wisdom God gave him. The king made him governor of Egypt and put him in charge of all the people in his palace.

11 "Then all the land of Egypt and Canaan became so dry that nothing would grow, and the people suffered very much. Jacob's sons, our ances-

tors, could not find anything to eat.
[12]But when Jacob heard there was
grain in Egypt, he sent his sons
there. This was their first trip to
Egypt. [13]When they went there a
second time, Joseph told his brothers who he was, and the king
learned about Joseph's family.
[14]Then Joseph sent messengers to
invite Jacob, his father, to come to
Egypt along with all his relatives
(seventy-five persons altogether).
[15]So Jacob went down to Egypt,
where he and his sons died. [16]Later
their bodies were moved to Shechem and put in a grave there. (It was the same grave Abraham had bought for a sum of money from the sons of Hamor in Shechem.)"

OLD TESTAMENT READING

Give thanks to the LORD and
pray to him.
Tell the nations what he has
done.
[2]Sing to him; sing praises to him.
Tell about all his miracles.
[3]Be glad that you are his;
let those who seek the LORD be
happy.
[4]Depend on the LORD and his
strength;
always go to him for help.

Psalm 105:1–4

INSIGHTS

What appears to be foolish in the eyes of society is often that which is most effective in the work of the kingdom. The ignorant, the uneducated, the despised of the world are sometimes God's choicest servants. So it was with Sophie "the scrubwoman" Lichtenfels, "whose sermons rose not from an exalted podium or pulpit but from callused hands and knees and with the rhythm of a lowly washtub and scrub brush." . . .

. . . Her testimony was simple.

"God called me to scrub and preach. I was born a preacher, but since I was poor I had to work. My work is good and I can be trusted, so they want me. But if they have me, they must hear me preach. No preach, no work. I scrub as unto the Lord and I preach to all in the house. When I am out of work I tell my father. He is the best employment office. You don't have to pay or wait. . . .

"Sometimes we pray so foolish. For 12 years I prayed the Lord make me a foreign missionary. One day I prayed like that and my Father said, 'Stop Sophie. Where were you born?' 'In Germany,' I replied. 'And where are you now?' 'In America.' 'Well, aren't you already a foreign missionary?' Then He said to me, 'Who lives on the floor above you?' 'A family of Swedes.' 'And above them?' 'Some Swiss.' . . .

"'Yes, and in back are Italians, and a block away Chinese. You have never spoken to them about My Son. Do you think I'll send you a thousand miles away when you've got foreigners, even heathen all around you?'"

Ruth Tucker

PAUSE FOR REFLECTION

Stephen was a powerful witness for God among Jews from many nations. What message did both Stephen and the psalmist have to share? What message has God given you to share to the "nations" around you?

WEEKEND

God Is Faithful to His People

Acts 7:17–42a

The promise God made to Abraham
was soon to come true, and the number of people in Egypt grew large.
18 Then a new king, who did not know
who Joseph was, began to rule Egypt.
19 This king tricked our people and
was cruel to our ancestors, forcing
them to leave their babies outside to
die. 20 At this time Moses was born,
and he was very beautiful. For three
months Moses was cared for in his
father's house. 21 When they put
Moses outside, the king's daughter
adopted him and raised him as if he
were her own son. 22 The Egyptians
taught Moses everything they knew,
and he was a powerful man in what
he said and did.

23 "When Moses was about forty
years old, he thought it would be good
to visit his own people, the people of
Israel. 24 Moses saw an Egyptian mis-
treating an Israelite, so he defended
the Israelite and punished the Egyptian by killing him. 25 Moses thought
his own people would understand that
God was using him to save them, but
they did not. 26 The next day when
Moses saw two men of Israel fighting,
he tried to make peace between them.
He said, 'Men, you are brothers. Why
are you hurting each other?' 27 The
man who was hurting the other
pushed Moses away and said, 'Who
made you our ruler and judge? 28 Are
you going to kill me as you killed the
Egyptian yesterday?' 29 When Moses
heard him say this, he left Egypt and
went to live in the land of Midian
where he was a stranger. While
Moses lived in Midian, he had two
sons.

30 "Forty years later an angel appeared to Moses in the flames of a
burning bush as he was in the desert
near Mount Sinai. 31 When Moses
saw this, he was amazed and went
near to look closer. Moses heard the
Lord's voice say, 32 'I am the God of
your ancestors, the God of Abraham,
Isaac, and Jacob.' Moses began to
shake with fear and was afraid to
look. 33 The Lord said to him, 'Take
off your sandals, because you are
standing on holy ground. 34 I have
seen the troubles my people have
suffered in Egypt. I have heard their
cries and have come down to save
them. And now, Moses, I am sending you back to Egypt.'

35 "This Moses was the same man
the two men of Israel rejected, saying, 'Who made you a ruler and
judge?' Moses is the same man God
sent to be a ruler and savior, with the
help of the angel that Moses saw in
the burning bush. 36 So Moses led
the people out of Egypt. He worked
miracles and signs in Egypt, at the
Red Sea, and then in the desert for
forty years. 37 This is the same
Moses that said to the people of Israel, 'God will give you a prophet like
me, who is one of your own people.'
38 This is the Moses who was with
the gathering of the Israelites in the
desert. He was with the angel that
spoke to him at Mount Sinai, and he
was with our ancestors. He received
commands from God that give life,
and he gave those commands to us.

39 "But our ancestors did not want
to obey Moses. They rejected him
and wanted to go back to Egypt.
40 They said to Aaron, 'Make us gods
who will lead us. Moses led us out

of Egypt, but we don't know what
has happened to him.' 41 So the
people made an idol that looked like
a calf. Then they brought sacrifices
to it and were proud of what they had
made with their own hands. 42 But
God turned against them and did not
try to stop them from worshiping the
sun, moon, and stars."

OLD TESTAMENT READING

The LORD sent darkness and
made the land dark,
but the Egyptians turned
against what he said.
29 So he changed their water into
blood
and made their fish die.
30 Then their country was filled with
frogs,
even in the bedrooms of their
rulers.
31 The LORD spoke and flies came,
and gnats were everywhere in
the country.
32 He made hail fall like rain
and sent lightning through their
land.
33 He struck down their grapevines
and fig trees,
and he destroyed every tree in
the country.
34 He spoke and grasshoppers came;
the locusts were too many to
count.
35 They ate all the plants in the land
and everything the earth
produced.
36 The LORD also killed all the
firstborn sons in the land,
the oldest son of each family.
37 Then he brought his people out,
and they carried with them
silver and gold.
Not one of his people stumbled.

Psalm 105:28–37

INSIGHTS

*Great is Thy faithfulness, O God
my Father,
There is no shadow of turning with
Thee;
Thou changest not, Thy compassions they fail not;
As Thou hast been Thou forever wilt
be.*

*Summer and winter, and springtime and harvest,
Sun, moon and stars in their courses
above
Join with all nature in manifold
witness
To Thy great faithfulness, mercy
and love.*

*Pardon for sin and a peace that
endureth,
Thy own dear presence to cheer and
to guide;
Strength for today and bright hope
for tomorrow,
Blessings all mine, with ten thousand beside!*

*Great is Thy faithfulness! Great is
Thy faithfulness!
Morning by morning new mercies I
see;
All I have needed Thy hand hath
provided.
Great is Thy faithfulness, Lord, unto
me!*

Thomas O. Chisholm

ACTION POINT

From what trials did God, in his faithfulness, deliver the people of Israel? List as many as you can. When you doubt his faithfulness in your life, reread your list and believe that God is and always will be faithful!

MONDAY

Some Refuse to Hear God's Messengers

Acts 7:42b—8:1

This is what is written in the book
of the prophets: God says,
'People of Israel, you did not
bring me sacrifices and
offerings
while you traveled in the
desert for forty years.
43 You have carried with you
the tent to worship Molech
and the idols of the star god
Rephan that you made to
worship.
So I will send you away beyond
Babylon.' *Amos 5:25-27*

44 "The Holy Tent where God
spoke to our ancestors was with
them in the desert. God told Moses
how to make this Tent, and he made
it like the plan God showed him.
45 Later, Joshua led our ancestors to
capture the lands of the other nations. Our people went in, and God
forced the other people out. When
our people went into this new land,
they took with them this same Tent
they had received from their ancestors. They kept it until the time of
David, 46 who pleased God and asked
God to let him build a house for him,
the God of Jacob. 47 But Solomon was
the one who built the Temple.

48 "But the Most High does not
live in houses that people build with
their hands. As the prophet says:
49 'Heaven is my throne,
and the earth is my footstool.
So do you think you can build a
house for me? says the Lord.
Do I need a place to rest?
50 Remember, my hand made all
these things!'" *Isaiah 66:1-2*

51 Stephen continued speaking:
"You stubborn people! You have not
given your hearts to God, nor will you
listen to him! You are always against
what the Holy Spirit is trying to tell
you, just as your ancestors were.
52 Your ancestors tried to hurt every
prophet who ever lived. Those prophets said long ago that the One who is
good would come, but your ancestors
killed them. And now you have turned
against and killed the One who is
good. 53 You received the law of
Moses, which God gave you through
his angels, but you haven't obeyed it."

Stephen Is Killed

When the leaders heard this, they
became furious. They were so mad
they were grinding their teeth at
Stephen. 55 But Stephen was full of
the Holy Spirit. He looked up to
heaven and saw the glory of God and
Jesus standing at God's right side.
56 He said, "Look! I see heaven open
and the Son of Man standing at
God's right side."

57 Then they shouted loudly and
covered their ears and all ran at
Stephen. 58 They took him out of the
city and began to throw stones at
him to kill him. And those who told
lies against Stephen left their coats
with a young man named Saul.
59 While they were throwing stones,
Stephen prayed, "Lord Jesus, receive
my spirit." 60 He fell on his knees and
cried in a loud voice, "Lord, do not
hold this sin against them." After
Stephen said this, he died.

8 Saul agreed that the killing of
Stephen was good.

Troubles for the Believers

On that day the church of Jerusalem began to be persecuted, and all the believers, except the apostles, were scattered throughout Judea and Samaria.

OLD TESTAMENT READING

The king and these leaders stopped worshiping in the Temple of the LORD, the God of their ancestors. Instead, they began to worship the Asherah idols and other idols. Because they did wrong, God was angry with the people of Judah and
Jerusalem. 19 Even though the LORD
sent prophets to the people to turn them back to him and even though the prophets warned them, they refused to listen.

20 Then the Spirit of God entered Zechariah son of Jehoiada the priest. Zechariah stood before the people and said, "This is what God says: 'Why do you disobey the LORD's commands? You will not be successful. Because you have left the LORD, he has also left you.'"

21 But the king and his officers made plans against Zechariah. At the king's command they threw stones at him in the courtyard of the Temple of the LORD until he died.

2 Chronicles 24:18–21

INSIGHTS

In his remarkable and eloquent sermon, Stephen revealed his accurate grasp of Jewish history and its relevance to the new faith he had embraced. He turned the tables on his attackers and charged them with being the guilty ones. He refuted their charges in a closely reasoned, eloquent speech that reviewed their history from the time of Abraham onward. From it he demonstrated that the presence of the eternal God cannot be localized and confined to an earthly temple, be it ever so magnificent.

He cited God's presence with Joseph even when he was in Egypt. He reminded them that as a nation they had persistently rejected and resisted the messengers of God. They had envied and mistreated Joseph, whom God had sent as their preserver. They had rebelled against Moses and rejected his message. They had stoned the prophets and abused the functions of the Temple. They boasted of the angelic mediation of the Law, yet they failed to keep it. . . .

When Stephen delivered his final, blistering denunciation, he did it with his eyes open. He knew what the inevitable reaction of those bigoted men would be when he told them that they were stiff-necked, uncircumcised in heart, and murderers and betrayers of the Righteous One (Acts 7:51–52).

J. Oswald Sanders

PAUSE FOR REFLECTION

Was Stephen's martyrdom a unique event in Jewish history? Why did the religious leaders kill him? Why did they kill those who had preceded him? Is your heart in any way hardened to God's message today?

TUESDAY

There Is No Room for Jealousy in God's Kingdom

Acts 8:2–25

And some religious people buried Stephen and cried loudly for him. 3 Saul was also trying to destroy the church, going from house to house, dragging out men and women and putting them in jail. 4 And wherever they were scattered, they told people the Good News.

Philip Preaches in Samaria

Philip went to the city of Samaria and preached about the Christ. 6 When the people there heard Philip and saw the miracles he was doing, they all listened carefully to what he said. 7 Many of these people had evil spirits in them, but Philip made the evil spirits leave. The spirits made a loud noise when they came out. Philip also healed many weak and crippled people there. 8 So the people in that city were very happy.

9 But there was a man named Simon in that city. Before Philip came there, Simon had practiced magic and amazed all the people of Samaria. He bragged and called himself a great man. 10 All the people—the least important and the most important—paid attention to Simon, saying, "This man has the power of God, called 'the Great Power'!" 11 Simon had amazed them with his magic so long that the people became his followers. 12 But when Philip told them the Good News about the kingdom of God and the power of Jesus Christ, men and women believed Philip and were baptized. 13 Simon himself believed, and after he was baptized, he stayed very close to Philip. When he saw the miracles and the powerful things Philip did, Simon was amazed.

14 When the apostles who were still in Jerusalem heard that the people of Samaria had accepted the word of God, they sent Peter and John to them. 15 When Peter and John arrived, they prayed that the Samaritan believers might receive the Holy Spirit. 16 These people had been baptized in the name of the Lord Jesus, but the Holy Spirit had not yet come upon any of them. 17 Then, when the two apostles began laying their hands on the people, they received the Holy Spirit.

18 Simon saw that the Spirit was given to people when the apostles laid their hands on them. So he offered the apostles money, 19 saying, "Give me also this power so that anyone on whom I lay my hands will receive the Holy Spirit."

20 Peter said to him, "You and your money should both be destroyed, because you thought you could buy God's gift with money. 21 You cannot share with us in this work since your heart is not right before God. 22 Change your heart! Turn away from this evil thing you have done, and pray to the Lord. Maybe he will forgive you for thinking this. 23 I see that you are full of bitter jealousy and ruled by sin."

24 Simon answered, "Both of you pray for me to the Lord so the things you have said will not happen to me."

25 After Peter and John told the people what they had seen Jesus do and after they had spoken the message of the Lord, they went back to

Jerusalem. On the way, they went through many Samaritan towns and preached the Good News to the people.

OLD TESTAMENT READING

Korah, Dathan, Abiram, and On turned against Moses. [2] These men gathered two hundred fifty other Israelite men, well-known leaders chosen by the community, and challenged Moses. [3] They came as a group to speak to Moses and Aaron and said, "You have gone too far. All the people are holy, every one of them, and the LORD is among them. So why do you put yourselves above all the people of the LORD?"

[8] Moses also said to Korah, "Listen, you Levites. [9] The God of Israel has separated you from the rest of the Israelites. He brought you near to himself to do the work in the LORD's Holy Tent and to stand before all the Israelites and serve them. Isn't that enough?"

[28] Then Moses said, "Now you will know that the LORD has sent me to do all these things; it was not my idea. [29] If these men die a normal death—the way men usually die—then the LORD did not really send me. [30] But if the LORD does something new, you will know they have insulted the LORD. The ground will open and swallow them. They will be buried alive and will go to the place of the dead, and everything that belongs to them will go with them."

Numbers 16:1a, 2–3, 8–9, 28–30

INSIGHTS

Delight yourself in the spiritual victories of others:

Delight in all triumphs
in Christ Jesus.
Rejoice when another's success is greater than yours:
Be glad when another receives what you need.
Remain at peace when another receives the attention
you think you deserve.
You must not strive:
You must war against
all jealousy and contention.

Say today:
I will not be jealous.
I will not contend.
I will not strive.
I will rejoice at another's victories.
I will delight in the success of others.
I will not think others less worthy or less important than I.
I will not see my work as more important than someone else's.
I will pray for those who are my competitors.
I will rejoice in my relationship with the Lord.

And so it will be.

Marie Chapian

ACTION POINT

Before reading Numbers 16, did you know that God considers jealousy of his chosen servants to be an insult to him, not an insult to his servants? God takes the bitter sin of jealousy quite seriously, doesn't he? For what sins of jealousy do you need to ask God's forgiveness?

WEDNESDAY

God's Word Brings Joy to Those Who Understand It

Acts 8:26—9:9

Philip Teaches an Ethiopian

An angel of the Lord said to Philip,
"Get ready and go south to the road
that leads down to Gaza from Jerusalem—the desert road." 27 So Philip
got ready and went. On the road he
saw a man from Ethiopia, a eunuch.
He was an important officer in the
service of Candace, the queen of the
Ethiopians; he was responsible for
taking care of all her money. He had
gone to Jerusalem to worship.
28 Now, as he was on his way home,
he was sitting in his chariot reading
from the Book of Isaiah, the prophet.
29 The Spirit said to Philip, "Go to that
chariot and stay near it."

30 So when Philip ran toward the
chariot, he heard the man reading
from Isaiah the prophet. Philip
asked, "Do you understand what you
are reading?"

31 He answered, "How can I understand unless someone explains it
to me?" Then he invited Philip to
climb in and sit with him. 32 The portion of Scripture he was reading was
this:

"He was like a sheep being led to
be killed.
He was quiet, as a lamb is quiet
while its wool is being cut;
he never opened his mouth.
33 He was shamed and was
treated unfairly.
He died without children to
continue his family.
His life on earth has ended."

Isaiah 53:7-8

34 The officer said to Philip,
"Please tell me, who is the prophet
talking about—himself or someone
else?" 35 Philip began to speak, and
starting with this same Scripture, he
told the man the Good News about
Jesus.

36 While they were traveling down
the road, they came to some water.
The officer said, "Look, here is water. What is stopping me from being
baptized?"

37 Philip answered, "If you believe
with all your heart, you can."

The officer said, "I believe that
Jesus Christ is the Son of God."

38 Then the officer commanded the
chariot to stop. Both Philip and the
officer went down into the water, and
Philip baptized him. 39 When they
came up out of the water, the Spirit
of the Lord took Philip away; the officer never saw him again. And the
officer continued on his way home,
full of joy. 40 But Philip appeared in a
city called Azotus and preached the
Good News in all the towns on the
way from Azotus to Caesarea.

Saul Is Converted

9 In Jerusalem Saul was still threat-
ening the followers of the Lord by
saying he would kill them. So he
went to the high priest 2 and asked
him to write letters to the synagogues in the city of Damascus.
Then if Saul found any followers of
Christ's Way, men or women, he
would arrest them and bring them
back to Jerusalem.

3 So Saul headed toward Damascus. As he came near the city, a
bright light from heaven suddenly

flashed around him. [4]Saul fell to the
ground and heard a voice saying to
him, "Saul, Saul! Why are you persecuting me?"
[5]Saul said, "Who are you, Lord?"
The voice answered, "I am Jesus,
whom you are persecuting. [6]Get up
now and go into the city. Someone
there will tell you what you must do."
[7]The people traveling with Saul
stood there but said nothing. They
heard the voice, but they saw no one.
[8]Saul got up from the ground and
opened his eyes, but he could not
see. So those with Saul took his hand
and led him into Damascus. [9]For
three days Saul could not see and did
not eat or drink.

OLD TESTAMENT READING

These Levites explained the Teachings to the people as they stood
there: Jeshua, Bani, Sherebiah,
Jamin, Akkub, Shabbethai, Hodiah,
Maaseiah, Kelita, Azariah, Jozabad,
Hanan, and Pelaiah. [8]They read
from the Book of the Teachings of
God and explained what it meant so
the people understood what was being read.
[9]Then Nehemiah the governor,
Ezra the priest and teacher, and the
Levites who were teaching said to all
the people, "This is a holy day to the
LORD your God. Don't be sad or cry."
All the people had been crying as
they listened to the words of the
Teachings.
[10]Nehemiah said, "Go and enjoy
good food and sweet drinks. Send
some to people who have none, because today is a holy day to the Lord.
Don't be sad, because the joy of the
LORD will make you strong."
[11]The Levites helped calm the
people, saying, "Be quiet, because
this is a holy day. Don't be sad."
[12]Then all the people went away
to eat and drink, to send some of
their food to others, and to celebrate
with great joy. They finally understood what they had been taught.

Nehemiah 8:7–12

INSIGHTS

The Word of God is a constant and continuing source of joy for the Christian. I don't think I've ever met a joyless Christian who was regularly employed in searching the Scriptures. The result of such searching is to see beyond the words the One who inspired them. Of all the habits the Christian can cultivate, this is one of the most blessed and profitable. Some books are exhausting and exhaustible. The Bible is the only Book that rewards the student with increasing insight as he allows the Word of God to flow through and cleanse him. Indeed, it is the only Book that can cleanse and purify the life of its reader. Other books can inform, but only the Scripture can transform, infill, and inspire.

Al Bryant

ACTION POINT

Why were the Israelites saddened when they first heard the Lord's teachings? What enabled them to be joyous? What brought great joy to the Ethiopian officer? Who has helped you understand God's Word? Thank God for that person and pray that you will experience the joy of living by God's Word.

THURSDAY

"Here I Am, Lord"

Acts 9:10–35

There was a follower of Jesus in Damascus named Ananias. The Lord spoke to Ananias in a vision, "Ananias!"

Ananias answered, "Here I am, Lord."

11 The Lord said to him, "Get up and go to Straight Street. Find the house of Judas, and ask for a man named Saul from the city of Tarsus. He is there now, praying. 12 Saul has seen a vision in which a man named Ananias comes to him and lays his hands on him. Then he is able to see again."

13 But Ananias answered, "Lord, many people have told me about this man and the terrible things he did to your holy people in Jerusalem. 14 Now he has come here to Damascus, and the leading priests have given him the power to arrest everyone who worships you."

15 But the Lord said to Ananias, "Go! I have chosen Saul for an important work. He must tell about me to those who are not Jews, to kings, and to the people of Israel. 16 I will show him how much he must suffer for my name."

17 So Ananias went to the house of Judas. He laid his hands on Saul and said, "Brother Saul, the Lord Jesus sent me. He is the one you saw on the road on your way here. He sent me so that you can see again and be filled with the Holy Spirit." 18 Immediately, something that looked like fish scales fell from Saul's eyes, and he was able to see again! Then Saul got up and was baptized. 19 After he ate some food, his strength returned.

Saul Preaches in Damascus

Saul stayed with the followers of Jesus in Damascus for a few days. 20 Soon he began to preach about Jesus in the synagogues, saying, "Jesus is the Son of God."

21 All the people who heard him were amazed. They said, "This is the man who was in Jerusalem trying to destroy those who trust in this name! He came here to arrest the followers of Jesus and take them back to the leading priests."

22 But Saul grew more powerful. His proofs that Jesus is the Christ were so strong that the Jewish people in Damascus could not argue with him.

23 After many days, some Jewish people made plans to kill Saul. 24 They were watching the city gates day and night, but Saul learned about their plan. 25 One night some followers of Saul helped him leave the city by lowering him in a basket through an opening in the city wall.

Saul Preaches in Jerusalem

When Saul went to Jerusalem, he tried to join the group of followers, but they were all afraid of him. They did not believe he was really a follower. 27 But Barnabas accepted Saul and took him to the apostles. Barnabas explained to them that Saul had seen the Lord on the road and the Lord had spoken to Saul. Then he told them how boldly Saul had preached in the name of Jesus in Damascus.

28 And so Saul stayed with the followers, going everywhere in

Jerusalem, preaching boldly in the
name of the Lord. 29 He would often
talk and argue with the Jewish
people who spoke Greek, but they
were trying to kill him. 30 When the
followers learned about this, they
took Saul to Caesarea and from
there sent him to Tarsus.
31 The church everywhere in
Judea, Galilee, and Samaria had a
time of peace and became stronger.
Respecting the Lord by the way they
lived, and being encouraged by the
Holy Spirit, the group of believers
continued to grow.

Peter Heals Aeneas

As Peter was traveling through all
the area, he visited God's people
who lived in Lydda. 33 There he met
a man named Aeneas, who was paralyzed and had not been able to leave
his bed for the past eight years. 34 Peter said to him, "Aeneas, Jesus
Christ heals you. Stand up and make
your bed." Aeneas stood up immediately. 35 All the people living in
Lydda and on the Plain of Sharon
saw him and turned to the Lord.

OLD TESTAMENT READING

The LORD said to Samuel, "Go, appoint him, because he is the one."
13 So Samuel took the container of
olive oil and poured it on Jesse's
youngest son to appoint him in front
of his brothers. From that day on,
the LORD's Spirit worked in David.
Samuel then went back to Ramah.

1 Samuel 16:12c–13

INSIGHTS

Blessed and happy are they who have a sweet faith in Jesus, intertwined with deep affection for Him, for this is a restful confidence. These lovers of Jesus are charmed with His character and delighted with His mission; they are carried away by the loving-kindness that He has manifested, and therefore they cannot help trusting Him because they so much admire, revere, and love Him. . . .

. . . We love Him and He loves us, and therefore we put ourselves into His hands, accept whatever He prescribes, and do whatever He bids. We feel that nothing can be wrongly ordered while He is the Director of our affairs, for He loves us too well to let us perish or suffer a single needless pang.

Faith is the root of obedience, and this may be clearly seen in the affairs of life. When a captain trusts a pilot to steer his vessel into port, he manages the vessel according to his direction. When a traveler trusts a guide to conduct him over a difficult pass, he follows the track which his guide points out. When a patient believes in a physician, he carefully follows his prescriptions and directions. Faith which refuses to obey the commands of the Saviour is a mere pretence and will never save the soul.

Charles Spurgeon

APPLICATION

What kind of faith is needed to earnestly say the words, "Here I am, Lord"? Is your faith sufficient to do anything your Savior may ask? What objections to complete obedience must you overcome?

FRIDAY

God Hears and Answers Our Prayers

Acts 9:36—10:23a

Peter Heals Tabitha

In the city of Joppa there was a follower named Tabitha (whose Greek
name was Dorcas). She was always
doing good deeds and kind acts.
37 While Peter was in Lydda, Tabitha
became sick and died. Her body was
washed and put in a room upstairs.
38 Since Lydda is near Joppa and the
followers in Joppa heard that Peter
was in Lydda, they sent two messengers to Peter. They begged him,
"Hurry, please come to us!" 39 So Peter got ready and went with them.
When he arrived, they took him to the
upstairs room where all the widows
stood around Peter, crying. They
showed him the shirts and coats
Tabitha had made when she was still
alive. 40 Peter sent everyone out of the
room and kneeled and prayed. Then
he turned to the body and said,
"Tabitha, stand up." She opened her
eyes, and when she saw Peter, she sat
up. 41 He gave her his hand and helped
her up. Then he called the saints and
the widows into the room and showed
them that Tabitha was alive. 42 People
everywhere in Joppa learned about
this, and many believed in the Lord.
43 Peter stayed in Joppa for many days
with a man named Simon who was a
tanner.

Peter Teaches Cornelius

10 At Caesarea there was a man
named Cornelius, an officer in
the Italian group of the Roman army.
2 Cornelius was a religious man. He
and all the other people who lived in
his house worshiped the true God.
He gave much of his money to the
poor and prayed to God often. 3 One
afternoon about three o'clock,
Cornelius clearly saw a vision. An
angel of God came to him and said,
"Cornelius!"

4 Cornelius stared at the angel. He
became afraid and said, "What do
you want, Lord?"

The angel said, "God has heard
your prayers. He has seen that you
give to the poor, and he remembers
you. 5 Send some men now to Joppa
to bring back a man named Simon
who is also called Peter. 6 He is staying with a man, also named Simon,
who is a tanner and has a house beside the sea." 7 When the angel who
spoke to Cornelius left, Cornelius
called two of his servants and a soldier, a religious man who worked for
him. 8 Cornelius explained everything
to them and sent them to Joppa.

9 About noon the next day as they
came near Joppa, Peter was going up
to the roof to pray. 10 He was hungry
and wanted to eat, but while the food
was being prepared, he had a vision.
11 He saw heaven opened and something coming down that looked like
a big sheet being lowered to earth
by its four corners. 12 In it were all
kinds of animals, reptiles, and birds.
13 Then a voice said to Peter, "Get up,
Peter; kill and eat."

14 But Peter said, "No, Lord! I have
never eaten food that is unholy or unclean."

15 But the voice said to him again,
"God has made these things clean so
don't call them 'unholy'!" 16 This happened three times, and at once the
sheet was taken back to heaven.

[17]While Peter was wondering what this vision meant, the men Cornelius sent had found Simon's house and were standing at the gate.
[18]They asked, "Is Simon Peter staying here?"

[19]While Peter was still thinking about the vision, the Spirit said to him, "Listen, three men are looking
for you. [20]Get up and go downstairs. Go with them without doubting, because I have sent them to you."

[21]So Peter went down to the men and said, "I am the one you are looking for. Why did you come here?"

[22]They said, "A holy angel spoke to Cornelius, an army officer and a good man; he worships God. All the Jewish people respect him. The angel told Cornelius to ask you to come to his house so that he can hear what
you have to say." [23]So Peter asked the men to come in and spend the night.

OLD TESTAMENT READING

Solomon finished building the Temple of the LORD and his royal palace and everything he wanted to
build. [2]Then the LORD appeared to him again just as he had done be-
fore, in Gibeon. [3]The LORD said to him: "I have heard your prayer and what you have asked me to do. You built this Temple, and I have made it a holy place. I will be worshiped there forever and will watch over it and protect it always."

1 Kings 9:1–3

INSIGHTS

The Lord God of the universe, the Creator and Sustainer of all things, . . . not only commands us to pray, but also invites us to make our requests known. Jesus says that we have not because we ask not. James tells us that the effectual, fervent prayer of a righteous man accomplishes much. Time and again the Bible says that prayer is an effective tool. It is useful; it works. . . .

Prayer, like everything else in the Christian life, is for God's glory and for our benefit, in that order. Everything that God does, everything that God allows and ordains, is in the supreme sense for His glory. It is also true that while God seeks His own glory supremely, man benefits when God is glorified. We pray to glorify God, but also to receive the benefits of prayer from His hand. . . .

One of the great themes of the Reformation was the idea that all of our life is to be lived under the authority of God, to the glory of God, in the presence of God. . . . Prayer is discourse with the personal God Himself. There, in the act and dynamic of praying, I bring my whole life under His gaze. Yes, He knows what is in my mind, but I still have the privilege of articulating to Him what is there. He says, "Come. Speak to Me. Make your requests known to Me." And so, we come in order to know Him and to be known by Him.

R. C. Sproul

ACTION POINT

Do you feel that your prayers are really in touch with God—powerful enough to raise the dead? No? Then take these Scriptures to heart. Pray as if God is the ultimate reality in your life. Then listen. His response will come!

WEEKEND

God Forgives All Who Come to Him

Acts 10:23b–48

The next day Peter got ready and
went with them, and some of the followers from Joppa joined him. 24 On
the following day they came to
Caesarea. Cornelius was waiting for
them and had called together his
relatives and close friends. 25 When
Peter entered, Cornelius met him,
fell at his feet, and worshiped him.
26 But Peter helped him up, saying,
"Stand up. I too am only a human."
27 As he talked with Cornelius, Peter
went inside where he saw many
people gathered. 28 He said, "You
people understand that it is against
our Jewish law for Jewish people to
associate with or visit anyone who is
not Jewish. But God has shown me
that I should not call any person 'unholy' or 'unclean.' 29 That is why I did
not argue when I was asked to come
here. Now, please tell me why you
sent for me."

30 Cornelius said, "Four days ago,
I was praying in my house at this
same time—three o'clock in the afternoon. Suddenly, there was a man
standing before me wearing shining
clothes. 31 He said, 'Cornelius, God
has heard your prayer and has seen
that you give to the poor and remembers you. 32 So send some men to
Joppa and ask Simon Peter to come.
Peter is staying in the house of a
man, also named Simon, who is a
tanner and has a house beside the
sea.' 33 So I sent for you immediately,
and it was very good of you to come.
Now we are all here before God to
hear everything the Lord has commanded you to tell us."

34 Peter began to speak: "I really
understand now that to God every
person is the same. 35 In every country God accepts anyone who worships him and does what is right.
36 You know the message that God
has sent to the people of Israel is the
Good News that peace has come
through Jesus Christ. Jesus is the
Lord of all people! 37 You know what
has happened all over Judea, beginning in Galilee after John preached
to the people about baptism. 38 You
know about Jesus from Nazareth,
that God gave him the Holy Spirit
and power. You know how Jesus
went everywhere doing good and
healing those who were ruled by the
devil, because God was with him.
39 We saw what Jesus did in Judea
and in Jerusalem, but the Jews in
Jerusalem killed him by hanging
him on a cross. 40 Yet, on the third
day, God raised Jesus to life and
caused him to be seen, 41 not by all
the people, but only by the witnesses
God had already chosen. And we are
those witnesses who ate and drank
with him after he was raised from
the dead. 42 He told us to preach to
the people and to tell them that he
is the one whom God chose to be the
judge of the living and the dead. 43 All
the prophets say it is true that all
who believe in Jesus will be forgiven
of their sins through Jesus' name."

44 While Peter was still saying this,
the Holy Spirit came down on all
those who were listening. 45 The Jewish believers who came with Peter
were amazed that the gift of the Holy
Spirit had been given even to those
who were not Jews. 46 These Jewish
believers heard them speaking in
different languages and praising

God. Then Peter said, [47] "Can anyone keep these people from being baptized with water? They have received the Holy Spirit just as we did!" [48] So Peter ordered that they be baptized in the name of Jesus Christ. Then they asked Peter to stay with them for a few days.

OLD TESTAMENT READING

The LORD says,
"Come, let us talk about these things.
Though your sins are like scarlet,
they can be as white as snow.
Though your sins are deep red,
they can be white like wool.
19 If you become willing and obey me,
you will eat good crops from the land.
20 But if you refuse to obey and if you turn against me,
you will be destroyed by your enemies' swords."
The LORD himself said these things.

Isaiah 1:18–20

INSIGHTS

At the heart of God is the desire to give and to forgive. Because of this, he set into motion the entire redemptive process that culminated in the cross and was confirmed in the resurrection. The usual notion of what Jesus did on the cross runs something like this: people were so bad and so mean and God was so angry with them that he could not forgive them unless somebody big enough took the rap for the whole lot of them.

Nothing could be further from the truth. Love, not anger, brought Jesus to the cross. Golgotha came as a result of God's great desire to forgive, not his reluctance. Jesus knew that by his vicarious suffering he could actually absorb all the evil of humanity and so heal it, forgive it, redeem it. . . .

Having accomplished this greatest of all his works, Jesus then took refreshment. "It is finished," he announced. That is, this great work of redemption was completed. He could feel the last dregs of the misery of humankind flow through him and into the care of the Father. The last twinges of evil, hostility, anger, and fear drained out of him, and he was able to turn again into the light of God's presence. . . .

This redemptive process is a great mystery hidden in the heart of God. But I know that it is true. I know this not only because the Bible says it is true, but because I have seen its effects in the lives of many people, including myself. It is the ground upon which we can know that confession and forgiveness are realities that transform us. Without the cross the Discipline of confession would be only psychologically therapeutic. But it is so much more. It involves an objective change in our relationship with God and a subjective change in us. It is a means of healing and transforming the inner spirit.

Richard Foster

PAUSE FOR REFLECTION

Peter was one of Jesus' closest disciples, yet we see here that he discovers a new, wonderful, and unexpected truth about God's forgiveness. What is it? Thank God for his awesome gift of salvation to you!

MONDAY

God's People Are to Care for One Another

Acts 11:1–30

Peter Returns to Jerusalem

11 The apostles and the believers in Judea heard that some who were not Jewish had accepted God's teaching too. 2 But when Peter came to Jerusalem, some Jewish believers argued with him. 3 They said, "You went into the homes of people who are not circumcised and ate with them!"

4 So Peter explained the whole story to them. 5 He said, "I was in the city of Joppa, and while I was praying, I had a vision. I saw something that looked like a big sheet being lowered from heaven by its four corners. It came very close to me. 6 I looked inside it and saw animals, wild beasts, reptiles, and birds. 7 I heard a voice say to me, 'Get up, Peter. Kill and eat.' 8 But I said, 'No, Lord! I have never eaten anything that is unholy or unclean.' 9 But the voice from heaven spoke again, 'God has made these things clean, so don't call them unholy.' 10 This happened three times. Then the whole thing was taken back to heaven. 11 Right then three men who were sent to me from Caesarea came to the house where I was staying. 12 The Spirit told me to go with them without doubting. These six believers here also went with me, and we entered the house of Cornelius. 13 He told us about the angel he saw standing in his house. The angel said to him, 'Send some men to Joppa and invite Simon Peter to come. 14 By the words he will say to you, you and all your family will be saved.' 15 When I began my speech, the Holy Spirit came on them just as he came on us at the beginning. 16 Then I remembered the words of the Lord. He said, 'John baptized with water, but you will be baptized with the Holy Spirit.' 17 Since God gave them the same gift he gave us who believed in the Lord Jesus Christ, how could I stop the work of God?"

18 When the Jewish believers heard this, they stopped arguing. They praised God and said, "So God is allowing even those who are not Jewish to turn to him and live."

The Good News Comes to Antioch

19 Many of the believers were scattered when they were persecuted after Stephen was killed. Some of them went as far as Phoenicia, Cyprus, and Antioch telling the message to others, but only to Jews. 20 Some of these believers were people from Cyprus and Cyrene. When they came to Antioch, they spoke also to Greeks, telling them the Good News about the Lord Jesus. 21 The Lord was helping the believers, and a large group of people believed and turned to the Lord.

22 The church in Jerusalem heard about all of this, so they sent Barnabas to Antioch. 23-24 Barnabas was a good man, full of the Holy Spirit and full of faith. When he reached Antioch and saw how God had blessed the people, he was glad. He encouraged all the believers in Antioch always to obey the Lord with

all their hearts, and many people
became followers of the Lord.
[25]Then Barnabas went to the city
of Tarsus to look for Saul, [26]and
when he found Saul, he brought him
to Antioch. For a whole year Saul
and Barnabas met with the church
and taught many people there. In
Antioch the followers were called
Christians for the first time.
[27]About that time some prophets
came from Jerusalem to Antioch.
[28]One of them, named Agabus, stood
up and spoke with the help of the
Holy Spirit. He said, "A very hard
time is coming to the whole world.
There will be no food to eat." (This
happened when Claudius ruled.)
[29]The believers all decided to help
the followers who lived in Judea, as
much as each one could. [30]They
gathered the money and gave it to
Barnabas and Saul, who brought it
to the elders in Judea.

OLD TESTAMENT READING

Generous people will be
blessed,
because they share their food
with the poor.

Proverbs 22:9

INSIGHTS

Someone has said, "We have no permission from Jesus to be selective in our compassion." It is our natural tendency, however, to choose whom we will reach out to. Perhaps this was the problem of the priest and the Levite in the parable of the good Samaritan. In any event, we know it is often our problem. Jesus mingled with all men, the rich and the poor, the socially acceptable and the backward and undesirable. This willingness to enter into others' lives is costly. . . .

Our God wants to dislodge us from our comfortable, smug existence, to move us to mingle with our needy brothers, to stir us to touch those we might otherwise shun. Another poet, whose name is lost in history, expresses the challenge well: "Love has a hem to her garment that trails in the very dust; it can reach the stains of the streets and lanes, and because it can, it must." This is clearly the brand of compassion Jesus exemplified, and it is the kind of loving outreach he calls us to in our modern world. Answering his call is often a struggle for us. We may pay lip service to such compassion, but the performance is often costly, and we're inclined to back away. . . .

True compassion is an expression of the life of our Lord Jesus Christ. It is always ready to give, and always willing to sacrifice.

William Fletcher

ACTION POINT

When has God shaken up your view of how you are to live for him or to care for others? Does your view of Christian compassion need some adjustment? Pray for a heart that will gladly give and sacrifice for Jesus' sake.

TUESDAY

God Intervenes to Save His People

Acts 12:1–25

Herod Agrippa Hurts the Church

12 During that same time King
Herod began to mistreat some
who belonged to the church. 2 He ordered James, the brother of John, to
be killed by the sword. 3 Herod saw
that the Jewish people liked this, so
he decided to arrest Peter, too. (This
happened during the time of the
Feast of Unleavened Bread.)
4 After Herod arrested Peter, he
put him in jail and handed him over
to be guarded by sixteen soldiers.
Herod planned to bring Peter before
the people for trial after the Passover
Feast. 5 So Peter was kept in jail, but
the church prayed earnestly to God
for him.

Peter Leaves the Jail

The night before Herod was to
bring him to trial, Peter was sleeping between two soldiers, bound
with two chains. Other soldiers were
guarding the door of the jail. 7 Suddenly, an angel of the Lord stood
there, and a light shined in the cell.
The angel struck Peter on the side
and woke him up. "Hurry! Get up!"
the angel said. And the chains fell off
Peter's hands. 8 Then the angel told
him, "Get dressed and put on your
sandals." And Peter did. Then the angel said, "Put on your coat and follow me." 9 So Peter followed him out,
but he did not know if what the angel was doing was real; he thought
he might be seeing a vision. 10 They
went past the first and second
guards and came to the iron gate
that separated them from the city.
The gate opened by itself for them,
and they went through it. When they
had walked down one street, the angel suddenly left him.
11 Then Peter realized what had
happened. He thought, "Now I know
that the Lord really sent his angel to
me. He rescued me from Herod and
from all the things the Jewish people
thought would happen."
12 When he considered this, he
went to the home of Mary, the
mother of John Mark. Many people
were gathered there, praying. 13 Peter knocked on the outside door, and
a servant girl named Rhoda came to
answer it. 14 When she recognized
Peter's voice, she was so happy she
forgot to open the door. Instead, she
ran inside and told the group, "Peter is at the door!"
15 They said to her, "You are
crazy!" But she kept on saying it was
true, so they said, "It must be Peter's
angel."
16 Peter continued to knock, and
when they opened the door, they
saw him and were amazed. 17 Peter
made a sign with his hand to tell
them to be quiet. He explained how
the Lord led him out of the jail, and
he said, "Tell James and the other
believers what happened." Then he
left to go to another place.
18 The next day the soldiers were
very upset and wondered what had
happened to Peter. 19 Herod looked
everywhere for him but could not
find him. So he questioned the
guards and ordered that they be
killed.

The Death of Herod Agrippa

Later Herod moved from Judea and
went to the city of Caesarea, where
he stayed. [20] Herod was very angry
with the people of Tyre and Sidon,
but the people of those cities all came
in a group to him. After convincing
Blastus, the king's personal servant,
to be on their side, they asked Herod
for peace, because their country got
its food from his country.

[21] On a chosen day Herod put on
his royal robes, sat on his throne,
and made a speech to the people.
[22] They shouted, "This is the voice
of a god, not a human!" [23] Because
Herod did not give the glory to God,
an angel of the Lord immediately
caused him to become sick, and he
was eaten by worms and died.

[24] God's message continued to
spread and reach people.

[25] After Barnabas and Saul finished their task in Jerusalem, they
returned to Antioch, taking John
Mark with them.

OLD TESTAMENT READING

But the Israelites crossed the sea
on dry land, with a wall of water on
their right and on their left. [30] So that
day the LORD saved the Israelites
from the Egyptians, and the Israelites saw the Egyptians lying dead on
the seashore. [31] When the Israelites
saw the great power the LORD had
used against the Egyptians, they
feared the LORD, and they trusted
him and his servant Moses.

Exodus 14:29–31

INSIGHTS

Interestingly, the Book of Daniel opens with a story of the Babylonian invasion of Judah. In the invasion the Babylonians were totally successful and a number of the children of Israel were deported into captivity, including Daniel and his three friends. . . . These young men understood that they were not in Babylon by chance. God had put them there. . . .

God knew what kind of persecution His children were facing and what He would have to do to deliver them out of it. . . . The fiery furnace, the intensity of the heat, and the anger of Nebuchadnezzar were all human efforts to thwart the will of God. But He overcame them all! At the moment of His children's greatest need, He sent His Son to deliver them from the fire. In so doing, God gives us a beautiful picture of His working in our lives. He does not always choose to keep us from the fire, but often brings about our deliverance while we are in the fire itself.

If God could deliver these young men from a fiery furnace, it should seem evident He can deliver us from whatever trouble we find ourselves in. . . .

. . . He may use these difficulties to teach us great lessons and to bring us to a point of repentance, but ultimately, He can also use these difficulties to produce a wonderful result that only He could bring to pass.

Richard Lee

PAUSE FOR REFLECTION

How did God's miraculous deliverance in each of these instances build up the faith of those involved? What result does his intervention bring about in your life?

WEDNESDAY

God's Miracles Can Lead Us Toward Faith

Acts 13:1–25

Barnabas and Saul Are Chosen

13 In the church at Antioch there
were these prophets and
teachers: Barnabas, Simeon (also
called Niger), Lucius (from the city
of Cyrene), Manaen (who had grown
up with Herod, the ruler), and Saul.
2 They were all worshiping the Lord
and giving up eating for a certain
time. During this time the Holy
Spirit said to them, "Set apart for me
Barnabas and Saul to do a special
work for which I have chosen them."
3 So after they gave up eating and
prayed, they laid their hands on
Barnabas and Saul and sent them out.

Barnabas and Saul in Cyprus

4 Barnabas and Saul, sent out by the
Holy Spirit, went to the city of
Seleucia. From there they sailed to
the island of Cyprus. 5 When they
came to Salamis, they preached the
Good News of God in the Jewish
synagogues. John Mark was with
them to help.
6 They went across the whole island to Paphos where they met a
Jewish magician named Bar-Jesus.
He was a false prophet 7 who always
stayed close to Sergius Paulus, the
governor and a smart man. He
asked Barnabas and Saul to come to
him, because he wanted to hear the
message of God. 8 But Elymas, the
magician, was against them.
(Elymas is the name for Bar-Jesus in
the Greek language.) He tried to
stop the governor from believing in
Jesus. 9 But Saul, who was also called
Paul, was filled with the Holy Spirit.
He looked straight at Elymas 10 and
said, "You son of the devil! You are
an enemy of everything that is right!
You are full of evil tricks and lies, always trying to change the Lord's
truths into lies. 11 Now the Lord will
touch you, and you will be blind. For
a time you will not be able to see anything—not even the light from the
sun."
Then everything became dark for
Elymas, and he walked around, trying to find someone to lead him by the
hand. 12 When the governor saw this,
he believed because he was amazed
at the teaching about the Lord.

Paul and Barnabas Leave Cyprus

13 Paul and those with him sailed from
Paphos and came to Perga, in
Pamphylia. There John Mark left
them to return to Jerusalem. 14 They
continued their trip from Perga and
went to Antioch, a city in Pisidia. On
the Sabbath day they went into the
synagogue and sat down. 15 After the
law of Moses and the writings of the
prophets were read, the leaders of
the synagogue sent a message to
Paul and Barnabas: "Brothers, if you
have any message that will encourage the people, please speak."
16 Paul stood up, raised his hand,
and said, "You Israelites and you
who worship God, please listen!
17 The God of the Israelites chose our
ancestors. He made the people great
during the time they lived in Egypt,
and he brought them out of that
country with great power. 18 And he

was patient with them for forty years
in the desert. 19 God destroyed seven
nations in the land of Canaan and
gave the land to his people. 20 All this
happened in about four hundred fifty
years.

"After this, God gave them judges
until the time of Samuel the prophet.
21 Then the people asked for a king,
so God gave them Saul son of Kish.
Saul was from the tribe of Benjamin
and was king for forty years. 22 After
God took him away, God made
David their king. God said about
him: 'I have found in David son of
Jesse the kind of man I want. He will
do all I want him to do.' 23 So God has
brought Jesus, one of David's descendants, to Israel to be its Savior,
as he promised. 24 Before Jesus
came, John preached to all the
people of Israel about a baptism of
changed hearts and lives. 25 When he
was finishing his work, he said,
'Who do you think I am? I am not
the Christ. He is coming later, and I
am not worthy to untie his sandals.'"

OLD TESTAMENT READING

Our ancestors in Egypt
did not learn from your
miracles.
They did not remember all your
kindnesses,
so they turned against you at
the Red Sea.
8 But the LORD saved them for his
own sake,
to show his great power.

Psalm 106:7, 8

Moses and Aaron gathered all the
older leaders of the Israelites, 30 and
Aaron told them everything that the
LORD had told Moses. Then Moses
did the miracles for all the people to
see, 31 and the Israelites believed.
When they heard that the LORD was
concerned about them and had seen
their troubles, they bowed down and
worshiped him.

Exodus 4:29–31

INSIGHTS

God, who made the visible heaven and earth, does not disdain to work visible miracles in heaven or earth, that He may thereby awaken the soul which is immersed in things visible to worship Himself, the Invisible. . . .

He restored to the blind those eyes which death was sure some time to close; He raised Lazarus from the dead, who was to die again. And whatever He did for the health of bodies, He did it not to the end that they should exist for evermore; whereas at the last He will give eternal health even to the body itself. But because those things which were not seen were not believed, by means of those temporal things which were seen He built up faith in those things which were not seen. Let no one therefore say that our Lord Jesus Christ doeth not those things now, and on this account prefer the former to the present ages of the Church. . . . The Lord did those things to invite us to the faith.

St. Augustine

PAUSE FOR REFLECTION

In each of these passages, what did the miracles reveal about God? What was the result? In what way has God revealed himself to you? How have you responded?

THURSDAY

Those Who Believe Are Happy

Acts 13:26–52

*B*rothers, sons of the family of
Abraham, and those of you who are
not Jews who worship God, listen!
The news about this salvation has
been sent to us. 27 Those who live in
Jerusalem and their leaders did not
realize that Jesus was the Savior.
They did not understand the words
that the prophets wrote, which are
read every Sabbath day. But they
made them come true when they
said Jesus was guilty. 28 They could
not find any real reason for Jesus to
be put to death, but they asked Pilate
to have him killed. 29 When they had
done to him all that the Scriptures
had said, they took him down from
the cross and laid him in a tomb.
30 But God raised him up from the
dead! 31 After this, for many days,
those who had gone with Jesus from
Galilee to Jerusalem saw him. They
are now his witnesses to the people.
32 We tell you the Good News about
the promise God made to our ancestors. 33 God has made this promise
come true for us, his children, by
raising Jesus from the dead. We read
about this also in Psalm 2:

'You are my Son.
Today I have become your
Father.' *Psalm 2:7*

34 God raised Jesus from the dead,
and he will never go back to the
grave and become dust. So God
said:

'I will give you the holy and sure
blessings
that I promised to David.'
Isaiah 55:3

35 But in another place God says:
'You will not let your Holy One
rot.' *Psalm 16:10*

36 David did God's will during his lifetime. Then he died and was buried
beside his ancestors, and his body
did rot in the grave. 37 But the One
God raised from the dead did not rot
in the grave. 38-39 Brothers, understand what we are telling you: You
can have forgiveness of your sins
through Jesus. The law of Moses
could not free you from your sins.
But through Jesus everyone who
believes is free from all sins. 40 Be
careful! Don't let what the prophets
said happen to you:

41 'Listen, you people who doubt!
You can wonder, and then die.
I will do something in your
lifetime
that you won't believe even
when you are told about it!'"
Habakkuk 1:5

42 While Paul and Barnabas were
leaving the synagogue, the people
asked them to tell them more about
these things on the next Sabbath.
43 When the meeting was over, many
Jews and those who had changed to
the Jewish religion and who worshiped God followed Paul and
Barnabas from that place. Paul and
Barnabas were persuading them to
continue trusting in God's grace.

44 On the next Sabbath day, almost
everyone in the city came to hear the
word of the Lord. 45 Seeing the
crowd, the Jewish people became
very jealous and said insulting
things and argued against what Paul
said. 46 But Paul and Barnabas spoke
very boldly, saying, "We must speak
the message of God to you first. But

you refuse to listen. You are judging
yourselves not worthy of having
eternal life! So we will now go to the
people of other nations. 47 This is
what the Lord told us to do, saying:

'I have made you a light for the
nations;
you will show people all over
the world the way to be
saved.'" *Isaiah 49:6*

48 When those who were not Jewish heard Paul say this, they were
happy and gave honor to the message of the Lord. And the people
who were chosen to have life forever
believed the message.
49 So the message of the Lord was
spreading through the whole country. 50 But the Jewish people stirred
up some of the important religious
women and the leaders of the city.
They started trouble against Paul
and Barnabas and forced them out
of their area. 51 So Paul and Barnabas
shook the dust off their feet and
went to Iconium. 52 But the followers
were filled with joy and the Holy
Spirit.

OLD TESTAMENT READING

Your words came to me, and I
listened carefully to them.
Your words made me very
happy,
because I am called by your name,
LORD God All-Powerful.

Jeremiah 15:16

INSIGHTS

I'm convinced that enjoyment is the ultimate stage of knowledge. When we set out to learn the basic truths of an intellectual discipline, we are confounded by all we don't know. Little by little, we become more secure in ideas and theories. Then one day, we suddenly realize that we have captured the subject and know how to use our knowledge. . . .

. . . Enjoyment of our faith grows in the same way. In the beginning, God seems distant and aloof. Biblical and theological terms are like a foreign language. Our prayers are strained and shallow. . . . And then, with the touch of the Father's hand, we discover how much He loves us and wants us to know Him personally. Secondary theories about Him are replaced by an intimate relationship with Him. None of our awe and adoration is lost as we begin to enjoy Him. . . .

Enjoying God is really a vital expression of glorifying Him. The glory of God is the manifestation and revelation of all that He is as Creator, Sustainer, Redeemer, and Lord of all. We glorify Him when we worship Him for His lovingkindness, goodness, and mercifulness. Our worship becomes intimate when we joyfully experience God's nature and attributes. From that joy springs our desire to glorify Him by serving Him. Our faithful obedience becomes an enjoyable response.

Lloyd Ogilvie

PAUSE FOR REFLECTION

How did the people respond when Paul and Barnabas spoke God's Word in Antioch? In what ways does the Lord make you happy? How has your happiness grown as you have come to know him better?

FRIDAY

Seek God's Guidance When Making Decisions

Acts 14:1–28

Paul and Barnabas in Iconium

14 In Iconium, Paul and Barnabas
went as usual to the Jewish
synagogue. They spoke so well that
a great many Jews and Greeks believed. 2 But some of the Jews who
did not believe excited the non-Jewish people and turned them against
the believers. 3 Paul and Barnabas
stayed in Iconium a long time and
spoke bravely for the Lord. He
showed that their message about his
grace was true by giving them the
power to work miracles and signs.
4 But the city was divided. Some of
the people agreed with the Jews, and
others believed the apostles.

5 Some who were not Jews, some
Jews, and some of their rulers wanted
to mistreat Paul and Barnabas and
to stone them to death. 6 When Paul
and Barnabas learned about this,
they ran away to Lystra and Derbe,
cities in Lycaonia, and to the areas
around those cities. 7 They announced the Good News there, too.

Paul in Lystra and Derbe

In Lystra there sat a man who had
been born crippled; he had never
walked. 9 As this man was listening to
Paul speak, Paul looked straight at him
and saw that he believed God could
heal him. 10 So he cried out, "Stand up
on your feet!" The man jumped up and
began walking around. 11 When the
crowds saw what Paul did, they
shouted in the Lycaonian language,
"The gods have become like humans
and have come down to us!" 12 Then
the people began to call Barnabas
"Zeus" and Paul "Hermes," because
he was the main speaker. 13 The priest
in the temple of Zeus, which was near
the city, brought some bulls and flowers to the city gates. He and the
people wanted to offer a sacrifice to
Paul and Barnabas. 14 But when the
apostles, Barnabas and Paul, heard
about it, they tore their clothes. They
ran in among the people, shouting,
15 "Friends, why are you doing these
things? We are only human beings
like you. We are bringing you the
Good News and are telling you to
turn away from these worthless
things and turn to the living God. He
is the One who made the sky, the
earth, the sea, and everything in them.
16 In the past, God let all the nations
do what they wanted. 17 Yet he proved
he is real by showing kindness, by giving you rain from heaven and crops
at the right times, by giving you food
and filling your hearts with joy."
18 Even with these words, they were
barely able to keep the crowd from offering sacrifices to them.

19 Then some Jewish people came
from Antioch and Iconium and persuaded the people to turn against
Paul. So they threw stones at him
and dragged him out of town, thinking they had killed him. 20 But the
followers gathered around him, and
he got up and went back into the
town. The next day he and Barnabas
left and went to the city of Derbe.

The Return to Antioch in Syria

Paul and Barnabas told the Good

News in Derbe, and many became followers. Paul and Barnabas returned to Lystra, Iconium, and
Antioch, [22] making the followers of Jesus stronger and helping them stay in the faith. They said, "We must suffer many things to enter
God's kingdom." [23] They chose elders for each church, by praying and giving up eating for a certain time. These elders had trusted the Lord, so Paul and Barnabas put them in the Lord's care.

[24] Then they went through Pisidia
and came to Pamphylia. [25] When
they had preached the message in Perga, they went down to Attalia.
[26] And from there they sailed away to Antioch where the believers had put them into God's care and had sent them out to do this work. Now they had finished.

[27] When they arrived in Antioch, Paul and Barnabas gathered the church together. They told the church all about what God had done with them and how God had made it possible for those who were
not Jewish to believe. [28] And they
stayed there a long time with the followers.

OLD TESTAMENT READING

Trust the LORD with all your
heart,
and don't depend on your own
understanding.
[6] Remember the LORD in all you do,
and he will give you success.

[7] Don't depend on your own
wisdom.
Respect the LORD and refuse to
do wrong.

Proverbs 3:5–7

INSIGHTS

When I was in my late teens I had life all figured out. . . . Now I realize how uncertain this world is, how limited my own experience is, how deceptive the evil one is, how easily I can be duped. I desperately need a guide though the maze of options every day. Don't you?

I need a guide who knows me, who understands me and has my best interests in mind. The best guide would understand my personality, my temperament, my gifts and abilities, my likes and dislikes. Wouldn't it be something to have a guide who takes all that into consideration as He charts a path for your life?

Such a guide exists, friend. God reaches out to you and says, in effect, "Take My hand. You matter to Me. I am trustworthy. I know you. I understand you. I know what will fulfill you. I created you." . . .

. . . He wants to guide your life. Will you let Him? Will you read and heed the Word? Will you be yielded and listen to and trust the leadings of the Holy Spirit? Will you submit your plans to others for their input? When you do, you'll find that life can truly be an adventure.

Bill Hybels

APPLICATION

Why do you think Paul and Barnabas especially sought God's guidance in choosing elders for the churches? For what decisions do you seek God's guidance? Should you be seeking his wisdom more?

WEEKEND

God Accepts Anyone Who Comes to Him

Acts 15:1–21

The Meeting at Jerusalem

15 Then some people came to
Antioch from Judea and began
teaching the non-Jewish believers:
"You cannot be saved if you are not
circumcised as Moses taught us."
2 Paul and Barnabas were against
this teaching and argued with them
about it. So the church decided to
send Paul, Barnabas, and some others to Jerusalem where they could
talk more about this with the
apostles and elders.

3 The church helped them leave
on the trip, and they went through
the countries of Phoenicia and
Samaria, telling all about how those
who were not Jewish had turned to
God. This made all the believers
very happy. 4 When they arrived in
Jerusalem, they were welcomed by
the apostles, the elders, and the
church. Paul, Barnabas, and the others told about everything God had
done with them. 5 But some of the
believers who belonged to the Pharisee group came forward and said,
"The non-Jewish believers must be
circumcised. They must be told to
obey the law of Moses."

6 The apostles and the elders gathered to consider this problem. 7 After a long debate, Peter stood up and
said to them, "Brothers, you know
that in the early days God chose me
from among you to preach the Good
News to those who are not Jewish.
They heard the Good News from
me, and they believed. 8 God, who
knows the thoughts of everyone,
accepted them. He showed this to us
by giving them the Holy Spirit, just
as he did to us. 9 To God, those
people are not different from us.
When they believed, he made their
hearts pure. 10 So now why are you
testing God by putting a heavy load
around the necks of the non-Jewish
believers? It is a load that neither we
nor our ancestors were able to carry.
11 But we believe that we and they too
will be saved by the grace of the
Lord Jesus."

12 Then the whole group became
quiet. They listened to Paul and
Barnabas tell about all the miracles
and signs that God did through them
among the non-Jewish people. 13 After they finished speaking, James
said, "Brothers, listen to me.
14 Simon has told us how God
showed his love for the non-Jewish
people. For the first time he is accepting from among them a people
to be his own. 15 The words of the
prophets agree with this too:

16 'After these things I will return.
The kingdom of David is like a
fallen tent.
But I will rebuild its ruins,
and I will set it up.
17 Then those people who are left
alive may ask the Lord for
help,
and the other nations that
belong to me,
says the Lord,
who will make it happen.
18 And these things have been
known for a long time.'

Amos 9:11-12

19 "So I think we should not bother
the non-Jewish people who are turn-

ing to God. [20] Instead, we should write a letter to them telling them these things: Stay away from food that has been offered to idols (which makes it unclean), any kind of sexual sin, eating animals that have been strangled, and blood. [21] They should do these things, because for a long time in every city the law of Moses has been taught. And it is still read in the synagogue every Sabbath day."

OLD TESTAMENT READING

God, have mercy on us and bless us
and show us your kindness *Selah*
2 so the world will learn your ways,
and all nations will learn that you can save.
3 God, the people should praise you;
all people should praise you.
4 The nations should be glad and sing
because you judge people fairly.
You guide all the nations on earth. *Selah*
5 God, the people should praise you;
all people should praise you.

Psalm 67:1–5

All people everywhere,
follow me and be saved.
I am God. There is no other God.

Isaiah 45:22

INSIGHTS

The Law came and in bold letters etched by the finger of God it read, "This is holiness! Honor My Name by keeping My Law!" But the fact is, nobody could keep it, which explains the statement in Romans 5:20 that says "sin increased." The Law arouses sin but never arrests it. So how can the tailspin stop? What hope is there? The answer is found in the same verse: ". . . but where sin increased, grace abounded all the more.". . .

Let me amplify the scriptural statement even more. Where sin overflowed, grace flooded in. Where sin measurably increased, grace immeasurably increased. Where sin was finite, grace was infinite. Where sin was colossal, grace was supercolossal. Where sin abounds, grace superabounds. The sin identified by the Law in no way stopped the flow of the grace of God. Jesus' death on the cross was the sufficient payment for sin, putting grace into action that was not simply adequate but abundant. . . .

. . . God, in grace, offers you the free gift of forgiveness. All you can do is take it. Once you take it, you will be given the power to give up, to put on, to take off, to quit, to start—whatever. But don't confuse the issue of salvation. It is yours strictly on the basis of God's free gift. In spite of all the stuff you may hear to the contrary, the emphasis is not on what we do for God; instead, it is on what God has done for us.

Charles Swindoll

PAUSE FOR REFLECTION

To whom was the law of Moses given? Why? What evidence in the Old and New Testaments reveals that God offers salvation through Jesus Christ to all people—Jew and non-Jew?

MONDAY

The Value of Encouragement

Acts 15:22—16:10

Letter to Non-Jewish Believers

The apostles, the elders, and the
whole church decided to send some
of their men with Paul and
Barnabas to Antioch. They chose
Judas Barsabbas and Silas, who
were respected by the believers.
23 They sent the following letter with
them:

From the apostles and elders,
your brothers.

To all the non-Jewish believers in
Antioch, Syria, and Cilicia:

Greetings!

24 We have heard that some of our
group have come to you and said
things that trouble and upset you.
But we did not tell them to do this.
25 We have all agreed to choose some
messengers and send them to you
with our dear friends Barnabas and
Paul—26 people who have given
their lives to serve our Lord Jesus
Christ. 27 So we are sending Judas
and Silas, who will tell you the same
things. 28 It has pleased the Holy
Spirit that you should not have a
heavy load to carry, and we agree.
You need to do only these things:
29 Stay away from any food that has
been offered to idols, eating any animals that have been strangled, and
blood, and any kind of sexual sin. If
you stay away from these things, you
will do well.

Good-bye.

30 So they left Jerusalem and went
to Antioch where they gathered the
church and gave them the letter.
31 When they read it, they were very
happy because of the encouraging
message. 32 Judas and Silas, who
were also prophets, said many
things to encourage the believers
and make them stronger. 33 After
some time Judas and Silas were sent
off in peace by the believers, and
they went back to those who had
sent them, 34 but Silas decided to remain there.

35 But Paul and Barnabas stayed
in Antioch and, along with many others, preached the Good News and
taught the people the message of the
Lord.

Paul and Barnabas Separate

After some time, Paul said to
Barnabas, "We should go back to all
those towns where we preached the
message of the Lord. Let's visit the
believers and see how they are doing."

37 Barnabas wanted to take John
Mark with them, 38 but he had left
them at Pamphylia; he did not continue with them in the work. So Paul
did not think it was a good idea to
take him. 39 Paul and Barnabas had
such a serious argument about this
that they separated and went different ways. Barnabas took Mark and
sailed to Cyprus, 40 but Paul chose
Silas and left. The believers in
Antioch put Paul into the Lord's
care, 41 and he went through Syria
and Cilicia, giving strength to the
churches.

Timothy Goes with Paul

16 Paul came to Derbe and
Lystra, where a follower

named Timothy lived. Timothy's mother was Jewish and a believer, but his father was a Greek.
[2]The believers in Lystra and Iconium respected Timothy and said good things about him. [3]Paul wanted Timothy to travel with him, but all the Jews living in that area knew that Timothy's father was Greek. So Paul circumcised Timothy to please the Jews. [4]Paul and those with him traveled from town to town and gave the decisions made by the apostles and elders in Jerusalem for the people to obey. [5]So the churches became stronger in the faith and grew larger every day.

Paul Is Called Out of Asia

Paul and those with him went through the areas of Phrygia and Galatia since the Holy Spirit did not let them preach the Good News in
the country of Asia. [7]When they
came near the country of Mysia, they tried to go into Bithynia, but the
Spirit of Jesus did not let them. [8]So
they passed by Mysia and went to
Troas. [9]That night Paul saw in a vision a man from Macedonia. The man stood and begged, "Come over
to Macedonia and help us." [10]After
Paul had seen the vision, we immediately prepared to leave for Macedonia, understanding that God had called us to tell the Good News to those people.

OLD TESTAMENT READING

The right word spoken at the
right time
is as beautiful as gold apples in
a silver bowl.

Proverbs 25:11

INSIGHTS

I was rushing around trying to get dinner ready for my husband and houseguests. . . .

. . . Just as I began last-minute preparations, the doorbell rang. I ran to answer it. A friend had stopped by to drop off a folder of information for my husband.

"How are you, Doris?"

I began to tell her that I was a little tired and frazzled around the edges, when I noticed she wasn't listening. Before I could finish my response, she said, "That's good. It's nice to see you." And with that she left.

I walked slowly back to my kitchen, feeling lonely and deflated. My friend had let me down when I could have used just a word of encouragement, maybe even a quick prayer.

Mechanically, I began to set the table. Why didn't she hear me? Doesn't she care how I am? I just needed a little of her time.

And then I heard the words: Doris, you've done this to people, too. Let this be a lesson to you. Listen to those I send across your path. Give them at least five minutes, even if you are in a hurry. Stop and pray with them.

Doris Greig

APPLICATION

Our Proverbs reading summarizes the beauty of encouragement well, doesn't it? What has been your most encouraging experience? What kind of encouragement is offered in each of these examples? How do they help you know how to encourage others?

TUESDAY

"Come Stay in My House"

Acts 16:11–34

Lydia Becomes a Christian

We left Troas and sailed straight to
the island of Samothrace. The next
day we sailed to Neapolis. [12]Then we
went by land to Philippi, a Roman
colony and the leading city in that
part of Macedonia. We stayed there
for several days.
[13]On the Sabbath day we went
outside the city gate to the river
where we thought we would find a
special place for prayer. Some
women had gathered there, so we
sat down and talked with them.
[14]One of the listeners was a woman
named Lydia from the city of
Thyatira whose job was selling
purple cloth. She worshiped God,
and he opened her mind to pay attention to what Paul was saying.
[15]She and all the people in her house
were baptized. Then she invited us
to her home, saying, "If you think I
am truly a believer in the Lord, then
come stay in my house." And she
persuaded us to stay with her.

Paul and Silas in Jail

Once, while we were going to the
place for prayer, a servant girl met
us. She had a special spirit in her,
and she earned a lot of money for
her owners by telling fortunes.
[17]This girl followed Paul and us,
shouting, "These men are servants
of the Most High God. They are telling you how you can be saved."
[18]She kept this up for many days.
This bothered Paul, so he turned
and said to the spirit, "By the power
of Jesus Christ, I command you to
come out of her!" Immediately, the
spirit came out.
[19]When the owners of the servant
girl saw this, they knew that now
they could not use her to make
money. So they grabbed Paul and
Silas and dragged them before the
city rulers in the marketplace.
[20]They brought Paul and Silas to the
Roman rulers and said, "These men
are Jews and are making trouble in
our city. [21]They are teaching things
that are not right for us as Romans
to do."
[22]The crowd joined the attack
against them. The Roman officers
tore the clothes of Paul and Silas and
had them beaten with rods. [23]Then
Paul and Silas were thrown into jail,
and the jailer was ordered to guard
them carefully. [24]When he heard this
order, he put them far inside the jail
and pinned their feet down between
large blocks of wood.
[25]About midnight Paul and Silas
were praying and singing songs to
God as the other prisoners listened.
[26]Suddenly, there was a strong
earthquake that shook the foundation of the jail. Then all the doors of
the jail broke open, and all the prisoners were freed from their chains.
[27]The jailer woke up and saw that the
jail doors were open. Thinking that
the prisoners had already escaped,
he got his sword and was about to
kill himself. [28]But Paul shouted,
"Don't hurt yourself! We are all
here."
[29]The jailer told someone to bring
a light. Then he ran inside and, shaking with fear, fell down before Paul

and Silas. 30 He brought them outside and said, "Men, what must I do
to be saved?"
31 They said to him, "Believe in the
Lord Jesus and you will be saved—
you and all the people in your
house." 32 So Paul and Silas told the
message of the Lord to the jailer and
all the people in his house. 33 At that
hour of the night the jailer took Paul
and Silas and washed their wounds.
Then he and all his people were baptized immediately. 34 After this the
jailer took Paul and Silas home and
gave them food. He and his family
were very happy because they now
believed in God.

OLD TESTAMENT READING

One day Elisha went to Shunem, where an important woman lived. She begged Elisha to stay and eat. So every time Elisha passed by, he stopped there to eat. 9 The woman said to her husband, "I know that this is a holy man of God who passes by our house all the time. 10 Let's make a small room on the roof and put a bed in the room for him. We can put a table, a chair, and a lampstand there. Then when he comes by, he can stay there."

2 Kings 4:8–10

INSIGHTS

THERE IS ROOM

You know how it happened, Lord:
She said, "May I live with you
Just a little while?
I have no place to go.
I'm lonely
And afraid."
I hastily glanced at the small room.
I thought of other rooms
Smaller and extremely crowded.
I said, "You see my small house.
There is really no room.
But I have room in my heart
For caring
For praying
I'll make phone calls—
There must be a family somewhere . . ."
That was this morning, Lord.
All day long
I prayed
I called
I waited . . .
Then You accomplished
What I cannot explain.
Through the hours
You pushed back the walls—
Until suddenly, tonight
There is room for her in my house
As well as in my heart
You are indeed a Master Builder!

Ruth Calkin

ACTION POINT

What do you find particularly interesting about these examples of hospitality? What do you think it means to express Christian hospitality to people today? Pray about how God wants you to use your home to serve him.

WEDNESDAY

It's Important to Know God's Powerful Word

Acts 16:35—17:15

The next morning, the Roman officers sent the police to tell the jailer,
"Let these men go free."
36 The jailer said to Paul, "The officers have sent an order to let you
go free. You can leave now. Go in
peace."
37 But Paul said to the police,
"They beat us in public without a
trial, even though we are Roman citizens. And they threw us in jail. Now
they want to make us go away quietly. No! Let them come themselves
and bring us out."
38 The police told the Roman officers what Paul said. When the officers heard that Paul and Silas were
Roman citizens, they were afraid.
39 So they came and told Paul and
Silas they were sorry and took them
out of jail and asked them to leave
the city. 40 So when they came out of
the jail, they went to Lydia's house
where they saw some of the believers and encouraged them. Then
they left.

Paul and Silas in Thessalonica

17 Paul and Silas traveled through
Amphipolis and Apollonia and
came to Thessalonica where there
was a Jewish synagogue. 2 Paul went
into the synagogue as he always did,
and on each Sabbath day for three
weeks, he talked with the Jews
about the Scriptures. 3 He explained
and proved that the Christ must die
and then rise from the dead. He said,
"This Jesus I am telling you about
is the Christ." 4 Some of the Jews
were convinced and joined Paul and
Silas, along with many of the Greeks
who worshiped God and many of the
important women.
5 But the Jews became jealous. So
they got some evil men from the
marketplace, formed a mob, and
started a riot. They ran to Jason's
house, looking for Paul and Silas,
wanting to bring them out to the
people. 6 But when they did not find
them, they dragged Jason and some
other believers to the leaders of the
city. The people were yelling, "These
people have made trouble everywhere in the world, and now they
have come here too! 7 Jason is keeping them in his house. All of them
do things against the laws of Caesar,
saying there is another king, called
Jesus."
8 When the people and the leaders of the city heard these things,
they became very upset. 9 They
made Jason and the others put up a
sum of money. Then they let the believers go free.

Paul and Silas Go to Berea

That same night the believers sent
Paul and Silas to Berea where they
went to the Jewish synagogue.
11 These Jews were more willing to
listen than the Jews in Thessalonica.
The Bereans were eager to hear
what Paul and Silas said and studied
the Scriptures every day to find out
if these things were true. 12 So, many
of them believed, as well as many
important Greek women and men.
13 But the Jews in Thessalonica
learned that Paul was preaching the

word of God in Berea, too. So they
came there, upsetting the people and
making trouble. 14The believers
quickly sent Paul away to the coast,
but Silas and Timothy stayed in
Berea. 15The people leading Paul
went with him to Athens. Then they
carried a message from Paul back to
Silas and Timothy for them to come
to him as soon as they could.

OLD TESTAMENT READING

Rain and snow fall from the sky
and don't return without
watering the ground.
They cause the plants to sprout
and grow,
making seeds for the farmer
and bread for the people.
11The same thing is true of the
words I speak.
They will not return to me
empty.
They make the things happen that
I want to happen,
and they succeed in doing what
I send them to do."

Isaiah 55:10–11

Your word is like a lamp for my feet
and a light for my path.
106I will do what I have promised
and obey your fair laws.
107I have suffered for a long time.
LORD, give me life by your
word.
108LORD, accept my willing praise
and teach me your laws.

Psalm 119:105–108

INSIGHTS

I never pretend to make but one book my study. I read them occasionally, but have little time or inclination to read other books much while I have so much to learn of my Bible. I find it like a deep mine, the more I work it, the richer it grows. We must read that more than any or all other books. We must pause and pray over it, verse after verse, and compare part with part, dwell on it, digest it, and get it into our minds, till we feel that the Spirit of God has filled us with the spirit of holiness.

Will you do it? Will you lay your hearts open to God, and not give him rest, till he has filled you with divine knowledge? Will you search the scriptures? I have often been asked by young converts, and young men preparing for the ministry, what they should read. Read the Bible. I would give the same answer five hundred times. Over and above all other things, study the Bible.

Charles Finney

ACTION POINT

What was unusual about the Jews in Berea? Is it, then, surprising that many of them believed? What does God say about his word in Isaiah? How much do you treasure and seek after God's Word? Will you begin today to search after it more diligently?

THURSDAY

Paul Tells Others About the True God

Acts 17:16—18:4

Paul Preaches in Athens

While Paul was waiting for Silas
and Timothy in Athens, he was
troubled because he saw that the city
was full of idols. 17 In the synagogue,
he talked with the Jews and the
Greeks who worshiped God. He also
talked every day with people in the
marketplace.

18 Some of the Epicurean and
Stoic philosophers argued with him,
saying, "This man doesn't know
what he is talking about. What is he
trying to say?" Others said, "He
seems to be telling us about some
other gods," because Paul was telling them about Jesus and his rising
from the dead. 19 They got Paul and
took him to a meeting of the Areopagus, where they said, "Please explain to us this new idea you have
been teaching. 20 The things you are
saying are new to us, and we want
to know what this teaching means."
21 (All the people of Athens and those
from other countries who lived there
always used their time to talk about
the newest ideas.)

22 Then Paul stood before the
meeting of the Areopagus and said,
"People of Athens, I can see you are
very religious in all things. 23 As I
was going through your city, I saw
the objects you worship. I found an
altar that had these words written
on it: TO A GOD WHO IS NOT KNOWN. You
worship a god that you don't know,
and this is the God I am telling you
about! 24 The God who made the
whole world and everything in it is
the Lord of the land and the sky. He
does not live in temples built by human hands. 25 This God is the One
who gives life, breath, and everything else to people. He does not
need any help from them; he has everything he needs. 26 God began by
making one person, and from him
came all the different people who
live everywhere in the world. God
decided exactly when and where
they must live. 27 God wanted them
to look for him and perhaps search
all around for him and find him,
though he is not far from any of us:
28 'We live in him. We walk in him.
We are in him.' Some of your own
poets have said: 'For we are his children.' 29 Since we are God's children, you must not think that God
is like something that people imagine or make from gold, silver, or
rock. 30 In the past, people did not
understand God, and he ignored
this. But now, God tells all people
in the world to change their hearts
and lives. 31 God has set a day that
he will judge all the world with fairness, by the man he chose long ago.
And God has proved this to everyone by raising that man from the
dead!"

32 When the people heard about
Jesus being raised from the dead,
some of them laughed. But others
said, "We will hear more about this
from you later." 33 So Paul went away
from them. 34 But some of the people
believed Paul and joined him.
Among those who believed was
Dionysius, a member of the Areopagus, a woman named Damaris, and
some others.

Paul in Corinth

18 Later Paul left Athens and
went to Corinth. [2] Here he met
a Jew named Aquila who had been
born in the country of Pontus. But
Aquila and his wife, Priscilla, had
recently moved to Corinth from Italy,
because Claudius commanded that
all Jews must leave Rome. Paul went
to visit Aquila and Priscilla. [3] Because
they were tentmakers, just as he
was, he stayed with them and
worked with them. [4] Every Sabbath
day he talked with the Jews and
Greeks in the synagogue, trying to
persuade them to believe in Jesus.

OLD TESTAMENT READING

This is the story of the creation of
the sky and the earth. When the
LORD God first made the earth and
the sky, [5] there were still no plants
on the earth. Nothing was growing
in the fields because the LORD God
had not yet made it rain on the land.
And there was no person to care for
the ground, [6] but a mist would rise
up from the earth and water all the
ground.
[7] Then the LORD God took dust
from the ground and formed a man
from it. He breathed the breath of
life into the man's nose, and the man
became a living person.

Genesis 2:4–7

INSIGHTS

I WILL WORSHIP

God, you are with me
and you can help me;
You were with me when I was
taken,
and you are with me now.
You strengthen me.

The God I serve is everywhere—
in heaven and earth and the sea,
but he is above them all,
for all live in him:
All were created by him,
and by him only do they remain.

I will worship only the true God;
you will I carry in my heart;
No one on earth shall be able to
separate me from you.

Quirinus of Siscia

MY COMFORT

Jesus Christ is my comfort.
It is you who created us all.
There is only you, one God,
Father, Son, and Holy Spirit,
to whom homage and praise are
due.

Januarius of Cordova

PAUSE FOR REFLECTION

In order to help them understand the Good News, what did Paul tell the philosophers and important people of Athens about the true God? What knowledge of God helps you to understand, trust, and worship him?

FRIDAY

"Don't Be Afraid . . . I Am with You"

Acts 18:5–28

Silas and Timothy came from Macedonia and joined Paul in Corinth. After this, Paul spent all his time telling people the Good News, showing the Jews that Jesus is the Christ. 6 But they would not accept Paul's teaching and said some evil things. So he shook off the dust from his clothes and said to them, "If you are not saved, it will be your own fault! I have done all I can do! After this, I will go only to those who are not Jewish." 7 Paul left the synagogue and moved into the home of Titius Justus, next to the synagogue. This man worshiped God. 8 Crispus was the leader of that synagogue, and he and all the people living in his house believed in the Lord. Many others in Corinth also listened to Paul and believed and were baptized.

9 During the night, the Lord told Paul in a vision: "Don't be afraid. Continue talking to people and don't be quiet. 10 I am with you, and no one will hurt you because many of my people are in this city." 11 Paul stayed there for a year and a half, teaching God's word to the people.

Paul Is Brought Before Gallio

When Gallio was the governor of the country of Southern Greece, some of the Jews came together against Paul and took him to the court. 13 They said, "This man is teaching people to worship God in a way that is against our law."

14 Paul was about to say something, but Gallio spoke to the Jews, saying, "I would listen to you Jews if you were complaining about a crime or some wrong. 15 But the things you are saying are only questions about words and names—arguments about your own law. So you must solve this problem yourselves. I don't want to be a judge of these things." 16 And Gallio made them leave the court.

17 Then they all grabbed Sosthenes, the leader of the synagogue, and beat him there before the court. But this did not bother Gallio.

Paul Returns to Antioch

Paul stayed with the believers for many more days. Then he left and sailed for Syria, with Priscilla and Aquila. At Cenchrea Paul cut off his hair, because he had made a promise to God. 19 Then they went to Ephesus, where Paul left Priscilla and Aquila. While Paul was there, he went into the synagogue and talked with the Jews. 20 When they asked him to stay with them longer, he refused. 21 But as he left, he said, "I will come back to you again if God wants me to." And so he sailed away from Ephesus.

22 When Paul landed at Caesarea, he went and gave greetings to the church in Jerusalem. After that, Paul went to Antioch. 23 He stayed there for a while and then left and went through the regions of Galatia and Phrygia. He traveled from town to town in these regions, giving strength to all the followers.

Apollos in Ephesus and Corinth

A Jew named Apollos came to

Ephesus. He was born in the city of
Alexandria and was a good speaker
who knew the Scriptures well. 25 He
had been taught about the way of the
Lord and was always very excited
when he spoke and taught the truth
about Jesus. But the only baptism
Apollos knew about was the baptism
that John taught. 26 Apollos began to
speak very boldly in the synagogue,
and when Priscilla and Aquila heard
him, they took him to their home
and helped him better understand
the way of God. 27 Now Apollos
wanted to go to the country of Southern Greece. So the believers helped
him and wrote a letter to the followers there, asking them to accept him.
These followers had believed in
Jesus because of God's grace, and
when Apollos arrived, he helped
them very much. 28 He argued very
strongly with the Jews before all the
people, clearly proving with the
Scriptures that Jesus is the Christ.

OLD TESTAMENT READING

The LORD guards you.
The LORD is the shade that
protects you from the sun.
6 The sun cannot hurt you during
the day,
and the moon cannot hurt you
at night.
7 The LORD will protect you from all
dangers;
he will guard your life.
8 The LORD will guard you as you
come and go,
both now and forever.

Psalm 121:5–8

I am with you and will protect you everywhere you go and will bring you back to this land. I will not leave you until I have done what I have promised you."

Genesis 28:15

INSIGHTS

How tenderly God soothes our fears! How sweetly He says, . . . "Fear thou not; for I am with thee: be not dismayed; for I am thy God: . . . I will uphold thee with the right hand of my righteousness" (Isaiah 41:10). And yet again, still with tender thoughtfulness, "I the Lord thy God will hold thy right hand, saying unto thee, Fear not; I will help thee" (Isaiah 41:13). He does not say it only once, but He keeps holding our right hand and repeating such promises.

The blessed Lord condensed it all into one single message of eternal comfort spoken to the disciples on the Sea of Galilee, It is I; be not afraid. He is the antidote to fear; He is the remedy for trouble; He is the substance and the sum of deliverance. We should, therefore, rise above fear. Let us keep our eyes fastened upon Him; let us abide continually in Him; let us be content with Him.

Let us cling closely to Him.

A. B. Simpson

ACTION POINT

What encouragement from the Lord have you received in times of fear? Which reading assures you that God is with you? Pray that you will always cling to God and feel the blessing of his presence!

WEEKEND

True Repentance Involves Abandoning Sinful Practices

Acts 19:1–22

Paul in Ephesus

19 While Apollos was in Corinth,
Paul was visiting some places
on the way to Ephesus. There he
found some followers 2 and asked
them, "Did you receive the Holy
Spirit when you believed?"
They said, "We have never even
heard of a Holy Spirit."
3 So he asked, "What kind of baptism did you have?"
They said, "It was the baptism
that John taught."
4 Paul said, "John's baptism was a
baptism of changed hearts and lives.
He told people to believe in the one
who would come after him, and that
one is Jesus."
5 When they heard this, they were
baptized in the name of the Lord
Jesus. 6 Then Paul laid his hands on
them, and the Holy Spirit came upon
them. They began speaking different languages and prophesying.
7 There were about twelve people in
this group.
8 Paul went into the synagogue
and spoke out boldly for three
months. He talked with the Jews and
persuaded them to accept the things
he said about the kingdom of God.
9 But some of the Jews became stubborn. They refused to believe and
said evil things about the Way of
Jesus before all the people. So Paul
left them, and taking the followers
with him, he went to the school of a
man named Tyrannus. There Paul
talked with people every day 10 for
two years. Because of his work, every Jew and Greek in the country of
Asia heard the word of the Lord.

The Sons of Sceva

11 God used Paul to do some very
special miracles. 12 Some people took
handkerchiefs and clothes that Paul
had used and put them on the sick.
When they did this, the sick were
healed and evil spirits left them.
13 But some Jews also were traveling around and making evil spirits
go out of people. They tried to use
the name of the Lord Jesus to force
the evil spirits out. They would say,
"By the same Jesus that Paul talks
about, I order you to come out!"
14 Seven sons of Sceva, a leading Jewish priest, were doing this.
15 But one time an evil spirit said
to them, "I know Jesus, and I know
about Paul, but who are you?"
16 Then the man who had the evil
spirit jumped on them. Because he
was so much stronger than all of
them, they ran away from the house
naked and hurt. 17 All the people in
Ephesus—Jews and Greeks—
learned about this and were filled
with fear and gave great honor to the
Lord Jesus. 18 Many of the believers
began to confess openly and tell all
the evil things they had done.
19 Some of them who had used magic
brought their magic books and
burned them before everyone.
Those books were worth about fifty
thousand silver coins.
20 So in a powerful way the word
of the Lord kept spreading and growing.
21 After these things, Paul decided

to go to Jerusalem, planning to go through the countries of Macedonia and Southern Greece and then on to Jerusalem. He said, "After I have been to Jerusalem, I must also visit Rome." [22] Paul sent Timothy and Erastus, two of his helpers, ahead to Macedonia, but he himself stayed in Asia for a while.

OLD TESTAMENT READING

Then Jehoiada made an agreement between the LORD and the king and the people that they would be the LORD's special people. He also made an agreement between the king and the people. [18] All the people of the land went to the temple of Baal and tore it down, smashing the altars and idols. They also killed Mattan, the priest of Baal, in front of the altars.

Then Jehoiada the priest placed guards at the Temple of the LORD.

2 Kings 11:17–18

INSIGHTS

When I was a boy, each Saturday my father would make a list of chores for me to do before I could go and play. When he came home in the evening, he would take the list and—walking with me beside him—check how each job had been done. Sometimes he would point out a hidden, unswept corner that I had missed or find a small, untrimmed area of the yard that I had overlooked. When he did so, I would take a brush or clippers right then and finish the job properly. And you can be sure that, the next week, I would remember to carefully check those places I'd missed.

In checking on my work, my father was not being unkind or critical of what I'd done. He was helping me learn to do a job right the first time. And when I did, he would always encourage me and say, "That's good work, son."

That's how we should be with the Lord. We need to learn to be quick to take care of everything we see on the Father's "list" in his Word and then be open and ready for him to point out the things we have overlooked or neglected. We must offer daily confession, both for known sins that blot a day's activities and for sins we overlooked.

When we do these things, we know that through the blood of Christ we have instant and complete forgiveness: "If we confess our sins to him, he can be depended on to forgive us and to cleanse us from every wrong" (1 John 1:9).

"Hidden corners" do slip by unnoticed, and there are many believers caught up in sinful habits that at first they don't even recognize as sin. We might find, as we open to the Lord, that he begins to confront and adjust a pattern of our relationships, an aspect of our daily activities or entertainment, or some continued practice from childhood. We need to bring all aspects of our lives, regardless of what the world says is right or acceptable, under the searching eyes of the Lord.

Jack Hayford

APPLICATION

What happens when God's people turn away from sin and truly seek to obey him? What sins in your life need to be put away?

MONDAY

God Can Defeat Those Who Stir Up Trouble for His People

Acts 19:23—20:6

Trouble in Ephesus

And during that time, there was
some serious trouble in Ephesus
about the Way of Jesus. 24 A man
named Demetrius, who worked with
silver, made little silver models that
looked like the temple of the goddess Artemis. Those who did this
work made much money. 25 Demetrius had a meeting with them
and some others who did the same
kind of work. He told them, "Men,
you know that we make a lot of
money from our business. 26 But look
at what this man Paul is doing. He
has convinced and turned away
many people in Ephesus and in almost all of Asia! He says the gods
made by human hands are not real.
27 There is a danger that our business will lose its good name, but
there is also another danger: People
will begin to think that the temple of
the great goddess Artemis is not
important. Her greatness will be destroyed, and Artemis is the goddess
that everyone in Asia and the whole
world worships."

28 When the others heard this,
they became very angry and
shouted, "Artemis, the goddess of
Ephesus, is great!" 29 The whole city
became confused. The people
grabbed Gaius and Aristarchus, who
were from Macedonia and were traveling with Paul, and ran to the theater. 30 Paul wanted to go in and talk
to the crowd, but the followers did
not let him. 31 Also, some leaders of
Asia who were friends of Paul sent
him a message, begging him not to
go into the theater. 32 Some people
were shouting one thing, and some
were shouting another. The meeting
was completely confused; most of
them did not know why they had
come together. 33 The Jews put a man
named Alexander in front of the
people, and some of them told him
what to do. Alexander waved his
hand so he could explain things to
the people. 34 But when they saw that
Alexander was a Jew, they all shouted
the same thing for two hours: "Great
is Artemis of Ephesus!"

35 Then the city clerk made the
crowd be quiet. He said, "People of
Ephesus, everyone knows that
Ephesus is the city that keeps the
temple of the great goddess Artemis
and her holy stone that fell from
heaven. 36 Since no one can say this
is not true, you should be quiet. Stop
and think before you do anything.
37 You brought these men here, but
they have not said anything evil
against our goddess or stolen anything from her temple. 38 If Demetrius and those who work with him
have a charge against anyone they
should go to the courts and judges
where they can argue with each
other. 39 If there is something else
you want to talk about, it can be decided at the regular town meeting of
the people. 40 I say this because some
people might see this trouble today
and say that we are rioting. We could
not explain this, because there is no
real reason for this meeting." 41 After the city clerk said these things,
he told the people to go home.

Paul in Macedonia and Greece

20 When the trouble stopped,
Paul sent for the followers to
come to him. After he encouraged
them and then told them good-bye,
he left and went to the country of
Macedonia. 2 He said many things to
strengthen the followers in the different places on his way through
Macedonia. Then he went to Greece,
3 where he stayed for three months.
He was ready to sail for Syria, but
some Jews were planning something
against him. So Paul decided to go
back through Macedonia to Syria.
4 The men who went with him were
Sopater son of Pyrrhus, from the city
of Berea; Aristarchus and Secundus,
from the city of Thessalonica; Gaius,
from Derbe; Timothy; and Tychicus
and Trophimus, two men from the
country of Asia. 5 These men went on
ahead and waited for us at Troas.
6 We sailed from Philippi after the
Feast of Unleavened Bread. Five
days later we met them in Troas,
where we stayed for seven days.

OLD TESTAMENT READING

What if the LORD had not been
on our side
when we were attacked?
3 When they were angry with us,
they would have swallowed us
alive.
6 Praise the LORD,
who did not let them chew us up.
7 We escaped like a bird
from the hunter's trap.
The trap broke,
and we escaped.
8 Our help comes from the LORD,
who made heaven and earth.

Psalm 124:2–3, 6–8

INSIGHTS

A mighty fortress is our God,
A bulwark never failing;
Our helper He amid the flood
Of mortal ills prevailing.
For still our ancient foe
Doth seek to work us woe—
His craft and pow'r are great,
And, armed with cruel hate,
On earth is not his equal.

Did we in our own strength confide,
Our striving would be losing,
Were not the right man on our side,
The man of God's own choosing.
Dost ask who that may be?
Christ Jesus, it is He—
Lord Sabaoth His name,
From age to age the same,
And He must win the battle.

And tho this world, with devils filled,
Should threaten to undo us,
We will not fear, for God hath willed
His truth to triumph thru us.
The prince of darkness grim,
We tremble not for him—
His rage we can endure,
For lo, his doom is sure:
One little word shall fell him.

Martin Luther

PAUSE FOR REFLECTION

What motivated Demetrius to start the trouble in Ephesus? For what other reasons do people cause trouble for God's people? What comfort and strength do you find in Psalm 124 and Luther's famous hymn?

TUESDAY

Serving God Is Most Important . . . Even If We Risk Our Lives

Acts 20:7–38

Paul's Last Visit to Troas

On the first day of the week, we all
met together to break bread, and
Paul spoke to the group. Because he
was planning to leave the next day,
he kept on talking until midnight.
8 We were all together in a room upstairs, and there were many lamps
in the room. 9 A young man named
Eutychus was sitting in the window.
As Paul continued talking, Eutychus
was falling into a deep sleep. Finally,
he went sound asleep and fell to the
ground from the third floor. When
they picked him up, he was dead.
10 Paul went down to Eutychus, knelt
down, and put his arms around him.
He said, "Don't worry. He is alive
now." 11 Then Paul went upstairs
again, broke bread, and ate. He
spoke to them a long time, until it
was early morning, and then he left.
12 They took the young man home
alive and were greatly comforted.

The Trip from Troas to Miletus

We went on ahead of Paul and
sailed for the city of Assos, where he
wanted to join us on the ship. Paul
planned it this way because he
wanted to go to Assos by land.
14 When he met us there, we took
him aboard and went to Mitylene.
15 We sailed from Mitylene and the
next day came to a place near Chios.
The following day we sailed to
Samos, and the next day we reached
Miletus. 16 Paul had already decided
not to stop at Ephesus, because he
did not want to stay too long in the
country of Asia. He was hurrying to
be in Jerusalem on the day of Pentecost, if that were possible.

The Elders from Ephesus

Now from Miletus Paul sent to
Ephesus and called for the elders of
the church. 18 When they came to
him, he said, "You know about my
life from the first day I came to Asia.
You know the way I lived all the time
I was with you. 19 The Jews made
plans against me, which troubled me
very much. But you know I always
served the Lord unselfishly, and I
often cried. 20 You know I preached
to you and did not hold back anything that would help you. You know
that I taught you in public and in
your homes. 21 I warned both Jews
and Greeks to change their lives and
turn to God and believe in our Lord
Jesus. 22 But now I must obey the
Holy Spirit and go to Jerusalem. I
don't know what will happen to me
there. 23 I know only that in every
city the Holy Spirit tells me that
troubles and even jail wait for me. 24 I
don't care about my own life. The
most important thing is that I complete my mission, the work that the
Lord Jesus gave me—to tell people
the Good News about God's grace.

25 "And now, I know that none of
you among whom I was preaching
the kingdom of God will ever see me
again. 26 So today I tell you that if any
of you should be lost, I am not responsible, 27 because I have told you
everything God wants you to know.

28 Be careful for yourselves and for
all the people the Holy Spirit has
given to you to care for. You must be
like shepherds to the church of God,
which he bought with the death of
his own son. 29 I know that after I
leave, some people will come like
wild wolves and try to destroy the
flock. 30 Also, some from your own
group will rise up and twist the truth
and will lead away followers after
them. 31 So be careful! Always remember that for three years, day
and night, I never stopped warning
each of you, and I often cried over
you.

32 "Now I am putting you in the
care of God and the message about
his grace. It is able to give you
strength, and it will give you the
blessings God has for all his holy
people. 33 When I was with you, I
never wanted anyone's money or
fine clothes. 34 You know I always
worked to take care of my own
needs and the needs of those who
were with me. 35 I showed you in all
things that you should work as I did
and help the weak. I taught you to
remember the words Jesus said: 'It
is more blessed to give than to receive.' "

36 When Paul had said this, he
knelt down with all of them and
prayed. 37-38 And they all cried because Paul had said they would
never see him again. They put their
arms around him and kissed him.
Then they went with him to the ship.

OLD TESTAMENT READING

Then Elijah said, "Capture the prophets of Baal! Don't let any of them run away!" The people captured all the prophets. Then Elijah led them down to the Kishon Valley, where he killed them.

1 Kings 18:40

INSIGHTS

David Brainerd, early missionary to the Indians of the United States, was so consumed with a passion for the glory of Christ in the salvation of souls that he claimed: "I cared not how or where I lived, or what hardships I endured, so that I could but gain souls for Christ."

Paul was a passionately ambitious man, even before his conversion. . . .

. . . Whereas his old ambition had been to efface the name of Jesus and exterminate His church, now he had a passion to exalt the name of Jesus and establish and edify His church. His new ambition found its center in the glory of Christ and the advancement of His kingdom. . . .

Our Lord was gripped by a master ambition that integrated the whole of His life. It can be summarized in a single sentence: "I have come to do your will, O God" (Hebrews 10:7). When at life's end He offered His wonderful high-priestly prayer, He was able to report the complete achievement of this ambition: "I have brought you glory on earth by completing the work you gave me to do" (John 17:4).

J. Oswald Sanders

PAUSE FOR REFLECTION

What was Paul's most important goal in life? What personal hardship did that commitment cost him? What sustains a person who makes such a commitment?

WEDNESDAY

God Requires Uncompromising Faithfulness

Acts 21:1–25

Paul Goes to Jerusalem

21 After we all said good-bye to them, we sailed straight to the island of Cos. The next day we reached Rhodes, and from there we went to Patara. [2]There we found a ship going to Phoenicia, so we went aboard and sailed away. [3]We sailed near the island of Cyprus, seeing it to the north, but we sailed on to Syria. We stopped at Tyre because the ship needed to unload its cargo there. [4]We found some followers in Tyre and stayed with them for seven days. Through the Holy Spirit they warned Paul not to go to Jerusalem. [5]When we finished our visit, we left and continued our trip. All the followers, even the women and children, came outside the city with us. After we all knelt on the beach and prayed, [6]we said good-bye and got on the ship, and the followers went back home.

[7]We continued our trip from Tyre and arrived at Ptolemais, where we greeted the believers and stayed with them for a day. [8]The next day we left Ptolemais and went to the city of Caesarea. There we went into the home of Philip the preacher, one of the seven helpers, and stayed with him. [9]He had four unmarried daughters who had the gift of prophesying. [10]After we had been there for some time, a prophet named Agabus arrived from Judea. [11]He came to us and borrowed Paul's belt and used it to tie his own hands and feet. He said, "The Holy Spirit says, 'This is how the Jews in Jerusalem will tie up the man who wears this belt. Then they will give him to those who are not Jews.' "

[12]When we all heard this, we and the people there begged Paul not to go to Jerusalem. [13]But he said, "Why are you crying and making me so sad? I am not only ready to be tied up in Jerusalem, I am ready to die for the Lord Jesus!"

[14]We could not persuade him to stay away from Jerusalem. So we stopped begging him and said, "We pray that what the Lord wants will be done."

[15]After this, we got ready and started on our way to Jerusalem. [16]Some of the followers from Caesarea went with us and took us to the home of Mnason, where we would stay. He was from Cyprus and was one of the first followers.

Paul Visits James

In Jerusalem the believers were glad to see us. [18]The next day Paul went with us to visit James, and all the elders were there. [19]Paul greeted them and told them everything God had done among the non-Jewish people through him. [20]When they heard this, they praised God. Then they said to Paul, "Brother, you can see that many thousands of Jews have become believers. And they think it is very important to obey the law of Moses. [21]They have heard about your teaching, that you tell the Jews who live among those who are not Jews to leave the law of Moses. They have heard that you tell them not to circumcise their children and not to obey Jewish customs. [22] What should we do? They will learn that you have come. [23] So we will tell you what to do: Four of our men have made a promise to God. [24] Take these men with you and share in their cleansing ceremony. Pay their expenses so they can shave their heads. Then it will prove to everyone that what they have heard about you is not true and that you follow the law of Moses in your own life. [25] We have already sent a letter to the non-Jewish believers. The letter said: 'Do not eat food that has been offered to idols, or blood, or animals that have been strangled. Do not take part in sexual sin.' "

OLD TESTAMENT READING

Then the LORD said to Moses, "Go down from this mountain, because your people, the people you brought out of the land of Egypt, have ruined themselves."

[26] So Moses stood at the entrance to the camp and said, "Let anyone who wants to follow the LORD come to me." And all the people from the family of Levi gathered around Moses.

[27] Then Moses said to them, "The LORD, the God of Israel, says this: 'Every man must put on his sword and go through the camp from one end to the other. Each man must kill his brother, his friend, and his neighbor.'" [29] Then Moses said, "Today you have been given for service to the LORD. You were willing to kill your own sons and brothers, and God has blessed you for this."

Exodus 32:7, 26–27, 29

INSIGHTS

Sometimes King Saul was among the prophets, easily turned into a prophet, and then afterwards among the witches; sometimes in one place and then another, and insincere in everything. How many such we have in every Christian assembly; men who are very easily molded. They have affectionate dispositions, very likely a tender conscience; but then the conscience is so remarkably tender, that when touched it seems to give, and you are afraid to probe deeper; it heals as soon as it is wounded. You may press then whichever way you wish, they are so elastic you can always win your purpose, but then they are not fixed in character and soon return to be what they were before.

Pray God to send a few men with "grit" in them; men, who when they know a thing to be right, will not turn away, or turn aside, or stop; men who will persevere all the more because there are difficulties to meet or foes to encounter; who stand all the more true to their Master because they are opposed; who, the more they are thrust into the fire, the hotter they become; who, just like the bow, the further the string is drawn the more powerfully it sends forth its arrows, and so the more they are trodden upon, the more mighty will they become in the cause of truth against error.

Charles Spurgeon

PAUSE FOR REFLECTION

Are you so convinced of the reality of God in your life that you would risk your life to serve him?

THURSDAY

Proclaim God's Truth Boldly

Acts 21:26—22:5

The next day Paul took the four
men and shared in the cleansing ceremony with them. Then he went to
the Temple and announced the time
when the days of the cleansing ceremony would be finished. On the
last day an offering would be given
for each of the men.

27 When the seven days were almost over, some Jews from Asia saw
Paul at the Temple. They caused all
the people to be upset and grabbed
Paul. 28 They shouted, "People of Israel, help us! This is the man who
goes everywhere teaching against
the law of Moses, against our people,
and against this Temple. Now he has
brought some Greeks into the
Temple and has made this holy place
unclean!" 29 (The Jews said this because they had seen Trophimus, a
man from Ephesus, with Paul in
Jerusalem. The Jews thought that
Paul had brought him into the
Temple.)

30 All the people in Jerusalem became upset. Together they ran, took
Paul, and dragged him out of the
Temple. The Temple doors were
closed immediately. 31 While they
were trying to kill Paul, the commander of the Roman army in
Jerusalem learned that there was
trouble in the whole city. 32 Immediately he took some officers and soldiers and ran to the place where the
crowd was gathered. When the
people saw them, they stopped beating Paul. 33 The commander went to
Paul and arrested him. He told his
soldiers to tie Paul with two chains.
Then he asked who he was and what
he had done wrong. 34 Some in the
crowd were yelling one thing, and
some were yelling another. Because
of all this confusion and shouting,
the commander could not learn what
had happened. So he ordered the
soldiers to take Paul to the army
building. 35 When Paul came to the
steps, the soldiers had to carry him
because the people were ready to
hurt him. 36 The whole mob was following them, shouting, "Kill him!"

37 As the soldiers were about to
take Paul into the army building, he
spoke to the commander, "May I say
something to you?"

The commander said, "Do you
speak Greek? 38 I thought you were
the Egyptian who started some
trouble against the government not
long ago and led four thousand kill-
ers out to the desert."

39 Paul said, "No, I am a Jew from
Tarsus in the country of Cilicia. I am
a citizen of that important city.
Please, let me speak to the people."

40 The commander gave permission, so Paul stood on the steps and
waved his hand to quiet the people.
When there was silence, he spoke to
them in the Jewish language.

Paul Speaks to the People

22 Paul said, "Friends, fellow
Jews, listen to my defense to
you." 2 When the Jews heard him
speaking the Jewish language, they
became very quiet. 3 Paul said, "I am
a Jew, born in Tarsus in the country
of Cilicia, but I grew up in this city. I
was a student of Gamaliel, who carefully taught me everything about the

law of our ancestors. I was very serious about serving God, just as are all of you here today. [4]I persecuted the people who followed the Way of Jesus, and some of them were even killed. I arrested men and women and put them in jail. [5]The high priest and the whole council of older Jewish leaders can tell you this is true. They gave me letters to the Jewish brothers in Damascus. So I was going there to arrest these people and bring them back to Jerusalem to be punished."

OLD TESTAMENT READING

He said, "Human, I am sending you to the people of Israel. That nation has turned against me and broken away from me. They and their ancestors have sinned against me until this very day. [4]I am sending you to people who are stubborn and who do not obey. You will say to them, 'This is what the Lord God says.' [5]They may listen, or they may not, since they are a people who have turned against me. But they will know that a prophet has been among them."

Ezekiel 2:3–5

INSIGHTS

Johan is young, tall, blond, and Dutch. I got to know him through my cousin, who attended the same Bible school in England. Gifted and handsome, Johan could have carved out a comfortable youth ministry in his native Netherlands—or most anywhere in the world, for that matter.

Comfort, however, isn't one of Johan's major goals. He chose to take the gospel of Christ to the bedouins and nomads near Israel's desolate Sinai desert. A forgotten people in one of the most desolate corners of the world.

Johan works by an oasis near the sea, attracting travelers and bedouins by offering hot meals, clothing, and first aid. . . .

From the bedouins, Johan learned it is considered worse than murder if you know of a water source and yet neglect to tell your fellow man.

Few of us will ever live in a wilderness like the one where young Johan has pitched his tent. Not many among us will ever proclaim salvation to desert nomads. But all around us, no matter where we reside or work, there are thirsty men and women. The neighbor down the street, the man at the service station, the boy who carries our groceries, the secretary who types and files, or even the distant aunt who occasionally comes by for visits.

If these people don't know Christ, they're going to die of thirst. . . .

Do you know the Source of living water? If you do, please don't withhold a drink from somebody who is thirsty.

It's not just a matter of hospitality. It's a matter of life and death.

Joni Eareckson Tada

APPLICATION

What difficulties did Paul and Ezekiel face in proclaiming God's message? Why did they speak God's Word, even at great personal risk? To whom is God leading you to share Christ? Will you take the risk?

FRIDAY

God Has Plans for Those He Has Chosen

Acts 22:6–29

About noon when I came near Damascus, a bright light from heaven suddenly flashed all around me. 7 I fell to the ground and heard a voice saying, 'Saul, Saul, why are you persecuting me?' 8 I asked, 'Who are you, Lord?' The voice said, 'I am Jesus from Nazareth whom you are persecuting.' 9 Those who were with me did not hear the voice, but they saw the light. 10 I said, 'What shall I do, Lord?' The Lord answered, 'Get up and go to Damascus. There you will be told about all the things I have planned for you to do.' 11 I could not see, because the bright light had made me blind. So my companions led me into Damascus.

12 "There a man named Ananias came to me. He was a religious man; he obeyed the law of Moses, and all the Jews who lived there respected him. 13 He stood by me and said, 'Brother Saul, see again!' Immediately I was able to see him. 14 He said, 'The God of our ancestors chose you long ago to know his plan, to see the Righteous One, and to hear words from him. 15 You will be his witness to all people, telling them about what you have seen and heard. 16 Now, why wait any longer? Get up, be baptized, and wash your sins away, trusting in him to save you.'

17 "Later, when I returned to Jerusalem, I was praying in the Temple, and I saw a vision. 18 I saw the Lord saying to me, 'Hurry! Leave Jerusalem now! The people here will not accept the truth about me.' 19 But I said, 'Lord, they know that in every synagogue I put the believers in jail and beat them. 20 They also know I was there when Stephen, your witness, was killed. I stood there agreeing and holding the coats of those who were killing him!' 21 But the Lord said to me, 'Leave now. I will send you far away to the non-Jewish people.' "

22 The crowd listened to Paul until he said this. Then they began shouting, "Kill him! Get him out of the world! He should not be allowed to live!" 23 They shouted, threw off their coats, and threw dust into the air.

24 Then the commander ordered the soldiers to take Paul into the army building and beat him. He wanted to make Paul tell why the people were shouting against him like this. 25 But as the soldiers were tying him up, preparing to beat him, Paul said to an officer nearby, "Do you have the right to beat a Roman citizen who has not been proven guilty?"

26 When the officer heard this, he went to the commander and reported it. The officer said, "Do you know what you are doing? This man is a Roman citizen."

27 The commander came to Paul and said, "Tell me, are you really a Roman citizen?"

He answered, "Yes."

28 The commander said, "I paid a lot of money to become a Roman citizen."

But Paul said, "I was born a citizen."

29 The men who were preparing to question Paul moved away from him

immediately. The commander was frightened because he had already tied Paul, and Paul was a Roman citizen.

OLD TESTAMENT READING

*A*ll the earth should worship the
  LORD;
 the whole world should fear him.
9 He spoke, and it happened.
 He commanded, and it appeared.
10 The LORD upsets the plans of
  nations;
 he ruins all their plans.
11 But the LORD's plans will stand
  forever;
 his ideas will last from now on.
12 Happy is the nation whose God is
  the LORD,
 the people he chose for his
  very own.

Psalm 33:8–12

*P*eople may make plans in their
  minds,
 but the LORD decides what they
  will do.

Proverbs 16:9

INSIGHTS

God is at work in all the kaleidoscoping family transitions: not only in the high points but in the endings, beginnings, detours, dead ends, and in-between times. His powerful tools are not just the promotions and graduations but the failures and firings and losses and sicknesses and shocks and periods of boredom. In them all He's silently, busily, unceasingly encouraging, punishing, shaping. . . .

. . . And during all His working—all God's silent activity in the disappointments, surprises, delights, irritations—transformations are taking place. . . .

Do you feel as if nothing is happening . . . ?

I guess so does a lobster, encased in that ridiculous armor. As he grows it even gets crowded inside. But he sheds it fourteen times during his first year of life. Each shedding takes ten days, and each time in the period between shells—when he's naked, exposed, vulnerable—he grows about seven percent.

You feel stifled, unfulfilled? You don't know when you'll break out into change?

Wait for God.

Wait on God.

Wait with God.

Life is not fixed. Let it happen; don't rush it. "It is God who works in you to will and to act according to his good purpose. Do everything without complaining or arguing" (Phil. 2:13, 14). Keep your eyes fixed on Him, live in obedience as you see it, and then just be there.

Anne Ortlund

APPLICATION

Imagine yourself as Paul. How would you have taken the news that God had very different plans than what you had chosen? Pray that you will trust God's plans and obey them as they are revealed to you.

WEEKEND

Be Brave; God Stands by His Own

Acts 22:30—23:22

Paul Speaks to Jewish Leaders

The next day the commander decided to learn why the Jews were accusing Paul. So he ordered the leading priests and the Jewish council to meet. The commander took Paul's chains off. Then he brought Paul out and stood him before their meeting.

23 Paul looked at the Jewish council and said, "Brothers, I have lived my life without guilt feelings before God up to this day." 2 Ananias, the high priest, heard this and told the men who were standing near Paul to hit him on the mouth. 3 Paul said to Ananias, "God will hit you, too! You are like a wall that has been painted white. You sit there and judge me, using the law of Moses, but you are telling them to hit me, and that is against the law."

4 The men standing near Paul said to him, "You cannot insult God's high priest like that!"

5 Paul said, "Brothers, I did not know this man was the high priest. It is written in the Scriptures, 'You must not curse a leader of your people.' "

6 Some of the men in the meeting were Sadducees, and others were Pharisees. Knowing this, Paul shouted to them, "My brothers, I am a Pharisee, and my father was a Pharisee. I am on trial here because I believe that people will rise from the dead."

7 When Paul said this, there was an argument between the Pharisees and the Sadducees, and the group was divided. 8 (The Sadducees do not believe in angels or spirits or that people will rise from the dead. But the Pharisees believe in them all.) 9 So there was a great uproar. Some of the teachers of the law, who were Pharisees, stood up and argued, "We find nothing wrong with this man. Maybe an angel or a spirit did speak to him."

10 The argument was beginning to turn into such a fight that the commander was afraid the Jews would tear Paul to pieces. So he told the soldiers to go down and take Paul away and put him in the army building.

11 The next night the Lord came and stood by Paul. He said, "Be brave! You have told people in Jerusalem about me. You must do the same in Rome."

12 In the morning some of the Jews made a plan to kill Paul, and they took an oath not to eat or drink anything until they had killed him. 13 There were more than forty Jews who made this plan. 14 They went to the leading priests and the older Jewish leaders and said, "We have taken an oath not to eat or drink until we have killed Paul. 15 So this is what we want you to do: Send a message to the commander to bring Paul out to you as though you want to ask him more questions. We will be waiting to kill him while he is on the way here."

16 But Paul's nephew heard about this plan and went to the army building and told Paul. 17 Then Paul called one of the officers and said, "Take this young man to the commander. He has a message for him."

[18]So the officer brought Paul's nephew to the commander and said, "The prisoner, Paul, asked me to bring this young man to you. He wants to tell you something."

[19]The commander took the young man's hand and led him to a place where they could be alone. He asked, "What do you want to tell me?"

[20]The young man said, "The Jews have decided to ask you to bring Paul down to their council meeting tomorrow. They want you to think they are going to ask him more questions. [21] But don't believe them! More than forty men are hiding and waiting to kill Paul. They have all taken an oath not to eat or drink until they have killed him. Now they are waiting for you to agree."

[22]The commander sent the young man away, ordering him, "Don't tell anyone that you have told me about their plan."

OLD TESTAMENT READING

God, we thank you;
we thank you because you are near.
We tell about the miracles you do.

[2]You say, "I set the time for trial,
and I will judge fairly.
[3]The earth with all its people may shake,
but I am the one who holds it steady." *Selah*

Psalm 75:1–3

INSIGHTS

Now on whom dost thou trust?" (2 Kings 18:20). Such was the challenge which the blatant Assyrian field-marshal, Rab-shakeh, flung at the beleagured king Hezekiah, more than two-and-a-half millenniums ago. Little did he guess that before many more sunrises 185,000 of his proud army would be corpses, cut down by an invisible scythe of the Almighty! Hezekiah did not reply to Rab-shakeh, but despite the hopeless-looking circumstances his heart was fixed, trusting in Jehovah (18:5). This was his secret of victory.

Even so today, the first mark of the true Christian is reliance on Jehovah-Jesus. We rely on Him exclusively as the vicarious Sinbearer through whom we have the salvation of our souls.

But we are to rely on Him continually as our victorious Champion through whom we have victory in our daily life. . . . So long as we rely on Him we have victory. Temper, fear, lust, pride, envy, grudging, moodiness, impatience, despondency, worry; over all such we gain victory as we really rely on Jesus.

Again, we are to rely on Him as our vigilant Provider, who "supplies all our need" (Phil. 4:19; Ps. 34:22). He does not always employ ravens to feed His Elijahs, but by one means or another He sustains them if they really rely on Him.

J. Sydlow Baxter

ACTION POINT

In what ways has the Lord stood next to you and encouraged you to be brave for his sake? For what in your life do you need confidence that he is standing with you? Pray for his protection. Trust him. He will supply the victory!

MONDAY

God Wants His People to Do What Is Right

Acts 23:23—24:16

Paul Is Sent to Caesarea

Then the commander called two officers and said, "I need some men to
go to Caesarea. Get two hundred
soldiers, seventy horsemen, and two
hundred men with spears ready to
leave at nine o'clock tonight. 24 Get
some horses for Paul to ride so he
can be taken to Governor Felix
safely." 25 And he wrote a letter that
said:

26 From Claudius Lysias.

To the Most Excellent Governor
Felix:

Greetings.

> 27 The Jews had taken this
> man and planned to kill him.
> But I learned that he is a Ro-
> man citizen, so I went with my
> soldiers and saved him. 28 I
> wanted to know why they were
> accusing him, so I brought him
> before their council meeting.
> 29 I learned that the Jews said
> Paul did some things that were
> wrong by their own laws, but
> no charge was worthy of jail or
> death. 30 When I was told that
> some of the Jews were plan-
> ning to kill Paul, I sent him to
> you at once. I also told those
> Jews to tell you what they have
> against him.

31 So the soldiers did what they
were told and took Paul and brought
him to the city of Antipatris that
night. 32 The next day the horsemen
went with Paul to Caesarea, but the
other soldiers went back to the army
building in Jerusalem. 33 When the
horsemen came to Caesarea and
gave the letter to the governor, they
turned Paul over to him. 34 The governor read the letter and asked Paul,
"What area are you from?" When he
learned that Paul was from Cilicia,
35 he said, "I will hear your case when
those who are against you come
here, too." Then the governor gave
orders for Paul to be kept under
guard in Herod's palace.

Paul Is Accused

24 Five days later Ananias, the
high priest, went to the city of
Caesarea with some of the older Jewish leaders and a lawyer named
Tertullus. They had come to make
charges against Paul before the governor. 2 Paul was called into the
meeting, and Tertullus began to accuse him, saying, "Most Excellent
Felix! Our people enjoy much peace
because of you, and many wrong
things in our country are being
made right through your wise help.
3 We accept these things always and
in every place, and we are thankful
for them. 4 But not wanting to take
any more of your time, I beg you to
be kind and listen to our few words.
5 We have found this man to be a
troublemaker, stirring up the Jews
everywhere in the world. He is a
leader of the Nazarene group. 6 Also,
he was trying to make the Temple
unclean, but we stopped him. And
we wanted to judge him by our own
law. 7 But the officer Lysias came and
used much force to take him from
us. 8 And Lysias commanded those
who wanted to accuse Paul to come

to you. By asking him questions
yourself, you can decide if all these
things are true." [9]The other Jews
agreed and said that all of this was
true.
[10]When the governor made a sign
for Paul to speak, Paul said, "Governor Felix, I know you have been a
judge over this nation for a long
time. So I am happy to defend myself before you. [11]You can learn for
yourself that I went to worship in
Jerusalem only twelve days ago.
[12]Those who are accusing me did
not find me arguing with anyone in
the Temple or stirring up the people
in the synagogues or in the city.
[13]They cannot prove the things they
are saying against me now. [14]But I
will tell you this: I worship the God
of our ancestors as a follower of the
Way of Jesus. The Jews say that the
Way of Jesus is not the right way. But
I believe everything that is taught in
the law of Moses and that is written
in the books of the Prophets. [15]I have
the same hope in God that they
have—the hope that all people, good
and bad, will surely be raised from
the dead. [16]This is why I always try
to do what I believe is right before
God and people."

OLD TESTAMENT READING

Your father was satisfied to have
  food and drink.
He did what was right and fair,
  so everything went well for him.
[16]He helped those who were poor
  and needy,
  so everything went well for him.
That is what it means to know
  God,"
  says the LORD.

Jeremiah 22:15b–16

INSIGHTS

Faithfully pleasing God is an activity, not just a nice set of beliefs. It must be a way of life.

. . . Twenty years ago, people were asking the question: Does God exist? Today that question has changed to: What difference does He make? The answer for too many people is: Not much. Even for many people who have an enormous amount of Bible knowledge, God makes little difference in how they actually live their lives.

. . . If Christ doesn't make any difference in my ethics and values at my job; if He doesn't affect my speech and attitudes toward co-workers; . . . if He makes absolutely no difference in the way I live and work, then pray tell, what difference does He make?! What's the point of playing a religious game that is all talk and no action?

I take the matter of obedience as an action quite seriously. I challenge you to do the same. Whenever you're exposed to Scripture, ask yourself: How can I apply this to my life? What practical thing can I do to embed this truth in my attitude, character, and behavior? Where does it need to make a difference? That's a commitment to life-change.

Doug Sherman
William Hendricks

ACTION POINT

Why did Paul try to do what was right before God and men? What does God say it means to know him (Jeremiah 22:16)? Pray that you will give yourself fully to obeying God's commands!

TUESDAY

The Unrighteous Fear God's Judgment

Acts 24:17—25:12

After being away from Jerusalem
for several years, I went back to
bring money to my people and to offer sacrifices. 18 I was doing this
when they found me in the Temple.
I had finished the cleansing ceremony and had not made any
trouble; no people were gathering
around me. 19 But there were some
Jews from the country of Asia who
should be here, standing before you.
If I have really done anything wrong,
they are the ones who should accuse
me. 20 Or ask these Jews here if they
found any wrong in me when I stood
before the Jewish council in Jerusalem. 21 But I did shout one thing
when I stood before them: 'You are
judging me today because I believe
that people will rise from the dead!' "

22 Felix already understood much
about the Way of Jesus. He stopped
the trial and said, "When commander Lysias comes here, I will
decide your case." 23 Felix told the
officer to keep Paul guarded but to
give him some freedom and to let his
friends bring what he needed.

Paul Speaks to Felix and His Wife

After some days Felix came with
his wife, Drusilla, who was Jewish,
and asked for Paul to be brought to
him. He listened to Paul talk about
believing in Christ Jesus. 25 But Felix
became afraid when Paul spoke
about living right, self-control, and
the time when God will judge the
world. He said, "Go away now. When
I have more time, I will call for you."
26 At the same time Felix hoped that
Paul would give him some money, so
he often sent for Paul and talked with
him.

27 But after two years, Felix was
replaced by Porcius Festus as governor. But Felix had left Paul in
prison to please the Jews.

Paul Asks to See Caesar

25 Three days after Festus became governor, he went from
Caesarea to Jerusalem. 2 There the
leading priests and the important
Jewish leaders made charges
against Paul before Festus. 3 They
asked Festus to do them a favor.
They wanted him to send Paul back
to Jerusalem, because they had a
plan to kill him on the way. 4 But
Festus answered that Paul would be
kept in Caesarea and that he himself
was returning there soon. 5 He said,
"Some of your leaders should go
with me. They can accuse the man
there in Caesarea, if he has really
done something wrong."

6 Festus stayed in Jerusalem another eight or ten days and then
went back to Caesarea. The next day
he told the soldiers to bring Paul
before him. Festus was seated on the
judge's seat 7 when Paul came into
the room. The Jewish people who
had come from Jerusalem stood
around him, making serious charges
against him, which they could not
prove. 8 This is what Paul said to defend himself: "I have done nothing
wrong against the Jewish law,
against the Temple, or against Caesar."

[9] But Festus wanted to please the
Jews. So he asked Paul, "Do you
want to go to Jerusalem for me to
judge you there on these charges?"
[10] Paul said, "I am standing at
Caesar's judgment seat now, where
I should be judged. I have done nothing wrong to the Jews; you know this
is true. [11] If I have done something
wrong and the law says I must die, I
do not ask to be saved from death.
But if these charges are not true,
then no one can give me to them. I
want Caesar to hear my case!"
[12] Festus talked about this with his
advisors. Then he said, "You have
asked to see Caesar, so you will go
to Caesar!"

OLD TESTAMENT READING

Then, it was as if their eyes were opened. They realized they were naked, so they sewed fig leaves together and made something to cover themselves.

[8] Then they heard the LORD God
walking in the garden during the
cool part of the day, and the man and
his wife hid from the LORD God
among the trees in the garden. [9] But
the LORD God called to the man and
said, "Where are you?"
[10] The man answered, "I heard
you walking in the garden, and I was
afraid because I was naked, so I hid."

Genesis 3:7–10

INSIGHTS

If our fathers emphasized God's "awful purity" at the expense of His love, we have emphasized His love at the expense of His "awful purity." We delight in these days to say, "Gentle, gentle, gentle, is the God and Father." We have almost forgotten that cherubim and seraphim, with veiled faces, continually cry, "Holy, holy, holy is the Lord of Hosts."

In our absorption in the thought of God as Father, we have almost lost sight of the fact that He is the Holy Sovereign, ruling the world in righteousness. The result has been that to a large extent we have lost the sense of religious awe, of reverence, and of godly fear. . . .

We have only to realize that God is the Holy Sovereign, and the awe is bound to come back. . . .

To believe that an Almighty God is on the throne, working out His own holy and perfect and acceptable righteousness—is there not enough in that to fill the hearts of sinful men with "godly fear"? Is there not enough in that to make us "tremble"?

The Puritan's religion was a serious religion. He was afraid of God—afraid of Him in a worthy sense. He conceived of God as with him and about him always, and he was afraid of sinning against His holiness.

And is there not enough in the mere realization of the fact that a Holy God sits upon the throne, a God who is actively and unceasingly asserting His holiness—is there not enough in that one fact to make us, who are so prone to sin, serious and fearful?

John Jones

ACTION POINT

How do you respond to God's insistence on purity and his declarations of coming judgment? Pray that God will convince you of his holiness and your need for him!

WEDNESDAY

The Testimony of a Blameless Life

Acts 25:13—26:8

Paul Before King Agrippa

A few days later King Agrippa and
Bernice came to Caesarea to visit
Festus. 14 They stayed there for some
time, and Festus told the king about
Paul's case. Festus said, "There is a
man that Felix left in prison. 15 When
I went to Jerusalem, the leading
priests and the older Jewish leaders
there made charges against him,
asking me to sentence him to death.
16 But I answered, 'When a man is
accused of a crime, Romans do not
hand him over until he has been allowed to face his accusers and defend himself against their charges.'
17 So when these Jews came here to
Caesarea for the trial, I did not waste
time. The next day I sat on the
judge's seat and commanded that the
man be brought in. 18 The Jews stood
up and accused him, but not of any
serious crime as I thought they
would. 19 The things they said were
about their own religion and about a
man named Jesus who died. But Paul
said that he is still alive. 20 Not knowing how to find out about these questions, I asked Paul, 'Do you want to
go to Jerusalem and be judged
there?' 21 But he asked to be kept in
Caesarea. He wants a decision from
the emperor. So I ordered that he be
held until I could send him to Caesar."
22 Agrippa said to Festus, "I would
also like to hear this man myself."
Festus said, "Tomorrow you will
hear him."
23 The next day Agrippa and
Bernice appeared with great show,
acting like very important people.
They went into the judgment room
with the army leaders and the important men of Caesarea. Then Festus
ordered the soldiers to bring Paul in.
24 Festus said, "King Agrippa and all
who are gathered here with us, you
see this man. All the Jewish people,
here and in Jerusalem, have complained to me about him, shouting
that he should not live any longer.
25 When I judged him, I found no reason to order his death. But since he
asked to be judged by Caesar, I decided to send him. 26 But I have nothing definite to write the emperor
about him. So I have brought him
before all of you—especially you,
King Agrippa. I hope you can question him and give me something to
write. 27 I think it is foolish to send a
prisoner to Caesar without telling
what charges are against him."

Paul Defends Himself

26 Agrippa said to Paul, "You
may now speak to defend
yourself."
Then Paul raised his hand and began to speak. 2 He said, "King
Agrippa, I am very happy to stand
before you and will answer all the
charges the Jewish people make
against me. 3 You know so much
about all the Jewish customs and the
things the Jews argue about, so
please listen to me patiently.
4 "All the Jewish people know
about my whole life, how I lived from
the beginning in my own country
and later in Jerusalem. 5 They have

known me for a long time. If they
want to, they can tell you that I was
a good Pharisee. And the Pharisees
obey the laws of the Jewish religion
more carefully than any other group.
6 Now I am on trial because I hope
for the promise that God made to
our ancestors. 7 This is the promise
that the twelve tribes of our people
hope to receive as they serve God
day and night. My king, the Jews
have accused me because I hope for
this same promise! 8 Why do any of
you people think it is impossible for
God to raise people from the dead?"

OLD TESTAMENT READING

*T*he LORD spared me because I
did what was right.
Because I have not done evil,
he has rewarded me.
22 I have followed the ways of the
LORD;
I have not done evil by turning
from my God.
23 I remember all his laws
and have not broken his rules.
24 I am innocent before him;
I have kept myself from doing
evil.
25 The LORD rewarded me because I
did what was right,
because I did what the LORD
said was right.

2 Samuel 22:21–25

*T*hen the LORD said to Satan, "Have you noticed my servant Job? No one else on earth is like him. He is an honest and innocent man, honoring God and staying away from evil. You caused me to ruin him for no good reason, but he continues to be without blame."

Job 2:3

INSIGHTS

We must show nonbelievers what it looks like to be at peace with ourselves, and to truly love other people. The best means of creating an interest in Christ and the Christian way of life is to so thoroughly live and enjoy it that others will want to know how they, too, can have it.

. . . Most Americans believe that you cannot tell a born-again Christian from nonbelievers because there is no difference in the way they live. The only distinction, people say, is that Christians are more religious, more fanatical or more closed-minded. There is no widespread sense that the religious experience of Christians has changed the fabric of our thinking or the nature of our life-styles (other than requiring regular participation in church activities).

To convince a hardened and cynical world that we are not just different, but better off for those differences, we must allow them to see how our struggles in life have been altered for the better as a result of our relationship with Christ.

George Barna

APPLICATION

How might Paul's testimony to King Agrippa have been different if he hadn't been so careful to live in a way that honored God? Is living in a way that pleases God most important to you? Pray that your life will make a positive difference in the world around you!

THURSDAY

Called to Be God's Witnesses

Acts 26:9–32

I, too, thought I ought to do many
things against Jesus from Nazareth.
10 And that is what I did in Jerusalem.
The leading priests gave me the
power to put many of God's people
in jail, and when they were being
killed, I agreed it was a good thing.
11 In every synagogue, I often punished them and tried to make them
speak against Jesus. I was so angry
against them I even went to other
cities to find them and punish them.
12 "One time the leading priests
gave me permission and the power
to go to Damascus. 13 On the way
there, at noon, I saw a light from
heaven. It was brighter than the sun
and flashed all around me and those
who were traveling with me. 14 We all
fell to the ground. Then I heard a
voice speaking to me in the Jewish
language, saying, 'Saul, Saul, why
are you persecuting me? You are
only hurting yourself by fighting
me.' 15 I said, 'Who are you, Lord?'
The Lord said, 'I am Jesus, the one
you are persecuting. 16 Stand up! I
have chosen you to be my servant
and my witness—you will tell people
the things that you have seen and
the things that I will show you. This
is why I have come to you today. 17 I
will keep you safe from your own
people and also from those who are
not Jewish. I am sending you to them
18 to open their eyes so that they may
turn away from darkness to the light,
away from the power of Satan and to
God. Then their sins can be forgiven,
and they can have a place with those
people who have been made holy by
believing in me.'
19 "King Agrippa, after I had this
vision from heaven, I obeyed it. 20 I
began telling people that they should
change their hearts and lives and
turn to God and do things to show
they really had changed. I told this
first to those in Damascus, then in
Jerusalem, and in every part of
Judea, and also to those who are not
Jewish. 21 This is why the Jews took
me and were trying to kill me in the
Temple. 22 But God has helped me,
and so I stand here today, telling all
people, small and great, what I have
seen. But I am saying only what
Moses and the prophets said would
happen—23 that the Christ would die,
and as the first to rise from the dead,
he would bring light to the Jewish
and non-Jewish people."

Paul Tries to Persuade Agrippa

While Paul was saying these
things to defend himself, Festus said
loudly, "Paul, you are out of your
mind! Too much study has driven
you crazy!"
25 Paul said, "Most excellent
Festus, I am not crazy. My words are
true and sensible. 26 King Agrippa
knows about these things, and I can
speak freely to him. I know he has
heard about all of these things, because they did not happen off in a
corner. 27 King Agrippa, do you believe what the prophets wrote? I
know you believe."
28 King Agrippa said to Paul, "Do
you think you can persuade me to
become a Christian in such a short
time?"
29 Paul said, "Whether it is a short

or a long time, I pray to God that not
only you but every person listening to
me today would be saved and be like
me—except for these chains I have."
30 Then King Agrippa, Governor
Festus, Bernice, and all the people
sitting with them stood up 31 and left
the room. Talking to each other, they
said, "There is no reason why this
man should die or be put in jail."
32 And Agrippa said to Festus, "We
could let this man go free, but he has
asked Caesar to hear his case."

OLD TESTAMENT READING

God Chose the Nation of Israel to Be His Witness

Are there any gods like you, LORD?
 There are no gods like you.
 You are wonderfully holy,
 amazingly powerful,
 a worker of miracles.
12 You reached out with your right
 hand,
 and the earth swallowed our
 enemies.
13 You keep your loving promise
 and lead the people you have
 saved.
 With your strength you will guide
 them
 to your holy place.
14 "The other nations will hear this
 and tremble with fear."

Exodus 15:11–14a

Obey these laws carefully, in order to show the other nations that you have wisdom and understanding. When they hear about these laws, they will say, "This great nation of Israel is wise and understanding."

Deuteronomy 4:6

INSIGHTS

The best instrument for evangelism is the ordinary church member bearing witness to a vital faith. It always has been; it always will be. . . .

There is a high probability that if you are a Christian, it is because a member of the church invited you and then some of the people of the church loved you into making a decision for Christ. Generally, people are led into a personal relationship with Christ because there have been church members who cared enough to talk to them and love them into the Kingdom. . . .

. . . Our lifestyle as Christians should be a testimony to the validity of our message, but if we had to be spiritually perfect in order to witness for Christ, no one would qualify. . . . According to Paul, we must share the gospel while we are still in the process of changing into truly Christianized people. He wanted us to know that if we wait until we are the kind of people we ought to be before witnessing, we will never get the evangelistic job done. As imperfect people who are heirs to the grace of God, we are called to invite people to join us as we strive together to become more and more like Christ.

Tony Campolo

APPLICATION

Have you ever felt unworthy to be God's witness? Despite your feelings, how is God making his name known through you? Pray to be a diligent and faithful witness!

FRIDAY

We Can Trust God to Keep His Promises

Acts 27:1–26

Paul Sails for Rome

27 It was decided that we would sail for Italy. An officer named Julius, who served in the emperor's army, guarded Paul and some other prisoners. 2 We got on a ship that was from the city of Adramyttium and was about to sail to different ports in the country of Asia. Aristarchus, a man from the city of Thessalonica in Macedonia, went with us. 3 The next day we came to Sidon. Julius was very good to Paul and gave him freedom to go visit his friends, who took care of his needs. 4 We left Sidon and sailed close to the island of Cyprus, because the wind was blowing against us. 5 We went across the sea by Cilicia and Pamphylia and landed at the city of Myra, in Lycia. 6 There the officer found a ship from Alexandria that was going to Italy, so he put us on it.

7 We sailed slowly for many days. We had a hard time reaching Cnidus because the wind was blowing against us, and we could not go any farther. So we sailed by the south side of the island of Crete near Salmone. 8 Sailing past it was hard. Then we came to a place called Fair Havens, near the city of Lasea.

9 We had lost much time, and it was now dangerous to sail, because it was already after the Day of Cleansing. So Paul warned them, 10 "Men, I can see there will be a lot of trouble on this trip. The ship, the cargo, and even our lives may be lost." 11 But the captain and the owner of the ship did not agree with Paul, and the officer believed what the captain and owner of the ship said. 12 Since that harbor was not a good place for the ship to stay for the winter, most of the men decided that the ship should leave. They hoped we could go to Phoenix and stay there for the winter. Phoenix, a city on the island of Crete, had a harbor which faced southwest and northwest.

The Storm

When a good wind began to blow from the south, the men on the ship thought, "This is the wind we wanted, and now we have it." So they pulled up the anchor, and we sailed very close to the island of Crete. 14 But then a very strong wind named the "northeaster" came from the island. 15 The ship was caught in it and could not sail against it. So we stopped trying and let the wind carry us. 16 When we went below a small island named Cauda, we were barely able to bring in the lifeboat. 17 After the men took the lifeboat in, they tied ropes around the ship to hold it together. The men were afraid that the ship would hit the sandbanks of Syrtis, so they lowered the sail and let the wind carry the ship. 18 The next day the storm was blowing us so hard that the men threw out some of the cargo. 19 A day later with their own hands they threw out the ship's equipment. 20 When we could not see the sun or the stars for many days, and the storm was very bad, we lost all hope of being saved.

21 After the men had gone without
food for a long time, Paul stood up
before them and said, "Men, you
should have listened to me. You
should not have sailed from Crete.
Then you would not have all this
trouble and loss. 22 But now I tell you
to cheer up because none of you will
die. Only the ship will be lost. 23 Last
night an angel came to me from the
God I belong to and worship. 24 The
angel said, 'Paul, do not be afraid.
You must stand before Caesar. And
God has promised you that he will
save the lives of everyone sailing
with you.' 25 So men, have courage. I
trust in God that everything will happen as his angel told me. 26 But we
will crash on an island."

OLD TESTAMENT READING

Joshua, be strong and brave! You
must lead these people so they can
take the land that I promised their
fathers I would give them. 7 Be
strong and brave. Be sure to obey all
the teachings my servant Moses
gave you. If you follow them exactly,
you will be successful in everything
you do. 8 Always remember what is
written in the Book of the Teachings.
Study it day and night to be sure to
obey everything that is written
there. If you do this, you will be wise
and successful in everything."

Joshua 1:6–8

INSIGHTS

The story of Jericho's conquest is a fine example of the completed promises of God. . . .

. . . On the seventh circuit of the seventh day the people shouted and the walls of Jericho fell down flat. The army of Israel entered the city unhindered and utterly destroyed all that was in the city, with one notable exception—the household of Rahab. Because they obeyed the Lord explicitly, the people saw two great promises of the Lord performed on the same day. The city of Jericho, the strongest outpost of the Canaanite defenses, had been utterly destroyed as God had promised. Likewise Rahab and her household had been spared destruction, as God had promised.

But there is one final promise of God that can be seen in the conquest of Jericho. . . . To show that God means business when He makes a promise, Joshua imprecated a solemn curse on anyone who would rebuild the now-destroyed Jericho. This curse was literally fulfilled in the fate of Heil, the Bethelite, who rebuilt Jericho in the reign of Ahab (about 925 B.C.). Heil's firstborn son, Abiram, died as he was laying the foundation for the rebuilding of Jericho. Also his youngest son, Segub, died while he was setting up the gates of the city (1 Kings 16:34). What God promises, God performs.

Whether the promise is for salvation, as in the case of Rahab, or for destruction, as in the case of Heil, the promises of God must never be taken lightly. Whatever God promises, God performs. You can count on it.

Woodrow Kroll

PAUSE FOR REFLECTION

How did Paul and Joshua respond to God's promises? How well do you face great challenges with only the hope offered by a yet-to-be-fulfilled promise?

WEEKEND

God Saves His Own to Accomplish His Purposes

Acts 27:27—28:11a

On the fourteenth night we were
still being carried around in the
Adriatic Sea. About midnight the
sailors thought we were close to
land, 28 so they lowered a rope with
a weight on the end of it into the
water. They found that the water was
one hundred twenty feet deep. They
went a little farther and lowered the
rope again. It was ninety feet deep.
29 The sailors were afraid that we
would hit the rocks, so they threw
four anchors into the water and
prayed for daylight to come. 30 Some
of the sailors wanted to leave the
ship, and they lowered the lifeboat,
pretending they were throwing
more anchors from the front of the
ship. 31 But Paul told the officer and
the other soldiers, "If these men do
not stay in the ship, your lives cannot be saved." 32 So the soldiers cut
the ropes and let the lifeboat fall into
the water.

33 Just before dawn Paul began persuading all the people to eat something. He said, "For the past fourteen
days you have been waiting and
watching and not eating. 34 Now I beg
you to eat something. You need it to
stay alive. None of you will lose even
one hair off your heads." 35 After he
said this, Paul took some bread and
thanked God for it before all of them.
He broke off a piece and began eating. 36 They all felt better and started
eating, too. 37 There were two hundred seventy-six people on the ship.
38 When they had eaten all they
wanted, they began making the ship
lighter by throwing the grain into the
sea.

The Ship Is Destroyed

When daylight came, the sailors
saw land. They did not know what
land it was, but they saw a bay with
a beach and wanted to sail the ship
to the beach if they could. 40 So they
cut the ropes to the anchors and left
the anchors in the sea. At the same
time, they untied the ropes that were
holding the rudders. Then they
raised the front sail into the wind and
sailed toward the beach. 41 But the
ship hit a sandbank. The front of the
ship stuck there and could not move,
but the back of the ship began to
break up from the big waves.

42 The soldiers decided to kill the
prisoners so none of them could
swim away and escape. 43 But Julius,
the officer, wanted to let Paul live
and did not allow the soldiers to kill
the prisoners. Instead he ordered
everyone who could swim to jump
into the water first and swim to land.
44 The rest were to follow using
wooden boards or pieces of the ship.
And this is how all the people made
it safely to land.

Paul on the Island of Malta

28 When we were safe on land,
we learned that the island
was called Malta. 2 The people who
lived there were very good to us. Because it was raining and very cold,
they made a fire and welcomed all
of us. 3 Paul gathered a pile of sticks
and was putting them on the fire
when a poisonous snake came out
because of the heat and bit him on
the hand. 4 The people living on the

island saw the snake hanging from
Paul's hand and said to each other,
"This man must be a murderer! He
did not die in the sea, but Justice
does not want him to live." 5 But Paul
shook the snake off into the fire and
was not hurt. 6 The people thought
that Paul would swell up or fall down
dead. They waited and watched him
for a long time, but nothing bad happened to him. So they changed their
minds and said, "He is a god!"
7 There were some fields around
there owned by Publius, an important man on the island. He welcomed
us into his home and was very good
to us for three days. 8 Publius' father
was sick with a fever and dysentery.
Paul went to him, prayed, and put his
hands on the man and healed him.
9 After this, all the other sick people
on the island came to Paul, and he
healed them, too. 10–11 The people on
the island gave us many honors.
When we were ready to leave, three
months later, they gave us the things
we needed.

OLD TESTAMENT READING

So they picked up Jonah and threw
him into the sea, and the sea became
calm. 16 Then they began to fear the
LORD very much; they offered a sacrifice to the LORD and made promises
to him.

Jonah 1:15–16

INSIGHTS

Job did not understand the trials that came to him, but he passed the test because he could say, "'Though He slay me, I will hope in Him . . .'" (Job 13:15). Mary and Martha did not understand why Jesus waited until after Lazarus died before He came to them (John 11:21). The disciples did not understand why Jesus took them through Samaria, or why He waited at the well rather than go with them to buy food (John 4:8). Peter did not understand why Jesus let the soldiers arrest Him (John 18:10–11). Today, we understand the reason for these things because we can see the end result.

Job was tested because Satan said Job loved and served God only because of the protection and blessing God gave him. Job stood the test and Satan was defeated (Job 42:10–17).

After Jesus had raised Lazarus from the dead, Mary and Martha understood how the sickness and death of their brother had brought glory to God (John 11:43–45).

By the time they left Samaria, the disciples realized why they had to go through Samaria. A whole city, which otherwise would have been closed to them, heard the gospel and believed in Christ, all because Jesus talked to a woman while he waited at the well (John 4:39–41).

When difficulties come, we can know they have a purpose. We need not be confused. If we are in right relationship with God, we may not understand at the time, but we can know He will make all that happens to us work out for our good and His glory.

Lucille Sollenberger

ACTION POINT

Notice how God used each of these adventures at sea to bring glory to himself. Pray for faithful confidence in God's perfect plan, even when you face the most difficult and confusing situations.

MONDAY

God's People Welcome All Who Visit Them

Acts 28:11b–31

Paul Goes to Rome

We got on a ship from Alexandria
that had stayed on the island during
the winter. On the front of the ship
was the sign of the twin gods. 12 We
stopped at Syracuse for three days.
13 From there we sailed to Rhegium.
The next day a wind began to blow
from the south, and a day later we
came to Puteoli. 14 We found some
believers there who asked us to stay
with them for a week. Finally, we
came to Rome. 15 The believers in
Rome heard that we were there and
came out as far as the Market of
Appius and the Three Inns to meet
us. When Paul saw them, he was
encouraged and thanked God.

Paul in Rome

When we arrived at Rome, Paul
was allowed to live alone, with the
soldier who guarded him.

17 Three days later Paul sent for
the Jewish leaders there. When they
came together, he said, "Brothers, I
have done nothing against our
people or the customs of our ancestors. But I was arrested in Jerusalem
and given to the Romans. 18 After
they asked me many questions, they
could find no reason why I should
be killed. They wanted to let me go
free, 19 but the Jewish people there
argued against that. So I had to ask
to come to Rome to have my trial
before Caesar. But I have no charge
to bring against my own people.
20 That is why I wanted to see you
and talk with you. I am bound with
this chain because I believe in the
hope of Israel."

21 They answered Paul, "We have
received no letters from Judea about
you. None of our Jewish brothers
who have come from there brought
news or told us anything bad about
you. 22 But we want to hear your
ideas, because we know that people
everywhere are speaking against
this religious group."

23 Paul and the Jewish people
chose a day for a meeting and on that
day many more of the Jews met with
Paul at the place he was staying. He
spoke to them all day long. Using the
law of Moses and the prophets' writings, he explained the kingdom of
God, and he tried to persuade them
to believe these things about Jesus.
24 Some believed what Paul said, but
others did not. 25 So they argued and
began leaving after Paul said one
more thing to them: "The Holy Spirit
spoke the truth to your ancestors
through Isaiah the prophet, saying,
26 'Go to this people and say:
You will listen and listen, but you
will not understand.
You will look and look, but you
will not learn,
27 because these people have
become stubborn.
They don't hear with their ears,
and they have closed their
eyes.
Otherwise, they might really
understand
what they see with their eyes
and hear with their ears.
They might really understand in
their minds

and come back to me and be
healed.' *Isaiah 6:9-10*
28 "I want you to know that God
has also sent his salvation to those
who are not Jewish, and they will listen!" 29 After Paul said this, the Jews
left. They were arguing very much
with each other.
30 Paul stayed two full years in his
own rented house and welcomed all
people who came to visit him. 31 He
boldly preached about the kingdom
of God and taught about the Lord
Jesus Christ, and no one tried to stop
him.

OLD TESTAMENT READING

Then Rebekah ran and told her
mother's family about all these
things. 29 She had a brother named
Laban. 30b So he ran out to the well,
and there was the man standing by
the camels at the spring. 31 Laban
said, "Sir, you are welcome to come
in; you don't have to stand outside. I
have prepared the house for you and
also a place for your camels."
32 So Abraham's servant went into
the house.

Genesis 24:28, 29a, 30b-32a

INSIGHTS

Recently I finally got around to inviting a couple from our home church over for Sunday lunch. Sandy and Mike are young college graduates with promising careers and an adorable new baby. They are busy people and had not yet gotten involved in our church. I was ashamed to discover that although they'd been members of our church for nearly three years, ours was the first personal invitation they had received from anyone in our congregation. . . .

. . . In addition to providing examples of hospitality, Scripture gives us specific instructions to practice this kind of loving care for others. In his letters to Timothy and Titus, Paul listed it as a necessary qualification of an elder of the church. He combined encouragement and hospitality as important Christian traits in Titus 1:8–9. . . .

Paul's instructions in Romans 12:9–13 emphasize that this ministry of love in action belongs not just to elders, but should be a trademark of all believers. . . .

The emphasis in our practice of hospitality should be on how we give of ourselves to minister to others—not on how we perform to entertain others. The Bible commands us to carry out this ministry; it does not set up requirements for housing or meals. We do not need a large, beautifully decorated, immaculately tidy house in order to invite others into our home. "Breaking bread" with others does not require serving filet mignon or lobster tails. The issue is not spending money, but spending our time—not giving things, but giving ourselves. . . .

. . . Focus on people, not preparations. In the Lord's hands, a few loaves and fishes go a long way.

Rachael Crabb

PAUSE FOR REFLECTION

Do you think Paul, a prisoner, offered his guests luxurious accommodations? What do you think are the biblical standards for hospitality?

TUESDAY

All of Creation Tells Us About God

Romans 1:1–27

1 From Paul, a servant of Christ Jesus. God called me to be an apostle and chose me to tell the Good News.

2 God promised this Good News long ago through his prophets, as it is written in the Holy Scriptures. 3-4 The Good News is about God's Son, Jesus Christ our Lord. As a man, he was born from the family of David. But through the Spirit of holiness he was appointed to be God's Son with great power by rising from the dead. 5 Through Christ, God gave me the special work of an apostle, which was to lead people of all nations to believe and obey. I do this work for him. 6 And you who are in Rome are also called to belong to Jesus Christ.

7 To all of you in Rome whom God loves and has called to be his holy people:

Grace and peace to you from God our Father and the Lord Jesus Christ.

A Prayer of Thanks

8 First I want to say that I thank my God through Jesus Christ for all of you, because people everywhere in the world are talking about your faith. 9 God, whom I serve with my whole heart by telling the Good News about his Son, knows that I always mention you 10 every time I pray. I pray that I will be allowed to come to you, and this will happen if God wants it. 11 I want very much to see you, to give you some spiritual gift to make you strong. 12 I mean that I want us to help each other with the faith we have. Your faith will help me, and my faith will help you. 13 Brothers and sisters, I want you to know that I planned many times to come to you, but this has not been possible. I wanted to come so that I could help you grow spiritually as I have helped the other non-Jewish people.

14 I have a duty to all people—Greeks and those who are not Greeks, the wise and the foolish. 15 That is why I want so much to preach the Good News to you in Rome.

16 I am proud of the Good News, because it is the power God uses to save everyone who believes—to save the Jews first, and also to save those who are not Jews. 17 The Good News shows how God makes people right with himself—that it begins and ends with faith. As the Scripture says, "But those who are right with God will live by trusting in him."

All People Have Done Wrong

18 God's anger is shown from heaven against all the evil and wrong things people do. By their own evil lives they hide the truth. 19 God shows his anger because some knowledge of him has been made clear to them. Yes, God has shown himself to them. 20 There are things about him that people cannot see—his eternal power and all the things that make him God. But since the beginning of the world those things have been easy to understand by what God has

made. So people have no excuse for
the bad things they do. 21 They
knew God, but they did not give
glory to God or thank him. Their
thinking became useless. Their foolish minds were filled with darkness.
22 They said they were wise, but they
became fools. 23 They traded the glory
of God who lives forever for the worship of idols made to look like earthly
people, birds, animals, and snakes.
24 Because they did these things,
God left them and let them go their
sinful way, wanting only to do evil.
As a result, they became full of sexual
sin, using their bodies wrongly with
each other. 25 They traded the truth
of God for a lie. They worshiped and
served what had been created instead of the God who created those
things, who should be praised forever. Amen.
26 Because people did those
things, God left them and let them
do the shameful things they wanted
to do. Women stopped having natural sex and started having sex with
other women. 27 In the same way,
men stopped having natural sex and
began wanting each other. Men did
shameful things with other men, and
in their bodies they received the
punishment for those wrongs.

OLD TESTAMENT READING

The heavens tell the glory of God,
and the skies announce what
his hands have made.
2 Day after day they tell the story;
night after night they tell it
again.
3 They have no speech or words;
they have no voice to be heard.
4 But their message goes out
through all the world;
their words go everywhere on
earth.

Psalm 19:1–4a

INSIGHTS

This is my Father's world,
And to my listening ears
All nature sings, and round me
rings
The music of the spheres.
This is my Father's world:
I rest me in the thought
Of rocks and trees, of skies and
seas—
His hand the wonders wrought.

This is my Father's world,
The birds their carols raise,
The morning light, the lily white,
Declare their Maker's praise.
This is my Father's world:
He shines in all that's fair;
In the rustling grass I hear Him
pass,
He speaks to me everywhere.

This is my Father's world,
O let me ne'er forget
That though the wrong seems oft
so strong,
God is the Ruler yet.
This is my Father's world:
The battle is not done;
Jesus who died shall be satisfied,
And earth and heav'n be one.

Maltbie Babcock

PAUSE FOR REFLECTION

According to Paul, what excuses do people have for not knowing God? What testifies to God's glory and goodness? Describe how God's creation has influenced your beliefs about God.

WEDNESDAY

People Do What They Want, but God Holds Them Accountable

Romans 1:28—2:16

People did not think it was important to have a true knowledge of God. So God left them and allowed them to have their own worthless thinking and to do things they should not do. 29 They are filled with every kind of sin, evil, selfishness, and hatred. They are full of jealousy, murder, fighting, lying, and thinking the worst about each other. They gossip 30 and say evil things about each other. They hate God. They are rude and conceited and brag about themselves. They invent ways of doing evil. They do not obey their parents. 31 They are foolish, they do not keep their promises, and they show no kindness or mercy to others. 32 They know God's law says that those who live like this should die. But they themselves not only continue to do these evil things, they applaud others who do them.

You People Also Are Sinful

2 If you think you can judge others, you are wrong. When you judge them, you are really judging yourself guilty, because you do the same things they do. 2 God judges those who do wrong things, and we know that his judging is right. 3 You judge those who do wrong, but you do wrong yourselves. Do you think you will be able to escape the judgment of God? 4 He has been very kind and patient, waiting for you to change, but you think nothing of his kindness. Perhaps you do not understand that God is kind to you so you will change your hearts and lives. 5 But you are stubborn and refuse to change, so you are making your own punishment even greater on the day he shows his anger. On that day everyone will see God's right judgments. 6 God will reward or punish every person for what that person has done. 7 Some people, by always continuing to do good, live for God's glory, for honor, and for life that has no end. God will give them life forever. 8 But other people are selfish. They refuse to follow truth and, instead, follow evil. God will give them his punishment and anger. 9 He will give trouble and suffering to everyone who does evil—to the Jews first and also to those who are not Jews. 10 But he will give glory, honor, and peace to everyone who does good—to the Jews first and also to those who are not Jews. 11 For God judges all people in the same way.

12 People who do not have the law and who are sinners will be lost, although they do not have the law. And, in the same way, those who have the law and are sinners will be judged by the law. 13 Hearing the law does not make people right with God. It is those who obey the law who will be right with him. 14 (Those who are not Jews do not have the law, but when they freely do what the law commands, they are the law for themselves. This is true even though they do not have the law. 15 They show that in their hearts they know what is right and wrong, just as the law commands. And they show this by their consciences.

Sometimes their thoughts tell them they did wrong, and sometimes their thoughts tell them they did right.)
16 All these things will happen on the day when God, through Christ Jesus, will judge people's secret thoughts. The Good News that I preach says this.

OLD TESTAMENT READING

The LORD hates what evil people do,
but he loves those who do what is right.
10 The person who quits doing what is right will be punished,
and the one who hates to be corrected will die.
11 The LORD knows what is happening in the world of the dead,
so he surely knows the thoughts of the living.

Proverbs 15:9–11

INSIGHTS

The Bible's proclamation of God's work as Judge is part of its witness to His character. It confirms what is said elsewhere of His moral perfection, His righteousness and justice, His wisdom, omniscience, and omnipotence. It shows us also that the heart of the justice which expresses God's nature is retribution, the rendering to men what they have deserved; for this is the essence of the judge's task. To reward good with good, and evil with evil, is natural to God. So, when the New Testament speaks of the final judgment, it always represents it in terms of retribution. God will judge all men, it says, 'according to their works' (Matthew 16:27; Revelation 20:12f.). Paul amplifies. 'God . . . will render to every man according to his deeds: to them who by patient continuance in well doing seek for glory and honour and immortality, eternal life; but unto them that are contentious, and do not obey the truth, but obey unrighteousness, indignation and wrath; tribulation and anguish, upon every soul of man that doeth evil . . . but glory, honour, and peace, to every man that worketh good . . . for there is no respect of persons throughout: Christians, as well as non-Christians, will receive 'according to their works'. . . .

Thus retribution appears as a natural and predetermined expression of the divine character. God has resolved to be every man's Judge, rewarding every man according to his works. Retribution is the inescapable moral law of creation; God will see that each man sooner or later receives what he deserves—if not here, then hereafter.

J. I. Packer

PAUSE FOR REFLECTION

What do people do when God gives them freedom to do as they please? What does God, in his kindness, wait for people to do? What will God, the Judge of the earth, do when people refuse to change their hearts and live in obedience to him?

THURSDAY

God Wants Us to Change Our Hearts and Lives

Romans 2:17—3:18

The Jews and the Law

What about you? You call yourself a Jew. You trust in the law of Moses and brag that you are close to God. 18 You know what he wants you to do and what is important, because you have learned the law. 19 You think you are a guide for the blind and a light for those who are in darkness. 20 You think you can show foolish people what is right and teach those who know nothing. You have the law; so you think you know everything and have all truth. 21 You teach others, so why don't you teach yourself? You tell others not to steal, but you steal. 22 You say that others must not take part in adultery, but you are guilty of that sin. You hate idols, but you steal from temples. 23 You brag about having God's law, but you bring shame to God by breaking his law, 24 just as the Scriptures say: "Those who are not Jews speak against God's name because of you."

25 If you follow the law, your circumcision has meaning. But if you break the law, it is as if you were never circumcised. 26 People who are not Jews are not circumcised, but if they do what the law says, it is as if they were circumcised. 27 You Jews have the written law and circumcision, but you break the law. So those who are not circumcised in their bodies, but still obey the law, will show that you are guilty. 28 They can do this because a person is not a true Jew if he is only a Jew in his physical body; true circumcision is not only on the outside of the body. 29 A person is a Jew only if he is a Jew inside; true circumcision is done in the heart by the Spirit, not by the written law. Such a person gets praise from God rather than from people.

3 So, do Jews have anything that other people do not have? Is there anything special about being circumcised? 2 Yes, of course, there is in every way. The most important thing is this: God trusted the Jews with his teachings. 3 If some Jews were not faithful to him, will that stop God from doing what he promised? 4 No! God will continue to be true even when every person is false. As the Scriptures say:

"So you will be shown to be right
when you speak,
and you will win your case."

Psalm 51:4

5 When we do wrong, that shows more clearly that God is right. So can we say that God is wrong to punish us? (I am talking as people might talk.) 6 No! If God could not punish us, he could not judge the world.

7 A person might say, "When I lie, it really gives him glory, because my lie shows God's truth. So why am I judged a sinner?" 8 It would be the same to say, "We should do evil so that good will come." Some people find fault with us and say we teach this, but they are wrong and deserve the punishment they will receive.

All People Are Guilty

So are we Jews better than others? No! We have already said that Jews

and those who are not Jews are all
guilty of sin. 10 As the Scriptures say:
"There is no one who always
does what is right,
not even one.
11 There is no one who understands.
There is no one who looks to
God for help.
12 All have turned away.
Together, everyone has
become useless.
There is no one who does
anything good;
there is not even one."
Psalm 14:1-3
13 "Their throats are like open
graves;
they use their tongues for
telling lies." *Psalm 5:9*
"Their words are like snake
poison." *Psalm 140:3*
14 "Their mouths are full of
cursing and hate." *Psalm 10:7*
15 "They are always ready to kill
people.
16 Everywhere they go they
cause ruin and misery.
17 They don't know how to live in
peace." *Isaiah 59:7-8*
18 "They have no fear of God."
Psalm 36:1

OLD TESTAMENT READING

This is what the LORD All-Powerful, the God of Israel, says: Change your lives and do what is right! Then I will let you live in this place. 5 You must change your lives and do what is right. Be fair to each other. 6 You must not be hard on strangers, orphans, and widows. Don't kill innocent people in this place! Don't follow other gods, or they will ruin your lives.

Jeremiah 7:3, 5–6

INSIGHTS

Everywhere Jesus went He proclaimed the twofold message of repentance and faith in God (Mark 1:15). The faith He proclaimed was not mere mental assent, but the kind of faith that produces change in people's lives. There is no such thing as biblical faith that does not produce obedience. . . .

It is important to note that the Bible identifies both a true and a false repentance. Second Corinthians 7:10 says, "Godly grief produces a repentance that leads to salvation and brings no regret, but worldly grief produces death." Godly grief is true repentance, and true repentance is more than contrition. A person may be sorrowful over his sins yet unrepentant because he is sorrowing for the wrong reasons. Instead of sorrowing because his sins have hurt and disappointed God, he may just feel bad because his sins have been personally painful, stressful, or costly, or because his sins have been found out. If there is no change in character, there has been no true repentance. . . .

The results of false repentance are seen everywhere in the church. Hearts are unbroken. Sin is covered up. . . . And many professing Christians do not walk in the light with God and one another. The fruit of true repentance is a change of mind, heart, and behavior.

Floyd McClung

PAUSE FOR REFLECTION

What value does God place on outward signs of obedience to his law? How does God want his people to live?

FRIDAY

Faith in God Is Our Salvation

Romans 3:19—4:12

We know that the law's commands
are for those who have the law. This
stops all excuses and brings the
whole world under God's judgment,
20 because no one can be made right
with God by following the law. The
law only shows us our sin.

How God Makes People Right

But God has a way to make people
right with him without the law, and
he has now shown us that way which
the law and the prophets told us
about. 22 God makes people right
with himself through their faith in
Jesus Christ. This is true for all who
believe in Christ, because all people
are the same: 23 All have sinned and
are not good enough for God's glory,
24 and all need to be made right with
God by his grace, which is a free gift.
They need to be made free from sin
through Jesus Christ. 25 God gave
him as a way to forgive sin through
faith in the blood of Jesus' death.
This showed that God always does
what is right and fair, as in the past
when he was patient and did not punish people for their sins. 26 And God
gave Jesus to show today that he
does what is right. God did this so
he could judge rightly and so he
could make right any person who
has faith in Jesus.

27 So do we have a reason to brag
about ourselves? No! And why not?
It is the way of faith that stops all
bragging, not the way of trying to
obey the law. 28 A person is made right
with God through faith, not through
obeying the law. 29 Is God only the
God of the Jews? Is he not also the
God of those who are not Jews? 30 Of
course he is, because there is only
one God. He will make Jews right
with him by their faith, and he will
also make those who are not Jews
right with him through their faith.
31 So do we destroy the law by following the way of faith? No! Faith causes
us to be what the law truly wants.

The Example of Abraham

4 So what can we say that
Abraham, the father of our
people, learned about faith? 2 If
Abraham was made right by the
things he did, he had a reason to
brag. But this is not God's view, 3 because the Scripture says, "Abraham
believed God, and God accepted
Abraham's faith, and that faith made
him right with God."

4 When people work, their pay is
not given as a gift, but as something
earned. 5 But people cannot do any
work that will make them right with
God. So they must trust in him, who
makes even evil people right in his
sight. Then God accepts their faith,
and that makes them right with him.
6 David said the same thing. He said
that people are truly blessed when
God, without paying attention to
good deeds, makes people right with
himself.

7 "Happy are they
whose sins are forgiven,
whose wrongs are pardoned.
8 Happy is the person
whom the Lord does not
consider guilty." *Psalm 32:1-2*

[9] Is this blessing only for those who
are circumcised or also for those
who are not circumcised? We have
already said that God accepted
Abraham's faith and that faith made
him right with God. [10] So how did
this happen? Did God accept
Abraham before or after he was circumcised? It was before his circumcision. [11] Abraham was circumcised
to show that he was right with God
through faith before he was circumcised. So Abraham is the father of all
those who believe but are not circumcised; he is the father of all believers who are accepted as being
right with God. [12] And Abraham is
also the father of those who have
been circumcised and who live following the faith that our father
Abraham had before he was circumcised.

OLD TESTAMENT READING

Wicked people have many
troubles,
but the LORD's love surrounds
those who trust him.
[11] Good people, rejoice and be
happy in the LORD.
Sing all you whose hearts are
right.

Psalm 32:10–11

INSIGHTS

Faith is believing that Christ is what He is said to be and that He will do what He has promised to do, and then to expect this of Him. The Scriptures speak of Jesus Christ as being God in human flesh, as being perfect in His character, as being made a sin offering on our behalf, as bearing our sins in His own body on the tree. . . . The sacred records further tell us that He "rose again" (1 Co 15:4) from the dead, that He "ever liveth to make intercession for us" (Heb 7:25), that He has gone up into glory and has taken possession of heaven on the behalf of His people, and that he will shortly come again "to judge the . . . world with righteousness, and the peoples with equity" (Ps 98:9, ASV). . . .

. . . Jesus is what He is said to be. Jesus will do what He says He will do. Therefore, we must each trust Him, saying, "He will be to me what He says He is, and He will do to me what He has promised to do. I leave myself in the hands of Him who is appointed to save, that he may save me. I rest upon His promise that He will do even as He has said." This is saving faith, and he that has it has everlasting life. Whatever his dangers and difficulties, whatever his darkness and depression, whatever his infirmities and sins, he that believes thus on Christ Jesus is not condemned, and shall never come into condemnation.

Charles Spurgeon

PAUSE FOR REFLECTION

How are people made right with God? Who can be made right with God? How did God enable us to be made right with him? How does God bless those who trust him? Have you received that blessing?

WEEKEND
God Has Great Love for Us

Romans 4:13—5:11

God Keeps His Promise

Abraham and his descendants received the promise that they would
get the whole world. He did not receive that promise through the law,
but through being right with God by
his faith. [14] If people could receive
what God promised by following the
law, then faith is worthless. And
God's promise to Abraham is worthless, [15] because the law can only
bring God's anger. But if there is no
law, there is nothing to disobey.
[16] So people receive God's promise by having faith. This happens so
the promise can be a free gift. Then
all of Abraham's children can have
that promise. It is not only for those
who live under the law of Moses but
for anyone who lives with faith like
that of Abraham, who is the father
of us all. [17] As it is written in the
Scriptures: "I am making you a father of many nations." This is true
before God, the God Abraham believed, the God who gives life to the
dead and who creates something
out of nothing.
[18] There was no hope that
Abraham would have children. But
Abraham believed God and continued hoping, and so he became the
father of many nations. As God told
him, "Your descendants also will be
too many to count." [19] Abraham was
almost a hundred years old, much
past the age for having children, and
Sarah could not have children.
Abraham thought about all this, but
his faith in God did not become
weak. [20] He never doubted that God
would keep his promise, and he
never stopped believing. He grew
stronger in his faith and gave praise
to God. [21] Abraham felt sure that God
was able to do what he had promised. [22] So, "God accepted Abraham's
faith, and that faith made him right
with God." [23] Those words ("God accepted Abraham's faith") were written not only for Abraham [24] but also
for us. God will accept us also because we believe in the One who
raised Jesus our Lord from the dead.
[25] Jesus was given to die for our sins,
and he was raised from the dead to
make us right with God.

Right with God

5 Since we have been made right
with God by our faith, we have
peace with God. This happened
through our Lord Jesus Christ, [2] who
has brought us into that blessing of
God's grace that we now enjoy. And
we are happy because of the hope we
have of sharing God's glory. [3] We
also have joy with our troubles, because we know that these troubles
produce patience. [4] And patience
produces character, and character
produces hope. [5] And this hope will
never disappoint us, because God
has poured out his love to fill our
hearts. He gave us his love through
the Holy Spirit, whom God has
given to us.
[6] When we were unable to help
ourselves, at the moment of our
need, Christ died for us, although we
were living against God. [7] Very few
people will die to save the life of
someone else. Although perhaps for

a good person someone might possibly die. 8 But God shows his great
love for us in this way: Christ died
for us while we were still sinners.
9 So through Christ we will surely
be saved from God's anger, because
we have been made right with God
by the blood of Christ's death.
10 While we were God's enemies, he
made friends with us through the
death of his Son. Surely, now that we
are his friends, he will save us
through his Son's life. 11 And not only
that, but now we are also very happy
in God through our Lord Jesus
Christ. Through him we are now
God's friends again.

OLD TESTAMENT READING

But I pray to you, LORD, for favor.
God, because of your great love,
answer me.
You are truly able to save.

Psalm 69:13

I will tell about the LORD's
kindness
and praise him for everything
he has done.
I will praise the LORD for the many
good things he has given us
and for his goodness to the
people of Israel.
He has shown great mercy to us
and has been very kind to us.
8 He said, "These are my people;
my children will not lie to me."
So he saved them.
9 When they suffered, he suffered
also.
He sent his own angel to save
them.
Because of his love and kindness,
he saved them.

Isaiah 63:7–9c

INSIGHTS

May God through His Holy Spirit teach you to cherish the unfathomable mystery of His love. Jesus said, "None is good save one, even God." The glory of God in heaven is that everything He wills and does is good. . . .

The God who wills only good is a God of love. He does not seek His own. He does not live for himself. He pours out His love upon all living creatures. . . .

Love "seeketh not her own." Love finds happiness in giving to others. Love sacrifices wholly for others. Therefore, God offered himself to us in the person of His Son. And the Son offered himself upon the cross to bring love to us and to win our hearts. The everlasting love with which the Father loves the Son is the same love with which the Son loves us. This same love of the Father, Jesus Christ has poured into our hearts through the Holy Spirit. God desires that our whole life be permeated with this love's vital power. . . .

. . . Love is the power of the Godhead: in the Father, Son, and Holy Spirit. All who are members of the body of Christ possess the love of God, and this love streams forth from them to take the whole world within its compass.

Andrew Murray

ACTION POINT

When we place our faith in God's love, what are the results? Write your own psalm of thanksgiving, praising God for his gift of love.

MONDAY

Christ Frees Us from the Power of Sin

Romans 5:12—6:14

Adam and Christ Compared

Sin came into the world because of
what one man did, and with sin came
death. This is why everyone must
die—because everyone sinned.
13 Sin was in the world before the law
of Moses, but sin is not counted
against us as breaking a command
when there is no law. 14 But from the
time of Adam to the time of Moses,
everyone had to die, even those who
had not sinned by breaking a command, as Adam had.

Adam was like the One who was
coming in the future. 15 But God's
free gift is not like Adam's sin. Many
people died because of the sin of that
one man. But the grace from God
was much greater; many people received God's gift of life by the grace
of the one man, Jesus Christ. 16 After
Adam sinned once, he was judged
guilty. But the gift of God is different. God's free gift came after many
sins, and it makes people right with
God. 17 One man sinned, and so death
ruled all people because of that one
man. But now those people who accept God's full grace and the great
gift of being made right with him will
surely have true life and rule
through the one man, Jesus Christ.

18 So as one sin of Adam brought
the punishment of death to all
people, one good act that Christ did
makes all people right with God. And
that brings true life for all. 19 One
man disobeyed God, and many became sinners. In the same way, one
man obeyed God, and many will be
made right. 20 The law came to make
sin worse. But when sin grew worse,
God's grace increased. 21 Sin once
used death to rule us, but God gave
people more of his grace so that
grace could rule by making people
right with him. And this brings life
forever through Jesus Christ our
Lord.

Dead to Sin but Alive in Christ

6 So do you think we should continue sinning so that God will
give us even more grace? 2 No! We
died to our old sinful lives, so how
can we continue living with sin? 3 Did
you forget that all of us became part
of Christ when we were baptized?
We shared his death in our baptism.
4 When we were baptized, we were
buried with Christ and shared his
death. So, just as Christ was raised
from the dead by the wonderful
power of the Father, we also can live
a new life.

5 Christ died, and we have been
joined with him by dying too. So we
will also be joined with him by rising from the dead as he did. 6 We
know that our old life died with
Christ on the cross so that our sinful selves would have no power over
us and we would not be slaves to sin.
7 Anyone who has died is made free
from sin's control.

8 If we died with Christ, we know
we will also live with him. 9 Christ
was raised from the dead, and we
know that he cannot die again.
Death has no power over him now.
10 Yes, when Christ died, he died to
defeat the power of sin one time—

enough for all time. He now has a
new life, and his new life is with God.
11 In the same way, you should see
yourselves as being dead to the
power of sin and alive with God
through Christ Jesus.
12 So, do not let sin control your
life here on earth so that you do
what your sinful self wants to do.
13 Do not offer the parts of your body
to serve sin, as things to be used in
doing evil. Instead, offer yourselves
to God as people who have died and
now live. Offer the parts of your
body to God to be used in doing
good. 14 Sin will not be your master,
because you are not under law but
under God's grace.

OLD TESTAMENT READING

So, say this to the people of Judah and those who live in Jerusalem: 'This is what the LORD says: I am preparing disaster for you and making plans against you. So stop doing evil. Change your ways and do what is right.' 12 But the people of Judah will answer, 'It won't do any good to try! We will continue to do what we want. Each of us will do what his stubborn, evil heart wants!'"

Jeremiah 18:11–12

INSIGHTS

If we would know what Christ wants to be to us, we must first of all know Him as our Saviour from sin. When the angel came down from heaven to proclaim that He was to be born into the world, you remember he gave His name, "He shall be called Jesus, for he shall save his people from their sins." HAVE WE BEEN DELIVERED FROM SIN? He did not come to save us in our sins, but from our sins. . . .

Let us look at Him as He hangs upon the Cross, and see how He has put away sin. He was manifested that He might take away our sins. . . .

But Christ is not only a Saviour. I might save a man from drowning and rescue him from an untimely grave; but I might probably not be able to do any more for him. Christ is something more than a Saviour. When the children of Israel were placed behind the blood, that blood was their salvation; but they would still have heard the crack of the slave-driver's whip, if they had not been delivered from the Egyptian yoke of bondage: then it was that God delivered them from the hand of the King of Egypt. I have little sympathy with the idea that God comes down to save us, and then leaves us in prison, the slaves of our besetting sins. No; He has come to deliver us, and to give us victory over our evil tempers, our passions, and our lusts. Are you a professed Christian, but one who is a slave to some besetting sin? If you want to get victory over that temper or that lust, go on to know Christ more intimately. He brings deliverance for the past, the present, and the future.

D. L. Moody

APPLICATION

In your own words, describe what the burden of sin does to people. How have you been enslaved to sin? Does your life give evidence that you are no longer a slave to sin? What can you do so that God will truly be your master?

TUESDAY

God's People Belong to Him

Romans 6:15—7:13

Be Slaves of Righteousness

So what should we do? Should we
sin because we are under grace and
not under law? No! 16 Surely you
know that when you give yourselves
like slaves to obey someone, then
you are really slaves of that person.
The person you obey is your master. You can follow sin, which brings
spiritual death, or you can obey
God, which makes you right with
him. 17 In the past you were slaves
to sin—sin controlled you. But
thank God, you fully obeyed the
things that you were taught. 18 You
were made free from sin, and now
you are slaves to goodness. 19 I use
this example because this is hard
for you to understand. In the past
you offered the parts of your body
to be slaves to sin and evil; you lived
only for evil. In the same way now
you must give yourselves to be
slaves of goodness. Then you will
live only for God.

20 In the past you were slaves to
sin, and goodness did not control
you. 21 You did evil things, and now
you are ashamed of them. Those
things only bring death. 22 But now
you are free from sin and have become slaves of God. This brings
you a life that is only for God, and
this gives you life forever. 23 When
people sin, they earn what sin
pays—death. But God gives us a
free gift—life forever in Christ
Jesus our Lord.

An Example from Marriage

7 Brothers and sisters, all of you
understand the law of Moses. So
surely you know that the law rules
over people only while they are alive.
2 For example, a woman must stay
married to her husband as long as
he is alive. But if her husband dies,
she is free from the law of marriage.
3 But if she marries another man
while her husband is still alive, the
law says she is guilty of adultery. But
if her husband dies, she is free from
the law of marriage. Then if she marries another man, she is not guilty
of adultery.

4 In the same way, my brothers
and sisters, your old selves died, and
you became free from the law
through the body of Christ. This
happened so that you might belong
to someone else—the One who was
raised from the dead—and so that
we might be used in service to God.
5 In the past, we were ruled by our
sinful selves. The law made us want
to do sinful things that controlled our
bodies, so the things we did were
bringing us death. 6 In the past, the
law held us like prisoners, but our
old selves died, and we were made
free from the law. So now we serve
God in a new way with the Spirit, and
not in the old way with written rules.

Our Fight Against Sin

You might think I am saying that
sin and the law are the same thing.
That is not true. But the law was the
only way I could learn what sin
meant. I would never have known
what it means to want to take something belonging to someone else if
the law had not said, "You must not

want to take your neighbor's things."
[8]And sin found a way to use that
command and cause me to want all
kinds of things I should not want.
But without the law, sin has no
power. [9]I was alive before I knew the
law. But when the law's command
came to me, then sin began to live,
[10]and I died. The command was
meant to bring life, but for me it
brought death. [11]Sin found a way to
fool me by using the command to
make me die.

[12]So the law is holy, and the command is holy and right and good.
[13]Does this mean that something
that is good brought death to me?
No! Sin used something that is good
to bring death to me. This happened
so that I could see what sin is really
like; the command was used to show
that sin is very evil.

OLD TESTAMENT READING

You are holy people who belong to the LORD your God. He has chosen you from all the people on earth to be his very own.

[7]The LORD did not care for you and choose you because there were many of you—you are the smallest nation of all. [8]But the LORD chose you because he loved you, and he kept his promise to your ancestors. So he brought you out of Egypt by his great power and freed you from the land of slavery, from the power of the king of Egypt.

Deuteronomy 7:6–8

INSIGHTS

We are chosen to be holy. This is what the word "saint" means. In Greek, the word is hagios, meaning holy, set apart, and belonging to God. It does not mean the spiritual elitism of a "Holy Joe" or the aloof smugness of a "Perfect Pat." Rather, it indicates ownership. God says to us, "You belong to Me!"

When Paul addressed the saints, he was not writing to church leaders or to spiritually advanced people. Rather, Paul wrote to all of God's people who stood equally with him as those chosen, called, and cherished.

We, then, can also enjoy our status as loved and forgiven people.

This is a lofty thought, but what does it mean practically? Nothing less than that all we are and have belongs to God. This means our minds, emotions, will and bodies belong to God. We expand God's reign in our lives to include the people, the possessions, and the plans of our lives. And we don't stop here. Our list grows to include the memories that shape our present and the values that etch our future. In addition, we must be sure to include our work world where we spend most of our days. We must also remember that our money is holy, too.

Choosing to be chosen means accepting Christ's lordship over our total lives. This requires our committed surrender to Him.

Lloyd Ogilvie

APPLICATION

Describe as fully as you can what it means to be a slave to sin. Describe what it means to belong to God. What difference does belonging to God make in a person's life? In your life? Have you surrendered to him as your Lord?

WEDNESDAY

We Must Choose Either to Follow Sin or Serve God

Romans 7:14—8:17

The War Within Us

We know that the law is spiritual,
but I am not spiritual since sin rules
me as if I were its slave. 15 I do not
understand the things I do. I do not
do what I want to do, and I do the
things I hate. 16 And if I do not want
to do the hated things I do, that
means I agree that the law is good.
17 But I am not really the one who is
doing these hated things; it is sin living in me that does them. 18 Yes, I
know that nothing good lives in
me—I mean nothing good lives in
the part of me that is earthly and sinful. I want to do the things that are
good, but I do not do them. 19 I do
not do the good things I want to do,
but I do the bad things I do not want
to do. 20 So if I do things I do not want
to do, then I am not the one doing
them. It is sin living in me that does
those things.

21 So I have learned this rule:
When I want to do good, evil is there
with me. 22 In my mind, I am happy
with God's law. 23 But I see another
law working in my body, which
makes war against the law that my
mind accepts. That other law working in my body is the law of sin, and
it makes me its prisoner. 24 What a
miserable man I am! Who will save
me from this body that brings me
death? 25 I thank God for saving me
through Jesus Christ our Lord!

So in my mind I am a slave to
God's law, but in my sinful self I am
a slave to the law of sin.

Be Ruled by the Spirit

8 So now, those who are in Christ
Jesus are not judged guilty.
2 Through Christ Jesus the law of the
Spirit that brings life made me free
from the law that brings sin and
death. 3 The law was without power,
because the law was made weak by
our sinful selves. But God did what
the law could not do. He sent his
own Son to earth with the same human life that others use for sin. By
sending his Son to be an offering to
pay for sin, God used a human life
to destroy sin. 4 He did this so that we
could be the kind of people the law
correctly wants us to be. Now we do
not live following our sinful selves,
but we live following the Spirit.

5 Those who live following their
sinful selves think only about things
that their sinful selves want. But
those who live following the Spirit are
thinking about the things the Spirit
wants them to do. 6 If people's thinking is controlled by the sinful self,
there is death. But if their thinking
is controlled by the Spirit, there is
life and peace. 7 When people's thinking is controlled by the sinful self,
they are against God, because they
refuse to obey God's law and really
are not even able to obey God's law.
8 Those people who are ruled by
their sinful selves cannot please God.

9 But you are not ruled by your
sinful selves. You are ruled by the
Spirit, if that Spirit of God really lives
in you. But the person who does not
have the Spirit of Christ does not
belong to Christ. 10 Your body will
always be dead because of sin. But

if Christ is in you, then the Spirit
gives you life, because Christ made
you right with God. 11 God raised
Jesus from the dead, and if God's
Spirit is living in you, he will also give
life to your bodies that die. God is
the One who raised Christ from the
dead, and he will give life through
his Spirit that lives in you.
12 So, my brothers and sisters, we
must not be ruled by our sinful
selves or live the way our sinful
selves want. 13 If you use your lives
to do the wrong things your sinful
selves want, you will die spiritually.
But if you use the Spirit's help to stop
doing the wrong things you do with
your body, you will have true life.
14 The true children of God are
those who let God's Spirit lead them.
15 The Spirit we received does not
make us slaves again to fear; it
makes us children of God. With that
Spirit we cry out, "Father." 16 And the
Spirit himself joins with our spirits
to say we are God's children. 17 If we
are God's children, we will receive
blessings from God together with
Christ. But we must suffer as Christ
suffered so that we will have glory
as Christ has glory.

OLD TESTAMENT READING

Then Joshua said to the people,
"Now respect the LORD and serve
him fully and sincerely. Throw away
the gods that your ancestors worshiped on the other side of the
Euphrates River and in Egypt. Serve
the LORD. 15 But if you don't want to
serve the LORD, you must choose for
yourselves today whom you will
serve. You may serve the gods that
your ancestors worshiped when they
lived on the other side of the
Euphrates River, or you may serve
the gods of the Amorites who lived
in this land. As for me and my family, we will serve the LORD."

Joshua 24:14–15

INSIGHTS

The Bible does not leave us floundering as to what is right and what is wrong in the basic areas of life. . . .

. . . Through Joshua God challenged the Israelites to choose among "the gods . . . on the other side of the River, or the gods of the Amorites," or the Lord. Elijah presented the choice on Mount Carmel, and made the difference very vivid. Choice continues to be important time after time for each of us, but there are crisis moments in each of our lives when we are tempted to make a tremendously wrong choice. . . .

What are your choices? Whom are your choices for? Not just for yourself. Choose now whom you will serve, and that choice is going to affect the next generation, and the next generation, and the next. Choice never affects one single person alone. It goes on and on and the effect goes out into geography and history. You are a part of history and your choices become a part of history.

Edith Schaeffer

ACTION POINT

In what ways are you aware of your life struggle between choosing God or the way of sin? Pray that you will see clearly the choices you must make and that you will unfailingly obey God's way of life.

THURSDAY

Nothing Can Separate Us from God's Love

Romans 8:18–39

Our Future Glory

The sufferings we have now are
nothing compared to the great glory
that will be shown to us. 19 Everything God made is waiting with excitement for God to show his
children's glory completely. 20 Everything God made was changed to become useless, not by its own wish
but because God wanted it and because all along there was this hope:
21 that everything God made would
be set free from ruin to have the freedom and glory that belong to God's
children.

22 We know that everything God
made has been waiting until now in
pain, like a woman ready to give
birth. 23 Not only the world, but we
also have been waiting with pain inside us. We have the Spirit as the
first part of God's promise. So we are
waiting for God to finish making us
his own children, which means our
bodies will be made free. 24 We were
saved, and we have this hope. If we
see what we are waiting for, that is
not really hope. People do not hope
for something they already have.
25 But we are hoping for something
we do not have yet, and we are waiting for it patiently.

26 Also, the Spirit helps us with our
weakness. We do not know how to
pray as we should. But the Spirit
himself speaks to God for us, even
begs God for us with deep feelings
that words cannot explain. 27 God can
see what is in people's hearts. And
he knows what is in the mind of the
Spirit, because the Spirit speaks to
God for his people in the way God
wants.

28 We know that in everything
God works for the good of those who
love him. They are the people he
called, because that was his plan.
29 God knew them before he made
the world, and he decided that they
would be like his Son so that Jesus
would be the firstborn of many
brothers. 30 God planned for them to
be like his Son; and those he planned
to be like his Son, he also called; and
those he called, he also made right
with him; and those he made right,
he also glorified.

God's Love in Christ Jesus

So what should we say about this?
If God is with us, no one can defeat
us. 32 He did not spare his own Son
but gave him for us all. So with
Jesus, God will surely give us all
things. 33 Who can accuse the people
God has chosen? No one, because God
is the One who makes them right.
34 Who can say God's people are
guilty? No one, because Christ Jesus
died, but he was also raised from the
dead, and now he is on God's right
side, begging God for us. 35 Can anything separate us from the love Christ
has for us? Can troubles or problems
or sufferings or hunger or nakedness or danger or violent death? 36 As
it is written in the Scriptures:

"For you we are in danger of
 death all the time.
People think we are worth no
 more than sheep to be
 killed." *Psalm 44:22*

[37] But in all these things we have
full victory through God who
showed his love for us. [38] Yes, I am
sure that neither death, nor life, nor
angels, nor ruling spirits, nothing
now, nothing in the future, no powers, [39] nothing above us, nothing below us, nor anything else in the
whole world will ever be able to separate us from the love of God that is
in Christ Jesus our Lord.

OLD TESTAMENT READING

The LORD looked and could not
find any justice,
and he was displeased.
[16] He could not find anyone to help
the people,
and he was surprised that
there was no one to help.
So he used his own power to save
the people;
his own goodness gave him
strength.
[17] He covered himself with goodness like armor.
He put the helmet of salvation
on his head.
He put on the clothes of punishment
and wrapped himself in the
coat of his strong love.

[21] The LORD says, "This is my
agreement with these people: My
Spirit and my words that I give you
will never leave you or your children
or your grandchildren, now and forever."

Isaiah 59:15b–17, 21

INSIGHTS

In the very nature of things we soon discover in life that in order to be loved either in a physical or filial dimension we must show ourselves lovable. Somehow we have to demonstrate to others that we are worth loving. We have to prove that we are worthy of their love. And, sad to say, in most cases, the moment we fail to do this we discover that we are being cut off. . . .

Now, amazing as it may sound, and incredible as it may seem, there is none of this in the love of God. The simple truth is that His love for me does not in any way depend on my worthiness of it. In other words, I do not have to merit His love. I do not, so to speak, have to earn His love.

Scripture repeats this theme again and again. For example, in that most poignant of all the stories told by Jesus, the account of the prodigal son, we see clearly portrayed for us what the love of God is like. . . .

No doubt the dear old man had died a thousand deaths after his son's departure. . . .

Yet his attitude of devotion, affection, and utter selflessness never altered. It mattered not what happened to himself as long as his son could be restored and redeemed and remade. His care and concern for this one's welfare never abated.

This is the love of God.

Phillip Keller

ACTION POINT

List the things (as many as you want) that, powerful and dreadful as they may be, cannot separate us from the love of God. Thank God that his love for you is greater than every one of those things!

FRIDAY

Is God Unfair?

Romans 9:1–29

God and the Jewish People

9 I am in Christ, and I am telling
you the truth; I do not lie. My
conscience is ruled by the Holy
Spirit, and it tells me I am not lying.
2 I have great sorrow and always feel
much sadness. 3 I wish I could help
my Jewish brothers and sisters, my
people. I would even wish that I were
cursed and cut off from Christ if that
would help them. 4 They are the
people of Israel, God's chosen children. They have seen the glory of
God, and they have the agreements
that God made between himself and
his people. God gave them the law
of Moses and the right way of worship and his promises. 5 They are the
descendants of our great ancestors,
and they are the earthly family into
which Christ was born, who is God
over all. Praise him forever! Amen.

6 It is not that God failed to keep
his promise to them. But only some
of the people of Israel are truly God's
people, 7 and only some of Abraham's descendants are true children
of Abraham. But God said to
Abraham: "The descendants I promised you will be from Isaac." 8 This
means that not all of Abraham's descendants are God's true children.
Abraham's true children are those
who become God's children because
of the promise God made to
Abraham. 9 God's promise to
Abraham was this: "At the right time
I will return, and Sarah will have a
son." 10 And that is not all. Rebekah's
sons had the same father, our father
Isaac. 11-12 But before the two boys
were born, God told Rebekah, "The
older will serve the younger." This
was before the boys had done anything good or bad. God said this so
that the one chosen would be chosen because of God's own plan. He
was chosen because he was the one
God wanted to call, not because of
anything he did. 13 As the Scripture
says, "I loved Jacob, but I hated
Esau."

14 So what should we say about
this? Is God unfair? In no way. 15 God
said to Moses, "I will show kindness
to anyone to whom I want to show
kindness, and I will show mercy to
anyone to whom I want to show
mercy." 16 So God will choose the
one to whom he decides to show
mercy; his choice does not depend
on what people want or try to do.
17 The Scripture says to the king of
Egypt: "I made you king for this reason: to show my power in you so that
my name will be talked about in all
the earth." 18 So God shows mercy
where he wants to show mercy, and
he makes stubborn the people he
wants to make stubborn.

19 So one of you will ask me:
"Then why does God blame us for
our sins? Who can fight his will?"
20 You are only human, and human
beings have no right to question
God. An object should not ask the
person who made it, "Why did you
make me like this?" 21 The potter can
make anything he wants to make.
He can use the same clay to make
one thing for special use and another thing for daily use.

22 It is the same way with God. He
wanted to show his anger and to let

people see his power. But he patiently stayed with those people he
was angry with—people who were
made ready to be destroyed. 23 He
waited with patience so that he could
make known his rich glory to the
people who receive his mercy. He
has prepared these people to have
his glory, 24 and we are those people
whom God called. He called us not
from the Jews only but also from
those who are not Jews. 25 As the
Scripture says in Hosea:

"I will say, 'You are my people'
to those I had called 'not my
people.'
And I will show my love
to those people I did not love."

Hosea 2:1, 23

26 "They were called,
'You are not my people,'
but later they will be called
'children of the living God.'"

Hosea 1:10

27 And Isaiah cries out about Israel:
"The people of Israel are many,
like the grains of sand by the
sea.
But only a few of them will be
saved,
28 because the Lord will quickly
and completely punish the
people on the earth."

Isaiah 10:22-23

29 It is as Isaiah said:
"The Lord All-Powerful
allowed a few of our descendants to live.
Otherwise we would have been
completely destroyed
like the cities of Sodom and
Gomorrah."

Isaiah 1:9

OLD TESTAMENT READING

The clay does not ask the potter,
'What are you doing?'
The thing that is made doesn't
say to its maker,
'You have no hands.'"

Isaiah 45:9c–d

INSIGHTS

Child, don't try to understand Me. Just love Me. Just let Me love you. You don't have to understand Me to open yourself to My love.

You're right—I do ride the wild winds into town sometimes. I do appear in forms you have never seen, sound notes you have never heard. This makes you wonder if I get My signals crossed, if I take you south in order to get you north. I seem to have plopped you down, reasonable creature that you are, into an unreasonable world. You do not understand all this because I am God and you are you.

May I remind you how different we really are? You are human; I am divine. You are finite; I am infinite. You need love; I delight in love but do not need it. You need to be understood; I am above the need to be understood. You cannot understand; I understand perfectly. You are of time; I am of eternity. You are of reason; I am above reason. You are blown by the wind; I blow the wind.

Ruth Senter

ACTION POINT

Are you comfortable with the fact that God is the potter and you are the clay? Pray for the humility to accept God's love for you in the way that he gives it.

WEEKEND

Salvation Comes to Those Who Believe

Romans 9:30—10:21

So what does all this mean? Those
who are not Jews were not trying to
make themselves right with God, but
they were made right with God because of their faith. 31 The people of
Israel tried to follow a law to make
themselves right with God. But they
did not succeed, 32 because they tried
to make themselves right by the
things they did instead of trusting in
God to make them right. They
stumbled over the stone that causes
people to stumble. 33 As it is written
in the Scripture:

"I will put in Jerusalem a stone
that causes people to
stumble,
a rock that makes them fall.
Anyone who trusts in him will
never be disappointed."

Isaiah 8:14; 28:16

10 Brothers and sisters, the thing
I want most is for all the Jews
to be saved. That is my prayer to
God. 2 I can say this about them:
They really try to follow God, but
they do not know the right way. 3 Because they did not know the way that
God makes people right with him,
they tried to make themselves right
in their own way. So they did not accept God's way of making people
right. 4 Christ ended the law so that
everyone who believes in him may
be right with God.

5 Moses writes about being made
right by following the law. He says,
"A person who obeys these things
will live because of them." 6 But this
is what the Scripture says about being made right through faith: "Don't
say to yourself, 'Who will go up into
heaven?'" (That means, "Who will go
up to heaven and bring Christ down
to earth?") 7 "And do not say, 'Who
will go down into the world below?'"
(That means, "Who will go down
and bring Christ up from the dead?")
8 This is what the Scripture says:
"The word is near you; it is in your
mouth and in your heart." That is the
teaching of faith that we are telling.
9 If you use your mouth to say, "Jesus
is Lord," and if you believe in your
heart that God raised Jesus from the
dead, you will be saved. 10 We believe
with our hearts, and so we are made
right with God. And we use our
mouths to say that we believe, and
so we are saved. 11 As the Scripture
says, "Anyone who trusts in him will
never be disappointed." 12 That Scripture says "anyone" because there is
no difference between those who are
Jews and those who are not. The
same Lord is the Lord of all and
gives many blessings to all who trust
in him, 13 as the Scripture says, "Anyone who calls on the Lord will be
saved."

14 But before people can ask the
Lord for help, they must believe in
him; and before they can believe in
him, they must hear about him; and
for them to hear about the Lord,
someone must tell them; 15 and before someone can go and tell them,
that person must be sent. It is written, "How beautiful is the person
who comes to bring good news."

16 But not all the Jews accepted
the good news. Isaiah said, "Lord,
who believed what we told them?"
17 So faith comes from hearing the

Good News, and people hear the
Good News when someone tells
them about Christ.
18 But I ask: Didn't people hear the
Good News? Yes, they heard—as the
Scripture says:

"Their message went out
through all the world;
their words go everywhere on
earth." *Psalm 19:4*

19 Again I ask: Didn't the people of
Israel understand? Yes, they did understand. First, Moses says:

"I will use those who are not a
nation to make you jealous.
I will use a nation that does not
understand to make you
angry." *Deuteronomy 32:21*

20 Then Isaiah is bold enough to say:

"I was found by those who were
not asking me for help.
I made myself known to people
who were not looking for
me." *Isaiah 65:1*

21 But about Israel God says,

"All day long I stood ready to
accept
people who disobey and are
stubborn." *Isaiah 65:2*

OLD TESTAMENT READING

Those Who Obey the Law Will Live

The LORD said to Moses, 2 "Tell the
people of Israel: 'I am the LORD your
God. 3 In the past you lived in Egypt,
but you must not do what was done
in that country. And you must not do
as they do in the land of Canaan,
where I am bringing you. Do not follow their customs. 4 You must obey
my rules and follow them. I am the
LORD your God. 5 Obey my laws and
rules; a person who obeys them will
live because of them. I am the
LORD.'"

Leviticus 18:1–5

INSIGHTS

It's not through wisdom that people come to the knowledge of God and their absolute equality before Him. It's not through endless arguments of fine points of theology that they will find a humble heart. The doorway into the kingdom is so low down that one must bend in humility to get through. I've never known a single person who has been convinced of the kingdom of God through head knowledge—a person just can't think his or her way into the kingdom of God. Nor can anyone come into the kingdom of God based on a religious experience. It is knowledge of and faith in Christ that enables the equality of life in the kingdom to be real. "For Jews request a sign, and Greeks seek after wisdom; but we preach Christ crucified, to the Jews a stumbling block and to the Greeks foolishness, but to those who are called, both Jews and Greeks, Christ the power of God and the wisdom of God" (1 Cor 1:22–25).

Terry Fullam

PAUSE FOR REFLECTION

Can a person successfully follow God in his or her own way (Romans 10:1–4)? What is the way of salvation? To whom does God offer it?

MONDAY

God's Mercy and Kindness Are Great

Romans 11:1–21

God Shows Mercy to All People

11 So I ask: Did God throw out his people? No! I myself am an Israelite from the family of Abraham, from the tribe of Benjamin. 2 God chose the Israelites to be his people before they were born, and he has not thrown his people out. Surely you know what the Scripture says about Elijah, how he prayed to God against the people of Israel. 3 "Lord," he said, "they have killed your prophets, and they have destroyed your altars. I am the only prophet left, and now they are trying to kill me, too." 4 But what answer did God give Elijah? He said, "But I have left seven thousand people in Israel who have never bowed down before Baal." 5 It is the same now. There are a few people that God has chosen by his grace. 6 And if he chose them by grace, it is not for the things they have done. If they could be made God's people by what they did, God's gift of grace would not really be a gift.

7 So this is what has happened: Although the Israelites tried to be right with God, they did not succeed, but the ones God chose did become right with him. The others were made stubborn and refused to listen to God. 8 As it is written in the Scriptures:

"God gave the people a dull mind
so they could not understand." *Isaiah 29:10*

"He closed their eyes so they
could not see
and their ears so they could
not hear.
This continues until today."

Deuteronomy 29:4

9 And David says:

"Let their own feasts trap them
and cause their ruin;
let their feasts cause them to
stumble and be paid back.
10 Let their eyes be closed so they
cannot see
and their backs be forever
weak from troubles."

Psalm 69:22-23

11 So I ask: When the Jews fell, did that fall destroy them? No! But their mistake brought salvation to those who are not Jews, in order to make the Jews jealous. 12 The Jews' mistake brought rich blessings for the world, and the Jews' loss brought rich blessings for the non-Jewish people. So surely the world will receive much richer blessings when enough Jews become the kind of people God wants.

13 Now I am speaking to you who are not Jews. I am an apostle to those who are not Jews, and since I have that work, I will make the most of it. 14 I hope I can make my own people jealous and, in that way, help some of them to be saved. 15 When God turned away from the Jews, he became friends with other people in the world. So when God accepts the Jews, surely that will bring them life after death.

16 If the first piece of bread is offered to God, then the whole loaf is made holy. If the roots of a tree are holy, then the tree's branches are holy too.

17 It is as if some of the branches from an olive tree have been broken off. You non-Jewish people are like the branch of a wild olive tree that

has been joined to that first tree. You now share the strength and life of the first tree, the Jews. [18] So do not brag about those branches that were broken off. If you brag, remember that you do not support the root, but the root supports you. [19] You will say, "Branches were broken off so that I could be joined to their tree." [20] That is true. But those branches were broken off because they did not believe, and you continue to be part of the tree only because you believe. Do not be proud, but be afraid. [21] If God did not let the natural branches of that tree stay, then he will not let you stay if you don't believe.

OLD TESTAMENT READING

But suppose the wicked stop doing all the sins they have done and obey all my rules and do what is fair and right. Then they will surely live; they will not die. [22] Their sins will be forgotten. Because they have done what is right, they will live. [23] I do not really want the wicked to die, says the Lord GOD. I want them to stop their bad ways and live."

Ezekiel 18:21–23

INSIGHTS

Kindness is invariably associated with mercy. It is impossible to be kind without being merciful. Likewise to be merciful is to be kind. It implies that there is a deep and genuine concern for another. This concern is one of compassion and mercy. . . .

Throughout the Scriptures the great theme of God's unrelenting kindness throbs like a powerful heartbeat. . . .

The kindness of God has drawn me to Him with bonds of love stronger than steel. The mercy of my Lord has endeared me to Him with enormous gratitude and thanksgiving. . . .

It is the kindness of God, expressed in Christ and revealed to us by His Spirit that supplies my salvation. His kindness makes provision for my pardon from sins and selfishness at the cost of His own laid down life. It is His kindness that forgives my faults and accepts me into His family as His dearly beloved child. His kindness enables me to stand acquitted of my wrongdoing, justified freely in His presence. God's kindness removes my guilt and I am at one with Him and others in peace. It is the kindness of God that enables Him to share Himself with me in the inner sanctuary of my spirit, soul, and body. His kindness enables me to be re-made, refashioned, re-formed gently into His likeness. His kindness gives enormous meaning and dignity to this life and endless delight in the life yet to come.

It is the constant, enduring, unchanging kindness of God that gives me every reason to rejoice and revel in life . . . all of life . . . this one and the next.

W. Phillip Keller

PAUSE FOR REFLECTION

Is there anyone to whom God doesn't want to offer his forgiveness? In what ways has God shown his forgiveness and mercy to the Jews? To non-Jews? Describe how God's unfailing kindness has touched your heart.

TUESDAY

God Wants Our Lives to Be a Sacrifice of Obedience

Romans 11:22—12:8

So you see that God is kind and
also very strict. He punishes those
who stop following him. But God is
kind to you, if you continue following in his kindness. If you do not,
you will be cut off from the tree.
23 And if the Jews will believe in God
again, he will accept them back. God
is able to put them back where they
were. 24 It is not natural for a wild
branch to be part of a good tree. And
you who are not Jews are like a
branch cut from a wild olive tree and
joined to a good olive tree. But since
those Jews are like a branch that
grew from the good tree, surely they
can be joined to their own tree again.
25 I want you to understand this
secret, brothers and sisters, so you
will understand that you do not know
everything: Part of Israel has been
made stubborn, but that will change
when many who are not Jews have
come to God. 26 And that is how all
Israel will be saved. It is written in
the Scriptures:

"The Savior will come from
Jerusalem;
he will take away all evil from
the family of Jacob.
27 And I will make this agreement
with those people
when I take away their sins."
Isaiah 59:20-21; 27:9

28 The Jews refuse to accept the
Good News, so they are God's enemies. This has happened to help
you who are not Jews. But the Jews
are still God's chosen people, and he
loves them very much because of
the promises he made to their ancestors. 29 God never changes his mind
about the people he calls and the
things he gives them. 30 At one time
you refused to obey God. But now
you have received mercy, because
those people refused to obey. 31 And
now the Jews refuse to obey, because God showed mercy to you.
But this happened so that they also
can receive mercy from him. 32 God
has given all people over to their
stubborn ways so that he can show
mercy to all.

Praise to God

Yes, God's riches are very great,
and his wisdom and knowledge have
no end! No one can explain the
things God decides or understand
his ways. 34 As the Scripture says,

"Who has known the mind of the
Lord,
or who has been able to give
him advice?" *Isaiah 40:13*
35 "No one has ever given God
anything
that he must pay back." *Job 41:11*

36 Yes, God made all things, and
everything continues through him
and for him. To him be the glory forever! Amen.

Give Your Lives to God

12 So brothers and sisters, since
God has shown us great
mercy, I beg you to offer your lives
as a living sacrifice to him. Your offering must be only for God and
pleasing to him, which is the spiritual way for you to worship. 2 Do not
change yourselves to be like the

people of this world, but be changed
within by a new way of thinking.
Then you will be able to decide what
God wants for you; you will know
what is good and pleasing to him and
what is perfect. 3 Because God has
given me a special gift, I have something to say to everyone among you.
Do not think you are better than you
are. You must decide what you really are by the amount of faith God
has given you. 4 Each one of us has
a body with many parts, and these
parts all have different uses. 5 In the
same way, we are many, but in Christ
we are all one body. Each one is a
part of that body, and each part belongs to all the other parts. 6 We all
have different gifts, each of which
came because of the grace God gave
us. The person who has the gift of
prophecy should use that gift in
agreement with the faith. 7 Anyone
who has the gift of serving should
serve. Anyone who has the gift of
teaching should teach. 8 Whoever
has the gift of encouraging others
should encourage. Whoever has the
gift of giving to others should give
freely. Anyone who has the gift of
being a leader should try hard when
he leads. Whoever has the gift of
showing mercy to others should do
so with joy.

INSIGHTS

Men would understand; they do not care to obey. They try to understand where it is impossible they could understand except by obeying. They would search into the work of the Lord instead of doing their part in it—thus making it impossible for the Lord to go on with his work, and for themselves to become capable of seeing and understanding what he does. Instead of immediately obeying the Lord of life, the one condition upon which he can help them, and in itself the beginning of their deliverance, they set themselves to question their unenlightened intellects as to his plans for their deliverance—and not merely how he means to carry it out, but whether he is able to carry it out. They would bind their Samson until they have scanned his limbs and muscles. They delay in setting their foot on the stair that alone can lead them to the house of wisdom until they shall have determined the material and mode of its construction. . . .

It is on them that do his will that the day dawns. To them the Daystar rises in their hearts. Obedience is the soul of knowledge.

George MacDonald

OLD TESTAMENT READING

But Samuel answered,
"What pleases the LORD more:
burnt offerings and sacrifices
or obedience to his voice?
It is better to obey than to
sacrifice.
It is better to listen to God than
to offer the fat of sheep."

1 Samuel 15:22

ACTION POINT

In what ways is your life an offering to God? In what ways are you tempted to fall short of full obedience? Pray that your deepest desire will be to give yourself fully as a living sacrifice to God.

WEDNESDAY

Owe Nothing but Love

Romans 12:9—13:14

Your love must be real. Hate what is evil, and hold on to what is good. 10 Love each other like brothers and sisters. Give each other more honor than you want for yourselves. 11 Do not be lazy but work hard, serving the Lord with all your heart. 12 Be joyful because you have hope. Be patient when trouble comes, and pray at all times. 13 Share with God's people who need help. Bring strangers in need into your homes.

14 Wish good for those who harm you; wish them well and do not curse them. 15 Be happy with those who are happy, and be sad with those who are sad. 16 Live in peace with each other. Do not be proud, but make friends with those who seem unimportant. Do not think how smart you are.

17 If someone does wrong to you, do not pay him back by doing wrong to him. Try to do what everyone thinks is right. 18 Do your best to live in peace with everyone. 19 My friends, do not try to punish others when they wrong you, but wait for God to punish them with his anger. It is written: "I will punish those who do wrong; I will repay them," says the Lord. 20 But you should do this:

"If your enemy is hungry, feed
him;
if he is thirsty, give him a drink.
Doing this will be like pouring
burning coals on his head."

Proverbs 25:21-22

21 Do not let evil defeat you, but defeat evil by doing good.

Christians Should Obey the Law

13 All of you must yield to the government rulers. No one rules unless God has given him the power to rule, and no one rules now without that power from God. 2 So those who are against the government are really against what God has commanded. And they will bring punishment on themselves. 3 Those who do right do not have to fear the rulers; only those who do wrong fear them. Do you want to be unafraid of the rulers? Then do what is right, and they will praise you. 4 The ruler is God's servant to help you. But if you do wrong, then be afraid. He has the power to punish; he is God's servant to punish those who do wrong. 5 So you must yield to the government, not only because you might be punished, but because you know it is right.

6 This is also why you pay taxes. Rulers are working for God and give their time to their work. 7 Pay everyone, then, what you owe. If you owe any kind of tax, pay it. Show respect and honor to them all.

Loving Others

Do not owe people anything, except always owe love to each other, because the person who loves others has obeyed all the law. 9 The law says, "You must not be guilty of adultery. You must not murder anyone. You must not steal. You must not want to take your neighbor's things." All these commands and all others are really only one rule: "Love your neighbor as you love yourself." 10 Love never hurts a neighbor, so loving is obeying all the law.

11 Do this because we live in an
important time. It is now time for you
to wake up from your sleep, because
our salvation is nearer now than
when we first believed. 12 The "night"
is almost finished, and the "day" is
almost here. So we should stop doing things that belong to darkness
and take up the weapons used for
fighting in the light. 13 Let us live in
a right way, like people who belong
to the day. We should not have wild
parties or get drunk. There should
be no sexual sins of any kind, no
fighting or jealousy. 14 But clothe
yourselves with the Lord Jesus
Christ and forget about satisfying
your sinful self.

OLD TESTAMENT READING

The wicked borrow and don't pay
    back,
  but those who do right give
    freely to others.
26 Good people always lend freely to
    others,
  and their children are a blessing.

Psalm 37:21, 26

INSIGHTS

The context of this passage does . . . set up a principle that says, "If I owe anyone anything, I am not free to give love to that person." Anyone who has borrowed money from another person, and especially another Christian, realizes the wall that immediately goes up from being in a debtor / lender relationship. Debtors and lenders are not really free to love one another. This verse suggests principles for both sides. Lending to another Christian needs to be considered very, very seriously before it is done. On the other side, before you borrow from anyone for anything, consider the ramifications of being in bondage to that person. Are you, in fact, free to love that person? . . .

. . . The reality is that whenever you have borrowed from anyone, you are a servant to that person. . . .

. . . "Why is so much written about debt in God's Word?" I believe there are three reasons. First of all, debt is extremely deceptive. As we said earlier, getting into debt is easy—getting out is next to impossible. Second, debt creates bondage, and if that bondage is to the world system, we are no longer free to be the witnesses in this world that God has called us to be. Third, debt is almost blasphemous when we use it and deny God an opportunity to work. . . .

. . . Being in debt is never the real problem; it is only symptomatic of the real problem, which is usually greed, self-indulgence, impatience, fear, poor self-image, lack of self-discipline, and perhaps others. So, if you find yourself in debt, your first question is not, "How do I get out of debt?" Ask first of all, "Why am I in this situation?" and answer that question. Then getting out of debt will become much easier.

Ron Blue

PAUSE FOR REFLECTION

What is Jesus' greatest commandment? Examine the relationships between love, debt, ministry, and giving in your life. How do your lifestyle choices hinder your obedience to Christ's commandment to love one another?

THURSDAY

Live in a Way that Pleases God; He Will Judge Our Actions

Romans 14:1—15:3

Do Not Criticize Other People

14 Accept into your group someone who is weak in faith, and do not argue about opinions. [2]One person believes it is right to eat all kinds of food. But another, who is weak, believes it is right to eat only vegetables. [3]The one who knows that it is right to eat any kind of food must not reject the one who eats only vegetables. And the person who eats only vegetables must not think that the one who eats all foods is wrong, because God has accepted that person. [4]You cannot judge another person's servant. The master decides if the servant is doing well or not. And the Lord's servant will do well because the Lord helps him do well.

[5]Some think that one day is more important than another, and others think that every day is the same. Let all be sure in their own mind. [6]Those who think one day is more important than other days are doing that for the Lord. And those who eat all kinds of food are doing that for the Lord, and they give thanks to God. Others who refuse to eat some foods do that for the Lord, and they give thanks to God. [7]We do not live or die for ourselves. [8]If we live, we are living for the Lord, and if we die, we are dying for the Lord. So living or dying, we belong to the Lord.

[9]The reason Christ died and rose from the dead to live again was so he would be Lord over both the dead and the living. [10]So why do you judge your brothers or sisters in Christ? And why do you think you are better than they are? We will all stand before God to be judged, [11]because it is written in the Scriptures:

"'As surely as I live,' says the
Lord,
'Everyone will bow before me;
everyone will say that I am
God.'" *Isaiah 45:23*

[12]So each of us will have to answer to God.

Do Not Cause Others to Sin

For that reason we should stop judging each other. We must make up our minds not to do anything that will make another Christian sin. [14]I am in the Lord Jesus, and I know that there is no food that is wrong to eat. But if a person believes something is wrong, that thing is wrong for him. [15]If you hurt your brother's or sister's faith because of something you eat, you are not really following the way of love. Do not destroy someone's faith by eating food he thinks is wrong, because Christ died for him. [16]Do not allow what you think is good to become what others say is evil. [17]In the kingdom of God, eating and drinking are not important. The important things are living right with God, peace, and joy in the Holy Spirit. [18]Anyone who serves Christ by living this way is pleasing God and will be accepted by other people.

[19]So let us try to do what makes peace and helps one another. [20]Do

not let the eating of food destroy the
work of God. All foods are all right
to eat, but it is wrong to eat food that
causes someone else to sin. 21 It is
better not to eat meat or drink wine
or do anything that will cause your
brother or sister to sin.
22 Your beliefs about these things
should be kept secret between you
and God. People are happy if they
can do what they think is right without feeling guilty. 23 But those who
eat something without being sure it
is right are wrong because they did
not believe it was right. Anything
that is done without believing it is
right is a sin.
15 We who are strong in faith
should help the weak with
their weaknesses, and not please
only ourselves. 2 Let each of us please
our neighbors for their good, to help
them be stronger in faith. 3 Even
Christ did not live to please himself.
It was as the Scriptures said: "When
people insult you, it hurts me."

OLD TESTAMENT READING

People will be rewarded for what
they say,
and they will also be rewarded
for what they do.

Proverbs 12:14

Now, everything has been
heard,
so I give my final advice:
Honor God and obey his commands,
because this is all people must
do.
14 God will judge everything,
even what is done in secret,
the good and the evil.

Ecclesiastes 12:13–14

Bring to me all the people who are
mine,
whom I made for my glory,
whom I formed and made."

Isaiah 43:7

INSIGHTS

When we please God, we have peace. We're not trying to juggle a dozen different things in order to please everyone around us. Instead, we have a single purpose—to please God.

When we try to please ourselves or others, however, things get out of balance. Far too many of us have become overly involved in various causes and have lost our perspective. Our priorities no longer are established by God, but by all the voices—many of which are sincere and good—clamoring around us. We have forgotten that our purpose is to please God.

But as spiritually renewed Christians who aim to please God, we can walk with security and confidence. We no longer view life and its problems with the short-sighted limitations of a merely human perspective. Instead, we view life with the long-term assurance that comes only from God's eternal perspective.

Luis Palau

PAUSE FOR REFLECTION

For whom do believers live and die? How does that affect our lifestyle? What is our guideline for living in a way that pleases God? Who exemplifies such a lifestyle? How are we to treat those whose faith is weak? Why?

FRIDAY

God Is the Source of Our Hope and Joy

Romans 15:4–29

Everything that was written in
the past was written to teach us.
The Scriptures give us patience
and encouragement so that we can
have hope. 5 Patience and encouragement come from God. And I
pray that God will help you all
agree with each other the way
Christ Jesus wants. 6 Then you will
all be joined together, and you will
give glory to God the Father of our
Lord Jesus Christ. 7 Christ accepted you, so you should accept
each other, which will bring glory
to God. 8 I tell you that Christ became a servant of the Jews to show
that God's promises to the Jewish
ancestors are true. 9 And he also
did this so that those who are not
Jews could give glory to God for
the mercy he gives to them. It is
written in the Scriptures:

"So I will praise you among the
non-Jewish people.
I will sing praises to your
name." *Psalm 18:49*

10 The Scripture also says,

"Be happy, you who are not Jews,
together with his people."
Deuteronomy 32:43

11 Again the Scripture says,

"All you who are not Jews, praise
the Lord.
All you people, sing praises to
him." *Psalm 117:1*

12 And Isaiah says,

"A new king will come from the
family of Jesse.
He will come to rule over the
non-Jewish people,
and they will have hope because
of him." *Isaiah 11:10*

13 I pray that the God who gives
hope will fill you with much joy and
peace while you trust in him. Then
your hope will overflow by the power
of the Holy Spirit.

Paul Talks About His Work

My brothers and sisters, I am sure
that you are full of goodness. I know
that you have all the knowledge you
need and that you are able to teach
each other. 15 But I have written to you
very openly about some things I
wanted you to remember. I did this
because God gave me this special gift:
16 to be a minister of Christ Jesus to
those who are not Jews. I served God
by teaching his Good News, so that
the non-Jewish people could be an
offering that God would accept—an
offering made holy by the Holy Spirit.

17 So I am proud of what I have
done for God in Christ Jesus. 18 I will
not talk about anything except what
Christ has done through me in leading those who are not Jews to obey
God. They have obeyed God because of what I have said and done,
19 because of the power of miracles
and the great things they saw, and
because of the power of the Holy
Spirit. I preached the Good News
from Jerusalem all the way around
to Illyricum, and so I have finished
that part of my work. 20 I always want
to preach the Good News in places
where people have never heard of
Christ, because I do not want to
build on the work someone else has
already started. 21 But it is written in
the Scriptures:

"Those who were not told about
him will see,
and those who have not heard
about him will understand."

Isaiah 52:15

Paul's Plan to Visit Rome

This is the reason I was stopped
many times from coming to you.
23 Now I have finished my work
here. Since for many years I have
wanted to come to you, 24 I hope to
visit you on my way to Spain. After
I enjoy being with you for a while, I
hope you can help me on my trip.
25 Now I am going to Jerusalem to
help God's people. 26 The believers in
Macedonia and Southern Greece
were happy to give their money
to help the poor among God's
people at Jerusalem. 27 They were
happy to do this, and really they
owe it to them. These who are not
Jews have shared in the Jews'
spiritual blessings, so they should
use their material possessions to
help the Jews. 28 After I am sure the
poor in Jerusalem get the money
that has been given for them, I will
leave for Spain and stop and visit
you. 29 I know that when I come to
you I will bring Christ's full blessing.

OLD TESTAMENT READING

So our hope is in the LORD.
He is our help, our shield to
protect us.
21 We rejoice in him,
because we trust his holy
name.
22 LORD, show your love to us
as we put our hope in you.

Psalm 33:20–22

INSIGHTS

As Jesus was entering into the last days of his life on earth, he prayed for his disciples and for all disciples to come. His petitions were for union with the Father, joy, protection, and usefulness. The sequence of those petitions is significant (John 17:11–17).

Friendship with Christ is the first priority and is basic for the qualities that follow. Out of that intimate, love relationship, joy is a logical consequence. Jesus knew, as he prayed for his disciples, that if they did indeed come into fellowship with him and exhibit the kind of full-fledged joy that he gives, there would be opposition from the world, and so he prayed not that his disciples would be protected from the world or taken out of it into a kind of insulated, holy huddle, but that they would be protected from anything that would destroy that union and joy. Then, out of that dynamic partnership, usefulness would naturally flow.

. . . The more I know Him, the more I experience that deep inner well of joy that is not dependent on external circumstances. This joy is present even in the midst of suffering and sorrow; it is a motivating power even in discouragement and dismay.

Jeanie Miley

ACTION POINT

Who does God fill with hope and joy? Why is God worthy of our trust and hope? What has God done that comforts you and brings you hope, even when life is difficult? Thank him. Rejoice in his unfailing love!

WEEKEND

Watch Out for False Prophets

Romans 15:30—16:27

Brothers and sisters, I beg you to
help me in my work by praying to
God for me. Do this because of our
Lord Jesus and the love that the Holy
Spirit gives us. 31 Pray that I will be
saved from the non-believers in
Judea and that this help I bring to
Jerusalem will please God's people
there. 32 Then, if God wants me to, I
will come to you with joy, and together you and I will have a time of
rest. 33 The God who gives peace be
with you all. Amen.

Greetings to the Christians

16 I recommend to you our sister
Phoebe, who is a helper in the
church in Cenchrea. 2 I ask you to accept her in the Lord in the way God's
people should. Help her with anything
she needs, because she has helped me
and many other people also.

3 Give my greetings to Priscilla
and Aquila, who work together with
me in Christ Jesus 4 and who risked
their own lives to save my life. I am
thankful to them, and all the non-
Jewish churches are thankful as
well. 5 Also, greet for me the church
that meets at their house.

Greetings to my dear friend
Epenetus, who was the first person
in the country of Asia to follow Christ.
6 Greetings to Mary, who worked
very hard for you. 7 Greetings to
Andronicus and Junia, my relatives,
who were in prison with me. They are
very important apostles. They were
believers in Christ before I was.
8 Greetings to Ampliatus, my dear
friend in the Lord. 9 Greetings to
Urbanus, a worker together with me
for Christ. And greetings to my dear
friend Stachys. 10 Greetings to
Apelles, who was tested and proved
that he truly loves Christ. Greetings
to all those who are in the family of
Aristobulus. 11 Greetings to Herodion,
my fellow citizen. Greetings to all
those in the family of Narcissus who
belong to the Lord. 12 Greetings to
Tryphena and Tryphosa, women
who work very hard for the Lord.
Greetings to my dear friend Persis,
who also has worked very hard for
the Lord. 13 Greetings to Rufus, who
is a special person in the Lord, and
to his mother, who has been like a
mother to me also. 14 Greetings to
Asyncritus, Phlegon, Hermes,
Patrobas, Hermas, and all the brothers who are with them. 15 Greetings
to Philologus and Julia, Nereus and
his sister, and Olympas, and to all
God's people with them. 16 Greet each
other with a holy kiss. All of Christ's
churches send greetings to you.

17 Brothers and sisters, I ask you
to look out for those who cause
people to be against each other and
who upset other people's faith. They
are against the true teaching you
learned, so stay away from them.
18 Such people are not serving our
Lord Christ but are only doing what
pleases themselves. They use fancy
talk and fine words to fool the minds
of those who do not know about evil.
19 All the believers have heard that
you obey, so I am very happy because of you. But I want you to be
wise in what is good and innocent in
what is evil.

[20] The God who brings peace will
soon defeat Satan and give you
power over him.
The grace of our Lord Jesus be
with you.
[21] Timothy, a worker together
with me, sends greetings, as well as
Lucius, Jason, and Sosipater, my
relatives.
[22] I am Tertius, and I am writing
this letter from Paul. I send greetings to you in the Lord.
[23] Gaius is letting me and the
whole church here use his home. He
also sends greetings to you, as do
Erastus, the city treasurer, and our
brother Quartus. [24] The grace of our
Lord Jesus Christ be with all of you.
Amen.
[25] Glory to God who can make you
strong in faith by the Good News
that I tell people and by the message
about Jesus Christ. The message
about Christ is the secret that was
hidden for long ages past but is now
made known. [26] It has been made
clear through the writings of the
prophets. And by the command of
the eternal God it is made known to
all nations that they might believe
and obey.
[27] To the only wise God be glory
forever through Jesus Christ!
Amen.

OLD TESTAMENT READING

This is what the Lord God says: How terrible it will be for foolish prophets who follow their own ideas and have not seen a vision from me! [7] You said, "This is the message of the LORD," but that is a false vision. Your prophecies are lies, because I have not spoken.

Ezekiel 13:3, 7

INSIGHTS

For the last sixty or so years professors and teachers in centers of theological training have had Satan's special attention, and so successful has he been that modernism has thoroughly penetrated the church. His ministers—yes, the devil's ministers, for he has many in the ministry!—are masquerading as ministers of truth and righteousness.

. . . Modern heresies and criticism are pitted against the infallible Word, the infallible Christ, the fact of sin, the redemptive works of the cross, the witness of the Holy Spirit. Knowing how completely the deity and death of Christ destroyed his works, Satan, through religious teachers, has been attacking the virgin birth, the sinlessness, the efficacious death, and the resurrection of our blessed Lord. . . .

By modernism, Satan has succeeded in robbing the church of her power in the world. With a humanized Christ, a mutilated Bible, and a glorified self, modernism is bankrupt. Nothing can damn evangelism like modernism, and Satan knows that—hence his untiring efforts to create an ever-increasing army of false teachers. . . . Let us pray for spiritual perception, whereby we can detect, and that immediately, the subtle error in a good deal we hear from some of the pulpits of our land.

Herbert Lockyer

APPLICATION

How seriously does God want his people to view the problem of false teachers? How can we guard against their deception?

MONDAY

God's Wisdom Defies Human Wisdom

1 Corinthians 1:1–25

1 From Paul. God called me to be an apostle of Christ Jesus because that is what God wanted. Also from Sosthenes, our brother in Christ.

2 To the church of God in Corinth, to you who have been made holy in Christ Jesus. You were called to be God's holy people with all people everywhere who pray in the name of the Lord Jesus Christ—their Lord and ours:

3 Grace and peace to you from God our Father and the Lord Jesus Christ.

Paul Gives Thanks to God

I always thank my God for you because of the grace God has given you in Christ Jesus. 5 I thank God because in Christ you have been made rich in every way, in all your speaking and in all your knowledge. 6 Just as our witness about Christ has been guaranteed to you, 7 so you have every gift from God while you wait for our Lord Jesus Christ to come again. 8 Jesus will keep you strong until the end so that there will be no wrong in you on the day our Lord Jesus Christ comes again. 9 God, who has called you to share everything with his Son, Jesus Christ our Lord, is faithful.

Problems in the Church

I beg you, brothers and sisters, by the name of our Lord Jesus Christ that all of you agree with each other and not be split into groups. I beg that you be completely joined together by having the same kind of thinking and the same purpose. 11 My brothers and sisters, some people from Chloe's family have told me quite plainly that there are quarrels among you. 12 This is what I mean: One of you says, "I follow Paul"; another says, "I follow Apollos"; another says, "I follow Peter"; and another says, "I follow Christ." 13 Christ has been divided up into different groups! Did Paul die on the cross for you? No! Were you baptized in the name of Paul? No! 14 I thank God I did not baptize any of you except Crispus and Gaius 15 so that now no one can say you were baptized in my name. 16 (I also baptized the family of Stephanas, but I do not remember that I baptized anyone else.) 17 Christ did not send me to baptize people but to preach the Good News. And he sent me to preach the Good News without using words of human wisdom so that the cross of Christ would not lose its power.

Christ Is God's Power and Wisdom

The teaching about the cross is foolishness to those who are being lost, but to us who are being saved it is the power of God. 19 It is written in the Scriptures:

"I will cause the wise men to lose
their wisdom;
I will make the wise men
unable to understand."

Isaiah 29:14

20 Where is the wise person? Where is the educated person? Where is the skilled talker of this world? God has made the wisdom of

the world foolish. 21 In the wisdom of
God the world did not know God
through its own wisdom. So God
chose to use the message that
sounds foolish to save those who
believe. 22 The Jews ask for miracles,
and the Greeks want wisdom. 23 But
we preach a crucified Christ. This is
a big problem to the Jews, and it is
foolishness to those who are not
Jews. 24 But Christ is the power of
God and the wisdom of God to those
people God has called—Jews and
Greeks. 25 Even the foolishness of
God is wiser than human wisdom,
and the weakness of God is stronger
than human strength.

OLD TESTAMENT READING

I, the LORD, made everything,
stretching out the skies by
myself
and spreading out the earth all
alone.
25 I show that the lying prophets'
signs are false;
I make fools of those who do
magic.
I confuse even wise men;
they think they know much,
but I make them look
foolish.
26 I make the messages of my
servants come true;
I make the advice of my
messengers come true."

Isaiah 44:24b–26a

INSIGHTS

The Jews sought after wonders, but the Greeks sought after wisdom. The Greeks were known for their great philosophers and their knowledge. They had come to the point where they literally deified wisdom. They were worshiping at the shrine of science and knowledge. Does that sound familiar today in the twentieth century?

We have people today who say, "If you can't put it into the test tube or in a mathematical equation, we will not believe it." But you can't put the Cross in a crucible, and you can't put faith in a formula. The great philosopher, Pascal, said, "The heart has its reasons that reason knows nothing of." . . .

. . . God is too wise to let man come to know Him by his own wisdom. Man cannot solve his problems because he will not recognize their source, which is sin. Furthermore, he will not recognize the solution, which is salvation. God is so wise that He is not going to let man come to Him by his own wisdom.

As a matter of fact, we are told in 1 Corinthians 3:19 that "the wisdom of this world is foolishness with God." Think about it, a world full of wisdom is just a thimble full of foolishness to God. The Prophet Jeremiah said, "The wise men are ashamed. They are dismayed and taken. Behold they have rejected the Word of the Lord; so what wisdom do they have?" (Jer. 8:9). . . .

. . . If a person is going to come to God, he or she will have to come as a little child (Matt. 18:3).

James Merritt

PAUSE FOR REFLECTION

Why would using worldly wisdom to tell the Good News cause the cross of Christ to lose its power? Why would God, the source of all wisdom, turn the world's wisdom into foolishness?

TUESDAY

God Is the Source of Wisdom

1 Corinthians 1:26–2:16

Brothers and sisters, look at what
you were when God called you. Not
many of you were wise in the way
the world judges wisdom. Not many
of you had great influence. Not many
of you came from important families.
27 But God chose the foolish things
of the world to shame the wise, and
he chose the weak things of the
world to shame the strong. 28 He
chose what the world thinks is unimportant and what the world looks
down on and thinks is nothing in order to destroy what the world thinks
is important. 29 God did this so that
no one can brag in his presence.
30 Because of God you are in Christ
Jesus, who has become for us wisdom from God. In Christ we are put
right with God, and have been made
holy, and have been set free from
sin. 31 So, as the Scripture says, "If
someone wants to brag, he should
brag only about the Lord."

The Message of Christ's Death

2 Dear brothers and sisters, when
I came to you, I did not come
preaching God's secret with fancy
words or a show of human wisdom.
2 I decided that while I was with you
I would forget about everything except Jesus Christ and his death on
the cross. 3 So when I came to you, I
was weak and fearful and trembling.
4 My teaching and preaching were
not with words of human wisdom
that persuade people but with proof
of the power that the Spirit gives.
5 This was so that your faith would
be in God's power and not in human
wisdom.

God's Wisdom

However, I speak a wisdom to
those who are mature. But this wisdom is not from this world or from
the rulers of this world, who are losing their power. 7 I speak God's secret wisdom, which he has kept hidden. Before the world began, God
planned this wisdom for our glory.
8 None of the rulers of this world
understood it. If they had, they
would not have crucified the Lord of
glory. 9 But as it is written in the
Scriptures:

"No one has ever seen this,
  and no one has ever heard
    about it.
No one has ever imagined
  what God has prepared for
    those
  who love him." *Isaiah 64:4*

10 But God has shown us these
things through the Spirit.

The Spirit searches out all things,
even the deep secrets of God. 11 Who
knows the thoughts that another
person has? Only a person's spirit
that lives within him knows his
thoughts. It is the same with God.
No one knows the thoughts of God
except the Spirit of God. 12 Now we
did not receive the spirit of the
world, but we received the Spirit that
is from God so that we can know all
that God has given us. 13 And we
speak about these things, not with
words taught us by human wisdom
but with words taught us by the
Spirit. And so we explain spiritual
truths to spiritual people. 14 A person

who does not have the Spirit does
not accept the truths that come from
the Spirit of God. That person thinks
they are foolish and cannot understand them, because they can only
be judged to be true by the Spirit.
15 The spiritual person is able to
judge all things, but no one can
judge him. The Scripture says:
16 "Who has known the mind of the
Lord?
Who has been able to teach
him?" *Isaiah 40:13*
But we have the mind of Christ.

OLD TESTAMENT READING

So from where does wisdom
come,
and where does understanding
live?
21 It is hidden from the eyes of
every living thing,
even from the birds of the air.
22 The places of destruction and
death say,
'We have heard reports about
it.'
23 Only God understands the way to
wisdom,
and he alone knows where it
lives,
24 because he looks to the farthest
parts of the earth
and sees everything under the
sky.
25 When God gave power to the
wind
and measured the water,
26 when he made rules for the rain
and set a path for a thunder-
storm to follow,
27 then he looked at wisdom and
decided its worth;
he set wisdom up and tested it.
28 Then he said to humans,
'The fear of the Lord is
wisdom;
to stay away from evil is
understanding.'"

Job 28:20–28

INSIGHTS

Men are always seeking for greater wisdom, but they usually bypass the Ultimate Source of wisdom. The Scriptures clearly point this direction. They reveal, "The fear of the Lord is the beginning of wisdom, and the knowledge of the Holy One is understanding" (Prov. 9:10). But what has man done with this tremendous resource at his fingertips? Ignored it! "For even though they knew God, they did not honor Him as God, or give thanks; but they became futile in their speculations, and their foolish heart was darkened. Professing to be wise, they became fools" (Rom. 1:21–22).

Since God's wisdom resides in His Word, it is imperative to know what He has revealed, but even many Christians ignore a regular time reading and studying the Scriptures. Therefore, many of their decisions are foolish, because they've not consulted the Ultimate Source of wisdom.

Rick Yohn

APPLICATION

How does Scripture define wisdom? How does a person gain wisdom? Does God need educated and wise teachers to communicate his message? What kind of person does God use? Are you willing to be that kind of person? How will you gain God's wisdom?

WEDNESDAY

Christ Is the Cornerstone of Our Faith, so Our Works Must Stand His Test

1 Corinthians 3:1—4:5

Following People Is Wrong

3 Brothers and sisters, in the past
I could not talk to you as I talk
to spiritual people. I had to talk to
you as I would to people without the
Spirit—babies in Christ. 2 The
teaching I gave you was like milk,
not solid food, because you were
not able to take solid food. And even
now you are not ready. 3 You are still
not spiritual, because there is jealousy and quarreling among you,
and this shows that you are not
spiritual. You are acting like people
of the world. 4 One of you says, "I
belong to Paul," and another says,
"I belong to Apollos." When you say
things like this, you are acting like
people of the world.

5 Is Apollos important? No! Is
Paul important? No! We are only
servants of God who helped you believe. Each one of us did the work
God gave us to do. 6 I planted the
seed, and Apollos watered it. But
God is the One who made it grow.
7 So the one who plants is not important, and the one who waters is not
important. Only God, who makes
things grow, is important. 8 The one
who plants and the one who waters
have the same purpose, and each
will be rewarded for his own work.
9 We are God's workers, working
together; you are like God's farm,
God's house.

10 Using the gift God gave me, I
laid the foundation of that house
like an expert builder. Others are
building on that foundation, but all
people should be careful how they
build on it. 11 The foundation that
has already been laid is Jesus
Christ, and no one can lay down any
other foundation. 12 But if people
build on that foundation, using gold,
silver, jewels, wood, grass, or straw,
13 their work will be clearly seen,
because the Day of Judgment will
make it visible. That Day will appear
with fire, and the fire will test
everyone's work to show what sort
of work it was. 14 If the building that
has been put on the foundation still
stands, the builder will get a reward. 15 But if the building is burned
up, the builder will suffer loss. The
builder will be saved, but it will be
as one who escaped from a fire.

16 Don't you know that you are
God's temple and that God's Spirit
lives in you? 17 If anyone destroys
God's temple, God will destroy that
person, because God's temple is
holy and you are that temple.

18 Do not fool yourselves. If you
think you are wise in this world, you
should become a fool so that you
can become truly wise, 19 because
the wisdom of this world is foolishness with God. It is written in the
Scriptures, "He catches those who
are wise in their own clever traps."
20 It is also written in the Scriptures,
"The Lord knows what wise people
think. He knows their thoughts are
just a puff of wind." 21 So you should
not brag about human leaders. All
things belong to you: 22 Paul,
Apollos, and Peter; the world, life,
death, the present, and the future—
all these belong to you. 23 And you

belong to Christ, and Christ belongs to God.

Apostles Are Servants of Christ

4 People should think of us as servants of Christ, the ones God has
trusted with his secrets. [2] Now in this
way those who are trusted with
something valuable must show they
are worthy of that trust. [3] As for myself, I do not care if I am judged by
you or by any human court. I do not
even judge myself. [4] I know of no
wrong I have done, but this does not
make me right before the Lord. The
Lord is the One who judges me. [5] So
do not judge before the right time;
wait until the Lord comes. He will
bring to light things that are now hidden in darkness, and will make
known the secret purposes of
people's hearts. Then God will
praise each one of them.

OLD TESTAMENT READING

The LORD says, "Two-thirds of
the people
through all the land will die.
They will be gone,
and one-third will be left.
[9] The third that is left I will test
with fire,
purifying them like silver,
testing them like gold.
Then they will call on me,
and I will answer them.
I will say, 'You are my people,'
and they will say, 'The LORD is
our God.'"

Zechariah 13:8–9

The stone that the builders
rejected
became the cornerstone.

Psalm 118:22

INSIGHTS

What does it mean to build your house on the rock or to dig deeply and lay a foundation? . . . It is a matter of building on Jesus Himself. . . . To practice His words means . . . to believe that He is who He says He is and to turn from sin to faith in Him as the way of salvation. . . .

Isaiah writes, "This is what the Sovereign LORD says: 'See I lay a stone in Zion, a tested stone, a precious cornerstone for a sure foundation'" (Isa. 28:16). Paul declares, "You are . . . built on the foundation of the apostles and prophets, with Christ Jesus himself as the chief cornerstone" (Eph 2:19–20). . . . That is the true sense of Christ's teaching: "If you want a life that will last for eternity, build on Me." We sing:

My hope is built on nothing less
Than Jesus' blood and righteousness;
I dare not trust the sweetest frame,
But wholly lean on Jesus' name.

On Christ, the solid rock, I stand;
All other ground is sinking sand. . . .

. . . A life built on Jesus and His teachings will stand—it will stand in the trials and testings of this life, and it will stand in eternity.

James Boice

ACTION POINT

On what foundation are you building your life's work? Is your work worthy of the foundation; will it stand the test? Pray that your works will be proven worthy.

THURSDAY

God Will Not Tolerate Sin Among His People

1 Corinthians 4:6—5:8

*B*rothers and sisters, I have used Apollos and myself as examples so you could learn through us the meaning of the saying, "Follow only what is written in the Scriptures." Then you will not be more proud of one person than another. 7 Who says you are better than others? What do you have that was not given to you? And if it was given to you, why do you brag as if you did not receive it as a gift?

8 You think you already have everything you need. You think you are rich. You think you have become kings without us. I wish you really were kings so we could be kings together with you. 9 But it seems to me that God has put us apostles in last place, like those sentenced to die. We are like a show for the whole world to see—angels and people. 10 We are fools for Christ's sake, but you are very wise in Christ. We are weak, but you are strong. You receive honor, but we are shamed. 11 Even to this very hour we do not have enough to eat or drink or to wear. We are often beaten, and we have no homes in which to live. 12 We work hard with our own hands for our food. When people curse us, we bless them. When they hurt us, we put up with it. 13 When they tell evil lies about us, we speak nice words about them. Even today, we are treated as though we were the garbage of the world—the filth of the earth.

14 I am not trying to make you feel ashamed. I am writing this to give you a warning as my own dear children. 15 For though you may have ten thousand teachers in Christ, you do not have many fathers. Through the Good News I became your father in Christ Jesus, 16 so I beg you, please follow my example. 17 That is why I am sending to you Timothy, my son in the Lord. I love Timothy, and he is faithful. He will help you remember my way of life in Christ Jesus, just as I teach it in all the churches everywhere.

18 Some of you have become proud, thinking that I will not come to you again. 19 But I will come to you very soon if the Lord wishes. Then I will know what the proud ones do, not what they say, 20 because the kingdom of God is present not in talk but in power. 21 Which do you want: that I come to you with punishment or with love and gentleness?

Wickedness in the Church

5 It is actually being said that there is sexual sin among you. And it is a kind that does not happen even among people who do not know God. A man there has his father's wife. 2 And you are proud! You should have been filled with sadness so that the man who did this should be put out of your group. 3 I am not there with you in person, but I am with you in spirit. And I have already judged the man who did that sin as if I were really there. 4 When you meet together in the name of our Lord Jesus, and I meet with you in spirit with the power of our Lord Jesus, 5 then hand this man over to Satan. So his sinful self will be de-

stroyed, and his spirit will be saved on the day of the Lord.

[6]Your bragging is not good. You know the saying, "Just a little yeast makes the whole batch of dough rise." [7]Take out all the old yeast so that you will be a new batch of dough without yeast, which you really are. For Christ, our Passover lamb, has been sacrificed. [8]So let us celebrate this feast, but not with the bread that has the old yeast—the yeast of sin and wickedness. Let us celebrate this feast with the bread that has no yeast—the bread of goodness and truth.

OLD TESTAMENT READING

A man or woman in one of the towns the LORD gave you might be found doing something evil and breaking the Agreement. [4b]If it is true that such a hateful thing has happened in Israel, [5]take the man or woman who has done the evil thing to the city gates and throw stones at that person until he dies.

[12]The person who does not show respect for the judge or priest who is there serving the LORD your God must be put to death. You must get rid of that evil from Israel.

Deuteronomy 17:2, 4b-5, 12

INSIGHTS

Can a Christian get away with sin? Some people seem to think so. However, a closer look points to another answer. God is always opposed to sin. He is never deceived and cannot be outwitted. He may allow sin to continue for a time, but there will be a day of accountability.

Nothing leads to evil quite as much as the idea that this world is all there is. Those who commit violent crimes and who harm the innocent have usually first convinced themselves that there will never be a day of judgment. Even the motorist speeding down the highway has convinced himself he will not receive a speeding ticket.

However, Jesus says that people who believe they will never be found out are wrong: "There is nothing covered up that will not be revealed, and hidden that will not be known" (Luke 12:2). . . .

. . . God totally opposes sin. Take a favorable attitude toward sin and God must take an unfavorable attitude toward you. No Christian can entertain sin and get away with it.

The Royal Canadian Mounted Police have taken as their motto, "We always get our man." The implication is that no matter where a wanted man runs, he will be found. Sin is the same way. No matter how hard we try, we cannot hide our sins. Regardless of how much good we do, it will not cover our disobedience.

God will not allow sin in the lives of His children to go unchecked.

George Sweeting
Donald Sweeting

APPLICATION

Why does God tell his people to punish the sinners among them? What was Paul's response to sin in the Corinthian church? What is your response to sin? How might your response be more pleasing to God?

FRIDAY

Honor God with Your Body; Keep Yourself from Sexual Sin

1 Corinthians 5:9—6:20

I wrote you in my earlier letter not
to associate with those who sin sexually. 10 But I did not mean you should
not associate with those of this world
who sin sexually, or with the greedy,
or robbers, or those who worship
idols. To get away from them you
would have to leave this world. 11 I
am writing to tell you that you must
not associate with those who call
themselves believers in Christ but
who sin sexually, or are greedy, or
worship idols, or abuse others with
words, or get drunk, or cheat people.
Do not even eat with people like that.
12-13 It is not my business to judge
those who are not part of the church.
God will judge them. But you must
judge the people who are part of the
church. The Scripture says, "You
must get rid of the evil person
among you."

Judging Problems Among Christians

6 When you have something
against another Christian, how
can you bring yourself to go before
judges who are not right with God?
Why do you not let God's people decide who is right? 2 Surely you know
that God's people will judge the
world. So if you are to judge the
world, are you not able to judge
small cases as well? 3 You know that
in the future we will judge angels, so
surely we can judge the ordinary
things of this life. 4 If you have ordinary cases that must be judged, are
you going to appoint people as
judges who mean nothing to the
church? 5 I say this to shame you.
Surely there is someone among you
wise enough to judge a complaint
between believers. 6 But now one
believer goes to court against another believer—and you do this in
front of unbelievers!
7 The fact that you have lawsuits
against each other shows that you
are already defeated. Why not let
yourselves be wronged? Why not let
yourselves be cheated? 8 But you
yourselves do wrong and cheat, and
you do this to other believers!
9-10 Surely you know that the
people who do wrong will not inherit
God's kingdom. Do not be fooled.
Those who sin sexually, worship
idols, take part in adultery, those
who are male prostitutes, or men
who have sexual relations with other
men, those who steal, are greedy,
get drunk, lie about others, or rob—
these people will not inherit God's
kingdom. 11 In the past, some of you
were like that, but you were washed
clean. You were made holy, and you
were made right with God in the
name of the Lord Jesus Christ and
in the Spirit of our God.

Use Your Bodies for God's Glory

I am allowed to do all things," but
all things are not good for me to do.
"I am allowed to do all things," but I
will not let anything make me its
slave. 13 "Food is for the stomach,
and the stomach for food," but God
will destroy them both. The body is
not for sexual sin but for the Lord,
and the Lord is for the body. 14 By his

power God has raised the Lord from the dead and will also raise us from the dead.
[15] Surely you know that your bodies are parts of Christ himself. So I must never take the parts of Christ and join them to a prostitute!
[16] It is written in the Scriptures, "The two will become one body." So you should know that anyone who joins with a prostitute becomes one body with the prostitute.
[17] But the one who joins with the Lord is one spirit with the Lord.

[18] So run away from sexual sin. Every other sin people do is outside their bodies, but those who sin sexually sin against their own bodies.
[19] You should know that your body is a temple for the Holy Spirit who is in you. You have received the Holy Spirit from God. So you do not belong to yourselves,
[20] because you were bought by God for a price. So honor God with your bodies.

OLD TESTAMENT READING

You cannot carry hot coals
against your chest
without burning your clothes,
[28] and you cannot walk on hot coals
without burning your feet.
[29] The same is true if you have
sexual relations with
another man's wife.
Anyone who does so will be
punished.

Proverbs 6:27–29

INSIGHTS

It's often said that people "fall" into immorality. The expression is as revealing as it is faulty and dangerous. The very term fall betrays a victim mentality. It sounds as if we were walking down a street and someone tripped us or kicked our feet out from under us. It implies that moral collapse comes out of nowhere, that there is little or nothing we could have done to prevent what happened.

We do not fall into immorality. We walk into it. Indeed, sometimes we run headlong into it. We must realize from the beginning that immorality is a choice. It is not something that happens to people. . . .

Sexual sin never comes out of the clear blue sky. It is often the result of a long process in which a mind susceptible to sin is granted unguarded exposure to immoral input.

"Sow a thought, reap an action. Sow an action, reap a habit. Sow a habit, reap a character. Sow a character, reap a destiny." Our thoughts are the fabric with which we weave our character and destiny. We must actively fight off thoughts of impurity. But the key to doing this is not simply saying "I will not lust, I will not lust"—that often has the same effect as saying, "I will not think of purple elephants." We must cultivate our hearts and minds with what is godly and pure. These better thoughts will displace others (Phil 4:8).

Randy Alcorn

PAUSE FOR REFLECTION

What does Paul say about judging the lifestyles of other Christians? What sins, in addition to sexual sins, does Paul take a hard line against? Why are we to run away from sin? What are the penalties for continuing in sin?

WEEKEND

Marriage Is a Gift from God Not to Be Taken Lightly

1 Corinthians 7:1–24

About Marriage

7 Now I will discuss the things you
wrote me about. It is good for a
man not to have sexual relations
with a woman. 2 But because sexual
sin is a danger, each man should
have his own wife, and each woman
should have her own husband. 3 The
husband should give his wife all that
he owes her as his wife. And the wife
should give her husband all that she
owes him as her husband. 4 The wife
does not have full rights over her
own body; her husband shares
them. And the husband does not
have full rights over his own body;
his wife shares them. 5 Do not refuse
to give your bodies to each other,
unless you both agree to stay away
from sexual relations for a time so
you can give your time to prayer.
Then come together again so Satan
cannot tempt you because of a lack
of self-control. 6 I say this to give you
permission to stay away from sexual
relations for a time. It is not a command to do so. 7 I wish that everyone were like me, but each person
has his own gift from God. One has
one gift, another has another gift.

8 Now for those who are not married and for the widows I say this: It
is good for them to stay unmarried
as I am. 9 But if they cannot control
themselves, they should marry. It is
better to marry than to burn with
sexual desire.

10 Now I give this command for
the married people. (The command
is not from me; it is from the Lord.)
A wife should not leave her husband.
11 But if she does leave, she must not
marry again, or she should make up
with her husband. Also the husband
should not divorce his wife.

12 For all the others I say this (I
am saying this, not the Lord): If a
Christian man has a wife who is not
a believer, and she is happy to live
with him, he must not divorce her.
13 And if a Christian woman has a
husband who is not a believer, and
he is happy to live with her, she must
not divorce him. 14 The husband who
is not a believer is made holy
through his believing wife. And the
wife who is not a believer is made
holy through her believing husband.
If this were not true, your children
would not be clean, but now your
children are holy.

15 But if those who are not believers decide to leave, let them leave.
When this happens, the Christian
man or woman is free. But God
called us to live in peace. 16 Wife, you
don't know; maybe you will save
your husband. And husband, you
don't know; maybe you will save
your wife.

Live as God Called You

*B*ut in any case each one of you
should continue to live the way God
has given you to live—the way you
were when God called you. This is a
rule I make in all the churches. 18 If
a man was already circumcised
when he was called, he should not
undo his circumcision. If a man was
without circumcision when he was
called, he should not be circum-

cised. [19] It is not important if a man
is circumcised or not. The important
thing is obeying God's commands.
[20] Each one of you should stay the
way you were when God called you.
[21] If you were a slave when God
called you, do not let that bother you.
But if you can be free, then make
good use of your freedom. [22] Those
who were slaves when the Lord
called them are free persons who
belong to the Lord. In the same way,
those who were free when they were
called are now Christ's slaves. [23] You
all were bought at a great price, so
do not become slaves of people.
[24] Brothers and sisters, each of you
should stay as you were when you
were called, and stay there with God.

OLD TESTAMENT READING

God made husbands and wives to become one body and one spirit for his purpose—so they would have children who are true to God.

So be careful, and do not break your promise to the wife you married when you were young.

[16] The LORD God of Israel says, "I hate divorce. And I hate people who do cruel things as easily as they put on clothes," says the LORD All-Powerful.

Malachi 2:15–16b

INSIGHTS

If Paul is writing anything . . . , he is writing this, "When you marry, you marry for life." He has permanence in mind.

- *The wife should not leave her husband (v. 10).*
- *The husband should not leave his wife (v. 11).*
- *Let him not send her away (v. 12).*
- *Let her not send him away (v. 13).*

To write it once would be sufficient. Twice would be extremely and unmistakably clear. Three times would be more than enough. But four times? The man means business!

Years ago Cynthia and I took the ugly word divorce out of our dialogues. We agreed we would not even store it in the arsenal of our argument vocabulary. No matter how heated our disagreements may be, we'd not threaten each other with that term. It does something to a marriage when you can count on your partner to stick around and hammer out your differences with each other instead of walking away from them.

What does it take to stick it out . . . to be permanently committed to each other? I repeat, it takes grace! It takes an enormous amount of grace to negotiate through the mine field of disagreements. It takes grace to forgive and go on. Grace to hang tough even though the same mistake is made over and over or the same sin committed again and again. A marriage well-oiled by grace is durable, longlasting—protected against the wear and tear of friction.

Charles Swindoll

APPLICATION

What do you learn about the seriousness of marriage from these Scripture readings? What adjustments need to be made in your thinking toward marriage? Will you make them?

MONDAY

To Marry or Not to Marry?

1 Corinthians 7:25—8:8

Questions About Getting Married

Now I write about people who are not married. I have no command from the Lord about this; I give my opinion. But I can be trusted, because the Lord has shown me mercy. 26 The present time is a time of trouble, so I think it is good for you to stay the way you are. 27 If you have a wife, do not try to become free from her. If you are not married, do not try to find a wife. 28 But if you decide to marry, you have not sinned. And if a girl who has never married decides to marry, she has not sinned. But those who marry will have trouble in this life, and I want you to be free from trouble.

29 Brothers and sisters, this is what I mean: We do not have much time left. So starting now, those who have wives should live as if they had no wives. 30 Those who are crying should live as if they were not crying. Those who are happy should live as if they were not happy. Those who buy things should live as if they own nothing. 31 Those who use the things of the world should live as if they were not using them, because this world in its present form will soon be gone.

32 I want you to be free from worry. A man who is not married is busy with the Lord's work, trying to please the Lord. 33 But a man who is married is busy with things of the world, trying to please his wife. 34 He must think about two things—pleasing his wife and pleasing the Lord. A woman who is not married or a girl who has never married is busy with the Lord's work. She wants to be holy in body and spirit. But a married woman is busy with things of the world, as to how she can please her husband. 35 I am saying this to help you, not to limit you. But I want you to live in the right way, to give yourselves fully to the Lord without concern for other things.

36 If a man thinks he is not doing the right thing with the girl he is engaged to, if she is almost past the best age to marry and he feels he should marry her, he should do what he wants. They should get married. It is no sin. 37 But if a man is sure in his mind that there is no need for marriage, and has his own desires under control, and has decided not to marry the one to whom he is engaged, he is doing the right thing. 38 So the man who marries his girl does right, but the man who does not marry will do better.

39 A woman must stay with her husband as long as he lives. But if her husband dies, she is free to marry any man she wants, but she must marry in the Lord. 40 The woman is happier if she does not marry again. This is my opinion, but I believe I also have God's Spirit.

About Food Offered to Idols

8 Now I will write about meat that is sacrificed to idols. We know that "we all have knowledge." Knowledge puffs you up with pride, but love builds up. 2 If you think you know something, you do not yet know anything as you should. 3 But

if any person loves God, that person is known by God.

[4] So this is what I say about eating meat sacrificed to idols: We know that an idol is really nothing in the world, and we know there is only one God. [5] Even though there are things called gods, in heaven or on earth (and there are many "gods" and "lords"), [6] for us there is only one God—our Father. All things came from him, and we live for him. And there is only one Lord—Jesus Christ. All things were made through him, and we also were made through him.

[7] But not all people know this. Some people are still so used to idols that when they eat meat, they still think of it as being sacrificed to an idol. Because their conscience is weak, when they eat it, they feel guilty. [8] But food will not bring us closer to God. Refusing to eat does not make us less pleasing to God, and eating does not make us better in God's sight.

OLD TESTAMENT READING

God Calls Jeremiah for Special Service, Not Marriage

The LORD spoke his word to me, saying:

[5] "Before I made you in your
mother's womb, I chose you.
Before you were born, I set you
apart for a special work.
I appointed you as a prophet to
the nations."

[9] Then the LORD reached out with his hand and touched my mouth. He said to me, "See, I am putting my words in your mouth. [10] Today I have put you in charge of nations and kingdoms. You will pull up and tear down, destroy and overthrow, build up and plant."

Then the LORD spoke his word to me: "You must not get married or have sons or daughters in this place."

Jeremiah 1:4–5, 9–10; 16:1–2

INSIGHTS

Jesus declared that there were those who were single "for the sake of the kingdom of heaven" (Matt. 19:12). And Paul builds on this foundation by suggesting that the unmarried can focus their energies toward the work of God in a way that the married simply cannot (1 Cor. 7:32–35).

Some have railed at Paul for urging people to seriously consider the single life, but the truth is that his words are filled with practical wisdom. He was not against marriage—in fact his great contribution to Christian sexual theology is the way he compares the sexual union in marriage to the union of Christ and his Church. But Paul did insist that we count the cost. You see, no one should enter the covenant of marriage without realizing the immense time and energy required to make that relationship work.

Richard Foster

APPLICATION

What does a person's marital status have to do with his or her spiritual service? What is more important than whether a person is married or single? Pray that you will be true to God's calling for you.

TUESDAY

Don't Do Anything to Cause Someone to Sin

1 Corinthians 8:9—9:18

*B*ut be careful that your freedom does not cause those who are weak in faith to fall into sin. [10]You have "knowledge," so you eat in an idol's temple. But someone who is weak in faith might see you eating there and be encouraged to eat meat sacrificed to idols while thinking it is wrong to do so. [11]This weak believer for whom Christ died is ruined because of your "knowledge." [12]When you sin against your brothers and sisters in Christ like this and cause them to do what they feel is wrong, you are also sinning against Christ. [13]So if the food I eat causes them to fall into sin, I will never eat meat again so that I will not cause any of them to sin.

Paul Is like the Other Apostles

9 I am a free man. I am an apostle. I have seen Jesus our Lord. You people are all an example of my work in the Lord. [2]If others do not accept me as an apostle, surely you do, because you are proof that I am an apostle in the Lord.

[3]This is the answer I give people who want to judge me: [4]Do we not have the right to eat and drink? [5]Do we not have the right to bring a believing wife with us when we travel as do the other apostles and the Lord's brothers and Peter? [6]Are Barnabas and I the only ones who must work to earn our living? [7]No soldier ever serves in the army and pays his own salary. No one ever plants a vineyard without eating some of the grapes. No person takes care of a flock without drinking some of the milk.

[8]I do not say this by human authority; God's law also says the same thing. [9]It is written in the law of Moses: "When an ox is working in the grain, do not cover its mouth to keep it from eating." When God said this, was he thinking only about oxen? No. [10]He was really talking about us. Yes, that Scripture was written for us, because it goes on to say: "The one who plows and the one who works in the grain should hope to get some of the grain for their work." [11]Since we planted spiritual seed among you, is it too much if we should harvest from you some things for this life? [12]If others have the right to get something from you, surely we have this right, too. But we do not use it. No, we put up with everything ourselves so that we will not keep anyone from believing the Good News of Christ. [13]Surely you know that those who work at the Temple get their food from the Temple, and those who serve at the altar get part of what is offered at the altar. [14]In the same way, the Lord has commanded that those who tell the Good News should get their living from this work.

[15]But I have not used any of these rights. And I am not writing this now to get anything from you. I would rather die than to have my reason for bragging taken away. [16]Telling the Good News does not give me any reason for bragging. Telling the Good News is my duty—something I must do. And how terrible it will be for me if I do not tell the Good

News. 17 If I preach because it is my
own choice, I have a reward. But if I
preach and it is not my choice to do
so, I am only doing the duty that was
given to me. 18 So what reward do I
get? This is my reward: that when I
tell the Good News I can offer it freely.
I do not use my full rights in my work
of preaching the Good News.

OLD TESTAMENT READING

I made some of your children to
be prophets
and some of your young people
to be Nazirites.
People of Israel, isn't this true?"
says the LORD.
12 "But you made the Nazirites
drink wine
and told the prophets not to
prophesy.
13 Now I will make you get stuck,
as a wagon loaded with grain
gets stuck.
14 No one will escape, not even the
fastest runner.
Strong people will not be
strong enough;
warriors will not be able to
save themselves."

Amos 2:11–14

INSIGHTS

Few would question the assertion that we should renounce the wrong things in our lives. It is self-evident that such things mar our lives, spoil our enjoyment of life, and limit our usefulness to God and man. But not everyone is equally convinced that in the interest of the gospel the disciple of Christ may need to renounce some things that are perfectly right and legitimate. . . .

Four times in 1 Corinthians 9 Paul asserts his rights in the gospel. Three times he claims that he has refrained from exercising these rights in the higher interests of spreading the gospel. He affirms that he is ready to forgo any right he may have, and forsake any privilege, out of love for Christ and in the interests of the progress of the gospel. . . .

Oswald Chambers had some trenchant words to say in this connection: "If we are willing to give up only wrong things for Jesus, never let us talk about being in love with Him. Anyone will give up wrong things if he knows how, but are we prepared to give up the best we have for Jesus Christ? The only right a Christian has is the right to give up his rights. If we are to be the best for God, there must be victory in the realm of legitimate desire as well as in the realm of unlawful indulgence." . . .

. . . The disciple must choose his priorities very carefully, even in things that are right in themselves. If we are aiming at the heights of Christian experience, there will always come the challenge to voluntary renunciation of some rights.

J. Oswald Sanders

APPLICATION

Define Christian freedom in your own words. What is the objective of Christian freedom? What legitimate freedoms did Paul sacrifice for the sake of the Gospel? How much freedom will you sacrifice for the cause of Christ?

WEDNESDAY

Stand Firm Against Temptation

1 Corinthians 9:19—10:22

Paul's Efforts to Win Others

I am free and belong to no one. But I make myself a slave to all people to win as many as I can. 20 To the Jews I became like a Jew to win the Jews. I myself am not ruled by the law. But to those who are ruled by the law I became like a person who is ruled by the law. I did this to win those who are ruled by the law. 21 To those who are without the law I became like a person who is without the law. I did this to win those people who are without the law. (But really, I am not without God's law—I am ruled by Christ's law.) 22 To those who are weak, I became weak so I could win the weak. I have become all things to all people so I could save some of them in any way possible. 23 I do all this because of the Good News and so I can share in its blessings.

24 You know that in a race all the runners run, but only one gets the prize. So run to win! 25 All those who compete in the games use self-control so they can win a crown. That crown is an earthly thing that lasts only a short time, but our crown will never be destroyed. 26 So I do not run without a goal. I fight like a boxer who is hitting something—not just the air. 27 I treat my body hard and make it my slave so that I myself will not be disqualified after I have preached to others.

Warnings from Israel's Past

10 Brothers and sisters, I want you to know what happened to our ancestors who followed Moses. They were all under the cloud and all went through the sea. 2 They were all baptized as followers of Moses in the cloud and in the sea. 3 They all ate the same spiritual food, 4 and all drank the same spiritual drink. They drank from that spiritual rock that followed them, and that rock was Christ. 5 But God was not pleased with most of them, so they died in the desert.

6 And these things happened as examples for us, to stop us from wanting evil things as those people did. 7 Do not worship idols, as some of them did. Just as it is written in the Scriptures: "They sat down to eat and drink, and then they got up and sinned sexually." 8 We must not take part in sexual sins, as some of them did. In one day twenty-three thousand of them died because of their sins. 9 We must not test Christ as some of them did; they were killed by snakes. 10 Do not complain as some of them did; they were killed by the angel that destroys.

11 The things that happened to those people are examples. They were written down to teach us, because we live in a time when all these things of the past have reached their goal. 12 If you think you are strong, you should be careful not to fall. 13 The only temptation that has come to you is that which everyone has. But you can trust God, who will not permit you to be tempted more than you can stand. But when you are tempted, he will also give you a way to escape so that you will be able to stand it.

[14]So, my dear friends, run away from the worship of idols. [15]I am speaking to you as to intelligent people; judge for yourselves what I say. [16]We give thanks for the cup of blessing, which is a sharing in the blood of Christ. And the bread that we break is a sharing in the body of Christ. [17]Because there is one loaf of bread, we who are many are one body, because we all share that one loaf.

[18]Think about the Israelites: Do not those who eat the sacrifices share in the altar? [19]I do not mean that the food sacrificed to an idol is important. I do not mean that an idol is anything at all. [20]But I say that what is sacrificed to idols is offered to demons, not to God. And I do not want you to share anything with demons. [21]You cannot drink the cup of the Lord and the cup of demons also. You cannot share in the Lord's table and the table of demons. [22]Are we trying to make the Lord jealous? We are not stronger than he is, are we?

OLD TESTAMENT READING

Then the LORD said to Satan, "Have you noticed my servant Job? No one else on earth is like him. He is an honest and innocent man, honoring God and staying away from evil. You caused me to ruin him for no good reason, but he continues to be without blame."

[4]"One skin for another!" Satan answered. "A man will give all he has to save his own life. [5]But reach out your hand and destroy his flesh and bones, and he will curse you to your face."

[6]The LORD said to Satan, "All right, then. Job is in your power, but you may not take his life."

[7]So Satan left the LORD's presence. He put painful sores on Job's body, from the top of his head to the soles of his feet. [8]Job took a piece of broken pottery to scrape himself, and he sat in ashes in misery.

[9]Job's wife said to him, "Why are you trying to stay innocent? Curse God and die!"

[10]Job answered, "You are talking like a foolish woman. Should we take only good things from God and not trouble?" In spite of all this Job did not sin in what he said.

Job 2:3–10

INSIGHTS

I have often heard my husband tell our teenagers, "Temptation is not only an opportunity to do the wrong thing, but an opportunity to do the right!" Although we usually consider temptation in negative terms, God allows us to be tempted in order to provide us with a chance to be obedient. If we are to learn to say no, and we are certainly supposed to say no sometimes to some things, then circumstances become life's workshop to that end. Saying no when you want to say yes strengthens you, produces endurance, and builds character—Christian character.

Jill Briscoe

APPLICATION

What did Paul mean when he said he made his body a slave? Why did he do that? What things does the example of the Israelites in the desert warn us against? How seriously do you take that warning?

THURSDAY

Everything We Do Should Honor God

1 Corinthians 10:23—11:22

How to Use Christian Freedom

We are allowed to do all things,"
but all things are not good for us to
do. "We are allowed to do all things,"
but not all things help others grow
stronger. 24 Do not look out only for
yourselves. Look out for the good of
others also.

25 Eat any meat that is sold in the
meat market. Do not ask questions
to see if it is meat you think is wrong
to eat. 26 You may eat it, "because the
earth belongs to the Lord, and everything in it."

27 Those who are not believers
may invite you to eat with them. If
you want to go, eat anything that is
put before you. Do not ask questions
to see if you think it might be wrong
to eat. 28 But if anyone says to you,
"That food was offered to idols," do
not eat it. Do not eat it because of
that person who told you and because eating it might be thought to
be wrong. 29 I don't mean you think
it is wrong, but the other person
might. But why, you ask, should my
freedom be judged by someone
else's conscience? 30 If I eat the meal
with thankfulness, why am I criticized because of something for
which I thank God?

31 The answer is, if you eat or
drink, or if you do anything, do it all
for the glory of God. 32 Never do anything that might hurt others—Jews,
Greeks, or God's church—33 just as
I, also, try to please everybody in every way. I am not trying to do what
is good for me but what is good for
most people so they can be saved.
11 Follow my example, as I follow
the example of Christ.

Being Under Authority

I praise you because you remember
me in everything, and you follow
closely the teachings just as I gave
them to you. 3 But I want you to understand this: The head of every
man is Christ, the head of a woman
is the man, and the head of Christ is
God. 4 Every man who prays or
prophesies with his head covered
brings shame to his head. 5 But every woman who prays or prophesies
with her head uncovered brings
shame to her head. She is the same
as a woman who has her head
shaved. 6 If a woman does not cover
her head, she should have her hair
cut off. But since it is shameful for a
woman to cut off her hair or to shave
her head, she should cover her head.
7 But a man should not cover his
head, because he is the likeness and
glory of God. But woman is man's
glory. 8 Man did not come from
woman, but woman came from man.
9 And man was not made for woman,
but woman was made for man. 10 So
that is why a woman should have a
symbol of authority on her head,
because of the angels.

11 But in the Lord women are not
independent of men, and men are
not independent of women. 12 This is
true because woman came from
man, but also man is born from
woman. But everything comes from
God. 13 Decide this for yourselves: Is
it right for a woman to pray to God

with her head uncovered? 14 Even
nature itself teaches you that wearing long hair is shameful for a man.
15 But long hair is a woman's glory.
Long hair is given to her as a covering. 16 Some people may still want to
argue about this, but I would add
that neither we nor the churches of
God have any other practice.

The Lord's Supper

In the things I tell you now I do not
praise you, because when you come
together you do more harm than
good. 18 First, I hear that when you
meet together as a church you are
divided, and I believe some of this.
19 (It is necessary to have differences
among you so that it may be clear
which of you really have God's ap-
proval.) 20 When you come together,
you are not really eating the Lord's
Supper. 21 This is because when you
eat, each person eats without waiting for the others. Some people do
not get enough to eat, while others
have too much to drink. 22 You can
eat and drink in your own homes!
You seem to think God's church is
not important, and you embarrass
those who are poor. What should I
tell you? Should I praise you? I do
not praise you for doing this.

OLD TESTAMENT READING

Eli's Sons Refuse to Honor God

Now Eli's sons were evil men; they
did not care about the Lord.

30 "So the Lord, the God of Israel,
says: 'I promised that your family
and your ancestor's family would
serve me always.' But now the Lord
says: 'This must stop! I will honor
those who honor me, but I will dishonor those who ignore me. 31 The
time is coming when I will destroy
the descendants of both you and
your ancestors. No man will grow
old in your family.'"

1 Samuel 2:12, 30–31

INSIGHTS

Everything created was through Christ and His power, and furthermore, it was created for His honor. That includes everyday things today. You have a good job? It's to be enjoyed for Him. You have a nice salary? It's to be enjoyed and invested for Him. You have good health? It is for Him. You have a family? The family members are for Him. You're planning a move? It's to be for Him. You're thinking about a career change? It needs to be for Him. That is true because He's the ruler of our kingdom. He is Lord. And that's not simply the title of a chorus Christians sing; it's a statement of faith. He has the right to take charge of our decisions so that He might be honored through them. Every day I live I must address that. Again, it is a matter of priorities. . . .

. . . Those who are really committed to excellence give Him top priority.

Charles Swindoll

APPLICATION

Think about Jesus' commandment to love God and to love one another. Notice how Paul's instructions fulfill his command. In what practical ways can you obey Christ's commandments and honor God in your daily life?

FRIDAY

The Holy Spirit Gives Gifts

1 Corinthians 11:23—12:13

The teaching I gave you is the same
teaching I received from the Lord:
On the night when the Lord Jesus
was handed over to be killed, he took
bread 24 and gave thanks for it. Then
he broke the bread and said, "This
is my body; it is for you. Do this to
remember me." 25 In the same way,
after they ate, Jesus took the cup. He
said, "This cup is the new agreement
that is sealed with the blood of my
death. When you drink this, do it to
remember me." 26 Every time you
eat this bread and drink this cup you
are telling others about the Lord's
death until he comes.

27 So a person who eats the bread
or drinks the cup of the Lord in a
way that is not worthy of it will be
guilty of sinning against the body
and the blood of the Lord. 28 Look
into your own hearts before you eat
the bread and drink the cup, 29 because all who eat the bread and
drink the cup without recognizing
the body eat and drink judgment
against themselves. 30 That is why
many in your group are sick and
weak, and many have died. 31 But if
we judged ourselves in the right way,
God would not judge us. 32 But when
the Lord judges us, he punishes us
so that we will not be destroyed
along with the world.

33 So my brothers and sisters,
when you come together to eat, wait
for each other. 34 Anyone who is too
hungry should eat at home so that
in meeting together you will not
bring God's judgment on yourselves.
I will tell you what to do about the
other things when I come.

Gifts from the Holy Spirit

12 Now, brothers and sisters, I
want you to understand about
spiritual gifts. 2 You know the way
you lived before you were believers.
You let yourselves be influenced and
led away to worship idols—things
that could not speak. 3 So I want you
to understand that no one who is
speaking with the help of God's
Spirit says, "Jesus be cursed." And
no one can say, "Jesus is Lord," without the help of the Holy Spirit.

4 There are different kinds of gifts,
but they are all from the same Spirit.
5 There are different ways to serve
but the same Lord to serve. 6 And
there are different ways that God
works through people but the same
God. God works in all of us in everything we do. 7 Something from the
Spirit can be seen in each person, for
the common good. 8 The Spirit gives
one person the ability to speak with
wisdom, and the same Spirit gives
another the ability to speak with
knowledge. 9 The same Spirit gives
faith to one person. And, to another,
that one Spirit gives gifts of healing.
10 The Spirit gives to another person
the power to do miracles, to another
the ability to prophesy. And he gives
to another the ability to know the difference between good and evil spirits. The Spirit gives one person the
ability to speak in different kinds of
languages and to another the ability
to interpret those languages. 11 One
Spirit, the same Spirit, does all these
things, and the Spirit decides what
to give each person.

The Body of Christ Works Together

A person's body is only one thing, but it has many parts. Though there are many parts to a body, all those parts make only one body. Christ is like that also. 13 Some of us are Jews, and some are Greeks. Some of us are slaves, and some are free. But we were all baptized into one body through one Spirit. And we were all made to share in the one Spirit.

OLD TESTAMENT READING

Gift of Speaking with Knowledge

Joshua son of Nun was then filled with wisdom, because Moses had put his hands on him. So the Israelites listened to Joshua, and they did what the LORD had commanded Moses.

Deuteronomy 34:9

Gift of Artistry

Then the LORD said to Moses,
2 "See, I have chosen Bezalel son of
Uri from the tribe of Judah. (Uri was
the son of Hur.) 3 I have filled
Bezalel with the Spirit of God and
have given him the skill, ability, and
knowledge to do all kinds of work.
4 He is able to design pieces to be
made from gold, silver, and bronze,
5 to cut jewels and put them in
metal, to carve wood, and to do all
kinds of work. 6 I have also chosen
Oholiab son of Ahisamach from the
tribe of Dan to work with Bezalel. I
have given skills to all the craftsmen, and they will be able to make
all these things I have commanded
you: 7 the Meeting Tent, the Ark of
the Agreement, the lid that covers
the Ark, and everything in the
Tent."

Exodus 31:1–7

INSIGHTS

It may take another Christian to pinpoint for us a particular talent we have. For instance, in the course of speaking at a meeting, I started, "I'm a one-talent person." . . . The meeting was scarcely over when a young woman dashed up to me and said, "That's not true what you said tonight. . . . I know about your writing and other things you do, but the best part is that you're good at sitting by the fire and being a friend."

It's evident, then, that we can be using a talent even when we do not recognize that we possess it. . . .

Perhaps we wish we could have had some choice as to which gift or ability would be ours. Maybe we would gladly trade ours off for something that has more appeal for us. But our all-wise God has apportioned His gifts as He wills, and one day He will require from each of us an accounting of our use of those gifts. . . .

If you and I really want to be used by our Lord, it will pay us to ferret out what our particular ability is, then get busy putting it to use.

Jeanette Lockerbie

PAUSE FOR REFLECTION

How are the gifts that the Spirit gives to different individuals intended to work together (1 Cor. 12:1–13)? What do the Scriptures reveal to you about the purpose of spiritual gifts?

WEEKEND

The Great Gift of Love

1 Corinthians 12:14—13:13

The human body has many parts. [15]The foot might say, “Because I am not a hand, I am not part of the body.” But saying this would not stop the foot from being a part of the body. [16]The ear might say, “Because I am not an eye, I am not part of the body.” But saying this would not stop the ear from being a part of the body. [17]If the whole body were an eye, it would not be able to hear. If the whole body were an ear, it would not be able to smell. [18-19]If each part of the body were the same part, there would be no body. But truly God put all the parts, each one of them, in the body as he wanted them. [20]So then there are many parts, but only one body.

[21]The eye cannot say to the hand, “I don’t need you!” And the head cannot say to the foot, “I don’t need you!” [22]No! Those parts of the body that seem to be the weaker are really necessary. [23]And the parts of the body we think are less are the parts to which we give the most honor. We give special respect to the parts we want to hide. [24]The more respectable parts of our body need no special care. But God put the body together and gave more honor to the parts that need it [25]so our body would not be divided. God wanted the different parts to care the same for each other. [26]If one part of the body suffers, all the other parts suffer with it. Or if one part of our body is honored, all the other parts share its honor.

[27]Together you are the body of Christ, and each one of you is a part of that body. [28]In the church God has given a place first to apostles, second to prophets, and third to teachers. Then God has given a place to those who do miracles, those who have gifts of healing, those who can help others, those who are able to govern, and those who can speak in different languages. [29]Not all are apostles. Not all are prophets. Not all are teachers. Not all do miracles. [30]Not all have gifts of healing. Not all speak in different languages. Not all interpret those languages. [31]But you should truly want to have the greater gifts.

Love Is the Greatest Gift

And now I will show you the best way of all.

13 I may speak in different languages of people or even angels. But if I do not have love, I am only a noisy bell or a crashing cymbal. [2]I may have the gift of prophecy. I may understand all the secret things of God and have all knowledge, and I may have faith so great I can move mountains. But even with all these things, if I do not have love, then I am nothing. [3]I may give away everything I have, and I may even give my body as an offering to be burned. But I gain nothing if I do not have love.

[4]Love is patient and kind. Love is not jealous, it does not brag, and it is not proud. [5]Love is not rude, is not selfish, and does not get upset with others. Love does not count up wrongs that have been done. [6]Love is not happy with evil but is happy with the truth. [7]Love patiently accepts all things. It always trusts, always hopes, and always remains strong.

8 Love never ends. There are gifts
of prophecy, but they will be ended.
There are gifts of speaking in different languages, but those gifts will
stop. There is the gift of knowledge,
but it will come to an end. 9 The reason is that our knowledge and our
ability to prophesy are not perfect.
10 But when perfection comes, the
things that are not perfect will end.
11 When I was a child, I talked like a
child, I thought like a child, I reasoned like a child. When I became a
man, I stopped those childish ways.
12 It is the same with us. Now we see
a dim reflection, as if we were looking into a mirror, but then we shall
see clearly. Now I know only a part,
but then I will know fully, as God has
known me. 13 So these three things
continue forever: faith, hope, and
love. And the greatest of these is love.

OLD TESTAMENT READING

Boaz Shows Love to Ruth

At mealtime Boaz told Ruth,
"Come here. Eat some of our bread
and dip it in our sauce."
So Ruth sat down beside the
workers. Boaz handed her some
roasted grain, and she ate until she
was full; she even had some food left
over. 15 When Ruth rose and went back
to work, Boaz commanded his workers, "Let her gather even around the
piles of cut grain. Don't tell her to go
away. 16 In fact, drop some full heads
of grain for her from what you have
in your hands, and let her gather
them. Don't tell her to stop."

Ruth 2:14–16

INSIGHTS

Jesus never wrote a book, yet the nature of his love was indelibly impressed upon the minds of his followers. They could never forget their three years experience with the Master. He was the Model. His very life clearly defined love for them. . . .

• Jesus was concerned about their families, homes, and health.

• Jesus was willing to take time for people in need even though he was engaged in a busy ministry.

• Jesus provided faithful support in the spiritual battle by intercessory prayer.

• Jesus extended complete forgiveness, even when it seemed undeserved.

• Jesus humbly served his followers, exemplified in his washing their feet.

• Jesus ultimately gave himself in his death on Calvary's cross.

In all of these acts of compassion, Jesus modeled a practical brand of love. His was a love that ministered to his disciples' pressing needs. Calvary, of course, tied it all together: The cross dealt finally with their sins and opened the way for them to experience all the blessings of God. . . .

So it is with us. If we are to love our brothers and sisters as Jesus commanded, we must learn to express a practical love for the whole person. It must be the kind of love our Master has shown to us.

William Fletcher

APPLICATION

What examples of Christian love that you have experienced stand out in your mind? What did those experiences teach you about love? What example of Jesus' love do you want to put into practice in your life?

MONDAY

Desire Spiritual Gifts that Strengthen the Church

1 Corinthians 14:1–25

Desire Spiritual Gifts

14 You should seek after love, and
you should truly want to have
the spiritual gifts, especially the gift
of prophecy. 2 I will explain why.
Those who have the gift of speaking
in different languages are not speaking to people; they are speaking to
God. No one understands them; they
are speaking secret things through
the Spirit. 3 But those who prophesy
are speaking to people to give them
strength, encouragement, and comfort. 4 The ones who speak in different languages are helping only themselves, but those who prophesy are
helping the whole church. 5 I wish all
of you had the gift of speaking in different kinds of languages, but more,
I wish you would prophesy. Those
who prophesy are greater than those
who can only speak in different languages—unless someone is there
who can explain what is said so that
the whole church can be helped.

6 Brothers and sisters, will it help
you if I come to you speaking in different languages? No! It will help you
only if I bring you a new truth or
some new knowledge, or prophecy,
or teaching. 7 It is the same as with
lifeless things that make sounds—
like a flute or a harp. If they do not
make clear musical notes, you will not
know what is being played. 8 And in a
war, if the trumpet does not give a
clear sound, who will prepare for
battle? 9 It is the same with you. Unless you speak clearly with your
tongue, no one can understand what
you are saying. You will be talking
into the air! 10 It may be true that
there are all kinds of sounds in the
world, and none is without meaning.
11 But unless I understand the meaning of what someone says to me, I
will be a foreigner to him, and he
will be a foreigner to me. 12 It is the
same with you. Since you want spiritual gifts very much, seek most of
all to have the gifts that help the
church grow stronger.

13 The one who has the gift of
speaking in a different language
should pray for the gift to interpret
what is spoken. 14 If I pray in a different language, my spirit is praying,
but my mind does nothing. 15 So
what should I do? I will pray with my
spirit, but I will also pray with my
mind. I will sing with my spirit, but
I will also sing with my mind. 16 If
you praise God with your spirit,
those persons there without understanding cannot say amen to your
prayer of thanks, because they do
not know what you are saying. 17 You
may be thanking God in a good way,
but the other person is not helped.

18 I thank God that I speak in different kinds of languages more than
all of you. 19 But in the church meetings I would rather speak five words
I understand in order to teach others than thousands of words in a different language.

20 Brothers and sisters, do not
think like children. In evil things be
like babies, but in your thinking you
should be like adults. 21 It is written
in the Scriptures:

"With people who use strange
words and foreign languages

I will speak to these people.
But even then they will not listen
to me," *Isaiah 28:11-12*
says the Lord.
[22] So the gift of speaking in different kinds of languages is a proof for those who do not believe, not for those who do believe. And prophecy is for people who believe, not for those who do not believe. [23] Suppose the whole church meets together and everyone speaks in different languages. If some people come in who do not understand or do not believe, they will say you are crazy. [24] But suppose everyone is prophesying and some people come in who do not believe or do not understand. If everyone is prophesying, their sin will be shown to them, and they will be judged by all that they hear. [25] The secret things in their hearts will be made known. So they will bow down and worship God saying, "Truly, God is with you."

OLD TESTAMENT READING

Josiah also broke down the altar at Bethel—the place of worship made by Jeroboam son of Nebat, who had led Israel to sin. Josiah burned that place, broke the stones of the altar into pieces, then beat them into dust. He also burned the Asherah idol. [16] When he turned around, he saw the graves on the mountain. He had the bones taken from the graves, and he burned them on the altar to ruin it. This happened as the LORD had said it would through the man of God.

2 Kings 23:15–16

INSIGHTS

The gifts of the Spirit . . . come to us from the Holy Spirit. He chooses who gets which gifts, and He dispenses them at His good pleasure. While we are held accountable for the use of any gifts He gives us, we have no responsibility for gifts we have not been given. Nor are we to covet what someone else has or be envious of that person. We may wish to have certain gifts and even ask for them, but if it is not the will of the Holy Spirit, we will not get what we ask for. And if we are dissatisfied because the Holy Spirit does not give us the gifts we want, we sin. . . .

Paul says that the purpose of these spiritual gifts is, "for the equipping of the saints for the work of service, to the building up of the body of Christ" (Eph. 4:12). In other words, God has given each of us a task to do, and supernatural gifts to equip us for it. . . .

In 1 Corinthians 12:7, the apostle Paul says the gifts are given "for the common good" so we are not to use them selfishly. Instead, we are to use them to help each other. . . .

God has also designed the gifts to help "unite" the body of Christ. . . .

Thus the gifts of the Spirit should never divide the body of Christ; they should unify it.

Billy Graham

APPLICATION

What is the purpose of spiritual gifts? What is the difference between prophesying and speaking in tongues? Why do you desire spiritual gifts? Pray that you will use your gift to God's glory.

TUESDAY

The Essentials of Christian Faith

1 Corinthians 14:26—15:11

Meetings Should Help the Church

So, brothers and sisters, what
should you do? When you meet together, one person has a song, and
another has a teaching. Another has
a new truth from God. Another
speaks in a different language, and
another person interprets that language. The purpose of all these
things should be to help the church
grow strong. 27 When you meet together, if anyone speaks in a different language, it should be only two,
or not more than three, who speak.
They should speak one after the
other, and someone else should interpret. 28 But if there is no inter-
preter, then those who speak in a
different language should be quiet
in the church meeting. They should
speak only to themselves and to
God.

29 Only two or three prophets
should speak, and the others should
judge what they say. 30 If a message
from God comes to another person
who is sitting, the first speaker
should stop. 31 You can all prophesy
one after the other. In this way all the
people can be taught and encouraged. 32 The spirits of prophets are
under the control of the prophets
themselves. 33 God is not a God of
confusion but a God of peace.

As is true in all the churches of
God's people, 34 women should keep
quiet in the church meetings. They
are not allowed to speak, but they
must yield to this rule as the law
says. 35 If they want to learn something, they should ask their own husbands at home. It is shameful for a
woman to speak in the church meeting. 36 Did God's teaching come from
you? Or are you the only ones to
whom it has come?

37 Those who think they are
prophets or spiritual persons should
understand that what I am writing to
you is the Lord's command. 38 Those
who ignore this will be ignored by
God.

39 So my brothers and sisters, you
should truly want to prophesy. But
do not stop people from using the
gift of speaking in different kinds of
languages. 40 But let everything be
done in a right and orderly way.

The Good News About Christ

15 Now, brothers and sisters, I
want you to remember the
Good News I brought to you. You received this Good News and continue
strong in it. 2 And you are being
saved by it if you continue believing
what I told you. If you do not, then
you believed for nothing.

3 I passed on to you what I received, of which this was most important: that Christ died for our sins,
as the Scriptures say; 4 that he was
buried and was raised to life on the
third day as the Scriptures say; 5 and
that he was seen by Peter and then
by the twelve apostles. 6 After that,
Jesus was seen by more than five
hundred of the believers at the same
time. Most of them are still living
today, but some have died. 7 Then he
was seen by James and later by all
the apostles. 8 Last of all he was seen
by me—as by a person not born at
the normal time. 9 All the other

apostles are greater than I am. I am
not even good enough to be called
an apostle, because I persecuted the
church of God. 10 But God's grace
has made me what I am, and his
grace to me was not wasted. I
worked harder than all the other
apostles. (But it was not I really; it
was God's grace that was with me.)
11 So if I preached to you or the other
apostles preached to you, we all
preach the same thing, and this is
what you believed.

OLD TESTAMENT READING

He was put to death;
he was punished for the sins of my people.
9 He was buried with wicked men,
and he died with the rich.

Isaiah 53:8c–9a

God has risen with a shout of joy;
the LORD has risen as the trumpets sounded.
6 Sing praises to God. Sing praises.
Sing praises to our King. Sing praises.
7 God is King of all the earth,
so sing a song of praise to him.
8 God is King over the nations.
God sits on his holy throne.

Psalm 47:5–8

INSIGHTS

In the guise of a man, Jesus the Christ, was born, lived, grew up, worked, was crucified, and rose from the grave among us, He ascended back to His splendor among us.

In all of this, though subject to the strains and stresses of our human society, he never sinned. His was a perfect performance. His was a life without a single stain. His was the "perfect doing" and "perfect dying" required to redeem all men for all time from all their wrongs and sins and stains. . . .

It was in my stead He did all this: He paid the penalty for all my wrongs. He bled and suffered and died for me. He took my sins to set me free. It was to satisfy His own righteousness that He became my substitute. He did this to impute to me His own wondrous righteousness.

This is a titanic transaction of eternal dimensions. God, very God, in Christ takes my sins and gives me His goodness . . . His own righteousness.

Nothing else can satisfy my searching spirit. I look away from myself to see the splendor of His supreme self-sacrifice for my salvation. I see that He has made me whole. He has enfolded and filled me with His righteousness. He has accepted me as His own son. He is my living Lord and Savior. He is my Father!

My spirit leaps for joy, where before it was sunk with sin and despair. His Spirit bears witness with my spirit that I am now His son. In overwhelming appreciation and gratitude, I look up and my spirit cries, "Abba Father!"

W. Phillip Keller

APPLICATION

What are the essential elements of the Christian faith? How fully was the Good News foretold in the Old Testament? Why must we continue believing the Good News? Pray that your faith will continue strong!

WEDNESDAY

God's People Will Be Raised to Life Again

1 Corinthians 15:12–44a

We Will Be Raised from the Dead

Now since we preached that Christ was raised from the dead, why do some of you say that people will not be raised from the dead? 13 If no one is ever raised from the dead, then Christ has not been raised. 14 And if Christ has not been raised, then our preaching is worth nothing, and your faith is worth nothing. 15 And also, we are guilty of lying about God, because we testified of him that he raised Christ from the dead. But if people are not raised from the dead, then God never raised Christ. 16 If the dead are not raised, Christ has not been raised either. 17 And if Christ has not been raised, then your faith has nothing to it; you are still guilty of your sins. 18 And those in Christ who have already died are lost. 19 If our hope in Christ is for this life only, we should be pitied more than anyone else in the world.

20 But Christ has truly been raised from the dead—the first one and proof that those who sleep in death will also be raised. 21 Death has come because of what one man did, but the rising from death also comes because of one man. 22 In Adam all of us die. In the same way, in Christ all of us will be made alive again. 23 But everyone will be raised to life in the right order. Christ was first to be raised. When Christ comes again, those who belong to him will be raised to life, 24 and then the end will come. At that time Christ will destroy all rulers, authorities, and powers, and he will hand over the kingdom to God the Father. 25 Christ must rule until he puts all enemies under his control. 26 The last enemy to be destroyed will be death. 27 The Scripture says that God put all things under his control. When it says "all things" are under him, it is clear this does not include God himself. God is the One who put everything under his control. 28 After everything has been put under the Son, then he will put himself under God, who had put all things under him. Then God will be the complete ruler over everything.

29 If the dead are never raised, what will people do who are being baptized for the dead? If the dead are not raised at all, why are people being baptized for them?

30 And what about us? Why do we put ourselves in danger every hour? 31 I die every day. That is true, brothers and sisters, just as it is true that I brag about you in Christ Jesus our Lord. 32 If I fought wild animals in Ephesus only with human hopes, I have gained nothing. If the dead are not raised, "Let us eat and drink, because tomorrow we will die."

33 Do not be fooled: "Bad friends will ruin good habits." 34 Come back to your right way of thinking and stop sinning. Some of you do not know God—I say this to shame you.

What Kind of Body Will We Have?

But someone may ask, "How are the dead raised? What kind of body will they have?" 36 Foolish person! When you sow a seed, it must die in the ground before it can live and

grow. 37 And when you sow it, it does
not have the same "body" it will have
later. What you sow is only a bare
seed, maybe wheat or something
else. 38 But God gives it a body that
he has planned for it, and God gives
each kind of seed its own body. 39 All
things made of flesh are not the same:
People have one kind of flesh, animals have another, birds have another, and fish have another. 40 Also
there are heavenly bodies and earthly
bodies. But the beauty of the heavenly bodies is one kind, and the
beauty of the earthly bodies is another. 41 The sun has one kind of
beauty, the moon has another beauty,
and the stars have another. And each
star is different in its beauty.

42 It is the same with the dead who
are raised to life. The body that is
"planted" will ruin and decay, but it is
raised to a life that cannot be destroyed. 43 When the body is "planted,"
it is without honor, but it is raised in
glory. When the body is "planted," it
is weak, but when it is raised, it is powerful. 44 The body that is "planted" is a
physical body. When it is raised, it is
a spiritual body.

OLD TESTAMENT READING

Many people who have already died
will live again. Some of them will
wake up to have life forever, but some
will wake up to find shame and disgrace forever. 3 The wise people will
shine like the brightness of the sky.
Those who teach others to live right
will shine like stars forever and ever."

Daniel 12:2–3

INSIGHTS

Often when we are racked with pain and unable to think or worship, we feel that this indeed is "the body of our humiliation," and when we are tempted by the passions which rise from the flesh we do not think the word "vile" at all too vigorous a translation. Our bodies humble us; and that is about the best thing they do for us. Oh, that we were duly lowly, because our bodies ally us with animals and even link us with the dust!

But our Savior, the Lord Jesus, shall change all this. We shall be fashioned like His own body of glory. This will take place in all who believe in Jesus. By faith their souls have been transformed, and their bodies will undergo such a renewal as shall fit them for their regenerated spirits. How soon this grand transformation will happen we cannot tell; but the thought of it should help us to bear the trials of today and all the woes of the flesh. In a little while we shall be as Jesus now is. No more aching brows, no more swollen limbs, no more dim eyes, no more fainting hearts. The old man shall be no more a bundle of infirmities, nor the sick man a mass of agony. "Like unto his glorious body" [Phil. 3:21]. What an expression! Even our flesh shall rest in hope of such a resurrection!

Charles Spurgeon

PAUSE FOR REFLECTION

What is the significance and what are the results of Christ's resurrection? What will all those who rise up in Christ be given? What about the resurrection gives you the greatest hope?

THURSDAY

Be Prepared for Opposition as You Serve God

1 Corinthians 15:44b—16:24

There is a physical body, and there is also a spiritual body. 45 It is written in the Scriptures: "The first man, Adam, became a living person." But the last Adam became a spirit that gives life. 46 The spiritual did not come first, but the physical and then the spiritual. 47 The first man came from the dust of the earth. The second man came from heaven. 48 People who belong to the earth are like the first man of earth. But those people who belong to heaven are like the man of heaven. 49 Just as we were made like the man of earth, so we will also be made like the man of heaven.

50 I tell you this, brothers and sisters: Flesh and blood cannot have a part in the kingdom of God. Something that will ruin cannot have a part in something that never ruins. 51 But look! I tell you this secret: We will not all sleep in death, but we will all be changed. 52 It will take only a second—as quickly as an eye blinks—when the last trumpet sounds. The trumpet will sound, and those who have died will be raised to live forever, and we will all be changed. 53 This body that can be destroyed must clothe itself with something that can never be destroyed. And this body that dies must clothe itself with something that can never die. 54 So this body that can be destroyed will clothe itself with that which can never be destroyed, and this body that dies will clothe itself with that which can never die. When this happens, this Scripture will be made true:

"Death is destroyed forever in
victory." *Isaiah 25:8*

55 "Death, where is your victory?
Death, where is your pain?"
Hosea 13:14

56 Death's power to hurt is sin, and the power of sin is the law. 57 But we thank God! He gives us the victory through our Lord Jesus Christ.

58 So my dear brothers and sisters, stand strong. Do not let anything change you. Always give yourselves fully to the work of the Lord, because you know that your work in the Lord is never wasted.

The Gift for Other Believers

16 Now I will write about the collection of money for God's people. Do the same thing I told the Galatian churches to do: 2 On the first day of every week, each one of you should put aside money as you have been blessed. Save it up so you will not have to collect money after I come. 3 When I arrive, I will send whomever you approve to take your gift to Jerusalem. I will send them with letters of introduction, 4 and if it seems good for me to go also, they will go along with me.

Paul's Plans

I plan to go through Macedonia, so I will come to you after I go through there. 6 Perhaps I will stay with you for a time or even all winter. Then you can help me on my trip, wherever I go. 7 I do not want to see you now just in passing. I hope to stay a longer time with you if the Lord allows it. 8 But I will stay at Ephesus until Pentecost, 9 because a good opportunity for a great and growing work has been

given to me now. And there are many
people working against me.
[10] If Timothy comes to you, see to
it that he has nothing to fear with you,
because he is working for the Lord
just as I am. [11] So none of you should
treat Timothy as unimportant, but
help him on his trip in peace so that
he can come back to me. I am expecting him to come with the brothers.
[12] Now about our brother Apollos:
I strongly encouraged him to visit
you with the other brothers. He did
not at all want to come now; he will
come when he has the opportunity.

Paul Ends His Letter

Be alert. Continue strong in the
faith. Have courage, and be strong.
[14] Do everything in love.
[15] You know that the family of
Stephanas were the first believers in
Southern Greece and that they have
given themselves to the service of
God's people. I ask you, brothers
and sisters, [16] to follow the leading
of people like these and anyone else
who works and serves with them.
[17] I am happy that Stephanas,
Fortunatus, and Achaicus have come.
You are not here, but they have filled
your place. [18] They have refreshed my
spirit and yours. You should recognize
the value of people like these.
[19] The churches in the country of
Asia send greetings to you. Aquila and
Priscilla greet you in the Lord, as does
the church that meets in their house.
[20] All the brothers and sisters here
send greetings. Give each other a holy
kiss when you meet.
[21] I, Paul, am writing this greeting
with my own hand.
[22] If anyone does not love the
Lord, let him be separated from
God—lost forever!
Come, O Lord!
[23] The grace of the Lord Jesus be
with you.
[24] My love be with all of you in
Christ Jesus.

OLD TESTAMENT READING

LORD, battle with those who
battle with me.
Fight against those who fight
against me.
[7] For no reason they spread out
their net to trap me;
for no reason they dug a pit for
me.

Psalm 35:1, 7

INSIGHTS

For many years as a struggling young Christian I was led to believe that if I was just good enough, and kind enough, and loving enough, the whole of the world would be bound to hug me to its heart. Unfortunately and unhappily one learns in time that simply is not so. It is one of the sobering shocks that comes to us as mature Christians.

If God, very God, who was all perfection, suffered such abuse at the hands of His adversaries when He was here among us as the Man Christ Jesus, how can we expect less? . . .

If in truth persecution does come to me because of my righteous character and commendable, Christlike conduct, it is proof positive that I am indeed God's person. . . .

W. Phillip Keller

APPLICATION

Why did Paul plan to stay in Ephesus? Do you gain or lose enthusiasm for the Lord's work when you face opposition?

FRIDAY

When Troubles Come, Trust in the God Who Comforts Us

2 Corinthians 1:1–17

Paul Answers His Accusers

1 From Paul, an apostle of Christ Jesus. I am an apostle because that is what God wanted. Also from Timothy our brother in Christ.

To the church of God in Corinth, and to all of God's people everywhere in Southern Greece:

2 Grace and peace to you from God our Father and the Lord Jesus Christ.

Paul Gives Thanks to God

Praise be to the God and Father of our Lord Jesus Christ. God is the Father who is full of mercy and all comfort. 4 He comforts us every time we have trouble, so when others have trouble, we can comfort them with the same comfort God gives us. 5 We share in the many sufferings of Christ. In the same way, much comfort comes to us through Christ. 6 If we have troubles, it is for your comfort and salvation, and if we have comfort, you also have comfort. This helps you to accept patiently the same sufferings we have. 7 Our hope for you is strong, knowing that you share in our sufferings and also in the comfort we receive.

8 Brothers and sisters, we want you to know about the trouble we suffered in Asia. We had great burdens there that were beyond our own strength. We even gave up hope of living. 9 Truly, in our own hearts we believed we would die. But this happened so we would not trust in ourselves but in God, who raises people from the dead. 10 God saved us from these great dangers of death, and he will continue to save us. We have put our hope in him, and he will save us again. 11 And you can help us with your prayers. Then many people will give thanks for us—that God blessed us because of their many prayers.

The Change in Paul's Plans

This is what we are proud of, and I can say it with a clear conscience: In everything we have done in the world, and especially with you, we have had an honest and sincere heart from God. We did this by God's grace, not by the kind of wisdom the world has. 13-14 We write to you only what you can read and understand. And I hope that as you have understood some things about us, you may come to know everything about us. Then you can be proud of us, as we will be proud of you on the day our Lord Jesus Christ comes again.

15 I was so sure of all this that I made plans to visit you first so you could be blessed twice. 16 I planned to visit you on my way to Macedonia and again on my way back. I wanted to get help from you for my trip to Judea. 17 Do you think that I made these plans without really meaning it? Or maybe you think I make plans as the world does, so that I say yes, yes and at the same time no, no.

OLD TESTAMENT READING

God, be merciful to me because
people are chasing me;

the battle has pressed me all
day long.
2 My enemies have chased me all
day;
there are many proud people
fighting me.
3 When I am afraid,
I will trust you.
4 I praise God for his word.
I trust God, so I am not afraid.
What can human beings do to
me?

Psalm 56:1–4

LORD, your love fills the earth.
Teach me your demands.
65 You have done good things for
your servant,
as you have promised, LORD.
66 Teach me wisdom and knowledge
because I trust your commands.
67 Before I suffered, I did wrong,
but now I obey your word.
68 You are good, and you do what is
good.
Teach me your demands.
76 Comfort me with your love,
as you promised me, your
servant.
77 Have mercy on me so that I may
live.
I love your teachings.

Psalm 119:64–68, 76–77

INSIGHTS

It has been well said that "earthly cares are a heavenly discipline." But they are even something better than discipline,—they are God's chariots, sent to take the soul to its high places of triumph. . . .

Everything that comes to us becomes a chariot the moment we treat it as such; and on the other hand, even the smallest trials may be a Juggernaut car to crush us into misery or despair if we so consider them. It lies with each of us to choose which they shall be. . . .

Look upon your chastenings then, no matter how grievous they may be for the present, as God's chariots sent to carry your souls into the "high places" of spiritual achievement and uplifting, and you will find that they are, after all, "paved with love."

The Bible tells us that when God went forth for the salvation of His people, then He "did ride upon His horses and chariots of salvation." And it is the same now. Everything becomes a "chariot of salvation" when God rides upon it. He maketh even the "clouds his chariot," we are told, and "rideth on the wings of the wind." Therefore the clouds and storms that darken our skies and seem to shut out the shining of the sun of righteousness are really only God's chariots, into which we may mount with Him, and "ride prosperously" over all the darkness.

Hannah Whitall Smith

ACTION POINT

How well acquainted are you with the God Paul describes in 2 Corinthians 1:3? The next time you are ready to give up hope, why not trust the God of comfort to turn your troubles into triumphs of his making?

WEEKEND

The Healing Power of Forgiveness

2 Corinthians 1:18—3:3

But if you can believe God, you can
believe that what we tell you is never
both yes and no. 19 The Son of God,
Jesus Christ, that Silas and Timothy
and I preached to you, was not yes
and no. In Christ it has always been
yes. 20 The yes to all of God's promises is in Christ, and through Christ
we say yes to the glory of God. 21 Remember, God is the One who makes
you and us strong in Christ. God
made us his chosen people. 22 He put
his mark on us to show that we are
his, and he put his Spirit in our
hearts to be a guarantee for all he
has promised.

23 I tell you this, and I ask God to
be my witness that this is true: The
reason I did not come back to
Corinth was to keep you from being
punished or hurt. 24 We are not trying to control your faith. You are
strong in faith. But we are workers
with you for your own joy.

2 So I decided that my next visit
to you would not be another one
to make you sad. 2 If I make you sad,
who will make me glad? Only you
can make me glad—particularly the
person whom I made sad. 3 I wrote
you a letter for this reason: that
when I came to you I would not be
made sad by the people who should
make me happy. I felt sure of all of
you, that you would share my joy.
4 When I wrote to you before, I was
very troubled and unhappy in my
heart, and I wrote with many tears.
I did not write to make you sad, but
to let you know how much I love you.

Forgive the Sinner

Someone there among you has
caused sadness, not to me, but to all
of you. I mean he caused sadness to
all in some way. (I do not want to
make it sound worse than it really
is.) 6 The punishment that most of
you gave him is enough for him.
7 But now you should forgive him
and comfort him to keep him from
having too much sadness and giving
up completely. 8 So I beg you to show
that you love him. 9 I wrote you to
test you and to see if you obey in everything. 10 If you forgive someone,
I also forgive him. And what I have
forgiven—if I had anything to forgive—I forgave it for you, as if Christ
were with me. 11 I did this so that
Satan would not win anything from
us, because we know very well what
Satan's plans are.

Paul's Concern in Troas

When I came to Troas to preach
the Good News of Christ, the Lord
gave me a good opportunity there.
13 But I had no peace, because I did
not find my brother Titus. So I said
good-bye to them at Troas and went
to Macedonia.

Victory Through Christ

But thanks be to God, who always
leads us in victory through Christ.
God uses us to spread his knowledge everywhere like a sweet-smelling perfume. 15 Our offering to God
is this: We are the sweet smell of
Christ among those who are being

saved and among those who are being lost. 16 To those who are lost, we
are the smell of death that brings
death, but to those who are being
saved, we are the smell of life that
brings life. So who is able to do this
work? 17 We do not sell the word of
God for a profit as many other people
do. But in Christ we speak the truth
before God, as messengers of God.

Servants of the New Agreement

3 Are we starting to brag about
ourselves again? Do we need letters of introduction to you or from
you, like some other people? 2 You
yourselves are our letter, written on
our hearts, known and read by everyone. 3 You show that you are a letter from Christ sent through us. This
letter is not written with ink but with
the Spirit of the living God. It is not
written on stone tablets but on human hearts.

OLD TESTAMENT READING

So they sent a message to Joseph
that said, "Your father gave this command before he died. 17 He said to us,
'You have done wrong and have
sinned and done evil to Joseph. Tell
Joseph to forgive you, his brothers.'
So now, Joseph, we beg you to forgive our wrong. We are the servants
of the God of your father." When
Joseph received the message, he
cried.
19 Then Joseph said to them,
"Don't be afraid. Can I do what only
God can do? 20 You meant to hurt me,
but God turned your evil into good
to save the lives of many people,
which is being done. 21 So don't be
afraid. I will take care of you and
your children." So Joseph comforted
his brothers and spoke kind words
to them.

Genesis 50:16–17, 19–21

INSIGHTS

Forgiveness of sins is a great all-embracing gift of God. In His mercy, God sets the sinner free and receives him back into His love and favor. When we are forgiven, we have confidence toward God in prayer. We can be thankful every day of our lives because we are free and nothing stands between us and God. With the door open to communion with Him, God desires that we spend time with Him in His Word each day as people whose sins are forgiven. We need to live in the light of His countenance daily.

And God desires that this assurance affect our relationship with others. Those who are forgiven are free to forgive others. If it is difficult to forgive, we should consider how freely God has forgiven us of every offense toward Him. . . .

Remember these words daily: "As I need God's forgiveness each day, so let me be ready each day to forgive my brother." God grant you grace to do it!

Andrew Murray

APPLICATION

What healing has God's forgiveness accomplished in your life? What are the consequences when God's people don't forgive one another? Who do you need to forgive? Pray that you will always follow God's merciful example in forgiving others.

MONDAY

God's Spirit Brings Glory and Understanding to Those Who Believe

2 Corinthians 3:4—4:15

We can say this, because through
Christ we feel certain before God.
5 We are not saying that we can do
this work ourselves. It is God who
makes us able to do all that we do.
6 He made us able to be servants of
a new agreement from himself to
his people. This new agreement is
not a written law, but it is of the
Spirit. The written law brings death,
but the Spirit gives life.

7 The law that brought death was
written in words on stone. It came
with God's glory, which made
Moses' face so bright that the Israelites could not continue to look at
it. But that glory later disappeared.
8 So surely the new way that brings
the Spirit has even more glory. 9 If
the law that judged people guilty of
sin had glory, surely the new way
that makes people right with God
has much greater glory. 10 That old
law had glory, but it really loses its
glory when it is compared to the
much greater glory of this new way.
11 If that law which disappeared came
with glory, then this new way which
continues forever has much greater
glory.

12 We have this hope, so we are
very bold. 13 We are not like Moses,
who put a covering over his face so
the Israelites would not see it. The
glory was disappearing, and Moses
did not want them to see it end. 14 But
their minds were closed, and even
today that same covering hides the
meaning when they read the old
agreement. That covering is taken
away only through Christ. 15 Even
today, when they read the law of
Moses, there is a covering over their
minds. 16 But when a person changes
and follows the Lord, that covering
is taken away. 17 The Lord is the
Spirit, and where the Spirit of the
Lord is, there is freedom. 18 Our
faces, then, are not covered. We all
show the Lord's glory, and we are
being changed to be like him. This
change in us brings ever greater
glory, which comes from the Lord,
who is the Spirit.

Preaching the Good News

4 God, with his mercy, gave us this
work to do, so we don't give up.
2 But we have turned away from secret and shameful ways. We use no
trickery, and we do not change the
teaching of God. We teach the truth
plainly, showing everyone who we
are. Then they can know in their
hearts what kind of people we are in
God's sight. 3 If the Good News that
we preach is hidden, it is hidden only
to those who are lost. 4 The devil who
rules this world has blinded the
minds of those who do not believe.
They cannot see the light of the
Good News—the Good News about
the glory of Christ, who is exactly
like God. 5 We do not preach about
ourselves, but we preach that Jesus
Christ is Lord and that we are your
servants for Jesus. 6 God once said,
"Let the light shine out of the darkness!" This is the same God who
made his light shine in our hearts by
letting us know the glory of God that
is in the face of Christ.

Spiritual Treasure in Clay Jars

We have this treasure from God,
but we are like clay jars that hold the
treasure. This shows that the great
power is from God, not from us. 8 We
have troubles all around us, but we
are not defeated. We do not know
what to do, but we do not give up the
hope of living. 9 We are persecuted,
but God does not leave us. We are
hurt sometimes, but we are not destroyed. 10 We carry the death of Jesus
in our own bodies so that the life of
Jesus can also be seen in our bodies. 11 We are alive, but for Jesus we
are always in danger of death so that
the life of Jesus can be seen in our
bodies that die. 12 So death is working in us, but life is working in you.
13 It is written in the Scriptures, "I
believed, so I spoke." Our faith is like
this, too. We believe, and so we
speak. 14 God raised the Lord Jesus
from the dead, and we know that
God will also raise us with Jesus.
God will bring us together with you,
and we will stand before him. 15 All
these things are for you. And so the
grace of God that is being given to
more and more people will bring increasing thanks to God for his glory.

OLD TESTAMENT READING

Those who fight against the light
do not know God's ways
or stay in his paths.

23 "God may let these evil people
feel safe,
but he is watching their ways.
24 For a little while they are important, and then they die;
they are laid low and buried
like everyone else;
they are cut off like the heads
of grain."

Job 24:13, 23–24

INSIGHTS

Glory, I've learned, is what God is all about. His essential being. Whenever you talk about His character or attributes—like holiness, love, compassion, justice, truth, or mercy—that's God's glory. . . .

So how is it that you and I can glorify God? It happens every time we reveal His attributes in the course of our daily lives. Every time you share the good news of Christ with another. Every time you reflect patience in the middle of an upsetting or perplexing problem. Every time you smile from the heart or offer an encouraging word. Whenever those around you see God's character displayed in your attitudes and responses, you are displaying His glory.

. . . God's glory isn't reserved for a temple of stone or some heavenly vista. It can shine out clearly while you're changing a flat on the freeway . . . or counseling an angry co-worker . . . or lying in a hospital bed . . . or balancing two crying babies in the church nursery.

Joni Eareckson Tada

APPLICATION

How is God's glory shown through believers different from that shown by Moses? How has God's Spirit opened up your mind? How is God's glory shining in your life?

TUESDAY

The Righteous Will Receive Eternal Glory

2 Corinthians 4:16—6:2

Living by Faith

So we do not give up. Our physical
body is becoming older and weaker,
but our spirit inside us is made new
every day. 17 We have small troubles
for a while now, but they are helping us gain an eternal glory that is
much greater than the troubles.
18 We set our eyes not on what we see
but on what we cannot see. What we
see will last only a short time, but
what we cannot see will last forever.
5 We know that our body—the
tent we live in here on earth—
will be destroyed. But when that happens, God will have a house for us.
It will not be a house made by human hands; instead, it will be a home
in heaven that will last forever. 2 But
now we groan in this tent. We want
God to give us our heavenly home,
3 because it will clothe us so we will
not be naked. 4 While we live in this
body, we have burdens, and we
groan. We do not want to be naked,
but we want to be clothed with our
heavenly home. Then this body that
dies will be fully covered with life.
5 This is what God made us for, and
he has given us the Spirit to be a
guarantee for this new life.

6 So we always have courage. We
know that while we live in this body,
we are away from the Lord. 7 We live
by what we believe, not by what we
can see. 8 So I say that we have courage. We really want to be away from
this body and be at home with the
Lord. 9 Our only goal is to please God
whether we live here or there, 10 because we must all stand before
Christ to be judged. Each of us will
receive what we should get—good
or bad—for the things we did in the
earthly body.

Becoming Friends with God

Since we know what it means to
fear the Lord, we try to help people
accept the truth about us. God
knows what we really are, and I hope
that in your hearts you know, too.
12 We are not trying to prove ourselves to you again, but we are telling you about ourselves so you will
be proud of us. Then you will have
an answer for those who are proud
about things that can be seen rather
than what is in the heart. 13 If we are
out of our minds, it is for God. If we
have our right minds, it is for you.
14 The love of Christ controls us, because we know that One died for all,
so all have died. 15 Christ died for all
so that those who live would not continue to live for themselves. He died
for them and was raised from the
dead so that they would live for him.

16 From this time on we do not
think of anyone as the world does.
In the past we thought of Christ as
the world thinks, but we no longer
think of him in that way. 17 If anyone
belongs to Christ, there is a new creation. The old things have gone; everything is made new! 18 All this is
from God. Through Christ, God
made peace between us and himself,
and God gave us the work of telling
everyone about the peace we can
have with him. 19 God was in Christ,
making peace between the world

and himself. In Christ, God did not hold the world guilty of its sins. And he gave us this message of peace.
[20] So we have been sent to speak for Christ. It is as if God is calling to you through us. We speak for Christ when we beg you to be at peace with God. [21] Christ had no sin, but God made him become sin so that in Christ we could become right with God.

6 We are workers together with God, so we beg you: Do not let the grace that you received from God be for nothing. [2] God says,

"At the right time I heard your
 prayers.
On the day of salvation I
 helped you." *Isaiah 49:8*

I tell you that the "right time" is now, and the "day of salvation" is now.

OLD TESTAMENT READING

Who may go up on the mountain of the LORD?
 Who may stand in his holy
  Temple?
[4] Only those with clean hands and
  pure hearts,
 who have not worshiped idols,
 who have not made promises
  in the name of a false god.
[5] They will receive a blessing from
  the LORD;
 the God who saves them will
  declare them right.
[6] They try to follow God;
 they look to the God of Jacob
  for help. *Selah*

Psalm 24:3–6

INSIGHTS

Man's place in creation was very remarkable. The Psalmist says, "For thou hast made him a little lower than the angels, and hast crowned him with glory and honor. Thou madest him to have dominion over the works of thy hands; thou hast put all things under his feet: all sheep and oxen, yea, and the beasts of the field; the fowl of the air, and the fish of the sea, and whatsoever passeth through the paths of the seas." . . .

What a man will become we can scarcely tell when he is remade in the image of God, and made like unto our divine Lord who is "the firstborn among many brethren." Our bodies are to be developed into something infinitely brighter and better than the bodies of men here below: and as for the soul, we cannot guess to what an elevation it shall be raised in Christ Jesus. There is room for the largest expectation here, as we conjecture what will be the full accomplishment of the vast intent of eternal love, an intent which has involved the sacrifice of the only-begotten Son of God. That can be no mean design which has been carried on at the expense of the best that heaven itself possessed.

Charles Spurgeon

ACTION POINT

Stop now and focus your eyes on what you cannot yet see. Imagine yourself standing in God's temple with clean hands and a pure heart. Imagine God as your glory and light forever. Praise him for his eternal glory that is to come!

WEDNESDAY

The Importance of Living a Pure Life

2 Corinthians 6:3—7:7

We do not want anyone to find fault
with our work, so nothing we do will
be a problem for anyone. 4 But in every way we show we are servants of
God: in accepting many hard things,
in troubles, in difficulties, and in
great problems. 5 We are beaten and
thrown into prison. We meet those
who become upset with us and start
riots. We work hard, and sometimes
we get no sleep or food. 6 We show
we are servants of God by our pure
lives, our understanding, patience,
and kindness, by the Holy Spirit, by
true love, 7 by speaking the truth,
and by God's power. We use our
right living to defend ourselves
against everything. 8 Some people
honor us, but others blame us. Some
people say evil things about us, but
others say good things. Some people
say we are liars, but we speak the
truth. 9 We are not known, but we are
well known. We seem to be dying,
but we continue to live. We are punished, but we are not killed. 10 We
have much sadness, but we are always rejoicing. We are poor, but we
are making many people rich in
faith. We have nothing, but really we
have everything.

11 We have spoken freely to you
in Corinth and have opened our
hearts to you. 12 Our feelings of love
for you have not stopped, but you
have stopped your feelings of love
for us. 13 I speak to you as if you
were my children. Do to us as we
have done—open your hearts to us.

Warning About Non-Christians

You are not the same as those who
do not believe. So do not join yourselves to them. Good and bad do not
belong together. Light and darkness
cannot share together. 15 How can
Christ and Belial, the devil, have any
agreement? What can a believer
have together with a nonbeliever?
16 The temple of God cannot have
any agreement with idols, and we
are the temple of the living God. As
God said: "I will live with them and
walk with them. And I will be their
God, and they will be my people."

17 "Leave those people,
and be separate, says the Lord.
Touch nothing that is unclean,
and I will accept you."

Isaiah 52:11; Ezekiel 20:34, 41

18 "I will be your father,
and you will be my sons and
daughters,
says the Lord Almighty."

2 Samuel 7:14; 7:8

7 Dear friends, we have these
promises from God, so we
should make ourselves pure—free
from anything that makes body or
soul unclean. We should try to become holy in the way we live, because we respect God.

Paul's Joy

Open your hearts to us. We have
not done wrong to anyone, we have
not ruined the faith of anyone, and
we have not cheated anyone. 3 I do
not say this to blame you. I told you
before that we love you so much we
would live or die with you. 4 I feel

very sure of you and am very proud of you. You give me much comfort, and in all of our troubles I have great joy.

[5] When we came into Macedonia, we had no rest. We found trouble all around us. We had fighting on the outside and fear on the inside. [6] But God, who comforts those who are troubled, comforted us when Titus came. [7] We were comforted, not only by his coming but also by the comfort you gave him. Titus told us about your wish to see me and that you are very sorry for what you did. He also told me about your great care for me, and when I heard this, I was much happier.

OLD TESTAMENT READING

Don't follow the ways of the
wicked;
don't do what evil people do.
[15] Avoid their ways, and don't follow
them.
Stay away from them and keep
on going.

Proverbs 4:14–15

INSIGHTS

Someone has said, "a belief is what you hold; a conviction is what holds you." A conviction is not truly a conviction unless it includes a commitment to live by what we claim to believe. A commitment is not a vow but a resolution—a determined purpose to live by God's word as he applies it to our lives. First, we need a commitment to holiness as a total way of life. We must decide that holiness is so important to God that it deserves priority attention in our lives. We must commit ourselves to obeying God in all of his commands. We cannot pick and choose according to our own values. A little bit of fudging on one's income tax return is sin just as much as outright theft; an unforgiving spirit toward someone else is sin just as much as murder. I am not suggesting that all sin is equally offensive to God; I am saying that all sin is offensive to God. The measure of sin is not just in its effect upon our neighbor, but in its affront to the majesty and holiness of a sovereign God.

Sin is serious to God, and it becomes serious business to us when we reflect upon the fact that every sin, regardless of how seemingly insignificant it appears to us, is an expression of contempt toward the sovereign authority of God. . . .

The psalmist recognized the seriousness of any and all sin when he said, "You have laid down precepts that are to be fully obeyed" (Psalm 119:4). He recognized that partial obedience—for example, refraining from outright theft of our neighbor's property while allowing our heart to covet it—is actually disobedience. God's precepts are to be fully obeyed.

Jerry Bridges

APPLICATION

List the lifestyle traits that are to characterize those who serve God. Why is purity so important to God? Why must God's people seek purity? What is the way to live a pure life? Is your desire for purity a belief or a conviction?

THURSDAY

Godly Sorrow Leads Us to Repentance

2 Corinthians 7:8—8:15

Even if my letter made you sad, I
am not sorry I wrote it. At first I was
sorry, because it made you sad, but
you were sad only for a short time.
9 Now I am happy, not because you
were made sad, but because your
sorrow made you change your lives.
You became sad in the way God
wanted you to, so you were not hurt
by us in any way. 10 The kind of sorrow God wants makes people
change their hearts and lives. This
leads to salvation, and you cannot be
sorry for that. But the kind of sorrow the world has brings death.
11 See what this sorrow—the sorrow
God wanted you to have—has done
to you: It has made you very serious.
It made you want to prove you were
not wrong. It made you angry and
afraid. It made you want to see me.
It made you care. It made you want
the right thing to be done. You
proved you were innocent in the
problem. 12 I wrote that letter, not
because of the one who did the
wrong or because of the person who
was hurt. I wrote the letter so you
could see, before God, the great care
you have for us. 13 That is why we
were comforted.

Not only were we very comforted, we were even happier to see
that Titus was so happy. All of you
made him feel much better. 14 I
bragged to Titus about you, and you
showed that I was right. Everything
we said to you was true, and you
have proved that what we bragged
about to Titus is true. 15 And his love
for you is stronger when he remembers that you were all ready to obey.
You welcomed him with respect and
fear. 16 I am very happy that I can
trust you fully.

Christian Giving

8 And now, brothers and sisters,
we want you to know about the
grace God gave the churches in
Macedonia. 2 They have been tested
by great troubles, and they are very
poor. But they gave much because
of their great joy. 3 I can tell you that
they gave as much as they were able
and even more than they could afford. No one told them to do it. 4 But
they begged and pleaded with us to
let them share in this service for
God's people. 5 And they gave in a
way we did not expect: They first
gave themselves to the Lord and to
us. This is what God wants. 6 So we
asked Titus to help you finish this
special work of grace since he is the
one who started it. 7 You are rich in
everything—in faith, in speaking, in
knowledge, in truly wanting to help,
and in the love you learned from us.
In the same way, be strong also in
the grace of giving.

8 I am not commanding you to
give. But I want to see if your love is
true by comparing you with others
that really want to help. 9 You know
the grace of our Lord Jesus Christ.
You know that Christ was rich, but
for you he became poor so that by
his becoming poor you might become rich.

10 This is what I think you should
do: Last year you were the first to
want to give, and you were the first

who gave. 11 So now finish the work
you started. Then your "doing" will
be equal to your "wanting to do."
Give from what you have. 12 If you
want to give, your gift will be accepted. It will be judged by what you
have, not by what you do not have.
13 We do not want you to have
troubles while other people are at
ease, but we want everything to be
equal. 14 At this time you have plenty.
What you have can help others who
are in need. Then later, when they
have plenty, they can help you when
you are in need, and all will be equal.
15 As it is written in the Scriptures,
"The person who gathered more did
not have too much, nor did the person who gathered less have too
little."

OLD TESTAMENT READING

As Ezra was praying and confessing and crying and throwing himself
down in front of the Temple, a large
group of Israelite men, women, and
children gathered around him who
were also crying loudly. 2 Then
Shecaniah son of Jehiel the Elamite
said to Ezra, "We have been unfaithful to our God by marrying women
from the peoples around us. But
even so, there is still hope for Israel.
3 Now let us make an agreement before our God. We will send away all
these women and their children as
you and those who respect the commands of our God advise."

Ezra 10:1–3b

INSIGHTS

Repentance is simply and precisely a change of mind. The original term denotes, a thinking again—a turning of the mind—as when one finds himself going wrong and turns about to pursue the opposite course. The term, when applied to evangelical repentance, means not merely a turning of the mind, but a change of the entire purposes of action, change in the entire attitude of the will. . . .

Conviction of sin as a wrong committed against God is implied in repentance. Without this there can be no rational repentance.

The sinner must become truly honest with God. He must honestly admit the truths affirmed by his reason and pressed on his soul by his conscience. Especially must he recognize God's rights: that he himself is God's property and belongs truly to God. . . .

Repentance implies a universal reformation of life, a reformation extending to all forms of sin. Penitent men turn from all sin as sin, because they regard it as sin, and therefore can have no sympathy with it. All known sin therefore they at once abandon. . . .

When I speak of abandoning sin, I do not imply that the penitent man never for even a moment relapses into it; but I imply that he sets himself against it in real honest earnestness.

Charles Finney

APPLICATION

What is the difference between godly sorrow and the world's sorrow? What feelings and actions does godly sorrow bring about? Pray that you will always respond appropriately to godly sorrow!

FRIDAY

God Encourages Us to Share Liberally with Others

2 Corinthians 8:16—9:15

Titus and His Companions Help

I thank God because he gave Titus the same love for you that I have. 17 Titus accepted what we asked him to do. He wanted very much to go to you, and this was his own idea. 18 We are sending with him the brother who is praised by all the churches because of his service in preaching the Good News. 19 Also, this brother was chosen by the churches to go with us when we deliver this gift of money. We are doing this service to bring glory to the Lord and to show that we really want to help.

20 We are being careful so that no one will criticize us for the way we are handling this large gift. 21 We are trying hard to do what the Lord accepts as right and also what people think is right.

22 Also, we are sending with them our brother, who is always ready to help. He has proved this to us in many ways, and he wants to help even more now, because he has much faith in you.

23 Now about Titus—he is my partner who is working with me to help you. And about the other brothers—they are sent from the churches, and they bring glory to Christ. 24 So show these men the proof of your love and the reason we are proud of you. Then all the churches can see it.

Help for Fellow Christians

9 I really do not need to write you about this help for God's people. 2 I know you want to help. I have been bragging about this to the people in Macedonia, telling them that you in Southern Greece have been ready to give since last year. And your desire to give has made most of them ready to give also. 3 But I am sending the brothers to you so that our bragging about you in this will not be empty words. I want you to be ready, as I said you would be. 4 If any of the people from Macedonia come with me and find that you are not ready, we will be ashamed that we were so sure of you. (And you will be ashamed, too!) 5 So I thought I should ask these brothers to go to you before we do. They will finish getting in order the generous gift you promised so it will be ready when we come. And it will be a generous gift—not one that you did not want to give.

6 Remember this: The person who plants a little will have a small harvest, but the person who plants a lot will have a big harvest. 7 Each one should give as you have decided in your heart to give. You should not be sad when you give, and you should not give because you feel forced to give. God loves the person who gives happily. 8 And God can give you more blessings than you need. Then you will always have plenty of everything—enough to give to every good work. 9 It is written in the Scriptures:

"He gives freely to the poor.
The things he does are right
and will continue forever."

Psalm 112:9

[10] God is the One who gives seed to
the farmer and bread for food. He
will give you all the seed you need
and make it grow so there will be a
great harvest from your goodness.
[11] He will make you rich in every way
so that you can always give freely.
And your giving through us will
cause many to give thanks to God.
[12] This service you do not only helps
the needs of God's people, it also
brings many more thanks to God.
[13] It is a proof of your faith. Many
people will praise God because you
obey the Good News of Christ—the
gospel you say you believe—and because you freely share with them
and with all others. [14] And when they
pray, they will wish they could be
with you because of the great grace
that God has given you. [15] Thanks be
to God for his gift that is too wonderful for words.

OLD TESTAMENT READING

Whoever gives to the poor will
have everything he needs,
but the one who ignores the
poor will receive many
curses.

Proverbs 28:27

Lazy people's desire for sleep
will kill them,
because they refuse to work.
[26] All day long they wish for more,
but good people give without
holding back.

Proverbs 21:25–26

INSIGHTS

We all know how subtle the materialistic temptations are and how convincing the rationalizations. Only by God's grace and with great effort can we escape the shower of luxuries which has almost suffocated our Christian compassion. All of us face this problem. Some years ago I spent about fifty dollars on an extra suit. That's not much of course. Besides, I persuaded myself, it was a wise investment (thanks to the 75 percent discount). But that money would have fed a starving child in India for about a year. In all honesty we have to ask ourselves: Dare we care at all about current fashions if that means reducing our ability to help hungry neighbors? Dare we care more about obtaining a secure economic future for our family than for living an uncompromisingly Christian lifestyle? . . .

. . . We have been brainwashed to believe that bigger houses, more prosperous businesses, more luxurious gadgets, are worthy goals in life. As a result, we are caught in an absurd, materialistic spiral. The more we make, the more we think we need in order to live decently and respectably. Somehow we have to break this cycle because it makes us sin against our needy brothers and sisters and, therefore, against our Lord. And it also destroys us. Sharing with others is the way to real joy.

Ronald Sider

APPLICATION

List what God promises those who give generously. What do you think it means to be made "rich in every way so that you can always give freely"? Is your giving such that it brings praise to God from others?

WEEKEND

Our Spiritual Weapons Are Empowered by God

2 Corinthians 10:1—11:4

Paul Defends His Ministry

10 I, Paul, am begging you with
the gentleness and the kindness of Christ. Some people say that
I am easy on you when I am with you
and bold when I am away. 2They
think we live in a worldly way, and I
plan to be very bold with them when
I come. I beg you that when I come
I will not need to use that same boldness with you. 3We do live in the
world, but we do not fight in the
same way the world fights. 4We fight
with weapons that are different from
those the world uses. Our weapons
have power from God that can destroy the enemy's strong places. We
destroy people's arguments 5and
every proud thing that raises itself
against the knowledge of God. We
capture every thought and make it
give up and obey Christ. 6We are
ready to punish anyone there who
does not obey, but first we want you
to obey fully.

7You must look at the facts before
you. If you feel sure that you belong
to Christ, you must remember that
we belong to Christ just as you do.
8It is true that we brag freely about
the authority the Lord gave us. But
this authority is to build you up, not
to tear you down. So I will not be
ashamed. 9I do not want you to think
I am trying to scare you with my letters. 10Some people say, "Paul's
letters are powerful and sound important, but when he is with us, he
is weak. And his speaking is nothing." 11They should know this: We
are not there with you now, so we
say these things in letters. But when
we are there with you, we will show
the same authority that we show in
our letters.

12We do not dare to compare ourselves with those who think they are
very important. They use themselves to measure themselves, and
they judge themselves by what they
themselves are. This shows that they
know nothing. 13But we will not brag
about things outside the work that
was given us to do. We will limit our
bragging to the work that God gave
us, and this includes our work with
you. 14We are not bragging too
much, as we would be if we had not
already come to you. But we have
come to you with the Good News of
Christ. 15We limit our bragging to
the work that is ours, not what others have done. We hope that as your
faith continues to grow, you will help
our work to grow much larger. 16We
want to tell the Good News in the
areas beyond your city. We do not
want to brag about work that has already been done in another person's
area. 17But, "If someone wants to
brag, he should brag only about the
Lord." 18It is not those who say they
are good who are accepted but those
who the Lord thinks are good.

Paul and the False Apostles

11 I wish you would be patient
with me even when I am a little
foolish, but you are already doing
that. 2I am jealous over you with a
jealousy that comes from God. I
promised to give you to Christ, as

your only husband. I want to give you as his pure bride. [3] But I am afraid that your minds will be led away from your true and pure following of Christ just as Eve was tricked by the snake with his evil ways. [4] You are very patient with anyone who comes to you and preaches a different Jesus from the one we preached. You are very willing to accept a spirit or gospel that is different from the Spirit and Good News you received from us.

OLD TESTAMENT READING

The Power of Faith

Jehoshaphat's army went out into the Desert of Tekoa early in the morning. As they were starting out, Jehoshaphat stood and said, "Listen to me, people of Judah and Jerusalem. Have faith in the LORD your God, and you will stand strong. Have faith in his prophets, and you will succeed." [21] Jehoshaphat listened to the people's advice. Then he chose men to be singers to the LORD, to praise him because he is holy and wonderful. As they marched in front of the army, they said,

"Thank the LORD,
because his love continues
forever."

[22] As they began to sing and praise God, the LORD set ambushes for the people of Ammon, Moab, and Edom who had come to attack Judah. And they were defeated.

2 Chronicles 20:20–22

INSIGHTS

We have no enemies but the enemies of God. Our fights are not against men but against spiritual wickednesses. We war with the devil and the blasphemy and error and despair which he brings into the field of battle. We fight with all the armies of sin—impurity, drunkenness, oppression, infidelity, and ungodliness. With these we contend earnestly, but not with sword or spear; the weapons of our warfare are not carnal.

Jehovah, our God, abhors everything which is evil, and, therefore, He goeth with us to fight for us in this crusade. He will save us, and He will give us grace to war a good warfare and win the victory. We may depend upon it that if we are on God's side God is on our side. With such an august ally the conflict is never in the least degree doubtful. It is not that truth is mighty and must prevail but that might lies with the Father who is almighty, with Jesus who has all power in heaven and in earth, and with the Holy Spirit who worketh His will among men.

Soldiers of Christ, gird on your armor. Strike home in the name of the God of holiness, and by faith grasp His salvation. Let not this day pass without striking a blow for Jesus and holiness.

Charles Spurgeon

ACTION POINT

Against what enemy does the believer fight? What weapons are in your spiritual arsenal? Are your weapons ready for battle and armed with the power of God? Pray that you will faithfully obey God and diligently fight against the enemy.

MONDAY

God Brings Good out of Our Suffering

2 Corinthians 11:5–33

I do not think that those "great apostles" are any better than I am. 6 I may not be a trained speaker, but I do have knowledge. We have shown this to you clearly in every way.

7 I preached God's Good News to you without pay. I made myself unimportant to make you important. Do you think that was wrong? 8 I accepted pay from other churches, taking their money so I could serve you. 9 If I needed something when I was with you, I did not trouble any of you. The brothers who came from Macedonia gave me all that I needed. I did not allow myself to depend on you in any way, and I will never depend on you. 10 No one in Southern Greece will stop me from bragging about that. I say this with the truth of Christ in me. 11 And why do I not depend on you? Do you think it is because I do not love you? God knows that I love you.

12 And I will continue doing what I am doing now, because I want to stop those people from having a reason to brag. They would like to say that the work they brag about is the same as ours. 13 Such men are not true apostles but are workers who lie. They change themselves to look like apostles of Christ. 14 This does not surprise us. Even Satan changes himself to look like an angel of light. 15 So it does not surprise us if Satan's servants also make themselves look like servants who work for what is right. But in the end they will be punished for what they do.

Paul Tells About His Sufferings

I tell you again: No one should think I am a fool. But if you think so, accept me as you would accept a fool. Then I can brag a little, too. 17 When I brag because I feel sure of myself, I am not talking as the Lord would talk but as a fool. 18 Many people are bragging about their lives in the world. So I will brag too. 19 You are wise, so you will gladly be patient with fools! 20 You are even patient with those who order you around, or use you, or trick you, or think they are better than you, or hit you in the face. 21 It is shameful to me to say this, but we were too "weak" to do those things to you!

But if anyone else is brave enough to brag, then I also will be brave and brag. (I am talking as a fool.) 22 Are they Hebrews? So am I. Are they Israelites? So am I. Are they from Abraham's family? So am I. 23 Are they serving Christ? I am serving him more. (I am crazy to talk like this.) I have worked much harder than they. I have been in prison more often. I have been hurt more in beatings. I have been near death many times. 24 Five times the Jews have given me their punishment of thirty-nine lashes with a whip. 25 Three different times I was beaten with rods. One time I was almost stoned to death. Three times I was in ships that wrecked, and one of those times I spent a night and a day in the sea. 26 I have gone on many travels and have been in danger from rivers, thieves, my own people, the Jews, and those who are not Jews. I have been in danger in cities, in places where no one lives, and on the sea. And I have been in danger with false Christians. 27 I have done hard and tiring work, and many times I did not sleep. I have been hungry and thirsty, and many times I have been without food. I have been cold and without clothes. 28 Besides all this, there is on me every day the load of my concern for all the churches. 29 I feel weak every time someone is weak, and I feel upset every time someone is led into sin.

30 If I must brag, I will brag about the things that show I am weak. 31 God knows I am not lying. He is the God and Father of the Lord Jesus Christ, and he is to be praised forever. 32 When I was in Damascus, the governor under King Aretas wanted to arrest me, so he put guards around the city. 33 But my friends lowered me in a basket through a hole in the city wall. So I escaped from the governor.

OLD TESTAMENT READING

So the king commanded all his people, "Every time a boy is born to the Hebrews, you must throw him into the Nile River, but let all the girl babies live."

Exodus 1:22

The king's daughter said to the woman, "Take this baby and nurse him for me, and I will pay you." So the woman took her baby and nursed him. 10 When the child grew older, the woman took him to the king's daughter, and she adopted the baby as her own son. The king's daughter named him Moses, because she had pulled him out of the water.

Exodus 2:9, 10

INSIGHTS

We grow in our understanding through difficulties, as God opens to us that which we could not have understood with any other background or in any other set of circumstances. Our assurance as children of the Living God is that He is able to bring beauty from ashes and to give the "oil of joy" for the spirit of mourning (see Isaiah 61:3). And, in addition, He refines, purifies, proves, and causes to grow in us something very precious and lasting in our attitudes toward Him and in our actions to other human beings. As He removed the hedge protecting Job (or any one of us . . .) he is also able to give us the grace to come through the onslaught that follows. However, there is much more than just "coming through," still hanging on to our trust and love of God. There is a "coming through," with a shinier, more gleaming sheen on our surface. We have the possibility during the hard time to have skimmed off more of the specks and scum which are hindering the more beautiful reality of love, joy, peace, longsuffering, and meekness.

Edith Schaeffer

APPLICATION

For Paul, preaching the Good News was "good" enough to willingly bear great suffering, wasn't it? Pray for total confidence that God is bringing about good through the suffering in your life, too.

TUESDAY

God's Power Is Made Perfect in Weakness

2 Corinthians 12:1—13:4

A Special Blessing in Paul's Life

12 I must continue to brag. It will do no good, but I will talk now about visions and revelations from the Lord. 2 I know a man in Christ who was taken up to the third heaven fourteen years ago. I do not know whether the man was in his body or out of his body, but God knows. 3–4 And I know that this man was taken up to paradise. I don't know if he was in his body or away from his body, but God knows. He heard things he is not able to explain, things that no human is allowed to tell. 5 I will brag about a man like that, but I will not brag about myself, except about my weaknesses. 6 But if I wanted to brag about myself, I would not be a fool, because I would be telling the truth. But I will not brag about myself. I do not want people to think more of me than what they see me do or hear me say.

7 So that I would not become too proud of the wonderful things that were shown to me, a painful physical problem was given to me. This problem was a messenger from Satan, sent to beat me and keep me from being too proud. 8 I begged the Lord three times to take this problem away from me. 9 But he said to me, "My grace is enough for you. When you are weak, my power is made perfect in you." So I am very happy to brag about my weaknesses. Then Christ's power can live in me. 10 For this reason I am happy when I have weaknesses, insults, hard times, sufferings, and all kinds of troubles for Christ. Because when I am weak, then I am truly strong.

Paul's Love for the Christians

I have been talking like a fool, but you made me do it. You are the ones who should say good things about me. I am worth nothing, but those "great apostles" are not worth any more than I am! 12 When I was with you, I patiently did the things that prove I am an apostle—signs, wonders, and miracles. 13 So you received everything that the other churches have received. Only one thing was different: I was not a burden to you. Forgive me for this!

14 I am now ready to visit you the third time, and I will not be a burden to you. I want nothing from you, except you. Children should not have to save up to give to their parents. Parents should save to give to their children. 15 So I am happy to give everything I have for you, even myself. If I love you more, will you love me less?

16 It is clear I was not a burden to you, but you think I was tricky and lied to catch you. 17 Did I cheat you by using any of the messengers I sent to you? No, you know I did not. 18 I asked Titus to go to you, and I sent our brother with him. Titus did not cheat you, did he? No, you know that Titus and I did the same thing and with the same spirit.

19 Do you think we have been defending ourselves to you all this time? We have been speaking in Christ and before God. You are our dear friends, and everything we do is to make you stronger. 20 I am afraid

that when I come, you will not be
what I want you to be, and I will not
be what you want me to be. I am
afraid that among you there may be
arguing, jealousy, anger, selfish
fighting, evil talk, gossip, pride, and
confusion. 21 I am afraid that when I
come to you again, my God will
make me ashamed before you. I may
be saddened by many of those who
have sinned because they have not
changed their hearts or turned from
their sexual sins and the shameful
things they have done.

Final Warnings and Greetings

13 I will come to you for the third
time. "Every case must be
proved by two or three witnesses."
2 When I was with you the second
time, I gave a warning to those who
had sinned. Now I am away from
you, and I give a warning to all the
others. When I come to you again, I
will not be easy with them. 3 You
want proof that Christ is speaking
through me. My proof is that he is
not weak among you, but he is powerful.
4 It is true that he was weak
when he was killed on the cross, but
he lives now by God's power. It is
true that we are weak in Christ, but
for you we will be alive in Christ by
God's power.

OLD TESTAMENT READING

Each man was sad and angry because his sons and daughters had been captured, but David found strength in the LORD his God.

8 Then David asked the LORD, "Should I chase the people who took our families? Will I catch them?"

The LORD answered, "Chase them. You will catch them, and you will succeed in saving your families."

1 Samuel 30:6b, 8

INSIGHTS

Upon examining the life of the apostle Paul, one hardly gets the impression that he was a weak man. On the contrary, he debated against Christ's apostles over the question of gentile salvation, and he won! He spent his life preaching in the most hostile of circumstances. He planted churches throughout the major cities of Asia Minor and in the port cities along the Aegean Sea. Paul trained the first pastors and elders of these early congregations. And to top it all off, he wrote half of the New Testament!

I don't know what you think, but that certainly doesn't sound like a weak man to me. . . . He was a mover and a shaker.

So how do we reconcile Paul's claim to weakness with his amazing accomplishments? Simple, the answer is in the phrase, "when I am weak, then I am strong." A paraphrase of his comment would go something like this: "When I, Paul, in and of my own strength, am weak, then I, Paul, relying of the power of Christ in me, become strong, capable of whatever the Lord requires of me, full of energy and zeal to accomplish His will."

Charles Stanley

APPLICATION

Why does Paul say that God allowed him to become weak? How did Paul respond to his weakness? What did David do in his time of weakness? What does this example of faith teach you?

WEDNESDAY

God Has Plans for His Own

2 Corinthians 13:5—Galatians 1:21

Look closely at yourselves. Test
yourselves to see if you are living in
the faith. You know that Jesus Christ
is in you—unless you fail the test.
6 But I hope you will see that we ourselves have not failed the test. 7 We
pray to God that you will not do anything wrong. It is not important to
see that we have passed the test, but
it is important that you do what is
right, even if it seems we have failed.
8 We cannot do anything against the
truth, but only for the truth. 9 We are
happy to be weak, if you are strong,
and we pray that you will become
complete. 10 I am writing this while I
am away from you so that when I
come I will not have to be harsh in
my use of authority. The Lord gave
me this authority to build you up, not
to tear you down.

11 Now, brothers and sisters, I say
good-bye. Try to be complete. Do
what I have asked you to do. Agree
with each other, and live in peace.
Then the God of love and peace will
be with you.

12 Greet each other with a holy
kiss. 13 All of God's holy people send
greetings to you.

14 The grace of the Lord Jesus
Christ, the love of God, and the fellowship of the Holy Spirit be with
you all.

Christians Are Saved by Grace

1 From Paul, an apostle. I was not
chosen to be an apostle by human
beings, nor was I sent from human beings. I was made an apostle through
Jesus Christ and God the Father who
raised Jesus from the dead. 2 This letter is also from all those of God's family who are with me.

To the churches in Galatia:

3 Grace and peace to you from
God our Father and the Lord Jesus
Christ. 4 Jesus gave himself for our
sins to free us from this evil world
we live in, as God the Father
planned. 5 The glory belongs to God
forever and ever. Amen.

The Only Good News

God, by his grace through Christ,
called you to become his people. So
I am amazed that you are turning
away so quickly and believing something different than the Good News.
7 Really, there is no other Good
News. But some people are confusing you; they want to change the
Good News of Christ. 8 We preached
to you the Good News. So if we ourselves, or even an angel from
heaven, should preach to you something different, we should be judged
guilty! 9 I said this before, and now I
say it again: You have already accepted the Good News. If anyone is
preaching something different to
you, he should be judged guilty!

10 Do you think I am trying to
make people accept me? No, God is
the One I am trying to please. Am I
trying to please people? If I still
wanted to please people, I would not
be a servant of Christ.

Paul's Authority Is from God

Brothers and sisters, I want you to
know that the Good News I preached
to you was not made up by human
beings. 12 I did not get it from humans

nor did anyone teach it to me, but Jesus Christ showed it to me.

[13]You have heard about my past life in the Jewish religion. I attacked the church of God and tried to destroy it. [14]I was becoming a leader in the Jewish religion, doing better than most other Jews of my age. I tried harder than anyone else to follow the teachings handed down by our ancestors.

[15]But God had special plans for me and set me apart for his work even before I was born. He called me through his grace [16]and showed his son to me so that I might tell the Good News about him to those who are not Jewish. When God called me, I did not get advice or help from any person. [17]I did not go to Jerusalem to see those who were apostles before I was. But, without waiting, I went away to Arabia and later went back to Damascus.

[18]After three years I went to Jerusalem to meet Peter and stayed with him for fifteen days. [19]I met no other apostles, except James, the brother of the Lord. [20]God knows that these things I write are not lies. [21]Later, I went to the areas of Syria and Cilicia.

OLD TESTAMENT READING

Now, tell my servant David: 'This is what the LORD All-Powerful says: I took you from the pasture and from tending the sheep and made you king of my people Israel. [8]I have been with you everywhere you have gone. I have defeated your enemies for you. I will make you as famous as any of the great people on the earth. [9]I will choose a place for my people Israel, and I will plant them so they can live in their own homes. They will not be bothered anymore. Wicked people will no longer hurt them as they have in the past [10]when I chose judges for my people Israel. I will defeat all your enemies.'"

1 Chronicles 17:7–10a

When Samuel first saw Saul, the LORD said to Samuel, "This is the man I told you about. He will organize my people."

1 Samuel 9:17

INSIGHTS

It is better we should not know our future. If we did, we should often spoil God's plan for our life. If we could see into tomorrow and know the troubles it will bring, we might be tempted to seek some way of avoiding them, while really they are God's way to new honor and blessing. God's thoughts for us are always thoughts of love, good, promotion; but sometimes the path to the hilltop lies through dark valleys or up rough paths. Yet to miss the hard bit of road is to fail of gaining the lofty height. It is better, therefore, to walk, not knowing, with God, than it would be to see the way and choose for ourselves. God's way for us is always better than our own.

J.R. Miller

ACTION POINT

David, Samuel, Saul, and Paul all knew that they were called by God to fulfill his plans. Is there any reason to believe that God has planned your life to a lesser degree? Are you willing to test yourself to see if you are following his plan for you? Pray that you will be faithful to his plan and calling for your life.

THURSDAY

"Remember to Help the Poor"

Galatians 1:22—2:21

In Judea the churches in Christ had never met me. 23 They had only heard it said, "This man who was attacking us is now preaching the same faith that he once tried to destroy." 24 And these believers praised God because of me.

Other Apostles Accepted Paul

2 After fourteen years I went to Jerusalem again, this time with Barnabas. I also took Titus with me. 2 I went because God showed me I should go. I met with the believers there, and in private I told their leaders the Good News that I preach to the non-Jewish people. I did not want my past work and the work I am now doing to be wasted. 3 Titus was with me, but he was not forced to be circumcised, even though he was a Greek. 4 We talked about this problem because some false believers had come into our group secretly. They came in like spies to overturn the freedom we have in Christ Jesus. They wanted to make us slaves. 5 But we did not give in to those false believers for a minute. We wanted the truth of the Good News to continue for you.

6 Those leaders who seemed to be important did not change the Good News that I preach. (It doesn't matter to me if they were "important" or not. To God everyone is the same.) 7 But these leaders saw that I had been given the work of telling the Good News to those who are not Jewish, just as Peter had the work of telling the Jews. 8 God gave Peter the power to work as an apostle for the Jewish people. But he also gave me the power to work as an apostle for those who are not Jews. 9 James, Peter, and John, who seemed to be the leaders, understood that God had given me this special grace, so they accepted Barnabas and me. They agreed that they would go to the Jewish people and that we should go to those who are not Jewish. 10 The only thing they asked us was to remember to help the poor—something I really wanted to do.

Paul Shows that Peter Was Wrong

When Peter came to Antioch, I challenged him to his face, because he was wrong. 12 Peter ate with the non-Jewish people until some Jewish people sent from James came to Antioch. When they arrived, Peter stopped eating with those who weren't Jewish, and he separated himself from them. He was afraid of the Jews. 13 So Peter was a hypocrite, as were the other Jewish believers who joined with him. Even Barnabas was influenced by what these Jewish believers did. 14 When I saw they were not following the truth of the Good News, I spoke to Peter in front of them all. I said, "Peter, you are a Jew, but you are not living like a Jew. You are living like those who are not Jewish. So why do you now try to force those who are not Jewish to live like Jews?"

15 We were not born as non-Jewish "sinners," but as Jews. 16 Yet we know that a person is made right with God not by following the law, but by trusting in Jesus Christ. So we, too, have put our faith in Christ

Jesus, that we might be made right
with God because we trusted in
Christ. It is not because we followed
the law, because no one can be made
right with God by following the law.
[17]We Jews came to Christ, trying
to be made right with God, and it
became clear that we are sinners,
too. Does this mean that Christ encourages sin? No! [18]But I would really be wrong to begin teaching
again those things that I gave up. [19]It
was the law that put me to death, and
I died to the law so that I can now
live for God. [20]I was put to death on
the cross with Christ, and I do not
live anymore—it is Christ who lives
in me. I still live in my body, but I
live by faith in the Son of God who
loved me and gave himself to save
me. [21]By saying these things I am
not going against God's grace. Just
the opposite, if the law could make
us right with God, then Christ's
death would be useless.

OLD TESTAMENT READING

Whoever ignores the poor when
they cry for help
will also cry for help and not
be answered.

Proverbs 21:13

If anyone from your country becomes too poor to support himself,
help him to live among you as you
would a stranger or foreigner. [36]Do
not charge him any interest on money
you loan to him, but respect your God;
let the poor live among you.'"

Leviticus 25:35–36

INSIGHTS

The Bible specifically commands believers to imitate God's special concern for the poor and oppressed. In the Old Testament, Yahweh frequently reminded the Israelites of their former oppression in Egypt when he commanded them to care for the poor. . . .

When Paul took up the collection for the poor in Jerusalem, he pointedly reminded the Corinthians that the Lord Jesus became poor so that they might become rich (2 Cor. 8:9). When the author of 1 John called on Christians to share with the needy, he first mentioned the example of Christ: "By this we know love, that he laid down his life for us; and we ought to lay down our lives for the brethren" (1 John 3:16). Then, in the very next verse, he urged Christians to give generously to the needy. It is the amazing self-sacrifice of Christ which Christians are to imitate as they relate to the poor and oppressed.

. . . God's Word commands believers to care for the poor. In fact the Bible underlines the command by teaching that when God's people care for the poor, they imitate God himself. But that is not all. God's Word teaches that those who neglect the poor and oppressed are really not God's people at all—no matter how frequent their religious rituals or how orthodox their creeds and confessions.

Ronald Sider

ACTION POINT

What do these passages reveal to you about God's attitude toward the poor? Deep in your heart, do you really want to help the poor? What more can you do to show God's compassion for the poor? Will you do it?

FRIDAY

God Will Bless Those Who Believe

Galatians 3:1–20

Blessing Comes Through Faith

3 You people in Galatia were told
very clearly about the death of
Jesus Christ on the cross. But you
were foolish; you let someone trick
you. 2 Tell me this one thing: How
did you receive the Holy Spirit? Did
you receive the Spirit by following
the law? No, you received the Spirit
because you heard the Good News
and believed it. 3 You began your life
in Christ by the Spirit. Now are you
trying to make it complete by your
own power? That is foolish. 4 Were all
your experiences wasted? I hope not!
5 Does God give you the Spirit and
work miracles among you because
you follow the law? No, he does
these things because you heard the
Good News and believed it.

6 The Scriptures say the same
thing about Abraham: "Abraham
believed God, and God accepted
Abraham's faith, and that faith made
him right with God." 7 So you should
know that the true children of
Abraham are those who have faith.
8 The Scriptures, telling what would
happen in the future, said that God
would make the non-Jewish people
right through their faith. This Good
News was told to Abraham before-
hand, as the Scripture says: "All nations will be blessed through you."
9 So all who believe as Abraham believed are blessed just as Abraham
was. 10 But those who depend on following the law to make them right
are under a curse, because the Scriptures say, "Anyone will be cursed
who does not always obey what is
written in the Book of the Law."
11 Now it is clear that no one can be
made right with God by the law, because the Scriptures say, "Those
who are right with God will live by
trusting in him." 12 The law is not
based on faith. It says, "A person
who obeys these things will live because of them." 13 Christ took away
the curse the law put on us. He
changed places with us and put himself under that curse. It is written in
the Scriptures, "Anyone whose body
is displayed on a tree is cursed."
14 Christ did this so that God's blessing promised to Abraham might
come through Jesus Christ to those
who are not Jews. Jesus died so that
by our believing we could receive
the Spirit that God promised.

The Law and the Promise

Brothers and sisters, let us think
in human terms: Even an agreement
made between two persons is firm.
After that agreement is accepted by
both people, no one can stop it or
add anything to it. 16 God made
promises both to Abraham and to his
descendant. God did not say, "and to
your descendants." That would
mean many people. But God said,
"and to your descendant." That
means only one person; that person
is Christ. 17 This is what I mean: God
had an agreement with Abraham
and promised to keep it. The law,
which came four hundred thirty
years later, cannot change that
agreement and so destroy God's
promise to Abraham. 18 If the law

could give us Abraham's blessing, then the promise would not be necessary. But that is not possible, because God freely gave his blessings to Abraham through the promise he had made.

[19] So what was the law for? It was given to show that the wrong things people do are against God's will. And it continued until the special descendant, who had been promised, came. The law was given through angels who used Moses for a mediator to give the law to people. [20] But a mediator is not needed when there is only one side, and God is only one.

OLD TESTAMENT READING

The angel of the LORD called to Abraham from heaven a second time [16] and said, "The LORD says, 'Because you did not keep back your son, your only son, from me, I make you this promise by my own name: [17] I will surely bless you and give you many descendants.'"

Genesis 22:15–17a

INSIGHTS

When upon life's billows you are tempest tossed,
When you are discouraged, thinking all is lost,
Count your many blessings, name them one by one,
And it will surprise you what the Lord hath done.

Are you ever burdened with a load of care?
Does the cross seem heavy you are called to bear?
Count your many blessings, ev'ry doubt will fly,
And you will be singing as the days go by.

When you look at others with their lands and gold,
Think that Christ has promised you His wealth untold;
Count your many blessings, money cannot buy
Your reward in heaven, nor your home on high.

So, amid the conflict, whether great or small,
Do not be discouraged, God is over all;
Count your many blessings, angels will attend,
Help and comfort give you to your journey's end.

Count your blessings, name them one by one;
Count your blessings, see what God hath done;
Count your blessings, name them one by one;
Count your many blessings, see what God hath done.

Johnson Oatman, Jr.

ACTION POINT

What are the differences between obeying the law and believing the Good News? What was the purpose of the law? What is promised to all who believe? Name the blessings God has bestowed on you!

WEEKEND

We Are God's Children

Galatians 3:21—4:20

The Purpose of the Law of Moses

Does this mean that the law is against God's promises? Never! That would be true only if the law could make us right. But God did not give a law that can bring life. 22 Instead, the Scriptures showed that the whole world is bound by sin. This was so the promise would be given through faith to people who believe in Jesus Christ.

23 Before this faith came, we were all held prisoners by the law. We had no freedom until God showed us the way of faith that was coming. 24 In other words, the law was our guardian leading us to Christ so that we could be made right with God through faith. 25 Now the way of faith has come, and we no longer live under a guardian.

26-27 You were all baptized into Christ, and so you were all clothed with Christ. This means that you are all children of God through faith in Christ Jesus. 28 In Christ, there is no difference between Jew and Greek, slave and free person, male and female. You are all the same in Christ Jesus. 29 You belong to Christ, so you are Abraham's descendants. You will inherit all of God's blessings because of the promise God made to Abraham.

4 I want to tell you this: While those who will inherit their fathers' property are still children, they are no different from slaves. It does not matter that the children own everything. 2 While they are children, they must obey those who are chosen to care for them. But when the children reach the age set by their fathers, they are free. 3 It is the same for us. We were once like children, slaves to the useless rules of this world. 4 But when the right time came, God sent his Son who was born of a woman and lived under the law. 5 God did this so he could buy freedom for those who were under the law and so we could become his children.

6 Since you are God's children, God sent the Spirit of his Son into your hearts, and the Spirit cries out, "Father." 7 So now you are not a slave; you are God's child, and God will give you the blessing he promised, because you are his child.

Paul's Love for the Christians

In the past you did not know God. You were slaves to gods that were not real. 9 But now you know the true God. Really, it is God who knows you. So why do you turn back to those weak and useless rules you followed before? Do you want to be slaves to those things again? 10 You still follow teachings about special days, months, seasons, and years. 11 I am afraid for you, that my work for you has been wasted.

12 Brothers and sisters, I became like you, so I beg you to become like me. You were very good to me before. 13 You remember that it was because of an illness that I came to you the first time, preaching the Good News. 14 Though my sickness was a trouble for you, you did not hate me or make me leave. But you welcomed me as an angel from God, as if I were Jesus Christ himself! 15 You were very happy then, but

where is that joy now? I am ready to
testify that you would have taken out
your eyes and given them to me if
that were possible. 16 Now am I your
enemy because I tell you the truth?
17 Those people are working hard
to persuade you, but this is not good
for you. They want to persuade you
to turn against us and follow only
them. 18 It is good for people to show
interest in you, but only if their purpose is good. This is always true, not
just when I am with you. 19 My little
children, again I feel the pain of
childbirth for you until you truly become like Christ. 20 I wish I could be
with you now and could change the
way I am talking to you, because I
do not know what to think about you.

OLD TESTAMENT READING

But LORD, you are our father.
We are like clay, and you are
the potter;
your hands made us all.
9 LORD, don't continue to be angry
with us;
don't remember our sins
forever.
Please, look at us,
because we are your people.

Isaiah 64:8–9

You are holy people, who belong to the LORD your God. He has chosen you from all the people on earth to be his very own.

Deuteronomy 14:2

INSIGHTS

Adoption, by its very nature, is an act of free kindness to the persons adopted. If you become a father by adopting a child, you do so because you choose to, not because you are bound to. Similarly, God adopts because he chooses to. He has no duty to do so. He need not have done anything about our sins save punish us as we deserved. But he loved us; he redeemed us, forgave us . . . gave himself to us as our Father.

Nor does his grace stop short with that initial act, any more than the love of human parents who adopt stops short with the completing of the legal process that makes the child theirs. The establishing of the child's status as a member of the family is only a beginning. The real task remains: to establish a filial relationship between your adopted child and yourself to win the child's love by loving it. You seek to excite affection by showing affection. And so it is with God. Throughout our life in this world, and to all eternity beyond, he will constantly be showing us in one way or another more and more of his love, and thereby increasing our love to him continually.

J. I. Packer

ACTION POINT

Think carefully about the implications of being made a child of God. How does one live as a child of a living, holy God? Pray that you will live like a child of God, not like a child of the world.

MONDAY

Christ Gives Us Freedom

Galatians 4:21—5:15

The Example of Hagar and Sarah

Some of you still want to be under the law. Tell me, do you know what the law says? 22 The Scriptures say that Abraham had two sons. The mother of one son was a slave woman, and the mother of the other son was a free woman. 23 Abraham's son from the slave woman was born in the normal human way. But the son from the free woman was born because of the promise God made to Abraham.

24 This story teaches something else: The two women are like the two agreements between God and his people. One agreement is the law that God made on Mount Sinai, and the people who are under this agreement are like slaves. The mother named Hagar is like that agreement. 25 She is like Mount Sinai in Arabia and is a picture of the earthly Jewish city of Jerusalem. This city and its people, the Jews, are slaves to the law. 26 But the heavenly Jerusalem, which is above, is like the free woman. She is our mother. 27 It is written in the Scriptures:

"Be happy, Jerusalem.
You are like a woman who
never gave birth to children.
Start singing and shout for joy.
You never felt the pain of
giving birth,
but you will have more children
than the woman who has a
husband." *Isaiah 54:1*

28 My brothers and sisters, you are God's children because of his promise, as Isaac was then. 29 The son who was born in the normal way treated the other son badly. It is the same today. 30 But what does the Scripture say? "Throw out the slave woman and her son. The son of the slave woman should not inherit anything. The son of the free woman should receive it all." 31 So, my brothers and sisters, we are not children of the slave woman, but of the free woman.

Keep Your Freedom

5 We have freedom now, because Christ made us free. So stand strong. Do not change and go back into the slavery of the law. 2 Listen, I Paul tell you that if you go back to the law by being circumcised, Christ does you no good. 3 Again, I warn every man: If you allow yourselves to be circumcised, you must follow all the law. 4 If you try to be made right with God through the law, your life with Christ is over—you have left God's grace. 5 But we have the true hope that comes from being made right with God, and by the Spirit we wait eagerly for this hope. 6 When we are in Christ Jesus, it is not important if we are circumcised or not. The important thing is faith—the kind of faith that works through love.

7 You were running a good race. Who stopped you from following the true way? 8 This change did not come from the One who chose you. 9 Be careful! "Just a little yeast makes the whole batch of dough rise." 10 But I trust in the Lord that you will not believe those different ideas. Whoever is confusing you with such ideas will be punished.

[11]My brothers and sisters, I do
not teach that a man must be circumcised. If I teach circumcision, why am I still being attacked? If I still taught circumcision, my preaching about the cross would not be a problem.
[12]I wish the people who are bothering you would castrate themselves!
[13]My brothers and sisters, God
called you to be free, but do not use your freedom as an excuse to do what pleases your sinful self. Serve each other with love.
[14]The whole law is made complete in this one command: "Love your neighbor as you love yourself."
[15]If you go on hurting each other and tearing each other apart, be careful, or you will completely destroy each other.

OLD TESTAMENT READING

*I*saac grew, and when he became old enough to eat food, Abraham gave a great feast.
[9]But Sarah saw Ishmael making fun of Isaac. (Ishmael was the son of Abraham by Hagar, Sarah's Egyptian slave.)
[10]So Sarah said to Abraham, "Throw out this slave woman and her son. Her son should not inherit anything; my son Isaac should receive it all."
[11]This troubled Abraham very
much because Ishmael was also his son.
[12]But God said to Abraham, "Don't be troubled about the boy and the slave woman. Do whatever Sarah tells you. The descendants I promised you will be from Isaac."

Genesis 21:8–12

INSIGHTS

Freedom is the privilege of those who are willing to obey. It is a privilege which carries many responsibilities. It is not an automatic right. . . .

Jesus said, ". . . You shall know the truth, and the truth shall make you free" (John 8:32). Truth makes us free because it gives understanding. Understanding helps us accept the necessary conditions, restrictions, and discipline which must prevail if there is to be true freedom. To obey the truth of God's Word makes us free from the slavery of evil habits, desires which harm us, and behavior which dishonors the Lord. Liberty is not the result of human achievement. It is the result of obedience to God. Disobedience means loss of freedom.

If freedom is to be real and lasting, it must be controlled by love. Freedom to do as one pleases, without regard for others or for the circumstances, is destructive. Christian liberty is freedom to love and to serve. It is abused when it is made an excuse for loveless behavior or inconsiderate action.

Real freedom is found in serving God. With our minds centered on Christ and what He would have us do, the self-centered desires and degrading habits of life are crowded out. Life is complete and happy when we surrender ourselves to God, whose yoke is easy and burden is light (Matthew 11:30).

Lucille Sollenberger

PAUSE FOR REFLECTION

What are the differences between the children of the slave woman and the free woman? Who gives true freedom? What privileges does freedom in Christ provide? Do you fully enjoy those privileges?

TUESDAY

We Harvest What We Plant

Galatians 5:16—6:18

The Spirit and Human Nature

So I tell you: Live by following the Spirit. Then you will not do what your sinful selves want. 17 Our sinful selves want what is against the Spirit, and the Spirit wants what is against our sinful selves. The two are against each other, so you cannot do just what you please. 18 But if the Spirit is leading you, you are not under the law.

19 The wrong things the sinful self does are clear: being sexually unfaithful, not being pure, taking part in sexual sins, 20 worshiping gods, doing witchcraft, hating, making trouble, being jealous, being angry, being selfish, making people angry with each other, causing divisions among people, 21 feeling envy, being drunk, having wild and wasteful parties, and doing other things like these. I warn you now as I warned you before: Those who do these things will not inherit God's kingdom. 22 But the Spirit produces the fruit of love, joy, peace, patience, kindness, goodness, faithfulness, 23 gentleness, self-control. There is no law that says these things are wrong. 24 Those who belong to Christ Jesus have crucified their own sinful selves. They have given up their old selfish feelings and the evil things they wanted to do. 25 We get our new life from the Spirit, so we should follow the Spirit. 26 We must not be proud or make trouble with each other or be jealous of each other.

Help Each Other

6 Brothers and sisters, if someone in your group does something wrong, you who are spiritual should go to that person and gently help make him right again. But be careful, because you might be tempted to sin, too. 2 By helping each other with your troubles, you truly obey the law of Christ. 3 If anyone thinks he is important when he really is not, he is only fooling himself. 4 Each person should judge his own actions and not compare himself with others. Then he can be proud for what he himself has done. 5 Each person must be responsible for himself.

6 Anyone who is learning the teaching of God should share all the good things he has with his teacher.

Life Is like Planting a Field

Do not be fooled: You cannot cheat God. People harvest only what they plant. 8 If they plant to satisfy their sinful selves, their sinful selves will bring them ruin. But if they plant to please the Spirit, they will receive eternal life from the Spirit. 9 We must not become tired of doing good. We will receive our harvest of eternal life at the right time if we do not give up. 10 When we have the opportunity to help anyone, we should do it. But we should give special attention to those who are in the family of believers.

Paul Ends His Letter

See what large letters I use to write this myself. 12 Some people are trying to force you to be circumcised so the Jews will accept them. They are afraid they will be attacked if

they follow only the cross of Christ.
13 Those who are circumcised do not
obey the law themselves, but they
want you to be circumcised so they
can brag about what they forced you
to do. 14 I hope I will never brag about
things like that. The cross of our
Lord Jesus Christ is my only reason
for bragging. Through the cross of
Jesus my world was crucified, and I
died to the world. 15 It is not important if a man is circumcised or
uncircumcised. The important thing
is being the new people God has
made. 16 Peace and mercy to those
who follow this rule—and to all of
God's people.

17 So do not give me any more
trouble. I have scars on my body that
show I belong to Christ Jesus.

18 My brothers and sisters, the
grace of our Lord Jesus Christ be
with your spirit. Amen.

OLD TESTAMENT READING

If people please God, God will give them wisdom, knowledge, and joy. But sinners will get only the work of gathering and storing wealth that they will have to give to the ones who please God. So all their work is useless, like chasing the wind.

Ecclesiastes 2:26

INSIGHTS

Our dividends in heaven are determined by what we invest in on earth. We can invest in eternal sureties, or we can invest in wind. . . .

. . . According to the law of the harvest you reap what you sow. If you sow wheat, you reap wheat; if you sow weeds, you reap weeds; if you sow wind, you reap wind. The law of the harvest operates in the spiritual and moral realms as well as the physical. "Do not be deceived, God is not mocked; for whatever a man sows, this he will also reap" (Galatians 6:7). . . . We should guard against sowing too much time, energy, and money on clothes and recreation and parties and other means of self-indulgence. We will reap nothing in terms of our eternal well-being from these seeds. No wonder growing Christians are exhorted to "guard yourselves from idols" (1 John 5:21). Idols are not just the wood and stone types that Israel turned to, but anything that steals our hearts and minds away from total commitment to the Lord. . . .

. . . If we invest our lives in the nothingness of what this world has to offer, we not only reap a harvest of nothing but we destroy our lives as well. Many Christians have lives that are disordered, chaotic, and shattered because of their investment in the wind of this world. . . .

. . . We must have a steady diet of the solid food of the Word of God now if we are going to avoid the stunted growth, starvation, and emptiness that are associated with feeding on wind.

David Reid

ACTION POINT

Examine your life and list what you have sown. Does what you have sown please the Spirit (Gal. 5:16–25)? What do you need to sow on earth in order to receive the heavenly dividends you desire?

WEDNESDAY

The Importance of Praying for One Another

Ephesians 1:1—2:3

1 From Paul, an apostle of Christ
Jesus. I am an apostle because
that is what God wanted.

To God's holy people living in
Ephesus, believers in Christ Jesus:
2 Grace and peace to you from God
our Father and the Lord Jesus Christ.

Spiritual Blessings in Christ

Praise be to the God and Father of
our Lord Jesus Christ. In Christ, God
has given us every spiritual blessing
in the heavenly world. 4 That is, in
Christ, he chose us before the world
was made so that we would be his
holy people—people without blame
before him. 5 Because of his love,
God had already decided to make us
his own children through Jesus
Christ. That was what he wanted and
what pleased him, 6 and it brings
praise to God because of his wonderful grace. God gave that grace to us
freely, in Christ, the One he loves.
7 In Christ we are set free by the
blood of his death, and so we have
forgiveness of sins. How rich is
God's grace, 8 which he has given to
us so fully and freely. God, with full
wisdom and understanding, 9 let us
know his secret purpose. This was
what God wanted, and he planned to
do it through Christ. 10 His goal was
to carry out his plan, when the right
time came, that all things in heaven
and on earth would be joined together in Christ as the head.

11 In Christ we were chosen to be
God's people, because from the very
beginning God had decided this in
keeping with his plan. And he is the
One who makes everything agree
with what he decides and wants. 12 We
are the first people who hoped in
Christ, and we were chosen so that we
would bring praise to God's glory. 13 So
it is with you. When you heard the
true teaching—the Good News about
your salvation—you believed in
Christ. And in Christ, God put his special mark of ownership on you by giving you the Holy Spirit that he had
promised. 14 That Holy Spirit is the
guarantee that we will receive what
God promised for his people until God
gives full freedom to those who are
his—to bring praise to God's glory.

Paul's Prayer

That is why since I heard about
your faith in the Lord Jesus and your
love for all God's people, 16 I have not
stopped giving thanks to God for
you. I always remember you in my
prayers, 17 asking the God of our
Lord Jesus Christ, the glorious Father, to give you a spirit of wisdom
and revelation so that you will know
him better. 18 I pray also that you will
have greater understanding in your
heart so you will know the hope to
which he has called us and that you
will know how rich and glorious are
the blessings God has promised his
holy people. 19 And you will know
that God's power is very great for us
who believe. That power is the same
as the great strength 20 God used to
raise Christ from the dead and put
him at his right side in the heavenly
world. 21 God has put Christ over all
rulers, authorities, powers, and

kings, not only in this world but also in the next. [22] God put everything under his power and made him the head over everything for the church, [23] which is Christ's body. The church is filled with Christ, and Christ fills everything in every way.

We Now Have Life

2 In the past you were spiritually dead because of your sins and the things you did against God. [2] Yes, in the past you lived the way the world lives, following the ruler of the evil powers that are above the earth. That same spirit is now working in those who refuse to obey God. [3] In the past all of us lived like them, trying to please our sinful selves and doing all the things our bodies and minds wanted. We should have suffered God's anger because of the way we were. We were the same as all other people.

OLD TESTAMENT READING

My servant Job will pray for you, and I will listen to his prayer. Then I will not punish you for being foolish. You have not said what is right about me, as my servant Job did." [9] So Eliphaz the Temanite, Bildad the Shuhite, and Zophar the Naamathite did as the LORD said, and the LORD listened to Job's prayer.

Job 42:8b–9

INSIGHTS

Compassion lies at the heart of intercession. . . .

When we promise to pray for someone, how often do we truly enter into the reality of what that means? The story of the paralytic borne by four friends to Jesus for healing is a powerful illustration of intercessory love. We 'carry' those for whom we pray (we even speak sometimes of having 'a burden' in prayer). Self is out of the picture, for we have become that other person experiencing his pain with him, suffering his fears for him, consumed with the same longings.

"Blessed are the merciful," said Jesus (Matt 5:7). Part of the meaning of being merciful is to get inside the skin of someone else, to feel as he feels, think as he thinks, see as he sees, to understand life the way he understands it. That, of course, is at the heart of the incarnation. It is precisely what Jesus did when he 'got inside the skin' of a human being and experienced life as we do.

This kind of intercession is contemplative rather than petitionary. It is gathered up in compassion and empathy more often than words—though words are sometimes helpful to us in focusing on a particular person or need. We can bear people to the Lord, as the friends of the paralytic did, and leave them with him. We do not need to inform him of all the facts or suggest how he should act. We are not able to pray, but the Holy Spirit can pray through and in us. We cannot heal, but God can heal through us.

Margaret Magdalen

PAUSE FOR REFLECTION

Do you feel the passion with which Paul prayed? Such prayers go far deeper than cursory "Lord bless" and "Lord forgive" prayers, don't they? Could your prayers perhaps flow from deeper in your heart?

THURSDAY

God Gives Mercy and Grace to His People

Ephesians 2:4—3:6

But God's mercy is great, and he loved us very much. 5 Though we were spiritually dead because of the things we did against God, he gave us new life with Christ. You have been saved by God's grace. 6 And he raised us up with Christ and gave us a seat with him in the heavens. He did this for those in Christ Jesus 7 so that for all future time he could show the very great riches of his grace by being kind to us in Christ Jesus. 8 I mean that you have been saved by grace through believing. You did not save yourselves; it was a gift from God. 9 It was not the result of your own efforts, so you cannot brag about it. 10 God has made us what we are. In Christ Jesus, God made us to do good works, which God planned in advance for us to live our lives doing.

One in Christ

You were not born Jewish. You are the people the Jews call "uncircumcised." Those who call you "uncircumcised" call themselves "circumcised." (Their circumcision is only something they themselves do on their bodies.) 12 Remember that in the past you were without Christ. You were not citizens of Israel, and you had no part in the agreements with the promise that God made to his people. You had no hope, and you did not know God. 13 But now in Christ Jesus, you who were far away from God are brought near through the blood of Christ's death. 14 Christ himself is our peace. He made both Jewish people and those who are not Jews one people. They were separated as if there were a wall between them, but Christ broke down that wall of hate by giving his own body. 15 The Jewish law had many commands and rules, but Christ ended that law. His purpose was to make the two groups of people become one new people in him and in this way make peace. 16 It was also Christ's purpose to end the hatred between the two groups, to make them into one body, and to bring them back to God. Christ did all this with his death on the cross. 17 Christ came and preached peace to you who were far away from God, and to those who were near to God. 18 Yes, it is through Christ we all have the right to come to the Father in one Spirit.

19 Now you who are not Jewish are not foreigners or strangers any longer, but are citizens together with God's holy people. You belong to God's family. 20 You are like a building that was built on the foundation of the apostles and prophets. Christ Jesus himself is the most important stone in that building, 21 and that whole building is joined together in Christ. He makes it grow and become a holy temple in the Lord. 22 And in Christ you, too, are being built together with the Jews into a place where God lives through the Spirit.

Paul's Work in Telling the Good News

3 So I, Paul, am a prisoner of Christ Jesus for you who are not Jews.

2 Surely you have heard that God
gave me this work through his grace
to help you. 3 He let me know his secret by showing it to me. I have already written a little about this. 4 If
you read what I wrote then, you can
see that I truly understand the secret
about the Christ. 5 People who lived
in other times were not told that secret. But now, through the Spirit,
God has shown that secret to his
holy apostles and prophets. 6 This is
that secret: that through the Good
News those who are not Jews will
share with the Jews in God's blessing. They belong to the same body,
and they share together in the promise that God made in Christ Jesus.

OLD TESTAMENT READING

There is no God like you.
You forgive those who are
guilty of sin;
you don't look at the sins of your
people
who are left alive.
You will not stay angry forever,
because you enjoy being kind.
19 You will have mercy on us again;
you will conquer our sins.

Micah 7:18–19a

INSIGHTS

In my own life I am acutely aware that I am a roughhewn man. Because of my rather tough, rough upbringing in a frontier environment, I simply do not possess the polish of the "man about the town." There are characteristics in my makeup which may seem harsh and unyielding. But, despite this, my life has been deeply touched by the mercy of those who took the time to try and understand me—who cared enough to forgive so many faults and who in mercy made me their friend.

Often these were people to whom I had shown no special kindness. Their bestowal of mercy on me was something totally unexpected and undeserved. Because of this, it has been a double delight. More than that, it has been an enormous inspiration that lifted and challenged me to respond in a measure beyond my wildest dreams.

Mercy does just that to people. It excites and stimulates their hope. It reassures them that life can be beautiful. It convinces them that there is good reason to carry on and push for better things if others care that much.

This all implies that if someone has extended mercy to me, surely I, in turn, can and must extend mercy to others.

But, to really find the true source of inner inspiration for this sort of conduct, the Christian simply must look beyond his fellow man. He must look away to the mercy of God our Father. Nothing else in all the world will so humble us. Nothing else will so move our stony spirits to extend mercy. Nothing else will so powerfully induce us to do the proper thing in extending genuine mercy to our contemporaries.

W. Phillip Keller

PAUSE FOR REFLECTION

What has God's mercy, as described in Ephesians, accomplished for all people? How has God's mercy touched your life? What has been the result of his merciful touch? How will you thank him?

FRIDAY

Christ's Love Is Greater than Anyone Can Fathom

Ephesians 3:7—4:16

By God's special gift of grace given to me through his power, I became a servant to tell that Good News. 8 I am the least important of all God's people, but God gave me this gift—to tell those who are not Jews the Good News about the riches of Christ, which are too great to understand fully. 9 And God gave me the work of telling all people about the plan for his secret, which has been hidden in him since the beginning of time. He is the One who created everything. 10 His purpose was that through the church all the rulers and powers in the heavenly world will now know God's wisdom, which has so many forms. 11 This agrees with the purpose God had since the beginning of time, and he carried out his plan through Christ Jesus our Lord. 12 In Christ we can come before God with freedom and without fear. We can do this through faith in Christ. 13 So I ask you not to become discouraged because of the sufferings I am having for you. My sufferings are for your glory.

The Love of Christ

So I bow in prayer before the Father 15 from whom every family in heaven and on earth gets its true name. 16 I ask the Father in his great glory to give you the power to be strong inwardly through his Spirit. 17 I pray that Christ will live in your hearts by faith and that your life will be strong in love and be built on love. 18 And I pray that you and all God's holy people will have the power to understand the greatness of Christ's love—how wide and how long and how high and how deep that love is. 19 Christ's love is greater than anyone can ever know, but I pray that you will be able to know that love. Then you can be filled with the fullness of God.

20 With God's power working in us, God can do much, much more than anything we can ask or imagine. 21 To him be glory in the church and in Christ Jesus for all time, forever and ever. Amen.

The Unity of the Body

4 I am in prison because I belong to the Lord. God chose you to be his people, so I urge you now to live the life to which God called you. 2 Always be humble, gentle, and patient, accepting each other in love. 3 You are joined together with peace through the Spirit, so make every effort to continue together in this way. 4 There is one body and one Spirit, and God called you to have one hope. 5 There is one Lord, one faith, and one baptism. 6 There is one God and Father of everything. He rules everything and is everywhere and is in everything.

7 Christ gave each one of us the special gift of grace, showing how generous he is. 8 That is why it says in the Scriptures,

"When he went up to the heights,
he led a parade of captives,
and he gave gifts to people."

Psalm 68:18

9 When it says, "He went up," what

does it mean? It means that he first
came down to the earth. [10] So Jesus
came down, and he is the same One
who went up above all the sky. Christ
did that to fill everything with his presence. [11] And Christ gave gifts to
people—he made some to be apostles,
some to be prophets, some to go and
tell the Good News, and some to have
the work of caring for and teaching
God's people. [12] Christ gave those gifts
to prepare God's holy people for the
work of serving, to make the body of
Christ stronger. [13] This work must
continue until we are all joined together in the same faith and in the
same knowledge of the Son of God.
We must become like a mature person, growing until we become like
Christ and have his perfection.

[14] Then we will no longer be babies. We will not be tossed about
like a ship that the waves carry one
way and then another. We will not be
influenced by every new teaching
we hear from people who are trying
to fool us. They make plans and try
any kind of trick to fool people into
following the wrong path. [15] No!
Speaking the truth with love, we will
grow up in every way into Christ,
who is the head. [16] The whole body
depends on Christ, and all the parts
of the body are joined and held together. Each part does its own work
to make the whole body grow and
be strong with love.

OLD TESTAMENT READING

Give thanks to the LORD because he is good.
His love continues forever.
[4] Only he can do great miracles.
His love continues forever.

Psalm 136:1, 4

INSIGHTS

Before we can have any right idea of the love of Jesus, we must understand His previous glory in its height of majesty, and His incarnation upon the earth in all its depths of shame. But who can tell us the majesty of Christ? When He was enthroned in the highest heavens He was very God of very God; by Him were the heavens made, and all the hosts thereof. His own almighty arm upheld the spheres; the praises of cherubim and seraphim perpetually surrounded Him; the full chorus of the hallelujahs of the universe unceasingly flowed to the foot of his throne: He reigned supreme above all His creatures, God over all, blessed for ever. Who can tell His height of glory then? And who, on the other hand, can tell how low He descended? To be a man was something, to be a man of sorrows was far more; to bleed, and die, and suffer, these were much for Him who was the Son of God; but to suffer such unparalleled agony—to endure a death of shame and desertion by His Father, this is a depth of condescending love which the most inspired mind must utterly fail to fathom. Herein is love! and truly it is love that "passeth knowledge." O let this love fill our hearts with adoring gratitude, and lead us to practical manifestations of its power.

Charles Spurgeon

ACTION POINT

Describe in the best way you can, how wide, long, high, and deep Christ's love is. Pray that you will know the fullness of God's love in your life.

WEEKEND

Guard Against Greed

Ephesians 4:17—5:14

The Way You Should Live

In the Lord's name, I tell you this. Do not continue living like those who do not believe. Their thoughts are worth nothing. [18]They do not understand, and they know nothing, because they refuse to listen. So they cannot have the life that God gives. [19]They have lost all feeling of shame, and they use their lives for doing evil. They continually want to do all kinds of evil. [20]But what you learned in Christ was not like this. [21]I know that you heard about him, and you are in him, so you were taught the truth that is in Jesus. [22]You were taught to leave your old self—to stop living the evil way you lived before. That old self becomes worse, because people are fooled by the evil things they want to do. [23]But you were taught to be made new in your hearts, [24]to become a new person. That new person is made to be like God—made to be truly good and holy.

[25]So you must stop telling lies. Tell each other the truth, because we all belong to each other in the same body. [26]When you are angry, do not sin, and be sure to stop being angry before the end of the day. [27]Do not give the devil a way to defeat you. [28]Those who are stealing must stop stealing and start working. They should earn an honest living for themselves. Then they will have something to share with those who are poor.

[29]When you talk, do not say harmful things, but say what people need—words that will help others become stronger. Then what you say will do good to those who listen to you. [30]And do not make the Holy Spirit sad. The Spirit is God's proof that you belong to him. God gave you the Spirit to show that God will make you free when the final day comes. [31]Do not be bitter or angry or mad. Never shout angrily or say things to hurt others. Never do anything evil. [32]Be kind and loving to each other, and forgive each other just as God forgave you in Christ.

Living in the Light

5 You are God's children whom he loves, so try to be like him. [2]Live a life of love just as Christ loved us and gave himself for us as a sweet-smelling offering and sacrifice to God.

[3]But there must be no sexual sin among you, or any kind of evil or greed. Those things are not right for God's holy people. [4]Also, there must be no evil talk among you, and you must not speak foolishly or tell evil jokes. These things are not right for you. Instead, you should be giving thanks to God. [5]You can be sure of this: No one will have a place in the kingdom of Christ and of God who sins sexually, or does evil things, or is greedy. Anyone who is greedy is serving a false god.

[6]Do not let anyone fool you by telling you things that are not true, because these things will bring God's anger on those who do not obey him. [7]So have nothing to do with them. [8]In the past you were full of darkness, but now you are full of

light in the Lord. So live like children
who belong to the light. [9] Light
brings every kind of goodness, right
living, and truth. [10] Try to learn what
pleases the Lord. [11] Have nothing to
do with the things done in darkness,
which are not worth anything. But
show that they are wrong. [12] It is
shameful even to talk about what
those people do in secret. [13] But the
light makes all things easy to see,
[14] and everything that is made easy
to see can become light. This is why
it is said:

"Wake up, sleeper!
Rise from death,
and Christ will shine on you."

OLD TESTAMENT READING

Greed has two daughters
named 'Give' and 'Give.'
There are three things that are
never satisfied,
really four that never say, 'I've
had enough!':
[16] the cemetery, the childless
mother,
the land that never gets
enough rain,
and fire that never says, 'I've
had enough!'"

Proverbs 30:15–16

INSIGHTS

Someone has well said, "Our pocketbooks have more to do with heaven and hell than our hymnbooks." Jesus told the story of the rich man who had everything, and a beggar who had nothing. The rich man, blinded by his abundance, neither saw his need for righteousness nor prepared himself for eternity. Lazarus, who had received only bad things, "crumbs from the rich man's table," had prepared well for his future. And their roles in the future life were completely reversed! (Luke 16:19–31) . . .

Cyprian, the third-century bishop of Carthage, wrote an amazingly up-to-date description of the affluent:

> *Their property held them in chains . . . which shackled their courage and choked their faith and hampered their judgment and throttled their souls. . . . If they stored up their treasure in heaven, they would not now have an enemy and a thief within their household. . . . They think of themselves as owners, whereas it is they rather who are owned: enslaved as they are to their own property, they are not the masters of their money but its slaves.*

How we need to hear the voice of the New Testament as it calls us to a life of responsible stewardship of our resources.

Art Beals

APPLICATION

Why is greed such a hindrance to spiritual growth? What other lifestyle choices are wrong for God's holy people? Why? What does your handling of possessions reveal about your heart?

MONDAY

Mutual Love in Marriage

Ephesians 5:15—6:4

So be very careful how you live. Do not live like those who are not wise, but live wisely. 16 Use every chance you have for doing good, because these are evil times. 17 So do not be foolish but learn what the Lord wants you to do. 18 Do not be drunk with wine, which will ruin you, but be filled with the Spirit. 19 Speak to each other with psalms, hymns, and spiritual songs, singing and making music in your hearts to the Lord. 20 Always give thanks to God the Father for everything, in the name of our Lord Jesus Christ.

Wives and Husbands

Yield to obey each other because you respect Christ.

22 Wives, yield to your husbands, as you do to the Lord, 23 because the husband is the head of the wife, as Christ is the head of the church. And he is the Savior of the body, which is the church. 24 As the church yields to Christ, so you wives should yield to your husbands in everything.

25 Husbands, love your wives as Christ loved the church and gave himself for it 26 to make it belong to God. Christ used the word to make the church clean by washing it with water. 27 He died so that he could give the church to himself like a bride in all her beauty. He died so that the church could be pure and without fault, with no evil or sin or any other wrong thing in it. 28 In the same way, husbands should love their wives as they love their own bodies. The man who loves his wife loves himself. 29 No one ever hates his own body, but feeds and takes care of it. And that is what Christ does for the church, 30 because we are parts of his body. 31 The Scripture says, "So a man will leave his father and mother and be united with his wife, and the two will become one body." 32 That secret is very important—I am talking about Christ and the church. 33 But each one of you must love his wife as he loves himself, and a wife must respect her husband.

Children and Parents

6 Children, obey your parents as the Lord wants, because this is the right thing to do. 2 The command says, "Honor your father and mother." This is the first command that has a promise with it—3 "Then everything will be well with you, and you will have a long life on the earth."

4 Fathers, do not make your children angry, but raise them with the training and teaching of the Lord.

OLD TESTAMENT READING

Be happy with the wife you
married when you were
young.
She gives you joy as your
fountain gives you water.
19 She is as lovely and graceful as a
deer.
Let her love always make you
happy;
let her love always hold you
captive.

[20] My son, don't be held captive by
a woman who takes part in
adultery.
Don't hug another man's wife.
Proverbs 5:18–20

My lover is mine, and I am his.
He feeds among the lilies
[17] until the day dawns
and the shadows disappear.
Turn, my lover.
Be like a gazelle or a young
deer
on the mountain valleys.
Song of Solomon 2:16–17

Laban and Bethuel answered,
"This is clearly from the LORD, and
we cannot change what must happen. [51] Rebekah is yours. Take her
and go. Let her marry your master's
son as the LORD has commanded."
[66] The servant told Isaac everything that had happened. [67] Then
Isaac brought Rebekah into the tent
of Sarah, his mother, and she became his wife. Isaac loved her very
much, and so he was comforted after his mother's death.
Genesis 24:50–51, 66–67

INSIGHTS

If you could enter a time machine and emerge back in the first century when Paul's letters hit the culture of the day, you would be in for some real excitement. His instruction to husbands in Ephesians 5:25–27 must have caused a riot! They went contrary to the way men treated women at that time. Paul's writing called the husband to a ministry of loving servanthood to his wife in a culture which treated women as little better than household furnishings!

A husband is to love his wife with the same sacrificial self-abandonment that Christ adopted toward each of us. When a man considers hardship in marriage, he needs to look at the life of Jesus. Jesus said, "The Son of Man came not to be served, but to serve" (Matthew 20:28). Jesus is presented in Scripture as both Head and Servant. He is the "head over everything for the church" (Ephesians 1:22) who took "the very nature of a servant" (Philippians 2:7). And Jesus instructed us, "The greatest among you will be your servant" (Matthew 23:11).

As believers, we are all called to servanthood as an expression of our new life in Christ. However, when it comes to marriage, modeling this attribute of God's Son is a calling extended to husbands. A husband expresses love to his wife by regarding her as a completely equal partner in everything that concerns their life together. He asserts his headship to see that this equal partnership works. Loving headship affirms and defers; it encourages and stimulates. Loving headship delights to delegate without demanding.

H. Norman Wright

PAUSE FOR REFLECTION

How do Paul's instructions about marriage fit in with the broader scope of instructions on Christian living that he offers in this passage (Ephesians 5:15–21)? What do his instructions reveal about God's desired intent for marriage?

TUESDAY

We Are Involved in a Spiritual Battle!

Ephesians 6:5–24

Slaves and Masters

Slaves, obey your masters here on earth with fear and respect and from a sincere heart, just as you obey Christ. 6 You must do this not only while they are watching you, to please them. With all your heart you must do what God wants as people who are obeying Christ. 7 Do your work with enthusiasm. Work as if you were serving the Lord, not as if you were serving only men and women. 8 Remember that the Lord will give a reward to everyone, slave or free, for doing good.

9 Masters, in the same way, be good to your slaves. Do not threaten them. Remember that the One who is your Master and their Master is in heaven, and he treats everyone alike.

Wear the Full Armor of God

Finally, be strong in the Lord and in his great power. 11 Put on the full armor of God so that you can fight against the devil's evil tricks. 12 Our fight is not against people on earth but against the rulers and authorities and the powers of this world's darkness, against the spiritual powers of evil in the heavenly world. 13 That is why you need to put on God's full armor. Then on the day of evil you will be able to stand strong. And when you have finished the whole fight, you will still be standing. 14 So stand strong, with the belt of truth tied around your waist and the protection of right living on your chest. 15 On your feet wear the Good News of peace to help you stand strong. 16 And also use the shield of faith with which you can stop all the burning arrows of the Evil One. 17 Accept God's salvation as your helmet, and take the sword of the Spirit, which is the word of God. 18 Pray in the Spirit at all times with all kinds of prayers, asking for everything you need. To do this you must always be ready and never give up. Always pray for all God's people.

19 Also pray for me that when I speak, God will give me words so that I can tell the secret of the Good News without fear. 20 I have been sent to preach this Good News, and I am doing that now, here in prison. Pray that when I preach the Good News I will speak without fear, as I should.

Final Greetings

I am sending to you Tychicus, our brother whom we love and a faithful servant of the Lord's work. He will tell you everything that is happening with me. Then you will know how I am and what I am doing. 22 I am sending him to you for this reason—so that you will know how we are, and he can encourage you.

23 Peace and love with faith to you from God the Father and the Lord Jesus Christ. 24 Grace to all of you who love our Lord Jesus Christ with love that never ends.

OLD TESTAMENT READING

One day the angels came to show

themselves before the LORD, and
Satan was with them. [7]The LORD said
to Satan, "Where have you come
from?"

Satan answered the LORD, "I have been wandering around the earth, going back and forth in it."
[8]Then the LORD said to Satan,
"Have you noticed my servant Job? No one else on earth is like him. He is an honest and innocent man, honoring God and staying away from evil."
[9]But Satan answered the LORD,
"Job honors God for a good reason.
[10]You have put a wall around him, his
family, and everything he owns. You have blessed the things he has done. His flocks and herds are so large they almost cover the land."

Job 1:6–10

You must destroy all the people the LORD your God hands over to you. Do not feel sorry for them, and do not worship their gods, or they will trap you.

Deuteronomy 7:16

INSIGHTS

Awareness that we are involved in a cosmic battle which is supernatural, personal, and futile if fought with natural weapons is the beginning of conquering wisdom. We must be convinced of these things if we are to succeed. We must go beyond evangelical lip service to a deep-souled conviction which bursts our simplistic religious shackles.

Paul is specific about the nature of our evil opponents: "our struggle is . . . against the rulers, against the authorities, against the powers of this dark world and against the spiritual forces of evil in the heavenly realms" (v. 12). . . .

The immediate implication is that Satan is terribly powerful. To be sure he does not possess anything near the power of God, but in God's inscrutable arrangement he temporarily dominates and drives the world, which on the whole is separated from God's grace. . .

. . . If we are filled with the Spirit (5:18), Satan's forces cannot subdue us. But those of us who neglect our resources, and especially those who give the enemies room in our lives, place ourselves in harm's way. . . .

. . . We cannot fight Satan ourselves. All our own doing will be in vain. Nevertheless there is something we can do, and that is to avail ourselves of the Lord's strength. . . . We are to acknowledge our weakness and invite his power. We must imitate Gideon's going from 32,000 warriors to 10,000 to 300 armed only with trumpets and lanterns (Judges 7). This divestment of natural strength enabled the putting on of God's power—and a mighty victory!

R. Kent Hughes

APPLICATION

What does Scripture say you need in order to fight spiritual battles? Identify the spiritual battlefields in your life. List the battles you most frequently fail to recognize as spiritual. How can you better avail yourself of God's resources to fight those battles?

WEDNESDAY

Be Humble and Give Honor to Others

Philippians 1:1—2:4

1 From Paul and Timothy, servants of Christ Jesus.
To all of God's holy people in
Christ Jesus who live in Philippi, including your elders and deacons:
2 Grace and peace to you from God
our Father and the Lord Jesus Christ.

Paul's Frayer

I thank my God every time I remember you, 4 always praying with joy for
all of you. 5 I thank God for the help
you gave me while I preached the
Good News—help you gave from
the first day you believed until now.
6 God began doing a good work in
you, and I am sure he will continue
it until it is finished when Jesus
Christ comes again.
7 And I know that I am right to
think like this about all of you, because I have you in my heart. All of
you share in God's grace with me
while I am in prison and while I am
defending and proving the truth of
the Good News. 8 God knows that I
want to see you very much, because
I love all of you with the love of
Christ Jesus.
9 This is my prayer for you: that
your love will grow more and more;
that you will have knowledge and
understanding with your love; 10 that
you will see the difference between
good and bad and will choose the
good; that you will be pure and without wrong for the coming of Christ;
11 that you will do many good things
with the help of Christ to bring glory
and praise to God.

Paul's Troubles Help the Work

I want you brothers and sisters to
know that what has happened to me
has helped to spread the Good
News. 13 All the palace guards and
everyone else knows that I am in
prison because I am a believer in
Christ. 14 Because I am in prison,
most of the believers have become
more bold in Christ and are not
afraid to speak the word of God.
15 It is true that some preach
about Christ because they are jealous and ambitious, but others
preach about Christ because they
want to help. 16 They preach because
they have love, and they know that
God gave me the work of defending
the Good News. 17 But the others
preach about Christ for selfish and
wrong reasons, wanting to make
trouble for me in prison.
18 But it doesn't matter. The important thing is that in every way,
whether for right or wrong reasons,
they are preaching about Christ. So I
am happy, and I will continue to be
happy. 19 Because you are praying for
me and the Spirit of Jesus Christ is
helping me, I know this trouble will
bring my freedom. 20 I expect and
hope that I will not fail Christ in anything but that I will have the courage
now, as always, to show the greatness
of Christ in my life here on earth,
whether I live or die. 21 To me the only
important thing about living is Christ,
and dying would be profit for me. 22 If
I continue living in my body, I will be
able to work for the Lord. I do not
know what to choose—living or dying.

[23] It is hard to choose between the two.
I want to leave this life and be with
Christ, which is much better, [24] but you
need me here in my body. [25] Since I am
sure of this, I know I will stay with you
to help you grow and have joy in your
faith. [26] You will be very happy in Christ
Jesus when I am with you again.
[27] Only one thing concerns me: Be
sure that you live in a way that brings
honor to the Good News of Christ. Then
whether I come and visit you or am
away from you, I will hear that you are
standing strong with one purpose, that
you work together as one for the faith
of the Good News, [28] and that you are
not afraid of those who are against you.
All of this is proof that your enemies
will be destroyed but that you will be
saved by God. [29] God gave you the
honor not only of believing in Christ
but also of suffering for him, both of
which bring glory to Christ. [30] When I
was with you, you saw the struggles I
had, and you hear about the struggles
I am having now. You yourselves are
having the same kind of struggles.

2 Does your life in Christ give you
strength? Does his love comfort
you? Do we share together in the
spirit? Do you have mercy and kindness? [2] If so, make me very happy by
having the same thoughts, sharing
the same love, and having one mind
and purpose. [3] When you do things,
do not let selfishness or pride be
your guide. Instead, be humble and
give more honor to others than to
yourselves. [4] Do not be interested
only in your own life, but be interested in the lives of others.

OLD TESTAMENT READING

The LORD has told you, human,
what is good;
he has told you what he wants
from you:
to do what is right to other people,
love being kind to others,
and live humbly, obeying your
God.

Micah 6:8

INSIGHTS

The humble person will renounce all the glory of the good he has or does and give it all to God. If there is anything good in him or any good done by him, he is not disposed to glorify himself or boast about it before God. . . . The disposition of the humble person is to wholly submit himself to God. He is content to be subject to the commands and laws of God, for he sees it is right and good that the creature be subject to His Creator. He wants to give God the honor that belongs to Him, and that is to reign over him and subject him to certain laws and commands that are designed for his own best interests.

Humility tends to prevent an inordinate aspiring to wealth or position—in short, ambitious behavior among people. A humble person is content with such a situation among others as God is pleased to allot to him and is not greedy for honor. Nor does he try to appear uppermost and exalted above his neighbors.

Jonathan Edwards

PAUSE FOR REFLECTION

Why is God opposed to the proud? What does God promise to the humble? In what ways is humility part of obeying Christ's commandment to love one another?

THURSDAY

Do Everything Without Complaining or Arguing

Philippians 2:5–30

Be Unselfish like Christ

In your lives you must think and act like Christ Jesus.

6 Christ himself was like God in
everything.
But he did not think that being
equal with God was some-
thing to be used for his own
benefit.
7 But he gave up his place with
God and made himself
nothing.
He was born to be a man
and became like a servant.
8 And when he was living as a man,
he humbled himself and was
fully obedient to God,
even when that caused his
death—death on a cross.
9 So God raised him to the highest
place.
God made his name greater
than every other name
10 so that every knee will bow to the
name of Jesus—
everyone in heaven, on earth,
and under the earth.
11 And everyone will confess that
Jesus Christ is Lord
and bring glory to God the
Father.

Be the People God Wants You to Be

My dear friends, you have always obeyed God when I was with you. It is even more important that you obey now while I am away from you. Keep on working to complete your salvation with fear and trembling,
13 because God is working in you to
help you want to do and be able to do what pleases him.

14 Do everything without complaining or arguing.
15 Then you will
be innocent and without any wrong. You will be God's children without fault. But you are living with crooked and mean people all around you, among whom you shine like stars in the dark world.
16 You offer the teaching that gives life. So when Christ comes again, I can be happy because my work was not wasted. I ran the race and won.

17 Your faith makes you offer your lives as a sacrifice in serving God. If I have to offer my own blood with your sacrifice, I will be happy and full of joy with all of you.
18 You also
should be happy and full of joy with me.

Timothy and Epaphroditus

I hope in the Lord Jesus to send Timothy to you soon. I will be happy to learn how you are.
20 I have no one
else like Timothy, who truly cares for you.
21 Other people are inter-
ested only in their own lives, not in the work of Jesus Christ.
22 You know
the kind of person Timothy is. You know he has served with me in telling the Good News, as a son serves his father.
23 I plan to send him to you
quickly when I know what will happen to me.
24 I am sure that the Lord
will help me to come to you soon.

25 Epaphroditus, my brother in Christ, works and serves with me in the army of Christ. When I needed help, you sent him to me. I think now

that I must send him back to you,
[26] because he wants very much to
see all of you. He is worried because
you heard that he was sick. [27] Yes, he
was sick, and nearly died, but God
had mercy on him and me too so that
I would not have more sadness. [28] I
want very much to send him to you
so that when you see him you can
be happy, and I can stop worrying
about you. [29] Welcome him in the
Lord with much joy. Give honor to
people like him, [30] because he almost
died for the work of Christ. He
risked his life to give me the help
you could not give in your service
to me.

OLD TESTAMENT READING

Foolish people are always
fighting,
but avoiding quarrels will
bring you honor.

Proverbs 20:3

Pleasant words are like a
honeycomb,
making people happy and
healthy.

Proverbs 16:24

People without good sense find
fault with their neighbors,
but those with understanding
keep quiet.

Proverbs 11:12

INSIGHTS

Whether we admit it or not, unbelief and disobedience are the underlying reasons for a complaining spirit.

God's Word is clear: "Do everything without complaining or arguing." This is a command, not an option. He doesn't qualify the statement and excuse us if things suddenly go wrong and it's not our fault. He says everything—and I take that to be all-inclusive. He is talking about every single circumstance whether desirable or not. When I complain, I am in essence saying, "I really don't believe God has arranged these circumstances or that He could change them if He desired." If I did believe it, I wouldn't need to complain. I'd know my only safety is in the center of His will no matter what happens.

The same God who told me not to complain also said, "In everything give thanks, for this is the will of God in Christ Jesus concerning you." How is it possible to give thanks and complain at the same time?

Is it hypocritical to say I'm thankful for my problems when I don't feel thankful? Not really, because God assures us that ". . . all things work together for good. . . ." Even when it looks disastrous, I can be certain that these self-same predicaments will be miraculously transformed under the skilled knife of the divine surgeon. He might do a little hurtful cutting on me through the process, but it will only be for my good.

Madalene Harris

PAUSE FOR REFLECTION

Did you realize that arguing and complaining are sins against God? Reread these Scripture passages and list the results of resisting the temptation to complain or argue—in your own life and in the lives of those around you.

FRIDAY

Pursue God and His Salvation

Philippians 3:1–21

The Importance of Christ

3 My brothers and sisters, be full of joy in the Lord. It is no trouble for me to write the same things to you again, and it will help you to be more ready. 2 Watch out for those who do evil, who are like dogs, who demand to cut the body. 3 We are the ones who are truly circumcised. We worship God through his Spirit, and our pride is in Christ Jesus. We do not put trust in ourselves or anything we can do, 4 although I might be able to put trust in myself. If anyone thinks he has a reason to trust in himself, he should know that I have greater reason for trusting in myself. 5 I was circumcised eight days after my birth. I am from the people of Israel and the tribe of Benjamin. I am a Hebrew, and my parents were Hebrews. I had a strict view of the law, which is why I became a Pharisee. 6 I was so enthusiastic I tried to hurt the church. No one could find fault with the way I obeyed the law of Moses. 7 Those things were important to me, but now I think they are worth nothing because of Christ. 8 Not only those things, but I think that all things are worth nothing compared with the greatness of knowing Christ Jesus my Lord. Because of him, I have lost all those things, and now I know they are worthless trash. This allows me to have Christ 9 and to belong to him. Now I am right with God, not because I followed the law, but because I believed in Christ. God uses my faith to make me right with him. 10 I want to know Christ and the power that raised him from the dead. I want to share in his sufferings and become like him in his death. 11 Then I have hope that I myself will be raised from the dead.

Continuing Toward Our Goal

I do not mean that I am already as God wants me to be. I have not yet reached that goal, but I continue trying to reach it and to make it mine. Christ wants me to do that, which is the reason he made me his. 13 Brothers and sisters, I know that I have not yet reached that goal, but there is one thing I always do. Forgetting the past and straining toward what is ahead, 14 I keep trying to reach the goal and get the prize for which God called me through Christ to the life above.

15 All of us who are spiritually mature should think this way, too. And if there are things you do not agree with, God will make them clear to you. 16 But we should continue following the truth we already have.

17 Brothers and sisters, all of you should try to follow my example and to copy those who live the way we showed you. 18 Many people live like enemies of the cross of Christ. I have often told you about them, and it makes me cry to tell you about them now. 19 In the end, they will be destroyed. They do whatever their bodies want, they are proud of their shameful acts, and they think only about earthly things. 20 But our homeland is in heaven, and we are

waiting for our Savior, the Lord Jesus Christ, to come from heaven. [21] By his power to rule all things, he will change our simple bodies and make them like his own glorious body.

OLD TESTAMENT READING

As a deer thirsts for streams of
water,
so I thirst for you, God.
2 I thirst for the living God.
When can I go to meet with him?

Psalm 42:1–2

God, you are my God.
I search for you.
I thirst for you
like someone in a dry, empty
land
where there is no water.
2 I have seen you in the Temple
and have seen your strength
and glory.
3 Because your love is better than
life,
I will praise you.
4 I will praise you as long as I live.
I will lift up my hands in prayer
to your name.

Psalm 63:1–4b

INSIGHTS

Recently, I saw a young New Zealand cyclist win a grueling race in which he broke the national record. In a subsequent interview by the TV sports commentator, he was asked the question, "And what do you aim at for the future?" With not a moment's hesitation the reply came back: "I aim to be one of the best cyclists in the world."

In order to realize his ambition, he was prepared to pay any price in training—grueling discipline, forfeiture of social life, self-denial in many areas—and all for a piece of gold, or even bronze. Why is it that so few disciples have a similar, fixed ambition to excel for Christ? Are we "taking time and trouble to keep spiritually fit," or have we grown soft and flabby? . . .

. . . Winning a race makes great demands on the stamina and perseverance of the athlete.

Once the race has begun, the athlete cannot afford to look back. He must press on to the tape without distraction. His eyes must be fixed on the umpire's stand at the end of the track if he is to win the prize. . . .

So must the disciple run his race with eyes steadfastly fixed on his encouraging Lord, who is at once Judge, Umpire, and Awarder. He is not to look back either wistfully or hopelessly but to resolutely forget what is behind—failures and disappointments as well as successes and victories. He must strain forward to the tape with eyes fixed on his welcoming Lord. It was He who initiated our faith, and it is He who will strengthen us to complete the course.

J. Oswald Sanders

PAUSE FOR REFLECTION

In what way does Paul say spiritual maturity changes a person's thinking? How diligently are you pursuing God's calling? May the psalmist's words be your prayer and praise to the Lord!

WEEKEND

Don't Worry About Anything; Ask God for What You Need

Philippians 4:1–23

What the Christians Are to Do

4 My dear brothers and sisters, I love you and want to see you. You bring me joy and make me proud of you, so stand strong in the Lord as I have told you.

2 I ask Euodia and Syntyche to agree in the Lord. 3 And I ask you, my faithful friend, to help these women. They served with me in telling the Good News, together with Clement and others who worked with me, whose names are written in the book of life.

4 Be full of joy in the Lord always. I will say again, be full of joy.

5 Let everyone see that you are gentle and kind. The Lord is coming soon. 6 Do not worry about anything, but pray and ask God for everything you need, always giving thanks. 7 And God's peace, which is so great we cannot understand it, will keep your hearts and minds in Christ Jesus.

8 Brothers and sisters, think about the things that are good and worthy of praise. Think about the things that are true and honorable and right and pure and beautiful and respected. 9 Do what you learned and received from me, what I told you, and what you saw me do. And the God who gives peace will be with you.

Paul Thanks the Christians

10 I am very happy in the Lord that you have shown your care for me again. You continued to care about me, but there was no way for you to show it. 11 I am not telling you this because I need anything. I have learned to be satisfied with the things I have and with everything that happens. 12 I know how to live when I am poor, and I know how to live when I have plenty. I have learned the secret of being happy at any time in everything that happens, when I have enough to eat and when I go hungry, when I have more than I need and when I do not have enough. 13 I can do all things through Christ, because he gives me strength.

14 But it was good that you helped me when I needed it. 15 You Philippians remember when I first preached the Good News there. When I left Macedonia, you were the only church that gave me help. 16 Several times you sent me things I needed when I was in Thessalonica. 17 Really, it is not that I want to receive gifts from you, but I want you to have the good that comes from giving. 18 And now I have everything, and more. I have all I need, because Epaphroditus brought your gift to me. It is like a sweet-smelling sacrifice offered to God, who accepts that sacrifice and is pleased with it. 19 My God will use his wonderful riches in Christ Jesus to give you everything you need. 20 Glory to our God and Father forever and ever! Amen.

21 Greet each of God's people in Christ. Those who are with me send greetings to you. 22 All of God's people greet you, particularly those from the palace of Caesar.

23 The grace of the Lord Jesus Christ be with you all.

OLD TESTAMENT READING

Give your worries to the LORD,
and he will take care of you.
He will never let good people
down.

Psalm 55:22

Give thanks to the LORD and
pray to him.
Tell the nations what he has
done.
2 Sing to him; sing praises to him.
Tell about all his miracles.
3 Be glad that you are his;
let those who seek the LORD be
happy.
4 Depend on the LORD and his
strength;
always go to him for help.

Psalm 105:1–4

Trust the LORD and do good.
Live in the land and feed on
truth.
4 Enjoy serving the LORD,
and he will give you what you
want.
5 Depend on the LORD;
trust him, and he will take care
of you.

Psalm 37:3–5

INSIGHTS

During the Great Depression the bank in which my father was an officer was forced to close. . . .

I was convinced my father would be out of work. I knew I had to get a job as a boy of twelve to help support the family. A nearby corner grocer hired me after school and Saturdays for a dollar a week to sweep the floors and deliver groceries.

When I told my father, he replied, "I appreciate your concern and desire to help, son, but I am trusting the Lord to meet our needs. We belong to Him and He will take care of His own."

God honored my father's faith. He never went a day without employment through the entire Depression.

With similar confidence Paul wrote to the Philippian Christians, "My God will meet all your needs" (4:19). This was the encouragement those believers needed because they were far from affluent (2 Cor. 8:1–5). Out of their meager resources they had sent an offering to Paul in Rome (Phil. 4:14–18). Paul assured them that God would reimburse them.

Two important details about this promise must be observed. First, God will meet "all your needs," not your desires. Jesus said, "Your Father knows what you need" (Matt. 6:8), and His understanding of our needs may be different from ours.

Second, God will meet our needs "according to His glorious riches in Christ Jesus." God's supply is not "out of" but "according to His glorious riches." God is "able to do immeasurably more than we ask or imagine" (Eph. 3:20). . . .

Whatever your needs are right now, trust God to meet them and look for His supply.

John Witmer

ACTION POINT

What does God's peace enable us to do? List the things on which God wants you to focus your thoughts. Will you ask God for what you need and trust him to care for you?

MONDAY

Christ's Preeminence in All of History

Colossians 1:1–23

1 From Paul, an apostle of Christ
Jesus. I am an apostle because
that is what God wanted. Also from
Timothy, our brother.
2 To the holy and faithful brothers
and sisters in Christ that live in
Colosse:

Grace and peace to you from God
our Father.

3 In our prayers for you we always
thank God, the Father of our Lord
Jesus Christ, 4 because we have
heard about the faith you have in
Christ Jesus and the love you have
for all of God's people. 5 You have
this faith and love because of your
hope, and what you hope for is kept
safe for you in heaven. You learned
about this hope when you heard the
message about the truth, the Good
News 6 that was told to you. Everywhere in the world that Good News
is bringing blessings and is growing.
This has happened with you, too,
since you heard the Good News and
understood the truth about the
grace of God. 7 You learned about
God's grace from Epaphras, whom
we love. He works together with us
and is a faithful servant of Christ for
us. 8 He also told us about the love
you have from the Holy Spirit.

9 Because of this, since the day we
heard about you, we have continued
praying for you, asking God that you
will know fully what he wants. We
pray that you will also have great wisdom and understanding in spiritual
things 10 so that you will live the kind
of life that honors and pleases the
Lord in every way. You will produce
fruit in every good work and grow in
the knowledge of God. 11 God will
strengthen you with his own great
power so that you will not give up
when troubles come, but you will be
patient. 12 And you will joyfully give
thanks to the Father who has made
you able to have a share in all that he
has prepared for his people in the
kingdom of light. 13 God has freed us
from the power of darkness, and he
brought us into the Kingdom of his
dear Son. 14 The Son paid for our sins,
and in him we have forgiveness.

The Importance of Christ

No one can see God, but Jesus
Christ is exactly like him. He ranks
higher than everything that has
been made. 16 Through his power all
things were made—things in heaven
and on earth, things seen and un-
seen, all powers, authorities, lords,
and rulers. All things were made
through Christ and for Christ. 17 He
was there before anything was
made, and all things continue because of him. 18 He is the head of the
body, which is the church. Everything comes from him. He is the first
one who was raised from the dead.
So in all things Jesus has first place.
19 God was pleased for all of himself
to live in Christ. 20 And through
Christ, God has brought all things
back to himself again—things on
earth and things in heaven. God
made peace through the blood of
Christ's death on the cross.

21 At one time you were separated
from God. You were his enemies in
your minds, and the evil things you

did were against God. [22]But now
God has made you his friends again.
He did this through Christ's death
in the body so that he might bring
you into God's presence as people
who are holy, with no wrong, and
with nothing of which God can judge
you guilty. [23]This will happen if you
continue strong and sure in your
faith. You must not be moved away
from the hope brought to you by the
Good News that you heard. That
same Good News has been told to
everyone in the world, and I, Paul,
help in preaching that Good News.

OLD TESTAMENT READING

Who caused the one to come
from the east?
Who gives him victories
everywhere he goes?
4 Who caused this to happen?
Who has controlled history
since the beginning?
I, the LORD, am the one. I was
here at the beginning,
and I will be here when all
things are finished."

Isaiah 41:2a–b, 4

INSIGHTS

Right through the Old Testament the conviction runs that God is managing all human history for the good of his people and that the climax will be the setting up of the kingdom of God under the Messiah, God's anointed King. In the New Testament, Jesus of Nazareth is shown to be that Messiah or Christ. But his role is not only a kingly one, but prophetic and priestly too. Jesus as prophet preached in God's name; as priest, he offered himself in sacrifice for the sins of the people; as king, having risen triumphantly from the dead, he now reigns at God's right hand. "All authority in heaven and on earth has been given to me," he told his disciples (Matt. 28:18). So the early Christians came to see Jesus of Nazareth as the Christ of God, their Teacher, Savior, and living Lord.

. . . As Christians we know that Christ is reigning until all things are put under his feet and that we are living in the last days—the period between his first coming, to bring salvation and set up his kingdom, and his second coming, to complete the work of his kingdom in royal triumph and final judgment.

There is increasing chaos and confusion as human history moves to its close, but as Christians we can find stability and hope in Jesus who is the sovereign Lord of history. The Father has promised the Son, "Thy throne, O God, is forever and ever" (Heb. 1:8), and the promise will never fail.

J. I. Packer

ACTION POINT

How does Christ's management of heaven and earth affect your view of history? Your hope for the future? Spend time in prayer, praising God for his incomparable greatness and his awesome love for you.

TUESDAY

Be Strong in Your Faith so No One Turns You Away from God

Colossians 1:24—2:15

Paul's Work for the Church

I am happy in my sufferings for you.
There are things that Christ must
still suffer through his body, the
church. I am accepting, in my body,
my part of these things that must be
suffered. 25 I became a servant of the
church because God gave me a special work to do that helps you, and
that work is to tell fully the message
of God. 26 This message is the secret
that was hidden from everyone since
the beginning of time, but now it is
made known to God's holy people.
27 God decided to let his people know
this rich and glorious secret which
he has for all people. This secret is
Christ himself, who is in you. He is
our only hope for glory. 28 So we continue to preach Christ to each person, using all wisdom to warn and
to teach everyone, in order to bring
each one into God's presence as a
mature person in Christ. 29 To do
this, I work and struggle, using
Christ's great strength that works so
powerfully in me.
2 I want you to know how hard I
work for you, those in Laodicea,
and others who have never seen me.
2 I want them to be strengthened and
joined together with love so that they
may be rich in their understanding.
This leads to their knowing fully
God's secret, that is, Christ himself.
3 In him all the treasures of wisdom
and knowledge are safely kept.
4 I say this so that no one can fool
you by arguments that seem good,
but are false. 5 Though I am absent
from you in my body, my heart is
with you, and I am happy to see your
good lives and your strong faith in
Christ.

Continue to Live in Christ

As you received Christ Jesus the
Lord, so continue to live in him.
7 Keep your roots deep in him and
have your lives built on him. Be
strong in the faith, just as you were
taught, and always be thankful.
8 Be sure that no one leads you
away with false and empty teaching
that is only human, which comes
from the ruling spirits of this world,
and not from Christ. 9 All of God lives
in Christ fully (even when Christ was
on earth), 10 and you have a full and
true life in Christ, who is ruler over
all rulers and powers.
11 Also in Christ you had a different kind of circumcision, a circumcision not done by hands. It was
through Christ's circumcision, that is,
his death, that you were made free
from the power of your sinful self.
12 When you were baptized, you were
buried with Christ, and you were
raised up with him through your faith
in God's power that was shown when
he raised Christ from the dead.
13 When you were spiritually dead because of your sins and because you
were not free from the power of your
sinful self, God made you alive with
Christ, and he forgave all our sins.
14 He canceled the debt, which listed
all the rules we failed to follow. He
took away that record with its rules
and nailed it to the cross. 15 God

stripped the spiritual rulers and powers of their authority. With the cross, he won the victory and showed the world that they were powerless.

OLD TESTAMENT READING

I waited patiently for the LORD.
He turned to me and heard my cry.
2 He lifted me out of the pit of destruction,
out of the sticky mud.
He stood me on a rock
and made my feet steady.
3 He put a new song in my mouth,
a song of praise to our God.
Many people will see this and worship him.
Then they will trust the LORD.

4 Happy is the person
who trusts the LORD,
who doesn't turn to those who are proud
or to those who worship false gods.

Psalm 40:1–4

Always remember what you have been taught,
and don't let go of it.
Keep all that you have learned;
it is the most important thing in life.
14 Don't follow the ways of the wicked;

Proverbs 4:13–14a

INSIGHTS

It is a grand thing to have a faith which cannot be shaken. I saw one day a number of beech trees which had formed a wood: they had all fallen to the ground through a storm. The fact was they leaned upon one another to a great extent, and the thickness of the wood prevented each tree from getting a firm hold of the soil. They kept each other up and also constrained each other to grow up tall and thin, to the neglect of root growth. When the tempest forced down the first few trees the others readily followed one after the other. Close to that same spot I saw another tree in the open, bravely defying the blast, in solitary strength. The hurricane had beaten upon it but it had endured all its force unsheltered. That lone, brave tree seemed to be better rooted than before the storm.

I thought, "Is it not so with professors?" They often hold together, and help each other to grow up, but if they have not firm personal roothold, when a storm arises they fall in rows. A minister dies, or certain leaders are taken away, and over go the members by departure from the faith and from holiness. I would have you be self-contained, growing each man into Christ for himself, rooted and grounded in love and faith and every holy grace. Then when the worst storm that ever blew on mortal man shall come, it will be said of your faith, "It could not shake it."

Charles Spurgeon

PAUSE FOR REFLECTION

Why must believers know and understand God's truth? How deep and strong are your roots in the faith? Can you clearly separate the ideas of humans from the teachings of God? Are his teachings safe within your heart?

WEDNESDAY

Put Away All Evil and Focus on the Holy Things of God

Colossians 2:16—3:17

Don't Follow People's Rules

So do not let anyone make rules for you about eating and drinking or about a religious feast, a New Moon Festival, or a Sabbath day. [17]These things were like a shadow of what was to come. But what is true and real has come and is found in Christ. [18]Do not let anyone disqualify you by making you humiliate yourself and worship angels. Such people enter into visions, which fill them with foolish pride because of their human way of thinking. [19]They do not hold tightly to Christ, the head. It is from him that all the parts of the body are cared for and held together. So it grows in the way God wants it to grow.

[20]Since you died with Christ and were made free from the ruling spirits of the world, why do you act as if you still belong to this world by following rules like these: [21]"Don't eat this," "Don't taste that," "Don't even touch that thing"? [22]These rules refer to earthly things that are gone as soon as they are used. They are only man-made commands and teachings. [23]They seem to be wise, but they are only part of a man-made religion. They make people pretend not to be proud and make them punish their bodies, but they do not really control the evil desires of the sinful self.

Your New Life in Christ

3 Since you were raised from the dead with Christ, aim at what is in heaven, where Christ is sitting at the right hand of God. [2]Think only about the things in heaven, not the things on earth. [3]Your old sinful self has died, and your new life is kept with Christ in God. [4]Christ is our life, and when he comes again, you will share in his glory.

[5]So put all evil things out of your life: sexual sinning, doing evil, letting evil thoughts control you, wanting things that are evil, and greed. This is really serving a false god. [6]These things make God angry. [7]In your past, evil life you also did these things.

[8]But now also put these things out of your life: anger, bad temper, doing or saying things to hurt others, and using evil words when you talk. [9]Do not lie to each other. You have left your old sinful life and the things you did before. [10]You have begun to live the new life, in which you are being made new and are becoming like the One who made you. This new life brings you the true knowledge of God. [11]In the new life there is no difference between Greeks and Jews, those who are circumcised and those who are not circumcised, or people who are foreigners, or Scythians. There is no difference between slaves and free people. But Christ is in all believers, and Christ is all that is important.

[12]God has chosen you and made you his holy people. He loves you. So always do these things: Show mercy to others, be kind, humble, gentle, and patient. [13]Get along with each other, and forgive each other.

If someone does wrong to you, forgive that person because the Lord
forgave you. 14 Do all these things;
but most important, love each other.
Love is what holds you all together
in perfect unity. 15 Let the peace that
Christ gives control your thinking,
because you were all called together
in one body to have peace. Always
be thankful. 16 Let the teaching of
Christ live in you richly. Use all wisdom to teach and instruct each other
by singing psalms, hymns, and spiritual songs with thankfulness in your
hearts to God. 17 Everything you do
or say should be done to obey Jesus
your Lord. And in all you do, give
thanks to God the Father through
Jesus.

OLD TESTAMENT READING

*B*e my holy people. Be holy because
I am the LORD your God. 8 Remember
and obey my laws. I am the LORD, and
I have made you holy.

26 " 'So you must be holy to me because I, the LORD, am holy, and I
have set you apart from other people
to be my own.' "

Leviticus 20:7–8, 26

INSIGHTS

The New Testament leaves no doubt that holiness is our responsibility. If we are to pursue holiness, we must take some decisive action. . . .

The action we are to take is to put to death the misdeeds of the body (Romans 8:13). Paul uses the same expression in another book: "Put to death, therefore, whatever belongs to your earthly nature" (Colossians 3:5). . . . To put to death the misdeeds of the body, then, is to destroy the strength and vitality of sin as it tries to reign in our bodies.

It must be clear to us that mortification, though it is something we do, cannot be carried out in our own strength. . . . Mortification must be done by the strength and under the direction of the Holy Spirit. . . .

. . . "How do we destroy the strength and vitality of sin?" If we are to work at this difficult task, we must first have conviction. We must be persuaded that a holy life of God's will for every Christian is important. . . .

Not only must we develop conviction for living a holy life in general, but we must also develop convictions in specific areas of obedience.

These convictions are developed through exposure to the Word of God. . . .

. . . Obedience is the pathway to holiness, but it is only as we have His commands that we can obey them. God's Word must be so strongly fixed in our minds that it becomes the dominant influence in our thoughts, our attitudes, and our actions.

Jerry Bridges

PAUSE FOR REFLECTION

What is the one and only reason that God's people are to be holy? What does a person need to know to be holy? What must a person do to be holy? How does a person have the strength to be holy? What do you need to focus on as you pursue holiness?

THURSDAY

Honor Your Parents

Colossians 3:18—4:18

Your New Life with Other People

Wives, yield to the authority of
your husbands, because this is the
right thing to do in the Lord.
19 Husbands, love your wives and
be gentle with them.
20 Children, obey your parents in
all things, because this pleases the
Lord.
21 Fathers, do not nag your children. If you are too hard to please,
they may want to stop trying.
22 Slaves, obey your masters in all
things. Do not obey just when they
are watching you, to gain their favor,
but serve them honestly, because
you respect the Lord. 23 In all the
work you are doing, work the best
you can. Work as if you were doing
it for the Lord, not for people. 24 Remember that you will receive your
reward from the Lord, which he
promised to his people. You are serving the Lord Christ. 25 But remember
that anyone who does wrong will be
punished for that wrong, and the
Lord treats everyone the same.
4 Masters, give what is good and
fair to your slaves. Remember
that you have a Master in heaven.

What the Christians Are to Do

Continue praying, keeping alert,
and always thanking God. 3 Also pray
for us that God will give us an opportunity to tell people his message.
Pray that we can preach the secret
that God has made known about
Christ. This is why I am in prison.
4 Pray that I can speak in a way that
will make it clear, as I should.
5 Be wise in the way you act with
people who are not believers, making the most of every opportunity.
6 When you talk, you should always
be kind and pleasant so you will be
able to answer everyone in the way
you should.

The People with Paul

Tychicus is my dear brother in
Christ and a faithful minister and
servant with me in the Lord. He will
tell you all the things that are happening to me. 8 This is why I am
sending him: so you may know how
we are and he may encourage you.
9 I send him with Onesimus, a faithful and dear brother in Christ, and
one of your group. They will tell you
all that has happened here.
10 Aristarchus, a prisoner with me,
and Mark, the cousin of Barnabas,
greet you. (I have already told you
what to do about Mark. If he comes,
welcome him.) 11 Jesus, who is called
Justus, also greets you. These are
the only Jewish believers who work
with me for the kingdom of God, and
they have been a comfort to me.
12 Epaphras, a servant of Jesus
Christ, from your group, also greets
you. He always prays for you that
you will grow to be spiritually mature and have everything God wants
for you. 13 I know he has worked
hard for you and the people in
Laodicea and in Hierapolis. 14 Demas
and our dear friend Luke, the doctor, greet you.
15 Greet the brothers in Laodicea.
And greet Nympha and the church

that meets in her house. [16] After this letter is read to you, be sure it is also read to the church in Laodicea. And you read the letter that I wrote to Laodicea. [17] Tell Archippus, "Be sure to finish the work the Lord gave you."

[18] I, Paul, greet you and write this with my own hand. Remember me in prison. Grace be with you.

OLD TESTAMENT READING

My son, keep your father's
  commands,
 and don't forget your mother's
  teaching.
21 Keep their words in mind forever
 as though you had them tied
  around your neck.
22 They will guide you when you
  walk.
 They will guard you when you
  sleep.
 They will speak to you when
  you are awake.

Proverbs 6:20–22

INSIGHTS

Much is being said and written these days about the care of the elderly. But what is being done in practical ways to relieve them of their ongoing fears for their future? Such fears as:

- *financial problems in a day of rising costs and a fixed income*
- *fears of sickness with no one to take care of them, in a day when families can be so scattered as to be unavailable to one another . . .*

Each of us, whatever our age, needs to remind himself that we are of great worth in the sight of God, that He has plans for each one. Speaking of the righteous, the psalmist writes, "They shall still bring forth fruit in old age" (Psalm 92:14).

Ironically, some countries to which we send missionaries with the gospel message can teach us much about honoring our fathers and our mothers. For example, a woman whom I met on one of my teaching trips to Asian countries confided to me, "My sister, who is much wealthier than I, felt that she should have the pleasure of taking care of our aged mother. But, as the youngest daughter, it is my privilege." . . .

. . . God knows our heart and our intentions. Where we treat the elderly around us with love and care, it will be counted as our obeying the fifth commandment.

And obedience is its own reward.

The Lord Jesus Himself set the pattern. From the cross, in the midst of His own agony, He remembered His mother and committed her to the care of "the disciple . . . whom he loved" (John 19:26–27).

Jeanette Lockerbie

PAUSE FOR REFLECTION

It is good to honor one's parents by caring for them, but Scripture reveals a broader perspective on what it means to honor one's parents. How does this reading expand your picture of honoring one's parents? How do you measure up?

FRIDAY

God Loves His Chosen People, Who May Endure Suffering

1 Thessalonians 1:1—2:16

1 From Paul, Silas, and Timothy.
To the church in Thessalonica,
the church in God the Father and
the Lord Jesus Christ:
Grace and peace to you.

The Faith of the Thessalonians

We always thank God for all of you
and mention you when we pray. 3 We
continually recall before God our
Father the things you have done because of your faith and the work you
have done because of your love. And
we thank him that you continue to
be strong because of your hope in
our Lord Jesus Christ.
4 Brothers and sisters, God loves
you, and we know he has chosen
you, 5 because the Good News we
brought to you came not only with
words, but with power, with the Holy
Spirit, and with sure knowledge that
it is true. Also you know how we
lived when we were with you in order to help you. 6 And you became
like us and like the Lord. You suffered much, but still you accepted
the teaching with the joy that comes
from the Holy Spirit. 7 So you became an example to all the believers
in Macedonia and Southern Greece.
8 And the Lord's teaching spread
from you not only into Macedonia
and Southern Greece, but now your
faith in God has become known everywhere. So we do not need to say
anything about it. 9 People everywhere are telling about the way you
accepted us when we were there
with you. They tell how you stopped
worshiping idols and began serving
the living and true God. 10 And you
wait for God's Son, whom God raised
from the dead, to come from heaven.
He is Jesus, who saves us from
God's angry judgment that is sure
to come.

Paul's Work in Thessalonica

2 Brothers and sisters, you know
our visit to you was not a failure.
2 Before we came to you, we suffered
in Philippi. People there insulted us,
as you know, and many people were
against us. But our God helped us
to be brave and to tell you his Good
News. 3 Our appeal does not come
from lies or wrong reasons, nor were
we trying to trick you. 4 But we speak
the Good News because God tested
us and trusted us to do it. When we
speak, we are not trying to please
people, but God, who tests our
hearts. 5 You know that we never
tried to influence you by saying nice
things about you. We were not trying to get your money; we had no
selfishness to hide from you. God
knows that this is true. 6 We were not
looking for human praise, from you
or anyone else, 7 even though as
apostles of Christ we could have
used our authority over you.

But we were very gentle with you,
like a mother caring for her little children. 8 Because we loved you, we were
happy to share not only God's Good
News with you, but even our own
lives. You had become so dear to us!
9 Brothers and sisters, I know you remember our hard work and difficul-

ties. We worked night and day so we
would not burden any of you while we
preached God's Good News to you.
10 When we were with you, we
lived in a holy and honest way, without fault. You know this is true, and
so does God. 11 You know that we
treated each of you as a father treats
his own children. 12 We encouraged
you, we urged you, and we insisted
that you live good lives for God, who
calls you to his glorious kingdom.
13 Also, we always thank God because when you heard his message
from us, you accepted it as the word
of God, not the words of humans. And
it really is God's message which
works in you who believe. 14 Brothers
and sisters, your experiences have
been like those of God's churches in
Christ that are in Judea. You suffered
from the people of your own country,
as they suffered from the Jews,
15 who killed both the Lord Jesus and
the prophets and forced us to leave
that country. They do not please God
and are against all people. 16 They try
to stop us from teaching those who
are not Jews so they may be saved.
By doing this, they are increasing
their sins to the limit. The anger of
God has come to them at last.

OLD TESTAMENT READING

The LORD did not care for you and choose you because there were many of you—you are the smallest nation of all. 8 But the LORD chose you because he loved you, and he kept his promise to your ancestors.

Deuteronomy 7:7–8a

INSIGHTS

If there be one place where our Lord Jesus most fully becomes the joy and comfort of His people, it is where He plunged deepest into the depths of woe. Come hither, gracious souls, and behold the Man in the garden of Gethsemane; behold His heart so brimming with love that He cannot hold it in—so full of sorrow that it must find a vent. Behold the Man as they drive the nails into His hands and feet. . . .

Most of us know what it is to be overwhelmed in heart. Disappointments and heartbreaks will do this when billow after billow rolls over us, and we are like a broken shell hurled to and fro by the surf. Blessed be God, at such seasons we are not without an all-sufficient solace; our Savior is the harbor of weather-beaten sails, the hospice of forlorn pilgrims. Higher than we are is our God, His mercy higher than our sins, His love higher than our thoughts. A rock He is since He changes not, and a high rock, because the tempests which overwhelm us roll far beneath at His feet. O Lord, our God, by Your Holy Spirit, teach us your way of faith, lead us unto Your rest.

Charles Spurgeon

ACTION POINT

How do you think Paul's words encouraged the Thessalonians? When has someone encouraged you with the assurance of God's love? Who can you encourage today?

WEEKEND

God Requires Holy Living

1 Thessalonians 2:17—4:12

Paul Wants to Visit Them Again

Brothers and sisters, though we
were separated from you for a short
time, our thoughts were still with
you. We wanted very much to see
you and tried hard to do so. [18]We
wanted to come to you. I, Paul, tried
to come more than once, but Satan
stopped us. [19]You are our hope, our
joy, and the crown we will take pride
in when our Lord Jesus Christ
comes. [20]Truly you are our glory
and our joy.

3 When we could not wait any
longer, we decided it was best to
stay in Athens alone [2]and send
Timothy to you. Timothy, our
brother, works with us for God and
helps us tell people the Good News
about Christ. We sent him to
strengthen and encourage you in
your faith [3]so none of you would be
upset by these troubles. You yourselves know that we must face these
troubles. [4]Even when we were with
you, we told you we all would have
to suffer, and you know it has happened. [5]Because of this, when I
could wait no longer, I sent Timothy
to you so I could learn about your
faith. I was afraid the devil had
tempted you, and then our hard
work would have been wasted.

[6]But Timothy now has come back
to us from you and has brought us
good news about your faith and love.
He told us that you always remember us in a good way and that you
want to see us just as much as we
want to see you. [7]So, brothers and
sisters, while we have much trouble
and suffering, we are encouraged
about you because of your faith.
[8]Our life is really full if you stand
strong in the Lord. [9]We have so
much joy before our God because of
you. We cannot thank him enough
for all the joy we feel. [10]Night and
day we continue praying with all our
heart that we can see you again and
give you all the things you need to
make your faith strong.

[11]Now may our God and Father
himself and our Lord Jesus prepare
the way for us to come to you. [12]May
the Lord make your love grow more
and multiply for each other and for
all people so that you will love others as we love you. [13]May your
hearts be made strong so that you
will be holy and without fault before
our God and Father when our Lord
Jesus comes with all his holy ones.

A Life that Pleases God

4 Brothers and sisters, we taught
you how to live in a way that will
please God, and you are living that
way. Now we ask and encourage you
in the Lord Jesus to live that way
even more. [2]You know what we told
you to do by the authority of the
Lord Jesus. [3]God wants you to be
holy and to stay away from sexual
sins. [4]He wants each of you to learn
to control your own body in a way
that is holy and honorable. [5]Don't
use your body for sexual sin like the
people who do not know God. [6]Also,
do not wrong or cheat another Christian in this way. The Lord will punish people who do those things as we
have already told you and warned

you. [7] God called us to be holy and does not want us to live in sin. [8] So the person who refuses to obey this teaching is disobeying God, not simply a human teaching. And God is the One who gives us his Holy Spirit.

[9] We do not need to write you about having love for your Christian family, because God has already taught you to love each other. [10] And truly you do love the Christians in all of Macedonia. Brothers and sisters, now we encourage you to love them even more.

[11] Do all you can to live a peaceful life. Take care of your own business, and do your own work as we have already told you. [12] If you do, then people who are not believers will respect you, and you will not have to depend on others for what you need.

OLD TESTAMENT READING

Remember my commands and obey them; I am the LORD. [32] Show respect for my holy name. You Israelites must remember that I am holy; I am the LORD, who has made you holy. [33] I brought you out of Egypt to be your God. I am the LORD."

Leviticus 22:31–33

I am the LORD your God. Keep yourselves holy for me because I am holy. Don't make yourselves unclean with any of these crawling animals. [45] I am the LORD who brought you out of Egypt to be your God; you must be holy because I am holy.'"

Leviticus 11:44–45

INSIGHTS

Our daily expression of holiness is a reflection of our faith in Christ. If we have no desire to be holy, we should seriously question the genuineness of our faith in the Lord Jesus.

Christ not only died to save us from the punishment for our sins, but also from slavery to sin in this worldly culture. To continue to live in sin as a Christian is contradictory to the most basic meaning of Christianity. Christ died to save us from our sins, not to let us remain in our sins (Matthew 1:21; 1 John 1:6, 7). What kind of person would want to follow Christ and not desire to live a holy life? . . .

Holiness, then, is not an option for the believer. Paul wrote to Titus, "For the grace of God has appeared for the salvation of all men, training us to renounce irreligion and worldly passions, and to live sober, upright, and godly lives in this world" (Titus 2:11, 12). Though holiness is not a condition for salvation, it is the natural consequence of salvation. We do not become holy in order to be saved, but because we are saved. We do not do good works to get to heaven, but because heaven has already come into our hearts.

To trust Christ for salvation is to trust him for holiness. If there is no desire for holiness within, then it is doubtful that the Holy Spirit has come to dwell within. The Holy Spirit does not save us without giving us the desire to live a holy life.

Floyd McClung

APPLICATION

What instruction does Paul give to those who please God? How does Scripture define holy living? If you are to live in a way that pleases God more and more, what is your next step?

MONDAY

The Hope of Christ's Second Coming

1 Thessalonians 4:13—5:28

The Lord's Coming

Brothers and sisters, we want you to know about those Christians who have died so you will not be sad, as others who have no hope. 14 We believe that Jesus died and that he rose again. So, because of him, God will raise with Jesus those who have died. 15 What we tell you now is the Lord's own message. We who are living when the Lord comes again will not go before those who have already died. 16 The Lord himself will come down from heaven with a loud command, with the voice of the archangel, and with the trumpet call of God. And those who have died believing in Christ will rise first. 17 After that, we who are still alive will be gathered up with them in the clouds to meet the Lord in the air. And we will be with the Lord forever. 18 So encourage each other with these words.

Be Ready for the Lord's Coming

5 Now, brothers and sisters, we do not need to write you about times and dates. 2 You know very well that the day the Lord comes again will be a surprise, like a thief that comes in the night. 3 While people are saying, "We have peace and we are safe," they will be destroyed quickly. It is like pains that come quickly to a woman having a baby. Those people will not escape. 4 But you, brothers and sisters, are not living in darkness, and so that day will not surprise you like a thief. 5 You are all people who belong to the light and to the day. We do not belong to the night or to darkness. 6 So we should not be like other people who are sleeping, but we should be alert and have self-control. 7 Those who sleep, sleep at night. Those who get drunk, get drunk at night. 8 But we belong to the day, so we should control ourselves. We should wear faith and love to protect us, and the hope of salvation should be our helmet. 9 God did not choose us to suffer his anger but to have salvation through our Lord Jesus Christ. 10 Jesus died for us so that we can live together with him, whether we are alive or dead when he comes. 11 So encourage each other and give each other strength, just as you are doing now.

Final Instructions and Greetings

Now, brothers and sisters, we ask you to appreciate those who work hard among you, who lead you in the Lord and teach you. 13 Respect them with a very special love because of the work they do.

Live in peace with each other. 14 We ask you, brothers and sisters, to warn those who do not work. Encourage the people who are afraid. Help those who are weak. Be patient with everyone. 15 Be sure that no one pays back wrong for wrong, but always try to do what is good for each other and for all people.

16 Always be joyful. 17 Pray continually, 18 and give thanks whatever happens. That is what God wants for you in Christ Jesus.

19 Do not hold back the work of
the Holy Spirit. 20 Do not treat prophecy as if it were unimportant. 21 But
test everything. Keep what is good,
22 and stay away from everything that
is evil.
23 Now may God himself, the
God of peace, make you pure, belonging only to him. May your
whole self—spirit, soul, and body—
be kept safe and without fault when
our Lord Jesus Christ comes. 24 You
can trust the One who calls you to
do that for you.
25 Brothers and sisters, pray for us.
26 Give each other a holy kiss
when you meet. 27 I tell you by the
authority of the Lord to read this letter to all the believers.
28 The grace of our Lord Jesus
Christ be with you.

OLD TESTAMENT READING

I know that my Defender lives,
and in the end he will stand
upon the earth.
26 Even after my skin has been
destroyed,
in my flesh I will see God.
27 I will see him myself;
I will see him with my very
own eyes.
How my heart wants that to
happen!

Job 19:25–27

INSIGHTS

What would you say about a person who had made a hundred promises to you and kept ninety-nine of them? You probably would think that he was honest enough to fulfill the last promise as well, wouldn't you?

Jesus Christ has fulfilled every promise He ever made, except one. He has not yet returned. Will He?

In both the Old and New Testaments there are references to the return of the Lord. . . . Ezekiel tells of a Jerusalem which is to be restored, a temple which is to be rebuilt, and a land which is to be reclaimed and blessed with prosperity at the Lord's return. Zephaniah gives us the new song that He will teach to Israel and describes the overthrow of the false Christ.

In the New Testament, Matthew likens Christ to a bridegroom coming to receive His bride. Mark sees Him as a householder going on a long journey and entrusting certain tasks to his servants until his return. To Luke, Jesus is a nobleman going to a far country to transact business and leaving his possessions with his servants that they may trade with them until he comes.

John quotes Christ as saying, "I go to prepare a place for you. I will come again to receive you unto myself." The entire book of Revelation tells of the glorious return of Christ. And we can say with the apostle John, who wrote that book, "Amen, even so, come, Lord Jesus."

Billy Graham

PAUSE FOR REFLECTION

What about Christ's second coming gives you hope? What difference does Paul say the hope of Christ's second coming should make in the believer's life? What difference does that hope make in your life?

TUESDAY

God's Righteous Judgment Will Destroy Those Who Refuse to Believe

2 Thessalonians 1:1—2:12

1 From Paul, Silas, and Timothy.
To the church in Thessalonica in
God our Father and the Lord Jesus
Christ:
2 Grace and peace to you from
God the Father and the Lord Jesus
Christ.

Paul Talks About God's Judgment

We must always thank God for you,
brothers and sisters. This is only
right, because your faith is growing
more and more, and the love that
every one of you has for each other
is increasing. 4 So we brag about you
to the other churches of God. We tell
them about the way you continue to
be strong and have faith even
though you are being treated badly
and are suffering many troubles.
5 This is proof that God is right in
his judgment. He wants you to be
counted worthy of his kingdom for
which you are suffering. 6 God will
do what is right. He will give trouble
to those who trouble you. 7 And he
will give rest to you who are troubled
and to us also when the Lord Jesus
appears with burning fire from
heaven with his powerful angels.
8 Then he will punish those who do
not know God and who do not obey
the Good News about our Lord
Jesus Christ. 9 Those people will be
punished with a destruction that
continues forever. They will be kept
away from the Lord and from his
great power. 10 This will happen on
the day when the Lord Jesus comes
to receive glory because of his holy
people. And all the people who have
believed will be amazed at Jesus. You
will be in that group, because you
believed what we told you.
11 That is why we always pray for
you, asking our God to help you live
the kind of life he called you to live.
We pray that with his power God will
help you do the good things you
want and perform the works that
come from your faith. 12 We pray all
this so that the name of our Lord
Jesus Christ will have glory in you,
and you will have glory in him. That
glory comes from the grace of our
God and the Lord Jesus Christ.

Evil Things Will Happen

2 Brothers and sisters, we have
something to say about the coming of our Lord Jesus Christ and the
time when we will meet together
with him. 2 Do not become easily
upset in your thinking or afraid if you
hear that the day of the Lord has already come. Someone may say this
in a prophecy or in a message or in
a letter as if it came from us. 3 Do not
let anyone fool you in any way. That
day of the Lord will not come until
the turning away from God happens
and the Man of Evil, who is on his
way to hell, appears. 4 He will be
against and put himself above anything called God or anything that
people worship. And that Man of Evil
will even go into God's Temple and
sit there and say that he is God.
5 I told you when I was with you
that all this would happen. Do you
not remember? 6 And now you know

what is stopping that Man of Evil so
he will appear at the right time. 7 The
secret power of evil is already working in the world, but there is one
who is stopping that power. And he
will continue to stop it until he is
taken out of the way. 8 Then that Man
of Evil will appear, and the Lord
Jesus will kill him with the breath
that comes from his mouth and will
destroy him with the glory of his
coming. 9 The Man of Evil will come
by the power of Satan. He will have
great power, and he will do many different false miracles, signs, and wonders. 10 He will use every kind of evil
to trick those who are lost. They will
die, because they refused to love the
truth. (If they loved the truth, they
would be saved.) 11 For this reason
God sends them something powerful that leads them away from the
truth so they will believe a lie. 12 So
all those will be judged guilty who
did not believe the truth, but enjoyed
doing evil.

OLD TESTAMENT READING

By doing what is fair,
    Jerusalem will be free again.
By doing what is right,
    her people who come back to
        the LORD will have freedom.
28 But sinners and those who turn
        against him will be de-
        stroyed;
    those who have left the LORD
        will die.

Isaiah 1:27–28

INSIGHTS

Death is the "wages of sin." It is just what sin deserves. Labour earns wages, and creates a rightful claim to such remuneration. So men are conceived as earning wages when they sin. They become entitled to their pay. God deems Himself holden to give them their well-deserved wages. . . .

We are informed that in the final consummation of earthly scenes, "the judgment shall sit and the books shall be opened." We shall be there, and what is more, there to close up our account with our Lord and receive our allotment. Which will you have on that final settlement day? The wages of sin? . . .

. . . O, sinner, think of hell, and of yourself thrust into it. It pours forth its volumes of smoke and flame forever, never ceasing, never exhausted. Upon that spectacle the universe can look and read—"The wages of sin is death! O, sin not, since such is the doom of the unpardoned sinner!" Think what a demonstration this is in the government of God! What an exhibition of His holy justice, of His inflexible purpose to sustain the interests of holiness and happiness in all His vast dominions! . . .

Sinner, you may now escape this fearful doom. This is the reason why God has revealed hell in His faithful Word.

Charles Finney

PAUSE FOR REFLECTION

When will God punish those who don't know him? How can one escape God's punishment? How will God treat those who believe? What will happen before Jesus comes again? How are believers to live until he comes?

WEDNESDAY

Called to Work for God's Service

2 Thessalonians 2:13—3:18

You Are Chosen for Salvation

Brothers and sisters, whom the
Lord loves, God chose you from the
beginning to be saved. So we must
always thank God for you. You are
saved by the Spirit that makes you
holy and by your faith in the truth.
14 God used the Good News that we
preached to call you to be saved so
you can share in the glory of our
Lord Jesus Christ. 15 So, brothers
and sisters, stand strong and continue to believe the teachings we
gave you in our speaking and in our
letter.

16-17 May our Lord Jesus Christ
himself and God our Father encourage you and strengthen you in every
good thing you do and say. God
loved us, and through his grace he
gave us a good hope and encouragement that continues forever.

Pray for Us

3 And now, brothers and sisters,
pray for us that the Lord's teaching will continue to spread quickly
and that people will give honor to
that teaching, just as happened with
you. 2 And pray that we will be protected from stubborn and evil
people, because not all people believe.

3 But the Lord is faithful and will
give you strength and will protect
you from the Evil One. 4 The Lord
makes us feel sure that you are doing and will continue to do the things
we told you. 5 May the Lord lead
your hearts into God's love and
Christ's patience.

The Duty to Work

Brothers and sisters, by the authority of our Lord Jesus Christ we command you to stay away from any believer who refuses to work and does
not follow the teaching we gave you.
7 You yourselves know that you
should live as we live. We were not
lazy when we were with you. 8 And
when we ate another person's food,
we always paid for it. We worked
very hard night and day so we would
not be an expense to any of you. 9 We
had the right to ask you to help us,
but we worked to take care of ourselves so we would be an example
for you to follow. 10 When we were
with you, we gave you this rule:
"Anyone who refuses to work should
not eat."

11 We hear that some people in
your group refuse to work. They do
nothing but busy themselves in
other people's lives. 12 We command
those people and beg them in the
Lord Jesus Christ to work quietly
and earn their own food. 13 But you,
brothers and sisters, never become
tired of doing good.

14 If some people do not obey what
we tell you in this letter, then take
note of them. Have nothing to do
with them so they will feel ashamed.
15 But do not treat them as enemies.
Warn them as fellow believers.

Final Words

Now may the Lord of peace give
you peace at all times and in every
way. The Lord be with all of you.

17 I, Paul, end this letter now in my own handwriting. All my letters have this to show they are from me. This is the way I write.

18 The grace of our Lord Jesus Christ be with you all.

OLD TESTAMENT READING

It is hard to find a good wife,
because she is worth more
than rubies.
11 Her husband trusts her completely.
With her, he has everything he
needs.
12 She does him good and not harm
for as long as she lives.
13 She looks for wool and flax
and likes to work with her
hands.
14 She is like a trader's ship,
bringing food from far away.
15 She gets up while it is still dark
and prepares food for her
family
and feeds her servant girls.
16 She inspects a field and buys it.
With money she earned, she
plants a vineyard.

Proverbs 31:10–16

INSIGHTS

The common drudgery of daily life can be a Divine Calling. We often speak of a young man as "being called to the Ministry"; but it is as fitting to speak of a carpenter being called to the bench, the blacksmith to the forge, and the shoemaker to his last. "Brethren," said the Apostle, "let every man wherein he is called, therein abide with God."

Remember that your life has been appointed by God's wise providence. God as much sent Joseph to the drudgery and discipline of the prison as to the glory and responsibility of the palace. Nothing happens to us which is not included in His plan for us; and the incidents which seem most tiresome are often contrived to give us opportunities to become nobler, stronger characters.

We are called to be faithful in performing our assigned duties. Not brilliance, not success, not notoriety which attracts the world's notice, but the regular, quiet, and careful performance of trivial and common duties; faithfulness in that which is least is as great an attainment in God's sight as in the greatest. . . .

Take up your work, then, you who seem to be the nobodies, the drudges, the maid-of-all-work, the clerk, or shop assistant. Do it with a brave heart, looking up to Him who for many years toiled at the carpenter's bench. Amid the many scenes and actions of life, set the Lord always before your face. Do all as in His presence, and to win His smile; and be sure to cultivate a spirit of love to God and man. Look out for opportunities of cheering your fellow-workers. Do not murmur or grumble, but let your heart rise from your toil to God your Maker, Saviour, and Friend. So the lowliest service will glisten, as grass-blades do when sun and dewdrops garnish them.

F. B. Meyer

ACTION POINT

Study these readings and describe what it means to be a diligent and faithful worker for God's service today. How well do you measure up? What changes will you make to bring greater honor to God?

THURSDAY

God Is Patient and Merciful to Sinners

1 Timothy 1:1–20

1 From Paul, an apostle of Christ Jesus, by the command of God our Savior and Christ Jesus our hope.

2 To Timothy, a true child to me because you believe:

Grace, mercy, and peace from God the Father and Christ Jesus our Lord.

Warning Against False Teaching

3 I asked you to stay longer in Ephesus when I went into Macedonia so you could command some people there to stop teaching false things. 4 Tell them not to spend their time on stories that are not true and on long lists of names in family histories. These things only bring arguments; they do not help God's work, which is done in faith. 5 The purpose of this command is for people to have love, a love that comes from a pure heart and a good conscience and a true faith. 6 Some people have missed these things and turned to useless talk. 7 They want to be teachers of the law, but they do not understand either what they are talking about or what they are sure about.

8 But we know that the law is good if someone uses it lawfully. 9 We also know that the law is not made for good people but for those who are against the law and for those who refuse to follow it. It is for people who are against God and are sinful, who are not holy and have no religion, who kill their fathers and mothers, who murder, 10 who take part in sexual sins, who have sexual relations with people of the same sex, who sell slaves, who tell lies, who speak falsely, and who do anything against the true teaching of God. 11 That teaching is part of the Good News of the blessed God that he gave me to tell.

Thanks for God's Mercy

12 I thank Christ Jesus our Lord, who gave me strength, because he trusted me and gave me this work of serving him. 13 In the past I spoke against Christ and persecuted him and did all kinds of things to hurt him. But God showed me mercy, because I did not know what I was doing. I did not believe. 14 But the grace of our Lord was fully given to me, and with that grace came the faith and love that are in Christ Jesus.

15 What I say is true, and you should fully accept it: Christ Jesus came into the world to save sinners, of whom I am the worst. 16 But I was given mercy so that in me, the worst of all sinners, Christ Jesus could show that he has patience without limit. His patience with me made me an example for those who would believe in him and have life forever. 17 To the King that rules forever, who will never die, who cannot be seen, the only God, be honor and glory forever and ever. Amen.

18 Timothy, my child, I am giving you a command that agrees with the prophecies that were given about you in the past. I tell you this so you can follow them and fight the good

fight. 19 Continue to have faith and do
what you know is right. Some people
have rejected this, and their faith has
been shipwrecked. 20 Hymenaeus
and Alexander have done that, and I
have given them to Satan so they will
learn not to speak against God.

OLD TESTAMENT READING

The wicked should stop doing
wrong,
and they should stop their evil
thoughts.
They should return to the LORD so
he may have mercy on them.
They should come to our God,
because he will freely
forgive them.

Isaiah 55:7

The LORD shows mercy and is
kind.
He does not become angry
quickly, and he has great
love.
9 He will not always accuse us,
and he will not be angry
forever.
10 He has not punished us as our
sins should be punished;
he has not repaid us for the
evil we have done.

Psalm 103:8–10

INSIGHTS

In amateur baseball, there is a rule known as the "mercy rule." This rule terminates a game after a certain number of innings (usually seven) when one team is ahead by a certain number of runs (usually ten). The "mercy rule" has relieved the misery of many inferior teams or of a team that just had a bad day.

Mercy is an attribute of God for which we should be especially thankful. How wonderful that He has not given us what we really deserve! We all have our "bad days." So many times we've "blown it" with God. But He is merciful! His patience is astounding! It's hard to fathom God's mercy as He looks down upon this wicked world. How many chances He has given us! How many times we have failed to obey! . . .

. . . It is God's mercy that gives us hope for a continued relationship with Him.

Because of his mercy, we are still here! We should be so grateful that God is merciful toward His children. Our God promises to complete what He began in us (Philippians 1:6), and by His mercy He shows compassion toward us in our weaknesses. Psalms 103:14 says, "For He knows how we are formed, He remembers that we are dust." God sees us in our lowly estate and extends His mercy. Our hearts should praise the God of mercy. . . .

. . . It's only by His mercy that we are not destroyed totally and completely. Therefore, we . . . should be imitators of God and show mercy to those God brings our way.

Elliot Johnson / Al Schierbaum

APPLICATION

Review the evidence in these readings that God is not begrudgingly merciful, but abundantly merciful! The next time someone accuses God of being harsh or unforgiving, tell about the evidence you have found of God's awesome, unfailing mercy.

FRIDAY

There Is Only One God, and He Alone Saves Us

1 Timothy 2:1—3:13

Some Rules for Men and Women

2 First, I tell you to pray for all people, asking God for what they need and being thankful to him. 2 Pray for rulers and for all who have authority so that we can have quiet and peaceful lives full of worship and respect for God. 3 This is good, and it pleases God our Savior, 4 who wants all people to be saved and to know the truth. 5 There is one God and one way human beings can reach God. That way is through Christ Jesus, who is himself human. 6 He gave himself as a payment to free all people. He is proof that came at the right time. 7 That is why I was chosen to tell the Good News and to be an apostle. (I am telling the truth; I am not lying.) I was chosen to teach those who are not Jews to believe and to know the truth.

8 So, I want the men everywhere to pray, lifting up their hands in a holy manner, without anger and arguments.

9 Also, women should wear proper clothes that show respect and self-control, not using braided hair or gold or pearls or expensive clothes. 10 Instead, they should do good deeds, which is right for women who say they worship God.

11 Let a woman learn by listening quietly and being ready to cooperate in everything. 12 But I do not allow a woman to teach or to have authority over a man, but to listen quietly, 13 because Adam was formed first and then Eve. 14 And Adam was not tricked, but the woman was tricked and became a sinner. 15 But she will be saved through having children if they continue in faith, love, and holiness, with self-control.

Elders in the Church

3 What I say is true: Anyone wanting to become an elder desires a good work. 2 An elder must not give people a reason to criticize him, and he must have only one wife. He must be self-controlled, wise, respected by others, ready to welcome guests, and able to teach. 3 He must not drink too much wine or like to fight, but rather be gentle and peaceable, not loving money. 4 He must be a good family leader, having children who cooperate with full respect. 5 (If someone does not know how to lead the family, how can that person take care of God's church?) 6 But an elder must not be a new believer, or he might be too proud of himself and be judged guilty just as the devil was. 7 An elder must also have the respect of people who are not in the church so he will not be criticized by others and caught in the devil's trap.

Deacons in the Church

*I*n the same way, deacons must be respected by others, not saying things they do not mean. They must not drink too much wine or try to get rich by cheating others. 9 With a clear conscience they must follow the secret of the faith that God made known to us. 10 Test them first. Then let them serve as deacons if you find nothing wrong in them. [11] In the same way, women must be respected by others. They must not speak evil of others. They must be self-controlled and trustworthy in everything. [12] Deacons must have only one wife and be good leaders of their children and their own families. [13] Those who serve well as deacons are making an honorable place for themselves, and they will be very bold in their faith in Christ Jesus.

OLD TESTAMENT READING

No other god has ever taken for himself one nation out of another. But the LORD your God did this for you in Egypt, right before your own eyes. He did it with tests, signs, miracles, war, and great sights, by his great power and strength.

[35] He showed you things so you would know that the LORD is God, and there is no other God besides him. [36] He spoke to you from heaven to teach you. He showed you his great fire on earth, and you heard him speak from the fire. [37] Because the LORD loved your ancestors, he chose you, their descendants, and he brought you out of Egypt himself by his great strength. [38] He forced nations out of their land ahead of you, nations that were bigger and stronger than you were. The LORD did this so he could bring you into their land and give it to you as your own, and this land is yours today.

Deuteronomy 4:34–38

INSIGHTS

Men have always stumbled over the simplicity of salvation. That is why there are so many cults. Each one has a unique slant on the doctrine of salvation, each corrupting the simplicity of the gospel revealed in God's Word (cf. 2 Corinthians 11:3) by espousing salvation by human works. . . .

From start to finish, God's Word disproves them all, and in a wonderfully consistent way. Its message, woven through sixty-six books, written over a span of fifteen hundred years by more than forty different authors, is marvelously unified and congruous. The message is simply that God graciously saves repentant sinners who come to Him in faith. There is no secret here, no mystery, no obscurity, no complexity. . . .

. . . God has come down from heaven and spoken to us by His Son (Hebrews 1:1–2). We can never gain the right to climb to heaven and find the answers for ourselves. . . .

. . . Jesus is the only source of salvation. Those who do not believe in His name are condemned, excluded from eternal life. No matter how sincere, how religious, how immersed in good works, everyone must be born again. There is no promise of life—only a guarantee of condemnation—for those who will not . . . turn from sin in obedient faith to the One who was lifted up so that they would not have to perish.

John F. MacArthur, Jr.

APPLICATION

What truth does God want all people to know? What evidence does Scripture give that God is the only true God? What is the one way of salvation? Do you personally know that way?

WEEKEND

Your Life Should Be a Godly Example

1 Timothy 3:14—4:16

The Secret of Our Life

Although I hope I can come to you soon, I am writing these things to you now. [15] Then, even if I am delayed, you will know how to live in the family of God. That family is the church of the living God, the support and foundation of the truth. [16] Without doubt, the secret of our life of worship is great:

He was shown to us in a human
body,
proved right in spirit,
and seen by angels.
He was preached to those who
are not Jews,
believed in by the world,
and taken up in glory.

A Warning About False Teachers

4 Now the Holy Spirit clearly says that in the later times some people will stop believing the faith. They will follow spirits that lie and teachings of demons. [2] Such teachings come from the false words of liars whose consciences are destroyed as if by a hot iron. [3] They forbid people to marry and tell them not to eat certain foods which God created to be eaten with thanks by people who believe and know the truth. [4] Everything God made is good, and nothing should be refused if it is accepted with thanks, [5] because it is made holy by what God has said and by prayer.

Be A Good Servant of Christ

By telling these things to the brothers and sisters, you will be a good servant of Christ Jesus. You will be made strong by the words of the faith and the good teaching which you have been following. [7] But do not follow foolish stories that disagree with God's truth, but train yourself to serve God. [8] Training your body helps you in some ways, but serving God helps you in every way by bringing you blessings in this life and in the future life, too. [9] What I say is true, and you should fully accept it. [10] This is why we work and struggle: We hope in the living God who is the Savior of all people, especially of those who believe.

[11] Command and teach these things. [12] Do not let anyone treat you as if you are unimportant because you are young. Instead, be an example to the believers with your words, your actions, your love, your faith, and your pure life. [13] Until I come, continue to read the Scriptures to the people, strengthen them, and teach them. [14] Use the gift you have, which was given to you through prophecy when the group of elders laid their hands on you. [15] Continue to do those things; give your life to doing them so your progress may be seen by everyone. [16] Be careful in your life and in your teaching. If you continue to live and teach rightly, you will save both yourself and those who listen to you.

OLD TESTAMENT READING

The king stood by the pillar and made an agreement in the presence of the LORD to follow the LORD and

obey his commands, rules, and laws with his whole being, and to obey the words of the agreement written in this book. Then all the people promised to obey the agreement.
[24] Josiah destroyed the mediums, fortune-tellers, house gods, and idols. He also destroyed all the hated gods seen in the land of Judah and Jerusalem. This was to obey the words of the teachings written in the book Hilkiah the priest had found in the Temple of the LORD.
[25] There was no king like Josiah before or after him. He obeyed the LORD with all his heart, soul, and strength, following all the Teachings of Moses.

2 Kings 23:3, 24–25

INSIGHTS

I frequently hear that the call to be holy and the call to demonstrate love to sinners are mutually exclusive. (As if love is the antithesis to holiness!) Jesus welcomed and loved sinners; he did not drive them away by too much affectation of righteousness. He showed genuine compassion for people, but he was also direct and uncompromising in denouncing sin. Jesus had compassion, but there was also toughness in this love. He won them without sacrificing the purity of his life.

The paradox of agape love is that we accept our neighbor unconditionally and with open arms and at the same time desire moral purity for their lives. If Jesus is our Lord, our compassion will be shaped by his moral absolutes. Christ both was merciful and made judgments. Some things, he said, were immoral and destructive, but he never ceased to love. Indeed, it was his love that prompted his judgment. The enemy of our age is our desire to be tolerant and open-minded. . . .

I know a Christian woman who has cared deeply for a non-Christian woman who has had every variety of sexual experience. One day the non-Christian woman said to the Christian, "It's funny, my non-Christian friends accept me. They say it doesn't matter what I do. I'm free. But it's only with you that I feel loved, that I know I could always come to you. But it's also only when I'm with you that I feel shame and remorse for what I'm doing."

That is holiness. It never abandons; it identifies deeply with individual people. But it also brings the reality of God's presence, the purity of his holiness.

Rebecca Pippert

PAUSE FOR REFLECTION

List the areas of life in which the believer ought to be an example. What happens when people have a godly example before them? To whom are you an example of godly living? Do you know what impact your example is having?

MONDAY

The Importance of Accountability Among God's People

1 Timothy 5:1–25

Rules for Living with Others

5 Do not speak angrily to an older
man, but plead with him as if he
were your father. Treat younger men
like brothers, 2 older women like
mothers, and younger women like
sisters. Always treat them in a pure
way.
3 Take care of widows who are
truly widows. 4 But if a widow has
children or grandchildren, let them
first learn to do their duty to their
own family and to repay their parents or grandparents. That pleases
God. 5 The true widow, who is all
alone, puts her hope in God and continues to pray night and day for
God's help. 6 But the widow who
uses her life to please herself is
really dead while she is alive. 7 Tell
the believers to do these things so
that no one can criticize them. 8 Whoever does not care for his own relatives, especially his own family members, has turned against the faith
and is worse than someone who
does not believe in God.
9 To be on the list of widows, a
woman must be at least sixty years
old. She must have been faithful to
her husband. 10 She must be known
for her good works—works such as
raising her children, welcoming
strangers, washing the feet of God's
people, helping those in trouble, and
giving her life to do all kinds of good
deeds.
11 But do not put younger widows
on that list. After they give themselves to Christ, they are pulled away
from him by their physical needs,
and then they want to marry again.
12 They will be judged for not doing
what they first promised to do. 13 Besides that, they learn to waste their
time, going from house to house.
And they not only waste their time
but also begin to gossip and busy
themselves with other people's lives,
saying things they should not say.
14 So I want the younger widows to
marry, have children, and manage
their homes. Then no enemy will
have any reason to criticize them.
15 But some have already turned
away to follow Satan.
16 If any woman who is a believer
has widows in her family, she should
care for them herself. The church
should not have to care for them.
Then it will be able to take care of
those who are truly widows.
17 The elders who lead the church
well should receive double honor,
especially those who work hard by
speaking and teaching, 18 because
the Scripture says: "When an ox is
working in the grain, do not cover
its mouth to keep it from eating," and
"A worker should be given his pay."
19 Do not listen to someone who
accuses an elder, without two or
three witnesses. 20 Tell those who
continue sinning that they are
wrong. Do this in front of the whole
church so that the others will have
a warning.
21 Before God and Christ Jesus
and the chosen angels, I command
you to do these things without showing favor of any kind to anyone.
22 Think carefully before you lay
your hands on anyone, and don't

share in the sins of others. Keep yourself pure.
[23] Stop drinking only water, but drink a little wine to help your stomach and your frequent sicknesses.
[24] The sins of some people are easy to see even before they are judged, but the sins of others are seen only later. [25] So also good deeds are easy to see, but even those that are not easily seen cannot stay hidden.

OLD TESTAMENT READING

Then Nathan said to David, "You are the man! This is what the LORD, the God of Israel, says: 'I appointed you king of Israel and saved you
from Saul. [9] So why did you ignore the LORD's command? Why did you do what he says is wrong? You killed Uriah the Hittite with the sword of the Ammonites and took his wife to be your wife!'"
[13] Then David said to Nathan, "I have sinned against the LORD."

Nathan answered, "The LORD has taken away your sin. You will not die.
[14] But what you did caused the LORD's enemies to lose all respect for him. For this reason the son who was born to you will die."

2 Samuel 12:7, 9, 13–14

INSIGHTS

Too often I have seen marriages go down the drain, relationships deteriorate to the point of destruction, people with glaring personal limitations go unchecked—all because Christians who know precisely what is wrong will not love sufficiently to tackle the problem.

"I was afraid I would hurt their future," is one lame excuse. But that is exactly what happens.

My mind recalls the words of our Lord to Peter when he veered off course; it seems a harsh slash to the disciple who had a short time before confessed him as Lord. "Out of my sight, Satan! You are a stumbling block to me; you do not have in mind the things of God, but the things of men." (Matthew 16:23) These words came from the lips of the One who loves with everlasting love.

A former pastor told me about his experience of sinking into an illicit sexual relationship. He said he felt like an exhausted swimmer battling alone in the pounding surf, unable to escape the strong undertow, about to go down for the last time. On shore he could see all the people of his church. Some were shaking their heads in weeping and despair; others were shouting and shaking their fists in anger and frustration. There were words of encouragement and gestures of good will. There they were, all lined up, watching and waiting for something to happen. Only one man stepped forward and risked everything to plunge into the water and help the victim to safety.

Howard and Jeanne Hendricks

PAUSE FOR REFLECTION

In what ways does Paul urge Christians to hold one another accountable? What are the results of a proper response to correction? Who holds you accountable to live in obedience to God?

TUESDAY

A Godly Attitude Toward Riches

1 Timothy 6:1–21

6 All who are slaves under a yoke
should show full respect to their
masters so no one will speak against
God's name and our teaching. 2 The
slaves whose masters are believers
should not show their masters any
less respect because they are believers. They should serve their masters
even better, because they are helping believers they love.

You must teach and preach these
things.

False Teaching and True Riches

Anyone who has a different teaching does not agree with the true
teaching of our Lord Jesus Christ
and the teaching that shows the true
way to serve God. 4 This person is
full of pride and understands nothing, but is sick with a love for arguing and fighting about words. This
brings jealousy, fighting, speaking
against others, evil mistrust, 5 and
constant quarrels from those who
have evil minds and have lost the
truth. They think that serving God
is a way to get rich.

6 Serving God does make us very
rich, if we are satisfied with what we
have. 7 We brought nothing into the
world, so we can take nothing out.
8 But, if we have food and clothes, we
will be satisfied with that. 9 Those who
want to become rich bring temptation
to themselves and are caught in a trap.
They want many foolish and harmful
things that ruin and destroy people.
10 The love of money causes all kinds
of evil. Some people have left the faith,
because they wanted to get more
money, but they have caused themselves much sorrow.

Some Things to Remember

But you, man of God, run away from
all those things. Instead, live in the
right way, serve God, have faith, love,
patience, and gentleness. 12 Fight the
good fight of faith, grabbing hold of
the life that continues forever. You
were called to have that life when you
confessed the good confession before
many witnesses. 13 In the sight of God,
who gives life to everything, and of
Christ Jesus, I give you a command.
Christ Jesus made the good confession when he stood before Pontius
Pilate. 14 Do what you were commanded to do without wrong or blame
until our Lord Jesus Christ comes
again. 15 God will make that happen at
the right time. He is the blessed and
only Ruler, the King of all kings and
the Lord of all lords. 16 He is the only
One who never dies. He lives in light
so bright no one can go near it. No
one has ever seen God, or can see
him. May honor and power belong to
God forever. Amen.

17 Command those who are rich
with things of this world not to be
proud. Tell them to hope in God, not
in their uncertain riches. God richly
gives us everything to enjoy. 18 Tell
the rich people to do good, to be rich
in doing good deeds, to be generous
and ready to share. 19 By doing that,
they will be saving a treasure for
themselves as a strong foundation
for the future. Then they will be able
to have the life that is true life.

[20]Timothy, guard what God has trusted to you. Stay away from foolish, useless talk and from the arguments of what is falsely called "knowledge." [21]By saying they have that "knowledge," some have missed the true faith.

Grace be with you.

OLD TESTAMENT READING

Be careful not to forget the LORD your God so that you fail to obey his commands, laws, and rules that I am giving to you today. [12]When you eat all you want and build nice houses and live in them, [13]when your herds and flocks grow large and your silver and gold increase, when you have more of everything, [14]then your heart will become proud. You will forget the LORD your God, who brought you out of the land of Egypt, where you were slaves.

[17]You might say to yourself, "I am rich because of my own power and strength," [18]but remember the LORD your God! It is he who gives you the power to become rich, keeping the agreement he promised to your ancestors, as it is today.

Deuteronomy 8:11–14, 17–18

God gives some people the ability to enjoy the wealth and property he gives them, as well as the ability to accept their state in life and enjoy their work. [20]They do not worry about how short life is, because God keeps them busy with what they love to do.

Ecclesiastes 5:19–20

INSIGHTS

There will be this difference between the rich that loves his riches and the poor that hates his poverty. When they die, the heart of the one will still be crowded with things and their pleasures, while the heart of the other will be relieved of their lack. The one has had his good things; the other, his sorrowful things.

But the rich man, on the other hand, who held his things lightly and who did not let them nestle in his heart, who was a channel and not a cistern, who was ever and always forsaking his money—this rich man starts in the new world side by side with the man who accepted, not hated, his poverty. Each will say, "I am free."

George MacDonald

God often allows people to accumulate property so they may have an opportunity to extend the cause of truth and righteousness in the earth. . . . Professing Christians acknowledge themselves to be but stewards for God, that everything they possess is His; consequently, their possessions are at His disposal. Now, is it a fact that these people act in harmony with what they profess? Well, God often tries them to see if they are hypocrites or not.

Charles Finney

PAUSE FOR REFLECTION

What traps await those who accumulate riches? Who is the source of wealth? Write down what it means for you to have a godly attitude toward riches. In what ways do riches tempt you? How well are you handling what God has given to you?

WEDNESDAY

Disciple One Another in the Teachings of God

2 Timothy 1:1—2:13

1 From Paul, an apostle of Christ
Jesus by the will of God. God sent
me to tell about the promise of life
that is in Christ Jesus.
2 To Timothy, a dear child to me:
Grace, mercy, and peace to you
from God the Father and Christ
Jesus our Lord.

Encouragement for Timothy

3 I thank God as I always mention you
in my prayers, day and night. I serve
him, doing what I know is right as my
ancestors did. 4 Remembering that
you cried for me, I want very much to
see you so I can be filled with joy. 5 I
remember your true faith. That faith
first lived in your grandmother Lois
and in your mother Eunice, and I
know you now have that same faith.
6 This is why I remind you to keep using the gift God gave you when I laid
my hands on you. Now let it grow, as
a small flame grows into a fire. 7 God
did not give us a spirit that makes us
afraid but a spirit of power and love
and self-control.
8 So do not be ashamed to tell
people about our Lord Jesus, and do
not be ashamed of me, in prison for
the Lord. But suffer with me for the
Good News. God, who gives us the
strength to do that, 9 saved us and
made us his holy people. That was not
because of anything we did ourselves
but because of God's purpose and
grace. That grace was given to us
through Christ Jesus before time began, 10 but it is now shown to us by the
coming of our Savior Christ Jesus. He
destroyed death, and through the
Good News he showed us the way to
have life that cannot be destroyed. 11 I
was chosen to tell that Good News
and to be an apostle and a teacher. 12 I
am suffering now because I tell the
Good News, but I am not ashamed,
because I know Jesus, the One in
whom I have believed. And I am sure
he is able to protect what he has
trusted me with until that day. 13 Follow the pattern of true teachings that
you heard from me in faith and love,
which are in Christ Jesus. 14 Protect
the truth that you were given; protect
it with the help of the Holy Spirit who
lives in us.
15 You know that everyone in the
country of Asia has left me, even
Phygelus and Hermogenes. 16 May
the Lord show mercy to the family
of Onesiphorus, who has often
helped me and was not ashamed that
I was in prison. 17 When he came to
Rome, he looked eagerly for me until he found me. 18 May the Lord allow him to find mercy from the Lord
on that day. You know how many
ways he helped me in Ephesus.

A Loyal Soldier of Christ Jesus

2 You then, Timothy, my child, be
strong in the grace we have in
Christ Jesus. 2 You should teach
people whom you can trust the
things you and many others have
heard me say. Then they will be able
to teach others. 3 Share in the
troubles we have like a good soldier
of Christ Jesus. 4 A soldier wants to
please the enlisting officer, so no one
serving in the army wastes time with
everyday matters. 5 Also an athlete
who takes part in a contest must

obey all the rules in order to win.
6 The farmer who works hard should
be the first person to get some of the
food that was grown. 7 Think about
what I am saying, because the Lord
will give you the ability to understand everything.
8 Remember Jesus Christ, who
was raised from the dead, who is
from the family of David. This is the
Good News I preach, 9 and I am suffering because of it to the point of being bound with chains like a criminal. But God's teaching is not in
chains. 10 So I patiently accept all
these troubles so that those whom
God has chosen can have the salvation that is in Christ Jesus. With that
salvation comes glory that never
ends.
11 This teaching is true:

If we died with him, we will
also live with him.
12 If we accept suffering, we will
also rule with him.
If we refuse to accept him, he
will refuse to accept us.
13 If we are not faithful, he will
still be faithful,
because he cannot be false to
himself.

OLD TESTAMENT READING

But be careful! Watch out and don't
forget the things you have seen.
Don't forget them as long as you live,
but teach them to your children and
grandchildren. 10 Remember the day
you stood before the LORD your God
at Mount Sinai. He said to me,
"Bring the people together so I can
tell them what I have to say. Then
they will respect me as long as they
live in the land, and they will teach
these things to their children."

Deuteronomy 4:9–10

INSIGHTS

The discipling ministry lacks the glamour and excitement of the platform or large meeting type of ministry. But we can hardly overemphasize the importance of investing the right kind of person, one of vision and discipline, totally committed to Jesus Christ, willing to pay any price to have the will of God fulfilled in his life. . . .

. . . The Great Commission given to us in Matthew 28:19–20 says, "Go therefore, and teach [make disciples of] all nations." It takes a disciple-maker to make disciples. Historically, the Church has believed that the Great Commission was not given to a select few people, but to all believers. If this is true, then all believers can be disciple-makers. . . .

. . . If you are not a disciple-maker, then I would suggest that you do the same thing that Timothy did with Paul, or that Peter, James, and John did with the Lord Jesus. Make yourself available to a disciple-maker who can help you to become a disciple-maker. Latch on to them. Learn from them the "how to" involved in developing those qualities needed to spiritually reproduce yourself in the lives of others.

Walter Henrichsen

PAUSE FOR REFLECTION

Is disciple-making a new phenomenon? What principles of discipleship did Moses outline for the Israelites? In what ways do those principles apply today?

THURSDAY

Those Who Follow God Must Flee Evil

2 Timothy 2:14—3:11

A Worker Pleasing to God

Continue teaching these things,
warning people in God's presence not
to argue about words. It does not help
anyone, and it ruins those who listen.
15 Make every effort to give yourself
to God as the kind of person he will
accept. Be a worker who is not
ashamed and who uses the true teaching in the right way. 16 Stay away from
foolish, useless talk, because that will
lead people further away from God.
17 Their evil teaching will spread like
a sickness inside the body. Hymenaeus and Philetus are like that.
18 They have left the true teaching, saying that the rising from the dead has
already taken place, and so they are
destroying the faith of some people.
19 But God's strong foundation continues to stand. These words are written
on the seal: "The Lord knows those
who belong to him," and "Everyone
who wants to belong to the Lord must
stop doing wrong."

20 In a large house there are not
only things made of gold and silver,
but also things made of wood and
clay. Some things are used for special purposes, and others are made
for ordinary jobs. 21 All who make
themselves clean from evil will be
used for special purposes. They will
be made holy, useful to the Master,
ready to do any good work.

22 But run away from the evil young
people like to do. Try hard to live right
and to have faith, love, and peace, together with those who trust in the
Lord from pure hearts. 23 Stay away
from foolish and stupid arguments,
because you know they grow into
quarrels. 24 And a servant of the Lord
must not quarrel but must be kind to
everyone, a good teacher, and patient.
25 The Lord's servant must gently
teach those who disagree. Then
maybe God will let them change their
minds so they can accept the truth.
26 And they may wake up and escape
from the trap of the devil, who catches
them to do what he wants.

The Last Days

3 Remember this! In the last days
there will be many troubles, 2 because people will love themselves,
love money, brag, and be proud. They
will say evil things against others and
will not obey their parents or be thankful or be the kind of people God wants.
3 They will not love others, will refuse
to forgive, will gossip, and will not control themselves. They will be cruel,
will hate what is good, 4 will turn
against their friends, and will do foolish things without thinking. They will
be conceited, will love pleasure instead of God, 5 and will act as if they
serve God but will not have his power.
Stay away from those people. 6 Some
of them go into homes and get control of silly women who are full of sin
and are led by many evil desires.
7 These women are always learning
new teachings, but they are never able
to understand the truth fully. 8 Just as
Jannes and Jambres were against
Moses, these people are against the
truth. Their thinking has been ruined,
and they have failed in trying to follow the faith. 9 But they will not be suc-

cessful in what they do, because as with Jannes and Jambres, everyone will see that they are foolish.

Obey the Teachings

But you have followed what I teach, the way I live, my goal, faith, patience, and love. You know I never give up. 11 You know how I have been hurt and have suffered, as in Antioch, Iconium, and Lystra. I have suffered, but the Lord saved me from all those troubles.

OLD TESTAMENT READING

I will sing of your love and
fairness;
LORD, I will sing praises to you.
2 I will be careful to live an innocent life.
When will you come to me?
I will live an innocent life in my house.
3 I will not look at anything wicked.
I hate those who turn against you;
they will not be found near me.
4 Let those who want to do wrong stay away from me;
I will have nothing to do with evil.
5 If anyone secretly says things against his neighbor,
I will stop him.
I will not allow people
to be proud and look down on others.

Psalm 101:1–5

INSIGHTS

The practice of godliness involves the pursuit of holiness because God has said, "Be holy, because I am holy" (1 Peter 1:16). Paul tells us that we have been called to a holy life; we have been redeemed for that purpose. Any Christian who is not earnestly pursuing holiness in every aspect of his life is flying in the face of God's purpose in saving him.

What is holiness? The best practical definition that I have heard is simply "without sin." . . .

John said he wrote his first letter so that his readers would not sin (1 John 2:1). Most Christians seem content not to sin very much, but John's goal was that we not sin at all. Every sin, no matter how small it may seem to us, is an affront to God's authority, a disregard for his law, a spurning of his love. Because of this, sin cannot be tolerated in any form, to any degree. . . .

. . . When Paul was instructing the Ephesian Christians about the importance of holiness he said, "So I tell you this, and insist on it in the Lord, that you must no longer live as the Gentiles do" (4:17). He insisted on holiness, and he did so with the Lord's authority. Holiness is not an option but a must for every Christian. . . .

. . . If we want to train ourselves to be godly, it must be holiness in every area of our lives.

Jerry Bridges

PAUSE FOR REFLECTION

What must everyone who believes in God stop doing—and start doing? How important is this teaching for Christians today? In what ways do you share the psalmist's delight in innocence and pure living expressed in Psalm 101?

FRIDAY

God Gave Us Scripture to Teach Us How to Live

2 Timothy 3:12—4:22

*E*veryone who wants to live as God desires, in Christ Jesus, will be hurt. 13 But people who are evil and cheat others will go from bad to worse. They will fool others, but they will also be fooling themselves.

14 But you should continue following the teachings you learned. You know they are true, because you trust those who taught you. 15 Since you were a child you have known the Holy Scriptures which are able to make you wise. And that wisdom leads to salvation through faith in Christ Jesus. 16 All Scripture is given by God and is useful for teaching, for showing people what is wrong in their lives, for correcting faults, and for teaching how to live right. 17 Using the Scriptures, the person who serves God will be capable, having all that is needed to do every good work.

4 I give you a command in the presence of God and Christ Jesus, the One who will judge the living and the dead, and by his coming and his kingdom: 2 Preach the Good News. Be ready at all times, and tell people what they need to do. Tell them when they are wrong. Encourage them with great patience and careful teaching, 3 because the time will come when people will not listen to the true teaching but will find many more teachers who please them by saying the things they want to hear. 4 They will stop listening to the truth and will begin to follow false stories. 5 But you should control yourself at all times, accept troubles, do the work of telling the Good News, and complete all the duties of a servant of God.

6 My life is being given as an offering to God, and the time has come for me to leave this life. 7 I have fought the good fight, I have finished the race, I have kept the faith. 8 Now, a crown is being held for me—a crown for being right with God. The Lord, the judge who judges rightly, will give the crown to me on that day—not only to me but to all those who have waited with love for him to come again.

Personal Words

*D*o your best to come to me as soon as you can, 10 because Demas, who loved this world, left me and went to Thessalonica. Crescens went to Galatia, and Titus went to Dalmatia. 11 Luke is the only one still with me. Get Mark and bring him with you when you come, because he can help me in my work here. 12 I sent Tychicus to Ephesus. 13 When I was in Troas, I left my coat there with Carpus. So when you come, bring it to me, along with my books, particularly the ones written on parchment.

14 Alexander the metalworker did many harmful things against me. The Lord will punish him for what he did. 15 You also should be careful that he does not hurt you, because he fought strongly against our teaching.

16 The first time I defended myself, no one helped me; everyone left me. May they be forgiven. 17 But the Lord

stayed with me and gave me strength so I could fully tell the Good News to all those who are not Jews. So I was saved from the lion's mouth. [18]The Lord will save me when anyone tries to hurt me, and he will bring me safely to his heavenly kingdom. Glory forever and ever be the Lord's. Amen.

Final Greetings

Greet Priscilla and Aquila and the family of Onesiphorus. [20]Erastus stayed in Corinth, and I left Trophimus sick in Miletus. [21]Try as hard as you can to come to me before winter.

Eubulus sends greetings to you. Also Pudens, Linus, Claudia, and all the brothers and sisters in Christ greet you.

[22]The Lord be with your spirit. Grace be with you.

OLD TESTAMENT READING

They read from the Book of the Teachings of God and explained what it meant so the people understood what was being read.

[14]This is what they found written in the Teachings: The LORD commanded through Moses that the people of Israel were to live in shelters during the feast of the seventh month. [15]The people were supposed to preach this message and spread it through all their towns and in Jerusalem: "Go out into the mountains, and bring back branches from olive and wild olive trees, myrtle trees, palms, and shade trees. Make shelters with them, as it is written."

Nehemiah 8: 8, 14–15

INSIGHTS

There are few joys like the joy of sudden discovery. Instantly, there is forgotten the pain and expense of the search, the inconveniences, the hours, the sacrifices. Bathed in the ecstasy of discovery, time stands still. . . .

Solomon talks about the greatest discovery of all. . . .

"My son, if you will receive my sayings,
And treasure my commandments within you,
Make your ear attentive to wisdom,
Incline your heart to understanding;
For if you cry for discernment,
Lift your voice for understanding;
If you seek her as silver,
And search for her as for hidden treasures;
Then you will discern the fear of the LORD,
And discover the knowledge of God."

(Proverbs 2:1–5)

Talk about a discovery! Hidden in the Scriptures are priceless verbal vaults. Silent. Hard to find. Easy to miss if you're in a hurry. But they are there, awaiting discovery. God's Word, like a deep, deep mine, stands ready to yield its treasures.

Charles Swindoll

PAUSE FOR REFLECTION

What are the results of learning and obeying God's Word? What are the results of rejecting it? Have you discovered the rich treasures of God's Word for yourself?

WEEKEND

God's Teachers Must Be Blameless and Trustworthy

Titus 1:1—2:8

1 From Paul, a servant of God and an apostle of Jesus Christ. I was sent to help the faith of God's chosen people and to help them know the truth that shows people how to serve God. 2 That faith and that knowledge come from the hope for life forever, which God promised to us before time began. And God cannot lie. 3 At the right time God let the world know about that life through preaching. He trusted me with that work, and I preached by the command of God our Savior.

4 To Titus, my true child in the faith we share:

Grace and peace from God the Father and Christ Jesus our Savior.

Titus' Work in Crete

5 I left you in Crete so you could finish doing the things that still needed to be done and so you could appoint elders in every town, as I directed you. 6 An elder must not be guilty of doing wrong, must have only one wife, and must have believing children. They must not be known as children who are wild and do not cooperate. 7 As God's manager, an elder must not be guilty of doing wrong, being selfish, or becoming angry quickly. He must not drink too much wine, like to fight, or try to get rich by cheating others. 8 An elder must be ready to welcome guests, love what is good, be wise, live right, and be holy and self-controlled. 9 By holding on to the trustworthy word just as we teach it, an elder can help people by using true teaching, and he can show those who are against the true teaching that they are wrong.

10 There are many people who refuse to cooperate, who talk about worthless things and lead others into the wrong way—mainly those who say all who are not Jews must be circumcised. 11 These people must be stopped, because they are upsetting whole families by teaching things they should not teach, which they do to get rich by cheating people. 12 Even one of their own prophets said, "Cretans are always liars, evil animals, and lazy people who do nothing but eat." 13 The words that prophet said are true. So firmly tell those people they are wrong so they may become strong in the faith, 14 not accepting Jewish false stories and the commands of people who reject the truth. 15 To those who are pure, all things are pure, but to those who are full of sin and do not believe, nothing is pure. Both their minds and their consciences have been ruined. 16 They say they know God, but their actions show they do not accept him. They are hateful people, they refuse to obey, and they are useless for doing anything good.

Following the True Teaching

2 But you must tell everyone what to do to follow the true teaching. 2 Teach older men to be self-controlled, serious, wise, strong in faith, in love, and in patience.

3 In the same way, teach older women to be holy in their behavior,

not speaking against others or enslaved to too much wine, but teaching what is good. [4]Then they can teach the young women to love their husbands, to love their children, [5]to be wise and pure, to be good workers at home, to be kind, and to yield to their husbands. Then no one will be able to criticize the teaching God gave us.

[6]In the same way, encourage young men to be wise. [7]In every way be an example of doing good deeds. When you teach, do it with honesty and seriousness. [8]Speak the truth so that you cannot be criticized. Then those who are against you will be ashamed because there is nothing bad to say about us.

OLD TESTAMENT READING

If the priests keep all the rules I have given, they will not become guilty; if they are careful, they will not die. I am the LORD who has made them holy.'"

Leviticus 22:9

A priest should teach what he knows, and people should learn the teachings from him, because he is the messenger of the LORD All-Powerful. [8]But you priests have stopped obeying me. With your teachings you have caused many people to do wrong. You have broken the agreement with the tribe of Levi!" says the LORD All-Powerful. [9]"You have not been careful to do what I say, but instead you take sides in court cases. So I have caused you to be hated and disgraced in front of everybody."

Malachi 2:7–9

INSIGHTS

Luke recorded that believers from Lystra and Iconium "spoke well of him" (Acts 16:2). In other words Timothy had a good reputation as a Christian. He was "blameless" in the eyes of those in the Christian community. There were no specific flaws in his life that would bring reproach to the cause of Christ. So Paul invited Timothy to be his missionary companion, and this resulted in a deep, lasting relationship and ministry together.

Titus was also this kind of man. Mature in many ways, he maintained pure motives, evidencing compassion and concern for people (2 Cor. 8:16) and demonstrating a positive attitude toward the ministry (v. 17). There is no better way in which to develop a good reputation among Christians and non-Christians alike.

Be blameless. This quality and the other qualifications for elders are standards all of us should strive for, whether we are in positions of church leadership or not.

Gene Getz

ACTION POINT

Why is it essential that those who teach others in the ways of God be blameless? How much do you want to be the kind of Christian Paul describes as an 'elder'? What changes must you make to be blameless and trustworthy? Are you willing?

MONDAY

Our Lives Are a Testimony to God

Titus 2:9—3:15

Slaves should yield to their own
masters at all times, trying to please
them and not arguing with them.
10 They should not steal from them
but should show their masters they
can be fully trusted so that in everything they do they will make the
teaching of God our Savior attrac-
tive.

11 That is the way we should live,
because God's grace that can save
everyone has come. 12 It teaches us
not to live against God nor to do the
evil things the world wants to do.
Instead, that grace teaches us to live
now in a wise and right way and in a
way that shows we serve God. 13 We
should live like that while we wait for
our great hope and the coming of the
glory of our great God and Savior
Jesus Christ. 14 He gave himself for
us so he might pay the price to free
us from all evil and to make us pure
people who belong only to him—
people who are always wanting to do
good deeds.

15 Say these things and encourage
the people and tell them what is
wrong in their lives, with all authority. Do not let anyone treat you as if
you were unimportant.

The Right Way to Live

3 Remind the believers to yield to
the authority of rulers and government leaders, to obey them, to be
ready to do good, 2 to speak no evil
about anyone, to live in peace, and
to be gentle and polite to all people.

3 In the past we also were foolish.
We did not obey, we were wrong,
and we were slaves to many things
our bodies wanted and enjoyed. We
spent our lives doing evil and being
jealous. People hated us, and we
hated each other. 4 But when the
kindness and love of God our Savior
was shown, 5 he saved us because of
his mercy. It was not because of
good deeds we did to be right with
him. He saved us through the washing that made us new people
through the Holy Spirit. 6 God
poured out richly upon us that Holy
Spirit through Jesus Christ our Savior. 7 Being made right with God by
his grace, we could have the hope
of receiving the life that never ends.

8 This teaching is true, and I want
you to be sure the people understand these things. Then those who
believe in God will be careful to use
their lives for doing good. These
things are good and will help everyone.

9 But stay away from those who
have foolish arguments and talk
about useless family histories and
argue and quarrel about the law.
Those things are worth nothing and
will not help anyone. 10 After a first
and second warning, avoid someone
who causes arguments. 11 You can
know that such people are evil and
sinful; their own sins prove them
wrong.

Some Things to Remember

When I send Artemas or Tychicus
to you, make every effort to come
to me at Nicopolis, because I have
decided to stay there this winter.

13 Do all you can to help Zenas the
lawyer and Apollos on their journey
so that they have everything they
need. 14 Our people must learn to use
their lives for doing good deeds to
provide what is necessary so that
their lives will not be useless.
15 All who are with me greet you.
Greet those who love us in the faith.
Grace be with you all.

OLD TESTAMENT READING

Daniel answered, "O king, live forever! 22 My God sent his angel to
close the lions' mouths. They have
not hurt me, because my God knows
I am innocent. I never did anything
wrong to you, O king."
25 Then King Darius wrote a letter
to all people and all nations, to those
who spoke every language in the
world:

I wish you great peace and wealth.
26 I am making a new law for
people in every part of my kingdom.
All of you must fear and respect the
God of Daniel.

Daniel's God is the living God;
he lives forever.
His kingdom will never be destroyed,
and his rule will never end.
27 God rescues and saves people
and does mighty miracles
in heaven and on earth.
He is the one who saved Daniel
from the power of the lions.

Daniel 6:21–22, 25–27

INSIGHTS

If you are a publisher or a pastor, a ditch-digger or a pilot, a fisherman or a fruit grower, a garage mechanic or a furniture maker, a writer or a homemaker, an office worker or a congressman . . . there are unique things involved in your moment-by-moment work since you are a child of the Creator of the universe. . . .

You are to do well, whatever you are doing, to the glory of God (see 1 Peter 4:11). Just as flowers that grow on the Alpine peaks, beauty in the cracks of rocks with perhaps no one ever passing that way, are not growing in vain because God sees them, so it is true of the human being. A person may live alone, walk alone, and feel that no one is recognizing that he or she is being patient in the tribulation of loneliness . . . but God does know, and is aware of the whisper, "I love you, God. Please accept my praise as I walk alone today." This is true of people in prisons, in concentration camps, in hospital beds, or in wheelchairs. . . . "Work" to the glory of God can be done in every part of life . . . which is what makes it all so fair. No one gets a bigger opportunity than another. And no one is "out of work"!

Edith Schaeffer

PAUSE FOR REFLECTION

What kind of people are we without Jesus? What kind of people does his death make us? How are believers supposed to use their lives? Who do you know who truly lives like a servant of the living God?

TUESDAY

All People Are Valuable in God's Eyes

Philemon 1–25

A Slave Becomes a Christian

From Paul, a prisoner of Christ
Jesus, and from Timothy, our brother.
To Philemon, our dear friend and
worker with us; 2 to Apphia, our sister; to Archippus, a worker with us;
and to the church that meets in your
home:
3 Grace and peace to you from
God our Father and the Lord Jesus
Christ.

Philemon's Love and Faith

I always thank my God when I mention you in my prayers, 5 because I
hear about the love you have for all
God's holy people and the faith you
have in the Lord Jesus. 6 I pray that
the faith you share may make you
understand every blessing we have
in Christ. 7 I have great joy and comfort, my brother, because the love
you have shown to God's people has
refreshed them.

Accept Onesimus as a Brother

So, in Christ, I could be bold and
order you to do what is right. 9 But
because I love you, I am pleading
with you instead. I, Paul, an old man
now and also a prisoner for Christ
Jesus, 10 am pleading with you for my
child Onesimus, who became my
child while I was in prison. 11 In the
past he was useless to you, but now
he has become useful for both you
and me.
12 I am sending him back to you,
and with him I am sending my own
heart. 13 I wanted to keep him with
me so that in your place he might
help me while I am in prison for the
Good News. 14 But I did not want to
do anything without asking you first
so that any good you do for me will
be because you want to do it, not
because I forced you. 15 Maybe
Onesimus was separated from you
for a short time so you could have
him back forever—16 no longer as a
slave, but better than a slave, as a
loved brother. I love him very much,
but you will love him even more,
both as a person and as a believer in
the Lord.
17 So if you consider me your partner, welcome Onesimus as you
would welcome me. 18 If he has done
anything wrong to you or if he owes
you anything, charge that to me. 19 I,
Paul, am writing this with my own
hand. I will pay it back, and I will say
nothing about what you owe me
for your own life. 20 So, my brother,
I ask that you do this for me in the
Lord: Refresh my heart in Christ. 21 I
write this letter, knowing that you
will do what I ask you and even
more.
22 One more thing—prepare a
room for me in which to stay, because
I hope God will answer your prayers
and I will be able to come to you.

Final Greetings

Epaphras, a prisoner with me for
Christ Jesus, sends greetings to you.
24 And also Mark, Aristarchus,
Demas, and Luke, workers together
with me, send greetings.

[25]The grace of our Lord Jesus Christ be with your spirit.

OLD TESTAMENT READING

So the king said to Joseph, "God has shown you all this. There is no one as wise and understanding as you are, so [40]I will put you in charge of my palace. All the people will obey your orders, and only I will be greater than you."

[42]Then the king took off from his own finger his ring with the royal seal on it, and he put it on Joseph's finger. He gave Joseph fine linen clothes to wear, and he put a gold
chain around Joseph's neck. [43]The
king had Joseph ride in the second royal chariot, and people walked ahead of his chariot calling, "Bow down!" By doing these things, the king put Joseph in charge of all of Egypt.

Genesis 41:39–40, 42–43

So Joseph said to them, "Come close to me." When the brothers came close to him, he said to them, "I am your brother Joseph, whom you sold as a slave to go to Egypt.
[5]Now don't be worried or angry with yourselves because you sold me here. God sent me here ahead of you to save people's lives.

[9]"So leave quickly and go to my father. Tell him, 'Your son Joseph says: God has made me master over all Egypt. Come down to me
quickly. [10]Live in the land of Goshen where you will be near me. Your children, your grandchildren, your flocks and herds, and all that you
have will also be near me. [11]I will
care for you during the next five years of hunger so that you and your family and all that you have will not starve.'"

Genesis 45:4–5, 9–11

INSIGHTS

Are you still running around trying to milk acceptance and self-esteem out of the world like lost people when you've already got both? Are you still employing the same old methods, such as trying to perform up to your flesh's standards to generate and maintain self-esteem moment by moment? You are of infinite worth. You are accepted. Not by people, perhaps, but of God! If you're rejected by certain people, welcome to the club. So was Jesus. But He didn't go around with His head down. Why? Because He knew it's not a feeling that matters; it's what you know. He knew He was accepted.

Do you know that? . . . You are not to strive to get love; we don't live that way. We live from a posture of knowing that we are loved.

. . . You can accept yourself now as the new person you truly are in Him, just as the Father accepts you—perfectly.

Bill Gillham

PAUSE FOR REFLECTION

In biblical times, who had less value than a slave? In what ways did God affirm the value of Joseph and Onesimus? How was each one received? Who do you need to accept as a beloved brother or sister before God?

WEDNESDAY

God Has Given Us a Great Salvation

Hebrews 1:1—2:4

God Spoke Through His Son

1 In the past God spoke to our ancestors through the prophets
many times and in many different
ways. 2 But now in these last days God
has spoken to us through his Son.
God has chosen his Son to own all
things, and through him he made the
world. 3 The Son reflects the glory of
God and shows exactly what God is
like. He holds everything together
with his powerful word. When the Son
made people clean from their sins, he
sat down at the right side of God, the
Great One in heaven. 4 The Son became much greater than the angels,
and God gave him a name that is
much greater than theirs.

5 This is because God never said
to any of the angels,

"You are my Son.
Today I have become your
Father." *Psalm 2:7*

Nor did God say of any angel,

"I will be his Father,
and he will be my Son."

2 Samuel 7:14

6 And when God brings his firstborn
Son into the world, he says,

"Let all God's angels worship
him." *Psalm 97:7*

7 This is what God said about the
angels:

"God makes his angels become
like winds.
He makes his servants become
like flames of fire." *Psalm 104:4*

8 But God said this about his Son:

"God, your throne will last
forever and ever.
You will rule your kingdom
with fairness.
9 You love right and hate evil,
so God has chosen you from
among your friends;
he has set you apart with much
joy." *Psalm 45:6-7*

10 God also says,

"Lord, in the beginning you made
the earth,
and your hands made the
skies.
11 They will be destroyed, but you
will remain.
They will all wear out like
clothes.
12 You will fold them like a coat.
And, like clothes, you will
change them.
But you never change,
and your life will never end."

Psalm 102:25-27

13 And God never said this to an angel:

"Sit by me at my right side
until I put your enemies under
your control." *Psalm 110:1*

14 All the angels are spirits who
serve God and are sent to help those
who will receive salvation.

Our Salvation Is Great

2 So we must be more careful to
follow what we were taught.
Then we will not stray away from the
truth. 2 The teaching God spoke
through angels was shown to be
true, and anyone who did not follow
it or obey it received the punishment
that was earned. 3 So surely we also
will be punished if we ignore this
great salvation. The Lord himself

first told about this salvation, and it was proven true to us by those who heard him. [4] God also proved it by using wonders, great signs, many kinds of miracles, and by giving people gifts through the Holy Spirit, just as he wanted.

OLD TESTAMENT READING

I will sing to the LORD,
because he is worthy of great honor.
He has thrown the horse and its rider
into the sea.
2 The LORD gives me strength and makes me sing;
he has saved me.
He is my God,
and I will praise him.

Exodus 15:1b–2b

LORD, teach me what you want me to do,
and I will live by your truth.
Teach me to respect you completely.
12 Lord, my God, I will praise you with all my heart,
and I will honor your name forever.
13 You have great love for me.
You have saved me from death.

Psalm 86:11–13

INSIGHTS

Our salvation is good reason to rejoice. Hannah rejoiced because of salvation in a song that Mary echoed when Jesus was born and salvation had come. The magi rejoiced when they saw the star that led them to the infant Jesus and salvation (Matthew 2:10). The Ethiopian eunuch rejoiced in the discovery of salvation through Philip's ministry of the Word (Acts 8:39). Christians rejoice in hope and even in suffering since they have peace with God (Romans 5:2–3).

Rejoicing and salvation belong together. The coming of Jesus into this world can never be a matter of academic aloofness or objective study. Because it is real and because it means so much it goes right to the heart to make it leap with joy. It is the emotion felt when a woman finds a lost coin or a shepherd finds a lost sheep or a waiting Father sees his lost son on the horizon (read Luke 15). It is not like a student poring over a book in the library. It is more like a student with a thousand others, rejoicing over a touchdown on the field. It is like oil drillers watching their first wild fountain of black gold after days of hard and fruitless labor. It is a soldier seeing a light in the window or a returning prisoner finding yellow ribbons tied all over the tree. In prayer let us remember all the joy we have drawn from the wells of salvation. It should make quite a list.

William Stoddard

ACTION POINT

If you risk living as if salvation were unimportant, take notice! What makes salvation great? Who revealed it? Who has proven it? Throughout the ages, God's people have rejoiced and celebrated his salvation. Go ahead, be amazed, and join them in praising God for his salvation!

THURSDAY

Jesus, Our Savior, Makes His People Holy

Hebrews 2:5—3:6

Christ Became like Humans

God did not choose angels to be
the rulers of the new world that was
coming, which is what we have been
talking about. 6 It is written in the
Scriptures,

"Why are people important to
you?
Why do you take care of
human beings?
7 You made them a little lower than
the angels
and crowned them with glory
and honor.
8 You put all things under their
control." *Psalm 8:4-6*

When God put everything under
their control, there was nothing left
that they did not rule. Still, we do not
yet see them ruling over everything.
9 But we see Jesus, who for a short
time was made lower than the angels. And now he is wearing a crown
of glory and honor because he suffered and died. And by God's grace,
he died for everyone.

10 God is the One who made all
things, and all things are for his
glory. He wanted to have many children share his glory, so he made the
One who leads people to salvation
perfect through suffering.

11 Jesus, who makes people holy,
and those who are made holy are
from the same family. So he is not
ashamed to call them his brothers
and sisters. 12 He says,

"Then, I will tell my fellow
Israelites about you;
I will praise you in the public
meeting." *Psalm 22:22*

13 He also says,

"I will trust in God." *Isaiah 8:17*

And he also says,

"I am here, and with me are the
children God has given me."
Isaiah 8:18

14 Since these children are people
with physical bodies, Jesus himself
became like them. He did this so
that, by dying, he could destroy the
one who has the power of death—
the devil— 15 and free those who
were like slaves all their lives because of their fear of death. 16 Clearly,
it is not angels that Jesus helps, but
the people who are from Abraham.
17 For this reason Jesus had to be
made like his brothers in every way
so he could be their merciful and
faithful high priest in service to God.
Then Jesus could bring forgiveness
for their sins. 18 And now he can help
those who are tempted, because he
himself suffered and was tempted.

Jesus Is Greater than Moses

3 So all of you holy brothers and
sisters, who were called by God,
think about Jesus, who was sent to
us and is the high priest of our faith.
2 Jesus was faithful to God as Moses
was in God's family. 3 Jesus has more
honor than Moses, just as the
builder of a house has more honor
than the house itself. 4 Every house
is built by someone, but the builder
of everything is God himself.
5 Moses was faithful in God's family
as a servant, and he told what God
would say in the future. 6 But Christ
is faithful as a Son over God's house.

And we are God's house if we keep on being very sure about our great hope.

OLD TESTAMENT READING

I will make them one nation in the land, on the mountains of Israel. One king will rule all of them. They will never again be two nations; they will not be divided into two kingdoms anymore. [23b] I will save them from all the ways they sin and turn against me, and I will make them clean. Then they will be my people, and I will be their God.

[24] "'My servant David will be their king, and they will all have one shepherd. They will live by my rules and obey my laws. [25] They will live on the land I gave to my servant Jacob, the land in which your ancestors lived. They will all live on the land forever: they, their children, and their grandchildren. David my servant will be their king forever. [26] I will make an agreement of peace with them, an agreement that continues forever. I will put them in their land and make them grow in number. Then I will put my Temple among them forever. [27] The place where I live will be with them. I will be their God, and they will be my people. [28] When my Temple is among them forever, the nations will know that I, the LORD, make Israel holy.'"

Ezekiel 37:22, 23b–28

INSIGHTS

Christ in us can manifest His holiness if we will yield our flesh to Him. This is not a human operation; it is a spiritual one. Jesus installs His holiness in us by grace. Not a once-for-all-time transaction, this is a daily, moment-by-moment striving to live more by the Spirit and less by the flesh.

Though becoming more holy is God's work in us, it is not a passive enterprise. Our part is active, to strive and strain toward the high calling we have received. God's part is to forgive our failings based on the merit of Christ's atoning death.

His will is that we become holy. . . . This kind of holiness is not the result of our own best effort. . . .

The forgiveness of Christ makes us holy; He washed away our sin. In reality, God in us—the Holy Spirit—makes us holy. There is no possibility of holiness apart from His grace. He calls us, He justifies us, He sanctifies us (makes us holy), and He will glorify us—all by His grace.

Our part is to surrender in faith; God's part is to implant the sanctifying Holy Spirit in us. "So I say, live by the Spirit, and you will not gratify the desires of the sinful nature" (Galatians 5:16). Because of His everlasting love, we know Him, and He is faithful to mold us into the character of His Son Jesus Christ—to make us holy.

Patrick Morley

ACTION POINT

Meditate on what Jesus did to make his people holy. How significant is it that Jesus considers his holy people to be his family—his brothers? How do these truths inspire you to yield to his holiness?

FRIDAY

God Demands Obedience and Punishes Unbelief

Hebrews 3:7—4:13

We Must Continue to Follow God

So it is as the Holy Spirit says:
"Today listen to what he says.
8 Do not be stubborn as in the past
when you turned against God,
when you tested God in the desert.
9 There your ancestors tried me
and tested me
and saw the things I did for
forty years.
10 I was angry with them.
I said, 'They are not loyal to me
and have not understood my
ways.'
11 I was angry and made a promise,
'They will never enter my
rest.'" *Psalm 95:7-11*
12 So brothers and sisters, be careful that none of you has an evil, unbelieving heart that will turn you
away from the living God. 13 But encourage each other every day while
it is "today." Help each other so none
of you will become hardened because sin has tricked you. 14 We all
share in Christ if we keep till the end
the sure faith we had in the beginning. 15 This is what the Scripture
says:
"Today listen to what he says.
Do not be stubborn as in the past
when you turned against God."
Psalm 95:7-8
16 Who heard God's voice and was
against him? It was all those people
Moses led out of Egypt. 17 And with
whom was God angry for forty
years? He was angry with those who
sinned, who died in the desert.
18 And to whom was God talking
when he promised that they would
never enter his rest? He was talking
to those who did not obey him. 19 So
we see they were not allowed to enter and have God's rest, because
they did not believe.
4 Now, since God has left us the
promise that we may enter his
rest, let us be very careful so none
of you will fail to enter. 2 The Good
News was preached to us just as it
was to them. But the teaching they
heard did not help them, because
they heard it but did not accept it
with faith. 3 We who have believed
are able to enter and have God's rest.
As God has said,
"I was angry and made a promise,
'They will never enter my rest.'"
Psalm 95:11
But God's work was finished from
the time he made the world. 4 In the
Scriptures he talked about the seventh day of the week: "And on the
seventh day God rested from all his
works." 5 And again in the Scripture
God said, "They will never enter my
rest."
6 It is still true that some people
will enter God's rest, but those who
first heard the way to be saved did
not enter, because they did not obey.
7 So God planned another day, called
"today." He spoke about that day
through David a long time later in
the same Scripture used before:
"Today listen to what he says.
Do not be stubborn." *Psalm 95:7-8*
8 We know that Joshua did not lead
the people into that rest, because
God spoke later about another day.
9 This shows that the rest for God's
people is still coming. 10 Anyone who

enters God's rest will rest from his
work as God did. [11] Let us try as hard
as we can to enter God's rest so that
no one will fail by following the example of those who refused to obey.
[12] God's word is alive and working
and is sharper than a double-edged
sword. It cuts all the way into us,
where the soul and the spirit are
joined, to the center of our joints and
bones. And it judges the thoughts
and feelings in our hearts. [13] Nothing in all the world can be hidden
from God. Everything is clear and
lies open before him, and to him we
must explain the way we have lived.

OLD TESTAMENT READING

If the LORD is pleased with us, he
will lead us into that land and give
us that fertile land. [9] Don't turn
against the LORD! Don't be afraid of
the people in that land! We will chew
them up. They have no protection,
but the LORD is with us. So don't be
afraid of them."
[20] The LORD answered, "I have forgiven them as you asked. [21] But, as
surely as I live and as surely as my
glory fills the whole earth, I make
this promise: [22] All these men saw
my glory and the miracles I did in
Egypt and in the desert, but they disobeyed me and tested me ten times.
[23] So not one of them will see the land
I promised to their ancestors. No
one who rejected me will see that
land."

Numbers 14:8–9, 20–23

INSIGHTS

How do we find God and grow in him? Jesus was adamant at this point. He said we must do what he says. We must put into practical obedience the knowledge that we have. He continually asked people to drop their nets, to sell all they had and to follow him.

We might say that Jesus had a theology of obedience. And the object of this obedience was a living person, not a historical norm, not a code of laws, but himself. He called people to be accountable to God whether they were believers or skeptics who were searching. For example, he told his disciples, "What is the point of calling me, 'Lord, Lord,' without doing what I tell you to do?" (Lk. 6:46 Phillips). . . .

Jesus knew that obedience to his and his Father's words yielded faith. . . . If I had to sum up one's response to the gospel message, I would say as William Pannell has said, "It's paint—or get off the ladder." Jesus approached people exactly like that. He told them to pick up their brush and paint something.

Do you want to discover who Jesus is and deal honestly with your doubts? Jesus' style is not to suggest that you go and ponder the virgin birth for three months but to begin doing what he says.

Rebecca Pippert

APPLICATION

What does an unbelieving heart lead us to do? What is the relationship between obedience and belief? When our life is over, what will God ask us to explain? Are you ready to answer him?

WEEKEND
Jesus Is Our High Priest

Hebrews 4:14—6:8

Since we have a great high priest,
Jesus the Son of God, who has gone
into heaven, let us hold on to the
faith we have. [15] For our high priest
is able to understand our weaknesses. When he lived on earth, he
was tempted in every way that we
are, but he did not sin. [16] Let us, then,
feel very sure that we can come before God's throne where there is
grace. There we can receive mercy
and grace to help us when we need
it.
5 Every high priest is chosen from
among other people. He is given
the work of going before God for
them to offer gifts and sacrifices for
sins. [2] Since he himself is weak, he
is able to be gentle with those who
do not understand and who are doing wrong things. [3] Because he is
weak, the high priest must offer sacrifices for his own sins and also for
the sins of the people.
[4] To be a high priest is an honor,
but no one chooses himself for this
work. He must be called by God as
Aaron was. [5] So also Christ did not
choose himself to have the honor of
being a high priest, but God chose
him. God said to him,

"You are my Son.
Today I have become your
Father." *Psalm 2:7*

[6] And in another Scripture God says,

"You are a priest forever,
a priest like Melchizedek."
Psalm 110:4

[7] While Jesus lived on earth, he
prayed to God and asked God for
help. He prayed with loud cries and
tears to the One who could save him
from death, and his prayer was
heard because he trusted God.
[8] Even though Jesus was the Son of
God, he learned obedience by what
he suffered. [9] And because his obedience was perfect, he was able to
give eternal salvation to all who obey
him. [10] In this way God made Jesus
a high priest, a priest like Melchizedek.

Warning Against Falling Away

[11] We have much to say about this,
but it is hard to explain because you
are so slow to understand. [12] By now
you should be teachers, but you
need someone to teach you again the
first lessons of God's message. You
still need the teaching that is like
milk. You are not ready for solid
food. [13] Anyone who lives on milk is
still a baby and knows nothing about
right teaching. [14] But solid food is for
those who are grown up. They have
practiced in order to know the difference between good and evil.
6 So let us go on to grown-up teaching. Let us not go back over the
beginning lessons we learned about
Christ. We should not again start
teaching about faith in God and
about turning away from those acts
that lead to death. [2] We should not
return to the teaching about bap-
tisms, about laying on of hands,
about the raising of the dead and
eternal judgment. [3] And we will go on
to grown-up teaching if God allows.
[4] Some people cannot be brought
back again to a changed life. They
were once in God's light, and enjoyed heaven's gift, and shared in the

Holy Spirit. 5 They found out how
good God's word is, and they received the powers of his new world.
6 But they fell away from Christ. It is
impossible to bring them back to a
changed life again, because they are
nailing the Son of God to a cross
again and are shaming him in front
of others.
7 Some people are like land that
gets plenty of rain. The land produces a good crop for those who
work it, and it receives God's blessings. 8 Other people are like land that
grows thorns and weeds and is
worthless. It is in danger of being
cursed by God and will be destroyed
by fire.

OLD TESTAMENT READING

God Chooses Priests for His Holy Work

Tell your brother Aaron to come to
you, along with his sons Nadab,
Abihu, Eleazar, and Ithamar. Separate them from the other Israelites
to serve me as priests. 2 Make holy
clothes for your brother Aaron to
give him honor and beauty. 3 Tell all
the skilled craftsmen to whom I have
given wisdom to make special
clothes for Aaron—clothes to show
that he belongs to me so that he may
serve me as a priest."

Exodus 28:1–3

INSIGHTS

At one time in history a "NO ACCESS" sign was posted at the gates of Paradise. Even in the Old Testament temple there was no access to the throne of God by the ordinary person. Even for the High Priest his access was "limited" to once a year under very guarded circumstances. A thick veil separated the Holy of Holies from the rest of the temple. It was off-limits. Restricted. No admission was permitted to the rank-and-file believer.

The moment Jesus was slain, the instant the Just One died for the unjust, the veil in the temple was torn. The presence of God became accessible to us. For the Christian the "NO ACCESS" sign was removed from the gates of Paradise. We may now trespass freely on holy ground. We have access to His grace, but even more, we have access to Him. Justified men need no longer say to the Holy, "Depart from me, for I am a sinful man." Now we can be comfortable in the presence of a holy God. We can take our questions to Him. He is not too remote to hear our cries. We come as those covered by the righteousness of Christ. I repeat: We can be comfortable in the presence of God. To be sure we still come in awe, in a spirit of reverence and adoration, but the tremendous news is that we can . . . approach the throne of grace with confidence.

R. C. Sproul

PAUSE FOR REFLECTION

From the Old Testament reading, do you begin to sense the vital role of God's priests? In what ways does your understanding of Christ's role as high priest (explained in Hebrews) help you realize how much he has done to save us?

MONDAY

God's Word Is True: He Keeps His Promises

Hebrews 6:9—7:10

Dear friends, we are saying this to
you, but we really expect better
things from you that will lead to your
salvation. 10 God is fair; he will not
forget the work you did and the love
you showed for him by helping his
people. And he will remember that
you are still helping them. 11 We want
each of you to go on with the same
hard work all your lives so you will
surely get what you hope for. 12 We
do not want you to become lazy. Be
like those who through faith and patience will receive what God has
promised.

13 God made a promise to
Abraham. And as there is no one
greater than God, he used himself
when he swore to Abraham, 14 saying,
"I will surely bless you and give you
many descendants." 15 Abraham
waited patiently for this to happen, and
he received what God promised.

16 People always use the name of
someone greater than themselves
when they swear. The oath proves
that what they say is true, and this
ends all arguing. 17 God wanted to
prove that his promise was true to
those who would get what he promised. And he wanted them to understand clearly that his purposes never
change, so he made an oath.
18 These two things cannot change:
God cannot lie when he makes a
promise, and he cannot lie when he
makes an oath. These things encourage us who came to God for
safety. They give us strength to hold
on to the hope we have been given.
19 We have this hope as an anchor for
the soul, sure and strong. It enters
behind the curtain in the Most Holy
Place in heaven, 20 where Jesus has
gone ahead of us and for us. He has
become the high priest forever, a
priest like Melchizedek.

The Priest Melchizedek

7 Melchizedek was the king of Salem and a priest for God Most
High. He met Abraham when
Abraham was coming back after defeating the kings. When they met,
Melchizedek blessed Abraham,
2 and Abraham gave him a tenth of
everything he had brought back
from the battle. First, Melchizedek's
name means "king of goodness," and
he is king of Salem, which means
"king of peace." 3 No one knows who
Melchizedek's father or mother was,
where he came from, when he was
born, or when he died. Melchizedek
is like the Son of God; he continues
being a priest forever.

4 You can see how great Melchizedek was. Abraham, the great father,
gave him a tenth of everything that
he won in battle. 5 Now the law says
that those in the tribe of Levi who
become priests must collect a tenth
from the people—their own
people—even though the priests and
the people are from the family of
Abraham. 6 Melchizedek was not
from the tribe of Levi, but he collected a tenth from Abraham. And he
blessed Abraham, the man who had
God's promises. 7 Now everyone
knows that the more important person blesses the less important person.
8 Priests receive a tenth, even though

they are only men who live and then die. But Melchizedek, who received a tenth from Abraham, continues living, as the Scripture says. [9] We might even say that Levi, who receives a tenth, also paid it when Abraham paid Melchizedek a tenth. [10] Levi was not yet born, but he was in the body of his ancestor when Melchizedek met Abraham.

OLD TESTAMENT READING

The LORD your God will force out the people living there. The LORD will push them out ahead of you. And you will own the land, as he has promised you.

[6] "Be strong. You must be careful to obey everything commanded in the Book of the Teachings of Moses. Do exactly as it says.

[14] "It's almost time for me to die. You know and fully believe that the LORD has done great things for you. You know that he has not failed to keep any of his promises. [15] Every good promise that the LORD your God made has come true, and in the same way, his other promises will come true. He promised that evil will come to you and that he will destroy you from this good land that he gave you. [16] This will happen if you don't keep your agreement with the LORD your God. If you go and serve other gods and worship them, the LORD will become very angry with you. Then none of you will be left in this good land he has given you."

Joshua 23:5–6, 14–16

INSIGHTS

The Bible is filled with the promises of God. We need to claim each one by faith and activate its truth in our lives. Some folks like to say, "If God said it, I believe it, and that settles it!" The fact of the matter is, if God said it, that settles it, whether we believe it or not.

Someone will question, "How can I be sure God really said this?" or, "How can I be sure this is what it means?" I realize we must interpret each promise in its proper context. But I also believe that we need to take those promises which apply to us and activate them by faith.

In Hebrews 4:3, we read an amazing truth. It says there that God's works were "finished from the foundation of the world." In other words, God had already provided the answer to your every need before the world was ever formed. With His divine foreknowledge He looked down the corridor of time to come, saw your coming problem and provided just exactly what you would need. . . .

. . . Think on the majesty and magnitude of God. Focus on the promises He has given you in His Word. Turn your attention to fulfilling His purpose for your life. Live in the confidence that He is in control. Now you can relax, for there is nothing to worry about. God cares and He keeps His promises to help.

Richard Lee

APPLICATION

What about God's character encourages us to trust in his promises? Of what did Joshua remind the Israelites before he died? Why is it important to remember that God keeps his promises? Will you remember to live by his promises?

TUESDAY

Jesus Is the High Priest of God's New Agreement

Hebrews 7:11—8:6

The people were given the law based on a system of priests from the tribe of Levi, but they could not be made perfect through that system. So there was a need for another priest to come, a priest like Melchizedek, not Aaron. 12 And when a different kind of priest comes, the law must be changed, too. 13 We are saying these things about Christ, who belonged to a different tribe. No one from that tribe ever served as a priest at the altar. 14 It is clear that our Lord came from the tribe of Judah, and Moses said nothing about priests belonging to that tribe.

Jesus Is like Melchizedek

And this becomes even more clear when we see that another priest comes who is like Melchizedek. 16 He was not made a priest by human rules and laws but through the power of his life, which continues forever. 17 It is said about him,

"You are a priest forever,
a priest like Melchizedek."

Psalm 110:4

18 The old rule is now set aside, because it was weak and useless. 19 The law of Moses could not make anything perfect. But now a better hope has been given to us, and with this hope we can come near to God. 20 It is important that God did this with an oath. Others became priests without an oath, 21 but Christ became a priest with God's oath. God said:

"The Lord has made a promise
and will not change his mind.
'You are a priest forever.'"

Psalm 110:4

22 This means that Jesus is the guarantee of a better agreement from God to his people.

23 When one of the other priests died, he could not continue being a priest. So there were many priests. 24 But because Jesus lives forever, he will never stop serving as priest. 25 So he is able always to save those who come to God through him because he always lives, asking God to help them.

26 Jesus is the kind of high priest we need. He is holy, sinless, pure, not influenced by sinners, and he is raised above the heavens. 27 He is not like the other priests who had to offer sacrifices every day, first for their own sins, and then for the sins of the people. Christ offered his sacrifice only once and for all time when he offered himself. 28 The law chooses high priests who are people with weaknesses, but the word of God's oath came later than the law. It made God's Son to be the high priest, and that Son has been made perfect forever.

Jesus Is Our High Priest

8 Here is the point of what we are saying: We have a high priest who sits on the right side of God's throne in heaven. 2 Our high priest serves in the Most Holy Place, the true place of worship that was made by God, not by humans.

3 Every high priest has the work of offering gifts and sacrifices to God. So our high priest must also

offer something to God. [4] If our high
priest were now living on earth, he
would not be a priest, because there
are already priests here who follow
the law by offering gifts to God. [5] The
work they do as priests is only a copy
and a shadow of what is in heaven.
This is why God warned Moses
when he was ready to build the Holy
Tent: "Be very careful to make everything by the plan I showed you
on the mountain." [6] But the priestly
work that has been given to Jesus is
much greater than the work that was
given to the other priests. In the
same way, the new agreement that
Jesus brought from God to his
people is much greater than the old
one. And the new agreement is
based on promises of better things.

OLD TESTAMENT READING

The LORD said to my Lord,
"Sit by me at my right side
until I put your enemies under
your control."
2The LORD will enlarge your
kingdom beyond Jerusalem,
and you will rule over your
enemies.
3Your people will join you on your
day of battle.
You have been dressed in
holiness from birth;
you have the freshness of a
child.

4The LORD has made a promise
and will not change his mind.
He said, "You are a priest forever,
a priest like Melchizedek."

Psalm 110:1–4

This is the agreement I will
make
with the people of Israel at that
time," says the LORD:
"I will put my teachings in their
minds
and write them on their hearts.
I will be their God,
and they will be my people."

Jeremiah 31:33

INSIGHTS

We need a priest such as Jesus is, to represent us in heaven. Although we are so completely absolved from guilt, and so fully "accepted in the beloved", yet in ourselves, while down here, we are still erring, sinning, feeble, needy creatures, exposed to trials and temptations, liable to stumble, and encompassed by infirmities. How we need the high priestly mediation of our dear heavenly Advocate, whose presence yonder keeps us in all the benefits of the New Covenant, maintains our standing in grace, and releases to us the paraclete ministries of the Holy Spirit. It has been well said, "We could not stand for a moment down here, if He were not living for us up there."

Thank God, "we have such an high priest"!

J. Sydlow Baxter

ACTION POINT

Identify the unique aspects of Christ's priesthood and describe why his unique role as high priest is significant. Pray now and thank God that he has sent a high priest—like no other— to offer the only perfect sacrifice for your sins.

WEDNESDAY

Jesus Takes Away Our Sins Forever

Hebrews 8:7—9:12

If there had been nothing wrong
with the first agreement, there
would have been no need for a second agreement. 8 But God found
something wrong with his people.
He says:

"Look, the time is coming, says
the Lord,
when I will make a new
agreement
with the people of Israel
and the people of Judah.
9 It will not be like the agreement
I made with their ancestors
when I took them by the hand
to bring them out of Egypt.
But they broke that agreement,
and I turned away from them,
says the Lord.
10 This is the agreement I will make
with the people of Israel at that
time, says the Lord.
I will put my teachings in their
minds
and write them on their hearts.
I will be their God,
and they will be my people.
11 People will no longer have to
teach their neighbors and
relatives
to know the Lord,
because all people will know me,
from the least to the most
important.
12 I will forgive them for the wicked
things they did,
and I will not remember their
sins anymore." *Jeremiah 31:31-34*

13 God called this a new agreement, so he has made the first agreement old. And anything that is old
and worn out is ready to disappear.

The Old Agreement

9 The first agreement had rules for
worship and a man-made place
for worship. 2 The Holy Tent was set
up for this. The first area in the Tent
was called the Holy Place. In it were
the lamp and the table with the
bread that was made holy for God.
3 Behind the second curtain was a
room called the Most Holy Place. 4 In
it was a golden altar for burning incense and the Ark covered with gold
that held the old agreement. Inside
this Ark was a golden jar of manna,
Aaron's rod that once grew leaves,
and the stone tablets of the old
agreement. 5 Above the Ark were the
creatures that showed God's glory,
whose wings reached over the lid.
But we cannot tell everything about
these things now.

6 When everything in the Tent
was made ready in this way, the
priests went into the first room every day to worship. 7 But only the
high priest could go into the second
room, and he did that only once a
year. He could never enter the inner
room without taking blood with him,
which he offered to God for himself
and for sins the people did without
knowing they did them. 8 The Holy
Spirit uses this to show that the way
into the Most Holy Place was not
open while the system of the old
Holy Tent was still being used. 9 This
is an example for the present time.
It shows that the gifts and sacrifices
offered cannot make the conscience
of the worshiper perfect. 10 These

gifts and sacrifices were only about food and drink and special washings. They were rules for the body, to be followed until the time of God's new way.

The New Agreement

But when Christ came as the high priest of the good things we now have, he entered the greater and more perfect tent. It is not made by humans and does not belong to this world. 12 Christ entered the Most Holy Place only once—and for all time. He did not take with him the blood of goats and calves. His sacrifice was his own blood, and by it he set us free from sin forever.

OLD TESTAMENT READING

But it was the LORD who decided
to crush him and make him
suffer.
The LORD made his life a
penalty offering,
but he will still see his descendants and live a long life.
He will complete the things the
LORD wants him to do.
11 "After his soul suffers many
things,
he will see life and be satisfied.
My good servant will make many
people right with God;
he will carry away their sins."

Isaiah 53:10–11

INSIGHTS

If we confess our sins, he is faithful and just and will forgive us our sins and purify us from all unrighteousness" (1 John 1:9). This verse tells us what to do when we've sinned—we must confess that we have sinned and need forgiveness.

Then if we confess, God promises to forgive. He takes care of that sin once and for all. He restores our relationship with him. . . .

. . . At the center of forgiveness is always the cross of Christ. Without his body on the cross, forgiveness would not even be available. Forgiveness is costly, and we need to see it from that perspective. There is no forgiveness without tears, without a price to be paid, without the sacrifice of Christ.

Because of Christ's sacrifice, sin need not defeat us. . . .

Though we cannot eliminate the temptation to sin, we are not left without redemptive resources. God is on our side, Jesus is advocating for us, and the Holy Spirit is making us aware of our weaknesses as our Teacher and Guide.

David McKenna

PAUSE FOR REFLECTION

Describe the many differences between the old and new agreements. What difference does it make that Jesus is now our high priest? Pray and thank God that the blood of Jesus takes away our sins forever.

THURSDAY

Christ's Blood: The Perfect Sacrifice

Hebrews 9:13—10:10

The blood of goats and bulls and the
ashes of a cow are sprinkled on the
people who are unclean, and this
makes their bodies clean again. 14 How
much more is done by the blood of
Christ. He offered himself through
the eternal Spirit as a perfect sacrifice
to God. His blood will make our consciences pure from useless acts so we
may serve the living God.
15 For this reason Christ brings a
new agreement from God to his
people. Those who are called by God
can now receive the blessings he has
promised, blessings that will last forever. They can have those things because Christ died so that the people
who lived under the first agreement
could be set free from sin.
16 When there is a will, it must be
proven that the one who wrote that
will is dead. 17 A will means nothing
while the person is alive; it can be used
only after the person dies. 18 This is
why even the first agreement could
not begin without blood to show
death. 19 First, Moses told all the
people every command in the law.
Next he took the blood of calves and
mixed it with water. Then he used red
wool and a branch of the hyssop plant
to sprinkle it on the book of the law
and on all the people. 20 He said, "This
is the blood that begins the Agreement that God commanded you to
obey." 21 In the same way, Moses
sprinkled the blood on the Holy Tent
and over all the things used in worship. 22 The law says that almost everything must be made clean by blood,
and sins cannot be forgiven without
blood to show death.

Christ's Death Takes Away Sins

So the copies of the real things in
heaven had to be made clean by animal sacrifices. But the real things in
heaven need much better sacrifices.
24 Christ did not go into the Most
Holy Place made by humans, which
is only a copy of the real one. He
went into heaven itself and is there
now before God to help us. 25 The
high priest enters the Most Holy
Place once every year with blood that
is not his own. But Christ did not offer himself many times. 26 Then he
would have had to suffer many times
since the world was made. But Christ
came only once and for all time at
just the right time to take away all
sin by sacrificing himself. 27 Just as
everyone must die once and be
judged, 28 so Christ was offered as a
sacrifice one time to take away the
sins of many people. And he will
come a second time, not to offer himself for sin, but to bring salvation to
those who are waiting for him.

10 The law is only an unclear picture of the good things coming
in the future; it is not the real thing.
The people under the law offer the
same sacrifices every year, but these
sacrifices can never make perfect
those who come near to worship
God. 2 If the law could make them
perfect, the sacrifices would have
already stopped. The worshipers
would be made clean, and they
would no longer have a sense of sin.
3 But these sacrifices remind them of
their sins every year, 4 because it is

impossible for the blood of bulls and
goats to take away sins.
5 So when Christ came into the
world, he said:

"You do not want sacrifices and
offerings,
but you have prepared a body
for me.
6 You do not ask for burnt offerings
and offerings to take away
sins.
7 Then I said, 'Look, I have come.
It is written about me in the
book.
God, I have come to do what
you want.'" *Psalm 40:6-8*

8 In this Scripture he first said, "You
do not want sacrifices and offerings.
You do not ask for burnt offerings and
offerings to take away sins." (These
are all sacrifices that the law commands.) 9 Then he said, "Look, I have
come to do what you want." God ends
the first system of sacrifices so he can
set up the new system. 10 And because
of this, we are made holy through the
sacrifice Christ made in his body once
and for all time.

OLD TESTAMENT READING

Then Aaron must kill the goat of
the sin offering for the people and
bring its blood into the room behind
the curtain. He must do with the
goat's blood as he did with the bull's
blood, sprinkling it on the lid and in
front of the lid. 17b So Aaron will perform the acts to remove sins from
himself, his family, and all the people
of Israel, so they will belong to the
LORD.
34 "That law for removing the sins
of the Israelites so they will belong
to the LORD will continue forever. You
will do these things once a year."

So they did the things the LORD had commanded Moses.

Leviticus 16:15, 17b, 34

INSIGHTS

When we sin, our only option is repentance. Without repentance there is no forgiveness. We must come before God in contrition. David put it this way:

"For thou has no delight in sacrifice. . . . The sacrifice acceptable to God is a broken spirit; a broken and contrite heart, O God, thou wilt not despise" [Psalm 51:16, 17].

Here David's profound thoughts reveal his understanding of what many Old Testament persons failed to grasp—that the offering of sacrifices in the temple did not gain merit for the sinner. Sacrifices pointed beyond themselves to the perfect Sacrifice. The perfect atonement was offered by the perfect Lamb without blemish. The blood of bulls and goats does not take away sin. The blood of Jesus does. To avail ourselves of the atonement of Christ, to gain that covering, requires that we come before God in brokenness and contrition. The true sacrifices of God are a broken spirit and a contrite heart.

R. C. Sproul

APPLICATION

What does the sacrifice of Christ's blood accomplish that no other sacrifice can do? What kind of sacrifice does God want from his people? What has Christ's sacrifice done for you personally?

FRIDAY

The Lord Will Judge His People

Hebrews 10:11–39

Every day the priests stand and do
their religious service, often offering
the same sacrifices. Those sacrifices
can never take away sins. 12 But after Christ offered one sacrifice for
sins, forever, he sat down at the right
side of God. 13 And now Christ waits
there for his enemies to be put under his power. 14 With one sacrifice
he made perfect forever those who
are being made holy.

15 The Holy Spirit also tells us
about this. First he says:

16 "This is the agreement I will make
with them at that time, says the
Lord.
I will put my teachings in their
hearts
and write them on their minds."

Jeremiah 31:33

17 Then he says:

"Their sins and the evil things
they do—
I will not remember anymore."

Jeremiah 31:34

18 Now when these have been forgiven, there is no more need for a
sacrifice for sins.

Continue to Trust God

So, brothers and sisters, we are
completely free to enter the Most
Holy Place without fear because of
the blood of Jesus' death. 20 We can
enter through a new and living way
that Jesus opened for us. It leads
through the curtain—Christ's body.
21 And since we have a great priest
over God's house, 22 let us come near
to God with a sincere heart and a sure
faith, because we have been made
free from a guilty conscience, and our
bodies have been washed with pure
water. 23 Let us hold firmly to the hope
that we have confessed, because we
can trust God to do what he promised.

24 Let us think about each other and
help each other to show love and do
good deeds. 25 You should not stay away
from the church meetings, as some are
doing, but you should meet together
and encourage each other. Do this even
more as you see the day coming.

26 If we decide to go on sinning
after we have learned the truth,
there is no longer any sacrifice for
sins. 27 There is nothing but fear in
waiting for the judgment and the terrible fire that will destroy all those
who live against God. 28 Anyone who
refused to obey the law of Moses
was found guilty from the proof
given by two or three witnesses. He
was put to death without mercy. 29 So
what do you think should be done
to those who do not respect the Son
of God, who look at the blood of the
agreement that made them holy as
no different from others' blood, who
insult the Spirit of God's grace?
Surely they should have a much
worse punishment. 30 We know that
God said, "I will punish those who
do wrong; I will repay them." And he
also said, "The Lord will judge his
people." 31 It is a terrible thing to fall
into the hands of the living God.

32 Remember those days in the
past when you first learned the
truth. You had a hard struggle with
many sufferings, but you continued
strong. 33 Sometimes you were hurt

and attacked before crowds of people, and sometimes you shared with those who were being treated
that way. 34 You helped the prisoners.
You even had joy when all that you owned was taken from you, because you knew you had something better and more lasting.
35 So do not lose the courage you had in the past, which has a great
reward. 36 You must hold on, so you can do what God wants and receive
what he has promised. 37 For in a
very short time,

"The One who is coming will
come
and will not be delayed.
38 The person who is right with me
will live by trusting in me.
But if he turns back with fear,
I will not be pleased with him."

Habakkuk 2:3-4

39 But we are not those who turn back and are lost. We are people who have faith and are saved.

OLD TESTAMENT READING

The LORD will judge the people
with fire,
and he will destroy many
people with his sword;
he will kill many people.

Isaiah 66:16

Try to do good, not evil,
so that you will live,
and the LORD God All-Powerful
will be with you
just as you say he is.

Amos 5:14

INSIGHTS

Without a physical order in the universe, there could be no science. Much of the genius of our space program involves achieving the most precise knowledge and conformity to this order. Failure means disaster.

Tens of thousands of man-hours, the most sophisticated technology, and the latest advances in space science are involved. . . . But all of it is helpless without an orderly universe to count on, and conform to.

God, who ordained physical order, also ordained moral and spiritual order.

Conformity guarantees fulfillment. Disobedience spells destruction. . . .

One can reject God's moral absolutes. But that does not get rid of them. The law of sin and death is just as inviolable as the law of gravity. Morality isn't arbitrary. It's part of the natural law of the universe. God's law stands whether we like it or not.

We ignore this fact to our doom. Violating God's physical law is destructive, but violating His moral law is infinitely more serious—for it has eternal consequences.

Every malfunction of the social order in America derives from our transgression of God's moral law. If we refuse to turn to God for mercy and grace, we condemn ourselves to His inexorable justice and judgment.

Richard Halverson

APPLICATION

What will happen to everyone who lives against God? What is promised to those who continue living by faith? Pray for the courage to live as God wants his people to live.

WEEKEND
Faith Pleases God

Hebrews 11:1–22

What Is Faith?

11 Faith means being sure of the
things we hope for and knowing that something is real even if we
do not see it. 2 Faith is the reason we
remember great people who lived in
the past.

3 It is by faith we understand that
the whole world was made by God's
command so what we see was made
by something that cannot be seen.

4 It was by faith that Abel offered
God a better sacrifice than Cain did.
God said he was pleased with the
gifts Abel offered and called Abel a
good man because of his faith. Abel
died, but through his faith he is still
speaking.

5 It was by faith that Enoch was
taken to heaven so he would not die.
He could not be found, because God
had taken him away. Before he was
taken, the Scripture says that he was
a man who truly pleased God.
6 Without faith no one can please
God. Anyone who comes to God
must believe that he is real and that
he rewards those who truly want to
find him.

7 It was by faith that Noah heard
God's warnings about things he
could not yet see. He obeyed God
and built a large boat to save his
family. By his faith, Noah showed
that the world was wrong, and he
became one of those who are made
right with God through faith.

8 It was by faith Abraham obeyed
God's call to go to another place
God promised to give him. He left
his own country, not knowing where
he was to go. 9 It was by faith that
he lived like a foreigner in the country God promised to give him. He
lived in tents with Isaac and Jacob,
who had received that same promise from God. 10 Abraham was waiting for the city that has real foundations—the city planned and built by
God.

11 He was too old to have children,
and Sarah could not have children.
It was by faith that Abraham was
made able to become a father, because he trusted God to do what he
had promised. 12 This man was so
old he was almost dead, but from
him came as many descendants as
there are stars in the sky. Like the
sand on the seashore, they could
not be counted.

13 All these great people died in
faith. They did not get the things
that God promised his people, but
they saw them coming far in the future and were glad. They said they
were like visitors and strangers on
earth. 14 When people say such
things, they show they are looking
for a country that will be their own.
15 If they had been thinking about
the country they had left, they could
have gone back. 16 But they were
waiting for a better country—a
heavenly country. So God is not
ashamed to be called their God, because he has prepared a city for
them.

17 It was by faith that Abraham,
when God tested him, offered his
son Isaac as a sacrifice. God made
the promises to Abraham, but
Abraham was ready to offer his own
son as a sacrifice. 18 God had said,

"The descendants I promised you
will be from Isaac." 19 Abraham believed that God could raise the dead,
and really, it was as if Abraham got
Isaac back from death.
20 It was by faith that Isaac
blessed the future of Jacob and
Esau. 21 It was by faith that Jacob, as
he was dying, blessed each one of
Joseph's sons. Then he worshiped
as he leaned on the top of his walking stick.
22 It was by faith that Joseph,
while he was dying, spoke about the
Israelites leaving Egypt and gave instructions about what to do with his
body.

OLD TESTAMENT READING

Then God led Abram outside and
said, "Look at the sky. There are so
many stars you cannot count them.
Your descendants also will be too
many to count."
6 Abram believed the Lord. And
the Lord accepted Abram's faith, and
that faith made him right with God.

Genesis 15:5–6

INSIGHTS

Faith is my deliberate and positive response to the good in another to the extent that I will act on his behalf in a personal, powerful way. . . .

. . . It means that I am willing to share my life along with all its capacities (time, strength, attention, talents, means, energy, affection, acceptance) with another. It means that I actively, energetically give of my best to another outside of and apart from myself.

To speak of faith in any other way than this is to indulge in mere "believism." It is to play around with pious platitudes that pack no punch at all. This sort of superficial spirituality is actually the great bane of Christianity. Literally hundreds of thousands of people claim they trust in God; they claim to have faith in Christ; they claim to be believers, yet their lives and personal conduct are a denial and travesty of true faith. . . .

. . . When our Lord lived amongst us He was continually looking for this dynamic trust and response to Himself. Whenever He found even the tiniest fragment of faith being exercised in Him He was delighted.

W. Phillip Keller

ACTION POINT

Is faith for things in the past, present, or future? In what ways is faith a catalyst in your life? Pray that your faith will be a delight to God.

MONDAY

God Corrects Those He Loves

Hebrews 11:23—12:6

It was by faith that Moses' parents
hid him for three months after he
was born. They saw that Moses was
a beautiful baby, and they were not
afraid to disobey the king's order.
24 It was by faith that Moses, when
he grew up, refused to be called the
son of the king of Egypt's daughter.
25 He chose to suffer with God's
people instead of enjoying sin for a
short time. 26 He thought it was better to suffer for the Christ than to
have all the treasures of Egypt, because he was looking for God's reward. 27 It was by faith that Moses
left Egypt and was not afraid of the
king's anger. Moses continued
strong as if he could see the God that
no one can see. 28 It was by faith that
Moses prepared the Passover and
spread the blood on the doors so the
one who brings death would not kill
the firstborn sons of Israel.
29 It was by faith that the people
crossed the Red Sea as if it were dry
land. But when the Egyptians tried
it, they were drowned.
30 It was by faith that the walls of
Jericho fell after the people had
marched around them for seven
days.
31 It was by faith that Rahab, the
prostitute, welcomed the spies and
was not killed with those who refused to obey God.
32 Do I need to give more examples? I do not have time to tell you
about Gideon, Barak, Samson,
Jephthah, David, Samuel, and the
prophets. 33 Through their faith they
defeated kingdoms. They did what
was right, received God's promises,
and shut the mouths of lions. 34 They
stopped great fires and were saved
from being killed with swords. They
were weak, and yet were made
strong. They were powerful in battle
and defeated other armies. 35 Women
received their dead relatives raised
back to life. Others were tortured
and refused to accept their freedom
so they could be raised from the
dead to a better life. 36 Some were
laughed at and beaten. Others were
put in chains and thrown into prison.
37 They were stoned to death, they
were cut in half, and they were killed
with swords. Some wore the skins
of sheep and goats. They were poor,
abused, and treated badly. 38 The
world was not good enough for
them! They wandered in deserts and
mountains, living in caves and holes
in the earth.
39 All these people are known for
their faith, but none of them received
what God had promised. 40 God
planned to give us something better
so that they would be made perfect,
but only together with us.

Follow Jesus' Example

12 We have around us many
people whose lives tell us what
faith means. So let us run the race
that is before us and never give up.
We should remove from our lives
anything that would get in the way
and the sin that so easily holds us
back. 2 Let us look only to Jesus, the
One who began our faith and who
makes it perfect. He suffered death
on the cross. But he accepted the

shame as if it were nothing because
of the joy that God put before him.
And now he is sitting at the right side
of God's throne. [3]Think about Jesus'
example. He held on while wicked
people were doing evil things to him.
So do not get tired and stop trying.

God Is like a Father

You are struggling against sin, but
your struggles have not yet caused
you to be killed. [5]You have forgotten the encouraging words that call
you his children:

"My child, don't think the Lord's
discipline is worth nothing,
and don't stop trying when he
corrects you.
[6]The Lord disciplines those he
loves,
and he punishes everyone he
accepts as his child."

Proverbs 3:11-12

OLD TESTAMENT READING

The one whom God corrects is
happy,
so do not hate being corrected
by the Almighty.
[18]God hurts, but he also bandages
up;
he injures, but his hands also
heal.

Job 5:17–18

INSIGHTS

Most of us don't want to be broken in the storms of life. We much prefer to protect our personalities from the stresses and strains of our days. We would rather, much rather, be tough and rugged and self-assured than contrite before Christ, repentant in soul before His Spirit. . . .

Many of us would like to avoid the mills of God. We are tempted to ask Him to deliver us from the upsetting, tumbling tides of time that knock off our rough corners and shape us to His design. We plead for release from the discipline of difficulties, the rub of routine responsibilities, the polish that comes from long perseverance.

We are a restless generation. We of the West want and insist on instant results. We demand a quick fix. We look for shortcuts and immediate results. We are quite sure we can be a rough slab of stone today and a polished gemstone tomorrow.

But God's ways and our ways are not the same. His patience is persistent. His work is meticulous. His years know no end. His perception of time is that one day is as a thousand years and a thousand years as but a single day.

The shattering of rock, the smoothing of stone, the polishing of a jewel in the sea requires eons of time. Can I then expect the breaking of my hard heart, the smoothing of my spirit, the shaping of my character as it is conformed to His own to be any less time-consuming?

W. Phillip Keller

APPLICATION

What is the relationship between having faith and receiving God's correction? In what way does correction help us remove sin from our lives? Pray that you will feel God's great love as he corrects you!

TUESDAY

Accept God's Correction so You Will Learn the Right Way to Live

Hebrews 12:7–29

So hold on through your sufferings, because they are like a father's discipline. God is treating you as children. All children are disciplined by their fathers. 8 If you are never disciplined (and every child must be disciplined), you are not true children. 9 We have all had fathers here on earth who disciplined us, and we respected them. So it is even more important that we accept discipline from the Father of our spirits so we will have life. 10 Our fathers on earth disciplined us for a short time in the way they thought was best. But God disciplines us to help us, so we can become holy as he is. 11 We do not enjoy being disciplined. It is painful, but later, after we have learned from it, we have peace, because we start living in the right way.

Be Careful How You Live

You have become weak, so make yourselves strong again. 13 Live in the right way so that you will be saved and your weakness will not cause you to be lost.

14 Try to live in peace with all people, and try to live free from sin. Anyone whose life is not holy will never see the Lord. 15 Be careful that no one fails to receive God's grace and begins to cause trouble among you. A person like that can ruin many of you. 16 Be careful that no one takes part in sexual sin or is like Esau and never thinks about God. As the oldest son, Esau would have received everything from his father, but he sold all that for a single meal. 17 You remember that after Esau did this, he wanted to get his father's blessing, but his father refused. Esau could find no way to change what he had done, even though he wanted the blessing so much that he cried.

18 You have not come to a mountain that can be touched and that is burning with fire. You have not come to darkness, sadness, and storms. 19 You have not come to the noise of a trumpet or to the sound of a voice like the one the people of Israel heard and begged not to hear another word. 20 They did not want to hear the command: "If anything, even an animal, touches the mountain, it must be put to death with stones." 21 What they saw was so terrible that Moses said, "I am shaking with fear."

22 But you have come to Mount Zion, to the city of the living God, the heavenly Jerusalem. You have come to thousands of angels gathered together with joy. 23 You have come to the meeting of God's firstborn children whose names are written in heaven. You have come to God, the judge of all people, and to the spirits of good people who have been made perfect. 24 You have come to Jesus, the One who brought the new agreement from God to his people, and you have come to the sprinkled blood that has a better message than the blood of Abel.

25 So be careful and do not refuse to listen when God speaks. Others refused to listen to him when he warned them on earth, and they did

not escape. So it will be worse for us
if we refuse to listen to God who
warns us from heaven. 26 When he
spoke before, his voice shook the
earth, but now he has promised,
"Once again I will shake not only the
earth but also the heavens." 27 The
words "once again" clearly show us
that everything that was made—
things that can be shaken—will be
destroyed. Only the things that cannot be shaken will remain.
28 So let us be thankful, because
we have a kingdom that cannot be
shaken. We should worship God in
a way that pleases him with respect
and fear, 29 because our God is like a
fire that burns things up.

OLD TESTAMENT READING

David felt ashamed after he had
counted the people. He said to the
LORD, "I have sinned greatly by what
I have done. LORD, I beg you to forgive me, your servant, because I
have been very foolish."
15a So the LORD sent a terrible disease on Israel.
17 When David saw the angel that
killed the people, he said to the
LORD, "I am the one who sinned and
did wrong. These people only followed me like sheep. They did nothing wrong. Please punish me and
my family."
18 That day Gad came to David
and said, "Go and build an altar to
the LORD on the threshing floor of
Araunah the Jebusite." 19 So David
did what Gad told him to do, just as
the LORD commanded.
25b Then the LORD answered his
prayer for the country, and the disease in Israel stopped.

2 Samuel 24:10, 15a, 17–19, 25b

INSIGHTS

Just as a caring parent will lovingly discipline and train his child, so God lovingly disciplines us. We live in a world of mystery and unexplained enigmas, so it is not surprising that the element of mystery should invade this realm too. Indeed, our Lord indicated that it would be so. "What I do you do not realize now; but you shall understand hereafter" (John 13:7). If we are to experience serenity in this turbulent world, we will need to take firmer grasp of God's sovereignty and trust His love even when we cannot discern His purpose. We must remember that the hand molding the clay is nail-pierced, and that our God's sovereignty will never clash with His paternity. "But now, O LORD, Thou art our Father, we are the clay, and Thou our potter" (Isa. 64:8). If we are to enjoy a deepening intimacy with God, we must react to His providential dealings in a spiritual way, even though they may be inscrutable. These dealings may take various forms, but all are planned in love, and with a view to cultivating a deeper intimacy with God.

J. Oswald Sanders

PAUSE FOR REFLECTION

Why does God punish his people? What did God's punishment accomplish in David's life (2 Samuel 24)? Do you think David realized how seriously he had sinned before God punished him? What causes you to recognize the seriousness of your sin?

WEDNESDAY

Live in a Way that Pleases God

Hebrews 13:1–25

13 Keep on loving each other as
brothers and sisters. 2 Remember to welcome strangers, because
some who have done this have welcomed angels without knowing it.
3 Remember those who are in prison
as if you were in prison with them.
Remember those who are suffering
as if you were suffering with them.
4 Marriage should be honored by
everyone, and husband and wife
should keep their marriage pure.
God will judge as guilty those who
take part in sexual sins. 5 Keep your
lives free from the love of money,
and be satisfied with what you have.
God has said,

"I will never leave you;
I will never forget you."

Deuteronomy 31:6

6 So we can be sure when we say,

"I will not be afraid, because the
Lord is my helper.
People can't do anything to me."

Psalm 118:6

7 Remember your leaders who
taught God's message to you. Remember how they lived and died, and copy
their faith. 8 Jesus Christ is the same
yesterday, today, and forever.
9 Do not let all kinds of strange
teachings lead you into the wrong
way. Your hearts should be strengthened by God's grace, not by obeying
rules about foods, which do not help
those who obey them.
10 We have a sacrifice, but the
priests who serve in the Holy Tent
cannot eat from it. 11 The high priest
carries the blood of animals into the
Most Holy Place where he offers
this blood for sins. But the bodies of
the animals are burned outside the
camp. 12 So Jesus also suffered outside the city to make his people holy
with his own blood. 13 So let us go to
Jesus outside the camp, holding on
as he did when we are abused.
14 Here on earth we do not have a
city that lasts forever, but we are
looking for the city that we will have
in the future. 15 So through Jesus let
us always offer to God our sacrifice
of praise, coming from lips that
speak his name. 16 Do not forget to
do good to others, and share with
them, because such sacrifices please
God.
17 Obey your leaders and act under their authority. They are watching over you, because they are responsible for your souls. Obey
them so that they will do this work
with joy, not sadness. It will not help
you to make their work hard.
18 Pray for us. We are sure that we
have a clear conscience, because we
always want to do the right thing. 19 I
especially beg you to pray so that
God will send me back to you soon.
20–21 I pray that the God of peace
will give you every good thing you
need so you can do what he wants.
God raised from the dead our Lord
Jesus, the Great Shepherd of the
sheep, because of the blood of his
death. His blood began the eternal
agreement that God made with his
people. I pray that God will do in us
what pleases him, through Jesus
Christ, and to him be glory forever
and ever. Amen.
22 My brothers and sisters, I beg
you to listen patiently to this mes-

sage I have written to encourage
you, because it is not very long. 23 I
want you to know that our brother
Timothy has been let out of prison.
If he arrives soon, we will both come
to see you.
24 Greet all your leaders and all of
God's people. Those from Italy send
greetings to you.
25 Grace be with you all.

OLD TESTAMENT READING

Respect the LORD your God, and do
what he has told you to do. Love him.
Serve the LORD your God with your
whole being, 13 and obey the LORD's
commands and laws that I am giving
you today for your own good.
16 Give yourselves completely to
serving him, and do not be stubborn
any longer.
18 He helps orphans and widows,
and he loves foreigners and gives
them food and clothes. 19 You also
must love foreigners, because you
were foreigners in Egypt. 20 Respect
the LORD your God and serve him.
Be loyal to him and make your promises in his name. 21 He is the one you
should praise; he is your God, who
has done great and wonderful things
for you, which you have seen with
your own eyes.

Deuteronomy 10:12b–13, 16, 18–21

INSIGHTS

In recent decades the phrase "easy believism" has surfaced. Unfortunately, it describes a large number of contemporary Christians who have received Christ as Savior but do not, in practice, regard Him as Lord. They seem to have received Him in order to reach heaven someday or to get help for their problems, but they have never fully committed to trust, obey, honor and serve Him as a way of life.

Our Lord never intended that we be His casual acquaintances. He wants us to be His disciples, fully dedicated to following Him and lifting up His holy name to the world. . . . Our Lord is repulsed by mediocre commitment. . . .

. . . When we acknowledge Christ as our Lord, we affirm that He is our Master for life and that we are dedicated to serving and glorifying Him. In all things, large and small, our deepest desire is to do what our Lord would want us to do. We ask for His guidance—not for our gain, but for His glory. We discipline ourselves in studying and obeying His written Word. We proclaim His love to the world around us. We try to think, speak and act in a way that will attract others to Him.

The misguided person who thinks all this is too difficult or irrelevant misses the point. The Christian life is far more than a fire escape from hell; it is the life of submission and obedience which result in joy and victory.

Bill Bright

ACTION POINT

Describe the kind of life God has called his people to live (in both Old and New Testaments). Pray that living such a life will be of utmost importance to you. Make that commitment today!

THURSDAY

God Gives Wisdom to Those Who Ask for It

James 1:1–27

1 From James, a servant of God and of the Lord Jesus Christ.

To all of God's people who are scattered everywhere in the world: Greetings.

Faith and Wisdom

My brothers and sisters, when you have many kinds of troubles, you should be full of joy, [3]because you know that these troubles test your faith, and this will give you patience. [4]Let your patience show itself perfectly in what you do. Then you will be perfect and complete and will have everything you need. [5]But if any of you needs wisdom, you should ask God for it. He is generous and enjoys giving to all people, so he will give you wisdom. [6]But when you ask God, you must believe and not doubt. Anyone who doubts is like a wave in the sea, blown up and down by the wind. [7-8]Such doubters are thinking two different things at the same time, and they cannot decide about anything they do. They should not think they will receive anything from the Lord.

True Riches

Believers who are poor should be proud, because God has made them spiritually rich. [10]Those who are rich should be proud, because God has shown them that they are spiritually poor. The rich will die like a wild flower in the grass. [11]The sun rises with burning heat and dries up the plants. The flower falls off, and its beauty is gone. In the same way the rich will die while they are still taking care of business.

Temptation Is Not from God

When people are tempted and still continue strong, they should be happy. After they have proved their faith, God will reward them with life forever. God promised this to all those who love him. [13]When people are tempted, they should not say, "God is tempting me." Evil cannot tempt God, and God himself does not tempt anyone. [14]But people are tempted when their own evil desire leads them away and traps them. [15]This desire leads to sin, and then the sin grows and brings death.

[16]My dear brothers and sisters, do not be fooled about this. [17]Every good action and every perfect gift is from God. These good gifts come down from the Creator of the sun, moon, and stars, who does not change like their shifting shadows. [18]God decided to give us life through the word of truth so we might be the most important of all the things he made.

Listening and Obeying

My dear brothers and sisters, always be willing to listen and slow to speak. Do not become angry easily, [20]because anger will not help you live the right kind of life God wants. [21]So put out of your life every evil thing and every kind of wrong. Then in gentleness accept God's teaching that is planted in your hearts, which can save you.

[22] Do what God's teaching says; when you only listen and do nothing, you are fooling yourselves. [23] Those who hear God's teaching and do nothing are like people who look at themselves in a mirror. [24] They see their faces and then go away and quickly forget what they looked like. [25] But the truly happy people are those who carefully study God's perfect law that makes people free, and they continue to study it. They do not forget what they heard, but they obey what God's teaching says. Those who do this will be made happy.

The True Way to Worship God

People who think they are religious but say things they should not say are just fooling themselves. Their "religion" is worth nothing. [27] Religion that God accepts as pure and without fault is this: caring for orphans or widows who need help, and keeping yourself free from the world's evil influence.

OLD TESTAMENT READING

The Lord was pleased that Solomon had asked this. [11] So God said to him, "You did not ask for a long life, or riches for yourself, or the death of your enemies. Since you asked for wisdom to make the right decisions, [12] I will do what you asked. I will give you wisdom and understanding that is greater than anyone has had in the past or will have in the future. I will also give you what you did not ask for: riches and honor. During your life no other king will be as great as you."

1 Kings 3:10–13

INSIGHTS

It has been said that the wisest man in the world is the man who knows he doesn't know.

In the midst of trials how often we say, "If only I knew what to do"; or we may say, "I don't know which way to turn or what to do."

God has promised to give us His wisdom. "If any of you is deficient in wisdom, let him ask of the giving God [Who gives] to every one liberally and ungrudgingly, without reproaching or faultfinding, and it will be given him" (Amplified). . . .

Not only are we to ask God for wisdom but we are to ask in faith. Someone has said, "Doubt is a nonconductor of grace."

We are not to be double-minded, wanting partly our way and partly God's way.

As we ask of God and ask in faith, God has promised to give liberally. We are to ask for wisdom to face serenely the trials of today, unwaveringly trusting in Him. We are to ask for wisdom to meet each trial of life and to face it triumphantly.

Millie Stamm

PAUSE FOR REFLECTION

For what reasons did Solomon and Daniel ask for God's wisdom? Did God's answer meet or exceed their expectations? For what in your life do you need God's wisdom? Have you asked him for it?

FRIDAY

Love Your Neighbor as Yourself

James 2:1–26

Love All People

2 My dear brothers and sisters, as
believers in our glorious Lord
Jesus Christ, never think some
people are more important than others. 2 Suppose someone comes into
your church meeting wearing nice
clothes and a gold ring. At the same
time a poor person comes in wearing old, dirty clothes. 3 You show special attention to the one wearing nice
clothes and say, "Please, sit here in
this good seat." But you say to the
poor person, "Stand over there," or,
"Sit on the floor by my feet." 4 What
are you doing? You are making some
people more important than others,
and with evil thoughts you are de-
ciding that one person is better.
5 Listen, my dear brothers and sisters! God chose the poor in the world
to be rich with faith and to receive
the kingdom God promised to those
who love him. 6 But you show no respect to the poor. The rich are always trying to control your lives.
They are the ones who take you to
court. 7 And they are the ones who
speak against Jesus, who owns you.
8 This royal law is found in the
Scriptures: "Love your neighbor as
you love yourself." If you obey this
law, you are doing right. 9 But if you
treat one person as being more important than another, you are sinning. You are guilty of breaking
God's law. 10 A person who follows all
of God's law but fails to obey even
one command is guilty of breaking
all the commands in that law. 11 The
same God who said, "You must not
be guilty of adultery," also said, "You
must not murder anyone." So if you
do not take part in adultery but you
murder someone, you are guilty of
breaking all of God's law. 12 In everything you say and do, remember that
you will be judged by the law that
makes people free. 13 So you must
show mercy to others, or God will
not show mercy to you when he
judges you. But the person who
shows mercy can stand without fear
at the judgment.

Faith and Good Works

My brothers and sisters, if people
say they have faith, but do nothing,
their faith is worth nothing. Can faith
like that save them? 15 A brother or
sister in Christ might need clothes
or food. 16 If you say to that person,
"God be with you! I hope you stay
warm and get plenty to eat," but you
do not give what that person needs,
your words are worth nothing. 17 In
the same way, faith that is alone—
that does nothing—is dead.
18 Someone might say, "You have
faith, but I have deeds." Show me
your faith without doing anything,
and I will show you my faith by what
I do. 19 You believe there is one God.
Good! But the demons believe that,
too, and they tremble with fear.
20 You foolish person! Must you be
shown that faith that does nothing
is worth nothing? 21 Abraham, our
ancestor, was made right with God
by what he did when he offered his
son Isaac on the altar. 22 So you see
that Abraham's faith and the things

he did worked together. His faith
was made perfect by what he did.
23 This shows the full meaning of the
Scripture that says: "Abraham believed God, and God accepted
Abraham's faith, and that faith made
him right with God." And Abraham
was called God's friend. 24 So you see
that people are made right with God
by what they do, not by faith only.
25 Another example is Rahab, a
prostitute, who was made right with God by something she did. She welcomed the spies into her home and helped them escape by a different road.
26 Just as a person's body that
does not have a spirit is dead, so faith that does nothing is dead!

OLD TESTAMENT READING

Do not enter the city gate of my
 people
 in their time of trouble,
or laugh at their problems
 in their time of trouble.
Do not take their treasures
 in their time of trouble.
14 Do not stand at the crossroads
 to destroy those who are
 trying to escape.
Do not capture those who escape
 alive and turn them over to
 their enemy
 in their time of trouble.

Obadiah 13–14

INSIGHTS

My life has been deeply touched by the mercy of those who took the time to try and understand me—who cared enough to forgive so many of my faults and who in mercy made me their friend.

Often these were people to whom I had shown no special kindness. Their bestowal of mercy on me was something totally unexpected and undeserved. Because of this, it has been a double delight. More than that, it has been an enormous inspiration that lifted and challenged me to respond in a measure beyond my wildest dreams. . . .

. . . To really find the true source of inner inspiration for this sort of conduct, the Christian simply must look beyond his fellow man. He must look away to the mercy of God our Father. Nothing else in all the world will so humble us. Nothing else will so move our stony spirits to extend mercy. Nothing else will so powerfully induce us to do the proper thing in extending genuine mercy to our contemporaries. . . .

Christ calls us to be merciful. He calls us to be forgiving and compassionate. This does not mean we wink at wrong and sweep sin under the carpet. Rather it demands that we care enough to bring others to the God of all mercy. And it is He who will cleanse, re-create, and renew them in His loving-kindness and tender mercy. Bless His dear name!

W. Phillip Keller

ACTION POINT

In what situations does James plead for believers to show mercy? In what ways does your normal human behavior lack God's mercy? How will you seek to demonstrate his mercy?

WEEKEND

Train Your Tongue for God's Service

James 3:1—4:10

Controlling the Things We Say

3 My brothers and sisters, not
many of you should become
teachers, because you know that we
who teach will be judged more
strictly. 2 We all make many mis-
takes. If people never said anything
wrong, they would be perfect and
able to control their entire selves,
too. 3 When we put bits into the
mouths of horses to make them
obey us, we can control their whole
bodies. 4 Also a ship is very big, and
it is pushed by strong winds. But a
very small rudder controls that big
ship, making it go wherever the pilot wants. 5 It is the same with the
tongue. It is a small part of the body,
but it brags about great things.

A big forest fire can be started
with only a little flame. 6 And the
tongue is like a fire. It is a whole
world of evil among the parts of our
bodies. The tongue spreads its evil
through the whole body. The tongue
is set on fire by hell, and it starts a
fire that influences all of life. 7 People
can tame every kind of wild animal,
bird, reptile, and fish, and they have
tamed them, 8 but no one can tame
the tongue. It is wild and evil and full
of deadly poison. 9 We use our
tongues to praise our Lord and Father, but then we curse people,
whom God made like himself.
10 Praises and curses come from the
same mouth! My brothers and sisters, this should not happen. 11 Do
good and bad water flow from the
same spring? 12 My brothers and sisters, can a fig tree make olives, or
can a grapevine make figs? No! And
a well full of salty water cannot give
good water.

True Wisdom

Are there those among you who
are truly wise and understanding?
Then they should show it by living
right and doing good things with a
gentleness that comes from wisdom.
14 But if you are selfish and have bitter jealousy in your hearts, do not
brag. Your bragging is a lie that
hides the truth. 15 That kind of "wisdom" does not come from God but
from the world. It is not spiritual; it
is from the devil. 16 Where jealousy
and selfishness are, there will be
confusion and every kind of evil.
17 But the wisdom that comes from
God is first of all pure, then peaceful, gentle, and easy to please. This
wisdom is always ready to help those
who are troubled and to do good for
others. It is always fair and honest.
18 People who work for peace in a
peaceful way plant a good crop of
right-living.

Give Yourselves to God

4 Do you know where your fights
and arguments come from?
They come from the selfish desires
that war within you. 2 You want
things, but you do not have them. So
you are ready to kill and are jealous
of other people, but you still cannot
get what you want. So you argue and
fight. You do not get what you want,
because you do not ask God. 3 Or

when you ask, you do not receive because the reason you ask is wrong. You want things so you can use them for your own pleasures.
4 So, you are not loyal to God! You should know that loving the world is the same as hating God. Anyone who wants to be a friend of the world becomes God's enemy. 5 Do you think the Scripture means nothing that says, "The Spirit that God made to live in us wants us for himself alone." 6 But God gives us even more grace, as the Scripture says,

"God is against the proud,
but he gives grace to the
humble." *Proverbs 3:34*

7 So give yourselves completely to God. Stand against the devil, and the devil will run from you. 8 Come near to God, and God will come near to you. You sinners, clean sin out of your lives. You who are trying to follow God and the world at the same time, make your thinking pure. 9 Be sad, cry, and weep! Change your laughter into crying and your joy into sadness. 10 Don't be too proud in the Lord's presence, and he will make you great.

OLD TESTAMENT READING

People will be rewarded for what
they say;
they will be rewarded by how
they speak.
21 What you say can mean life or
death.
Those who speak with care will
be rewarded.

Proverbs 18:20–21

INSIGHTS

No man can tame the tongue, but the Word of God encourages us to recognize that the Holy Spirit can transform and tie the tongue. . . .

. . . The tongue is the temperature gauge on the heart's engine. If the engine overheats, then the temperature gauge warns us of engine trouble. If the tongue gets out of control, it is a sure sign that we need to check our heart. . . . We need to constantly fill the heart with good things from God's Word in order to tie our tongues.

One must also concede to the Spirit's control to tie the tongue successfully. It always interested me that when James describes the tongue as a horse's bit that controls the horse or a ship's rudder that directs the ship, he, perhaps purposefully, fails to mention that a horse's bit must, in reality, be controlled by the rider and the ship's rudder must be controlled by the helmsman. I daily remind myself that the Lord, through the Holy Spirit, must be the rider or the helmsman controlling my tongue. Who is your helmsman?

If you have difficulty yielding control to the Lord, ask Him for the desire to give Him control. . . . When you have the willingness to concede control of your tongue, you'll soon discover you also have the strength to do it as well.

Vicki Lake

PAUSE FOR REFLECTION

What does your tongue reveal about your heart? Think about your experiences with the good and evil things people have said, and write your own proverb about the tongue.

MONDAY

God Answers the Prayers of His People

James 4:11—5:20

You Are Not the Judge

Brothers and sisters, do not tell evil
lies about each other. If you speak
against your fellow believers or
judge them, you are judging and
speaking against the law they follow.
And when you are judging the law,
you are no longer a follower of the
law. You have become a judge. 12 God
is the only Lawmaker and Judge. He
is the only One who can save and
destroy. So it is not right for you to
judge your neighbor.

Let God Plan Your Life

Some of you say, "Today or tomorrow we will go to some city. We will
stay there a year, do business, and
make money." 14 But you do not know
what will happen tomorrow! Your life
is like a mist. You can see it for a short
time, but then it goes away. 15 So you
should say, "If the Lord wants, we will
live and do this or that." 16 But now you
are proud and you brag. All of this
bragging is wrong. 17 Anyone who
knows the right thing to do, but does
not do it, is sinning.

A Warning to the Rich

5 You rich people, listen! Cry and be
very sad because of the troubles
that are coming to you. 2 Your riches
have rotted, and your clothes have
been eaten by moths. 3 Your gold and
silver have rusted, and that rust will
be a proof that you were wrong. It will
eat your bodies like fire. You saved
your treasure for the last days. 4 The
pay you did not give the workers who
mowed your fields cries out against
you, and the cries of the workers have
been heard by the Lord All-Powerful.
5 Your life on earth was full of rich living and pleasing yourselves with everything you wanted. You made yourselves fat, like an animal ready to be
killed. 6 You have judged guilty and
then murdered innocent people, who
were not against you.

Be Patient

Brothers and sisters, be patient until the Lord comes again. A farmer
patiently waits for his valuable crop
to grow from the earth and for it to
receive the autumn and spring rains.
8 You, too, must be patient. Do not
give up hope, because the Lord is
coming soon. 9 Brothers and sisters,
do not complain against each other
or you will be judged guilty. And the
Judge is ready to come! 10 Brothers
and sisters, follow the example of the
prophets who spoke for the Lord.
They suffered many hard things, but
they were patient. 11 We say they are
happy because they did not give up.
You have heard about Job's patience,
and you know the Lord's purpose for
him in the end. You know the Lord
is full of mercy and is kind.

Be Careful What You Say

My brothers and sisters, above all,
do not use an oath when you make
a promise. Don't use the name of
heaven, earth, or anything else to
prove what you say. When you mean

yes, say only yes, and when you mean no, say only no so you will not be judged guilty.

The Power of Prayer

Anyone who is having troubles should pray. Anyone who is happy should sing praises. 14 Anyone who is sick should call the church's elders. They should pray for and pour oil on the person in the name of the Lord. 15 And the prayer that is said with faith will make the sick person well; the Lord will heal that person. And if the person has sinned, the sins will be forgiven. 16 Confess your sins to each other and pray for each other so God can heal you. When a believing person prays, great things happen. 17 Elijah was a human being just like us. He prayed that it would not rain, and it did not rain on the land for three and a half years! 18 Then Elijah prayed again, and the rain came down from the sky, and the land produced crops again.

Saving a Soul

My brothers and sisters, if one of you wanders away from the truth, and someone helps that person come back, 20 remember this: Anyone who brings a sinner back from the wrong way will save that sinner's soul from death and will cause many sins to be forgiven.

OLD TESTAMENT READING

Then Esther sent this answer to Mordecai: 16 "Go and get all the Jewish people in Susa together. For my sake, give up eating; do not eat or drink for three days, night and day. I and my servant girls will also give up eating. Then I will go to the king, even though it is against the law, and if I die, I die."

Esther 4:15–16

INSIGHTS

God honors prayer. . . . He longs to demonstrate His power in the tremendous trials that jar us like thunder, and in the pinprick troubles that annoy us. Giant needs are never too great for His power; dwarf-sized ones are never too small for His love. . . .

God can answer prayer because He is the supreme ruler of all. . . . He governs both world events and our individual lives, ready at our request to act, to intervene, to overrule for our good, His glory, and the progress of the gospel. He has decreed that prayer is the way to secure His aid and move His mighty hand. Therefore even in sickness, failure, rejection, or financial distress, we can pray and experience His peace which transcends human understanding. Through prayer we can open a window to let God's love shine into our lives; we can open our hands to receive His riches; we can open our hearts to let His presence fill and empower us. Through it we can also allow Him to provide answers to prayer that are important to Him and to us.

Warren Myers

PAUSE FOR REFLECTION

What great powers does James attribute to prayer? Do you believe God answers prayer—enough to risk your life on the power of prayer as Esther did?

TUESDAY

God Will Purify Our Faith

1 Peter 1:1–21

1 From Peter, an apostle of Jesus Christ.

To God's chosen people who are away from their homes and are scattered all around the countries of Pontus, Galatia, Cappadocia, Asia, and Bithynia. 2 God planned long ago to choose you by making you his holy people, which is the Spirit's work. God wanted you to obey him and to be made clean by the blood of the death of Jesus Christ.

Grace and peace be yours more and more.

We Have a Living Hope

Praise be to the God and Father of our Lord Jesus Christ. In God's great mercy he has caused us to be born again into a living hope, because Jesus Christ rose from the dead. 4 Now we hope for the blessings God has for his children. These blessings, which cannot be destroyed or be spoiled or lose their beauty, are kept in heaven for you. 5 God's power protects you through your faith until salvation is shown to you at the end of time. 6 This makes you very happy, even though now for a short time different kinds of troubles may make you sad. 7 These troubles come to prove that your faith is pure. This purity of faith is worth more than gold, which can be proved to be pure by fire but will ruin. But the purity of your faith will bring you praise and glory and honor when Jesus Christ is shown to you. 8 You have not seen Christ, but still you love him. You cannot see him now, but you believe in him. So you are filled with a joy that cannot be explained, a joy full of glory. 9 And you are receiving the goal of your faith—the salvation of your souls.

10 The prophets searched carefully and tried to learn about this salvation. They prophesied about the grace that was coming to you. 11 The Spirit of Christ was in the prophets, telling in advance about the sufferings of Christ and about the glory that would follow those sufferings. The prophets tried to learn about what the Spirit was showing them, when those things would happen, and what the world would be like at that time. 12 It was shown them that their service was not for themselves but for you, when they told about the truths you have now heard. Those who preached the Good News to you told you those things with the help of the Holy Spirit who was sent from heaven—things into which angels desire to look.

A Call to Holy Living

So prepare your minds for service and have self-control. All your hope should be for the gift of grace that will be yours when Jesus Christ is shown to you. 14 Now that you are obedient children of God do not live as you did in the past. You did not understand, so you did the evil things you wanted. 15 But be holy in all you do, just as God, the One who called you, is holy. 16 It is written in the Scriptures: "You must be holy, because I am holy."

17 You pray to God and call him

Father, and he judges each person's work equally. So while you are here on earth, you should live with respect for God. [18]You know that in the past you were living in a worthless way, a way passed down from the people who lived before you. But you were saved from that useless life. You were bought, not with something that ruins like gold or silver,
[19]but with the precious blood of Christ, who was like a pure and perfect lamb. [20]Christ was chosen before the world was made, but he was shown to the world in these last times for your sake. [21]Through Christ you believe in God, who raised Christ from the dead and gave him glory. So your faith and your hope are in God.

OLD TESTAMENT READING

The third that is left I will test with fire,
purifying them like silver,
testing them like gold.
Then they will call on me,
and I will answer them.
I will say, 'You are my people,'
and they will say, 'The LORD is our God.'"

Zechariah 13:9

INSIGHTS

What is trouble but that very influence that brings you nearer to the heart of God than prayers or hymns? I think sorrows usually bring us closer to God than joys do. But sorrows, to be of use, must be borne, as Christ's were, victoriously, carrying with them intimations and sacred prophecies to the heart of hope. This is not only so we will not be overcome by them, but also so we will be strengthened and ennobled and enlarged by them. . . .

. . . By fire, by anvil-strokes, by the hammer that breaks the flinty rock, you are made what you are. You were gold in the rock, and God played miner, and blasted you out of the rock. Then He played stamper, and crushed you. Then He played smelter, and melted you.

Now you are gold, free from the rock by the grace of God's severity to you. As you look back upon those experiences of 5, 10, or 20 years ago and see what they have done for you, and what you are now, you say, "I would not exchange what I learned from these things for all the world." . . .

When God comes to you wrapped and wreathed in clouds, and in storms, why should we not recognize Him, and say, "I know you, God; and I will not flee you; though you slay me, I will trust thee"? If a man could see God in his troubles and take sorrow to be the . . . sweet discipline of a bitter medicine that brings health, though the taste is not agreeable—if one could so look upon his God, how sorrows would make him strong!

Henry Beecher

APPLICATION

What is the value of a pure faith? What are its rewards? How does our faith become pure? How is God purifying your faith today? Welcome his testing!

WEDNESDAY

The Lives of God's People Bring Glory to Him

1 Peter 1:22—2:17

Now that you have made your souls
pure by obeying the truth, you can
have true love for your Christian
brothers and sisters. So love each
other deeply with all your heart.
23 You have been born again, and this
new life did not come from something that dies, but from something
that cannot die. You were born again
through God's living message that
continues forever. 24 The Scripture
says,

"All people are like the grass,
and all their glory is like the
flowers of the field.
The grass dies and the flowers
fall,
25 but the word of the Lord will live
forever." *Isaiah 40:6-8*

And this is the word that was
preached to you.

Jesus Is the Living Stone

2 So then, rid yourselves of all evil,
all lying, hypocrisy, jealousy, and
evil speech. 2 As newborn babies
want milk, you should want the pure
and simple teaching. By it you can
grow up and be saved, 3 because you
have already examined and seen
how good the Lord is.
4 Come to the Lord Jesus, the
"stone" that lives. The people of the
world did not want this stone, but he
was the stone God chose, and he was
precious. 5 You also are like living
stones, so let yourselves be used to
build a spiritual temple—to be holy
priests who offer spiritual sacrifices
to God. He will accept those sacrifices through Jesus Christ. 6 The
Scripture says:

"I will put a stone in the ground in
Jerusalem.
Everything will be built on this
important and precious
rock.
Anyone who trusts in him
will never be disappointed."

Isaiah 28: 16

7 This stone is worth much to you
who believe. But to the people who
do not believe,

"the stone that the builders
rejected
has become the cornerstone."

Psalm 118:22

8 Also, he is

"a stone that causes people to
stumble,
a rock that makes them fall."

Isaiah 8:14

They stumble because they do not
obey what God says, which is what
God planned to happen to them.
9 But you are a chosen people,
royal priests, a holy nation, a people
for God's own possession. You were
chosen to tell about the wonderful
acts of God, who called you out of
darkness into his wonderful light.
10 At one time you were not a people,
but now you are God's people. In the
past you had never received mercy,
but now you have received God's
mercy.

Live for God

Dear friends, you are like foreigners and strangers in this world. I beg
you to avoid the evil things your bodies want to do that fight against your

soul. 12 People who do not believe are
living all around you and might say
that you are doing wrong. Live such
good lives that they will see the good
things you do and will give glory to
God on the day when Christ comes
again.

Yield to Every Human Authority

For the Lord's sake, yield to the
people who have authority in this
world: the king, who is the highest
authority, 14 and the leaders who
are sent by him to punish those who
do wrong and to praise those who do
right. 15 It is God's desire that by doing good you should stop foolish
people from saying stupid things
about you. 16 Live as free people, but
do not use your freedom as an excuse to do evil. Live as servants of
God. 17 Show respect for all people:
Love the brothers and sisters of
God's family, respect God, honor the
king.

OLD TESTAMENT READING

Then Nebuchadnezzar said, "Praise
the God of Shadrach, Meshach, and
Abednego. Their God has sent his
angel and saved his servants from
the fire! These three men trusted
their God and refused to obey my
command. They were willing to die
rather than serve or worship any
god other than their own. 29 So I now
give this command: Anyone from
any nation or language who says
anything against the God of Shadrach, Meshach, and Abednego will
be torn apart and have his house
turned into a pile of stones. No other
god can save his people like this."

Daniel 3:28–29

INSIGHTS

God considers himself honored by the high attainments of His children and dishonored by their low attainments. He is honored in the fact that their graces so shine forth that it shall be seen by all around that they have partaken largely of His Spirit.

Exalted piety is honorable to God. Manifestations of great grace and spirituality of mind honor God. He is greatly honored by the fruits of righteousness His people bring forth. Christ himself says, "Herein is my Father glorified that ye bring forth much fruit." Ministers should be greatly fruitful. They should bring forth the fruits of the Spirit in their tempers, in their lives, in the strength of their faith and labors of love. Can you doubt that God has great interest in these things? Indeed His great desire, that you should bring forth fruit to His glory, is shown in the fact that He says, "open thy mouth wide, and I will fill it."

Charles Finney

PAUSE FOR REFLECTION

What do you think it means to be made "pure by obeying the truth"? What purpose is served when believers live good lives? What have you learned from the lives of those who honor God in such a way? Are you willing to get rid of everything in your life that doesn't bring honor to the King?

THURSDAY

Live in Peace!

1 Peter 2:18—3:12

Follow Christ's Example

Slaves, yield to the authority of your
masters with all respect, not only
those who are good and kind, but
also those who are dishonest. 19 A
person might have to suffer even
when it is unfair, but if he thinks of
God and stands the pain, God is
pleased. 20 If you are beaten for doing wrong, there is no reason to
praise you for being patient in your
punishment. But if you suffer for
doing good, and you are patient,
then God is pleased. 21 This is what
you were called to do, because
Christ suffered for you and gave you
an example to follow. So you should
do as he did.

22 "He had never sinned,
and he had never lied." *Isaiah 53:9*

23 People insulted Christ, but he did
not insult them in return. Christ suffered, but he did not threaten. He let
God, the One who judges rightly, take
care of him. 24 Christ carried our sins
in his body on the cross so we would
stop living for sin and start living for
what is right. And you are healed because of his wounds. 25 You were like
sheep that wandered away, but now
you have come back to the Shepherd
and Protector of your souls.

Wives and Husbands

3 In the same way, you wives
should yield to your husbands.
Then, if some husbands do not obey
God's teaching, they will be persuaded to believe without anyone's
saying a word to them. They will be
persuaded by the way their wives
live. 2 Your husbands will see the
pure lives you live with your respect
for God. 3 It is not fancy hair, gold
jewelry, or fine clothes that should
make you beautiful. 4 No, your
beauty should come from within
you—the beauty of a gentle and
quiet spirit that will never be destroyed and is very precious to God.
5 In this same way the holy women
who lived long ago and followed God
made themselves beautiful, yielding
to their own husbands. 6 Sarah
obeyed Abraham, her husband, and
called him her master. And you
women are true children of Sarah if
you always do what is right and are
not afraid.

7 In the same way, you husbands
should live with your wives in an
understanding way, since they are
weaker than you. But show them
respect, because God gives them the
same blessing he gives you—the
grace that gives true life. Do this so
that nothing will stop your prayers.

Suffering for Doing Right

8 Finally, all of you should be in
agreement, understanding each
other, loving each other as family,
being kind and humble. 9 Do not do
wrong to repay a wrong, and do not
insult to repay an insult. But repay
with a blessing, because you yourselves were called to do this so that
you might receive a blessing. 10 The
Scripture says,

"A person must do these things
to enjoy life and have many
happy days.

He must not say evil things,
and he must not tell lies.
11 He must stop doing evil and do good.
He must look for peace and work for it.
12 The Lord sees the good people
and listens to their prayers.
But the Lord is against
those who do evil." *Psalm 34:12-16*

OLD TESTAMENT READING

Abimelech came from Gerar to see
Isaac. He brought with him Ahuz-
zath, who advised him, and Phicol,
the commander of his army. 27 Isaac
asked them, "Why have you come
to see me? You were my enemy and
forced me to leave your country."
28 They answered, "Now we know
that the LORD is with you. Let us
swear an oath to each other. Let us
make an agreement with you 29 that
since we did not hurt you, you will
not hurt us. We were good to you
and sent you away in peace. Now the
LORD has blessed you."
30 So Isaac prepared food for
them, and they all ate and drank.
31 Early the next morning the men
swore an oath to each other. Then
Isaac sent them away, and they left
in peace.

Genesis 26:26–31

INSIGHTS

If the life is opened to receive the divine presence of the risen Christ, He comes in, speaking peace—just as He came again and again to His distraught disciples after His resurrection, saying, "Peace be unto you!"

He comes into our lives there to shed abroad a new love, His own life, that expresses itself in peace. When He enters my experience; when He penetrates my personality; when He becomes Sovereign in my spirit, I in turn become a person of peace. It is then that I begin to know what it means to be at peace with God, at peace with others, at peace with myself.

Increasingly as He is given control of my life the entire complexion of my character, conduct, and conversation alters. I discover that He can change me dramatically. Peace, good will, good cheer, and serenity replace animosity, bitterness, hostility, belligerence, jealousy, bad temper, quarreling, and rivalry. . . .

. . . The peace of God, which is self-sacrificing and self-foregoing, produces healing. It comes to bind up the wounds; to pour in the oil of consolation; to bring repose and quietness; to still the troubled soul; to speak peace to stormy spirits. This peace comes only from Christ. It is one of the genuine, indisputable marks of God's presence in a person's life.

W. Phillip Keller

ACTION POINT

Who set the standard for living in peace? What does living in peace look like? How full of Christ's peace is your life? Pray that God will give you a fuller love and more intimate understanding of his peace and that it will touch every area of your life.

FRIDAY

Always Be Ready to Explain the Hope of Your Salvation

1 Peter 3:13—4:11

If you are trying hard to do good,
no one can really hurt you. 14 But
even if you suffer for doing right, you
are blessed.

"Don't be afraid of what they fear;
do not dread those things."

Isaiah 8:12-13

15 But respect Christ as the holy Lord
in your hearts. Always be ready to
answer everyone who asks you to
explain about the hope you have,
16 but answer in a gentle way and
with respect. Keep a clear conscience so that those who speak evil
of your good life in Christ will be
made ashamed. 17 It is better to suffer for doing good than for doing
wrong if that is what God wants.
18 Christ himself suffered for sins
once. He was not guilty, but he suffered for those who are guilty to
bring you to God. His body was
killed, but he was made alive in the
spirit. 19 And in the spirit he went and
preached to the spirits in prison
20 who refused to obey God long ago
in the time of Noah. God was waiting patiently for them while Noah
was building the boat. Only a few
people—eight in all—were saved by
water. 21 And that water is like baptism that now saves you—not the
washing of dirt from the body, but
the promise made to God from a
good conscience. And this is because Jesus Christ was raised from
the dead. 22 Now Jesus has gone into
heaven and is at God's right side ruling over angels, authorities, and
powers.

Change Your Lives

4 Since Christ suffered while he
was in his body, strengthen yourselves with the same way of thinking Christ had. The person who has
suffered in the body is finished with
sin. 2 Strengthen yourselves so that
you will live here on earth doing
what God wants, not the evil things
people want. 3 In the past you wasted
too much time doing what nonbelievers enjoy. You were guilty of sexual
sins, evil desires, drunkenness, wild
and drunken parties, and hateful idol
worship. 4 Nonbelievers think it is
strange that you do not do the many
wild and wasteful things they do, so
they insult you. 5 But they will have
to explain this to God, who is ready
to judge the living and the dead. 6 For
this reason the Good News was
preached to those who are now
dead. Even though they were judged
like all people, the Good News was
preached to them so they could live
in the spirit as God lives.

Use God's Gifts Wisely

The time is near when all things will
end. So think clearly and control
yourselves so you will be able to
pray. 8 Most importantly, love each
other deeply, because love will cause
many sins to be forgiven. 9 Open
your homes to each other, without
complaining. 10 Each of you has received a gift to use to serve others.
Be good servants of God's various
gifts of grace. 11 Anyone who speaks
should speak words from God. Anyone who serves should serve with

the strength God gives so that in everything God will be praised through Jesus Christ. Power and glory belong to him forever and ever. Amen.

OLD TESTAMENT READING

God, don't be far off.
My God, hurry to help me.
13 Let those who accuse me
be ashamed and destroyed.
Let those who are trying to hurt me
be covered with shame and disgrace.
14 But I will always have hope
and will praise you more and more.
15 I will tell how you do what is right.
I will tell about your salvation all day long,
even though it is more than I can tell.
16 I will come and tell about your powerful works, Lord GOD.
I will remind people that only you do what is right.

Psalm 71:12–16

INSIGHTS

Christians have a corner on hope. Why? Because the basis of all hope is knowing who God is. There is no hope without a God who controls the universe and promises to bring us to heaven.

Hope designates a future—that is what we hope in. Time, our period on this earth, can be seen in various ways, but only one way offers hope. Some see time as cyclical: history repeats itself and will continue to repeat itself only to get worse (and finally burn itself up). Others see time in the modern secular view that immortality exists as each generation gives birth to the next, which then gives birth to the next. But Christians see time in a straight line—God began time, has a specific purpose for each person within his divine plan, and he will bring it to an end when he returns as he promised.

Hope is not in most of the things our fellow humans hope in. It cannot be found in possessions, in our own strength or supposed "immortality," in people's love, in the past. Neither can it be found in human achievement, in who we are or what we have done, or in this life itself.

So where is hope? Our hope lies in our Christian growth here on earth—that we are doing what God wants for us in our particular place in time. We hope in the new heaven and new earth God has promised for us (Hebrews 13:14). We hope in Christ's second coming, in eternal life, and in resurrection (1 John 3:2, 3). We hope in the fact that this world is not all there is (Revelation 21:2, 3). And the great thing about our hope is that it is based on fact. It will happen because our hope is based on God, not on us.

YFC Editors

ACTION POINT

Describe the hope of your salvation. Be specific. How might your hope affect the heart of a nonbeliever? What should be your purpose in everything you do? Ask God to fulfill his purpose through you.

WEEKEND

Give All Your Worries to God; He Cares for You

1 Peter 4:12—5:14

Suffering as a Christian

My friends, do not be surprised at
the terrible trouble which now
comes to test you. Do not think that
something strange is happening to
you. 13 But be happy that you are
sharing in Christ's sufferings so that
you will be happy and full of joy
when Christ comes again in glory.
14 When people insult you because
you follow Christ, you are blessed,
because the glorious Spirit, the Spirit
of God, is with you. 15 Do not suffer
for murder, theft, or any other crime,
nor because you trouble other
people. 16 But if you suffer because
you are a Christian, do not be
ashamed. Praise God because you
wear that name. 17 It is time for judgment to begin with God's family. And
if that judging begins with us, what
will happen to those people who do
not obey the Good News of God?
18 "If it is very hard for a good
person to be saved,
the wicked person and the
sinner will surely be lost!"
19 So those who suffer as God
wants should trust their souls to the
faithful Creator as they continue to
do what is right.

The Flock of God

5 Now I have something to say to
the elders in your group. I also
am an elder. I have seen Christ's sufferings, and I will share in the glory
that will be shown to us. I beg you
to 2 shepherd God's flock, for whom
you are responsible. Watch over
them because you want to, not because you are forced. That is how
God wants it. Do it because you are
happy to serve, not because you
want money. 3 Do not be like a ruler
over people you are responsible for,
but be good examples to them.
4 Then when Christ, the Chief Shepherd, comes, you will get a glorious
crown that will never lose its beauty.
5 In the same way, younger people
should be willing to be under older
people. And all of you should be
very humble with each other.
"God is against the proud,
but he gives grace to the
humble." *Proverbs 3:34*
6 Be humble under God's powerful hand so he will lift you up when
the right time comes. 7 Give all your
worries to him, because he cares
about you.
8 Control yourselves and be careful! The devil, your enemy, goes
around like a roaring lion looking for
someone to eat. 9 Refuse to give in
to him, by standing strong in your
faith. You know that your Christian
family all over the world is having
the same kinds of suffering.
10 And after you suffer for a short
time, God, who gives all grace, will
make everything right. He will make
you strong and support you and
keep you from falling. He called you
to share in his glory in Christ, a
glory that will continue forever. 11 All
power is his forever and ever. Amen.

Final Greetings

I wrote this short letter with the

help of Silas, who I know is a faithful brother in Christ. I wrote to encourage you and to tell you that this is the true grace of God. Stand strong in that grace.

13 The church in Babylon, who was chosen like you, sends you greetings. Mark, my son in Christ, also greets you. 14 Give each other a kiss of Christian love when you meet.

Peace to all of you who are in Christ.

OLD TESTAMENT READING

Then the LORD spoke his word to
Elijah: 3 "Leave this place and go east
and hide near Kerith Ravine east of
the Jordan River. 4 You may drink
from the stream, and I have commanded ravens to bring you food
there." 6 The birds brought Elijah
bread and meat every morning and
evening, and he drank water from
the stream.
7 After a while the stream dried
up because there was no rain.
8 Then the LORD spoke his word to
Elijah, 9 "Go to Zarephath in Sidon
and live there. I have commanded
a widow there to take care of you."

1 Kings 17:2–4, 6–9

INSIGHTS

One winter I worked as secretary and receptionist at a mortuary. . . .

My husband had just been affected by a large company layoff, so I had needed to work. One particularly dark and dreary day I sat all by myself in the large office of the mortuary. While I typed a letter, my thoughts drifted to the house payment and utility bills. I soon felt overwhelmed. Tears came as I thought about the fact that we also needed groceries. Furthermore, Christmas was coming.

Suddenly, my thoughts were interrupted by a noise at the window. I walked over to see what it was. Through my tears, I saw that a sparrow had flown into the window and, stunned by the blow, had fallen to the ground.

This little incident reminded me of what God has to say in His Word about the birds of the air. He's aware of and provides for all of their needs. How much more is He aware of His children in need.

I felt so encouraged as I recalled sermons on this topic. I could almost hear the gospel singer: "His Eye Is On the Sparrow." I hummed the song the rest of the day. My faith increased, as I learned to trust God for my every need.

Then one morning a friend stood at the front door. "The Lord laid it on my heart to give you this money," he said. He didn't know it, but it was our house payment. Later, several checks came in the mail from a loving friend, signed, "Love, Jesus." One week we were invited out to dinner every night. And the children ended up having a delightful Christmas.

Barbara Hyatt

APPLICATION

What worry did Peter's readers face? For what reasons does he tell them not to worry? What reassurance of God's loving care does the Old Testament reading provide? Will you trust in his care?

MONDAY

Add Knowledge to Your Faith

2 Peter 1:1–21

1 From Simon Peter, a servant and
apostle of Jesus Christ.
To you who have received a faith
as valuable as ours, because our God
and Savior Jesus Christ does what is
right.
2 Grace and peace be given to you
more and more, because you truly
know God and Jesus our Lord.

God Has Given Us Blessings

Jesus has the power of God, by
which he has given us everything we
need to live and to serve God. We
have these things because we know
him. Jesus called us by his glory and
goodness. 4 Through these he gave
us the very great and precious promises. With these gifts you can share
in being like God, and the world will
not ruin you with its evil desires.
5 Because you have these blessings, do your best to add these
things to your lives: to your faith, add
goodness; and to your goodness,
add knowledge; 6 and to your knowledge, add self-control; and to your
self-control, add patience; and to
your patience, add service for God;
7 and to your service for God, add
kindness for your brothers and sisters in Christ; and to this kindness,
add love. 8 If all these things are in
you and are growing, they will help
you to be useful and productive in
your knowledge of our Lord Jesus
Christ. 9 But anyone who does not
have these things cannot see clearly.
He is blind and has forgotten that he
was made clean from his past sins.
10 My brothers and sisters, try
hard to be certain that you really are
called and chosen by God. If you do
all these things, you will never fall.
11 And you will be given a very great
welcome into the eternal kingdom of
our Lord and Savior Jesus Christ.
12 You know these things, and you
are very strong in the truth, but I will
always help you remember them. 13 I
think it is right for me to help you
remember as long as I am in this
body. 14 I know I must soon leave this
body, as our Lord Jesus Christ has
shown me. 15 I will try my best so
that you may be able to remember
these things even after I am gone.

We Saw Christ's Glory

When we told you about the powerful coming of our Lord Jesus
Christ, we were not telling just smart
stories that someone invented. But
we saw the greatness of Jesus with
our own eyes. 17 Jesus heard the
voice of God, the Greatest Glory,
when he received honor and glory
from God the Father. The voice said,
"This is my Son, whom I love, and I
am very pleased with him." 18 We
heard that voice from heaven while
we were with Jesus on the holy
mountain.
19 This makes us more sure about
the message the prophets gave. It is
good for you to follow closely what
they said as you would follow a light
shining in a dark place, until the day
begins and the morning star rises in
your hearts. 20 Most of all, you must
understand this: No prophecy in the
Scriptures ever comes from the

prophet's own interpretation. [21] No prophecy ever came from what a person wanted to say, but people led by the Holy Spirit spoke words from God.

OLD TESTAMENT READING

Only the LORD gives wisdom;
he gives knowledge and
understanding.

Proverbs 2:6

These are the wise words of Solomon son of David, king of Israel.

[3] They will teach you how to be
wise and self-controlled
and will teach you to do what is
honest and fair and right.

[7] Knowledge begins with respect
for the LORD,
but fools hate wisdom and self-control.

Proverbs 1:1, 3, 7

INSIGHTS

We are to make every effort to increase our faith, knowledge, self-control, steadfastness and brotherly affection. Each of us is expected to be spiritually self-sustaining. We cannot rely on pastors or Christian leaders to keep our faith propped up.

Some Christians live from Sunday to Sunday. They start their week ready for action, but by Saturday are drained of their enthusiasm and can barely drag themselves to church the next day for another boost. Paul talks of digesting the milk of the Word (1 Cor 3:2). Babies need someone to feed them milk, and in the same way, new Christians need someone to help them understand biblical truth. Yet, we have all seen retarded adults who are incapable of feeding themselves. Behavior that is natural and cute in an infant is saddening to watch in these adults. Sadly, there are Christians who have not made "every effort to supplement their faith," and they too are retarded in their spiritual development.

Prayer and Bible study are important in supplementing our faith. God reveals himself to us in the Bible, and through prayer we have direct access to him with our problems and questions. . . .

. . . Once Bible study is a regular part of our lives, we will begin to reap the rewards of a more stable and mature relationship with the Lord. We will also have the personal confidence to go to the Bible and find our own answers to life's questions.

God does not want us to be spiritually retarded and unable to sustain the new life he has given us. He wants us to reach a place of maturity where we can spiritually feed ourselves and be able to stand firm in the face of any adversity.

Floyd McClung

PAUSE FOR REFLECTION

What things does Peter say to add to your faith? What is the purpose and the result of doing these things? Consider your own life, and write down what you think will be accomplished if you add each of these things to your faith. Be specific.

TUESDAY

God Condemns False Teachers Who Lead People into Evil

2 Peter 2:1–22

False Teachers

2 There used to be false prophets
among God's people, just as you
will have some false teachers in your
group. They will secretly teach
things that are wrong—teachings
that will cause people to be lost.
They will even refuse to accept the
Master, Jesus, who bought their
freedom. So they will bring quick
ruin on themselves. 2 Many will follow their evil ways and say evil
things about the way of truth.
3 Those false teachers only want your
money, so they will use you by telling you lies. Their judgment spoken
against them long ago is still coming, and their ruin is certain.

4 When angels sinned, God did
not let them go free without punishment. He sent them to hell and put
them in caves of darkness where
they are being held for judgment.
5 And God punished the world long
ago when he brought a flood to the
world that was full of people who
were against him. But God saved
Noah, who preached about being
right with God, and seven other
people with him. 6 And God also destroyed the evil cities of Sodom and
Gomorrah by burning them until
they were ashes. He made those cities an example of what will happen
to those who are against God. 7 But
he saved Lot from those cities. Lot,
a good man, was troubled because
of the filthy lives of evil people. 8 (Lot
was a good man, but because he
lived with evil people every day, his
good heart was hurt by the evil
things he saw and heard.) 9 So the
Lord knows how to save those who
serve him when troubles come. He
will hold evil people and punish
them, while waiting for the Judgment Day. 10 That punishment is especially for those who live by doing
the evil things their sinful selves
want and who hate authority.

These false teachers are bold and
do anything they want. They are not
afraid to speak against the angels.
11 But even the angels, who are much
stronger and more powerful than false
teachers, do not accuse them with insults before the Lord. 12 But these
people speak against things they do
not understand. They are like animals
that act without thinking, animals
born to be caught and killed. And, like
animals, these false teachers will be
destroyed. 13 They have caused many
people to suffer, so they themselves
will suffer. That is their pay for what
they have done. They take pleasure
in openly doing evil, so they are like
dirty spots and stains among you.
They delight in trickery while eating
meals with you. 14 Every time they
look at a woman they want her, and
their desire for sin is never satisfied.
They lead weak people into the trap
of sin, and they have taught their
hearts to be greedy. God will punish
them! 15 These false teachers left the
right road and lost their way, following the way Balaam went. Balaam was
the son of Beor, who loved being paid
for doing wrong. 16 But a donkey, which
cannot talk, told Balaam he was sinning. It spoke with a man's voice and
stopped the prophet's crazy thinking.

[17] Those false teachers are like springs without water and clouds blown by a storm. A place in the blackest darkness has been kept for them. [18] They brag with words that mean nothing. By their evil desires they lead people into the trap of sin—people who are just beginning to escape from others who live in error. [19] They promise them freedom, but they themselves are not free. They are slaves of things that will be destroyed. For people are slaves of anything that controls them. [20] They were made free from the evil in the world by knowing our Lord and Savior Jesus Christ. But if they return to evil things and those things control them, then it is worse for them than it was before. [21] Yes, it would be better for them to have never known the right way than to know it and to turn away from the holy teaching that was given to them. [22] What they did is like this true saying: "A dog goes back to what it has thrown up," and, "After a pig is washed, it goes back and rolls in the mud."

OLD TESTAMENT READING

They are like hungry dogs
that are never satisfied.
They are like shepherds
who don't know what they are doing.
They all have gone their own way;
all they want to do is satisfy themselves.

Isaiah 56:11

INSIGHTS

Deception is on the rise within the Christian church and we ignore it to our peril.

Sometimes it is difficult—even for a Christian—to recognize the deceivers. Jesus spoke of false prophets who "perform great signs and miracles to deceive even the elect." . . .

Satan does not want to build a church and call it "The First Church of Satan." He is far too clever for that. He invades the Sunday school, the youth department, the Christian education program, the pulpit and the seminary classroom.

The apostle Paul warned that many will follow false teachers, not knowing that in feeding upon what these people say they are taking the devil's poison into their own lives. Thousands of uninstructed Christians are being deceived today. False teachers use high-sounding words that seem like the height of logic, scholarship and culture. They are intellectually clever and crafty in their sophistry. They are adept at beguiling thoughtless, untaught men and women. . . .

The best advice against deception that I can give is to urge you to spend your time looking at the real Christ. Then, when a counterfeit appears, you'll have less trouble spotting him.

Billy Graham

ACTION POINT

List the lifestyle patterns that serve as clues that a false teacher is at work. How can a person guard against the practiced deception of false teachers? How do you plan to learn God's truth?

WEDNESDAY

But Be Strong in Your Faith

2 Peter 3:1–18

Jesus Will Come Again

3 My friends, this is the second letter I have written you to help your honest minds remember. 2 I want you to think about the words the holy prophets spoke in the past, and remember the command our Lord and Savior gave us through your apostles. 3 It is most important for you to understand what will happen in the last days. People will laugh at you. They will live doing the evil things they want to do. 4 They will say, "Jesus promised to come again. Where is he? Our fathers have died, but the world continues the way it has been since it was made." 5 But they do not want to remember what happened long ago. By the word of God heaven was made, and the earth was made from water and with water. 6 Then the world was flooded and destroyed with water. 7 And that same word of God is keeping heaven and earth that we now have in order to be destroyed by fire. They are being kept for the Judgment Day and the destruction of all who are against God.

8 But do not forget this one thing, dear friends: To the Lord one day is as a thousand years, and a thousand years is as one day. 9 The Lord is not slow in doing what he promised—the way some people understand slowness. But God is being patient with you. He does not want anyone to be lost, but he wants all people to change their hearts and lives.

10 But the day of the Lord will come like a thief. The skies will disappear with a loud noise. Everything in them will be destroyed by fire, and the earth and everything in it will be burned up. 11 In that way everything will be destroyed. So what kind of people should you be? You should live holy lives and serve God, 12 as you wait for and look forward to the coming of the day of God. When that day comes, the skies will be destroyed with fire, and everything in them will melt with heat. 13 But God made a promise to us, and we are waiting for a new heaven and a new earth where goodness lives.

14 Dear friends, since you are waiting for this to happen, do your best to be without sin and without fault. Try to be at peace with God. 15 Remember that we are saved because our Lord is patient. Our dear brother Paul told you the same thing when he wrote to you with the wisdom that God gave him. 16 He writes about this in all his letters. Some things in Paul's letters are hard to understand, and people who are ignorant and weak in faith explain these things falsely. They also falsely explain the other Scriptures, but they are destroying themselves by doing this.

17 Dear friends, since you already know about this, be careful. Do not let those evil people lead you away by the wrong they do. Be careful so you will not fall from your strong faith. 18 But grow in the grace and knowledge of our Lord and Savior Jesus Christ. Glory be to him now and forever! Amen.

OLD TESTAMENT READING

You sit as the Holy One.

The praises of Israel are your
throne.
4 Our ancestors trusted you;
they trusted, and you saved
them.
5 They called to you for help
and were rescued.
They trusted you
and were not disappointed.
6 But I am like a worm instead of a
man.
People make fun of me and
hate me.
7 Those who look at me laugh.
They stick out their tongues
and shake their heads.
8 They say, "Turn to the LORD for
help.
Maybe he will save you.
If he likes you,
maybe he will rescue you."

Psalm 22:3–8

INSIGHTS

They laughed at me and made fun of me because I wouldn't participate in what they were doing."

"I lost the promotion at work because I refused to take my clients to that sleazy nightclub."

"I lost several 'friends' because I didn't go along with their gossiping when we got together."

Modern day persecution because of our faith? Perhaps. It hurts to be misunderstood and not accepted. Believers in China and other parts of the world still face intense persecution. They lose their homes, some end up in prison, and many are killed because of their faith.

Most of us have never really felt the piercing sting of persecution. It could happen to us as it does in other countries like China. It could happen in ways hard to imagine if our democratic society were overturned. You never know. But whatever type of persecution you experience, do you know how Jesus wants you to respond? It's quite simple. Rejoice and be glad. That's all. Be glad. Don't retaliate. Don't sulk. Don't complain. Don't just grin and bear it. Rejoice and actually "leap for joy" (Luke 6:23).

. . . Expect opposition to your Christian stance. That's normal. If you are persecuted because of your stance for Jesus Christ, it means you are really committed to Him and your commitment is evident to others. You are having an impact in the world around you. Isn't it strange that living for Him brings discomfort? But why not? Living for Christ means confronting a world that is living contrary to the way God intended. Your Christian life bothers them. It's convicting. So they will react to you. But I guess Jesus understands that pretty well, doesn't He? Look at what it cost Him.

H. Norman Wright

APPLICATION

What perspective does Peter offer to help his readers bear persecution? Will God hurry to fulfill his plan for anyone? In what ways does focusing on God—his eternal timelessness and omnipotent power—help you face the challenges of unbelievers?

THURSDAY

Live in the Light!

1 John 1:1—2:14

1 We write you now about what has
always existed, which we have
heard, we have seen with our own
eyes, we have looked at, and we have
touched with our hands. We write to
you about the Word that gives life.
2 He who gives life was shown to us.
We saw him and can give proof about
it. And now we announce to you that
he has life that continues forever. He
was with God the Father and was
shown to us. 3 We announce to you
what we have seen and heard, because we want you also to have fellowship with us. Our fellowship is
with God the Father and with his
Son, Jesus Christ. 4 We write this to
you so you can be full of joy with us.

God Forgives Our Sins

*H*ere is the message we have heard
from Christ and now announce to
you: God is light, and in him there
is no darkness at all. 6 So if we say
we have fellowship with God, but we
continue living in darkness, we are
liars and do not follow the truth.
7 But if we live in the light, as God is
in the light, we can share fellowship
with each other. Then the blood of
Jesus, God's Son, cleanses us from
every sin.

8 If we say we have no sin, we are
fooling ourselves, and the truth is
not in us. 9 But if we confess our sins,
he will forgive our sins, because we
can trust God to do what is right. He
will cleanse us from all the wrongs
we have done. 10 If we say we have
not sinned, we make God a liar, and
we do not accept God's teaching.

Jesus Is Our Helper

2 My dear children, I write this letter to you so you will not sin. But
if anyone does sin, we have a helper
in the presence of the Father—Jesus
Christ, the One who does what is
right. 2 He is the way our sins are
taken away, and not only our sins but
the sins of all people.

3 We can be sure that we know
God if we obey his commands. 4 Anyone who says, "I know God," but
does not obey God's commands is
a liar, and the truth is not in that
person. 5 But if someone obeys God's
teaching, then in that person God's
love has truly reached its goal. This
is how we can be sure we are living in God: 6 Whoever says that he
lives in God must live as Jesus lived.

The Command to Love Others

*M*y dear friends, I am not writing
a new command to you but an old
command you have had from the
beginning. It is the teaching you
have already heard. 8 But also I am
writing a new command to you, and
you can see its truth in Jesus and in
you, because the darkness is passing away, and the true light is already shining.

9 Anyone who says, "I am in the
light," but hates a brother or sister,
is still in the darkness. 10 Whoever
loves a brother or sister lives in the
light and will not cause anyone to
stumble in his faith. 11 But whoever
hates a brother or sister is in darkness, lives in darkness, and does not

know where to go, because the darkness has made that person blind.
12 I write to you, dear children,
because your sins are forgiven through Christ.
13 I write to you, parents,
because you know the One who existed from the beginning.
I write to you, young people,
because you have defeated the Evil One.
14 I write to you, children,
because you know the Father.
I write to you, parents,
because you know the One who existed from the beginning.
I write to you, young people,
because you are strong;
the teaching of God lives in you,
and you have defeated the Evil One.

OLD TESTAMENT READING

Send me your light and truth
to guide me.
Let them lead me to your holy mountain,
to where you live.
4 Then I will go to the altar of God,
to God who is my joy and happiness.
I will praise you with a harp,
God, my God.

Psalm 43:3–4

Light is not given to evil people.

Job 38:15a

INSIGHTS

Servants of Christ shine with His light in a society that is hopelessly lost. . .

We pose a weird phenomenon to those in darkness. They cannot figure us out! And that is exactly as Jesus planned it. Think of some distinctive characteristics of light:

- *Light is silent. No noise, no big splash, no banners—light simply shines. It's like a single lighthouse along a rugged shoreline. All it does is shine as it turns.*
- *Light gives direction. No words, no sermon. Jesus says that others "see" our actions—but nothing is said of their hearing.*
- *Light attracts attention. You don't have to ask people to look at you when you turn a light on in a dark room. It happens automatically. . . . If you are a Christian family in a non-Christian neighborhood, you are the light in that darkness. The same is true if you are the only Christian nurse on your floor, or student in your school, or professional in your firm or group, or salesman in your district. You are a light in darkness—a servant of God who is being watched, who gives off a very distinct message . . . often with hardly a word being said. . . . Let it shine! Don't attempt to show off how bright and sparkling you are, just shine!*

Charles Swindoll

APPLICATION

What feelings does the God of light bring into your life? Describe what it means for you to "live in the light." What corners of darkness in your life do you need to open up to God's cleansing light?

FRIDAY

You Have Been Forgiven, so Don't Love the World's Fleeting Pleasures

1 John 2:15—3:10

Do not love the world or the things
in the world. If you love the world,
the love of the Father is not in you.
16 These are the ways of the world:
wanting to please our sinful selves,
wanting the sinful things we see, and
being too proud of what we have.
None of these come from the Father,
but all of them come from the world.
17 The world and everything that
people want in it are passing away,
but the person who does what God
wants lives forever.

Reject the Enemies of Christ

My dear children, these are the
last days. You have heard that the enemy of Christ is coming, and now
many enemies of Christ are already
here. This is how we know that these
are the last days. 19 These enemies
of Christ were in our fellowship, but
they left us. They never really belonged to us; if they had been a part
of us, they would have stayed with
us. But they left, and this shows that
none of them really belonged to us.
20 You have the gift that the Holy
One gave you, so you all know the
truth. 21 I do not write to you because
you do not know the truth but because you do know the truth. And
you know that no lie comes from the
truth.
22 Who is the liar? It is the person
who does not accept Jesus as the
Christ. This is the enemy of Christ:
the person who does not accept the
Father and his Son. 23 Whoever does
not accept the Son does not have the
Father. But whoever confesses the
Son has the Father, too.
24 Be sure you continue to follow
the teaching you heard from the beginning. If you continue to follow
what you heard from the beginning,
you will stay in the Son and in the
Father. 25 And this is what the Son
promised to us—life forever.
26 I am writing this letter about
those people who are trying to lead
you the wrong way. 27 Christ gave
you a special gift that is still in you,
so you do not need any other
teacher. His gift teaches you about
everything, and it is true, not false.
So continue to live in Christ, as his
gift taught you.
28 Yes, my dear children, live in
him so that when Christ comes back,
we can be without fear and not be
ashamed in his presence. 29 If you
know that Christ is all that is right,
you know that all who do right are
God's children.

We Are God's Children

3 The Father has loved us so much
that we are called children of
God. And we really are his children.
The reason the people in the world
do not know us is that they have not
known him. 2 Dear friends, now we
are children of God, and we have not
yet been shown what we will be in
the future. But we know that when
Christ comes again, we will be like
him, because we will see him as he
really is. 3 Christ is pure, and all who
have this hope in Christ keep themselves pure like Christ.

4 The person who sins breaks
God's law. Yes, sin is living against
God's law. 5 You know that Christ
came to take away sins and that
there is no sin in Christ. 6 So anyone
who lives in Christ does not go on
sinning. Anyone who goes on sinning has never really understood
Christ and has never known him.

7 Dear children, do not let anyone
lead you the wrong way. Christ is all
that is right. So to be like Christ a
person must do what is right. 8 The
devil has been sinning since the beginning, so anyone who continues to
sin belongs to the devil. The Son of
God came for this purpose: to destroy the devil's work.

9 Those who are God's children do
not continue sinning, because the new
life from God remains in them. They
are not able to go on sinning, because
they have become children of God.
10 So we can see who God's children
are and who the devil's children are:
Those who do not do what is right
are not God's children, and those who
do not love their brothers and sisters
are not God's children.

OLD TESTAMENT READING

Anything I saw and wanted, I
got for myself;
I did not miss any pleasure I
desired.
I was pleased with everything I
did,
and this pleasure was the
reward for all my hard work.
11 But then I looked at what I had
done,
and I thought about all the
hard work.
Suddenly I realized it was useless, like chasing the wind.
There is nothing to gain from
anything we do here on
earth.

Ecclesiastes 2:10–11

INSIGHTS

When I look back on my life nowadays, which I sometimes do, what strikes me forcibly about it is that what seemed at the time most significant and seductive, seems now most futile and absurd. For instance, success in all of its various guises; being known and being praised; ostensible pleasures, like acquiring money or seducing women, or travelling, going to and fro in the world and up and down in it like Satan, exploring and experiencing whatever Vanity Fair has to offer.

In retrospect all these exercises in self-gratification seem pure fantasy, what Pascal called "licking the earth." They are diversions designed to distract our attention from the true purpose of our existence in this world, which is, quite simply, to look for God, and, in looking, to find Him, and having found Him, to love Him, thereby establishing a harmonious relationship with His purposes for His creation.

Malcolm Muggeridge

ACTION POINT

Write down what you believe to be your true purpose in life. What things are important according to that purpose? Pray that God will help you focus on the important things and put aside everything else—no matter how tempting it may appear!

WEEKEND

God's People Must Show Their Love for One Another

1 John 3:11—4:12

We Must Love Each Other

This is the teaching you have heard
from the beginning: We must love
each other. 12 Do not be like Cain
who belonged to the Evil One and
killed his brother. And why did he
kill him? Because the things Cain
did were evil, and the things his
brother did were good.
13 Brothers and sisters, do not be
surprised when the people of the
world hate you. 14 We know we have
left death and have come into life because we love each other. Whoever
does not love is still dead. 15 Everyone who hates a brother or sister is
a murderer, and you know that no
murderers have eternal life in them.
16 This is how we know what real
love is: Jesus gave his life for us. So
we should give our lives for our
brothers and sisters. 17 Suppose
someone has enough to live and
sees a brother or sister in need, but
does not help. Then God's love is not
living in that person. 18 My children,
we should love people not only with
words and talk, but by our actions
and true caring.
19-20 This is the way we know that
we belong to the way of truth. When
our hearts make us feel guilty, we
can still have peace before God. God
is greater than our hearts, and he
knows everything. 21 My dear
friends, if our hearts do not make us
feel guilty, we can come without fear
into God's presence. 22 And God
gives us what we ask for because we
obey God's commands and do what
pleases him. 23 This is what God commands: that we believe in his Son,
Jesus Christ, and that we love each
other, just as he commanded. 24 The
people who obey God's commands
live in God, and God lives in them.
We know that God lives in us because of the Spirit God gave us.

Warning Against False Teachers

4 My dear friends, many false
prophets have gone out into the
world. So do not believe every spirit,
but test the spirits to see if they are
from God. 2 This is how you can
know God's Spirit: Every spirit who
confesses that Jesus Christ came to
earth as a human is from God. 3 And
every spirit who refuses to say this
about Jesus is not from God. It is the
spirit of the enemy of Christ, which
you have heard is coming, and now
he is already in the world.
4 My dear children, you belong to
God and have defeated them; because God's Spirit, who is in you, is
greater than the devil, who is in the
world. 5 And they belong to the world,
so what they say is from the world,
and the world listens to them. 6 But
we belong to God, and those who
know God listen to us. But those
who are not from God do not listen
to us. That is how we know the Spirit
that is true and the spirit that is false.

Love Comes from God

Dear friends, we should love each
other, because love comes from God.
Everyone who loves has become
God's child and knows God. 8 Who-

ever does not love does not know God, because God is love. [9]This is how God showed his love to us: He sent his one and only Son into the world so that we could have life through him. [10]This is what real love is: It is not our love for God; it is God's love for us in sending his Son to be the way to take away our sins.

[11]Dear friends, if God loved us that much we also should love each other. [12]No one has ever seen God, but if we love each other, God lives in us, and his love is made perfect in us.

OLD TESTAMENT READING

The king asked, "Is anyone left in Saul's family? I want to show God's kindness to that person."

Ziba answered the king, "Jonathan has a son still living who is crippled in both feet."

[5]Then King David had servants bring Jonathan's son from the house of Makir son of Ammiel in Lo Debar. [6]Mephibosheth, Jonathan's son, came before David and bowed facedown on the floor.

David said, "Mephibosheth!"

Mephibosheth said, "I am your servant."

[7]David said to him, "Don't be afraid. I will be kind to you for your father Jonathan's sake. I will give you back all the land of your grandfather Saul, and you will always eat at my table."

2 Samuel 9:3, 5–7

INSIGHTS

There is more to becoming a Christian than accepting a set of doctrines and striving to live out a particular lifestyle. Being a Christian involves allowing God to become a living presence in your life. . . . A Christian is a person who is possessed by Christ in such a way that feelings, thoughts, and attitudes are all changed. For the Christian person, loving becomes a spiritual exercise because God is love, and the Christian knows that "every one that loveth is born of God." God wants to indwell you and affect your consciousness for many reasons, but above them all is His desire to be able to reach other people with His love through you. . . . If you will pray and ask Him to be an indwelling reality and if you are willing to yield to His will in all things, He will enter into your consciousness and begin to effect a transformation in your life. Most important, you will, little by little, begin to relate to other people as He would relate to them. You will recognize that being a Christian involves a commitment to treat others as He would treat them. . . .

If you want to do something that will cause you to become a more loving person, surrender yourself to Jesus. He has a way of making lovers out of people.

Tony Campolo

APPLICATION

Why is love characteristic of God's children? What does a lack of love reveal about a person's heart? How much should God's children love each other? In what ways do God's children demonstrate their love? To whom can you show the kind of godly love that David showed Mephibosheth?

MONDAY

God Listens to the Prayers of His People

1 John 4:13—5:21

We know that we live in God and he lives in us, because he gave us his Spirit. 14 We have seen and can testify that the Father sent his Son to be the Savior of the world. 15 Whoever confesses that Jesus is the Son of God has God living inside, and that person lives in God. 16 And so we know the love that God has for us, and we trust that love.

God is love. Those who live in love live in God, and God lives in them. 17 This is how love is made perfect in us: that we can be without fear on the day God judges us, because in this world we are like him. 18 Where God's love is, there is no fear, because God's perfect love drives out fear. It is punishment that makes a person fear, so love is not made perfect in the person who fears.

19 We love because God first loved us. 20 If people say, "I love God," but hate their brothers or sisters, they are liars. Those who do not love their brothers and sisters, whom they have seen, cannot love God, whom they have never seen. 21 And God gave us this command: Those who love God must also love their brothers and sisters.

Faith in the Son of God

5 Everyone who believes that Jesus is the Christ is God's child, and whoever loves the Father also loves the Father's children. 2 This is how we know we love God's children: when we love God and obey his commands. 3 Loving God means obeying his commands. And God's commands are not too hard for us, 4 because everyone who is a child of God conquers the world. And this is the victory that conquers the world—our faith. 5 So the one who wins against the world is the person who believes that Jesus is the Son of God.

6 Jesus Christ is the One who came by water and blood. He did not come by water only, but by water and blood. And the Spirit says that this is true, because the Spirit is the truth. 7 So there are three witnesses that tell us about Jesus: 8 the Spirit, the water, and the blood; and these three witnesses agree. 9 We believe people when they say something is true. But what God says is more important, and he has told us the truth about his own Son. 10 Anyone who believes in the Son of God has the truth that God told us. Anyone who does not believe makes God a liar, because that person does not believe what God told us about his Son. 11 This is what God told us: God has given us eternal life, and this life is in his Son. 12 Whoever has the Son has life, but whoever does not have the Son of God does not have life.

We Have Eternal Life Now

I write this letter to you who believe in the Son of God so you will know you have eternal life. 14 And this is the boldness we have in God's presence: that if we ask God for anything that agrees with what he wants, he

hears us. [15] If we know he hears us
every time we ask him, we know we
have what we ask from him.

[16] If anyone sees a brother or sister sinning (sin that does not lead to
eternal death), that person should
pray, and God will give the sinner
life. I am talking about people whose
sin does not lead to eternal death.
There is sin that leads to death. I do
not mean that a person should pray
about that sin. [17] Doing wrong is always sin, but there is sin that does
not lead to eternal death.

[18] We know that those who are
God's children do not continue to
sin. The Son of God keeps them safe,
and the Evil One cannot touch them.
[19] We know that we belong to God,
but the Evil One controls the whole
world. [20] We also know that the Son
of God has come and has given us
understanding so that we can know
the True One. And our lives are in
the True One and in his Son, Jesus
Christ. He is the true God and the
eternal life.

[21] So, dear children, keep yourselves away from gods.

OLD TESTAMENT READING

But God has listened;
he has heard my prayer.
[20] Praise God,
who did not ignore my prayer.
or hold back his love from me.

Psalm 66:19–20

INSIGHTS

PLEASE INTERRUPT

Sometimes I feel like an interruption,
and then I want to shrink
back into my shell
and never come out again.
I want to walk away and say,
"I'm sorry I took your time."

Being an interruption hurts.
It tells me
something is more important than I am.
It tells me
to hurry up and move along.
It tells me
you are looking
but don't see me.
It tells me
you are listening
but don't hear me.
And so I move along.
But, God says,
"Don't hurry away.
Stick around.
Tell me how it is with you.
Tell me what you're feeling
right this minute.
Tell me why you feel that way.
I want to know you.
You count with me.
I care about you.
Tell me what I can do for you."

And I go away feeling
He was glad I called.

Ruth Senter

PAUSE FOR REFLECTION

Who listens to you every time you speak? How do you know that God hears your prayers? What would you tell others that he has done for you?

TUESDAY

Encourage and Support One Another in the Faith

2 John 1—3 John 15

From the Elder.

To the chosen lady and her children:

I love all of you in the truth, and all those who know the truth love you. 2 We love you because of the truth that lives in us and will be with us forever.

3 Grace, mercy, and peace from God the Father and his Son, Jesus Christ, will be with us in truth and love.

4 I was very happy to learn that some of your children are following the way of truth, as the Father commanded us. 5 And now, dear lady, this is not a new command but is the same command we have had from the beginning. I ask you that we all love each other. 6 And love means living the way God commanded us to live. As you have heard from the beginning, his command is this: Live a life of love.

7 Many false teachers are in the world now who do not confess that Jesus Christ came to earth as a human. Anyone who does not confess this is a false teacher and an enemy of Christ. 8 Be careful yourselves that you do not lose everything you have worked for, but that you receive your full reward.

9 Anyone who goes beyond Christ's teaching and does not continue to follow only his teaching does not have God. But whoever continues to follow the teaching of Christ has both the Father and the Son. 10 If someone comes to you and does not bring this teaching, do not welcome or accept that person into your house. 11 If you welcome such a person, you share in the evil work.

12 I have many things to write to you, but I do not want to use paper and ink. Instead, I hope to come to you and talk face to face so we can be full of joy. 13 The children of your chosen sister greet you.

Help Christians Who Teach Truth

From the Elder.

To my dear friend Gaius, whom I love in the truth:

2 My dear friend, I know your soul is doing fine, and I pray that you are doing well in every way and that your health is good. 3 I was very happy when some brothers and sisters came and told me about the truth in your life and how you are following the way of truth. 4 Nothing gives me greater joy than to hear that my children are following the way of truth.

5 My dear friend, it is good that you help the brothers and sisters, even those you do not know. 6 They told the church about your love. Please help them to continue their trip in a way worthy of God. 7 They started out in service to Christ, and they have been accepting nothing from nonbelievers. 8 So we should help such people; when we do, we share in their work for the truth.

9 I wrote something to the church, but Diotrephes, who loves to be their leader, will not listen to us. 10 So if I come, I will talk about what Diotrephes is doing, about how he lies and says evil things about us. But more than that, he refuses to accept the other brothers and sisters; he even stops those who do want to accept them and puts them out of the church.

11 My dear friend, do not follow
what is bad; follow what is good. The
one who does good belongs to God.
But the one who does evil has never
known God.
12 Everyone says good things
about Demetrius, and the truth
agrees with what they say. We also
speak well of him, and you know
what we say is true.
13 I have many things I want to
write you, but I do not want to use
pen and ink. 14 I hope to see you soon
and talk face to face. 15 Peace to you.
The friends here greet you. Please
greet each friend there by name.

OLD TESTAMENT READING

Then Moses called Joshua and said
to him in front of the people, "Be
strong and brave, because you will
lead these people into the land the
LORD promised to give their ancestors, and help them take it as their
own. 8 The LORD himself will go before you. He will be with you; he will
not leave you or forget you. Don't be
afraid and don't worry."

Deuteronomy 31:7–8

INSIGHTS

I decided to take a break and hit the slopes (emphasis on hit, since it was my first time in all my life to attempt to ski). . . .

It was unbelievable! You have heard of the elephant man? On skis, I'm the rhinoceros man. It is doubtful that anyone else on planet earth has ever come down any ski slope more ways than I did. Or landed in more positions. Or did more creative things in the air before landing. . . .

Working with me that humiliating day was the world's most encouraging ski instructor (yes, I had an instructor!) who set the new record in patience. . . .

Never once did she lose her cool.

Never once did she laugh at me.

Never once did she yell, scream, threaten, or swear.

Never once did she call me "dummy." . . .

. . . That day God gave me a living, never-to-be-forgotten illustration of the value of encouragement. . . .

What is true for a novice on the snow once a year is all the more true for the people we meet every day. Harassed by demands and deadlines; bruised by worry, adversity, and failure; broken by disillusionment; and defeated by sin, they live somewhere between dull discouragement and sheer panic. Even Christians are not immune! We may give off this "I've got it all together" air of confidence, much like I did when I first snapped on the skis. But realistically, we also struggle, lose our balance, slip and slide, tumble, and fall flat on our faces.

All of us need encouragement—somebody to believe in us. To reassure and reinforce us. To help us pick up the pieces and go on. To provide us with increased determination in spite of the odds.

Charles Swindoll

APPLICATION

Describe the kinds of encouragement in faith revealed through these Scripture readings. When have you been blessed by spiritual encouragement? Who could use your encouragement today?

WEDNESDAY

God Will Punish Everyone Who Is Against Him

Jude 1–13

From Jude, a servant of Jesus Christ and a brother of James.

To all who have been called by God. God the Father loves you, and you have been kept safe in Jesus Christ:

2 Mercy, peace, and love be yours richly.

God Will Punish Sinners

Dear friends, I wanted very much to write you about the salvation we all share. But I felt the need to write you about something else: I want to encourage you to fight hard for the faith that was given the holy people of God once and for all time. 4 Some people have secretly entered your group. Long ago the prophets wrote about these people who will be judged guilty. They are against God and have changed the grace of our God into a reason for sexual sin. They also refuse to accept Jesus Christ, our only Master and Lord.

5 I want to remind you of some things you already know: Remember that the Lord saved his people by bringing them out of the land of Egypt. But later he destroyed all those who did not believe. 6 And remember the angels who did not keep their place of power but left their proper home. The Lord has kept these angels in darkness, bound with everlasting chains, to be judged on the great day. 7 Also remember the cities of Sodom and Gomorrah and the other towns around them. In the same way they were full of sexual sin and people who desired sexual relations that God does not allow. They suffer the punishment of eternal fire, as an example for all to see.

8 It is the same with these people who have entered your group. They are guided by dreams and make themselves filthy with sin. They reject God's authority and speak against the angels. 9 Not even the archangel Michael, when he argued with the devil about who would have the body of Moses, dared to judge the devil guilty. Instead, he said, "The Lord punish you." 10 But these people speak against things they do not understand. And what they do know, by feeling, as dumb animals know things, are the very things that destroy them. 11 It will be terrible for them. They have followed the way of Cain, and for money they have given themselves to doing the wrong that Balaam did. They have fought against God as Korah did, and like Korah, they surely will be destroyed. 12 They are like dirty spots in your special Christian meals you share. They eat with you and have no fear, caring only for themselves. They are clouds without rain, which the wind blows around. They are autumn trees without fruit that are pulled out of the ground. So they are twice dead. 13 They are like wild waves of the sea, tossing up their own shameful actions like foam. They are like stars that wander in the sky. A place in the blackest darkness has been kept for them forever.

OLD TESTAMENT READING

Cry, because the LORD's day of
judging is near;
the Almighty is sending
destruction.
7 People will be weak with fear,
and their courage will melt
away.
8 Everyone will be afraid.
Pain and hurt will grab them;
they will hurt like a woman
giving birth to a baby.
They will look at each other in
fear,
with their faces red like fire.

9 Look, the LORD's day of judging is
coming—
a terrible day, a day of God's
anger.
He will destroy the land
and the sinners who live in it.
10 The stars will not show their
light;
the skies will be dark.
The sun will grow dark as it rises,
and the moon will not give its
light.

11 The LORD says, "I will punish the
world for its evil
and wicked people for their
sins.
I will cause proud people to lose
their pride,
and I will destroy the pride of
those who are cruel to
others."

Isaiah 13:6–11

INSIGHTS

You have a "lake of fire and brimstone," and you see lost sinners thrown into its waves of rolling fire; and they lash its burning shore, and gnaw their tongues for pain. There the worm dieth not, and their fire is not quenched, and "not one drop of water" can reach them to "cool their tongues"—"tormented in that flame."

What think you? Has God said these things to frighten our poor souls? Did He mean to play on our fears for His own amusement? Can you think so? Nay, does it not rather grieve His heart that He must build such a hell, and must plunge therein the sinners who will not honour His law—will not embrace salvation from sinning through His grace? Ah, the waves of death roll darkly under the eye of the Holy and compassionate One! He has no pleasure in the death of the sinner! But He must sustain His throne, and save His loyal subjects if He can. . . .

God would have us understand what an awful thing sin is, and what fearful punishment it deserves. He would fain show us by such figures how terrible must be the doom of the determined sinner.

Charles Finney

PAUSE FOR REFLECTION

Why must God punish those who are against him? List the sins of those who are against God. How can God's people stand strong against them? How are God's people to treat those who have doubts?

THURSDAY

God Is a Merciful Judge

Jude 14–25

Enoch, the seventh descendant
from Adam, said about these people:
"Look, the Lord is coming with many
thousands of his holy angels to
15 judge every person. He is coming
to punish all who are against God for
all the evil they have done against
him. And he will punish the sinners
who are against God for all the evil
they have said against him."

16 These people complain and
blame others, doing the evil things
they want to do. They brag about
themselves, and they flatter others
to get what they want.

A Warning and Things to Do

Dear friends, remember what the
apostles of our Lord Jesus Christ
said before. 18 They said to you, "In
the last times there will be people
who laugh about God, following
their own evil desires which are
against God." 19 These are the people
who divide you, people whose
thoughts are only of this world, who
do not have the Spirit.

20 But dear friends, use your most
holy faith to build yourselves up,
praying in the Holy Spirit. 21 Keep
yourselves in God's love as you wait
for the Lord Jesus Christ with his
mercy to give you life forever.

22 Show mercy to some people
who have doubts. 23 Take others out
of the fire, and save them. Show
mercy mixed with fear to others,
hating even their clothes which are
dirty from sin.

Praise God

God is strong and can help you not
to fall. He can bring you before his
glory without any wrong in you and
can give you great joy. 25 He is the
only God, the One who saves us. To
him be glory, greatness, power, and
authority through Jesus Christ our
Lord for all time past, now, and forever. Amen.

OLD TESTAMENT READING

The Truth About Bragging

This is what the LORD says:
"The wise must not brag about
their wisdom.
The strong must not brag
about their strength.
The rich must not brag about
their money.
24 But if someone wants to brag, let
him brag
that he understands and knows
me.
Let him brag that I am the LORD,
and that I am kind and fair,
and that I do things that are
right on earth.
This kind of bragging pleases
me," says the LORD.

Jeremiah 9:23–24

Those Who Have Faith in God Will Receive His Mercy

Give happiness to me, your
servant,
because I give my life to you,
Lord.
5 Lord, you are kind and forgiving

and have great love for those
who call to you.
11 LORD, teach me what you want me
to do,
and I will live by your truth.
Teach me to respect you completely.
12 Lord, my God, I will praise you
with all my heart,
and I will honor your name
forever.
13 You have great love for me.
You have saved me from death.
14 God, proud men are attacking
me;
a gang of cruel men is trying
to kill me.
They do not respect you.
16 Turn to me and have mercy.

Psalm 86:4–5, 11–14, 16a

INSIGHTS

God is a just God, One who shows no partiality. Outside of grace, God's penalty falls on all. "The wages of sin is death" (Romans 6:23). Sin is sin. The consequences have been posted; He gives fair warning. No excuses accepted. No variations on the rules. Man is accountable. Rebellion, be it active or passive, calls for justice.

I understand God's justice because I remember rebellion—ten-year-old rebellion. My father was the dispenser of justice. "No swimming in the creek today," he said. I had plenty of excuses: "Jimmy went in." "I was so hot." "It isn't fair when everybody else's dad lets them go."

Excuses didn't matter because the standard had been violated. The penalty was swift and sure. Justice was done. But then the father who had just administered justice reached for his big white handkerchief and wiped the tears from his eyes. That day, justice and love were forever linked in my mind.

My father's actions pointed me toward a heavenly Father who sits in the hall of justice, calls His creation to accountability, but weeps over waywardness even as He pronounces sentence. "Oh, Jerusalem, Jerusalem . . . how often I have longed to gather your children together, as a hen gathers her chicks under her wings, but you were not willing!" (Luke 13:34, NIV). Justice and love exist in the same person.

. . . I can be at peace about God's system of justice, for I have confidence in the Judge. There will be no payoffs. He judges clean.

As a sinner who knew where to find grace, I know God today not as my judge but as a loving Father who continually calls me to accountability. One day He was my judge. But I can almost see a white handkerchief dabbing tears as He wept over my rebellion, issued the sentence, and then took my penalty upon Himself. I am acquitted. Justice has been done. My debt has been paid. I can rest my case. . . .

"God is fair," I said to myself, "whether or not I understand His ways. For He is a God of justice."

Ruth Senter

APPLICATION

How does God want his people to treat those who have doubts? Do you have complete trust in God, who is both Judge and Savior? Are you at rest in his love?

FRIDAY

God Is the Great I AM— the Beginning and the End

Revelation 1:1–20

John Tells About This Book

1 This is the revelation of Jesus Christ, which God gave to him, to show his servants what must soon happen. And Jesus sent his angel to show it to his servant John, [2] who has told everything he has seen. It is the word of God; it is the message from Jesus Christ. [3] Happy is the one who reads the words of God's message, and happy are the people who hear this message and do what is written in it. The time is near when all of this will happen.

Jesus' Message to the Churches

From John.

To the seven churches in the country of Asia:

Grace and peace to you from the One who is and was and is coming, and from the seven spirits before his throne, [5] and from Jesus Christ. Jesus is the faithful witness, the first among those raised from the dead. He is the ruler of the kings of the earth.

He is the One who loves us, who made us free from our sins with the blood of his death. [6] He made us to be a kingdom of priests who serve God his Father. To Jesus Christ be glory and power forever and ever! Amen.

[7] Look, Jesus is coming with the clouds, and everyone will see him, even those who stabbed him. And all peoples of the earth will cry loudly because of him. Yes, this will happen! Amen.

[8] The Lord God says, "I am the Alpha and the Omega. I am the One who is and was and is coming. I am the Almighty."

[9] I, John, am your brother. All of us share with Christ in suffering, in the kingdom, and in patience to continue. I was on the island of Patmos, because I had preached the word of God and the message about Jesus. [10] On the Lord's day I was in the Spirit, and I heard a loud voice behind me that sounded like a trumpet. [11] The voice said, "Write what you see in a book and send it to the seven churches: to Ephesus, Smyrna, Pergamum, Thyatira, Sardis, Philadelphia, and Laodicea."

[12] I turned to see who was talking to me. When I turned, I saw seven golden lampstands [13] and someone among the lampstands who was "like a Son of Man." He was dressed in a long robe and had a gold band around his chest. [14] His head and hair were white like wool, as white as snow, and his eyes were like flames of fire. [15] His feet were like bronze that glows hot in a furnace, and his voice was like the noise of flooding water. [16] He held seven stars in his right hand, and a sharp double-edged sword came out of his mouth. He looked like the sun shining at its brightest time.

[17] When I saw him, I fell down at his feet like a dead man. He put his right hand on me and said, "Do not be afraid. I am the First and the Last. [18] I am the One who lives; I was dead, but look, I am alive forever and ever! And I hold the keys to death and to

the place of the dead. [19] So write the
things you see, what is now and what
will happen later. [20] Here is the secret
of the seven stars that you saw in my
right hand and the seven golden
lampstands: The seven lampstands
are the seven churches, and the
seven stars are the angels of the
seven churches."

OLD TESTAMENT READING

People of Jacob, listen to me.
People of Israel, I have called
you to be my people.
I am God;
I am the beginning and the
end.
13 I made the earth with my own
hands.
With my right hand I spread
out the skies.
When I call them,
they come together before
me."

Isaiah 48:12–13

INSIGHTS

I am the beginning;
I am the end.
You are very concerned with beginnings.
You hesitate to reach
the end.
The Alpha / beginning,
the Omega / end,
means that I am your all-in-all.
Do you want to stay
an Alpha person—
always at the starting line of faith?
That is a safe place—
where you say you believe Me,
where you champion truth,
but you don't move.
Move, I say!
Feel the wind of trials and victories in Me.
I am the Finisher, the Omega.
Lift your eyes from the starting line
and focus on all that lies before you—
on the intelligent golden faith
awaiting you at the finish.

Learn of me; digest My Word,
always in communion with Me.
I am your health, your energy:
I bring you to a "finish"
that is not the end of all things;
not a place where you collapse,
emptied out, done.
It is the place where you
allow Me freely
to live through you.

My finish means new development,
new discoveries,
new victories,
new holy charges.
My dearest and most effective servants
are those who move
in "finished" faith.

Marie Chapian

APPLICATION

As you read about the awesome power and greatness of God, the I AM, fear seems to be an appropriate response, doesn't it? Yet when John fell down in fear before God, God gently and compassionately reached out to him and told him what he was to do (Rev. 1:17–20). What is the great I AM moving you to do today?

WEEKEND

Repent and Regain Your Love for Christ

Revelation 2:1–17

To the Church in Ephesus

2 "Write this to the angel of the
church in Ephesus:
"The One who holds the seven
stars in his right hand and walks
among the seven golden lampstands
says this: 2 I know what you do, how
you work hard and never give up. I
know you do not put up with the
false teachings of evil people. You
have tested those who say they are
apostles but really are not, and you
found they are liars. 3 You have patience and have suffered troubles for
my name and have not given up.
4 "But I have this against you: You
have left the love you had in the beginning. 5 So remember where you
were before you fell. Change your
hearts and do what you did at first. If
you do not change, I will come to you
and will take away your lampstand
from its place. 6 But there is something
you do that is right: You hate what the
Nicolaitans do, as much as I.
7 "Every person who has ears
should listen to what the Spirit says
to the churches. To those who win
the victory I will give the right to eat
the fruit from the tree of life, which
is in the garden of God.

To the Church in Smyrna

Write this to the angel of the
church in Smyrna:
"The One who is the First and the
Last, who died and came to life
again, says this: 9 I know your
troubles and that you are poor, but
really you are rich! I know the bad
things some people say about you.
They say they are Jews, but they are
not true Jews. They are a synagogue
that belongs to Satan. 10 Do not be
afraid of what you are about to suffer. I tell you, the devil will put some
of you in prison to test you, and you
will suffer for ten days. But be faithful, even if you have to die, and I will
give you the crown of life.
11 "Everyone who has ears should
listen to what the Spirit says to the
churches. Those who win the victory
will not be hurt by the second death.

To the Church in Pergamum

Write this to the angel of the
church in Pergamum:
"The One who has the sharp,
double-edged sword says this: 13 I know
where you live. It is where Satan has
his throne. But you are true to me. You
did not refuse to tell about your faith
in me even during the time of Antipas,
my faithful witness who was killed in
your city, where Satan lives.
14 "But I have a few things against
you: You have some there who follow
the teaching of Balaam. He taught
Balak how to cause the people of Israel to sin by eating food offered to
idols and by taking part in sexual sins.
15 You also have some who follow the
teaching of the Nicolaitans. 16 So
change your hearts and lives. If you
do not, I will come to you quickly and
fight against them with the sword that
comes out of my mouth.
17 "Everyone who has ears should
listen to what the Spirit says to the
churches.
"I will give some of the hidden
manna to everyone who wins the

victory. I will also give to each one who wins the victory a white stone with a new name written on it. No one knows this new name except the one who receives it."

OLD TESTAMENT READING

Jeremiah Delivers a Message of Repentance

'Come back, unfaithful people of
Israel,' says the Lord.
'I will stop being angry at you,
because I am full of mercy,' says
the Lord.
'I will not be angry with you
forever.'

Jeremiah 3:12

INSIGHTS

A few years ago, in a commencement address at Harvard University, Alexander Solzhenitsyn tried to summarize the root problem facing capitalism and Marxism. He said that the trouble with both systems is that men have forgotten God. One system does it by its materialist philosophy; the other system by its materialist economy.

But "the sin of forgetting God" is not just the sin of economics and governments. It can be the sin of religion as well. Religious people forget God by setting up a religious system in His place.

Stephen was up against such a system in Acts 7. Stephen charged that the religion of Jerusalem had turned bad. The supreme court of that city did not take Stephen's words lightly. They were furious. They tried to silence him by running him out of town, and finally they killed him by stoning. Stephen's hot piety was a threat to the council's cold religion.

A fire dies unless it is fed. The most natural thing in this world is for a person to lose his zeal, fervor, and drive. . . .

Each of us forgets too soon. We all have the inherent tendency to drift from God.

The constant call of the Bible is to be on guard—to remember! Continually we are told to turn around, to repent, to draw near to God and submit to Him. . . .

The first lesson we must learn is the one Stephen tried to teach the Sanhedrin: "The Most High does not dwell in houses [or structures, or systems] made by human hands" (v. 48). He is God, Maker of heaven and earth, Alpha and Omega. He is the One to whom every man shall one day give account.

The second lesson that Stephen preached, by his words and life, is that God wants a personal relationship with His people. He does not want a system or a dead religion. He wants you. He wants to be your God and your friend. He wants a partnership with His creatures. He wants them to love Him and enjoy Him forever.

George Sweeting
Donald Sweeting

ACTION POINT

How much does God treasure the faithful love of his followers? What does he promise to those who love him faithfully? What is his warning to those who forsake him? In what ways have you forsaken God? How will you regain your love for him?

MONDAY

God Calls Us to Get Rid of Sin and Walk with Him

Revelation 2:18—3:6

To the Church in Thyatira

Write this to the angel of the church in Thyatira:

"The Son of God, who has eyes that blaze like fire and feet like shining bronze, says this: [19] I know what you do. I know about your love, your faith, your service, and your patience. I know that you are doing more now than you did at first.

[20] "But I have this against you: You let that woman Jezebel spread false teachings. She says she is a prophetess, but by her teaching she leads my people to take part in sexual sins and to eat food that is offered to idols. [21] I have given her time to change her heart and turn away from her sin, but she does not want to change. [22] So I will throw her on a bed of suffering. And all those who take part in adultery with her will suffer greatly if they do not turn away from the wrongs she does. [23] I will also kill her followers. Then all the churches will know I am the One who searches hearts and minds, and I will repay each of you for what you have done.

[24] "But others of you in Thyatira have not followed her teaching and have not learned what some call Satan's deep secrets. I say to you that I will not put any other load on you. [25] Only continue in your loyalty until I come.

[26] "I will give power over the nations to everyone who wins the victory and continues to be obedient to me until the end.

[27] 'You will rule over them with an
iron rod,
as when pottery is broken into
pieces.' *Psalm 2:9*

[28] This is the same power I received from my Father. I will also give him the morning star. [29] Everyone who has ears should listen to what the Spirit says to the churches.

To the Church in Sardis

3 "Write this to the angel of the church in Sardis:

"The One who has the seven spirits and the seven stars says this: I know what you do. People say that you are alive, but really you are dead. [2] Wake up! Make yourselves stronger before what you have left dies completely. I have found that what you are doing is less than what my God wants. [3] So do not forget what you have received and heard. Obey it, and change your hearts and lives. So you must wake up, or I will come like a thief, and you will not know when I will come to you. [4] But you have a few there in Sardis who have kept their clothes unstained, so they will walk with me and will wear white clothes, because they are worthy. [5] Those who win the victory will be dressed in white clothes like them. And I will not erase their names from the book of life, but I will say they belong to me before my Father and before his angels. [6] Everyone who has ears should listen to what the Spirit says to the churches."

OLD TESTAMENT READING

Now, Israel, this is what the LORD

your God wants you to do: Respect the LORD your God, and do what he has told you to do. Love him. Serve the LORD your God with your whole being.

Deuteronomy 10:12

Today you have said that the LORD is your God, and you have promised to do what he wants you to do—to keep his rules, commands, and laws. You have said you will obey him. [18]And today the LORD has said that you are his very own people, as he has promised you. But you must obey his commands.

Deuteronomy 26:17–18

Prophets or those who tell the future with dreams might come to you and say they will show you a miracle or a sign. [2]The miracle or sign might even happen, and then they might say, "Let's serve other gods" (gods you have not known) "and let's worship them." [5]The prophets or dreamers must be killed, because they said you should turn against the LORD your God, who brought you out of Egypt and saved you from the land where you were slaves. They tried to turn you from doing what the LORD your God commanded you to do. You must get rid of the evil among you.

Deuteronomy 13:1–2, 5

INSIGHTS

The older I get and the better acquainted I am with Christ, the more I'm aware of His insistence on holiness. This seems to be a matter about which He's not open to negotiation even in the slightest.

I guess somebody could consider bringing up this subject for discussion, "Ah, Jesus, I feel You're a bit too stubborn on this righteousness issue. I mean, I figure I've made some pretty big concessions Your way. On the matter of this one pet sin, couldn't You compromise a little? Accommodate me? Maybe 3 or 4 percent darkness allowable, and all the rest light?"

I warn you, the Lord won't budge even one millimeter. . . .

The absolute truth is: Anyone who wants to be close friends with Christ needs to achieve this victory-over-sin mindset, needs to learn to keep short accounts with God, needs to refuse to allow sins of long standing to go unconfessed day after day, week after week, even year after year. . . .

The hour must come when the church as a body and the individuals who compose the corporate entity reach for holiness. We must ask God for determination to overcome sin; we must pray for conviction for our unrighteousness. We must understand that we will never experience that overwhelming sense of the presence of Christ if we are not intent on striving to be 100 percent light-walkers.

David Mains

APPLICATION

What attitude do these readings say God's people must have toward sin? What action does he require? What does God promise to those who win the victory? How determined are you to overcome the sin in your life?

TUESDAY

God Saves and Honors Those Who Follow Him Faithfully

Revelation 3:7—4:5

To the Church in Philadelphia

Write this to the angel of the
church in Philadelphia:

"This is what the One who is holy
and true, who holds the key of
David, says. When he opens a door,
no one can close it. And when he
closes it, no one can open it. 8 I know
what you do. I have put an open door
before you, which no one can close.
I know you have a little strength, but
you have obeyed my teaching and
were not afraid to speak my name.
9 Those in the synagogue that belongs to Satan say they are Jews, but
they are not true Jews; they are liars. I will make them come before
you and bow at your feet, and they
will know that I have loved you.
10 You have obeyed my teaching
about not giving up your faith. So I
will keep you from the time of
trouble that will come to the whole
world to test those who live on earth.

11 "I am coming soon. Continue
strong in your faith so no one will take
away your crown. 12 I will make those
who win the victory pillars in the
temple of my God, and they will never
have to leave it. I will write on them
the name of my God and the name of
the city of my God, the new Jerusalem, that comes down out of heaven
from my God. I will also write on them
my new name. 13 Everyone who has
ears should listen to what the Spirit
says to the churches.

To the Church in Laodicea

Write this to the angel of the
church in Laodicea:

"The Amen, the faithful and true
witness, the beginning of all God has
made, says this: 15 I know what you
do, that you are not hot or cold. I
wish that you were hot or cold! 16 But
because you are lukewarm—neither
hot, nor cold—I am ready to spit you
out of my mouth. 17 You say, 'I am
rich, and I have become wealthy and
do not need anything.' But you do
not know that you are really miserable, pitiful, poor, blind, and naked.
18 I advise you to buy from me gold
made pure in fire so you can be truly
rich. Buy from me white clothes so
you can be clothed and so you can
cover your shameful nakedness. Buy
from me medicine to put on your
eyes so you can truly see.

19 "I correct and punish those
whom I love. So be eager to do right,
and change your hearts and lives.
20 Here I am! I stand at the door and
knock. If you hear my voice and
open the door, I will come in and eat
with you, and you will eat with me.

21 "Those who win the victory will
sit with me on my throne in the same
way that I won the victory and sat
down with my Father on his throne.
22 Everyone who has ears should listen to what the Spirit says to the
churches."

John Sees Heaven

4 After the vision of these things I
looked, and there before me was
an open door in heaven. And the
same voice that spoke to me before,
that sounded like a trumpet, said,
"Come up here, and I will show you

what must happen after this." [2]Im-
mediately I was in the Spirit, and
before me was a throne in heaven,
and someone was sitting on it. [3]The
One who sat on the throne looked
like precious stones, like jasper and
carnelian. All around the throne was
a rainbow the color of an emerald.
[4]Around the throne there were
twenty-four other thrones with
twenty-four elders sitting on them.
They were dressed in white and had
golden crowns on their heads.
[5]Lightning flashes and noises and
thundering came from the throne.
Before the throne seven lamps were
burning, which are the seven spirits
of God.

OLD TESTAMENT READING

God Will Save and Honor His People

At that time Michael, the great
prince who protects your people, will
stand up. There will be a time of
much trouble, the worst time since
nations have been on earth, but your
people will be saved. Everyone
whose name is written in God's book
will be saved. [2]Many people who
have already died will live again.
Some of them will wake up to have
life forever, but some will wake up
to find shame and disgrace forever.
[3]The wise people will shine like the
brightness of the sky. Those who
teach others to live right will shine
like stars forever and ever.

Daniel 12:1–3

INSIGHTS

Ray Stedman tells the story of an old missionary couple who had been working in Africa for many years and were returning to New York City to retire. With no pension and broken in health, they were discouraged, fearful of the future.

They happened to be booked on the same ship as Teddy Roosevelt, who was returning from a big-game hunting expedition. They watched the passengers trying to glimpse the great man, the crew fussing over him. . . .

At the dock in New York a band was waiting to greet the President. . . . But the missionary couple slipped off the ship unnoticed.

That night, in a cheap flat they found on the East Side, the man's spirit broke. He said to his wife, "I can't take this; God is not treating us fairly." His wife suggested he go in the bedroom and tell the Lord.

A short time later he came out of the bedroom with a face completely changed. His wife asked, "Dear, what happened?"

"The Lord settled it with me," he said. "I told him how bitter I was that the President should receive this tremendous homecoming, when no one met us as we returned home. And when I finished, it seemed as though the Lord put his hand on my shoulder and simply said, 'But you're not home yet!'"

Donald McCullough

APPLICATION

To whom does Jesus promise salvation? What kind of a 'homecoming' does he promise to those who belong to him? Ask God to help you, like the old missionary, keep perspective on what is to come!

WEDNESDAY

A Glimpse of Heaven's Holiness

Revelation 4:6—6:2

Also before the throne there was
something that looked like a sea of
glass, clear like crystal.

In the center and around the
throne were four living creatures with
eyes all over them, in front and in
back. 7 The first living creature was
like a lion. The second was like a calf.
The third had a face like a man. The
fourth was like a flying eagle. 8 Each
of these four living creatures had six
wings and was covered all over with
eyes, inside and out. Day and night
they never stop saying:

"Holy, holy, holy is the Lord God
Almighty.
He was, he is, and he is
coming."

9 These living creatures give
glory, honor, and thanks to the One
who sits on the throne, who lives forever and ever. 10 Then the twenty-
four elders bow down before the
One who sits on the throne, and they
worship him who lives forever and
ever. They put their crowns down
before the throne and say:

11 "You are worthy, our Lord and
God,
to receive glory and honor and
power,
because you made all things.
Everything existed and was
made,
because you wanted it."

5 Then I saw a scroll in the right hand
of the One sitting on the throne.
The scroll had writing on both sides
and was kept closed with seven seals.
2 And I saw a powerful angel calling
in a loud voice, "Who is worthy to
break the seals and open the scroll?"
3 But there was no one in heaven or
on earth or under the earth who could
open the scroll or look inside it. 4 I
cried hard because there was no one
who was worthy to open the scroll or
look inside. 5 But one of the elders said
to me, "Do not cry! The Lion from the
tribe of Judah, David's descendant,
has won the victory so that he is able
to open the scroll and its seven seals."

6 Then I saw a Lamb standing in
the center of the throne and in the
middle of the four living creatures
and the elders. The Lamb looked as
if he had been killed. He had seven
horns and seven eyes, which are the
seven spirits of God that were sent
into all the world. 7 The Lamb came
and took the scroll from the right
hand of the One sitting on the
throne. 8 When he took the scroll,
the four living creatures and the
twenty-four elders bowed down before the Lamb. Each one of them had
a harp and golden bowls full of incense, which are the prayers of
God's holy people. 9 And they all
sang a new song to the Lamb:

"You are worthy to take the scroll
and to open its seals,
because you were killed,
and with the blood of your
death you bought people for
God
from every tribe, language,
people, and nation.
10 You made them to be a kingdom
of priests for our God,
and they will rule on the earth."

11 Then I looked, and I heard the
voices of many angels around the
throne, and the four living creatures,

and the elders. There were thousands and thousands of angels,
12 saying in a loud voice:

"The Lamb who was killed is
worthy
to receive power, wealth, wisdom,
and strength,
honor, glory, and praise!"

13 Then I heard all creatures in heaven and on earth and under the earth and in the sea saying:

"To the One who sits on the
throne
and to the Lamb
be praise and honor and glory
and power
forever and ever."

14 The four living creatures said, "Amen," and the elders bowed down and worshiped.

6 Then I watched while the Lamb opened the first of the seven
seals. I heard one of the four living
creatures say with a voice like thunder, "Come!"
2 I looked, and there before me was a white horse. The rider on the horse held a bow, and he was given a crown, and he rode out, determined to win the victory.

OLD TESTAMENT READING

In the year that King Uzziah died, I saw the Lord sitting on a very high throne. His long robe filled the
Temple.
2 Heavenly creatures of fire stood above him. Each creature had six wings: It used two wings to cover its face, two wings to cover its feet, and two wings for flying.
3 Each creature was calling to the others:

"Holy, holy, holy is the LORD All-
Powerful.
His glory fills the whole earth."

4 Their calling caused the frame around the door to shake, as the Temple filled with smoke.

5 I said, "Oh, no! I will be destroyed. I am not pure, and I live among people who are not pure, but I have seen the King, the Lord All-Powerful."

Isaiah 6:1–5

INSIGHTS

For this one moment in time, the old apostle was ushered into the presence of the Mystery behind the universe. There is no way to describe God. John could only describe the response to God. . . . Even as he stood before Him, God remained a mystery to John and to us—the Mystery who was and is and will always be, the Mystery behind our creation and our preservation, the Mystery worthy of our glory and honor and power.

The risen Christ had called John into the presence of God so that the old man could know, and through him we could know, this fact: Behind the universe there is a Power worthy of our praise and of our trust. In spite of rumors to the contrary, we are not creatures abandoned on a planet spinning madly through the universe. . . . We are the children of a great and wonderful God who even now sits in power accomplishing His purposes in His creation.

Billy Graham

APPLICATION

Reread each detail John uses to describe heaven's holiness. Imagine the sights, the sounds, and magnitude of God's powerful holiness! Praise God for his holiness.

THURSDAY

Who Can Stand Against the Lord's Anger?

Revelation 6:3—7:8

When the Lamb opened the second seal, I heard the second living
creature say, "Come!" 4 Then another
horse came out, a red one. Its rider
was given power to take away peace
from the earth and to make people
kill each other, and he was given a
big sword.
5 When the Lamb opened the
third seal, I heard the third living
creature say, "Come!" I looked, and
there before me was a black horse,
and its rider held a pair of scales in
his hand. 6 Then I heard something
that sounded like a voice coming
from the middle of the four living
creatures. The voice said, "A quart of
wheat for a day's pay, and three quarts
of barley for a day's pay, and do not
damage the olive oil and wine!"
7 When the Lamb opened the
fourth seal, I heard the voice of the
fourth living creature say, "Come!"
8 I looked, and there before me was
a pale horse. Its rider was named
death, and Hades was following
close behind him. They were given
power over a fourth of the earth to
kill people by war, by starvation, by
disease, and by the wild animals of
the earth.
9 When the Lamb opened the fifth
seal, I saw under the altar the souls
of those who had been killed because they were faithful to the word
of God and to the message they had
received. 10 These souls shouted in
a loud voice, "Holy and true Lord,
how long until you judge the people
of the earth and punish them for killing us?" 11 Then each one of them
was given a white robe and was told
to wait a short time longer. There
were still some of their fellow servants and brothers and sisters in the
service of Christ who must be killed
as they were. They had to wait until
all of this was finished.
12 Then I watched while the Lamb
opened the sixth seal, and there was
a great earthquake. The sun became
black like rough black cloth, and the
whole moon became red like blood.
13 And the stars in the sky fell to the
earth like figs falling from a fig tree
when the wind blows. 14 The sky disappeared as a scroll when it is rolled
up, and every mountain and island
was moved from its place.
15 Then the kings of the earth, the
rulers, the generals, the rich people,
the powerful people, the slaves, and the
free people hid themselves in caves
and in the rocks on the mountains.
16 They called to the mountains and the
rocks, "Fall on us. Hide us from the
face of the One who sits on the throne
and from the anger of the Lamb! 17 The
great day for their anger has come, and
who can stand against it?"

The 144,000 People of Israel

7 After the vision of these things I
saw four angels standing at the
four corners of the earth. The angels
were holding the four winds of the
earth to keep them from blowing on
the land or on the sea or on any tree.
2 Then I saw another angel coming
up from the east who had the seal of
the living God. And he called out in
a loud voice to the four angels to
whom God had given power to harm

the earth and the sea. [3]He said to
them, "Do not harm the land or the
sea or the trees until we mark with
a sign the foreheads of the people
who serve our God." [4]Then I heard
how many people were marked with
the sign. There were one hundred
forty-four thousand from every tribe
of the people of Israel.

5 From the tribe of Judah twelve
thousand were marked with
the sign,
from the tribe of Reuben
twelve thousand,
from the tribe of Gad twelve
thousand,
6 from the tribe of Asher twelve
thousand,
from the tribe of Naphtali
twelve thousand,
from the tribe of Manasseh
twelve thousand,
7 from the tribe of Simeon
twelve thousand,
from the tribe of Levi twelve
thousand,
from the tribe of Issachar
twelve thousand,
8 from the tribe of Zebulun
twelve thousand,
from the tribe of Joseph twelve
thousand,
and from the tribe of Benjamin
twelve thousand were
marked with the sign.

OLD TESTAMENT READING

God Declares His Anger Against Nineveh

The LORD is a jealous God who
punishes;
the LORD punishes and is filled
with anger.

[5]The mountains shake in front of
him,
and the hills melt.
The earth trembles when he comes;
the world and all who live in it
shake with fear.
[6]No one can stay alive when he is
angry;
no one can survive his strong
anger.

Nahum 1:2a, 5–6a

INSIGHTS

The Sixth Seal Judgment (Rev. 6:12–17) . . unleashes universal havoc on the earth. . . .

These judgments will produce terror in the hearts of all living men. Their hearts will be filled with fear—not primarily because of the physical disturbances or the awful wars and pestilences, but because they will see God on His throne. Men will plead to be hidden "from the face of Him that sitteth on the throne, and from the wrath of the Lamb." They will go to any length to avoid facing their Creator and Judge, even to seeking death under the rocks and mountains in which they will try to hide. All classes of people (v. 15) will be affected. As has been true throughout history, there will be no general or mass turning to God in repentance, but only a turning from God's face.

Charles Ryrie

ACTION POINT

What does God promise to those who are guilty of sin? Pray that you will be faithful so you will not hide from God's presence.

FRIDAY

The Glorious Reward of Those Washed Clean by the Blood of the Lamb

Revelation 7:9—8:13

The Great Crowd Worships God

After the vision of these things I
looked, and there was a great number of people, so many that no one
could count them. They were from
every nation, tribe, people, and language of the earth. They were all
standing before the throne and before the Lamb, wearing white robes
and holding palm branches in their
hands. 10They were shouting in a
loud voice, "Salvation belongs to our
God, who sits on the throne, and to
the Lamb." 11All the angels were
standing around the throne and the
elders and the four living creatures.
They all bowed down on their faces
before the throne and worshiped
God, 12saying, "Amen! Praise, glory,
wisdom, thanks, honor, power, and
strength belong to our God forever
and ever. Amen!"

13Then one of the elders asked
me, "Who are these people dressed
in white robes? Where did they
come from?"

14I answered, "You know, sir."

And the elder said to me, "These
are the people who have come out
of the great distress. They have
washed their robes and made them
white in the blood of the Lamb. 15Be-
cause of this, they are before the
throne of God. They worship him
day and night in his temple. And the
One who sits on the throne will be
present with them. 16Those people
will never be hungry again, and they
will never be thirsty again. The sun
will not hurt them, and no heat will
burn them, 17because the Lamb at
the center of the throne will be their
shepherd. He will lead them to
springs of water that give life. And
God will wipe away every tear from
their eyes."

The Seventh Seal

8 When the Lamb opened the seventh seal, there was silence in
heaven for about half an hour. 2And
I saw the seven angels who stand
before God and to whom were given
seven trumpets.

3Another angel came and stood at
the altar, holding a golden pan for
incense. He was given much incense
to offer with the prayers of all
God's holy people. The angel put
this offering on the golden altar before the throne. 4The smoke from
the incense went up from the angel's
hand to God with the prayers of
God's people. 5Then the angel filled
the incense pan with fire from the
altar and threw it on the earth, and
there were flashes of lightning, thunder and loud noises, and an earthquake.

The Seven Angels and Trumpets

Then the seven angels who had the
seven trumpets prepared to blow
them.

7The first angel blew his trumpet,
and hail and fire mixed with blood
were poured down on the earth. And
a third of the earth, and all the green
grass, and a third of the trees were
burned up.

[8]Then the second angel blew his trumpet, and something that looked like a big mountain, burning with fire, was thrown into the sea. And a third of the sea became blood, [9]a third of the living things in the sea died, and a third of the ships were destroyed.

[10]Then the third angel blew his trumpet, and a large star, burning like a torch, fell from the sky. It fell on a third of the rivers and on the springs of water. [11]The name of the star is Wormwood. And a third of all the water became bitter, and many people died from drinking the water that was bitter.

[12]Then the fourth angel blew his trumpet, and a third of the sun, and a third of the moon, and a third of the stars were struck. So a third of them became dark, and a third of the day was without light, and also the night.

[13]While I watched, I heard an eagle that was flying high in the air cry out in a loud voice, "Trouble! Trouble! Trouble for those who live on the earth because of the remaining sounds of the trumpets that the other three angels are about to blow!"

OLD TESTAMENT READING

The LORD makes me very
happy;
all that I am rejoices in my
God.
He has covered me with clothes
of salvation
and wrapped me with a coat of
goodness,
like a bridegroom dressed for his
wedding,
like a bride dressed in jewels.

Isaiah 61:10

INSIGHTS

How many achievements and how many blessings for men the Scripture ascribes to the power of the Blood of the Lord Jesus! By the power of His Blood peace is made between man and God. By its power there is forgiveness of sins and eternal life for all who put their faith in the Lord Jesus. By the power of His Blood Satan is overcome. By its power there is continual cleansing from all sin for us. By the power of His Blood we may be set free from the tyranny of an evil conscience to serve the living God. By its infinite power with God the most unworthy have liberty to enter the Holy of Holies of God's presence and live there all the day. . . .

. . . That which gives the precious Blood its power with God for men is the lamb-like disposition of the One who shed it. . . . The title "the Lamb" so frequently given to the Lord Jesus in Scripture is first of all descriptive of His work—that of being a sacrifice for our sin. . . . But the title "the Lamb" has a deeper meaning. It describes His character. He is the Lamb in that He is meek and lowly in heart, gentle and unresisting, and all the time surrendering His own will to the Father's for the blessing and saving of men.

Roy and Revel Hession

ACTION POINT

Who is the Lamb of God? What does the blood of the Lamb do? List the ways God will bless those who are washed clean by the blood of the Lamb. Pray now and thank him for such a glorious salvation!

WEEKEND

God Sends Punishment in Order to Turn People from Sin

Revelation 9:1—10:4

9 Then the fifth angel blew his trumpet, and I saw a star fall from the
sky to the earth. The star was given
the key to the deep hole that leads to
the bottomless pit. 2 Then it opened up
the hole that leads to the bottomless
pit, and smoke came up from the hole
like smoke from a big furnace. Then
the sun and sky became dark because
of the smoke from the hole. 3 Then
locusts came down to the earth out of
the smoke, and they were given the
power to sting like scorpions. 4 They
were told not to harm the grass on the
earth or any plant or tree. They could
harm only the people who did not
have the sign of God on their foreheads. 5 These locusts were not given
the power to kill anyone, but to cause
pain to the people for five months. And
the pain they felt was like the pain a
scorpion gives when it stings someone. 6 During those days people will
look for a way to die, but they will not
find it. They will want to die, but death
will run away from them.

7 The locusts looked like horses
prepared for battle. On their heads
they wore what looked like crowns of
gold, and their faces looked like human faces. 8 Their hair was like
women's hair, and their teeth were
like lions' teeth. 9 Their chests looked
like iron breastplates, and the sound
of their wings was like the noise of
many horses and chariots hurrying
into battle. 10 The locusts had tails with
stingers like scorpions, and in their
tails was their power to hurt people
for five months. 11 The locusts had a
king who was the angel of the bottomless pit. His name in the Hebrew language is Abaddon and in the Greek
language is Apollyon.

12 The first trouble is past; there
are still two other troubles that will
come.

13 Then the sixth angel blew his
trumpet, and I heard a voice coming
from the horns on the golden altar
that is before God. 14 The voice said
to the sixth angel who had the trumpet, "Free the four angels who are
tied at the great river Euphrates."
15 And they let loose the four angels
who had been kept ready for this
hour and day and month and year so
they could kill a third of all people
on the earth. 16 I heard how many
troops on horses were in their
army—two hundred million.

17 The horses and their riders I saw
in the vision looked like this: They had
breastplates that were fiery red, dark
blue, and yellow like sulfur. The heads
of the horses looked like heads of lions, with fire, smoke, and sulfur coming out of their mouths. 18 A third of all
the people on earth were killed by
these three terrible disasters coming
out of the horses' mouths: the fire, the
smoke, and the sulfur. 19 The horses'
power was in their mouths and in their
tails; their tails were like snakes with
heads, and with them they hurt people.

20 The other people who were not
killed by these terrible disasters still
did not change their hearts and turn
away from what they had made with
their own hands. They did not stop
worshiping demons and idols made
of gold, silver, bronze, stone, and
wood—things that cannot see or
hear or walk. 21 These people did not

change their hearts and turn away from murder or evil magic, from their sexual sins or stealing.

The Angel and the Small Scroll

10 Then I saw another powerful angel coming down from
heaven dressed in a cloud with a rain-
bow over his head. His face was like
the sun, and his legs were like pillars
of fire. 2 The angel was holding a small
scroll open in his hand. He put his
right foot on the sea and his left foot
on the land. 3 Then he shouted loudly
like the roaring of a lion. And when
he shouted, the voices of seven thunders spoke. 4 When the seven thunders spoke, I started to write. But I
heard a voice from heaven say, "Keep
hidden what the seven thunders said,
and do not write them down."

OLD TESTAMENT READING

Let all the people who live in the
land shake with fear,
because the LORD's day of
judging is coming;
it is near.

10 Before them, earth and sky shake.
The sun and the moon become
dark,
and the stars stop shining.
11 The LORD shouts out orders
to his army.
His army is very large!
Those who obey him are very
strong!
The LORD's day of judging
is an overwhelming and
terrible day.
No one can stand up against it!

12 The LORD says, "Even now, come
back to me with all your heart.
Go without food, and cry and be
sad."

Joel 2:1b, 10–12

INSIGHTS

How terrible it is to witness the approach of a tempest: to note the forewarnings of the storm; to mark the birds of heaven as they droop their wings; to see the cattle as they lay their heads low in terror; to discern the face of the sky as it groweth black, and look to the sun which shineth not, and the heavens which are angry and frowning! . . . And yet, sinner, this is your present position. No hot drops have as yet fallen, but a shower of fire is coming. No terrible winds howl around you, but God's tempest is gathering its dread artillery. As yet the water-floods are dammed up by mercy, but the flood-gates shall soon be opened: the thunderbolts of God are yet in His storehouse, but lo! the tempest hastens, and how awful shall that moment be when God, robed in vengeance, shall march forth in fury! Where, where, where, O sinner, wilt thou hide thy head, or whither wilt thou flee? O that the hand of mercy may now lead you to Christ! He is freely set before you in the gospel: His riven side is the rock of shelter. Thou knowest thy need of Him; believe in Him, cast thyself upon Him, and then the fury shall be overpast for ever.

Charles Spurgeon

PAUSE FOR REFLECTION

What is the sole reason for the horrible punishment that is promised on God's day of judgment? What does God want from every person?

MONDAY

God's Prophets Are Empowered to Deliver His Message

Revelation 10:5—11:14

Then the angel I saw standing on the sea and on the land raised his right hand to heaven, 6 and he made a promise by the power of the One who lives forever and ever. He is the One who made the skies and all that is in them, the earth and all that is in it, and the sea and all that is in it. The angel promised, "There will be no more waiting! 7 In the days when the seventh angel is ready to blow his trumpet, God's secret will be finished. This secret is the Good News God told to his servants, the prophets."

8 Then I heard the same voice from heaven again, saying to me: "Go and take the open scroll that is in the hand of the angel that is standing on the sea and on the land."

9 So I went to the angel and told him to give me the small scroll. And he said to me, "Take the scroll and eat it. It will be sour in your stomach, but in your mouth it will be sweet as honey." 10 So I took the small scroll from the angel's hand and ate it. In my mouth it tasted sweet as honey, but after I ate it, it was sour in my stomach. 11 Then I was told, "You must prophesy again about many peoples, nations, languages, and kings."

The Two Witnesses

11 I was given a measuring stick like a rod, and I was told, "Go and measure the temple of God and the altar, and count the people worshiping there. 2 But do not measure the yard outside the temple. Leave it alone, because it has been given to those who are not God's people. And they will trample on the holy city for forty-two months. 3 And I will give power to my two witnesses to prophesy for one thousand two hundred sixty days, and they will be dressed in rough cloth to show their sadness."

4 These two witnesses are the two olive trees and the two lampstands that stand before the Lord of the earth. 5 And if anyone tries to hurt them, fire comes from their mouths and kills their enemies. And if anyone tries to hurt them in whatever way, in that same way that person will die. 6 These witnesses have the power to stop the sky from raining during the time they are prophesying. And they have power to make the waters become blood, and they have power to send every kind of trouble to the earth as many times as they want.

7 When the two witnesses have finished telling their message, the beast that comes up from the bottomless pit will fight a war against them. He will defeat them and kill them. 8 The bodies of the two witnesses will lie in the street of the great city where the Lord was killed. This city is named Sodom and Egypt, which has a spiritual meaning. 9 Those from every race of people, tribe, language, and nation will look at the bodies of the two witnesses for three and one-half days, and they will refuse to bury them. 10 People who live on the earth will rejoice and be happy because these

two are dead. They will send each other gifts, because these two prophets brought much suffering to those who live on the earth.

[11] But after three and one-half days, God put the breath of life into the two prophets again. They stood on their feet, and everyone who saw them became very afraid. [12] Then the two prophets heard a loud voice from heaven saying, "Come up here!" And they went up into heaven in a cloud as their enemies watched.

[13] In the same hour there was a great earthquake, and a tenth of the city was destroyed. Seven thousand people were killed in the earthquake, and those who did not die were very afraid and gave glory to the God of heaven.

[14] The second trouble is finished. Pay attention: The third trouble is coming soon.

OLD TESTAMENT READING

Now Elijah the Tishbite was a prophet from the settlers in Gilead. "I serve the LORD, the God of Israel," Elijah said to Ahab. "As surely as the LORD lives, no rain or dew will fall during the next few years unless I command it."

[1] During the third year without rain, the LORD spoke his word to Elijah: "Go and meet King Ahab, and I will soon send rain." So Elijah went to meet Ahab.

[2] By this time there was no food in Samaria.

1 Kings 17:1; 18:1–2

INSIGHTS

During the darkest ages, men have been raised up to testify against the prevailing corruption of their time, and especially the corruption of the apostate church. Their opponents have endeavored to silence their voice and blacken their character, but God has ever vindicated them and given life out of death. Always when the enemies of the truth have deemed themselves triumphant, there has been a rekindling of gospel testimony. A few years before Luther appeared, a medal was struck to commemorate the extinction of so-called heresy. Such witness-bearing as is suggested by the comparison with Zechariah's vision is fed from the heart of Christ. He is the root of the martyr line; his Spirit is the life-breath of his witnesses. All through the centuries, commonly called Christian though generally very un-Christian, there has been an unbroken succession of pure and noble souls who have stood for Jesus Christ even unto death. Let us dare to stand with them and our Lord, that he may not be ashamed of us at his coming.

F. B. Meyer

ACTION POINT

At what times does God call special prophets? What powers does he give them? Who controls their fate? What has God called you to do? Pray that you will trust him to care for you and enable you to accomplish his work.

TUESDAY

Satan Is Defeated by Christ's Coming

Revelation 11:15—12:12

The Seventh Trumpet

Then the seventh angel blew his trumpet. And there were loud voices in heaven, saying:

"The power to rule the world
now belongs to our Lord and his Christ,
and he will rule forever and ever."

[16]Then the twenty-four elders, who sit on their thrones before God, bowed down on their faces and worshiped God. [17]They said:

"We give thanks to you, Lord God Almighty,
who is and who was,
because you have used your great power
and have begun to rule!
[18]The people of the world were angry,
but your anger has come.
The time has come to judge the dead
and to reward your servants the prophets
and your holy people,
all who respect you, great and small.
The time has come to destroy those who destroy the earth!"

[19]Then God's temple in heaven was opened. The Ark that holds the agreement God gave to his people could be seen in his temple. Then there were flashes of lightning, noises, thunder, an earthquake, and a great hailstorm.

The Woman and the Dragon

12 And then a great wonder appeared in heaven: A woman was clothed with the sun, and the moon was under her feet, and a crown of
twelve stars was on her head. [2]She
was pregnant and cried out with pain, because she was about to give birth.
[3]Then another wonder appeared in
heaven: There was a giant red dragon with seven heads and seven crowns on each head. He also had ten horns.
[4]His tail swept a third of the stars out
of the sky and threw them down to the earth. He stood in front of the woman who was ready to give birth so he could eat her baby as soon as it was
born. [5]Then the woman gave birth to
a son who will rule all the nations with an iron rod. And her child was taken
up to God and to his throne. [6]The
woman ran away into the desert to a place God prepared for her where she would be taken care of for one thousand two hundred sixty days.
[7]Then there was a war in heaven.
Michael and his angels fought against the dragon, and the dragon
and his angels fought back. [8]But the
dragon was not strong enough, and he and his angels lost their place in
heaven. [9]The giant dragon was
thrown down out of heaven. (He is that old snake called the devil or Satan, who tricks the whole world.) The dragon with his angels was thrown down to the earth.
[10]Then I heard a loud voice in
heaven saying:

"The salvation and the power and the kingdom of our God
and the authority of his Christ have now come.
The accuser of our brothers and sisters,

who accused them day and
night before our God,
has been thrown down.
11 And our brothers and sisters
defeated him
by the blood of the Lamb's
death
and by the message they
preached.
They did not love their lives so
much
that they were afraid of death.
12 So rejoice, you heavens
and all who live there!
But it will be terrible for the earth
and the sea,
because the devil has come
down to you!
He is filled with anger,
because he knows he does not
have much time."

OLD TESTAMENT READING

As I watched, the little horn began making war against God's holy people and was defeating them
22 until God, who has been alive forever, came. He judged in favor of the holy people who belong to the Most High God; then the time came for them to receive the power to rule."

Daniel 7:21–22

INSIGHTS

What is this celestial conflict all about? The fact that Michael led God's angels to victory is significant, because Michael is identified with the nation Israel. . . . Apparently, the devil's hatred of Israel will spur him to make one final assault against the throne of God, but he will be defeated by Michael and a heavenly host. . . .

How does this future war apply to the church today? The same serpent who accuses the saints in heaven also deceives . . . the nations into thinking that the people of God are dangerous, deluded, even destructive. . . . God's people in every age must expect the world's opposition, but the church can always defeat the enemy by being faithful to Jesus Christ. . . .

. . . Satan is not equal to God; he is not omnipotent, omnipresent, or omniscient. His power is limited and his tactics must fail when God's people trust the power of the blood and of the Word. . . .

Believers in any age or situation can rejoice in this victory, no matter how difficult their experiences may be. Our warfare is not against flesh and blood, but against the spiritual forces of the wicked one; and these have been defeated by our Saviour (Eph. 6:10ff; note also 1:15–23).

Warren Wiersbe

ACTION POINT

What persepective do you gain on your struggles today from this account of ultimate struggle in heaven? Thank God he has already won the battle! Pray that you will remain faithful to him as you fight the battles in your life.

WEDNESDAY

God's People Must Fight Satan with Patience and Faith

Revelation 12:13—13:18

When the dragon saw he had been thrown down to the earth, he hunted for the woman who had given birth to the son. 14 But the woman was given the two wings of a great eagle so she could fly to the place prepared for her in the desert. There she would be taken care of for three and one-half years, away from the snake. 15 Then the snake poured water out of its mouth like a river toward the woman so the flood would carry her away. 16 But the earth helped the woman by opening its mouth and swallowing the river that came from the mouth of the dragon. 17 Then the dragon was very angry at the woman, and he went off to make war against all her other children—those who obey God's commands and who have the message Jesus taught.

18 And the dragon stood on the seashore.

The Two Beasts

13 Then I saw a beast coming up out of the sea. It had ten horns and seven heads, and there was a crown on each horn. A name against God was written on each head. 2 This beast looked like a leopard, with feet like a bear's feet and a mouth like a lion's mouth. And the dragon gave the beast all of his power and his throne and great authority. 3 One of the heads of the beast looked as if it had been killed by a wound, but this death wound was healed. Then the whole world was amazed and followed the beast. 4 People worshiped the dragon because he had given his power to the beast. And they also worshiped the beast, asking, "Who is like the beast? Who can make war against it?"

5 The beast was allowed to say proud words and words against God, and it was allowed to use its power for forty-two months. 6 It used its mouth to speak against God, against God's name, against the place where God lives, and against all those who live in heaven. 7 It was given power to make war against God's holy people and to defeat them. It was given power over every tribe, people, language, and nation. 8 And all who live on earth will worship the beast—all the people since the beginning of the world whose names are not written in the Lamb's book of life. The Lamb is the One who was killed.

9 Anyone who has ears should listen:

10 If you are to be a prisoner,
then you will be a prisoner.
If you are to be killed with the sword,
then you will be killed with the sword.

This means that God's holy people must have patience and faith.

11 Then I saw another beast coming up out of the earth. It had two horns like a lamb, but it spoke like a dragon. 12 This beast stands before the first beast and uses the same power the first beast has. By this power it makes everyone living on earth worship the first beast, who had the death wound that was healed. 13 And the second beast does

great miracles so that it even makes fire come down from heaven to earth while people are watching. [14] It fools those who live on earth by the miracles it has been given the power to do. It does these miracles to serve the first beast. The second beast orders people to make an idol to honor the first beast, the one that was wounded by the deadly sword but sprang to life again. [15] The second beast was given power to give life to the idol of the first one so that the idol could speak. And the second beast was given power to command all who will not worship the image of the beast to be killed. [16] The second beast also forced all people, small and great, rich and poor, free and slave, to have a mark on their right hand or on their forehead. [17] No one could buy or sell without this mark, which is the name of the beast or the number of its name. [18] This takes wisdom. Let the one who has understanding find the meaning of the number, which is the number of a person. Its number is six hundred sixty-six.

OLD TESTAMENT READING

The king of the North will tell lies and cause those who have not obeyed God to be ruined. But those who know God and obey him will be strong and fight back.

[33] "Those who are wise will help the others understand what is happening. But they will be killed with swords, or burned, or taken captive, or robbed of their homes and possessions. These things will continue for many days. [34] When the wise ones are suffering, they will get a little help, but many who join the wise ones will not help them in their time of need. [35] Some of the wise ones will be killed. But the hard times must come so they can be made stronger and purer and without faults until the time of the end comes. Then, at the right time, the end will come."

Daniel 11:32–35

INSIGHTS

We must be entrenched in the strength of the Lord. We must be enclosed "in the power of his might," or, as one has paraphrased it, "in the energy of him, the strong." It is in vain we engage in the conflict if that preliminary condition has not been fulfilled. In earthly warfare the soldier does not provide his own means of defense or weapons of assault. So in Christian conflict our whole equipment is divinely provided for us. He gives us a position that is impregnable—strength in the Lord; an armor that is impenetrable; and a weapon that is infallible—"the sword of the Spirit." We have by faith to take that position and continually to abide in it. We have by faith to put on that armor and wear it constantly.

Evan Hopkins

ACTION POINT

What difficulties will God's people face in the end times? How must they respond to Satan? What are their weapons, and what must they be prepared to give up? What will be accomplished by those who remain strong? Pray that your faith will be purified through the battles you face!

THURSDAY

God Will Pour Out His Holy Anger Against the Wicked

Revelation 14:1–20

The Song of the Saved

14 Then I looked, and there before me was the Lamb standing on Mount Zion. With him were
one hundred forty-four thousand
people who had his name and his
Father's name written on their foreheads. 2 And I heard a sound from
heaven like the noise of flooding
water and like the sound of loud
thunder. The sound I heard was like
people playing harps. 3 And they
sang a new song before the throne
and before the four living creatures
and the elders. No one could learn
the new song except the one hundred forty-four thousand who had
been bought from the earth. 4 These
are the ones who did not do sinful
things with women, because they
kept themselves pure. They follow
the Lamb every place he goes.
These one hundred forty-four thousand were bought from among the
people of the earth as people to be
offered to God and the Lamb. 5 They
were not guilty of telling lies; they
are without fault.

The Three Angels

Then I saw another angel flying
high in the air. He had the eternal
Good News to preach to those who
live on earth—to every nation, tribe,
language, and people. 7 He preached
in a loud voice, "Fear God and give
him praise, because the time has
come for God to judge all people. So
worship God who made the heavens,
and the earth, and the sea, and the
springs of water."

8 Then the second angel followed
the first angel and said, "Ruined, ruined is the great city of Babylon! She
made all the nations drink the wine
of the anger of her adultery."

9 Then a third angel followed the
first two angels, saying in a loud
voice: "If anyone worships the beast
and his idol and gets the beast's
mark on the forehead or on the
hand, 10 that one also will drink the
wine of God's anger, which is prepared with all its strength in the cup
of his anger. And that person will be
put in pain with burning sulfur before the holy angels and the Lamb.
11 And the smoke from their burning
pain will rise forever and ever. There
will be no rest, day or night, for those
who worship the beast and his idol
or who get the mark of his name."
12 This means God's holy people
must be patient. They must obey
God's commands and keep their
faith in Jesus.

13 Then I heard a voice from
heaven saying, "Write this: Happy
are the dead who die from now on
in the Lord."

The Spirit says, "Yes, they will
rest from their hard work, and the
reward of all they have done stays
with them."

The Earth Is Harvested

Then I looked, and there before me
was a white cloud, and sitting on the
white cloud was One who looked
like a Son of Man. He had a gold
crown on his head and a sharp sickle

in his hand. 15 Then another angel came out of the temple and called out in a loud voice to the One who was sitting on the cloud, "Take your sickle and harvest from the earth, because the time to harvest has come, and the fruit of the earth is ripe." 16 So the One who was sitting on the cloud swung his sickle over the earth, and the earth was harvested.

17 Then another angel came out of the temple in heaven, and he also had a sharp sickle. 18 And then another angel, who has power over the fire, came from the altar. This angel called to the angel with the sharp sickle, saying, "Take your sharp sickle and gather the bunches of grapes from the earth's vine, because its grapes are ripe." 19 Then the angel swung his sickle over the earth. He gathered the earth's grapes and threw them into the great winepress of God's anger. 20 They were trampled in the winepress outside the city, and blood flowed out of the winepress as high as horses' bridles for a distance of about one hundred eighty miles.

OLD TESTAMENT READING

The LORD, the God of Israel, said this to me: "My anger is like the wine in a cup. Take it from my hand and make all the nations, to whom I am sending you, drink all of my anger from this cup. 16 They will drink my anger and stumble about and act like madmen because of the war I am going to send among them."

17 So I took the cup from the LORD's hand and went to those nations and made them drink from it. 26b I made all the kingdoms on earth drink from the cup of the LORD's anger, but the king of Babylon will drink from this cup after all the others.

Jeremiah 25:15–17, 26b

INSIGHTS

The sinner's peace is that terribly prophetic calm that the traveler occasionally experiences on the higher Alps. Everything is still. The birds suspend their notes, fly low, and cower down with fear. The hum of bees among the flowers is hushed. A horrible stillness rules the hour, as if death had silenced all things by stretching his awful scepter over them. But the tempest is preparing—the lightning will soon cast abroad its flames of fire. Earth will rock with thunder-blasts; granite peaks will be dissolved. All nature will tremble beneath the fury of the storm. That calm is what the sinner is experiencing. He should not rejoice in it, because the hurricane of wrath is coming, the whirlwind and the tribulation that can sweep him away and utterly destroy him.

Charles Spurgeon

PAUSE FOR REFLECTION

In light of these Scripture readings, the "sinner's peace" that Spurgeon refers to certainly is ominous, isn't it? What does God's merciful forgiveness that he repeatedly offers to all people, contrasted with his guarantee of final, unchangeable punishment, teach you about the divine nature?

FRIDAY

God's People Praise Their Righteous and Faithful God

Revelation 15:1—16:11

The Last Troubles

15 Then I saw another wonder in
heaven that was great and
amazing. There were seven angels
bringing seven disasters. These are
the last disasters, because after
them, God's anger is finished.
2 I saw what looked like a sea of
glass mixed with fire. All of those
who had won the victory over the
beast and his idol and over the number of his name were standing by the
sea of glass. They had harps that
God had given them. 3 They sang the
song of Moses, the servant of God,
and the song of the Lamb:

"You do great and wonderful
things, *Psalm 111:2*
Lord God Almighty. *Amos 3:13*
Everything the Lord does is right
and true, *Psalm 145:17*
King of the nations.
4 Everyone will respect you, Lord, *Jeremiah 10:7*
and will honor you.
Only you are holy.
All the nations will come
and worship you, *Psalm 86:9-10*
because the right things you have
done
are now made known." *Deuteronomy 32:4*

5 After this I saw that the temple
(the Tent of the Agreement) in
heaven was opened. 6 And the seven
angels bringing the seven disasters
came out of the temple. They were
dressed in clean, shining linen and
wore golden bands tied around their
chests. 7 Then one of the four living
creatures gave to the seven angels
seven golden bowls filled with the
anger of God, who lives forever and
ever. 8 The temple was filled with
smoke from the glory and the power
of God, and no one could enter the
temple until the seven disasters of
the seven angels were finished.

The Bowls of God's Anger

16 Then I heard a loud voice from
the temple saying to the seven
angels, "Go and pour out the seven
bowls of God's anger on the earth."
2 The first angel left and poured
out his bowl on the land. Then ugly
and painful sores came upon all
those who had the mark of the beast
and who worshiped his idol.
3 The second angel poured out his
bowl on the sea, and it became blood
like that of a dead man, and every
living thing in the sea died.
4 The third angel poured out his
bowl on the rivers and the springs of
water, and they became blood. 5 Then
I heard the angel of the waters saying:

"Holy One, you are the One who
is and who was.
You are right to decide to
punish these evil people.
6 They have poured out the blood
of your holy people and
your prophets.
So now you have given them
blood to drink as they
deserve."

7 And I heard a voice coming from
the altar saying:

"Yes, Lord God Almighty,
the way you punish evil people
is right and fair."

[8]The fourth angel poured out his
bowl on the sun, and he was given
power to burn the people with fire.
[9]They were burned by the great
heat, and they cursed the name of
God, who had control over these disasters. But the people refused to
change their hearts and lives and
give glory to God.
[10]The fifth angel poured out his
bowl on the throne of the beast, and
darkness covered its kingdom.
People gnawed their tongues because of the pain. [11]They also cursed
the God of heaven because of their
pain and the sores they had, but they
refused to change their hearts and
turn away from the evil things they
did.

OLD TESTAMENT READING

The LORD saw this and rejected
them;
his sons and daughters had
made him angry.
[20]He said, "I will turn away from
them
and see what will happen to
them.
They are evil people,
unfaithful children.

[23]"I will pile troubles upon them
and shoot my arrows at them.
[24]They will be starved and sick,
destroyed by terrible diseases.
I will send them vicious animals
and gliding, poisonous snakes."

Deuteronomy 32:19–20, 23–24

INSIGHTS

How glorious must He [Christ] have been in the eyes of seraphs, when a cloud received Him out of mortal sight, and He ascended up to heaven! Now He wears the glory which He had with God or ever the earth was, and yet another glory above all—that which He has well earned in the fight against sin, death, and hell. As victor He wears the illustrious crown. . . . He wears the glory of an Intercessor who can never fail, of a Prince who can never be defeated, of a Conqueror who has vanquished every foe, of a Lord who has the heart's allegiance of every subject. Jesus wears all the glory which the pomp of heaven can bestow upon Him, which ten thousand times ten thousand angels can minister to Him. You cannot with your utmost stretch of imagination conceive His exceeding greatness; yet there will be a further revelation of it when He shall descend from heaven in great power, with all the holy angels—"Then shall He sit upon the throne of His glory." Oh, the splendour of that glory! It will ravish His people's hearts. Nor is this the close, for eternity shall sound His praise, "Thy throne, O God, is for ever and ever!" Reader, if you would joy in Christ's glory hereafter, He must be glorious in your sight now. Is He so?

Charles Spurgeon

APPLICATION

Study the contrasts between the praises of God's people and the evil of those who reject God and his salvation. On which side of the battle will you stand firm? Do you delight to sing God's praises?

WEEKEND

God Reveals His Holiness Through His Anger Against Evil

Revelation 16:12—17:8

The sixth angel poured out his bowl on the great river Euphrates so that the water in the river was dried up to prepare the way for the kings from the east to come. [13]Then I saw three evil spirits that looked like frogs coming out of the mouth of the dragon, out of the mouth of the beast, and out of the mouth of the false prophet. [14]These evil spirits are the spirits of demons, which have power to do miracles. They go out to the kings of the whole world to gather them together for the battle on the great day of God Almighty.

[15]"Listen! I will come as a thief comes! Happy are those who stay awake and keep their clothes on so that they will not walk around naked and have people see their shame."

[16]Then the evil spirits gathered the kings together to the place that is called Armageddon in the Hebrew language.

[17]The seventh angel poured out his bowl into the air. Then a loud voice came out of the temple from the throne, saying, "It is finished!" [18]Then there were flashes of lightning, noises, thunder, and a big earthquake—the worst earthquake that has ever happened since people have been on earth. [19]The great city split into three parts, and the cities of the nations were destroyed. And God remembered the sins of Babylon the Great, so he gave that city the cup filled with the wine of his terrible anger. [20]Then every island ran away, and mountains disappeared. [21]Giant hailstones, each weighing about a hundred pounds, fell from the sky upon people. People cursed God for the disaster of the hail, because this disaster was so terrible.

The Woman on the Animal

17 Then one of the seven angels who had the seven bowls came and spoke to me. He said, "Come, and I will show you the punishment that will be given to the great prostitute, the one sitting over many waters. [2]The kings of the earth sinned sexually with her, and the people of the earth became drunk from the wine of her sexual sin."

[3]Then the angel carried me away by the Spirit to the desert. There I saw a woman sitting on a red beast. It was covered with names against God written on it, and it had seven heads and ten horns. [4]The woman was dressed in purple and red and was shining with the gold, precious jewels, and pearls she was wearing. She had a golden cup in her hand, a cup filled with evil things and the uncleanness of her sexual sin. [5]On her forehead a title was written that was secret. This is what was written:

THE GREAT BABYLON
MOTHER OF PROSTITUTES
AND OF THE EVIL THINGS OF THE EARTH

[6]Then I saw that the woman was drunk with the blood of God's holy people and with the blood of those who were killed because of their faith in Jesus.

When I saw the woman, I was very amazed. [7]Then the angel said to me, "Why are you amazed? I will tell you the secret of this woman and the beast she rides—the one with seven heads and ten horns. [8]The beast you saw was once alive but is not alive now. But soon it will come up out of the bottomless pit and go away to be destroyed. There are people who live on earth whose names have not been written in the book of life since the beginning of the world. They will be amazed when they see the beast, because he was once alive, is not alive now, but will come again."

OLD TESTAMENT READING

This is what will happen: On the day Gog attacks the land of Israel, [19]I will become very angry, says the Lord God. With jealousy and great anger I tell you that at that time there will surely be a great earthquake in Israel. [20]The fish of the sea, the birds of the sky, the wild animals, everything that crawls on the ground, and all the people on the earth will shake with fear before me. Also the mountains will be thrown down, the cliffs will fall, and every wall will fall to the ground. [21]Then I will call for a war against Gog on all my mountains, says the Lord God. Everyone's sword will attack the soldier next to him. [22]I will punish Gog with disease and death. I will send a heavy rain with hailstones and burning sulfur on Gog, his army, and the many nations with him. [23]Then I will show how great I am. I will show my holiness, and I will make myself known to the many nations that watch. Then they will know that I am the Lord.'"

Ezekiel 38:18–23

INSIGHTS

If men and women will not yield to the love of God, and be changed by the grace of God, then there is no way for them to escape the wrath of God.

Rank and wealth will not deliver anyone in that terrible day. John's list included kings, captains, and slaves, the rich and the poor. "Who shall be able to stand?"

. . . We are so accustomed to emphasizing the meekness and gentleness of Christ (Matt. 11:28–30) that we forget His holiness and justice. The same Christ who welcomed the children in the temple also drove merchants from that same temple. God's wrath is not like a child's temper tantrum or punishment meted out by an impatient parent. God's wrath is the evidence of His holy love for all that is right and His holy hatred for all that is evil. Only a soft and sentimental person would want to worship a God who did not deal justly with evil in the world.

Warren Wiersbe

PAUSE FOR REFLECTION

What are God's purposes in punishing the evil nations? How will the people on earth respond when the last of God's angels pours out his anger? Pray that God will give you greater insight into his perfect holiness as you study these passages.

MONDAY

God Calls His People to Run Away from Evil

Revelation 17:9—18:10

You need a wise mind to understand
this. The seven heads on the beast
are seven mountains where the
woman sits. 10 And they are seven
kings. Five of the kings have already
been destroyed, one of the kings
lives now, and another has not yet
come. When he comes, he must stay
a short time. 11 The beast that was
once alive, but is not alive now, is
also an eighth king. He belongs to
the first seven kings, and he will go
away to be destroyed.

12 "The ten horns you saw are ten
kings who have not yet begun to
rule, but they will receive power to
rule with the beast for one hour. 13 All
ten of these kings have the same
purpose, and they will give their
power and authority to the beast.
14 They will make war against the
Lamb, but the Lamb will defeat
them, because he is Lord of lords
and King of kings. He will defeat
them with his called, chosen, and
faithful followers."

15 Then the angel said to me, "The
waters that you saw, where the prostitute sits, are peoples, races, nations, and languages. 16 The ten
horns and the beast you saw will
hate the prostitute. They will take
everything she has and leave her
naked. They will eat her body and
burn her with fire. 17 God made the
ten horns want to carry out his purpose by agreeing to give the beast
their power to rule, until what God
has said comes about. 18 The woman
you saw is the great city that rules
over the kings of the earth."

Babylon Is Destroyed

18 After the vision of these
things, I saw another angel
coming down from heaven. This angel had great power, and his glory
made the earth bright. 2 He shouted
in a powerful voice:

"Ruined, ruined is the great city
of Babylon!
She has become a home for
demons
and a prison for every evil spirit,
and a prison for every unclean
bird and unclean beast.
3 She has been ruined, because all
the peoples of the earth
have drunk the wine of the
desire of her sexual sin.
She has been ruined also because
the kings of the earth
have sinned sexually with her,
and the merchants of the earth
have grown rich from the great
wealth of her luxury."

4 Then I heard another voice from
heaven saying:

"Come out of that city, my people,
so that you will not share in
her sins,
so that you will not receive the
disasters that will come to her.
5 Her sins have piled up as high as
the sky,
and God has not forgotten the
wrongs she has done.
6 Give that city the same as she
gave to others.
Pay her back twice as much as
she did.
Prepare wine for her that is twice
as strong

as the wine she prepared for
others.
7 She gave herself much glory and
rich living.
Give her that much suffering
and sadness.
She says to herself, 'I am a queen
sitting on my throne.
I am not a widow; I will never
be sad.'
8 So these disasters will come to
her in one day:
death, and crying, and great
hunger,
and she will be destroyed by fire,
because the Lord God who
judges her is powerful."
9 The kings of the earth who
sinned sexually with her and shared
her wealth will see the smoke from
her burning. Then they will cry and
be sad because of her death. 10 They
will be afraid of her suffering and
stand far away and say:
"Terrible! How terrible for you,
great city,
powerful city of Babylon,
because your punishment has
come in one hour!"

OLD TESTAMENT READING

At dawn the next morning, the angels begged Lot to hurry. They said, "Go! Take your wife and your two daughters with you so you will not be destroyed when the city is punished."

Genesis 19:15

INSIGHTS

Through our union with Christ in His death we are delivered from the dominion of sin. But we still find sin struggling to gain mastery over us. . . . We may not like the fact that we have this lifelong struggle with sin, but the more we realize and accept it, the better equipped we will be to deal with it. . . .

The Bible tells us that the heart is deceitful and unsearchable to any but God alone (Jeremiah 17:9–10). Even as believers we do not know our own hearts (1 Corinthians 4:3–5). . . .

Knowing that indwelling sin occupies a heart that is deceitful and unsearchable should make us extremely wary. . . .

. . . Though sin no longer has dominion over us, it wages its guerrilla warfare against us. If left unchecked, it will defeat us. Our recourse against this warfare is to deal swiftly and firmly with the first motions of indwelling sin. . . .

. . . We must never consider that our fight against sin is at an end. The heart is unsearchable, our evil desires are insatiable, and our reason is constantly in danger of being deceived. Well did Jesus say, "Watch and pray so that you will not fall into temptation" (Matthew 26:41).

Jerry Bridges

APPLICATION

Why is it important for God's people to do everything they can to separate themselves from sin? What punishment will come to those who linger when God tells them to run? Are you listening for his warning?

TUESDAY

God Will Punish Babylon

Revelation 18:11–24

And the merchants of the earth will
cry and be sad about her, because
now there is no one to buy their cargoes—12 cargoes of gold, silver, jewels, pearls, fine linen, purple cloth,
silk, red cloth; all kinds of citron
wood and all kinds of things made
from ivory, expensive wood, bronze,
iron, and marble; 13 cinnamon, spice,
incense, myrrh, frankincense, wine,
olive oil, fine flour, wheat, cattle,
sheep, horses, carriages, slaves, and
human lives.

14 The merchants will say,

"Babylon, the good things you
wanted are gone from you.
All your rich and fancy things
have disappeared.
You will never have them again."

15 The merchants who became rich
from selling to her will be afraid of her
suffering and will stand far away. They
will cry and be sad 16 and say:

"Terrible! How terrible for the
great city!
She was dressed in fine linen,
purple and red cloth,
and she was shining with gold,
precious jewels, and pearls!
17 All these riches have been
destroyed in one hour!"

Every sea captain, every passen-
ger, the sailors, and all those who
earn their living from the sea stood
far away from Babylon. 18 As they
saw the smoke from her burning,
they cried out loudly, "There was
never a city like this great city!"
19 And they threw dust on their heads
and cried out, weeping and being
sad. They said:

"Terrible! How terrible for the
great city!
All the people who had ships on
the sea
became rich because of her
wealth!
But she has been destroyed in
one hour!
20 Be happy because of this, heaven!
Be happy, God's holy people
and apostles and prophets!
God has punished her because of
what she did to you."

21 Then a powerful angel picked
up a large stone, like one used for
grinding grain, and threw it into the
sea. He said:

"In the same way, the great city of
Babylon will be thrown down,
and it will never be found again.
22 The music of people playing
harps and other instru-
ments, flutes, and trumpets,
will never be heard in you again.
No workman doing any job
will ever be found in you again.
The sound of grinding grain
will never be heard in you
again.
23 The light of a lamp
will never shine in you again,
and the voices of a bridegroom
and bride
will never be heard in you
again.
Your merchants were the world's
great people,
and all the nations were
tricked by your magic.
24 You are guilty of the death of the
prophets and God's holy
people
and all who have been killed
on earth."

OLD TESTAMENT READING

The LORD says,
"Babylon, you are a destroying
mountain,
and I am against you.
You have destroyed the whole
land.
I will put my hand out against
you.
I will roll you off the cliffs,
and I will make you a burned-
out mountain.
26 People will not find any rocks in
Babylon big enough for
cornerstones.
People will not take any rocks
from Babylon to use for the
foundation of a building,
because your city will be just a
pile of ruins forever," says
the LORD.

36 So this is what the LORD says:
"I will soon defend you, Judah,
and make sure that Babylon is
punished."

Jeremiah 51:25–26, 36a

INSIGHTS

In spite of what people often think, no one is getting away with anything. Payday someday! God's vengeance will be revealed, even against false religion in whose name and under whose influence millions have suffered and died. God's judgment will fall and vindicate His people. . . .

The extent of Babylon's payment: The law of retribution is applied; what we sow, we shall reap. It is doubled to emphasize the enormity of the woman's sins and the justice behind her judgment and fall. The "cup which she has mixed," containing the wine of her wrath against the people of God, is now mixed for her with a double portion of God's wrath (14:10).

The experience of Babylon's sorrow: Like so many unbelievers today, this woman believes she will never experience sorrow or torment for her lifestyle and luxurious living. She boasts "I sit as queen, and am no widow." After all, she reasons, the kings of the earth are her lovers. But she is a widow in that God has forsaken her. . . .

Two things characterize the harlot's lifestyle: self-glorification and sensuous living. For this, she will receive torment and sorrow. So will all who choose to follow her path. . . .

The hunger for achievement and accumulation of wealth remains as the dominant factor of people's lifestyles and desires. The "fools" of this world are found daily in every marketplace and place of business. . . . But judgment day is coming! The merchants of the world, along with the kings of the earth, will mourn the sudden destruction of the woman who helped them become prosperous.

David Hocking

PAUSE FOR REFLECTION

Why is God against Babylon? Why will the people of earth mourn the destruction of Babylon? What does her defeat symbolize? Where is your heart's loyalty? Will you shed even one tear over Babylon's loss?

WEDNESDAY

All the People of Heaven Worship God!

Revelation 19:1–16

People in Heaven Praise God

19 After this vision and announcement I heard what sounded like a great many people in heaven saying:

"Hallelujah!
Salvation, glory, and power
belong to our God,
2 because his judgments are
true and right.
He has punished the prostitute
who made the earth evil with
her sexual sin.
He has paid her back for the
death of his servants."

3 Again they said:
"Hallelujah!
She is burning, and her smoke
will rise forever and ever."

4 Then the twenty-four elders and the four living creatures bowed down and worshiped God, who sits on the throne. They said:
"Amen, Hallelujah!"

5 Then a voice came from the throne, saying:
"Praise our God, all you who
serve him
and all you who honor him,
both small and great!"

6 Then I heard what sounded like a great many people, like the noise of flooding water, and like the noise of loud thunder. The people were saying:
"Hallelujah!
Our Lord God, the Almighty,
rules.
7 Let us rejoice and be happy
and give God glory,
because the wedding of the Lamb
has come,
and the Lamb's bride has made
herself ready
8 Fine linen, bright and clean, was
given to her to wear."

(The fine linen means the good things done by God's holy people.)

9 And the angel said to me, "Write this: Happy are those who have been invited to the wedding meal of the Lamb!" And the angel said, "These are the true words of God."

10 Then I bowed down at the angel's feet to worship him, but he said to me, "Do not worship me! I am a servant like you and your brothers and sisters who have the message of Jesus. Worship God, because the message about Jesus is the spirit that gives all prophecy."

The Rider on the White Horse

Then I saw heaven opened, and there
before me was a white horse. The
rider on the horse is called Faithful
and True, and he is right when he
judges and makes war. 12 His eyes are
like burning fire, and on his head are
many crowns. He has a name written
on him, which no one but himself
knows. 13 He is dressed in a robe
dipped in blood, and his name is the
Word of God. 14 The armies of heaven,
dressed in fine linen, white and clean,
were following him on white horses.
15 Out of the rider's mouth comes a
sharp sword that he will use to defeat
the nations, and he will rule them with
a rod of iron. He will crush out the
wine in the winepress of the terrible
anger of God the Almighty. 16 On his
robe and on his upper leg was written

this name: KING OF KINGS AND LORD OF LORDS.

OLD TESTAMENT READING

Are there any gods like you,
LORD?
There are no gods like you.
You are wonderfully holy,
amazingly powerful,
a worker of miracles.
12 You reached out with your right
hand,
and the earth swallowed our
enemies.
13 You keep your loving promise
and lead the people you have
saved.
With your strength you will guide
them
to your holy place.

17 "You will lead your people and
place them
on your very own mountain,
the place that you, LORD, made for
yourself to live,
the temple, Lord, that your
hands have made.
18 The LORD will be king forever!"

Exodus 15:11–13, 17–18

INSIGHTS

There is a party in heaven because the party that meant destruction for so many has been ended. A new celebration sponsored by God has gotten under way. According to this scripture, those allied with the Lamb of God cannot help but shout, "Hallelujah!" at this incredible turn of events. . . .

. . . Many of the most credible biblical scholars have agreed that Babylon in the Book of Revelation always refers to the dominant society in which Christians have to live. . . .

. . . When our Babylon falls (and it, like all Babylons, will one day fall), how will you react? Will you react like the merchants described in Revelation 18:3 who "grew rich from her excessive luxuries" and those political potentates who conspired with her to exploit the weak and the poor? Or will you be able to join the angels on that day and sing praises to God?

. . . Have you given your time and energy to get those things that go with living in Babylon so that, when it falls, all that you have ever worked for will fall with it? Or have you so invested your life in the Kingdom of God that, even if heaven and earth shall pass away, what is important to you will endure? In the end, will you be able to shout and sing in that eternal party that will be shared by those who have laid up their treasures in heaven (Matt. 6:19–21)?

Tony Campolo

PAUSE FOR REFLECTION

Reread the praises to God in these passages—several times, if you'd like. Can you imagine anything more wonderful than praising God in heaven? Have you accepted your invitation to join his everlasting party?

THURSDAY

God's Triumph over Satan and Sin Is Complete

Revelation 19:17—20:15

Then I saw an angel standing in the sun, and he called with a loud voice to all the birds flying in the sky: "Come and gather together for the great feast of God 18 so that you can eat the bodies of kings, generals, mighty people, horses and their riders, and the bodies of all people—free, slave, small, and great."

19 Then I saw the beast and the kings of the earth. Their armies were gathered together to make war against the rider on the horse and his army. 20 But the beast was captured and with him the false prophet who did the miracles for the beast. The false prophet had used these miracles to trick those who had the mark of the beast and worshiped his idol. The false prophet and the beast were thrown alive into the lake of fire that burns with sulfur. 21 And their armies were killed with the sword that came out of the mouth of the rider on the horse, and all the birds ate the bodies until they were full.

The Thousand Years

20 I saw an angel coming down from heaven. He had the key to the bottomless pit and a large chain in his hand. 2 The angel grabbed the dragon, that old snake who is the devil and Satan, and tied him up for a thousand years. 3 Then he threw him into the bottomless pit, closed it, and locked it over him. The angel did this so he could not trick the people of the earth anymore until the thousand years were ended. After a thousand years he must be set free for a short time.

4 Then I saw some thrones and people sitting on them who had been given the power to judge. And I saw the souls of those who had been killed because they were faithful to the message of Jesus and the message from God. They had not worshiped the beast or his idol, and they had not received the mark of the beast on their foreheads or on their hands. They came back to life and ruled with Christ for a thousand years. 5 (The others that were dead did not live again until the thousand years were ended.) This is the first raising of the dead. 6 Happy and holy are those who share in this first raising of the dead. The second death has no power over them. They will be priests for God and for Christ and will rule with him for a thousand years.

7 When the thousand years are over, Satan will be set free from his prison. 8 Then he will go out to trick the nations in all the earth—Gog and Magog—to gather them for battle. There are so many people they will be like sand on the seashore. 9 And Satan's army marched across the earth and gathered around the camp of God's people and the city God loves. But fire came down from heaven and burned them up. 10 And Satan, who tricked them, was thrown into the lake of burning sulfur with the beast and the false prophet. There they will be punished day and night forever and ever.

People of the World Are Judged

Then I saw a great white throne

and the One who was sitting on it.
Earth and sky ran away from him
and disappeared. 12 And I saw the
dead, great and small, standing before the throne. Then books were
opened, and the book of life was
opened. The dead were judged by
what they had done, which was written in the books. 13 The sea gave up
the dead who were in it, and Death
and Hades gave up the dead who
were in them. Each person was
judged by what he had done. 14 And
Death and Hades were thrown into
the lake of fire. The lake of fire is
the second death. 15 And anyone
whose name was not found written
in the book of life was thrown into
the lake of fire.

OLD TESTAMENT READING

Human, prophesy against Gog
and say, 'This is what the Lord God
says: I am against you, Gog, chief
ruler of Meshech and Tubal. 4 You,
all your troops, and the nations
with you will fall dead on the mountains of Israel. I will let you be food
for every bird that eats meat and
every wild animal. 5 You will lie
fallen on the ground, because I
have spoken, says the Lord God. 6 I
will send fire on Magog and those
who live in safety on the coastlands.
Then they will know that I am the
Lord.

7 "'I will make myself known
among my people Israel, and I will
not let myself be dishonored anymore. Then the nations will know
that I am the Lord, the Holy One in
Israel. 8 It is coming! It will happen,
says the Lord God. The time I talked
about is coming.'"

Ezekiel 39:1, 4–8

INSIGHTS

For thousands of years, Satan has seduced nations and people into thinking that they can build a world of peace and love without Christ. Sometimes he has deceived people into thinking that education or money would solve personal problems. But his dirty work is over, for a time. At the end of the thousand years "he must be set free for a short time" (Revelation 20:3).

During the Millennium, believers will continue to populate the earth. However, their offspring, living in an ideal environment with King Jesus as the loving, benevolent ruler, can still rebel against God, and some will.

When Satan is released for a time, he will gather some of his old cohorts, Gog and Magog, the nations that hated Israel, and march on Jerusalem once more. This battle will not last long, for fire will come down from heaven and zap them. Then Satan will have his final place of unrest; he will be thrown "into the lake of burning sulfur, where the beast and the false prophet had been thrown. They will be tormented day and night for ever and ever" (Revelation 20:10).

David Jeremiah

APPLICATION

What amazing events are promised for future times in this portion of Scripture? What is the penalty for those who are not faithful to God? Pray that you, no matter what happens in your lifetime, will remain faithful to your Lord.

FRIDAY

God Makes All Things New and Comes to Live with His People

Revelation 21:1–27

The New Jerusalem

21 Then I saw a new heaven and
a new earth. The first heaven
and the first earth had disappeared,
and there was no sea anymore. 2 And
I saw the holy city, the new Jerusalem,
coming down out of heaven from God.
It was prepared like a bride dressed
for her husband. 3 And I heard a loud
voice from the throne, saying, "Now
God's presence is with people, and he
will live with them, and they will be
his people. God himself will be with
them and will be their God. 4 He will
wipe away every tear from their eyes,
and there will be no more death, sadness, crying, or pain, because all the
old ways are gone."

5 The One who was sitting on the
throne said, "Look! I am making everything new!" Then he said, "Write
this, because these words are true
and can be trusted."

6 The One on the throne said to
me, "It is finished. I am the Alpha
and the Omega, the Beginning and
the End. I will give free water from
the spring of the water of life to anyone who is thirsty. 7 Those who win
the victory will receive this, and I will
be their God, and they will be my
children. 8 But cowards, those who
refuse to believe, who do evil things,
who kill, who sin sexually, who do
evil magic, who worship idols, and
who tell lies—all these will have a
place in the lake of burning sulfur.
This is the second death."

9 Then one of the seven angels
who had the seven bowls full of the
seven last troubles came to me, saying, "Come with me, and I will show
you the bride, the wife of the Lamb."
10 And the angel carried me away by
the Spirit to a very large and high
mountain. He showed me the holy
city, Jerusalem, coming down out of
heaven from God. 11 It was shining
with the glory of God and was bright
like a very expensive jewel, like a jasper, clear as crystal. 12 The city had
a great high wall with twelve gates
with twelve angels at the gates, and
on each gate was written the name
of one of the twelve tribes of Israel.
13 There were three gates on the
east, three on the north, three on the
south, and three on the west. 14 The
walls of the city were built on twelve
foundation stones, and on the stones
were written the names of the twelve
apostles of the Lamb.

15 The angel who talked with me
had a measuring rod made of gold
to measure the city, its gates, and its
wall. 16 The city was built in a square,
and its length was equal to its width.
The angel measured the city with
the rod. The city was twelve thousand stadia long, twelve thousand
stadia wide, and twelve thousand stadia high. 17 The angel also measured
the wall. It was one hundred forty-
four cubits high, by human measure-
ments, which the angel was using.
18 The wall was made of jasper, and
the city was made of pure gold, as
pure as glass. 19 The foundation
stones of the city walls were decorated with every kind of jewel. The
first foundation was jasper, the second was sapphire, the third was chal-

cedony, the fourth was emerald,
[20] the fifth was onyx, the sixth was carnelian, the seventh was chrysolite, the eighthy was beryl, the ninth was topaz, the tenth was chrysoprase, the eleventh was jacinth, and the twelfth was amethyst.
[21] The twelve gates were twelve pearls, each gate having been made from a single pearl. And the street of the city was made of pure gold as clear as glass.

[22] I did not see a temple in the city, because the Lord God Almighty and the Lamb are the city's temple.
[23] The city does not need the sun or the moon to shine on it, because the glory of God is its light, and the Lamb is the city's lamp.
[24] By its light the people of the world will walk, and the kings of the earth will bring their glory into it.
[25] The city's gates will never be shut on any day, because there is no night there.
[26] The glory and the honor of the nations will be brought into it.
[27] Nothing unclean and no one who does shameful things or tells lies will ever go into it. Only those whose names are written in the Lamb's book of life will enter the city.

OLD TESTAMENT READING

Shout and be glad, Jerusalem. I am coming, and I will live among you," says the LORD.
[11] "At that time people from many nations will join with the LORD and will become my people. Then I will live among you, and you will know that the LORD All-Powerful has sent me to you.
[12] The LORD will take Judah as his own part of the holy land, and Jerusalem will be his chosen city again.
[13] Be silent, everyone, in the presence of the LORD. He is coming out of the holy place where he lives."

Zechariah 2:10–13

INSIGHTS

The longing for a future glorious city of God can be traced back as far as the Old Testament patriarchs. Abraham ". . . was looking forward to the city with foundations, whose architect and builder is God" (Hebrews 11:10).

Paul mentioned this city in his letter to the Galatians. He called it "the Jerusalem which is above" (Galatians 4:26).

The "New Jerusalem" (Revelation 21:2; 3:12) is just one of the several names given to this future city of God. It is also called The Holy City, the Heavenly Jerusalem, and Mount Zion. Whatever it is named, it will be a holy and beautiful place, more perfect than the Garden of Eden. . . .

Jesus is preparing the New Jerusalem for us now. . . .

. . . His light will be among us forevermore.

In our eternal home there will be no sadness, no more tears. . . .

. . . For all eternity He will be with us and we will know and see Him.

David Jeremiah

ACTION POINT

Study what God promises to his children in the New Jerusalem. Do you have any doubts that God deeply loves you and fully knows your every pain and sorrow? Trust your heavenly Father's promise. Thank him for his goodness.

WEEKEND

Come to the Water of Life, for Jesus Is Coming Soon

Revelation 22:1–21

22 Then the angel showed me
the river of the water of life.
It was shining like crystal and was
flowing from the throne of God and
of the Lamb 2 down the middle of the
street of the city. The tree of life was
on each side of the river. It produces
fruit twelve times a year, once each
month. The leaves of the tree are for
the healing of all the nations. 3 Nothing that God judges guilty will be in
that city. The throne of God and of
the Lamb will be there, and God's
servants will worship him. 4 They
will see his face, and his name will
be written on their foreheads.
5 There will never be night again.
They will not need the light of a lamp
or the light of the sun, because the
Lord God will give them light. And
they will rule as kings forever and
ever.
6 The angel said to me, "These
words can be trusted and are true."
The Lord, the God of the spirits of
the prophets, sent his angel to show
his servants the things that must
happen soon.
7 "Listen! I am coming soon!
Happy is the one who obeys the
words of prophecy in this book."
8 I, John, am the one who heard
and saw these things. When I heard
and saw them, I bowed down to worship at the feet of the angel who
showed these things to me. 9 But the
angel said to me, "Do not worship
me! I am a servant like you, your
brothers the prophets, and all those
who obey the words in this book.
Worship God!"
10 Then the angel told me, "Do not
keep secret the words of prophecy
in this book, because the time is near
for all this to happen. 11 Let whoever
is doing evil continue to do evil. Let
whoever is unclean continue to be
unclean. Let whoever is doing right
continue to do right. Let whoever is
holy continue to be holy."
12 "Listen! I am coming soon! I will
bring my reward with me, and I
will repay each one of you for what
you have done. 13 I am the Alpha and
the Omega, the First and the Last,
the Beginning and the End.
14 "Happy are those who wash
their robes so that they will receive
the right to eat the fruit from the tree
of life and may go through the gates
into the city. 15 Outside the city are
the evil people, those who do evil
magic, who sin sexually, who murder, who worship idols, and who love
lies and tell lies.
16 "I, Jesus, have sent my angel to
tell you these things for the
churches. I am the descendant from
the family of David, and I am the
bright morning star."
17 The Spirit and the bride say,
"Come!" Let the one who hears this
say, "Come!" Let whoever is thirsty
come; whoever wishes may have the
water of life as a free gift.
18 I warn everyone who hears the
words of the prophecy of this book:
If anyone adds anything to these
words, God will add to that person
the disasters written about in this
book. 19 And if anyone takes away
from the words of this book of
prophecy, God will take away that
one's share of the tree of life and of

the holy city, which are written about
in this book.

20 Jesus, the One who says these
things are true, says, "Yes, I am coming soon."

Amen. Come, Lord Jesus!

21 The grace of the Lord Jesus be
with all. Amen.

OLD TESTAMENT READING

The LORD says, "All you who are thirsty,
come and drink.
Those of you who do not have money,
come, buy and eat!
Come buy wine and milk
without money and without cost.
3 Come to me and listen;
listen to me so you may live."

Isaiah 55:1, 3a

There is a river that brings joy to the city of God,
the holy place where God Most High lives.
5 God is in that city, and so it will not be shaken.

Psalm 46:4–5a

INSIGHTS

Come celebrate the living water that flows for you from an eternal spring. You need not fear stagnation. You need only draw nearer—put your roots down deep, settle in, and be at home in My love. Then every day will be a new day. Every day you will wonder at the richness of life that has come to you by My grace. Every day you will watch eagerly for My sunrise, search eagerly for My presence in the mundane activities of your world. Every day you will know Me better, and every day you will want to know Me more.

And every day you will live in joyful anticipation of My presence. You will think of My love for you as it is now, and as it will be on that day when I carry you across the threshold into the New Jerusalem—the home I am preparing for you.

Every day you will count the days until the wedding, when you and I will sit down together at the marriage supper of the Lamb. . . .

On that day, child, I will call you by a new name. You will be a crown of splendor in My hand, a royal diadem in the hand of your God. I will delight in you, I will rejoice over you as a bridegroom rejoices over his bride.

Come to the spring and drink deeply of My love. Let it flow over you, bringing a foretaste of that day when the river of life will flow for you through the New Jerusalem and love will be forever fresh.

Until then, turn from your fears and relax in My love. Here at the source you will find your renewal.

Ruth Senter

PAUSE FOR REFLECTION

What to you is the most meaningful aspect of God's salvation, of his endless river of life? Meditate on this glorious gift. Thank him for what he has done for you and for anyone who will forsake sin and come to him.

INDEX

ACKNOWLEDGMENTS

Alcorn, Randy C., taken from *Sexual Temptation.* © 1989 by Randy Alcorn. Used by permission of InterVarsity Press, P.O. Box 1400, Downers Grove, IL 60515.

Anderson, Lynn, *Finding the Heart to Go On,* Here's Life Publishers, San Bernadino, CA, © 1991.

Arnold, Duane W. H., taken from the book *Prayers of the Martyrs.* Copyright © 1991 by Duane W. H. Arnold. Used by permission of Zondervan Publishing House.

Augsburger, David W., taken from *Freedom of Forgiveness.* Copyright ©1970, 1988. Moody Bible Institute of Chicago. Moody Press. Used by permission.

Avila, St. Theresa of, from the book *A Life of Prayer,* copyright 1983 by Multnomah Press. Published by Multnomah Press, Portland, Oregon, 97206. Used by permission.

Babcock, Maltbie, *This Is My Father's World* in *The Hymnal for Worship and Celebration,* copyright © 1986, Word Music, Waco, Texas.

Barna, George, *The Frog in the Kettle,* copyright © 1990 by Regal Books, a division of Gospel Light Publications. Used by permission.

Baxter, J. Sidlow, taken from the book *Awake My Heart.* Copyright © 1959 by J. Sidlow Baxter. Used by permission of the Zondervan Publishing House.

Beals, Art, *Beyond Hunger,* copyright © 1985, Multnomah Press, Portland, Oregon 97266.

Beckwith, Mary, *Still Moments,* copyright © 1989 by Regal Books, a division of Gospel Light Publications. Used by permission.

Blue, Ron, *Master Your Money,* copyright © 1986, Thomas Nelson Publishers, Nashville, TN.

Boice, James Montgomery, taken from *The Parables of Jesus.* Copyright © 1983. Moody Bible Institute of Chicago. Moody Press. Used by permission.

Bridges, Jerry, *The Practice of Godliness,* copyright © 1983 by Jerry Bridges, NavPress, Colorado Springs, Colorado.

Bridges, Jerry, *The Pursuit of Holiness,* copyright © 1978 by the Navigators, NavPress, Colorado Springs, Colorado.

Bright, Bill, *Promises — A Daily Guide to Supernatural Living,* Here's Life Publishers, San Bernadino, CA, © 1983.

Bright, Bill, *The Secret: How to Live with Purpose and Power,* Here's Life Publishers, San Bernadino, CA, © 1989.

Briscoe, Jill, *Running on Empty,* copyright © 1988, Word, Inc., Dallas, Texas.

Bruce, F. F., taken from *The Hard Sayings of Jesus.* © 1983 by F. F. Bruce. Used by permission of InterVarsity Press, P.O. Box 1400, Downers Grove, IL 60515. Worldwide permission granted by Hodder & Stoughton Limited, England.

Bryant, Al, (Compiler) *Day By Day With C. H. Spurgeon,* copyright © 1980, Word, Inc., Dallas, Texas.

Bryant, Al, *Keep in Touch,* copyright © 1981, Word, Inc., Dallas, Texas.

Bryant, Al, *Strength for the Day: Daily Meditations with F. B. Meyer,* copyright © 1979, Word, Inc., Dallas, Texas.

Buechner, Frederick, excerpt from *Wishful Thinking.* Copyright © 1973 by Frederick Buechner. Reprinted by permission of HarperCollins Publishers.

Calkins, Ruth Harms, from *Tell Me Again Lord, I Forget,* © 1974. Used by permission of Tyndale House Publishers, Inc. All rights reserved.

Campolo, Anthony, *The Kingdom of God is a Party,* copyright © 1990, Word, Inc., Dallas, Texas.

Campolo, Anthony, *Who Switched the Price Tags?,* copyright © 1986, Word, Inc., Dallas, Texas.

Chapian, Marie, *Discovering Joy,* Bethany House Publishers, © 1990.

Chisholm, Thomas O. (Words) and Runyan, William M. (Music), *Great Is Thy Faithfulness* in *The Hymnal for Worship and Celebration,* copyright © 1923. Renewal 1951 by Hope Publishing Co., Carol Stream, IL 60188. All rights reserved. Used by permission.

Crabb, Rachael, *The Personal Touch,* copyright © 1990 by Rachael Crabb and Raeann Hart, NavPress, Colorado Springs, Colorado.

Evans, Anthony T., taken from *America's Only Hope.* Copyright © 1990. Moody Bible Institute of Chicago. Moody Press. Used by permission.

Fickett, Harold L., *Walking What You're Talking (Principles of James),* copyright © 1988 by Regal Books, a division of Gospel Light Publications. Used by permission.

Finney, Charles G., *God's Love for a Sinning World.* © 1966 by Kregel Publications: Grand Rapids, Michigan. Used by permission.

Finney, Charles G., *Principles of Consecration,* Bethany House Publishers, © 1990.

Finney, Charles Grandison, *Principles of Devotion,* Bethany House Publishers, © 1987.

Finney, Charles G., *Victory Over the World.* © 1966 by Kregel Publications: Grand Rapids, Michigan. Used by permission.

Fletcher, William M., *The Second Greatest Commandment.* Copyright © 1983. NavPress, Colorado Springs, Colorado. (Dr. William M. Fletcher is Minister-at-Large, Rocky Mountain Conservative Baptist Association.)

Foster, Richard J., excerpts from *Celebration of Discipline.* Copyright © 1978 by Richard J. Foster. Reprinted by permission of HarperCollins Publishers.

Foster, Richard J., excerpts from *Money, Sex and Power.* Copyright © 1985 by Richard J. Foster. Reprinted by permission of HarperCollins Publishers.

Fullham, Terry L., *Thirsting,* copyright © 1989, Thomas Nelson Publishers, Nashville, TN.

Gaither, Gloria, *We Have This Moment,* copyright © 1988, Word, Inc., Dallas, Texas.

Geisler, Norman L., (Editor), *What Augustine Says,* Baker Book House, © 1982.

Gillham, Bill, *Lifetime Guarantee,* Wolgemuth & Hyatt, Publishers, Inc. Used by permission.

Graham, Billy, *Answers to Life's Problems,* copyright © 1960, 1988, Word, Inc., Dallas, Texas.

Graham, Billy, *Approaching Hoofbeats,* copyright © 1983, Word, Inc., Dallas, Texas.

Graham, Billy, *The Holy Spirit,* copyright © 1978, 1988, Word, Inc., Dallas, Texas.

Graham, Billy, *Unto the Hills: A Devotional Treasury from Billy Graham,* copyright © 1986, Word, Inc., Dallas, Texas.

Gregory, Joel C., *Growing Pains of the Soul,* copyright © 1987, Word, Inc., Dallas, Texas.

Guiness, Os, taken from *The Devil's Gauntlet.* © 1989 by Os Guiness. Used by permission of InterVarsity Press, P.O. Box 1400, Downers Grove, IL 60515.

Halverson, Richard C., *No Greater Power,* copyright © 1986, Multnomah Press, Portland, Oregon 97266.

Harris, Madalene, *Climbing Higher,* Here's Life Publishers, San Bernadino, CA, © 1989.

Hayford, Jack, from *Daybreak,* © 1984. Used by permission of Tyndale House Publishers, Inc. All rights reserved.

Hendrichson, Walter A., Reprinted by permission from *Disciples are Made — Not Born.* Published by Victor Books and © 1974 by SP Publications, Inc., Wheaton, IL.

Hendricks, Howard G. and Jeanne W., from the book *Footprints,* copyright © 1981, Multnomah Press, Portland, Oregon, 97266. (Howard Hendricks is a distinguished professor at Dallas Theological Seminary; Jeanne Hendricks is an author, mother of four, and grandmother of six.)

Hession, Roy, from *The Calvary Road,* copyright 1952 Christian Literature Crusade, London (Ft. Washington, PA and Alresford, Hants: Christian Literature Crusade). Used by permission.

Hocking, David L., from the book *The Coming World Leader,* copyright 1988 by Calvary Communications, Inc. Published by Multnomah Press, Portland, Oregon 97266. Used by permission.

Hughes, R. Kent, taken from *Ephesians,* copyright 1990. Used with permission by Good News Publishers/Crossway Books, Wheaton, IL.

Hybels, Bill, *Seven Wonders of the Spiritual World,* copyright © 1988, Word, Inc., Dallas, Texas.

Hybels, Bill, taken from *Too Busy Not to Pray.* © 1988 by Bill Hybels. Used by permission of InterVarsity Press, P.O. Box 1400, Downers Grove, IL 60515.

Jeremiah, David and Carlson, Carole C., *Escape the Coming Night,* copyright © 1990, Word, Inc., Dallas, Texas.

Johnson, Elliott and Schierbaum, Al, *Our Great and Awesome God: Meditations for Athletes.* Wolgemuth & Hyatt, Publishers, Inc. Used by permission.

Keller, W. Phillip, *A Gardener Looks at the Fruits of the Spirit,* copyright © 1986, Word, Inc., Dallas, Texas.

Keller, W. Phillip, *Salt for Society,* copyright © 1981, Word, Inc., Dallas, Texas.

Keller, W. Phillip, *Songs of My Soul,* copyright © 1989, Word, Inc., Dallas, Texas.

Keller, W. Phillip, *Taming Tension,* Baker Book House, © 1979.

Kempis, Thomas a, taken from *The Imitation of Christ.* Copyright © 1984. Moody Bible Institute of Chicago. Moody Press. Used by permission.

Kroll, Woodrow Michael, *Early in the Morning, Book Two.* Used by permission of Loizeaux Brothers, Inc., Neptune, New Jersey.

Lake, Vicki, reprinted by permission from *Firming Up Your Flabby Faith.* Published by Victor Books and © 1990 by SP Publications, Inc., Wheaton, IL.

Larson, Bruce, reprinted from *A Call to Holy Living,* copyright © 1988 Augsburg Publishing House. Used by permission of Augsburg Fortress.

Lee, Richard, *The Unfailing Promise,* copyright © 1988, Word, Inc., Dallas, Texas.

Lockerbie, Jeanette, taken from *Springtime of Faith.* Copyright © 1990. Moody Bible Institute of Chicago. Moody Press. Used by permission.

Lockyer, Herbert, *Satan: His Person and Power,* copyright © 1980, Word, Inc., Dallas, Texas.

Lucado, Max, *The Applause of Heaven,* copyright © 1990, Word, Inc., Dallas, Texas.

Lucado, Max, from the book *God Came Near,* copyright 1987 by Max Lucado. Published by Multnomah Press, Portland, Oregon 97266. Used by permission.

Lucado, Max, from *On the Anvil,* © 1985. Used by permission of Tyndale House Publishers, Inc. All rights reserved.

Luther, Martin, *A Mighty Fortress Is Our God* in *The Hymnal for Worship and Celebration,* copyright © 1986, Word Music, Waco, Texas.

MacArthur, John Jr., taken from the book *The Gospel According to Jesus.* Copyright © 1988 by John F. MacArthur, Jr. Used by permission of Zondervan Publishing House.

MacDonald, George, *Knowing the Heart of God,* Bethany House Publishers, © 1990.

MacDonald, Gordon, *Ordering Your Private World,* copyright © 1984, 1985, Thomas Nelson Publishers, Nashville, TN.

MacDonald, Gordon, *Rebuilding Your Broken World,* copyright © 1988, 1990, Thomas Nelson Publishers, Nashville, TN.

McClung, Floyd, *Holiness and the Spirit of the Age.* Copyright © 1990 by Harvest House Publishers, Eugene, OR 97402.

McClung, Floyd, taken from *Wholehearted.* © 1988, 1990 by Floyd McClung. Used by permission of InterVarsity Press, P.O. Box 1400, Downers Grove, IL 60515. Worldwide permission granted by HarperCollins Publishers, London, England.

McCullough, Donald W., taken from *Finding Happiness in the Most Unlikely Places.* © 1990 by Donald W. McCullough. Used by permission of InterVarsity Press, P.O. Box 1400, Downers Grove, IL 60515.

McKenna, David, from *Practical Christianity*; LaVonne Neff, Ron Beers, Bruce Barton, Linda Taylor, Dave Veerman, and Jim Galvin (Compilers and Editors), © 1987 by Youth for Christ/USA. Used by permission of Tyndale House Publishers. All rights reserved.

Magdalen, Margaret, taken from *Jesus, Man of Prayer.* © 1987 by Sister Margaret Magdalen. Used by permission of InterVarsity Press, P.O. Box 1400, Downers Grove, IL 60515. Worldwide permission granted by Hodder & Stoughton Limited, England.

Mains, David R., *The Sense of His Presence,* copyright © 1988, Word, Inc., Dallas, Texas.

Mains, Karen Burton, taken from the book *You Are What You Say.* Copyright © 1988 by Karen Burton Mains. Used by permission of the Zondervan Publishing House.

Merritt, James Gregory, reprinted by permission from *God's Prescription for a Healthy*

Christian. Published by Victor Books and © 1990 by SP Publications, Inc., Wheaton, IL.

Meyer, F. B., from *Devotional Commentary by F. B. Meyer* (1989) Tyndale House Publishers, Inc. Used by permission. All rights reserved.

Meyer, F. B., taken from *Our Daily Walk.* Copyright © 1951, 1972 by the Zondervan Publishing House. Used by permission.

Miley, Jeanie, *Creative Silence: Keys to the Deeper Life,* copyright © 1989, Word, Inc., Dallas, Texas.

Mitchell, John G., from the book *An Everlasting Love,* copyright 1982 by Multnomah Press. Published by Multnomah Press, Portland, Oregon 97206. Used by permission.

Moody, D. L., taken from *The Way to God and How to Find It.* Copyright © 1983. Moody Bible Institute of Chicago. Moody Press. Used by permission.

Morley, Patrick, *I Surrender.* Wolgemuth & Hyatt, Publishers, Inc. Used by permission.

Mote, Edward, *The Solid Rock* in *The Hymnal for Worship and Celebration,* copyright © 1986, Word Music, Waco, Texas.

Muggeridge, Malcolm, from *The End of Christendom,* copyright 1980 by William B. Eerdmans Publishing Co., pp. 51-54. Used by permission.

Muggeridge, Malcolm, *A Twentieth Century Testimony,* copyright © 1978, Thomas Nelson Publishers, Nashville, TN.

Murray, Andrew, from *Abide in Christ* (Ft. Washington, PA: Christian Literature Crusade).

Murray, Andrew, *The Believer's Secret of Living Like Christ,* Bethany House Publishers, © 1985.

Murray, Andrew, *The Believer's Secret of Waiting on God,* Bethany House Publishers, © 1986.

Murray, Andrew, taken from *The True Vine.* Copyright © 1983. Moody Bible Institute of Chicago. Moody Press. Used by permission.

Murray, Andrew, and Edwards, Jonathan; Parkhurst, Louis Gifford (Compiler and Editor), *The Believer's Secret of Christian Love,* Bethany House Publishers, © 1990.

Murray, Andrew, and Finney, Charles G.; Parkhurst, L. G. (Compiler and Editor), *The Believer's Secret of Spiritual Power,* Bethany House Publishers, © 1987.

Myers, Warren and Ruth, *Pray: How to Be Effective in Prayer,* copyright © 1983, Navpress, Colorado Springs, Colorado.

Oatman, Johnson Jr., *Count Your Blessings* in *The Hymnal for Worship and Celebration,* copyright © 1986, Word Music, Waco, Texas.

Ogilvie, Lloyd, *Enjoying God,* copyright © 1989, Word, Inc., Dallas, Texas.

Ogilvie, Lloyd John, taken from *Silent Strength for My Life.* Copyright © 1990 by Harvest House Publishers, Eugene, OR 97402. Used by permission.

Ortlund, Anne, *Disciplines of the Home,* copyright © 1990, Word, Inc., Dallas, Texas.

Packer, J. I., taken from *Knowing God.* © 1973 by J. I. Packer. Used by permission of InterVarsity Press, P.O. Box 1400, Downers Grove, IL 60515. Worldwide permission granted by Hodder & Stoughton Limited, England.

Packer, James and Watson, Jean, reprinted from *Your Father Loves You,* © 1986 by James Packer and Jean Watson. Used by permission of Harold Shaw Publishers, Wheaton, IL. Worldwide permission granted by Hodder & Stoughton Limited, England.

Palau, Luis, reprinted by permission from *Time to Stop Pretending.* Published by Victor Books and © 1985 by SP Publications, Inc., Wheaton, IL.

Pinnock, Clark H., from *Practical Christianity*; LaVonne Neff, Ron Beers, Bruce Barton, Linda Taylor, Dave Veerman, and Jim Galvin (Compilers and Editors), © 1987 by Youth for Christ/USA. Used by permission of Tyndale House Publishers. All rights reserved.

Pippert, Rebecca Manley, taken from *Out of the Saltshaker and Into the World.* © 1979 by Inter-Varsity Christian Fellowship of the USA. Used by permission of InterVarsity Press, P.O. Box 1400, Downers Grove, IL 60515.

Reid, David, *Devotions for Growing Christians.* Used by permission of Loizeaux Brothers, Inc., Neptune, New Jersey.

Ryrie, Charles C., reprinted by permission from *The Final Countdown.* Published by Victor Books and © 1982 by SP Publications, Inc., Wheaton, IL.

Sanders, J. Oswald, taken from *Enjoying Intimacy With God.* Copyright © 1980. Moody Bible Institute of Chicago. Moody Press. Used by permission.

Sanders, J. Oswald, taken from *Just Like Us.* Copyright © 1978. Moody Bible Institute of Chicago. Moody Press. Used by permission.

Sanders, J. Oswald, taken from *Shoe Leather Commitment.* Copyright © 1990. Moody Bible Institute of Chicago. Moody Press. Used by permission.

Schaeffer, Edith, from the book *Affliction,* copyright © 1978 by Edith Schaeffer. Used by permission of Fleming H. Revell Company.

Schaeffer, Edith, *Common Sense Christian Living,* copyright © 1983, Thomas Nelson Publishers, Nashville, TN.

Schmidt, Thomas E., taken from the book *Trying to Be Good.* Copyright © 1990 by Thomas E. Schmidt. Used by permission of the Zondervan Publishing House.

Senter, Ruth, taken from *The Attributes of God.* Copyright © 1987. Moody Bible Institute of Chicago. Moody Press. Used by permission.

Senter, Ruth, *Longing for Love,* copyright © 1991 by Ruth Senter, NavPress, Colorado Springs, Colorado.

Senter, Ruth, taken from the book *Startled by Silence.* Copyright © 1986 by Ruth Senter. Used by permission of the Zondervan Publishing House.

Shaw, Luci, reprinted from *Postcard from the Shore,* © 1985 by Luci Shaw. Used by permission of Harold Shaw Publishers, Wheaton, IL.

Sherman, Doug and Hendricks, William, *How to Succeed Where It Really Counts,* copyright © 1989 by Doug Sherman and William Hendricks, NavPress, Colorado Springs, Colorado.

Sider, Ronald J., *Rich Christians in an Age of Hunger,* copyright © 1990, Word, Inc., Dallas, Texas.

Simpson, A. B., taken from the book *Days of Heaven on Earth.* Copyright © 1984 by Christian Publications. Used by permission of the Zondervan Publishing House.

Smith, F. LaGard, *The Daily Gospels* (formerly *The Intimate Jesus*). Copyright © 1988 by Harvest House Publishers, Eugene, OR 97402.

Smith, Hannah Whitall, from the book *The Christian's Secret of a Happy Life.* Copyright © 1952 by Fleming H. Revell Company. Used by permission of Fleming H. Revell Company.

Sollenberger, Lucille Fern, *My Daily Appointment with God,* copyright © 1988, Word, Inc., Dallas, Texas.

Sproul, R. C., from *Effective Prayer,* © 1984. Used by permission of Tyndale House Publishers, Inc. All rights reserved.

Sproul, R. C., from *The Holiness of God,* © 1985. Used by permission of Tyndale House Publishers, Inc. All rights reserved.

Sproul, R. C., *One Holy Passion,* copyright © 1987, Thomas Nelson Publishers, Nashville, TN.

Spurgeon, C. H., taken from *All of Grace.* Copyright © 1984. Moody Bible Institute of Chicago. Moody Press. Used by permission.

Spurgeon, Charles H., taken from *Faith's Checkbook.* Copyright © 1987. Moody Bible Institute of Chicago. Moody Press. Used by permission.

Spurgeon, Charles H., *Morning and Evening,* copyright © 1991, Hendrickson Publishers, Inc. Peabody, MA.

Spurgeon, C. H., reprinted from *The Quotable Spurgeon,* © 1990 by Harold Shaw Publishers, Wheaton, IL. Used by permission.

Stamm, Mildred, taken from the book *Meditation Moments for Women.* Copyright © 1967 by the Zondervan Publishing House. Used by permission.

Stamm, Millie, taken from the book *Beside Still Waters.* Copyright © 1984 by Christian Women's Club. Used by permission of the Zondervan Publishing House.

Stamm, Millie, taken from the book *Be Still and Know.* Copyright © 1978 by Millie Stamm. Used by permission of the Zondervan Publishing House.

Stanley, Charles, *How to Handle Adversity,* copyright © 1989, Thomas Nelson Publishers, Nashville, TN.

Steer, Roger, reprinted from *Spiritual Secrets of George Müller,* © 1985 by Roger Steer. U.S.A. rights granted by permission of Harold Shaw Publishers, Wheaton, IL. Worldwide permission granted by Hodder & Stoughton Limited, England.

Steinberger, G., *In the Footprints of the Lamb,* Bethany House Publishers, © 1936.

Stoddard, William S., from the book *First Light,* copyright 1990 by Multnomah Press. Published by Multnomah Press, Portland, Oregon 97266. Used by permission.

Stott, John, from *Basic Christianity.* Copyright 1958, 1971. Inter-Varsity Press, London. Published in the U.S.A. by William B. Eerdmans Publishing Co. and in the U.K. by InterVarsity Press. Used by permission. Worldwide permission granted by InterVarsity Press, London, England. Second edition.

Sweeting, George, taken from *The Acts of God.* Copyright © 1986. Moody Bible Institute of Chicago. Moody Press. Used by permission.

Swindoll, Charles R., *The Grace Awakening,* copyright © 1990, Word, Inc., Dallas, Texas.

Swindoll, Charles R., *Improving Your Serve: The Art of Unselfish Living,* copyright © 1981, Word, Inc., Dallas, Texas.

Swindoll, Charles R., *Living Above the Level of Mediocrity: A Commitment to Excellence.* Copyright © 1987, Word, Inc., Dallas, Texas.

Swindoll, Charles R., from the book *Make Up Your Mind,* copyright 1981. Published by Multnomah Press, Portland, Oregon 97266. Used by permission.

Swindoll, Charles R., *Strengthening Your Grip: Essentials in an Aimless World,* copyright © 1982, Word, Inc., Dallas, Texas.

Tada, Joni Eareckson, from the book *Secret Strength,* copyright 1988 by Joni, Inc. Published by Multnomah Press, Portland, Oregon 97266. Used by permission.

Tamasy, Robert J., (General Editor), *The Complete Christian Businessman,* Wolgemuth & Hyatt, Publishers, Inc. Used by permission.

Tucker, Ruth A., taken from the book *Stories of Faith.* Copyright © 1989 by Ruth A. Tucker. Used by permission of Zondervan Publishing House.

Webber, Robert, *Worship is a Verb,* copyright © 1985, Word, Inc., Dallas, Texas. (Second edition by Abbott Martyn Press, Nashville, TN).

Wenham, David, taken from *The Parables of Jesus.* © 1989 by David Wenham. Used by permission of InterVarsity Press, P.O. Box 1400, Downers Grove, IL 60515. Worldwide permission granted by Hodder & Stoughton Limited, England.

White, John, taken from *The Fight.* © 1976 by Inter-Varsity Christian Fellowship of the U.S.A. Used by permission of InterVarsity Press, P.O. Box 1400, Downers Grove, IL 60515.

Wiersbe, Warren W., Reprinted by permission from *Be Alert.* Published by Victor Books and © 1984 by SP Publications, Inc., Wheaton, IL.

Wiersbe, Warren W., Reprinted by permission from *Be Victorious.* Published by Victor Books and © by 1985 SP Publications, Inc., Wheaton, IL.

Wiersbe, Warren W. (Compiler), *Classic Sermons on the Attributes of God.* © 1989 by Kregel Publications: Grand Rapids, Michigan. Used by permission.

Wiersbe, Warren W., taken from *Thoughts for Men on the Move.* Copyright © 1970, 1988. Moody Bible Institute of Chicago. Moody Press. Used by permission.

Wiersbe, Warren W., Reprinted by permission from *Windows on the Parables.* Published by Victor Books and © 1979 by SP Publications, Inc., Wheaton, IL.

Wirt, Sherwood E., *Your Mighty Fortress: Cultivating Your Inner Life With God,* Here's Life Publishers, San Bernadino, CA, © 1989.

Wright, H. Norman, *Quiet Times for Couples.* Copyright © 1990 by Harvest House Publishers, Eugene, OR 97402.

YFC Editors, from *Practical Christianity*; LaVonne Neff, Ron Beers, Bruce Barton, Linda Taylor, Dave Veerman, and Jim Galvin (Compilers and Editors), © 1987 by Youth for Christ/USA. Used by permission of Tyndale House Publishers. All rights reserved.

Yancey, Philip, taken from the book *Where Is God When It Hurts?* Copyright © 1990, 1977 by Philip Yancey. Used by permission of the Zondervan Publishing House.

Yohn, Rick, *Finding Time,* copyright © 1984, Word, Inc., Dallas, Texas.

Zuck, Roy B. (Editor), reprinted by permission from *Devotions for Kindred Spirits.* Published by Victor Books and © 1990 by SP Publications, Inc., Wheaton, IL.

Notes

Notes

Notes

Notes